For Students

- Three Web appendices entitled *An Overview of Transaction Processing; Requirements and Specifications;* and *Design, Coding, and Testing*
- Additional practice problems and solutions
- Online PowerPoint slides for all figures in the textbook
- A Practice Case Study
- Glossary

These student supplements are available at www.aw-bc.com/kifer.

Database Place, a series of online database tutorials, offers additional help mastering SQL, normalization, and modeling. A complimentary subscription is offered when an access code is bundled with a new copy of this text. Subscriptions may also be purchased online. For more information, visit www.aw-bc.com/databaseplace.

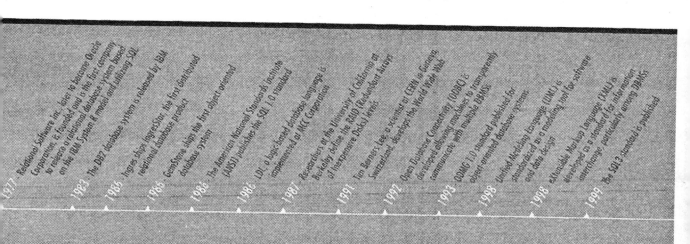

16

Distributed Databases

An increasing number of applications require access to multiple databases located at different sites, perhaps widely separated geographically. These applications fall into two broad categories, each illustrated with an example.

- *Category 1.* An Internet grocer has established a nationwide network of warehouses to speed delivery of its products. Each warehouse has its own local database, and the merchant has a database at its headquarters. An application that determines the total inventory in all warehouses might execute at headquarters and access all warehouse databases.

- *Category 2.* When a customer makes a purchase from the Internet grocer, the transaction might involve both the merchant and a credit card company. Information about the purchase might have to be recorded in both the merchant's and the credit card company's databases.

Distributed data is involved in both of these applications. The difference lies in the way each accesses the databases at the individual sites. In category 1, the application is written in terms of a schema that allows it to access the sites at the level of SQL statements. Thus, it might send SELECT statements to each warehouse to obtain the desired information and then take the union of the returned tuples.

Applications in category 2 do not access data in this way. The merchant and the credit card company are separate enterprises, and their databases contain sensitive information that neither is willing to share. Furthermore, neither is willing to allow the other to (perhaps inadvertently) introduce inconsistencies into its database. Therefore, the credit card company provides a subroutine (perhaps a stored procedure executed as a transaction) that can be invoked to update its database to record the charges made to a customer's account. Since the credit card company creates the routine, it has more control over the security and integrity of its data.

In this chapter we discuss efficient strategies for accessing distributed data. Efficiency is affected by the location of the data items in the network and the algorithm used to manipulate the items (given that their location has been determined). Unfortunately, the techniques we discuss are not applicable to applications in category 2: the location of the data is determined by the individual companies, and the data is accessed by company-controlled routines. An application can be built that invokes these routines and manipulates the data they return, but it cannot access the databases directly, so the application programmer has little flexibility in designing an efficient strategy.

Hence, our focus is on applications in category 1. They access data directly and can employ database-oriented strategies to improve performance and availability. In this chapter, we discuss such strategies. For example,

- How should a distributed database be designed?
- At what site should individual data items or tables be stored?
- Which data items should be replicated, and at what sites should replicas be stored?
- How are queries that access multiple databases processed?
- What issues are involved in distributed query optimization?
- How do the techniques used for query optimization affect database design?

Why data might be distributed.   Since distribution introduces new problems, why distribute data at all? Why not gather all of the data of a distributed enterprise into a single, central site? There are a number of (possibly conflicting) reasons why data might be distributed and, if so, for its locations.

- Data might be placed in such a way as to minimize communication costs and/or response time. This generally means that data is kept at the site that accesses it most often.
- Data might be distributed to equalize the workload so that individual sites are not overloaded to such a degree that throughput is impaired.
- Data might be kept at the site at which it was created so that its creators can maintain control and guarantee security.
- Certain data items might be replicated at multiple sites to increase their availability in the event of system crashes (if one replica becomes unavailable, an alternate can be accessed) or to increase throughput and reduce response time (since the data can be more quickly accessed using a local or nearby copy).

16.1 The Application Designer's View of the Database

An application that directly accesses a database submits SQL statements that have been constructed with some schema in mind. The schema describes the structure of the database seen by the application. We consider three kinds of schemas: multiple local, global, and restricted global.

Multiple local schemas.   The distributed database looks to the application program like a collection of individual databases, each with its own schema, as shown in Figure 16.1(a). Such a system is an example of a **multidatabase**. If the individual DBMSs have been supplied by different vendors, the system is referred to as **heterogeneous**; if by the same vendor, it is referred to as **homogeneous**.

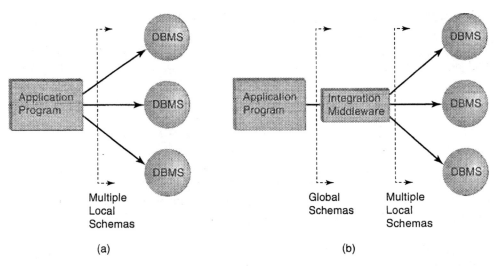

FIGURE 16.1 Views of a distributed database: (a) multidatabase with local schemas; (b) integrated distributed database supporting a global schema.

The application program must explicitly set up a connection to each site that contains data items to be accessed. After a connection has been established, the program can access the database using SQL statements constructed using the site's schema. If data items are moved from one site to another, the program must be changed.

A single SQL statement that refers to tables at different sites—for example, a global join—is not supported. If the application wants to join tables at different sites, it must read the tuples from each table into buffers at the application site (with separate **SELECT** statements) and explicitly test the join condition for each pair of tuples.

Data at different sites might be stored in different formats. For example, at one site an individual's last name might be stored first; at another it might be stored last. In addition, the types in the individual schema might be different. For example, at one site an Id might be stored as a sequence of characters; at another, as an integer. In these cases, the application must provide conversion routines that can be used at run time to integrate the data.

The application must manage replication. If a replicated item is being queried, the application must decide which replica should be accessed, and, if the item is being updated, it must ensure that the update occurs at all replicas.

The methods we discussed in Chapter 8 for accessing a distributed database using embedded SQL, JDBC, SQLJ, and ODBC all see a distributed database in this way.

Global schema. The local schema approach provides little support for the application programmer. All of the issues arising from the distributed nature of the database must be handled explicitly in the program. The opposite extreme, in which all issues are hidden from the application and handled automatically, is interesting since it provides an ideal against which distributed database systems can be measured.

In this approach, the application designer sees a single schema that integrates all local schemas. Therefore, we refer to it as a **global schema** and refer to the system as an **integrated** distributed database system.

The integration is done by middleware (as shown in Figure 16.1(b)). **Middleware** is software that supports the interaction of clients and servers, often in heterogeneous systems. It performs general utility functions that can assist in the construction of a wide variety of applications. In this case, the middleware unifies the individual schemas into a single global schema that includes data from all sites. The global schema might include tables that do not appear in any local schema but can be computed from tables in local schemas using appropriate SQL statements. In other words, the global schema is a view of the local schemas.

Connections to individual sites are made automatically by the middleware when elements of the global schema are accessed. Hence, the locations of tables are hidden from the application program (this is called **location transparency**). If data items are moved from one site to another, the global schema remains the same and the application program need not be changed. The mapping from global to local schema does need to be changed in the middleware, but doing so is easier than changing all the application programs that access the data.

As with local schemas, related data at different sites can be stored in different formats and types, which might not match those of the global schema. The middleware provides the conversion routines to integrate the systems under these circumstances.

A related problem is **semantic integration**, which involves at least the issues of value conversion and name conversion. Consider a distributed database that has sites in Europe, Japan, and the United States. Monetary values at all sites can be represented as double-precision numbers, so no format conversion is required. However, 1000 yen is different from 1000 euro, as 1000 euro is different from 1000 dollars. Thus, a request originating in Tokyo for a total sales figure might require currency conversion into yen, while the same request originating in Amsterdam might require conversion into euro. Attribute-name conversion has to deal with cultural differences and individual habits. Even ignoring the possibility that a site in Amsterdam might use a different language from one in New York, we still must deal with the possibility that two different U.S. sites refer to the same attribute as item# and part#.

Application programs execute SQL statements against the global schema. For example, the application might request the join of two tables, T_1 and T_2, in the global schema. If the tables are stored at the same site, the statement is passed on to that site for processing. If they are stored at different sites (a global join), the middleware must translate the join into a sequence of steps executed by the individual DBMSs and perform any other operations needed to compute the join. In a more complex case, both T_1 and T_2 can be views that are populated by the middleware using queries that join relations stored at different sites.

An important aspect of this is query optimization: the middleware attempts to choose a sequence of steps that constitutes a least-cost plan for evaluating the SQL statement submitted by the application. Cost is frequently measured in terms of the amount of data that must be transmitted between sites since this is generally the most time-consuming aspect of the plan. In this regard there is a significant difference between homogeneous and heterogeneous systems. With a heterogeneous system, each DBMS presents an SQL interface to the middleware, and hence a step performed by a DBMS is the execution of an SQL statement submitted by the middleware. As a result, data is transmitted between the middleware and each DBMS, but not directly between two DBMSs. Since the DBMSs of a homogeneous system are all produced by the same vendor, they can be built to support direct communication among themselves. Hence, the integration module shown in Figure 16.1(b) can be distributed among the individual DBMSs, and the opportunity to optimize the plan is much greater. We discuss some optimization techniques in Section 16.3.1.

The application designer might choose to replicate certain data items and designate the sites at which the replicas are to reside. However, replication is hidden from the application program. The program accesses a logical data item, and the middleware automatically manages the replication, supplying an appropriate replica to satisfy a query and updating all replicas when appropriate. This is referred to as **replication transparency** and is discussed in more detail in Section 16.2.3.

Restricted global schema.   The application designer sees a single global schema, but the schema is the union (as contrasted with a view) of the schemas of individual databases. Thus, the restricted global schema consists of all the tables of the individual databases.

Restricted global schemas are supported by the vendors of some homogeneous systems. The database servers supplied by such a vendor cooperate directly, eliminating the need for middleware, but still function as shown in Figure 16.1(b).[1]

Applications use a naming convention to refer to the tables in each database. Thus, the location of the tables can be hidden from the application (location transparency). A connection to a site is made automatically when a table at that site is accessed.

The application can execute an SQL statement that refers to tables at different sites—for example, a global join. The system includes a global query optimizer to design efficient query plans and provides replication transparency.

16.2 Distributing Data among Different Databases

In many cases, the distribution of data among different sites is not under the control of the application designer. For example, certain data items might have to be stored at a particular site for security reasons. In other situations, the designer can participate in the decision as to where data is stored or replicated. In this section, we describe several issues related to data distribution.

---

[1] The view described here is similar to that supplied by Oracle except that the Oracle implementation supports a certain amount of heterogeneity by allowing limited access to databases from other vendors.

16.2.1 Partitioning

The simplest way to distribute data is to store individual tables at different sites. However, a table is not necessarily the best choice as the unit of distribution. Frequently a transaction accesses only a subset of the rows of a table, or a view of a table, rather than the table as a whole. If different transactions access different portions of the table and run at different sites, performance can be improved by storing a portion of the table at the site where the corresponding transaction is executed. When a table is decomposed in this way, we refer to the portions as **partitions**. For such applications, partitions are a better unit of data distribution than tables.

Distributing the partitions of a table has other potential advantages. For example, the time to process a single query over a large table can be reduced by distributing the execution over a number of sites at which partitions are stored. Consider, for example, the query that produces the names and grade point averages of all students at a university with multiple campuses. If the STUDENT and TRANSCRIPT tables are stored at the central administrative site, all processing takes place there. If, instead, the tables are partitioned and stored at individual campuses, the DBMSs at each campus can execute in parallel and together produce the result in less time. Furthermore, distributing partitions might make it possible to improve throughput, provided that a query executed at a site accesses the partition local to that site. Partitioning can be either horizontal or vertical.

Horizontal partitioning. A single table, T, is partitioned into several tables, called **partitions**

$$T_1, T_2, \ldots, T_r$$

where each partition contains a subset of the rows of T and each row of T is in exactly one partition. For example, the Internet grocer might have a relation

```
INVENTORY(StockNum, Amount, Price, Location)
```

to describe its inventory, together with the location of the warehouse where it is stored. The grocer might horizontally partition the relation by city so that, for example, it stores all the tuples satisfying

```
Location = 'Chicago'
```
16.1

in a partition named INVENTORY_CH at the Chicago warehouse, with the schema

```
INVENTORY_CH(StockNum, Amount, Price)
```

(The attribute Location is now redundant and so could be omitted.) Because each tuple is stored in some partition, horizontal partitioning is lossless. The table can be reconstructed by taking the union of its partitions.

More generally, each partition satisfies

$$T_i = \sigma_{C_i}(T)$$

where C_i is a selection condition and each tuple in T satisfies C_i for exactly one value of i and

$$T = \bigcup_i T_i$$

Expression (16.1) is an example of a selection condition.

Vertical partitioning. A table, T, is divided into partitions

$$T_1, T_2, \ldots, T_r$$

where each partition contains a subset of the columns of T. Each column must be included in at least one partition, and each partition must include the columns of a candidate key (the same for all partitions).

Thus, the Internet grocer might have a relation

EMPLOYEE(SSnum, Name, Salary, Title, Location)

to describe its employees at all warehouses. It might vertically partition EMPLOYEE as

EMP1 (SSnum, Name, Salary)
EMP2 (SSnum, Name, Title, Location)

where EMP1 is stored at the headquarters site (where the payroll is computed) and EMP2 is stored elsewhere. More generally

$$T_i = \pi_{attr\_list_i}(T)$$

Because each column must be in at least one partition and all partitions include the same candidate key, vertical partitioning is lossless: by taking the natural join of its partitions the original table can be reconstructed.

$$T = T_1 \bowtie T_2 \cdots \bowtie T_r$$

Because the candidate key is included in each partition, vertical partitioning involves replication. Other columns might be replicated as well. In our case, Name is included in both partitions because it is used by local applications at each site.

Note that the rationale behind vertical partitioning in the above case is very different from that behind relational normalization, which we discussed in Chapter 6.

Indeed, all three relations, EMPLOYEE, EMP1, and EMP2, are in Boyce-Codd normal form, so the algorithms proposed in Chapter 6 leave EMPLOYEE alone.

Mixed partitioning. Combinations of horizontal and vertical partitioning are also possible, but care must be taken to ensure that the original table can be reconstructed from its partitions. One approach is to do one type of partitioning and then the other. Thus, after our Internet grocer vertically partitions EMPLOYEE into EMP1 and EMP2, it might horizontally partition EMP2 by location. The partitions corresponding to the Chicago and Buffalo warehouses become

```
EMP2_CH (SSnum, Name, Title, Location)
EMP2_BU (SSnum, Name, Title, Location)
```

(Once again, the attribute Location might be omitted.) EMP1 is stored at the headquarters site, and EMP2_CH and EMP2_BU are stored at the corresponding warehouse sites.

Derived horizontal partitioning. In some situations, it might be desirable to horizontally partition a relation, but the information needed to decide which rows belong in which partition is not contained in the relation itself. Suppose, for example, that the Internet grocer has more than one warehouse in each city and each warehouse is identified by a warehouse number. Conceptually the database contains two tables:

```
INVENTORY(StockNum, Amount, Price, WarehouseNum)
WAREHOUSE(WarehouseNum, Capacity, Street-address, Location)
```

The grocer has one database site in each city and wants to horizontally partition INVENTORY so that a partition in a particular city contains information about all the items in all the warehouses in that city. The problem is that Location, which identifies the city in which a warehouse is located, is not an attribute of INVENTORY, and so it is not clear how the tuples are to be partitioned.

To solve this problem, we need to know the location of the warehouse that has been identified by a warehouse number. That information is contained in WAREHOUSE. Thus, we need to join the information in the two tables before we can do the partitioning. We use the *natural join* since the warehouse number is stored in the two tables using the same attribute name. The rows contained in the partition of INVENTORY describing Chicago, which we call INVENTORY_CH, are those that join with the rows of WAREHOUSE that satisfy the predicate Location = 'Chicago'. Hence,

$$INVENTORY\_CH = \pi_A(INVENTORY \bowtie (\sigma_{Location='Chicago'}(WAREHOUSE)))$$

where A is the set of all attributes of INVENTORY. The join is used only to *locate* the rows of INVENTORY that we want to include in INVENTORY_CH. Because we do not want to retain any columns of WAREHOUSE, we project the result of the join on the attributes in A. Since

$$\sigma_{\text{Location = 'Chicago'}} (\text{WAREHOUSE})$$

is a partition of WAREHOUSE, the partitioning of INVENTORY is derived from a partitioning of WAREHOUSE, and we refer to this type of partitioning as **derived partitioning**. INVENTORY_CH is a *semi-join* of INVENTORY with a partition of WAREHOUSE. We discuss semi-joins in Section 16.3.1.

Horizontal partitioning is used when (most) applications at each site need to access only a *subset of the tuples* in a relation. Vertical partitioning is used when (most) applications at each site need to access only a *subset of the attributes* in a relation. We discuss methods for numerically comparing various possible database designs involving partitioning in Section 16.3.

Architectures based on the global schema can provide **partition transparency**. This means that the relation appears in its original unpartitioned form in the global schema and the middleware transforms any accesses to it into appropriate accesses to its partitions stored in different databases. In contrast, multidatabase systems do not provide partition transparency—each application program must be aware of the partitioning and use it appropriately in its queries.

> *Brain Teaser:* Can horizontal partitioning into disjoint sets of tuples decrease the overall storage requirements? Can it increase these requirements? How about the vertical partitioning of BCNF tables? Of 3NF tables?

16.2.2 Updates and Partitioning

Although our main interest has been in queries, we note that when relations are partitioned, update operations sometimes require tuples to be moved from one partition to another and hence from one database site to another. Suppose that an employee of the Internet grocer is transferred from the Chicago warehouse to the Buffalo warehouse. In the unpartitioned EMPLOYEE relation

```
EMPLOYEE (SSnum, Name, Salary, Title, Location)
```

the value of the Location attribute for that employee's tuple must be changed. If EMPLOYEE is partitioned into EMP2_CH and EMP2_BU, as described earlier, updating the Location attribute for that employee requires moving the corresponding tuple from the Chicago database to the Buffalo database.

The possibility that updates as well as queries might require moving data from one site to another must be taken into account when deciding where to place the data in a distributed database.

16.2.3 Replication

Replication is one of the most used, and most useful, mechanisms in distributed databases. Replicating data at several sites provides increased availability because the data can still be accessed if some of the sites fail. It also has the potential for improving performance: queries can be executed more efficiently because the data can be read from a local or nearby copy. However, updates are usually slower because all replicas of the data must be updated. Hence, performance is improved in applications in which updates occur substantially less often than queries. In this section, we discuss performance issues related to the execution of individual SQL statements.

Example 16.2.1 (Internet Grocer). To keep track of its customers, the Internet grocer might have a relation

CUSTOMER(CustNum, Address, Location)

where Location specifies an area serviced by a particular warehouse. The relation is queried by an application at the headquarters site that sends monthly mailings to all customers. An application at each warehouse site queries the relation to obtain information about deliveries in its area. The relation is updated by an application at the headquarters site when (1) a new customer registers with the company or (2) information about a particular customer changes (which happens infrequently). ▪

Intuitively, it seems appropriate to horizontally partition the relation by Location so that a particular partition is stored both at the corresponding warehouse and at headquarters. Thus the relation would be replicated, with a complete copy at the headquarters site. We perform an analysis to evaluate that design choice compared to two others in which data is not replicated. The three choices are as follows:

1. Store the entire relation at the headquarters site and nothing at the warehouses.

2. Store all partitions at the warehouse sites with nothing at headquarters.

3. Replicate the partitions at both sites.

One way to compare the alternatives is to estimate the amount of information that must be transmitted between sites in each case when the specified applications are executed. To do this, we make the following assumptions about table sizes and the frequency with which each application is executed:

▪ The CUSTOMER relation has about 100,000 tuples.

▪ The mailing application at headquarters sends each customer one mailing each month.

▪ About 500 deliveries per day (over all warehouses) are performed, and a single tuple must be read for each delivery.

▪ The company gets about 100 new customers a day (and the number of changes to individual customers' information is negligible by comparison).

Now we can evaluate the three alternatives.

1. If we store the relation at the headquarters site, information must be transmitted from there to the appropriate warehouse site whenever a delivery is made—about 500 tuples per day.

2. If we store the partitions at the warehouse sites, information must be transmitted as follows:

   • From the warehouses to headquarters when the mailing application is executed—about 100,000 tuples per month or 3300 per day
   • From headquarters to the warehouses when a new customer registers—about 100 tuples per day

   In total, then, about 3400 tuples per day must be transmitted.

3. If we replicate the partitions at both headquarters and the warehouses, information must be sent from the headquarters site to the appropriate warehouse site when a new customer registers—about 100 tuples per day.

By this measure, replication appears to be the best alternative. We might also want to compare the alternatives using other measures, such as the response time of transactions.

1. If we store the relation at headquarters, the time to handle deliveries suffers because of the required remote access. This might not be viewed as important.

2. If we store the partitions at the warehouses and the monthly mailing is done by a single application, the 100,000 tuples that must be sent from the warehouses to headquarters might clog the communication system and slow down other applications. This can be avoided by running the mailing application late at night or over the weekend when few other applications are executing.

3. If we replicate the partitions, the time to register a new customer suffers because of the time required to update the tables at both the headquarters and the appropriate warehouse. This might be viewed as important because the customer is online when the update occurs and the time required to update the remote table might make the registration time unacceptably long. However, for this application the customer interaction can be considered complete when the headquarters database is updated. The update at the warehouse site can be performed later because the information is not needed there until some delivery transaction is executed. We discuss such **asynchronous-update replication** in Section A.3.3.

We see from this that replicating the partitions still seems to be the best alternative.

> Replication may reduce network traffic for queries, but it slows down updates. Potential benefits of replication must be evaluated on a case-by-case basis.

16.3 Query Planning Strategies

A multidatabase system is composed of a set of independent DBMSs. Typically, each DBMS exports an SQL interface, and an application is confronted with multiple local schemas. In order for the application to query information stored at multiple sites, it must decompose the query into a sequence of SQL statements, each of which is processed by a particular DBMS. On receiving an SQL statement, the query optimizer at the DBMS develops a query execution plan, the statement is executed, and results are returned to the application.

Systems that support a global schema contain a global query optimizer, which analyzes a query using the global schema and translates it into an appropriate sequence of steps to be executed at individual sites. Each step can be further optimized by the local query optimizer at a site and then executed. In this section we will assume a homogeneous distributed database. Since direct communication between individual DBMSs is supported in such systems, the query optimizer has a lot more flexibility and the difference between the cost of a good plan and a bad one can be substantial. Global query processing thus involves a distributed algorithm that involves the direct exchange of data between DBMSs.

In both cases, we are interested in executing the query efficiently. Since the cost of I/O is so much greater than that of computation, our measure of the efficiency of a query execution plan in Chapter 10 was an estimate of the number of I/O operations it requires. By similar reasoning, the cost of evaluating a query over a distributed database is based on the communication costs involved since communication is both expensive and time consuming. Communication costs will be measured by the number of bytes that have to be transmitted.

Our interest in query optimization is threefold. A familiarity with algorithms for global query optimization helps in designing

- Global queries that will execute efficiently for a given distribution of data
- Algorithms for efficiently evaluating global queries in multidatabase systems (Section 16.3.2)
- The distribution of data that will be accessed by global queries (Section 16.3.3)

16.3.1 Global Query Optimization

We will now discuss the techniques that are commonly used in optimizing distributed queries.

Planning with joins. Queries that involve a join of tables at different sites (a global join) are particularly expensive since information must be exchanged between sites in order to determine the tuples in the result. For example, suppose that an application at site A wants to join tables at sites B and C, with the result to be returned to site A. Two straightforward ways to execute the join that might be evaluated by a global query optimizer are

1. Transmit both tables to site A and execute the join there. The application program at site A then explicitly tests the join condition. This is the approach used in multidatabase systems that do not support global joins.

2. Transmit the smaller of the tables—for example, the table at site B, to site C, execute the join at site C, and then transmit the result to site A.

Example 16.3.1 (Distributed Student Database). To be more specific, we consider two tables, STUDENT(Id, Major) and TRANSCRIPT(StudId, CrsCode), where STUDENT records the major of each student and TRANSCRIPT records the courses in which a student is registered *this semester*. These tables are stored at sites B and C, respectively. Suppose that an application at site A wants to compute an equi-join with the join condition

$$Id = StudId \qquad 16.2$$

To compare alternative query plans, we must make certain assumptions about table sizes and, in some cases, about the relative frequency of operations on those tables. For this example, we assume that

- The lengths of the attributes are
  - Id and StudId: 9 bytes
  - Major: 3 bytes
  - CrsCode: 6 bytes
- STUDENT has about 15,000 tuples, each of length 12 bytes $(9 + 3)$.
- Approximately 5000 students are registered for at least one course, and, on average, each student is registered for four courses. Thus, TRANSCRIPT has about 20,000 tuples, each of length 15 bytes $(= 9 + 6)$. Note that 10,000 students are not registered for any course (this is the summer session).

The join then has about 20,000 tuples (each tuple in TRANSCRIPT corresponds to a tuple in the join), each of length 18 bytes $(= 9 + 3 + 6)$.

Based on these assumptions, we can compare three alternative plans.

1. If we send both tables to site A to perform the join, we have to send 480,000 bytes $(= 15,000 * 12 + 20,000 * 15)$.
2. If we send STUDENT to site C, compute the join there, and then send the result to site A, we have to send 540,000 bytes $(= 15,000 * 12 + 20,000 * 18)$.
3. If we send TRANSCRIPT to site B, compute the join there, and then send the result to site A, we have to send 660,000 bytes $(= 20,000 * 15 + 20,000 * 18)$.

Thus, we see that the best of the three is alternative (1). ∎

Planning with semi-joins. Another, often more efficient approach that a global query optimizer might consider is to transmit from site B to site C only those tuples from STUDENT that will actually participate in the join, and then perform the join at site C between those tuples and TRANSCRIPT. This approach involves performing what is called a *semi-join*. The procedure involves three steps:

1. At site C, compute a table, **P**, that is the projection of TRANSCRIPT on StudId—the column involved in the join condition—and then send **P** to site B. Hence, **P** contains the Ids of students who are currently registered for at least one course. In this step we are sending $5000 * 9 = 45{,}000$ bytes.

2. At site B, form the join of STUDENT with **P** using join condition (16.2) and then send the resulting table, **Q**, to site C. **Q** contains all of the tuples in STUDENT that participate in the join. In the example, **Q** consists of all tuples in STUDENT that represent students who registered for at least one course. In this step we are sending $5000 * 12 = 60{,}000$ bytes.

3. At site C, join TRANSCRIPT with **Q** using the join condition. The result is the join of STUDENT and TRANSCRIPT, which is then sent to site A. Since the size of the join is 20,000 tuples $* 18$ bytes, we are sending 360,000 bytes.

In total we are sending 465,000 bytes ($= 45{,}000 + 60{,}000 + 360{,}000$). Hence, in terms of communication costs, this latest alternative is better than those we have investigated earlier. In fact, we can do even better. Instead of sending **Q** to C, we can send both **Q** and TRANSCRIPT to site A:

2′. At site B, form the join of STUDENT with **P** using join condition (16.2) and then send the resulting table, **Q**, to site A ($5000 * 12 = 60{,}000$ bytes).

3′. Send TRANSCRIPT to site A and join it there with **Q**. The communication cost of this operation is $20000 * 15 = 300{,}000$ bytes.

The total cost of the last plan is $45000 + 60000 + 300000 = 405{,}000$ bytes. This is the best among all the plans we have analyzed. Notice that the reason for the cost reduction in the last two cases is that we have managed to pare down STUDENT to only the subset of tuples that can possibly join with a tuple of TRANSCRIPT. In this way, we avoided the need to send STUDENT to site C (and TRANSCRIPT to site B) and instead sent only portions of these relations.

The result of step 2 (or step 2′), the relation **Q**, is called the *semi-join* of STUDENT with TRANSCRIPT. More generally, the **semi-join** $T_1 \ltimes_{join\text{-}condition} T_2$ is defined to be the projection over the columns of T_1 of the join of T_1 and T_2:

$$\pi_{attributes(T_1)} (T_1 \bowtie_{join\text{-}condition} T_2)$$

Some tuples of T_1 do not join with any tuple of T_2 and hence are not a part of any tuple in $(T_1 \bowtie_{join\text{-}condition} T_2)$. Hence, when the result of the join is projected on the attributes of T_1, only a subset of the tuples of T_1 are produced. In other words, the semi-join consists of the tuples of T_1 that participate in the join with T_2. Note that semi-join is not a symmetric operator: $P \ltimes_{cond} Q$ is not equivalent to $Q \ltimes_{cond} P$. One contains a subset of the tuples of **P** and the other a subset of the tuples of **Q**.

Armed with the concept of a semi-join, we can compute the join of the form

$$T_1 \bowtie_{join\text{-}condition} T_2$$

by first computing a semi-join and then joining it with T_2:

$$(T_1 \ltimes_{join\text{-}condition} T_2) \bowtie_{join\text{-}condition} T_2$$

It is left to Exercise 16.10 to show that the above two expressions are equivalent.

> *Brain Teaser:* We just saw that $(T_1 \ltimes T_2) \bowtie T_2 = T_1 \bowtie T_2$. What can you say about $T_1 \bowtie (T_1 \ltimes T_2)$?

It might seem that we have made a step backward by replacing one join with two. However, step 1 provides a clue—namely, the potential savings in performing a semi-join that lie in the following equivalence:

$$T_1 \ltimes_{join\text{-}condition} T_2 = \pi_{attributes(T_1)} (T_1 \bowtie_{join\text{-}condition} T_2)$$
$$= \pi_{attributes(T_1)} (T_1 \bowtie_{join\text{-}condition} \pi_{attributes(join\text{-}condition)}(T_2))$$

In other words, in computing a semi-join of T_1 and T_2 we can first take the projection of T_2 on the attributes mentioned in the join condition and then join the result with T_1 (using the same join condition). We leave the proof of this equivalence to Exercise 16.9. This first step potentially cuts communication costs because the projection of T_2 can be substantially smaller than T_2, so we avoid sending large chunks of data over the communication link. However, we do have to pay for performing the additional join between the result of the semi-join and T_2. If the savings in communication dominate the overhead of the extra join, we come out on top.

In our example, the three steps of the computation correspond to the following algebraic expression:

$$\pi_{attributes(STUDENT)} \ (\pi_{attributes(join\text{-}condition)}(TRANSCRIPT)$$
$$\bowtie_{join\text{-}condition} STUDENT)$$
$$\bowtie_{join\text{-}condition} TRANSCRIPT$$ **16.3**

Step 1, computed at site C, corresponds to the table **P**:

$$\pi_{attributes(join\text{-}condition)}(TRANSCRIPT)$$

This is sent to site B where it is used in step 2 in the computation

$$\pi_{attributes(STUDENT)} (P \bowtie_{join\text{-}condition} STUDENT)$$

The result, **Q**, is sent back to site C and step 3, consisting of the computation

$$Q \bowtie_{join\text{-}condition} TRANSCRIPT$$

is performed there. Query (16.3) can be expressed using the semi-join operator as

$$(STUDENT \ltimes_{join\text{-}condition} TRANSCRIPT) \bowtie_{join\text{-}condition} TRANSCRIPT$$

According to the previous discussion, this is equivalent to computing the join of STUDENT and TRANSCRIPT.

> Semi-joins may reduce network traffic, but this technique requires more locally performed joins. The overall benefits must be evaluated for each query plan.

Implementing global joins with replication. Still another way to implement a global join is to store a replica of one of the tables at the site of the other, thus turning the global join into a local join. In the example, we might store a replica of STUDENT at site C. We can then perform the join of STUDENT and TRANSCRIPT at site C and send the result, 360,000 bytes, to site A.

This approach speeds up the join operation but slows down updates of the replicated table. In the example, such updates might be rare because students seldom change their major.

Queries that involve joins and projections. Most queries involve not only joins but also other relational operators. In the above example, suppose that an application at site A executes a query that returns the majors and course codes of all students who are registered for at least one course. Thus, the row (CS, CS305) will be in the result table if there is at least one computer science (CS) student taking CS305. The query first takes the join of the two tables, STUDENT and TRANSCRIPT, and then projects on Major and CrsCode to obtain the result table, **R**. Our plan is to do the projection at the site at which the join is performed and then send **R** to site A.

In order to reevaluate the communication costs of the five alternatives we considered in the last section, we need to make one additional assumption—that **R** has 1000 tuples. Each tuple has a length of 9 bytes, so the size of **R** is 9000 bytes, making it much smaller than the joined table. That is common in real queries.

1. If we send both tables to site A and do all operations there, we have to send, as before, 480,000 bytes.

2. If we send the STUDENT table to site C, do the operations there, and then send **R** to site A, we have to send 189,000 bytes ($= 15,000 * 12 + 1000 * 9$).

3. If we send the TRANSCRIPT table to site B, do the operations there, and then send **R** to site A, we have to send 309,000 bytes ($= 20,000 * 15 + 1000 * 9$).

4. If we perform the semi-join at site B as previously described, we again have two options:

   (a) Send the result of the semi-join, **Q**, to site C; join it with STUDENT; project on Major and CrsCode; then send the result, **R**, to site A. The cost would be 114,000 bytes ($= 5000 * 9 + 5000 * 12 + 1000 * 9$).

   (b) Send both **Q**, and TRANSCRIPT to site A and complete the computation there. The cost of this is 405,000 bytes, as before.

Hence, the semi-join approach is still the best alternative, although now option (a) is better than option (b).

We can optimize this procedure by changing step 2 so that, after performing the semi-join to obtain **Q**, we do a projection on **Q** to retain only the columns of STUDENT needed for the query. Only those columns are sent from site B to site C. For example, suppose that STUDENT has additional attributes (such as `Address`, `Date_of_Birth`, `Entrance_date`,) and that, as before, the query requests the `Id`, `CrsCode`, and `Major` of students for each course in which a student is registered. Then, in step 2, we can project on those attributes named in the WHERE and SELECT clauses and send only those to site C.

This idea can be used in all of the approaches discussed so far. Before a table is sent from one site to another to perform a join, all unnecessary attributes can be eliminated.

Queries that involve joins and selections. A similar idea can be used when the query involves joins and selections. Suppose that there is only one warehouse in the Internet grocer application and that the EMPLOYEE relation is vertically partitioned as

```
EMP1 (SSnum, Name, Salary)
EMP2 (SSnum, Title, Location)
```
                                                                        16.4

EMP1 is stored at site B (headquarters) and EMP2 is stored at site C (warehouse). Suppose that a query at a third site, A, requests the names of all employees with title "manager" whose salary is more than $20,000. (If we had assumed more than one warehouse, the reasoning would have been similar but the arithmetic would have been a bit more complex—see Exercise 16.14.)

A straightforward approach is to first perform the join of the tables (to regenerate the EMPLOYEE table) and then use the selection and projection operators on the result to obtain

$$\pi_{\text{Name}}(\sigma_{\text{Title='manager' AND Salary>'20000'}} (\text{EMP1} \bowtie \text{EMP2}))$$

Unfortunately, using the semi-join procedure to optimize the join will not reduce communication costs. This is because the two tables are the vertical partitions of the joined table, so EMP1 and EMP2 both contain SSnum, the key of EMPLOYEE. Hence all tuples of each table must be brought together to reconstruct EMPLOYEE.

Note, however, that the selection condition can be partitioned into selection conditions on the individual tables.

■ Selection condition `Salary > '20000'` on EMP1
■ Selection condition `Title = 'manager'` on EMP2

Now we can use the mathematical properties of the relational operators to change the order of the join and selection operators (recall the cascading and pushing rules for selection in Section 11.2):

$$\pi_{\text{NAME}}((\sigma_{\text{Salary>'20000'}} (\text{EMP1})) \bowtie (\sigma_{\text{Title='manager'}} (\text{EMP2})))$$

Specifically,

1.   At site B, select all tuples from EMP1 for which the salary is more than $20,000. Call the result R_1.
2.   At site C, select all tuples from EMP2 for which the title is manager. Call the result R_2.
3.   At some site (to be determined below), perform the join of R_1 and R_2 and project on the result using the Name attribute. Call the result R_3. If this site is not site A, send R_3 to site A.

The only remaining issue is where to perform the join in step 3. There are three possibilities:

1.   Plan 1: Send R_2 to site B, and do the join there. Then send the names to site A.
2.   Plan 2: Send R_1 to site C, and do the join there. Then send the names to site A.
3.   Plan 3: Send R_1 and R_2 to site A, and do the join there.

As before, to determine the best plan we must take into account the sizes of the various tables and the size of the result. We make the following assumptions:

■   The lengths of the attributes are
   - SSnum: 9 bytes;
   - Salary: 6 bytes;
   - Title: 7 bytes;
   - Location: 10 bytes;
   - Name: 15 bytes.

   Thus, the length of each tuple in EMP1 is 30 bytes and in EMP2 is 26 bytes.
■   EMP1 (and hence EMP2) has about 100,000 tuples.
■   About 5000 employees have a salary of more than $20,000. Therefore, R_1 has about 5000 tuples (each of length 30 bytes), for a total of 150,000 bytes.
■   There are about 50 managers. Therefore, R_2 has about 50 tuples (each of length 26 bytes), for a total of 1300 bytes.
■   About 90% of the managers have a salary of more than $20,000. Therefore, R_3 has about 45 tuples, each of length 15 bytes, for a total of 675 bytes.

We can now evaluate the cost of each plan.

1.   If we do the join at site B, we have to send 1300 bytes from site C to site B, and then 675 bytes from site B to site A, for a total of 1975 bytes.
2.   If we do the join at site C, we have to send 150,000 bytes from site B to site C, and then 675 bytes from site C to site A, for a total of 150,675 bytes.

3. If we do the join at site A, we have to send 150,000 bytes from site B to site A, and 1300 bytes from site C to site A, for a total of 151,300 bytes.

As you can see, the first plan is substantially better than the other two.[2]

To fully appreciate a well-designed query plan, compare the cost of this plan with the cost of the unoptimized plan in which EMP1 and EMP2 are sent, in their entirety, to site A and the query is evaluated there. In that case, 5,600,000 bytes ($= 2,600,000 + 3,000,000$) have to be transmitted!

16.3.2 Strategies for a Multidatabase System

An application accessing a multidatabase system does not have a global schema to work with. Instead, a query involving data at several sites must be constructed using a sequence of SQL statements, each of which is formulated over the schema of a particular DBMS and processed at that site. Although global query optimizers do not exist in such an environment, the application designer can use some of the ideas discussed in Section 16.3.1 to choose a suitable sequence of statements for query evaluation. Unfortunately, the designer is limited because of the following considerations:

1. In a multidatabase system, data can be communicated only between a database site and the site at which a query is submitted—site A in the example. With a global query optimizer, on the other hand, database sites cooperate with one another and communicate directly.

2. Even though data cannot be transmitted directly between database sites, we might consider transferring data from one site to another indirectly through site A. This approach is not possible, however. Although site A can receive data from a DBMS (as a result of submitting a SELECT statement), it cannot send data to a DBMS because the application interface is concerned only with processing SQL statements (not receiving data).

This makes it essentially impossible to mimic step 1 of the semi-join procedure (page 700), in which a projection of a table (**P** in that step) is transmitted from one database site to another (see Exercise 16.15 for a somewhat impractical exception to this statement).

Example 16.3.2 (Global Optimization). Let us reconsider the partitioned EMPLOYEE table of the previous section and the query at site A that requests the names of all managers whose salary is more than $20,000. If the query were executed in a system with a global optimizer, we would expect the optimizer to choose plan 1, which has a communication cost of 1975 bytes.

If the same query were executed in a multidatabase system, the application designer could first execute SELECT statements at each site that returned R_1 and R_2

---

[2] By projecting R_2 at site C on SSnum before sending it to site B, we can further reduce the cost of communication.

to site A. The program would then perform the necessary processing on these tuples to implement the join operation. The communication cost would be the same as plan 3: 151,300 bytes. Although this strategy would not be as efficient as the best strategy that can be chosen by a global query optimizer, it would certainly be an improvement over a naive strategy that brings EMP1 and EMP2 in their entirety to site A, at the cost of 5,600,000 bytes. ▪

16.3.3 Tuning Issues: Database Design and Query Planning in a Distributed Environment

As in the centralized case, query planning for distributed databases involves evaluating alternatives, among which are

- Performing operations at different sites
- Sending partial results or entire tables from one site to another during query execution
- Performing semi-joins
- Using the heuristic optimization rules for relational algebra (Section 11.2) to reorder operations

Application designers do not have any significant control over the strategies used by a global query optimizer. However, the designer often does have control over the design of the distributed database, and that design can have a significant effect on query planning by changing the alternatives available to the global query optimizer. This is also true if query planning is done manually by the application designer for a multidatabase system.

In the centralized case, the application designer might change the database schema by, for example, adding indices or denormalizing tables (see Sections 6.13 and 12.2). In the distributed case, the designer might have additional choices, such as

- Placing tables at different sites
- Partitioning tables in different ways and placing the partitions at different sites
- Replicating tables, or data within tables (e.g., denormalizing), and placing the replicas at different sites

As in the centralized case, these choices might speed up certain operations and slow down others. Thus, the designer must evaluate a proposed database design based on the relative frequency of each operation in the application and the importance of throughput and response time for that operation.

In the Internet grocer application, partitioning the INVENTORY relation speeds up local applications involving delivery of merchandise but slows down global applications that require joining the partitions—for example, computing the total inventory for the company. In evaluating these alternatives, the enterprise might decide that the delivery application must execute quickly but that the total inventory application might execute infrequently with no significant demand on its response time.

The application designer might then consider speeding up the global inventory application by replicating the warehouse inventory information in the headquarters database. But this alternative will probably be rejected because the warehouse inventory information is updated frequently—every time a delivery is made—and the communication cost of updating the replicas is much greater than that of performing the global inventory application. Evaluating such tradeoffs is essential in designing an application that executes efficiently and meets the needs of the enterprise.

BIBLIOGRAPHIC NOTES

Our description of distributed query processing is based on the implementations of two systems, SDD-1 [Wong 1977; Bernstein et al. 1981] and System R* [Griffiths-Selinger and Adiba 1980]. The theory of semi-joins is discussed in [Bernstein and Chiu 1981]. Partitioning is discussed in [Chang and Cheng 1980; Ceri et al. 1982]. More in-depth study of a number of issues in distributed databases (especially database design and query processing) can be found in specialized texts, such as [Ceri and Pelagatti 1984; Bell and Grimson 1992; Ozsu and Valduriez 1999].

EXERCISES

16.1 Discuss the advantages to the application designer of designing an application as a homogeneous system in which all databases are supplied by the same vendor.

16.2 Explain why a table might be partitioned in the schema of a centralized system.

16.3 Explain whether or not the following statement is true: the join of two tables obtained by a (vertical or horizontal) partitioning of a table, T, can never contain more tuples than are contained in T.

16.4 Consider the two examples of query design in a multidatabase system given in Section 16.3.2. Write programs in Java and JDBC that implement both.

16.5 Give an example of a program at site A that requires the join of two tables, one at site B and one at site C. State the assumptions needed to justify the result that, as far as communication costs are concerned, the best implementation is to ship the table at site B to site C, do the join there, and then send the result to site A.

16.6 You are considering the possibility of horizontally partitioning the relation

EMPLOYEE (SSN, Name, Salary, Title, Location)

by location and storing each partition in the database at that location, with the possibility of replicating some partitions at different sites. Discuss the types of queries and updates (and their frequencies) that might influence your decision.

16.7   Suppose that we have a relation

> EMPLOYEE2 (SSnum, Name, Salary, Age, Title, Location)

which is partitioned as

> EMP21 (SSnum, Name, Salary)
> EMP22 (SSnum, Title, Age, Location)

where EMP21 is stored at site B and EMP22 is stored at site C. A query at site A wants the names of all managers in the accounting department whose salary is greater than their age. Design a plan for this query, using the assumptions on page 704 for table and attribute sizes. Assume that the items in the Age column are two bytes long.

16.8   Design a multidatabase query plan and a set of SQL statements that implement the query of the previous exercise.

16.9   Show that step 2 of the method used in Section 16.3.1 to perform a join using a semi-join does in fact generate the semi-join. For simplicity, assume that the join we are attempting is a natural join. That is, prove that

$$\pi_{attributes(T_1)} (T_1 \bowtie T_2) = \pi_{attributes(T_1)}(T_1 \bowtie \pi_{attributes(join\text{-}condition)}(T_2))$$

16.10   Show that step 3 of the method used in Section 16.3.1 to perform a join using a semi-join does in fact generate the join. For simplicity, assume that the join we are attempting is a natural join. In other words, show that

$$(T_1 \ltimes T_2) \bowtie T_2 = (T_1 \bowtie T_2)$$

16.11   Design a query plan for the join example in Section 16.3.1, assuming the same table sizes as in that section, but with the following differences:

a. An application at site B requested the join.
b. An application at site C requested the join.

16.12   Show that the method of designing horizontal partitions described in Section 16.2.1 works as advertised.

16.13   Show that the semi-join operation is not commutative, that is, T_1 semi-joined with T_2 is not the same as T_2 semi-joined with T_1.

16.14   Use the example schema (16.4) on page 703 to design a query for finding the names of all managers (employees with Title = 'manager') whose salary is more than $20,000, but assume that there are three warehouses. Also assume that the total number of employees is 100,000, that 5000 of them make over $20,000, that the total number of managers is 50, and that 90% of the managers make more than $20,000.

16.15   In Section 16.3.2 we pointed out that in a multidatabase system, data could not be communicated directly from one database site to another and that even indirect communication was difficult since a query site cannot send data to a database site.

However, the following "end run" might be considered for computing a semi-join. The query site, A, executes a SELECT statement at the first database site, B, which returns the projection, P, used in computing the semi-join. Site A then uses the projection to dynamically construct another SELECT statement whose result set is the semi-join. Using Example 16.3.1 on page 699 of Section 16.3.1 involving tables STUDENT and TRANSCRIPT, give the two queries. Under what circumstances could such an approach be considered?

17

OLAP and Data Mining

This chapter is an introduction to the concepts and techniques from the fields of *online analytical processing* (OLAP), *data warehousing*, and *data mining*. Recall from our discussion in Section 1.4 that while online transaction processing (OLTP) is concerned with using a database to maintain an accurate model of some real-world situation, OLAP and data mining are concerned with using the information in a database to guide strategic decisions. OLAP is concerned with obtaining specific information, while data mining can be viewed as knowledge discovery. Data warehouses are used to accumulate and store the information needed for OLAP and data mining queries.

In Sections 17.2 and 17.3, you will learn about the multidimensional model for OLAP and related notions, such as CUBE and ROLLUP. In Sections 17.7 and beyond, you will be introduced to a number of important techniques, including the a priori algorithm for computing associations, the ID3 and C4.5 algorithms for training decision trees using the information gain measure, the perceptron and back propagation learning algorithms for neural nets, and the K-means and hierarchical algorithms (using dendrograms) for clustering.

17.1 OLAP and Data Warehouses—Old and New

Why is so much free material available on the Internet—all for just filling out a form? In fact, the goodies you receive are not free—you are paying for them by providing information about yourself, and, when you buy on the Internet, you are providing even more information about yourself—your buying habits.

You also provide information about yourself when you purchase items in a department store or supermarket with your credit card. In these cases, you are inputting information into a transaction processing system, and the system is saving that information for future use.

What is done with this information? In many situations, it is combined with what is known about you from other sources, stored in a database, and then

■ It might be combined with information about the purchases of other people to help an enterprise plan its inventory, advertising, or other aspects of its future strategy.

■ It might be used to produce an individualized profile of your buying (or browsing) habits so that an enterprise can target its marketing to you through the mail or in other ways. Perhaps in the future, the people in your zip code area will see different TV commercials based on information about their purchasing habits. Or perhaps you will see TV commercials personalized for you.

These trends in information gathering and assimilation have serious implications for personal privacy. Do you want strangers to be able to access this information and use it in ways of which you might not approve? However, that is not our concern in this text. Our concern is to understand the techniques that might be used to analyze this data.

The applications that use data of this type are referred to as **online analytic processing**, or **OLAP**, in contrast with **online transaction processing**, or OLTP. The two types of applications have different goals and different technical requirements.

■ The goal of OLTP is to maintain a database that is an accurate model of some real-world enterprise. The system must provide sufficiently large transaction throughput and low response time to keep up with the load and avoid user frustration. OLTP applications are characterized by

- Short, simple transactions
- Relatively frequent updates
- Transactions that access only a tiny fraction of the database

■ The goal of OLAP is to use the information in a database to guide strategic decisions. The databases involved are usually very large and often need not be completely accurate or up to date. Nor is fast response always required. OLAP applications are characterized by

- Complex queries
- Infrequent updates
- Transactions that access a significant fraction of the database

One might say that OLTP is *operational* in that it deals with the everyday operations of the enterprise, while OLAP is *decisional* in that it deals with decision making by the managers of the enterprise.

The example of an OLAP application in Section 1.4 involved managers of a supermarket chain who want to make one-time (not preprogrammed) queries to the database to gather information they need in order to make a specific decision. This illustrates the traditional use of OLAP—ad hoc queries, often made by people who are not highly technical.

The OLAP examples at the beginning of this section describe some of the newer uses. Businesses are using preprogrammed queries against OLAP databases on an ongoing operational basis to customize marketing and other aspects of their business. These queries are often complex and, since they are key to the business and used operationally (perhaps daily or weekly), are designed and implemented by professionals.

In traditional OLAP applications, the information in the OLAP database is often just the data the business happens to gather during day-to-day operations—perhaps in its OLTP systems. In newer applications, the business often makes an active effort to gather—perhaps even to purchase—the additional information needed for its planned application.

As the *A* in OLAP implies, the goal of an OLAP application is to *analyze* data for use in some application. Thus, there are often two separate but related subjects.

- *The analysis to be performed.* For example, a company wants to decide the mix of products to manufacture during the next accounting period. It develops an analysis procedure that requires as input the sales for the last period and the history of sales for the equivalent periods over the past five years.

- *The methods to efficiently obtain the large amounts of data required for the analysis.* For example, how can the company extract the required sales data from databases in its subsidiary departments? In what form should it store this data in the OLAP database? How can it retrieve the data efficiently when needed for the analysis?

The first issue, analysis, is not a database problem since it requires algorithms specific to the particular business in which the company engages. Our interest is primarily in the second issue—database support for these analytical procedures. For our purposes, we assume that the retrieved data is simply displayed on the screen. However, in many situations—particularly in newer applications—this data is input to sophisticated analysis procedures.

Data warehouses. OLAP databases are usually stored in special OLAP servers, often called **data warehouses**, which are structured to support the OLAP queries that will be made against them. OLAP queries are often so complex that if they were run in an OLTP environment, they would slow down OLTP transactions to an unacceptable degree.

We will discuss some of the issues involved in populating a data warehouse in Section 17.6. First, we will look at the kinds of data we might want to store in the warehouse.

17.2 A Multidimensional Model for OLAP Applications

Fact tables and dimension tables. Many OLAP applications are similar to the supermarket example of Section 1.4: analysis of sales of different products in different supermarkets over different time periods. We might describe this sales data with a relational table such as that shown in Figure 17.1. Market_Id identifies a particular supermarket, Product_Id identifies a particular product, Time_Id identifies a particular time interval, and Sales_Amt identifies the dollar value of the sales of that product at that supermarket in that time period. Such a table is called a **fact table** because it contains all of the facts about the data to be analyzed.

We can view this data as **multidimensional**. The Market_Id, Product_Id, and Time_Id attributes are the dimensions and correspond to the arguments of a function. The Sales_Amt attribute corresponds to the value of the function.

SALES	Market_Id	Product_Id	Time_Id	Sales_Amt
	M1	P1	T1	1000
	M1	P2	T1	2000
	M1	P3	T1	1500
	M1	P4	T1	2500
	M2	P1	T1	500
	M2	P2	T1	800
	M2	P3	T1	0
	M2	P4	T1	3333
	M3	P1	T1	5000
	M3	P2	T1	8000
	M3	P3	T1	10
	M3	P4	T1	3300
	M1	P1	T2	1001
	M1	P2	T2	2001
	M1	P3	T2	1501
	M1	P4	T2	2501
	M2	P1	T2	501
	M2	P2	T2	801
	M2	P3	T2	1
	M2	P4	T2	3334
	M3	P1	T2	5001
	M3	P2	T2	8001
	M3	P3	T2	11
	M3	P4	T2	3301
	M1	P1	T3	1002
	M1	P2	T3	2002
	M1	P3	T3	1502
	M1	P4	T3	2502
	M2	P1	T3	502
	M2	P2	T3	802
	M2	P3	T3	2
	M2	P4	T3	333
	M3	P1	T3	5002
	M3	P2	T3	8002
	M3	P3	T3	12
	M3	P4	T3	3302

FIGURE 17.1 The fact table for the supermarket application.

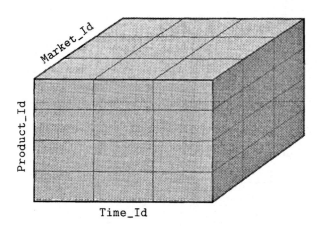

FIGURE 17.2 Three-dimensional cube for the supermarket application.

We can also think of the data in a fact table as being arranged in a multi-dimensional cube. Thus, in the supermarket example, the data is arranged in the three-dimensional cube shown in Figure 17.2, where the dimensions of the cube are Market_Id, Product_Id, and Time_Id and the vertices, or **cells**, of the cube contain the corresponding Sales_Amt. Such a multidimensional view can be an intuitive way to think about OLAP queries and their results.

Additional information about the dimensions can be stored in **dimension tables**, which describe dimension attributes. For the supermarket example, these tables might be called MARKET, PRODUCT, and TIME, as shown in Figure 17.3. The MARKET table describes the market: its city, state, and region. In a more realistic example, the MARKET table would contain a row for each supermarket in the chain, which might include many markets in each city, many cities in each state, and many states in each region.

Star schema. The relations corresponding to the supermarket example can be displayed in a diagram, as in Figure 17.4. The figure suggests a star, with the fact table at the center and the dimension tables radiating from it. This type of schema, called a **star schema**, is very common in OLAP applications. It is interesting to note that a star schema corresponds to a very common fragment of an entity-relation diagram, where the fact table is a relationship and the dimension tables are entities.

If the dimension tables are normalized (so that each might become several tables), the figure gets a bit more complex and is called a **snowflake schema**. However, for two reasons, dimension tables are rarely normalized:

1. They are so small compared with the fact table that the space saved due to the elimination of redundancy is negligible.

2. They are updated so infrequently that update anomalies are not an issue. Moreover, in this situation, decomposing the relations into 3NF or BCNF might lead to significant query overhead, as explained in Section 6.13.

MARKET	Market_Id	City	State	Region
	M1	Stony Brook	New York	East
	M2	Newark	New Jersey	East
	M3	Oakland	California	West

PRODUCT	Product_Id	Name	Category	Price
	P1	Beer	Drink	1.98
	P2	Diapers	Soft Goods	2.98
	P3	Cold Cuts	Meat	3.98
	P4	Soda	Drink	1.25

TIME	Time_Id	Week	Month	Quarter
	T1	Wk-1	January	First
	T2	Wk-24	June	Second
	T3	Wk-52	December	Fourth

FIGURE 17.3 Dimension tables for the supermarket application.

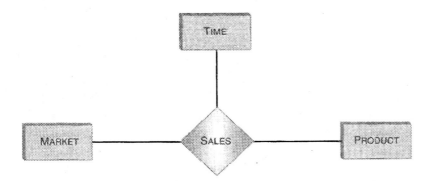

FIGURE 17.4 Star schema for the supermarket example.

Instead of a star schema, many OLAP applications use a **constellation schema**, which consists of several fact tables that might share one or more dimension tables. For example, the supermarket application might maintain a fact table called INVENTORY, with dimension tables WAREHOUSE, PRODUCT, and TIME, as shown in Figure 17.5. Note that the PRODUCT and TIME dimension tables are shared with the SALES fact table, whereas the WAREHOUSE table, which describes where the inventory is stored, is not shared.

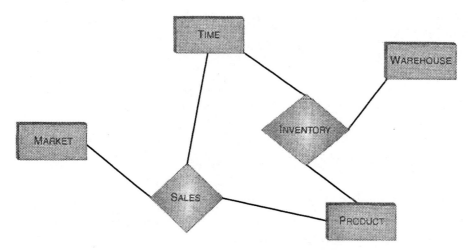

FIGURE 17.5 Constellation schema for the expanded supermarket example.

SUM(Sales_Amt)		Market_Id		
		M1	M2	M3
	P1	3003	1503	15003
Product_Id	P2	6003	2402	24003
	P3	4503	3	33
	P4	7503	7000	9903

FIGURE 17.6 Query result that aggregates `Sales_Amt` on the time dimension.

17.3 Aggregation

Many OLAP queries involve **aggregation** of the data in the fact table. For example, a query that produces the total sales (over time) of each product in each market can be expressed with the SQL statement

```
SELECT      S.Market_Id, S.Product_Id, SUM(S.Sales_Amt)
FROM        SALES S
GROUP BY    S.Market_Id, S.Product_Id
```

which returns the result table shown in Figure 17.6. Here we depict the result table as a two-dimensional cube with the values of the aggregation over `Sales_Amt` placed in the cells. Since this aggregation is over the entire time dimension (i.e., the result does not depend on the time coordinate), it produces a reduced-dimensional view of the data—two dimensions instead of three.

SUM(Sales_Amt)		Region			
		North	South	East	West
	P1	0	0	4506	15003
Product_Id	P2	0	0	8405	24003
	P3	0	0	4506	33
	P4	0	0	14503	9903

FIGURE 17.7 Query result that drills down on regions.

17.3.1 Drilling, Slicing, Rolling, and Dicing

Some dimension tables represent an **aggregation hierarchy**. For example, the MAR-KET table represents the hierarchy

```
Market_Id → City → State → Region
```

meaning that supermarkets are in cities, cities are in states, and states are in regions. We can perform queries at different levels of a hierarchy, as shown here:

```
SELECT      S.Product_Id, M.Region, SUM(S.Sales_Amt)
FROM        SALES S,    MARKET M
WHERE       M.Market_Id = S.Market_Id                      17.1
GROUP BY    S.Product_Id, M.Region
```

This produces the table of Figure 17.7, which aggregates total sales per product for each region over all time.

When we execute a sequence of queries that move down a hierarchy—from general to specific, such as moving from aggregation over regions to aggregation over states—we are said to be **drilling down**. Drilling down, of course, requires access to more specific information than is contained in the result of a more general query. Thus, in order to aggregate over states, we must either use the fact table or a previously computed table that aggregates over cities. Thus, we might use the fact table to drill down to states with

```
SELECT      S.Product_Id, M.State, SUM(S.Sales_Amt)
FROM        SALES S,    MARKET M
WHERE       M.Market_Id = S.Market_Id                      17.2
GROUP BY    S.Product_Id, M.State
```

When we move up the hierarchy (for example, from aggregation over states to aggregation over regions), we are said to be **rolling up**. For example, if we were to save the result of executing the query (17.2) as a table called STATE_SALES, then we could roll up the hierarchy using the query

SUM(Sales_Amt)		Quarter			
		First	Second	Third	Fourth
	P1	6500	6503	0	6506
Product_Id	P2	10800	10803	0	10806
	P3	1510	1513	0	1516
	P4	9133	9136	0	6137

FIGURE 17.8 Query result that presents total product sales for each quarter.

```
SELECT       T.Product_Id, M.Region, SUM(T.Sales_Amt)
FROM         STATE_SALES T,   MARKET M
WHERE        R.State = T.State
GROUP BY     T.Product_Id, R.Region
```

While this is not an efficient way to aggregate over regions, it demonstrates the ability to use previously computed results when rolling up. This is an important optimization and has motivated the inclusion in SQL of special features, which we will discuss shortly. It is very common to roll up or drill down using the time dimension—for example, to summarize sales on a daily, monthly, or quarterly basis.

Here is a bit more OLAP terminology. When we view the data in the form of a multidimensional cube and then select a subset of the axes, we are said to be performing a **pivot** (we are reorienting the multidimensional cube). The selected axes correspond to the list of attributes in the GROUP BY clause. Pivoting is usually followed by aggregation on the remaining axes.

As an example, the following query performs a pivot of the multidimensional cube to view it from the product and time dimensions. It finds the total sales (over all markets) of each product for each quarter (of the current year) and produces the table of Figure 17.8:

```
SELECT       S.Product_Id, T.Quarter,   SUM(S.Sales_Amt)
FROM         SALES S,   TIME T
WHERE        T.Time_Id = S.Time_Id
GROUP BY     S.Product_Id, T.Quarter
```
17.3

If we next ask the same query, but use the GROUP BY clause to group by years instead of by quarters, we are rolling up the time hierarchy. *grouped by years instead of quarters - rollup*

```
SELECT       S.Product_Id, T.Year, SUM(S.Sales_Amt)
FROM         SALES S,   TIME T
WHERE        T.Time_Id = S.Time_Id
GROUP BY     S.Product_Id, T.Year
```

SQL:1999/2003 and some OLAP vendors support a new SQL clause, **ROLLUP**, to simplify this process (see Section 17.3.2). However, notice that a corresponding drill-down clause is usually *not* provided. The reason is that rollup is not only a convenience but also an optimization device. If the user first asks to aggregate over quarters and then rolls up the result to years, the OLAP system does not need to compute from scratch but can aggregate to the year using the previously computed aggregation results for each quarter. No such optimization is possible for drilling down. However, OLAP systems typically let the user precompute and cache certain aggregations in order to speed up the drilling down process. For instance, if we are expected to drill down to weeks and quarters, we might ask the system to precompute aggregations of the data cube grouping by weeks in the time dimension. Then when we drill down to weeks or quarters we will not need to sum up the sales figures for each particular value of the `Time_Id` attribute. Instead, when we group by `Week` or `Quarter` we will be summing up the already precomputed weekly sales figures—a much smaller number of items.

> Rollup can be optimized through the reuse of the results of previous requests. Drilling down can be sped up by precomputing and caching certain carefully selected aggregations.

Not all aggregation hierarchies are linear, as is the location hierarchy. The time hierarchy shown in Figure 17.9, for example, is a lattice. Weeks are not fully contained in months—the same week can fall on the boundary for two different months. Thus, we can roll up days into either weeks or months, but we can only roll up weeks into quarters.

Note that all of the above queries access a significant fraction of the data in the fact table. By contrast, the OLTP query to the database at your local supermarket *How many cans of tomato juice are in stock?* accesses only a single tuple.

Slicing and dicing.   We can imagine that the hierarchy for each dimension partitions the multidimensional cube into subcubes. Thus, for example, the `Quarter`

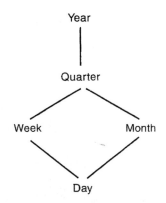

FIGURE 17.9 Time hierarchy as a lattice.

level of the time dimension partitions the cube into subcubes, one for each quarter. Queries that return information about those subcubes are said to **slice and dice**.

■ When we pivot, that is, use a GROUP BY clause in a query to specify a level in a hierarchy, we are partitioning the multidimensional cube into subcubes: all the elements in the contained level are grouped together. For example, if we group by product Id and quarter, as in the query (17.3), all transactions for the same product in the same quarter are grouped together. Thus, pivoting creates the effect of **dicing** the data cube into subcubes.

■ When we use a WHERE clause that equates a dimension attribute to a constant, we are specifying a particular value for that dimension and so are performing a **slice**.

Typically pivoting and slicing are used together, so it has become known as "slicing and dicing." For example, a query that requests the total product sales in each market in the first quarter

```
SELECT      S.Product_Id, SUM(S.Sales_Amt)
FROM        SALES S, TIME T
WHERE       T.Time_Id = S.Time_Id AND T.Quarter = 'First'
GROUP BY    S.Product_Id
```

is an example of a slice in the time dimension and dice in the product dimension. Thus, pivoting "dices" (partitions) the cube into subcubes along the specified dimensions and slicing selects a cross section that cuts across these subcubes.

17.3.2 The CUBE Operator

Many OLAP queries use the aggregate functions and the GROUP BY clause of the SELECT statement to perform aggregation. However, the standard options for the SELECT statement limit the types of OLAP queries that can be easily formulated in SQL. A number of OLAP vendors (as well as SQL:1999/2003) extend SQL with additional aggregate functions, and some vendors even allow programmers to specify their own aggregate functions.

One extension in this direction is the ROLLUP operator; another is the CUBE operator introduced in [Gray et al. 1997]. Suppose that we want to obtain a table such as that in Figure 17.10. This table is similar to the one in Figure 17.6 except that, in addition, it has totals for each row and each column. To construct such a table, we would need to use four standard SQL SELECT statements to retrieve the necessary information. The following statement returns the data needed for the table entries (without the totals).

```
SELECT      S.Market_Id, S.Product_Id, SUM(S.Sales_Amt)
FROM        SALES S
GROUP BY    S.Market_Id, S.Product_Id
```

SUM(Sales_Amt)		Market_Id			
		M1	M2	M3	Total
Product_Id	P1	3003	1503	15003	19509
	P2	6003	2402	24003	32408
	P3	4503	3	33	4539
	P4	7503	7000	9903	24406
	Total	21012	10908	48942	80862

FIGURE 17.10 Query result for the sales application in the form of a spreadsheet.

The next statement computes the row totals:

```
SELECT      S.Product_Id, SUM(S.Sales_Amt)
FROM        SALES S
GROUP BY    S.Product_Id
```

This statement computes the totals for the columns:

```
SELECT      S.Market_Id, SUM(S.Sales_Amt)
FROM        SALES S
GROUP BY    S.Market_Id
```

and the last statement computes the grand total of 80862 in the lower right corner:

```
SELECT      SUM(S.Sales_Amt)
FROM        SALES S
```

Four statements are required because the table needs four aggregations—by time, by product Id and time, by market Id and time, and by all attributes together. Each such aggregation is produced by a different GROUP BY clause.

Computing all of these queries *independently* is wasteful of both time and computing resources. The first query does much of the work needed for the other three queries, so, if we save the result and then use it to aggregate over Market_Id and Product_Id, we can compute the second and third queries more efficiently. Efficient computation of such "data cubes" is important in OLAP, and much research has been dedicated to this issue. See, for example, [Agrawal et al. 1996; Harinarayan et al. 1996; Ross and Srivastava 1997; Zhao et al. 1998].

Economy of scale is the main motivation for the CUBE clause [Gray et al. 1997], which is included in the SQL:1999/2003 standard. When CUBE is used in a GROUP BY clause,

```
GROUP BY CUBE(v1, v2, ..., vn)
```

it is equivalent to a collection of GROUP BYs, one for each of the $2^n - 1$ non-empty subsets of $v1, v2, \ldots, vn$, plus the query that does not have the GROUP BY clause, which corresponds to the empty subset. For example, the statement

```
SELECT   S.Market_Id, S.Product_Id, SUM(S.Sales_Amt)
FROM     SALES S
GROUP BY CUBE(S.Market_Id, S.Product_Id)
```

returns the result set of Figure 17.11, which is equivalent to all four of the above SELECT statements and includes all of the values required for the table of Figure 17.10. Note the NULL entries in the columns that are being aggregated. For example, the

RESULT SET	Market_Id	Product_Id	Sales_Amt
	M1	P1	3003
	M1	P2	6003
	M1	P3	4503
	M1	P4	7503
	M2	P1	1503
	M2	P2	2402
	M2	P3	3
	M2	P4	7000
	M3	P1	15003
	M3	P2	24003
	M3	P3	33
	M3	P4	9903
	M1	NULL	21012
	M2	NULL	10908
	M3	NULL	48942
	NULL	P1	19509
	NULL	P2	32408
	NULL	P3	4539
	NULL	P4	24406
	NULL	NULL	80862

FIGURE 17.11 Result set returned with the CUBE operator.

first NULL in the `Product_Id` column means that the sales for market M1 are being aggregated over all products.[1]

ROLLUP is similar to CUBE except that instead of aggregating all subsets of its arguments, it creates subsets by moving from right to left. Like CUBE, the ROLLUP option to the GROUP BY clause is included in SQL:1999/2003.

Consider the above SELECT statement in which CUBE has been replaced with ROLLUP:

```
SELECT   S.Market_Id, S.Product_Id, SUM(S.Sales_Amt)
FROM     SALES S                                              17.4
GROUP BY ROLLUP(S.Market_Id, S.Product_Id)
```

The syntax here says that aggregation should be computed first with the finest granularity, using GROUP BY S.Market_Id, S.Product_Id, and then with the next level of granularity, using GROUP BY S.Market_Id. Finally, the grand total is computed, which corresponds to the empty GROUP BY clause. The result set is depicted in Figure 17.12. In a larger example (with more attributes in the ROLLUP clause), the result set table would contain some rows with NULL in the last column, some with NULL in the last two columns, some with NULL in the last three columns, and so on.

Note that the ROLLUP operator of OLAP-extended SQL is a generalization of the idea of rolling up the aggregation hierarchy described on page 718. Moreover, the cost savings from reusing the results of fine-grained aggregations to compute coarser levels of aggregation apply to the general ROLLUP operator. For instance, in query (17.4), aggregations computed for the clause GROUP BY S.Market_Id, S.Product_Id can be reused in the computation of aggregates for the clause GROUP BY S.Market_Id. These aggregates can then be reused in the computation of the grand total.

Materialized views using the CUBE operator. The CUBE operator can be used to precompute aggregations on all dimensions of a fact table and then save them for use in future queries. Thus, the statement

```
SELECT   S.Market_Id, S.Product_Id, SUM(S.Sales_Amt)
FROM     SALES S
GROUP BY CUBE(S.Market_Id, S.Product_Id, S.Time_Id)
```

produces a result set that is the table of Figure 17.1 with the addition of rows corresponding to aggregations on all subsets of the dimensions. The *additional* rows

---

[1] The use of SQL NULL in this context might be confusing because in this context NULL actually means "all" (it is the aggregation of one of the dimensions).

RESULT SET	Market_ Id	Product_Id	Sales_Amt
	M1	P1	3003
	M1	P2	6003
	M1	P3	4503
	M1	P4	7503
	M2	P1	1503
	M2	P2	2402
	M2	P3	3
	M2	P4	7000
	M3	P1	15003
	M3	P2	24003
	M3	P3	33
	M3	P4	9903
	M1	NULL	21012
	M2	NULL	10908
	M3	NULL	48092
	NULL	NULL	80862

FIGURE **17.12** Result set returned with the ROLLUP operator.

are shown in Figure 17.13. If this result set is saved as a materialized view (see Section 5.2.9), it can speed up subsequent queries.

Several materialized views can be prepared (with or without the CUBE operator) and used to speed up queries throughout the entire OLAP application. Of course, each such materialized view requires additional storage space, so there is some limit on the number of materialized views that can be constructed. Since updates are infrequent, the view update problem is not an issue.

17.4 ROLAP and MOLAP

We have been assuming that the OLAP data is stored in a relational database as one (or more) star schemas. Such an implementation is referred to as **relational OLAP** (ROLAP).

Some vendors provide OLAP servers that implement the fact table as a **data cube** using some sort of multidimensional (nonrelational) implementation, often with a substantial amount of precomputed aggregation. Such implementations are referred to as **multidimensional OLAP** (MOLAP). Note that in ROLAP implementations, a data cube is a way to think about the data; in MOLAP implementations, the data is actually stored in some representation of a data cube.

RESULT SET	Market_Id	Product_Id	Time_Id	Sales_Amt
	. . .	. . .	. . .	. . .
	NULL	P1	T1	6500
	NULL	P2	T1	10800
	NULL	P3	T1	1510
	NULL	P4	T1	9133
	NULL	P1	T2	6503
	NULL	P2	T2	10803
	NULL	P3	T2	1513
	NULL	P4	T2	9136
	NULL	P1	T3	6506
	NULL	P2	T3	10806
	NULL	P3	T3	1516
	NULL	P4	T3	6137
	M1	NULL	T1	7000
	M2	NULL	T1	4633
	M3	NULL	T1	4610
	M1	NULL	T2	7004
	M2	NULL	T2	4634
	M3	NULL	T2	16314
	M1	NULL	T3	7008
	M2	NULL	T3	1639
	M3	NULL	T3	16318
	M1	P1	NULL	3003
	M1	P2	NULL	6003
	M1	P3	NULL	4503
	M1	P4	NULL	7503
	M2	P1	NULL	1503
	M2	P2	NULL	2402
	M2	P3	NULL	3
	M2	P4	NULL	7000
	M3	P1	NULL	15003
	M3	P2	NULL	24003
	M3	P3	NULL	33
	M3	P4	NULL	9903
	NULL	NULL	T1	16243
	NULL	NULL	T2	27952

FIGURE 17.13 Tuples added to the fact table by the CUBE operator.

RESULT SET	Market_Id	Product_Id	Time_Id	Sales_Amt
	NULL	NULL	T3	24967
	NULL	P1	NULL	19509
	NULL	P2	NULL	32408
	NULL	P3	NULL	4539
	NULL	P4	NULL	24406
	M1	NULL	NULL	31012
	M2	NULL	NULL	10908
	M3	NULL	NULL	48942
	NULL	NULL	NULL	80862

FIGURE 17.13 (continued)

One use of the CUBE operator is to compute the aggregations needed to load a MOLAP database from an SQL database. Many MOLAP systems also allow the user to specify certain other aggregations that are to be stored as materialized views. Their databases provide efficient implementations of certain (perhaps nonrelational) operations often used in OLAP, such as aggregations at different levels of a hierarchy.

There is no standard query language for MOLAP implementations, but a number of MOLAP (and ROLAP) vendors provide proprietary, sometimes visual, languages that allow technically unsophisticated users to compute tables such as that in Figure 17.10 with a single query, and then to pivot, drill down, or roll up on any table dimension, sometimes with a single click of a mouse.

Not all commercial decision support applications use ROLAP (with star schemas) or MOLAP database servers. Many use conventional relational databases with schemas designed for their particular application. For example, several complex SQL queries used throughout this book can be viewed as OLAP queries (e.g., *List all professors who have taught all courses* . . .). Indeed, any query that uses complicated joins or nested SELECT statements is probably useful only for analysis since its execution time is too long for an OLTP system.

17.5 Implementation Issues

Most of the specialized implementation techniques for OLAP systems are derived from the key technical characteristic of OLAP applications:

> OLAP applications deal with very large amounts of data, but that data is relatively static and updates are infrequent.

Moreover, many of these techniques involve precomputing partial results or indices, which makes them particularly appropriate when queries are known in advance—for example, when they are embedded into an operational OLAP application. They can also be used for ad hoc (nonprogrammed) queries if the database designer or administrator has some idea as to what those queries will be.

One technique is to precompute some often-used aggregations and store them in the database. These include aggregations over some of the dimension hierarchies. Since the data does not change often, the overhead of maintaining the aggregation values is small.

Another technique is to use indices particularly oriented toward the queries that will be made. Since data updates are infrequent, the usual overhead of index maintenance is minimal. Two examples of such indices are *join* and *bitmap* indices.

Star joins and join indices. A join of the relations in a star schema, called a **star join**, can be optimized using a special index structure, called a **join index**, as discussed in Section 9.7.2. All recent releases of major commercial DBMSs are capable of recognizing and optimizing star joins.

Bitmap indices. Bitmap indices, introduced in Section 9.7.1, are particularly useful for indexing attributes that can take only a small number of values. Such attributes occur frequently in OLAP applications. For example, Region in the MARKET table might take only four values: North, South, East, and West. If the MARKET table has a total of 10,000 rows, a bitmap index on Region contains four bit vectors, with a total storage requirement of 40,000 bits or 5K bytes. An index of this size can easily fit in main memory and can provide quick access to records with corresponding values.

17.6 Populating a Data Warehouse

Data for both OLAP and data mining is usually stored in a special database often called a **data warehouse**. Data warehouses are usually very large, perhaps containing terabytes of data that have been gathered at different times from a number of sources, including databases from different vendors and with different schemas. Merging such data into a single OLAP database is not trivial. Additional problems arise when that data has to be periodically updated.

Two important operations must be performed on the data before it can be loaded into the warehouse.

1. *Transformation*. The data from the different source DBMSs must be transformed, both syntactically and semantically, into the common format required by the warehouse.

   (a) *Syntactic transformation*. The syntax used by the different DBMSs to represent the same data might be different. For example, the schema in one DBMS might represent Social Security numbers with the attribute SSN while another might use SSnum. One might represent it as a character string, another as an integer.

(b) *Semantic transformation.* The semantics used by the different DBMSs to represent the same data might be different. For example, the warehouse might summarize sales on a daily basis, while one DBMS summarizes them on an hourly basis and another does not summarize sales at all but merely provides information about individual transactions.

2. *Data cleaning.* The data must be examined to correct any errors and missing information. We might think that data obtained from an OLTP database should be correct, but experience indicates otherwise. Moreover, some erroneous data might have been obtained from sources other than an OLTP database—for example, an incorrect zip code on a form filled in on the Internet.

Often the term "data cleaning" is used to describe both types of operations. Although there is no general design theory for performing these operations, a number of vendors supply tools that do a decent job for concrete domains such as postal addresses, product descriptions, and the like.

If no data cleaning is necessary and the sources are relational databases that have schemas sufficiently similar to that of the warehouse, the data can sometimes be extracted from the sources and inserted into the warehouse with a single SQL statement. For example, assume that each store, M, in the supermarket chain has an M_SALES table with schema M_SALES(Product_Id, Time_Id, Sales_Amt), which records M's sales of each product for each time period. Then, after time period T4, we can update the fact table (Figure 17.1) stored in the data warehouse with the sales information for market M in time period T4 with the statement

```
INSERT INTO SALES(Market_Id, Product_Id, Time_Id, Sales_Amt)
    SELECT Market_Id = 'M', S.Product_Id, S.Time_Id, S.Sales_Amt
    FROM M_SALES  S
    WHERE S.Time_Id = 'T4'
```

If data cleaning or reformatting is needed, the data to be extracted can be represented as nonmaterialized views over the source databases. A cleansing program can then retrieve the data through the views (without requiring knowledge of the individual database schemas) for further processing before inserting it into the warehouse database.

As with other types of databases, an OLAP database must include a **metadata repository** containing information about the physical and logical organization of the data, including its schema, indices, and the like. For data warehouses, the repository must also include information about the source of all data and the dates on which it was loaded and refreshed.

The large volume of data in an OLAP database makes loading and updating a significant task. For the sake of efficiency, updating is usually incremental. Different parts of the database are updated at different times. Unfortunately, however, incremental updating might leave the database in an inconsistent state. It might

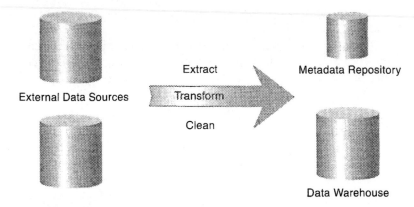

FIGURE 17.14 Loading data into an OLAP database.

not satisfy certain integrity constraints or it might not exactly describe the current state of the enterprise at the current instant. Usually, this is not an important issue for OLAP queries because much of the data analysis involves only summaries and statistical analyses, which are not significantly affected by such inconsistencies.

Figure 17.14 summarizes the processes involved in loading an OLAP database.

17.7 Data Mining Tasks

Data mining is an attempt at knowledge discovery—searching for patterns and structure in large data sets, as contrasted with requesting specific information. If OLAP is about confirming the known, we might say that data mining is about exploring the unknown.

Data mining uses techniques from many disciplines, such as statistical analysis, pattern recognition, machine learning, and artificial intelligence. Our main interest is in understanding these techniques and how they are used to process large data sets. Data mining with its associated data warehousing, data displaying, etc. is sometimes called *Knowledge Discovery in Databases* (KDD).

Among the goals of data mining are

- *Association*. Finding patterns in data that associate instances of that data with other related instances of that data. For example, *Amazon.com* associates the information about books purchased by its customers so that if a particular customer purchases some book, it then suggests other books that this customer might also want to purchase.

- *Classification*. Finding patterns in data that can be used to classify that data (and possibly the people it describes) into certain interesting categories. For example, a company might classify its customers based on their past purchases as either "high-end buyers" or "low-end buyers." This information might then be used to target specific advertisements to those customers.

One important application of classification is for *prediction*. For example, a bank might gather data about the customers who did or did not default on their mortgages over the past five years: their net worth, their income, their marital status, etc. and use that data to classify each customer as a *defaulter* or a *nondefaulter* based on this data. When new customers apply for a mortgage, the bank might use the data on their net worth, income, and marital status to predict whether or not they would default on their mortgage if the application were approved.

■ *Clustering.* As with classification, clustering involves finding patterns in data that can be used to classify that data (and possibly the people it describes) into certain interesting categories. However, in contrast with classification, in which the categories are specified by the analyst, in clustering, the categories are discovered by the clustering algorithm.

17.8 Mining Associations

One of the more important applications of data mining is finding associations. An **association** is a correlation between certain values in the database. We gave an example of such a correlation in Section 1.4:

In a convenience store in the early evening, a high percentage of customers who bought diapers also bought beer.

This association can be described using the **association rule**

Purchase_diapers $\Rightarrow$ *Purchase_ beer* **17.5**

An association can involve more than two items. For example, it might assert that, if a customer buys cream cheese and lox, she is likely to also buy bagels (if the customer buys only cream cheese, she might be planning to use it for a different purpose and therefore not buy bagels).

Purchase_creamcheese AND *Purchase_lox* $\Rightarrow$ *Purchase_bagels*

To see how the association (17.5) might have been discovered, assume that the convenience store maintains a PURCHASES table, shown in Figure 17.15, which it computes from its OLTP system. Based on this table, the data mining system can compute two measures:

1. *The* **confidence** *for an association.* The percentage of transactions that contain the items on the right side of the association among the transactions that contain the items on the left side of the association. The first three transactions of Figure 17.15 contain diapers, and of these, the first two also contain beer. Hence the confidence for association (17.5) is 66.66%.

PURCHASES	Transaction_Id	Product
	001	diapers
	001	beer
	001	popcorn
	001	bread
	002	diapers
	002	cheese
	002	soda
	002	beer
	002	juice
	003	diapers
	003	cold cuts
	003	cookies
	003	napkins
	004	cereal
	004	beer
	004	cold cuts

FIGURE 17.15 PURCHASES table used for data mining.

2. *The* **support** *for an association*. The percentage of transactions that contain all items (on both the left and right sides) of the association. Two of the four transactions in Figure 17.15 contain both items. Hence the support for association (17.5) is 50%. We also define the support for a single item as the percentage of transactions that contain that item.

The purpose of the confidence factor is to certify that there is certain probability that if a transaction includes all items on the left side of the association—*Purchase_diapers* in (17.5)—then the item on the right side will appear as well—*Purchase_beer*. If the confidence factor is high enough, the convenience store manager might want to put a beer display at the end of the diaper aisle.

However, confidence alone might not provide reliable information. We need to make sure that the correlation it represents is statistically significant. For instance, the confidence for the association *Purchase_cookies* $\Rightarrow$ *Purchase_napkins* is 100%, but there is only one transaction where napkins and cookies are involved, so this association is most likely not statistically significant. The support of an association deals with this issue by measuring the fraction of transactions in which the association is actually demonstrated.

To assert that the association exists, both of the above measures must be above a certain threshold. Selecting appropriate thresholds is part of the discipline of statistical analysis and is beyond the scope of this book.

It is relatively easy for the system to compute the support and confidence for a particular association. That is an OLAP query. However, it is much more difficult for the system to return all possible associations for which the confidence and support are above a certain threshold. That is a data mining query. The idea of mining for association rules and some early algorithms were first introduced in [Agrawal et al. 1993].

We present an efficient algorithm for retrieving the data needed to determine all associations for which the support is larger than a given threshold, T. As we will see, once we have found those associations it is easy to determine which of them has a confidence factor greater than some given threshold.

Assume that we are trying to find all associations $A \Rightarrow B$ for which the support is greater than T. The naive approach is to compute the support for $A_i \Rightarrow B_j$ for all pairs of distinct items, A_i and B_j. However, if there are n items, $n(n-1)$ pairs have to be tried. This is usually too costly. The situation is even more difficult if we are interested in associations in which the left side contains more than one item, for example A AND $C \Rightarrow B$. Now we would have to compute the support for all triples of items, A_i, B_i, and C_i. It would be still more difficult if we are interested in associations with *any* number of items on the left side.

We call such sets of items $(A_i, B_i, \ldots)$ **itemsets**. Our goal is to find all itemsets for which the support is greater than T. The plan is to first find all single items for which the support is greater than T, then use that information to find all pairs of items with support greater than T, and so on. We consider only the case of associations among two items, but the same ideas generalize to associations with more than one item on the left side

The algorithm we use, called the **a priori algorithm**, is based on the following observation, which follows from the fact that if A and B appear together in R rows, then A and B each appear in at least R rows—and perhaps even more.

> *If the support for an association* A ⇒ B *(or an itemset* A, B*) is larger than* T, *then the support for both* A *and* B *separately must be larger than* T.

Based on this observation, the a priori algorithm for pairs of items can be described as follows:

1. *Find all individual items whose support is greater than* T. This requires examining n items. The number of items with high enough support, m, is likely to be much less than n.

2. *Among these* m *items, find all distinct pairs of items whose support is greater than* T. This requires examining $m * (m-1)$ pairs of items. Assume the number of such pairs with high enough support is p.

3. *Compute the confidence factor for these* p *associations.*

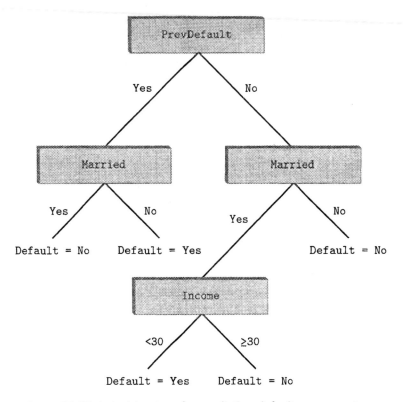

FIGURE 17.17 A decision tree for predicting defaults on a mortgage.

from the training set so that those rules can be used to predict, hopefully with a high success rate, the future behavior of new customers.

One measure of the quality of the decision tree is the percentage of errors that occur when the tree is used to make decisions using all the entries in the training set table, the so-called **training-set error**. Often, some of the historical entries in such a table are not used as part of the training set but are used as a **test set**. After the decision tree has been constructed, the data in the test set is used to test the tree. The percentage of errors using these entries is called the **test-set error**.

Sometimes the test-set error is significantly larger than the training-set error. One reason for this might be that the classification rules implied by the resulting decision tree **overfit** the training data by being tuned to some features peculiar to the particular training set that happened to be selected and not present in the general data. One approach to dealing with such overfitting is to ignore some of the data in the training set—particularly the data that provides the least information about the decision (see the discussion in the next few paragraphs). This can result in the decision tree being **pruned**, that is, all the nodes below a given node (or nodes) are removed, and the best possible decision is made at each such node, again based on the information provided by the remaining data in the training set. We discuss

pruning might be done later in this section. As we shall see, frequently
ng is accomplished with still another subset of the historical entries in the
the **validation set**, which is disjoint from both the training set and the

n decision trees. A number of algorithms have been developed for
decision tree from a training set, and many of these algorithms have
ented in commercial systems. We discuss one of these algorithms, **ID3**
decision trees) [Quinlan 1986]. The ID3 algorithm is "top down." It
ing an attribute to be used at the top level of the tree to make the first
hus produce the second-level nodes in the tree. Each value of that
a new level of the tree, and the process repeats on each level. A key
thm is how to pick the attribute on each level that best differentiates
training set.

e want to pick the attribute that maximizes the "purity" of the
levotees of the field would say). A selection is "pure" if it contains
of one outcome, and it is "impure" if it contains many instances
espond to both outcomes ("yes" and "no" in the example). The
that is used in the ID3 algorithm is **entropy**, which is defined as

$$-\sum_{i=1}^{n} p_i \, log_2 \, p_i$$

robability that an item has the outcome *i*) is approximated by the
as that have outcome *i*. This measure is borrowed from the field of
eory, where it is used to measure randomness or lack of information
n a set of data is, the less information it implies). Thus, again
v that we want to select the attribute that gives us the most
final decision.

he entries in a training table have an outcome of "yes" and
no." Then the entropy for the table would be

$$/2 \, log_2 \, 1/2 + 1/2 \, log_2 \, 1/2) = 1$$

ind corresponds to zero information. By contrast if all
of "no," the entropy for the table would be

$$-(1 \, log_2 \, 1) = 0$$

random and implies a maximum amount of information
s "no").

re 17.16, six entries have an outcome of "yes" and fourteen
no," so the entropy of the table is

$$-(6/20 \, log_2 \, 6/20 + 14/20 \, log_2 \, 14/20) = .881$$

to make the decision tree using the table in Figure 17.16 as a
initial goal is to find what attribute should be used to make the

CUSTOMER	Id	Married	Income	Default
	C3	no	135	yes
	C7	yes	10	no
	C10	yes	45	no
	C12	no	125	yes
	C13	yes	20	no
	C18	no	160	yes

FIGURE 17.18 The table used as the training set at the second level of the tree whe PrevDefault is "yes."

decision at the top level in the tree. We investigate, one at a time, each of attributes—PrevDefault, Married, and Income—to see which attribute provi the most information about the outcome.

If the topmost attribute were selected to be PrevDefault, the second level the tree would consist of two nodes, one corresponding to when PrevDefault "yes" and the other to when PrevDefault is "no." Each of these nodes would the topmost node of a subtree of the decision tree. The training sets for these tv subtrees would be the two tables: Figure 17.18 (for the subtree where PrevDefaul is "yes") and Figure 17.19 (for the subtree where PrevDefault is "no"). Each these tables is a subset of the table in Figure 17.16 consisting of those entries whe PrevDefault has the specified value and with the column for PrevDefault omitte

Now let us investigate how much information would be gained by usi PrevDefault as the topmost attribute. We start by computing the entropy of ea of the resulting subtables. When PrevDefault is "yes," four of the six outcomes "yes" and two are "no," so the entropy of that subtable is

$$-(4/6 \; log_2 \; 4/6 + 2/6 \; log_2 \; 2/6) = .918$$

When PrevDefault is "no," two of the fourteen outcomes are "yes" and twelve "no," so the entropy of that subtable is

$$-(2/14 \; log_2 \; 2/14 + 12/14 \; log_2 \; 12/14) = .592$$

Since the first subtable has six entries and the second has fourteen entri weighted average entropy of the two subtables is

$$(6/20 * .918) + (14/20 * .592) = .690$$

The measure used by the ID3 algorithm to determine which attribute t called the **information gain**. The algorithm compares the information ga by using each of the attributes and selects the attribute with the largest in gain. The information gain when using some attribute, A, as the topm how such pruning might be done later in this section. As we shall see, frequently this pruning is accomplished with still another subset of the historical entries in the table, called the **validation set**, which is disjoint from both the training set and the test set.

Induction on decision trees. A number of algorithms have been developed for producing a decision tree from a training set, and many of these algorithms have been implemented in commercial systems. We discuss one of these algorithms, **ID3** (induction of decision trees) [Quinlan 1986]. The ID3 algorithm is "top down." It starts by selecting an attribute to be used at the top level of the tree to make the first decision and thus produce the second-level nodes in the tree. Each value of that attribute starts a new level of the tree, and the process repeats on each level. A key part of the algorithm is how to pick the attribute on each level that best differentiates the items in the training set.

Intuitively we want to pick the attribute that maximizes the "purity" of the selection (as the devotees of the field would say). A selection is "pure" if it contains mainly instances of one outcome, and it is "impure" if it contains many instances of items that correspond to both outcomes ("yes" and "no" in the example). The measure of purity that is used in the ID3 algorithm is **entropy**, which is defined as

$$-\sum_{i=1}^{n} p_i \, log_2 \, p_i$$

where p_i (the probability that an item has the outcome i) is approximated by the fraction of items that have outcome i. This measure is borrowed from the field of information theory, where it is used to measure randomness or lack of information (the more random a set of data is, the less information it implies). Thus, again intuitively, we can say that we want to select the attribute that gives us the most information about the final decision.

Suppose that half of the entries in a training table have an outcome of "yes" and half have an outcome of "no." Then the entropy for the table would be

$$-(1/2 \, log_2 \, 1/2 + 1/2 \, log_2 \, 1/2) = 1$$

which is maximally random and corresponds to zero information. By contrast if all the entries have an outcome of "no," the entropy for the table would be

$$-(1 \, log_2 \, 1) = 0$$

which is maximally nonrandom and implies a maximum amount of information (that the only decision is "no").

In the table of Figure 17.16, six entries have an outcome of "yes" and fourteen have an outcome of "no," so the entropy of the table is

$$-(6/20 \, log_2 \, 6/20 + 14/20 \, log_2 \, 14/20) = .881$$

Now we begin to make the decision tree using the table in Figure 17.16 as a training set. Our initial goal is to find what attribute should be used to make the

CUSTOMER	Id	Married	Income	Default
	C3	no	135	yes
	C7	yes	10	no
	C10	yes	45	no
	C12	no	125	yes
	C13	yes	20	no
	C18	no	160	yes

FIGURE 17.18 The table used as the training set at the second level of the tree when PrevDefault is "yes."

decision at the top level in the tree. We investigate, one at a time, each of the attributes—PrevDefault, Married, and Income—to see which attribute provides the most information about the outcome.

If the topmost attribute were selected to be PrevDefault, the second level of the tree would consist of two nodes, one corresponding to when PrevDefault is "yes" and the other to when PrevDefault is "no." Each of these nodes would be the topmost node of a subtree of the decision tree. The training sets for these two subtrees would be the two tables: Figure 17.18 (for the subtree where PrevDefault is "yes") and Figure 17.19 (for the subtree where PrevDefault is "no"). Each of these tables is a subset of the table in Figure 17.16 consisting of those entries where PrevDefault has the specified value and with the column for PrevDefault omitted.

Now let us investigate how much information would be gained by using PrevDefault as the topmost attribute. We start by computing the entropy of each of the resulting subtables. When PrevDefault is "yes," four of the six outcomes are "yes" and two are "no," so the entropy of that subtable is

$$-(4/6 \; log_2 \; 4/6 + 2/6 \; log_2 \; 2/6) = .918$$

When PrevDefault is "no," two of the fourteen outcomes are "yes" and twelve are "no," so the entropy of that subtable is

$$-(2/14 \; log_2 \; 2/14 + 12/14 \; log_2 \; 12/14) = .592$$

Since the first subtable has six entries and the second has fourteen entries, the weighted average entropy of the two subtables is

$$(6/20 * .918) + (14/20 * .592) = .690$$

The measure used by the ID3 algorithm to determine which attribute to select is called the **information gain**. The algorithm compares the information gain implied by using each of the attributes and selects the attribute with the largest information gain. The information gain when using some attribute, A, as the topmost node in

CUSTOMER	Id	Married	Income	Default
	C1	yes	50	no
	C2	yes	100	no
	C4	yes	125	no
	C5	yes	50	no
	C6	no	30	no
	C8	yes	10	yes
	C9	yes	75	no
	C11	yes	60	yes
	C14	no	15	no
	C15	no	60	no
	C16	yes	15	yes
	C17	yes	35	no
	C19	yes	40	no
	C20	yes	30	no

FIGURE 17.19 The table used as the training set at the second level of the tree when `PrevDefault` is "no."

the tree constructed using a table, T, is the entropy of T minus the average entropy of the subtables determined by A:

> **Information gain**$(A, T) = entropy(T) - average(entropy(T_i)*weight(T_i))$

The average in the computation of the information gain is taken over all subtables T_i of T that are determined by the values of the attribute A. The weight of each subtable is the relative contribution of the rows of that subtable to the pool of rows in T: $weight(T_i) = |T_i|/|T|$, where $|\cdot|$ denotes the number of rows in a table. Thus the information gain for the attribute `PrevDefault` is

$$.881 - .690 = .191$$

Note that the attribute that provides the largest information gain is always the attribute whose subtables have the smallest average entropy (since for all calculations of information gain for different attributes, the average entropy corresponding to each attribute is subtracted from the same value of entropy for the complete table).

Now we compute the information gain implied by each of the other attributes. If we repeat the information gain calculation assuming the topmost attribute of the tree is Married, the information gain would be .056.[2] Clearly PrevDefault provides more information gain and would be a better choice for the topmost attribute.

Now consider the possibility of using Income as the topmost attribute. There is a complication since Income has continuous values, whereas a decision tree makes its decision based on discrete values. Therefore, to use an attribute with continuous values, we have to divide its possible values into discrete ranges. This process is called **discretization**. (Actually this approach to dealing with continuous values is not in ID3 but in its extension C4.5 [Quinlan 1986].)

If we decide to divide Income into two ranges, Income $< X$ and Income $\geq X$, we have two choices. We can just pick *some* value of X based on our intuitive knowledge of the application, or we can try *all* values for X that are mentioned in the table and compute the entropy for each to see if any of those ranges provide more information gain than PrevDefault. The second choice is usually preferable. For example, if we try $X = 50$, the information gain would be .035. In fact, it turns out that no value of X provides more information gain than does PrevDefault.

Thus, based on the information-gain measure, we decide to use PrevDefault as the toplevel attribute of the tree. We therefore label the topmost node in the tree PrevDefault and construct a branch descending from that node for each of the possible values of PrevDefault going to a node at the second level. These second-level nodes are each the topmost node of a subtree. The tables of Figures 17.18 and 17.19 are the training sets for these subtrees.

Now we repeat the entire procedure on each of these subtrees. When we use the information gain measure on each of the training tables for these subtrees to determine the attributes to be used to make the decisions at the second level, either of the following situations might (or might not) happen.

1. The attribute selected might be different for the two tables.
2. The range selected for some attributes with continuous values (such as the Income attribute in the example) might be different for the two tables (and different from that in analysis at the topmost level).

In our example, neither of these situations occur, and the attribute with the largest information gain for both second-level nodes is Married. Thus we label both of the second-level nodes Married and construct branches going to nodes at the third level of the tree. The tables to be used as the training sets for these third-level nodes are shown in Figures 17.20, 17.21, 17.22, and 17.23.

Note that in the tables shown in Figures 17.20, 17.21, and 17.23, all entries have the same outcome and therefore the tables have an entropy of 0. Thus these tables correspond to leaf nodes of the decision tree, each labelled with its unique outcome.

---

[2] The subtable determined by Married = yes has 11 tuples with Default = no and 3 tuples with Default = yes. Therefore, this table's entropy is 0.7496. The subtable determined by Married = no has 3 tuples with Default = no and 3 tuples with Default = yes. Its entropy is therefore 1. The average weighted by the relative number of tuples in these tables ($14/20 = 0.7$ and $6/20 = 0.3$) is thus $0.7 * 0.7496 + 0.3 * 1 = 0.8247$. Therefore, the information gain is $.881 - .8247 = .0563$.

CUSTOMER	Id	Income	Default
	C7	10	no
	C10	45	no
	C13	20	no

FIGURE 17.20 The table used as the training set at the third level of the tree when PrevDefault is "yes" and Married is "yes."

CUSTOMER	Id	Income	Default
	C3	135	yes
	C12	125	yes
	C18	160	yes

FIGURE 17.21 The table used as the training set at the third level of the tree when PrevDefault is "yes" and Married is "no."

CUSTOMER	Id	Income	Default
	C1	50	no
	C2	100	no
	C4	125	no
	C5	50	no
	C8	10	yes
	C9	75	no
	C11	60	yes
	C16	15	yes
	C17	35	no
	C19	40	no
	C20	30	no

FIGURE 17.22 The table used as the training set at the third level of the tree when PrevDefault is "no" and Married is "yes."

We then repeat the procedure on the remaining table, Figure 17.22. The only remaining attribute is Income. When we investigate all the possible ranges for Income, we find that the maximum information (minimum entropy) is obtained when X is 30. For that value of X, the average entropy is .412. Thus we decide

CUSTOMER	Id	Income	Default
	C6	30	no
	C14	15	no
	C15	60	no

FIGURE 17.23 The table used as the training set at the third level of the tree when PrevDefault is "no" and Married is "no."

CUSTOMER	Id	Default
	C8	yes
	C16	yes

FIGURE 17.24 The table used as the training set at the fourth level of the tree when PrevDefault is "no" and Married is "yes" and Income is less than 30.

CUSTOMER	Id	Default
	C1	no
	C2	no
	C4	no
	C5	no
	C9	no
	C11	yes
	C17	no
	C19	no
	C20	no

FIGURE 17.25 The table used as the training set at the fourth level of the tree when PrevDefault is "no" and Married is "yes" and Income is greater than or equal to 30.

to use the ranges, Income < 30 and Income ≥ 30, and obtain the tables shown in Figures 17.24 and 17.25.

The table shown in Figure 17.24 has an entropy of 0 and corresponds to a leaf node labelled with outcome "yes."

However, the table shown in Figure 17.25 does not have an entropy of 0 because all the outcomes are not the same. However, we have run out of attributes and cannot continue the procedure. Thus we say that this table corresponds to a leaf with outcome "no" (because "no" is the most frequently occurring outcome in this table). We have to settle for the fact that this leaf does not make the correct decision for customer C11. That completes the design of the decision tree.

Summary of the ID3 algorithm. The ID3 procedure can be described recursively as follows. Given a table, T, to be used as a training set to construct a decision tree d:

1. If T has entropy equal to 0, construct d with only a single node, which is a leaf node labelled with the (only) outcome in T.

2. If T has no attributes, construct d with only a single node, which is a leaf node labelled with the most frequently occurring outcome in T.

3. Otherwise

   (a) Find the attribute, A, in T that provides the maximum information gain. Specifically, find the attribute, A, that divides T into n subtables, $T_1, T_2, \ldots, T_n$ (assuming that A has n possible values, $v_1, \ldots, v_n$), such that the information gain is the largest of all the information gains obtained from all the other attributes in T. Each subtable T_i is $\sigma_{a=v_i}(T)$ with the column corresponding to the attribute A projected out.

   (b) Label the topmost node in d with the name A.

   (c) Construct n branches descending from that node, where each branch corresponds to one of the n values of A and is labelled with that value.

   (d) At the end of each branch, for example, the branch corresponding to the value v_i of A, start a subtree, d_i, and use T_i as its training set.

   (e) Repeat this procedure on each of the subtrees, $d_1, \ldots, d_n$, starting at step 1.

Brain Teaser: The algorithm ID3 is guaranteed to terminate. Why?

If we are concerned about possible overfitting of the data and want to consider the possibility of pruning the decision tree, one approach is to use the validation set, which (as you might recall) is a subset of the historical data that is disjoint from both the training set and the test set. We first construct the complete decision tree using the training set and compute the training-set error. Then we test the tree with the validation set. If the validation-set error is significantly greater than the training-set error, we can assume that some overfitting has taken place. We then make a series of pruned versions of the tree by deleting each of the leaf nodes. We apply the validation set to each of these pruned versions. If we find that the validation set error has been decreased, we assume that some overfitting has taken place. We then continue the pruning process until the new pruned versions do not have less validation-set error. When we are done, we apply the test set to the final version to compute the test-set error.

The information-gain measure is not the only measure than can be used to produce a decision tree from a training set. Two other measures that have been proposed and used in commercial products are

- **Gain ratio** [Quinlan 1986]. The **gain ratio** is defined as follows:

$$Gain\ Ratio = (Information\ Gain)/SplitInfo$$

where information gain is as defined earlier and

$$SplitInfo = -\sum_{i=1}^{n} |T_i| / |T| \ log_2(|T_i| / |T|)$$

where $|T|$ is the number of entries in the table being decomposed by the attribute and $|T_i|$ is the number of entries in the ith table produced by the decomposition. The idea is to normalize the information-gain measure to compensate for the fact that it favors attributes that have a large number of values.

Since the information gain obtained when using PrevDefault is .191, and since there are six entries in the table of Figure 17.18 and fourteen entries in the table of Figure 17.19, the gain ratio for the PrevDefault attribute is

$$Gain\ Ratio = .191/(6/20\ log_2(6/20) + 14/20\ log_2(14/20)) = .217$$

- **Gini index** [Breiman et al. 1984]. The **Gini index** is defined as

$$Gini = 1 - \sum_{i=1}^{k} p_i^2$$

where p_i is the probability that a tuple in the training set table has outcome i. Thus, if all of the entries in the training table had outcome "no," the Gini index would be 0, and if half of the entries had outcome "yes" and half had outcome "no," the Gini index would be 1/2.

Since the number of "yes" outcomes in the table of Figure 17.16 is six and the number of "no" outcomes is fourteen, the Gini index of that table is

$$Gini = 1 - ((6/20)^2 + (14/20)^2)) = .42$$

Each measure has its advocates and its share of successes in specific applications.

17.10 Classification and Prediction Using Neural Nets

One might say that the decision tree algorithm just discussed is a learning algorithm that *learns* how to make predictions based on the data in its training set. The field of machine learning, which is a subfield of artificial intelligence, provides a number of other techniques that are useful in classification and prediction. Suppose that the mortgage lender wants to determine which applicants are likely to default on their mortgage but believes that the classification depends on a larger number of factors than in the previous example and that these factors should be weighted differently.

To see how a bank might use weights in making a decision, assume it wants to consider only two factors: PrevDefault and Married. Then it might associate a weight w_1 with the predicate PrevDefault = yes and a weight w_2 with the predicate Married = yes. The bank might then evaluate the expression

$$w_1 * x_1 + w_2 * x_2$$

where x_1 has value 1 if PrevDefault = yes is true and 0 otherwise; x_2 is defined similarly using the predicate Married = yes. A customer is considered a bad risk if the value of that expression exceeds some threshold, t, that is, if

$$w_1 * x_1 + w_2 * x_2 \geq t.$$

If $w_1 * x_1 + w_2 * x_2 < t$, the customer is considered a good risk. In practice, the lender might want to include a number of other possible factors in this computation. The question is, how should the weights and the threshold be determined?

A technique called **neural nets** allows the lender to use the information in a training set derived from an OLAP database about past customers to "learn" a set of weights that would have predicted their behavior and thus will (hopefully) predict the behavior of new customers. By "learning" we mean that the system uses examples of the characteristics of past customers who did or did not default on their loans to incrementally adjust the weights to give a better prediction of whether or not customers will default.

The above inequality can be viewed as modeling the behavior of a primitive **neuron** (or nerve cell). In general, a neuron can have any number of inputs, $x_1, \ldots, x_n$, and each input has a weight, w_i. The neuron is said to be **activated** if the weighted sum of its inputs, $\sum_{i=1}^{n} w_i * x_i$, exceeds or equals some threshold, t, which can be specific to that particular neuron. When a neuron is activated, it **emits** the value 1; otherwise it is said to emit the value 0.

Our discussion of neurons can be simplified if we introduce w_0 so that $w_0 = t$ and rewrite the equation

$$\sum_{i=1}^{n} w_i * x_1 \geq t$$

as

$$\sum_{i=1}^{n} w_i * x_i - w_0 * 1 \geq 0$$

(We can assume there is a new input x_0, which always has a value of -1.) The expression $\sum_{i=1}^{n} w_i * x_i - w_0 * 1$ is sometimes called the **normalized weighted input**. The **activation function** of the neuron is a monotonic function that takes the normalized weighted input, X, and returns a real number, $f(X)$, such that $0 \leq f(X) \leq 1$.

A typical activation function (and the one used above) is a **step function** where $f(X) = 0$, if $X < 0$, and $f(X) = 1$, if $X \geq 0$. The step activation function tells us when the neuron is "active" (emits 1) or "inactive" (emits 0). In general, however, the activation function can be continuous, such as the *sigmoid* function depicted in Figure 17.27, which will be discussed shortly. In such a case the neuron can emit any real number between 0 and 1, and the activation function indicates the "degree of activation" of the neuron.

The perceptron learning algorithm. Based on this notation, we can define a learning algorithm for a single neuron that has the step function activation. This algorithm is sometimes called the **perceptron learning algorithm** because the authors of that algorithm referred to such neuron models as perceptrons.

1. Initially set the values of all the weights and the threshold to some small random number.

2. Apply the inputs corresponding to each item in the training set one at a time to the neuron model. For each input, compute the output of the neuron.

3. If the desired output of the neuron for that input is d and the actual output is y, change each weight, w_i, by Δw_i where

$$\Delta w_i = \eta * x_i * (d - y)$$

(assuming $x_0 = -1$) where η is some small positive number called the **learning rate**. Note that if for this input, the neuron does not make an error (the desired output equals the actual output), no weights are changed. If the neuron emits a value higher than d, then the weight w_i is decreased in order to try to lower the emitted value (observe that the activation function is monotonically growing). If the emitted value is less than d, then w_i is increased in order to raise the emitted value.

4. Continue the training until some termination condition is met. For example, the data in the training set has been used some fixed number of times, the number of errors has stopped decreasing significantly, the weights have stopped changing significantly, or the number of errors reaches some predetermined level.

If the neuron has n inputs, each of which can be 1 or 0, then there are 2^n possible combinations of these inputs. If we assume that the training set includes each of these 2^n combinations of inputs, the perceptron learning algorithm has the property that if the decision can *always* be correctly made by a single neuron, the values of the weights and threshold will converge to correct values after only a bounded number of weight adjustments [Novikoff 1962].

Neural networks: the sigmoid function. In practice the perceptron learning algorithm is not very useful because for most applications the required decisions cannot be made (even approximately) by a single neuron. Therefore, a network of neurons, such as the one depicted in Figure 17.26, is used.

The network shown has three layers: the input layer, the middle or hidden layer, and the output layer. The input layer does not consist of neurons that can adjust their weights. It just gathers the inputs and presents them to the neurons in the middle layer. The neurons in the middle layer make some intermediate decisions and then send those decisions to the neurons in the output layer, which makes the final decisions.

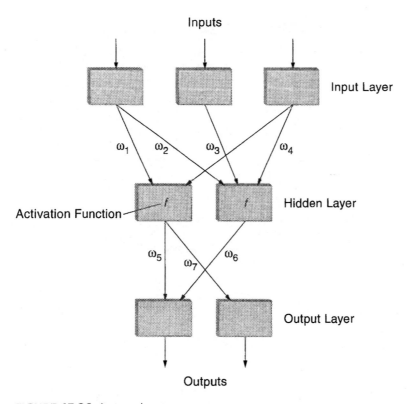

FIGURE 17.26 A neural net.

Learning algorithms for such neural networks are more complex than those for a single neuron because it is not immediately apparent how to adjust the weights of the neurons in the middle layer when one or more of the neurons in the output layer gives an output different than its desired output. More specifically it is not apparent how each such weight in the middle layer affects the output of the network. A mathematical analysis of this situation is difficult because such an analysis usually requires taking derivatives of the activation function, and the step function that we used so far is discontinuous and does not have a derivative. For this reason, neural networks usually use differentiable activation functions.

A commonly used activation function is the **sigmoid function**, shown in Figure 17.27, which is defined as

$$1/(1 + e^{-X})$$

where X denotes the normalized weighted input to the neuron:

$$X = \sum_{i=1}^{n} w_i * x_i - w_0 * 1$$

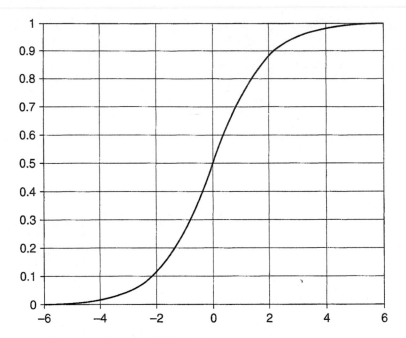

FIGURE 17.27 The sigmoid function.

Note that the value of the sigmoid function is 1/2 for $X = 0$. It becomes asymptotic to 1 for large positive values of X and asymptotic to 0 for large negative values of X. Thus it is a continuous (and differentiable) approximation of the step activation function.

The sigmoid function has an interesting property that we will use later: if the output of the neuron is denoted as y, so that

$$y = 1/(1 + e^{-X})$$

then the partial derivative of y with respect to X is

$$\frac{\partial y}{\partial X} = e^{-X}/(1 + e^{-X})^2 = (1/(1 + e^{-X})) * (1 - (1/(1 + e^{-X}))) = y * (1 - y)$$

and then if we use the definition of X given above, the partial derivative of y with respect to any particular weight, w_i, is

$$\frac{\partial y}{\partial w_i} = \frac{\partial y}{\partial X} * \frac{\partial X}{\partial w_i} = y * (1 - y) * x_i \qquad \textbf{17.6}$$

Using this result, we can now derive the learning procedure for a single neuron that uses the sigmoid activation function. Assume that for some input in the training set, the output of the neuron is y and the desired output is d. The error is then $(d - y)$, and the squared error is $(d - y)^2$. (We could also consider the mean squared error for all the inputs, but now we are just considering a single input.) Consider the squared error as an *n*-dimensional function of the weights $w_1, \ldots, w_n$. The plan is to take the partial derivative of that function with respect to each of the weights. We will then adjust each weight by some small fraction, η, of the negative of that partial derivative. This is called the **gradient descent** approach to finding the minimum of that function. Thus we change the weight of w_i to $w_i + \Delta w_i$ where

$$\Delta w_i = -\eta \frac{\partial (d - y)^2}{\partial w_i}$$

To see why gradient descent is a good heuristic for finding a local minimum of a function, we need to observe two things:

1. If we change w_i to $w_i + \Delta w_i$, we are moving towards a local minimum of the function $(d - y)^2$. Indeed, if this function is increasing at this value of w_i, the above derivative is positive and so we need to decrease w_i to approach the local minimum. In this case $\Delta w_i < 0$ and $w_i + \Delta w_i$ is an adjustment in the right direction. If the derivative is negative, it means that the function is decreasing, so we need to increase w_i in order to approach the local minimum. In this case $\Delta w_i > 0$ and, again, $w_i + \Delta w_i$ is an adjustment in the right direction. We can imagine that, as we change the weights, we are sliding down a hill.

2. As w_i approaches the local minimum, the value of the derivative decreases to zero and therefore the adjustment step, Δw_i, becomes smaller and smaller. In this way, we avoid overshooting the local minimum by large amounts and the process eventually converges.

The derivative of the square of the error with respect to w_i is

$$\frac{\partial (d - y)^2}{\partial w_i} = -2 * (d - y) * \frac{\partial y}{\partial w_i} = -2 * (d - y) * y * (1 - y) * x_i$$

Thus, to adjust the weights and decrease the error, the learning algorithm needs to change w_i by some fraction of the negative of that derivative.

$$\Delta w_i = \eta * x_i * y * (1 - y) * (d - y) \qquad \textbf{17.7}$$

(Note that we have incorporated the constant 2 that appears in the derivative into the learning rate η. Note also that we have changed the order of the multipliers to what is common in the literature.)

The back-propagation learning algorithms for neural networks. Next we present a learning algorithm for networks of neurons, each described by the sigmoid activation function. Specifically we discuss one of the most popular learning algorithms for such neural networks: the **back-propagation algorithm**. We present the algorithm for three-layer networks, such as that in Figure 17.26, but this algorithm can be adapted for networks with any number of layers.

It is called the back-propagation algorithm because, for each input in the training set, the algorithm first goes forward to compute the output of each neuron in

OPTIONAL

the output layer. Then it goes backward to adjust the weights in each layer one at a time. It initially adjusts the weights of the neurons in the output layer, and then it uses the result of that adjustment to adjust the weights of the neurons in the middle layer (and, if there are more layers, it goes further backward to adjust the weights in those layers one at a time).

1. Initially set the values of all the weights and thresholds of all the neurons in the network to some small random number.

2. Apply the inputs corresponding to each item in the training set one at a time to the network. For each input, compute the output of each neuron in the output layer.

3. Adjust the value of the weights in each neuron in the output layer. Consider one such neuron, v_{out}, and assume it emits y^{out} (for the given input) while the desired output is d^{out}. We can use the same reasoning for v_{out} as we did for the case of a single neuron earlier. Thus we can apply the equation (17.7) to v_{out} and adjust each weight, w_i^{out}, associated with input x_i^{out}, according to the formula

$$\Delta w_i^{out} = \eta * x_i^{out} * y^{out} * (1 - y^{out}) * (d^{out} - y^{out})$$

For reasons that will become clear in the next step, it is convenient to rewrite this formula as

$$\Delta w_i^{out} = \eta * x_i^{out} * \delta^{out}$$

where

$$\delta^{out} = y^{out} * (1 - y^{out}) * (d^{out} - y^{out}) \qquad \textbf{17.8}$$

4. Adjust the value of the weights in each middle-layer neuron. Consider one such neuron—let us denote it v_{mid}. Assume its output for the given input is y^{mid}. A problem is that we do not know what is the *desired* output of v_{mid}. However we do know the desired outputs of the output-layer neurons to which v_{mid} is connected. We are interested in determining how the input weights in the middle-layer neuron v_{mid} affect the output of the outer-layer neurons. As a simple example, suppose our middle-layer neuron is connected to only one output-layer neuron, such as v_{out} above, and the weight of that connection is $w^{mid/out}$. Suppose that for the given training set input, the output neuron v_{out} emits y^{out} while its desired output is d^{out}. Using the same reasoning as before, for each input weight w_i^{mid} of the middle-layer neuron v_{mid} with input x_i^{mid}, we want to adjust w_i^{mid} by some fraction of the negative of the derivative of $(d^{out} - y^{out})^2$ with respect to w_i^{mid}

$$\Delta w_i^{mid} = -\eta * \frac{\partial (d^{out} - y^{out})^2}{\partial w_i^{mid}}$$

Then we note that

$$\frac{\partial(d^{out} - y^{out})^2}{\partial w_i^{mid}} = \frac{\partial(d^{out} - y^{out})^2}{\partial X^{out}} * \frac{\partial X^{out}}{\partial w_i^{mid}}$$

where X^{out} is the X of the output-layer neuron. As before

$$\frac{\partial(d^{out} - y^{out})^2}{\partial X^{out}} = -2 * (d^{out} - y^{out}) * y^{out} * (1 - y^{out})$$

Then we observe that the inputs x_k^{out} of the output neuron v_{out} are the outputs of the middle-layer neurons connected to v_{out}. Therefore, we have

$$X^{out} = \sum_k w_k^{mid/out} * y_k^{mid}$$

where the y_k^{mid} are the outputs of all the middle-layer neurons connected to v_{out}, and the $w_k^{mid/out}$ are the corresponding weights of the connection. Note that since v_{mid} is connected to v_{out}, $w^{mid/out}$ is one of these $w_k^{mid/out}$ and y^{mid} is one of these y_k^{mid}. Returning to our derivatives, we can see that $\frac{\partial y_k^{mid}}{\partial w_i^{mid}} \neq 0$ only when y_k^{mid} is y^{mid}, since w_i^{mid} in an input weight to v_{mid} and thus it affects v_{mid}'s output only. We also know from (17.6) that $\frac{\partial y^{mid}}{\partial w_i^{mid}} = x_i^{mid} * y^{mid} * (1 - y^{mid})$. Therefore we can then write

$$\frac{\partial X^{out}}{\partial w_i^{mid}} = w^{mid/out} * \frac{\partial y^{mid}}{\partial w_i^{mid}} = w^{mid/out} * x_i^{mid} * y^{mid} * (1 - y^{mid})$$

Putting all this together we get

$$\frac{\partial(d^{out} - y^{out})^2}{\partial w_i^{mid}} =$$
$$- 2 * (d^{out} - y^{out}) * y^{out} * (1 - y^{out}) * w^{mid/out} * x_i^{mid} * y^{mid} * (1 - y^{mid})$$

Therefore, we can use the following learning rule for our middle-layer neuron v_{mid} connected to the single output-layer neuron v_{out}. For each weight w_i^{mid} of v_{mid} associated with input x_i^{mid}, adjust that weight using the formula

$$\Delta w_i^{mid} = \eta * x_i^{mid} * \delta^{mid}$$

where δ^{mid} is defined as

$$\delta^{mid} = y^{mid} * (1 - y^{mid}) * w^{mid/out} * y^{out} * (1 - y^{out}) * (d^{out} - y^{out})$$

The formula for δ^{mid} can be rewritten as

$$\delta^{mid} = y^{mid} * (1 - y^{mid}) * w^{mid/out} * \delta^{out}$$

where δ^{out} was previously computed for the output neuron v_{out} in (17.8). There-fore, δ^{mid} can be computed from δ^{out}, whence the name back propagation.

If the v_{mid} is connected to several output-layer neurons, we can use the same reasoning based on the negative of the derivative of the sum of the squares of the errors of all the output-layer neurons to which v_{mid} is connected:

$$\Delta w_i^{mid} = -\eta * \frac{\partial \sum_j (d_j^{out} - y_j^{out})^2}{\partial w_i^{mid}}$$

Here y_j^{out} and d_j^{out} are, respectively, the outputs and the desired outputs of all the output-layer neurons that receive input from v_{mid}. The computations are a bit more complex, but the result is that the formula for Δw_i^{mid} is the same as when v_{mid} is connected to a single output-layer neuron except that the formula for δ^{mid} involves the weighted sum of the δ^{out}s of all the output-layer neurons in question:

$$\Delta w_i^{mid} = \eta * x_i^{mid} * \delta^{mid}$$

where

$$\delta^{mid} = y^{mid} * (1 - y^{mid}) * \sum_j (w_j^{wid/out} * \delta_j^{out})$$

5. Continue the training until some termination condition is met. For example, the data in the training set has been used some fixed number of times, the number of errors has stopped decreasing significantly, the weights have stopped changing significantly, or the number of errors reaches some predetermined level.

17.11 Clustering

Suppose we examine the addresses of all the people in the United States who have a certain form of lung cancer. We might find that many of those addresses are clustered in a few areas that are near certain chemical plants. We might then conclude that those chemical plants are somehow involved in causing that cancer.

In a more general situation, suppose we are given a set of data items, each with certain attributes, and a similarity measure based on those attributes. In the above example, the items contain information about cancer patients, the attribute is Address, and the similarity measure is *nearness* (as measured by Euclidean distance). **Clustering** involves placing those data items into *clusters* such that the items in each cluster are similar to each other and the items in different clusters are less similar. The clusters are usually disjoint. Thus in the example, we are finding clusters of cancer patients who are similar in that they live near each other.

Note that clustering is different than the classification rules and decision trees that we discussed earlier because in those cases the categories into which the data items are to be classified are known in advance. In clustering, the categories are determined by the clustering algorithm.

An important issue in clustering is the similarity measure that is used. When the attributes are numeric, a similarity measure based on Euclidean distance is often used. Thus if two cancer patients have addresses that can be represented using location coordinates as x_1, y_1 and x_2, y_2, the Euclidean distance between them is $\sqrt{(x_1 - x_2)^2 + (y_1 - y_2)^2}$. If the attributes are not numeric, an analyst must develop an appropriate similarity measure. Sometimes this involves converting a nonnumeric attribute into a numeric attribute.

The K-means algorithm.   Many algorithms have been proposed for clustering. We first present one of the most popular, the **K-means** algorithm. The inputs to the algorithm are: the dataset of items to be clustered, the desired number of clusters k, and the similarity measure. The algorithms proceeds as follows:

1. Select k of the items at random as the centers of the (initial versions) of the k clusters.

2. Put each item in the dataset into the cluster for which that item is closest to the center, based on the similarity measure. (Initially, when the cluster has only one item, the center is the location of that member.)

3. Recalculate the center of each cluster as the mean of the locations (similarity measures) of all the items in that cluster.

4. Repeat the procedure starting at step 2 until there is no change in the membership in all clusters.

> *Brain Teaser:* The K-means algorithm is guaranteed to eventually terminate. Why?

The final version of the clusters produced by the K-means algorithm is not necessarily unique—there can be several states where equilibrium is achieved. Hence the final version of the clusters might depend on the initial selection of the items in step 1.

As a simple example, consider the table of students' ages and GPAs shown in Figure 17.28. Suppose we are interested in investigating whether older students do better or worse in college than younger ones. As a part of that investigation, we want to cluster these items by age and then see the average GPA in each cluster. Note that the similarity measure (age) is just one-dimensional, so the calculation of distances is particularly easy.

Suppose we want to place the students into two clusters: cluster 1 (younger students) and cluster 2 (older students), so we set k equal to 2. Then suppose in step 1 of the algorithm, we randomly select students S_1 and S_4 as the centers of our initial clusters. Thus the (initial) centers are at ages 17 and 20.

STUDENT	Id	Age	GPA
	S_1	17	3.9
	S_2	17	3.5
	S_3	18	3.1
	S_4	20	3.0
	S_5	23	3.5
	S_6	26	3.6

FIGURE 17.28 Table of student ages and GPAs for clustering example.

Then we examine each student row and place it in one of the clusters. For example, student S_2 is at a distance of 0 from cluster 1 and at a distance of 3 from cluster 2, so it is placed in cluster 1. On the other hand, student S_5 is at a distance of 6 from cluster 1 and at a distance of 3 from cluster 2, so it is placed in cluster 2. Thus the initial version of the clusters is

Cluster 1: S_1, S_2, S_3
Cluster 2: S_4, S_5, S_6

The new centers of these clusters are

Cluster 1: $(17 + 17 + 18)/3 = 17.333$
Cluster 2: $(20 + 23 + 26)/3 = 23.0$

Then we recompute in which cluster each student is to be placed. The only interesting computation is for student S_4, who is at a distance of 2.677 from the center of cluster 1 and a distance of 3 from the center of cluster 2 and so is placed in cluster 1 (perhaps counter-intuitively since this student was chosen as the initial center of cluster 2). The other students remain in their original clusters. Thus the second version of the clusters is

Cluster 1: S_1, S_2, S_3, S_4
Cluster 2: S_5, S_6

If we now repeat step 2 of the algorithm, the clusters remain the same, and so the algorithm has completed. The average GPA of the students in each cluster is then:

Cluster 1 (younger students): $(3.9 + 3.5 + 3.1 + 3.0)/4 = 3.375$
Cluster 2 (older students): $(3.5 + 3.6)/2 = 3.55$

Whether or not that is a significant difference is a subject for further analysis.

Since the final value of the clusters might depend on the initial selection of items in step 1, some authors suggest that the algorithm be repeated with different initial selections or that a nonrandom selection be made of items that are far apart. Other authors suggest that a better set of final clusters is often obtained if, in step 2, the items are moved one at a time and the cluster centers are recalculated after each move.

In some applications, it might not be obvious what value to use for k. One approach is to try different values of k and calculate the average distance to the center of each cluster as k increases. Usually the average decreases rapidly until the "correct" value of k has been reached and then decreases more slowly.

The hierarchical algorithm.   Another algorithm for clustering, in which the value of k need not be selected in advance, is the **hierarchical** algorithm (sometimes called the **agglomerative** hierarchical algorithm). The algorithm proceeds as follows:

1.   Start with each item in the dataset as a separate cluster.
2.   Select two clusters to merge into a single cluster. The goal is to pick the two clusters that are "closest." Various measures have been proposed for closeness. One measure, and the one we will use, is that the distance between clusters is the distance between their centers. The center of a cluster is the mean (the numeric average) of the locations of all the items in the cluster. We therefore merge the two clusters for which the centers are closest. (Another measure is that the distance between groups is the distance between the "nearest neighbors," the closest two items in each group.)
3.   Repeat step 2 until some termination condition is reached. One condition is that some predetermined number of k clusters has been obtained. Another condition might be to continue as long as the average distance to the center of each cluster is decreasing rapidly and terminate when it begins to decrease more slowly. Still another, as we shall see below, is to continue until there is only one cluster and then analyze the result to select an appropriate set of clusters.

One way to implement this algorithm is with a matrix of all the pairwise distances between the clusters. Initially, the matrix contains the pairwise distances between the individual items in the data set. The matrix is then used in step 2 to determine which clusters to merge. After this determination is made, the matrix is updated by inactivating (or deleting) one of the clusters being merged and updating the information about the other cluster (now representing the new cluster) with the distances between that cluster and the other clusters. If there are n items in the dataset, this implementation requires $O(n^2)$ space and $O(n^3)$ time.

If we use this algorithm on the items in the table of Figure 17.28, we would get the following sequence of clusters. Here we denote each cluster by its age attribute and separate different clusters with space.

      17   17   18   20   23   26

      17, 17   18   20   23   26

      17, 17, 18   20   23   26

      17, 17, 18, 20   23   26

      17, 17, 18, 20   23, 26

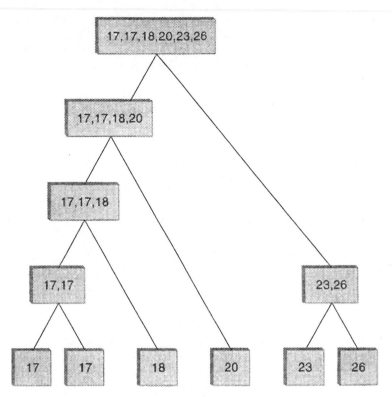

FIGURE 17.29 A dendrogram corresponding to the example of the hierarchical clustering algorithm.

The first row depicts clusters where each item is in a cluster of its own. In the last row we have only two clusters. If we stop at this point, the final set of clusters is the same as with the K-means algorithm. If we continue one more step, we would reduce the set of clusters to a single cluster

$$17, 17, 18, 20, 23, 26$$

One way to analyze the results of the hierarchical clustering algorithm is with a tree, usually called a **dendrogram**, that represents the progress of the algorithm, assuming it continues until there is only one cluster. The dendrogram for the above example is shown in Figure 17.29. The cluster generated by each step in the algorithm is denoted by a node in the tree.

Any set of nodes whose children include all the leaves in the tree exactly once represents a possible set of clusters. For example the three nodes denoted as

$$17, 17, 18 \quad 20 \quad 23, 26$$

is a set of clusters that did not appear at any time in the hierarchical algorithm but might be appropriate for certain applications.

The analyst can then analyze such a dendrogram in the light of her knowledge of the application and select a set of clusters that is appropriate for that application.

BIBLIOGRAPHIC NOTES

The term "OLAP" was coined by Codd in [Codd 1995]. A good survey of OLAP appears in [Chaudhuri and Dayal 1997]. A collection of articles on applications and current research in data mining can be found in [Fayyad et al. 1996]. The CUBE operator was introduced in [Gray et al. 1997]. Efficient computation of data cubes is discussed in [Agrawal et al. 1996; Harinarayan et al. 1996; Ross and Srivastava 1997; Zhao et al. 1998]. The idea of mining for association rules and some early algorithms was first introduced in [Agrawal et al. 1993]. The ID3 algorithm for decision trees, including both the information gain and gain ratio measures, was introduced in [Quinlan 1986]. The Gini index was introduced in [Breiman et al. 1984]. A textbook-style coverage of data mining can be found in [Han and Kamber 2001] and [Hand et al. 2001].

EXERCISES

17.1 Is a typical fact table in BCNF? Explain.

17.2 Explain why, in an E-R model of a star schema, the fact table is a relationship and the dimension tables are entities.

17.3 Design another fact table and related dimension tables that a supermarket might want to use for an OLAP application.

17.4 Explain why it is not appropriate to model the database for the Student Registration System as a star schema.

17.5 Design SQL queries for the supermarket example that will return the information needed to make a table similar to that of Figure 17.10, except that markets are aggregated by state, and time is aggregated by months.

a. Use CUBE or ROLLUP operators.
b. Do not use CUBE or ROLLUP operators.
c. Compute the result table.

17.6 a. Design a query for the supermarket example that will return the total sales (over time) for each supermarket.
b. Compute the result table.

17.7 Suppose that an application has four dimension tables, each of which contains 100 rows.

a. Determine the maximum number of rows in the fact table.
b. Suppose that a one-dimension table has an attribute that can take on 10 values. Determine the size in bytes of a bit index on that attribute.

c. Determine the maximum number of tuples in a join index for a join between one of the dimension tables and the fact table.

d. Suppose that we use the CUBE operator on this fact table to perform aggregations on all four dimensions. Determine the number of rows in the resulting table.

e. Suppose that we use the ROLLUP operator on this fact table. Determine the number of rows in the resulting table.

17.8 Design a query evaluation algorithm for the ROLLUP operator. The objective of such an algorithm should be that the results of the previously computed aggregations are *reused* in subsequent aggregations and *not* recomputed from scratch.

17.9 Design a query evaluation algorithm for the CUBE operator that uses the results of the previously computed aggregations to compute new aggregations. (*Hint*: Organize the GROUP BY clauses used in the computation of a data cube into a lattice, that is, a partial order with the least upper bound and the greatest lower bound for each pair of elements. Here is an example of such a partial order: GROUP BY A > GROUP BY A,B > GROUP BY A,B,C and GROUP BY B > GROUP BY B,C > GROUP BY A,B,C. Describe how aggregates computed for the lower parts of the lattice can be used in the computation of the upper parts.)

17.10 Suppose that the fact table of Figure 17.1 has been cubed and the result has been stored as a view, SALES_v1. Design queries against SALES_v1 that will return the tables of Figure 17.10 and Figure 17.7.

17.11 We are interested in building an OLAP application with which we can analyze the grading at our university, where grades are represented as integers from 0 to 4 (4 representing an A). We want to ask questions about average grades for different courses, professors, and departments during different semesters and years. Design a star schema for this application.

17.12 Discuss the difference in storage requirements for a data cube implemented as a multidimensional array and a fact table.

17.13 Give examples, different from those in the text, of syntactic and semantic transformations that might have to be made while loading data into a data warehouse.

17.14 Perform the a priori algorithm on the table of Figure 17.15 to determine all reasonable two-item associations.

17.15 Show that, when evaluating possible associations, the confidence is always larger than the support.

17.16 Apply the gain ratio measure to the table in Figure 17.16 to design a decision tree.

17.17 Apply the Gini measure to the table in Figure 17.16 to design a decision tree.

17.18 Show how the K-mean clustering algorithm would have worked on the table of Figure 17.28 if the original choice for cluster centers had been 17 and 18.

17.19 a. Give an example of a set of three items on a straight line for which the K-mean algorithm, with $k = 2$, would give a different answer for the two clusters depending on the choice of items for the initial clusters.

b. Which of these final clusters would have been obtained by the hierarchical algorithm?

17.20 Suppose the table of Figure 17.16 is stored in a relational database. Use SQL to compute the probabilities needed to compute the information gain when using the PrevDefault attribute as the topmost attribute of a decision tree based on that table.

PART FIVE

Transaction Processing

Now we are ready to begin our study of transaction processing.

In Chapter 18 we give a detailed description of the ACID properties of transactions and how transactions differ from ordinary programs.

In Chapter 19 we describe a variety of transaction models. A transaction need not be simply a program wrapped in the ACID properties. It can provide additional features or, alternatively, compromise on the properties in different ways. A workflow represents the ultimate compromise and is discussed in this chapter.

Chapter 20 discusses isolation in general terms and the theory on which it rests. However, for performance reasons, isolation need not be absolute in a relational database. Instead, several degrees of isolation, referred to as isolation levels, are generally offered. While this provides needed flexibility, it adds significantly to the complexity of the design. Chapter 21 discusses this issue at length.

Chapter 22 discusses the implementation of atomicity and durability in situations in which a transaction aborts, the system crashes, or the media on which the database is stored fails.

18

ACID Properties of Transactions

A transaction is a very special kind of program. It executes within an application in which a database models the state of some real-world enterprise. For example, if the enterprise is a bank, then the value of the balance attribute in the row corresponding to your account is the net amount of money held for you in that account by the bank. In fact, since the database is so central to the functioning of the bank, one might say that the database determines the state of the real world.

The job of the transaction is to maintain this model as the state of the enterprise changes. Thus, whenever the state of the real world changes, a transaction is executed that updates the database to reflect that change. The transaction is said to perform a "unit of work" because it does all the work required to update the database to reflect the real-world change.

Specifically a transaction can perform one or more of the following functions:

1. It can update a database to reflect the occurrence of a real-world event that affects the state of the enterprise the database is modeling. An example is a deposit transaction at a bank. The event is that the customer gives the teller cash. After that event occurs, the transaction updates the customer's account information in the database to reflect the deposit.

2. It can ensure that one or more real-world events occur. An example is a withdrawal transaction at an automated teller machine (ATM). The transaction actuates the mechanical device that dispenses the cash, and that event occurs if and only if the transaction successfully completes.

3. It can return information derived from the database about the current state of the enterprise. An example is a transaction that displays a customer's balance.

The difference between the first two functions is that, in the first, the real-world event has already occurred and the transaction simply updates the database to reflect that fact; in the second, the real-world event is triggered from within the transaction.

A single transaction can perform all three functions. For example, a deposit transaction might

1. Update the database in response to a real-world event in which the customer gives cash to the teller

2. Cause the real-world event in which a deposit slip is printed if and only if the transaction successfully completes

3. Return information from the database about the customer's account

Because of the requirement that a transaction processing application must maintain an accurate model of the state of the enterprise, the execution of transactions is constrained by certain properties that do not apply to ordinary programs. For example, the state of the enterprise must be correctly maintained even if the system crashes while transactions are executing or even if hundreds of transactions are attempting to update the database at the same time.

These special properties are frequently referred to using the acronym ACID: Atomic, Consistent, Isolated, Durable. In this chapter, we define these properties (but not in the order of the acronym) and explain why they are needed.

18.1 Consistency

Think of a database as playing both an active and a passive role in relation to the real-world enterprise that it models. In its passive role, it maintains the correspondence between the database state and the enterprise state. For example, the Student Registration System must accurately maintain the identity and number of students who have registered for each course since there is no paper record of the registration. In its active role, it enforces certain rules of the enterprise—for example, the number of students registered for a course must not exceed another number stored in the database, the maximum enrollment for that course. A transaction that attempts to register a student for a course that is already full must not complete successfully.

Consistency is the term that is used to describe these issues, and it has two aspects.

The database must satisfy all integrity constraints. Not all database states are allowable. There are two reasons for this.

1. *Internal consistency.* It is often convenient to store the same information in different forms. For example, we might store the number of students registered for a course as well as a list whose entries name each student registered for the course. A database state in which the length of the list is not equal to the number of registrants is not allowed.

2. *Enterprise rules.* Enterprise rules restrict the possible states of the enterprise. When such a rule exists, the possible states of the database are similarly restricted. The rule relating the number of registrants and the maximum enrollment in a course is one example. A state in which the number of registrants is greater than the maximum enrollment is not allowed.

The restrictions are referred to as **integrity constraints** (or sometimes **consistency constraints**). The execution of each transaction must maintain all integrity constraints. Assuming that all constraints are satisfied when execution starts, the constraints will be satisfied in the new state produced by the transaction when it terminates. (If the constraints are not satisfied when the transaction starts, the transaction is not required to execute correctly and no guarantees can be made about the new state produced by the transaction.)

The database must model the state of the real-world enterprise. The transaction must be **correct** in the sense that it updates the database in such a way as to have the effect stated in its specification. The new database state must reflect the new real-world state—for example, a registration transaction must increment the database variable that stores the number of students registered for a course and must add that student to the list of registrants. A registration transaction that completes successfully but does not update the database leaves the database in a consistent state, but that state does not show the student as registered. Similarly, a deposit transaction that records your deposit as being in someone else's account leaves the database in a consistent state, but that state clearly does not correspond to the state of the real world.

We can determine whether or not all integrity constraints are satisfied by examining the values of the data items in a snapshot of the database (perhaps at a time when no transactions are executing). Unfortunately, this does not tell us whether or not the database state is an accurate reflection of the real-world state of the enterprise. Hence, in addition to the database state being consistent, we require that each transaction must be consistent as well.

> **Transaction consistency.** The transaction designer can assume that, when execution of the transaction is initiated, the database is in a state in which all integrity constraints are satisfied. The designer has the responsibility of ensuring that when execution has completed, the database is once again in a state in which all integrity constraints are satisfied and that the new state reflects the transformation described in the transaction's specification.

Note that we are using the word "consistent" in two ways. The database is consistent when all integrity constraints are satisfied; a transaction is consistent if it maintains the consistency of the database and produces a new database state that satisfies the requirements of the transaction's specifications.

Keep in mind that constructing consistent transactions is the sole responsibility of the application programmer. The remainder of the transaction processing system takes consistency as a given and provides atomicity, isolation, and durability—the properties needed to ensure that concurrent execution of consistent transactions preserves the relationship between the state of the database and the state of the enterprise in spite of failures.

18.1.1 Checking Integrity Constraints

SQL provides some support for maintaining integrity constraints. When the database is designed, certain integrity constraints can be incorporated as SQL assertions, key constraints, and the like. For example, a PRIMARY KEY constraint can eliminate the possibility that two students are recorded in the database with the same student

Id. A CHECK constraint can enforce the relationship between the number of registrants in a class and its maximum enrollment. An ASSERTION can ensure that the room assigned to a particular course is larger than the maximum enrollment. If a transaction updates data that is included in a constraint specified in the schema, the database management system (DBMS) automatically checks that the constraint is not violated and prevents the transaction from completing if that is not the case.

Unfortunately, not all integrity constraints can be encoded in the schema. Even when a constraint can be encoded, the design decision is sometimes made not to do so. Instead, it is checked within the transaction program itself. For example, the constraint that asserts that the maximum enrollment in a class should not be exceeded might be checked by the registration transaction instead of being included in the schema. One reason for such a decision is that constraint checking takes time. When encoded in the schema, constraints are checked automatically whenever a table they reference is modified. As a result, the check might be performed unnecessarily often. By placing constraint checking in the transactions, it can be carried out only in transactions that might cause a violation. For example, a limitation on the number of students who can register for a course cannot be violated by a transaction that deregisters a student. Thus, despite the fact that the number of students in the course is modified, no check need be made (either automatically or otherwise) when this transaction is executed. The advantage of such an approach is that the transaction designer includes constraint-checking code only in transactions where constraint violations can occur.

Checking constraints inside transactions has important drawbacks of its own. It increases the possibility of programming errors and makes it more difficult to maintain the system as rules change. For example, if at some point the limitation on enrollment is changed to say that the number of students in a course should not exceed the room capacity, several transactions might have to be modified, recompiled, and retested. However, if the constraint is specified in the schema, independently of any transaction, changing it is easy and no transaction needs to be modified.

18.1.2 A Transaction as a Unit of Work

The requirement that every transaction preserve integrity constraints limits the designer in specifying the tasks to be done by each of the transactions within an application. To explain this limitation, some authors have defined a transaction as a program that does a "unit of work," meaning that each transaction within an application must do *all* the work required to update the database in a way that maintains the integrity constraints when a real-world event occurs. Thus, for example, it is incorrect to specify that when a student wants to register for a course, two transactions should be executed—one that updates the count of registrants and one that updates the course roster—because neither of these "transactions" is consistent. The "unit of work" in this case requires updating both, and it must be done by a single transaction that then preserves the constraints.

18.2 Atomicity

In addition to consistency, the transaction processing system must provide certain guarantees concerning how transactions are executed. One such guarantee is *atomicity*.

> **Atomicity.** The system must ensure that either the transaction runs to completion or, if it does not complete, it has no effect at all (as if it had never been started).

Conventional operating systems usually do not guarantee atomicity. If during the execution of a (conventional) program, the system crashes, whatever partial changes the program made to files before the crash might still be there when the system restarts. If those changes leave the files in some incorrect state, the operating system takes no responsibility for correcting them.

Such behavior is unacceptable in a transaction processing system. Either a student has or has not registered for a course. Partial registration makes no sense and might leave the database in an inconsistent state. If the system were to crash while a registration transaction was executing, the number of students registered might have been incremented, but the registrant's name might not have been added to the roster, and hence the resulting database state is inconsistent.

If a transaction successfully completes and the system agrees to preserve its effects, we say that it has **committed**. If the transaction does not successfully complete, we say that it has **aborted** and the system must ensure that whatever changes the transaction made to the database are undone, or **rolled back**. A transaction processing system includes sophisticated mechanisms for aborting transactions and rolling back their effects.

The above discussion leads to the following important conclusion:

> Atomic execution implies that every transaction either commits or aborts.

Let us look at another example. A withdrawal transaction at an ATM involves (at least) two actions: The account is debited by the amount of the withdrawal, and the appropriate amount of cash is dispensed. Its atomic execution implies that if the transaction commits, both actions occur; if it aborts, neither occurs. Similarly, the atomic execution of a banking transaction that transfers money between two accounts guarantees that if the transaction commits, both updates occur; if it aborts, neither occurs.

Why transactions abort. A transaction might be aborted for several reasons. One possibility is that the system crashes during its execution (before it commits), or, in the case of a distributed transaction, the system on which one of the databases resides crashes. Other possibilities include the following:

1. Allowing the transaction to complete would cause a violation of an integrity constraint.

2. Allowing the transaction to complete would violate the *isolation requirement,* meaning that there is a possibility of a "bad interaction" with another executing transaction (as described in Section 18.4).

3. The transaction is involved in a deadlock, meaning that two or more transactions are each waiting for the others to complete, and hence none would complete if the system did not abort one of them (as described in Section 20.4.2).

Finally, the transaction itself might decide to abort. For example, the user might push the *cancel* button, or the transaction program might encounter some (application-related) condition that causes it to abandon its computation. Most transaction processing systems have an abort procedure that a transaction can invoke in such cases. Strictly speaking, such a procedure is unnecessary. The transaction can cause the equivalent of an abort by itself, undoing any changes it made to the database and then committing. However, this is a delicate and error-prone task that requires the transaction to remember what database items it has changed and to have sufficient information to enable it to return those items to their previous values. Since the system must contain an abort procedure for dealing with crashes and other conditions anyway, this procedure can be made available to all transactions. The transaction designer can thus avoid having to program the abort.

Programming conventions for bracketing a transaction. Each transaction processing system must provide a set of programming conventions so that the programmer can specify a transaction's boundaries. These conventions differ from one system to another. For example, the start of a transaction might be denoted by a `begin_transaction` command, and its successful completion might be denoted by a `commit` command.

The execution of the `commit` command at run time is a *request* to commit. The system might decide to commit the transaction or, for the reasons previously discussed, to abort it. A `rollback` command is provided so that a transaction can abort itself. In contrast to the request to commit, a request to roll back is always honored by the system.

Before the commit is executed, the transaction must be in an uncommitted state (and can still be aborted). After it is executed, the transaction is in a committed state (and can no longer be aborted). The commit operation must be atomic in the sense that no intermediate state separates the uncommitted and committed states. As a result, if the system crashes while the commit is in progress, on recovery the transaction will be either committed or uncommitted.

18.3 Durability

A second requirement of the transaction processing system is that it not lose information. For example, if you register for a course and your transaction commits, you expect the system to remember that fact despite subsequent hardware or software failures. Even if an ice storm causes a power blackout the next day and the computer crashes (or even if the crash occurs one microsecond after your transaction commits), you still want to be able to attend class. Conventional operating systems usually do not guarantee durability. Backups might be kept, but no assurances are given that the most recent changes are durable. Hardware failures are not restricted to the central processing unit (CPU) and its local memory. The data stored on a mass storage device can also be lost if the device malfunctions. For these reasons, we require *durability*.

> **Durability.** The system must ensure that once the transaction commits, its effects remain in the database even if the computer or the medium on which the database is stored subsequently fails.

Durability can be achieved by storing data redundantly on different backup devices. The characteristics of these devices lead to different degrees of system **availability**. If the devices are fast, the system might provide **nonstop** availability. For example, with **mirrored disks** two identical copies of the database are maintained on different mass storage devices, and updates are made immediately to both devices. Even though one device might fail, the information in the database is still readily available on the other and service can be provided. As a result, the malfunction might be imperceptible to users. The telephone system has this requirement (although in practice the requirement cannot always be met).

If the backup device is slow, service might be unavailable to users for some period of time after a failure while a **recovery** procedure, which restores the database, is executed. Most airline reservation systems are of this type, much to the chagrin of air travelers who want to make reservations when the system is temporarily unavailable. The Student Registration System is also of this type.

In the real world, durability is relative. What kinds of events do we want the committed data in our system to survive?

- CPU crash
- Disk failure
- Multiple disk failures
- Fire
- Malicious attacks

Different costs are involved in achieving durability for each of these events. Each enterprise must decide the degree of durability that is essential to its business, the probability of specific failures that might affect durability, and the level of durability for which it is willing to pay. Many enterprises keep backup copies of their databases in different cities or even in different countries to support a high level of durability.

18.4 Isolation

In discussing atomicity, consistency, and durability, we concentrated on the effect of a single transaction. We next examine the effect of executing a set of transactions. We say that a set of transactions is executed sequentially, or **serially**, if one transaction in it is executed to completion before another is started. Hence, at any given time only one transaction is being processed. The nice thing about serial execution is that, if all transactions are consistent and the database is initially in a consistent state, consistency is maintained. When the first transaction in the set starts, the database is in a consistent state and, since the transaction is consistent, the database will be consistent when the transaction completes. Since the database is consistent when the second transaction starts, it too will perform correctly, and the argument repeats.

Serial execution is adequate for applications that have modest performance requirements, but it is insufficient for applications that have strict requirements on response time and throughput. Fortunately, modern computer systems consist of a collection of processors—CPUs and input/output (I/O) processors—that are capable of the **concurrent execution** of a number of computations and I/O transfers. A transaction, on the other hand, is generally a **sequential program** that alternates between computation on local variables, which requires the use of a CPU, and reading or writing information to or from the database, which requires the use of an I/O device. In either case, the service of only a single processor at a time is needed. Modern computing systems are therefore capable of servicing more than one transaction simultaneously, and we refer to this mode of execution as **concurrent execution**. Concurrent execution is appropriate in a transaction processing system serving many users. In this case, there are many active, partially completed transactions at any given time.

In concurrent execution, the database operations of different transactions are effectively interleaved in time, as shown in Figure 18.1. Transaction T_1 alternately computes (using local variables) and sends requests (SQL statements) to the database system to perform operations on the database. For example, an operation might transfer data between the database and local variables or it might perform some specific update on a database variable. The requests are made in the sequence $op_{1,1}$, $op_{1,2}$. We refer to this as a **transaction schedule**. T_2 behaves in a similar way. Since the executions of the two transactions are not synchronized, the order of operations arriving at the database, called a **schedule**, is an arbitrary merge of the two sequences. In Figure 18.1, this sequence is $op_{1,1}$, $op_{2,1}$, $op_{2,2}$, $op_{1,2}$.

When transactions are executed concurrently, the consistency of each transaction is not sufficient to guarantee that the database remains consistent. For example, although a consistent transaction that starts in a consistent state leaves the database in a consistent state when it commits, its intermediate states during execution need not be consistent. Another (consistent) transaction that reads the values of variables in such an intermediate state can thus behave unpredictably because it assumes that it starts in a consistent state. Suppose, for example, that the registrar periodically executes an audit transaction that prints student and course records. If that transaction executes after a registration transaction updates the course count and before it updates the class roster, the information printed will be inconsistent: the total number of student records indicating enrollment in the course will be one less than the number of students shown in the course record as enrolled in the course. In this example, the database ultimately reaches a consistent state even though the information printed by the audit transaction is inconsistent.

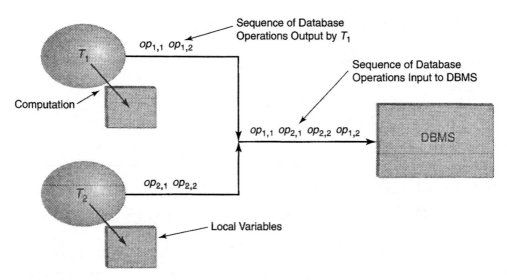

FIGURE 18.1 Database operations output by two transactions in a concurrent schedule might be interleaved in time. Note that the figure should be interpreted as meaning that $op_{1,1}$ arrives first at DBMS followed by $op_{2,1}$, etc.

Concurrent execution can also destroy consistency. In Figure 2.4 on page 23, we showed a concurrent schedule of two registration transactions that destroys consistency. Each transaction read from the database that there were 29 students currently registered in the course, and since the allowable number of students was 30, they each allowed a student to register. After both transactions completed, the count of the number of students registered for the course did not reflect the state of the real world since it said that 30 students were registered when in fact there were 31. In addition, the database state did not satisfy one of the integrity constraints because there were 31 entries on the class roster, although the integrity constraint said there could be no more than 30.

Figure 18.2 illustrates a similar situation. In this case, the execution of two bank deposit transactions is interleaved. Assume that the only integrity constraint asserts that the balance of each account is greater than zero. T_1 is attempting to deposit $5, and T_2 is attempting to deposit $20. In its first step, each transaction reads the balance as 10. In their second steps, T_2 writes 30 and T_1 writes 15. Since the final value is 15, T_2's update is lost. Note that the final database state is consistent, because the value of the balance is greater than zero. It is just incorrect: the value of the balance should be 35. If the transactions had executed sequentially, T_1 would have completed before T_2 was allowed to start, T_2 would have read a starting balance of 15, and both updates would have been reflected in the final database.

The failures we have been describing result from the fact that concurrent transactions are accessing shared data—the database (this is exactly the *critical section* problem discussed in the context of operating systems). For this reason, in studying the correctness of concurrent transactions, we are justified in concentrating on the

FIGURE 18.2 A schedule in which two deposit transactions are not isolated from one another.

T_1:   *step* 1:   *step* 2:
         r(*bal*: 10)   *w*(*bal*: 15)

T_2:   *step* 1:   *step* 2:
                            r(*bal*: 10)   *w*(*bal*: 30)

FIGURE 18.3 Schedule illustrating the failure of atomicity when transactions are not isolated.

T_1 : *w*(*prereq*: *new_list*)   *abort*

T_2:   *r*(*prereq*: *new_list*)   *commit*

---

operations that access the shared data—the database operations—rather than on the internal operations within the transaction.

Atomicity is also complicated by concurrent execution. For example, in Figure 18.3, T_1 is a transaction that eliminates a prerequisite, $course_1$, from another course, $course_2$. T_1 writes the new list of prerequisites to the database with the operation *w*(*prereq*: *new_list*). The new list is read by the registration transaction T_2, and, based on it, the student is successfully registered. However, after T_2 commits, T_1 aborts and the original list is reinstated. The fact that the student might successfully register for $course_2$ without having taken $course_1$ implies that T_1 has had an effect despite having aborted. Thus, T_1's execution is not atomic.

As these examples demonstrate, we must specify some restriction on concurrent execution that guarantees consistency and atomicity. One such *sufficient* restriction is *isolation*.

Isolation. Even though transactions are executed concurrently, the overall effect of the schedule is the same as if the transactions had executed serially in some order.

The exact meaning of this requirement will be made more clear in Chapters 20 and 21. However, it should be evident that if the transactions are consistent and if the overall effect of a concurrent schedule is the same as that of some serial schedule, the concurrent schedule will maintain consistency. Concurrent schedules that satisfy this condition are called **serializable**.

Note that conventional operating systems usually do not guarantee isolation. Different programs might read and write shared files maintained by the file system. Since the operating system enforces no restriction on the order in which these reads and writes are performed, isolation is not guaranteed when the programs are run concurrently.

18.5 The ACID Properties

The features that distinguish transactions from ordinary programs are frequently abbreviated by the acronym ACID [Haerder and Reuter 1983], which denotes the following four properties of transactions.

- *Atomic*. Each transaction is executed completely or not at all.
- *Consistent*. The execution of each transaction in isolation maintains database consistency and moves it to a new state that correctly models the new state of the enterprise.
- *Isolated*. The concurrent execution of a set of transactions has the same effect as that of some serial execution of that set.
- *Durable*. The results of committed transactions are permanent.

It is the transaction designer's job to design consistent transactions. It is the transaction processing system's job to guarantee that transactions are atomic, isolated, and durable. This guarantee greatly simplifies the designer's task since there is no need to be concerned with failures or concurrent execution.

The ACID properties guarantee that each schedule maintains database consistency in the following sense:

> The ACID properties guarantee that the database is a correct, consistent, and up-to-date model of the real world.

Many applications require such a guarantee of correctness.

ACID properties in the real world.   In later chapters, we will show that implementing atomicity, isolation, and durability can cause system performance to suffer. For example,

- Isolation is usually implemented by requiring transactions to obtain locks on the database items they access. These locks prevent other transactions from accessing the items until the locks are released. If locks are held for long periods of time, long waits result and the performance of the system suffers.
- Atomicity and durability are generally implemented by maintaining a log of update operations. Log maintenance involves overhead.
- The atomicity of a distributed transaction requires that the transaction either commit at all sites or abort at all sites. Thus, when the transaction completes at one site it cannot unilaterally commit there. Instead, it must wait until accesses at all sites have completed. Since locks cannot be released until commit time, this might cause a significant delay.

Even though implementation of the ACID properties involves performance penalties, many transaction processing applications are designed to execute in this way. For some applications, however, the penalties are unacceptable—the system cannot achieve the desired throughput or response time. In such situations, isolation is often sacrificed. It is weakened in order to improve performance. For example,

- Some applications do not require exact information about the real world. For example, a decision support system for a nationwide chain of department stores might allow store managers to obtain information about the inventory held in each store. Such information is useful in deciding when to purchase additional merchandise. When transactions are completely isolated, the system produces a snapshot of the inventory of all the stores as it exists at some instant of time. However, managers might be able to make adequate purchasing decisions with an approximate snapshot, in which the inventory reported for some stores is an hour or so old while that reported for others is up to date, or in which a few stores do not supply their inventory at all.

- Some transaction processing applications must model the real world exactly but execute correctly even though transactions are not completely isolated. Complete isolation guarantees that *any* application executes correctly: it is *sufficient* but not *necessary*. *Some* applications model the real world exactly even though some transactions are not isolated. (We will give examples of such applications in Section 21.2.2.)

To improve the performance of such applications, most commercial systems implement weaker levels of isolation that do not guarantee schedules that are equivalent to serial schedules. Designers must choose the level of isolation appropriate for their application. One goal of the following chapters is to explore this issue.

BIBLIOGRAPHIC NOTES

Excellent treatments of transactions and their implementation are given in [Gray and Reuter 1993; Lynch et al. 1994; Bernstein and Newcomer 1997]. The term "ACID" was coined in [Haerder and Reuter 1983], but the individual components of ACID were introduced in earlier papers, for example [Gray et al. 1976; Eswaran et al. 1976].

EXERCISES

18.1 Some distributed transaction processing systems replicate data at two or more sites separated geographically. A common technique for organizing replicated systems is one in which transactions that update a data item must change all replicas. Hence, one possible integrity constraint in a replicated system is that the values of all of the replicas of an item be the same. Explain how transactions running on such a system might violate

    a. Atomicity
    b. Consistency
    c. Isolation
    d. Durability

18.2 Consider the replicated system described in the previous problem.

    a. What is the impact of replication on the performance of a read-only transaction?

b. What is the impact of replication on the performance of a transaction that both reads and writes the data?

c. What is the impact of replication on the communication system?

18.3 Give three examples of transactions, other than an ATM bank withdrawal, in which a real-world event occurs if and only if the transaction commits.

18.4 The schema of the Student Registration System includes the number of current registrants and a list of registered students in each course.

a. What integrity constraint relates this data?

b. How might a registration transaction that is not atomic violate this constraint?

c. Suppose the system also implements a transaction that displays the current information about a course. Give a nonisolated schedule in which the transaction displays inconsistent information.

18.5 Give three examples of applications in which certain transactions need not be totally isolated and, as a result, might return data which, although not the result of a serializable schedule, is adequate for the needs of the applications.

18.6 Describe a situation in which the execution of a program under your local operating system is not

a. Atomic

b. Isolated

c. Durable

18.7 At exactly noon on a particular day, 100 people at 100 different ATM terminals attempt to withdraw cash from their bank accounts at the same bank. Suppose their transactions are run sequentially and each transaction takes .25 seconds of compute and I/O time. Estimate how long it takes to execute all 100 transactions and what the average response time is for all 100 customers.

18.8 You have the choice of running a single transaction to transfer $300 from one of your savings accounts to another savings account at the same bank or of running two transactions, one to withdraw $300 from one account and a second to deposit $300 in the other. In the first choice the transfer is made atomically; in the second it is not. Describe a scenario in which after the transfer, the sum of the balances in the two accounts is different (from what it was when both transactions started) at the instant the transfer is complete. *Hint:* Other transactions might be executing at the same time that you are doing the funds transfer.

18.9 A distributed transaction consists of subtransactions that execute at different sites and access local DBMSs at those sites. For example, a distributed transaction that transfers money from a bank account at site A to a bank account at site B executes a subtransaction at A that does the withdrawal and then a subtransaction at B that does the deposit.

Such a distributed transaction must satisfy the ACID properties in a global sense: it must be globally atomic, isolated, consistent, and durable. The issue is, if the subtransactions at each site individually satisfy the ACID properties, does the distributed transaction necessarily satisfy the ACID properties? Certainly if the subtransactions at each site are individually durable, the distributed transaction is durable. Give examples of situations in which

a. The subtransactions at each site are atomic, but the distributed transaction is not atomic.

       b. The subtransactions at each site are consistent, but the distributed transaction is not consistent.

       c. The subtransactions at each site are isolated, but the distributed transaction is not isolated.

18.10 Isolation is a sufficient but not necessary condition to achieve correctness. Consider an application that reserves seats for a concert. Each reservation transaction (1) reads the list of seats that have not yet been reserved, (2) presents them to a potential customer who selects one of them, and (3) marks the selected seat as reserved. An integrity constraint asserts that the same seat cannot be reserved by two different customers. Describe a situation in which two such transactions that reserve two different seats execute in a nonisolated fashion but are nevertheless correct.

18.11 Assume a schedule consists of consistent transactions that execute in an isolated fashion except for one transaction that performs a single update that is lost (as in Figure 18.2). Show that the final state of the database satisfies all integrity constraints but nevertheless is incorrect.

19

Models of Transactions

All of the transactions in the Student Registration System are short and make only a small number of accesses to data stored in a single database server. However, many applications involve long transactions that make many database accesses. For example, in a student billing system a single transaction might prepare the tuition and housing bills for all 10,000 students in a university, and in truly large systems a transaction might access millions of records stored in multiple database servers running at different sites in a network. To deal with such long and complex transactions, many transaction processing systems provide mechanisms for imposing some structure on transactions or for breaking up a single task into several related transactions. In this chapter, we describe some of these structuring mechanisms from the point of view of the application designer. In later chapters, we will describe how the mechanisms can be implemented.

19.1 Flat Transactions

The transaction model we have discussed involves a database on a single server. It has no internal structure and so is called a **flat transaction**, which has the form

```
begin_transaction();
    S;
commit();
```

We introduce the `begin_transaction()` statement here, although, if you recall our discussion of transactions in Section 8.2.3, no such statement exists in the SQL-92 standard (a transaction is implicitly started when the previous transaction ends). It does exist, however, in SQL:1999. In this and later sections in this chapter we talk about transactions in a more general context, and it is useful to describe the abstraction of a transaction explicitly and to use a new syntax for that purpose. `begin_transaction()` informs the DBMS that a new transaction has begun and that the subsequent SQL statements contained in S are part of it.

A transaction alternates between computation using local variables and the execution of SQL statements. These statements cause data and status information to be passed between the database and local variables—which include the in and out parameters of the SQL statements and descriptors. The computation completes when the transaction requests that the server commit or abort the changes to the database that have been made. The DBMS guarantees the transaction's atomicity, isolation, and durability.

To understand the limitations of this model, consider the following situations.

1. Suppose that a travel-planning transaction must make flight reservations for a trip from London to Des Moines. The strategy might be to make a reservation from London to New York, then a reservation from New York to Chicago, and finally a reservation from Chicago to Des Moines. Now suppose that, after making the first two reservations, it is found that there are no seats available on the flight from Chicago to Des Moines. The transaction might decide to give up the New York to Chicago reservation and instead choose a route from New York to St. Louis and then to Des Moines.

    There are several options for designing such a transaction. The transaction might abort when it fails to get the Chicago-to-Des Moines reservation, and a subsequent transaction might be used to route the trip through St. Louis. The difficulty with this approach is that the computation to get a reservation from London to New York (and the resulting reservation) will be lost, and the subsequent transaction might find that there are no longer seats available on that flight. Another approach is for the transaction to cancel the New York-to-Chicago reservation and route the trip through St. Louis. While this is a viable approach, in a more involved situation in which a number of computations must be undone, the code for doing this can be quite complex. Furthermore, it seems that with relatively little effort the transaction processing system itself might be able to provide a mechanism for undoing some part of the computation. The system already provides the abstraction of total rollback (abort). What is needed here is a generalization of that abstraction for partial rollback.

2. Since Des Moines does not handle international flights, our traveler must change planes at some point and will probably have to make hotel and auto reservations. Hence, the transaction has to access multiple databases involving different database servers running on machines that might be spread around the world. Despite this multiplicity of database servers, we still want to maintain the ACID abstraction. For example, if we succeed in reserving a seat on the international flight, but the server maintaining the domestic airline's database crashes (making it impossible to arrange a complete trip), we need to abort that reservation. In general, new techniques are needed to guarantee the atomicity, isolation, and durability of transactions that access multiple servers.

3. Arranging a trip includes not only making the necessary reservations but printing and mailing the tickets as well. It is necessary that these jobs get done, but they need not all be done at the same time, particularly since some jobs require mechanical operations and the intervention of humans. Thus, the activities performed by a transaction might be spread out in time as well as in space. Useful here are models that allow a transaction to create other transactions to be executed at a later time. More generally, a model is needed to describe an entire

enterprise-wide activity, involving multiple, related jobs performed at different locations and at different times by both computers and humans.

4. Banks post interest at the end of each quarter. One way to do this is to execute a separate transaction that updates the balance and other relevant account information for each account. If there are 10,000 accounts, 10,000 transactions must be executed. The problem with this approach is that between two successive transactions, the database is in an inconsistent state. Interest has been posted in some accounts but not in others. If at that point an auditor were to run a transaction that summed the balances in all accounts, the total would be a meaningless number. A better approach is to post interest to all accounts in a single transaction. Suppose that this is done with a flat transaction and that after it has posted interest to the first 9,000 accounts, the system crashes. Since the transaction is aborted, all the time and compute cycles it has expended are lost. A model is needed in which a transaction is allowed to preserve partial results in spite of system failures.

The next sections present transaction models that address these and other related issues.

19.2 Providing Structure within a Transaction

With the introduction of flat transactions, the application designer was essentially given an all-or-nothing choice: use flat transactions to get atomicity, isolation, and durability, or design the application without relying on these abstractions. In the remainder of this chapter (and in the following chapters), we will describe models and mechanisms that provide a more refined access to these abstractions. Atomicity, isolation, and durability are made available in different degrees. This flexibility is achieved by introducing structure within a transaction. Structuring implies decomposition. A transaction is broken into parts that relate to each other in various ways. In some cases, the internal structure of a transaction is not visible to other transactions. In other cases it is, and the abstraction of isolation, which is enshrined in ACID, is breached.

In this section we describe models in which the transaction is conceived as a single, tightly integrated unit of work. In Section 19.3 we describe models in which the subtasks of an application are more loosely connected.

19.2.1 Savepoints

Database systems generally provide **savepoints** [Astrahan et al. 1976], which are points in a transaction that serve as the targets of partial rollbacks of the database. A savepoint marks a particular point in the execution of a transaction. The transaction can specify several different savepoints, which are numbered consecutively, so that they can be distinguished and so that the transaction can refer to a specific one at a later time. A savepoint is created using a call to the database server, such as

$$sp := \texttt{create\_savepoint()}$$

The value returned is the savepoint's index, which names the point in the program at which the savepoint was created. A transaction with several savepoints has the form

```
begin_transaction();
    S₁;
    sp1 := create_savepoint();
    S₂;
    sp2 := create_savepoint();
    . . .
    Sₙ;
    spn := create_savepoint();
    . . .
    if (condition) {
        rollback(spi);
        . . .
    }
    . . .
commit();
```

A transaction can request a rollback to a particular previously created savepoint using

```
rollback(sp)
```

where the variable *sp* contains the target savepoint's index.

The semantics of rollback is that the values of the database items accessed by the transaction, called its **database context**, are returned to the state they had when the savepoint was created—any database changes that the transaction made after that savepoint was created are undone. The execution of the transaction then continues at the statement after the rollback statement (not the statement after `create_savepoint()`).

For example, the travel-planning transaction might create a savepoint after each individual flight reservation is made. When it is discovered that there are no seats available on the flight from Chicago to Des Moines, the transaction rolls back to the savepoint created after the London-to-New York reservation was made, causing reversal of the database changes made by the New York-to-Chicago reservation. The desired effect is that the database is in the same state it would have been in if the transaction had never attempted to route the passenger through Chicago. We will discuss the implementation of savepoints (and, particularly, how isolation is maintained) in Section 20.8.1.

Note that, although the database is returned to the state it had at the time the savepoint was created, the state of the transaction's local variables is not affected by the rollback call (i.e., the variables are not rolled back). Hence, they might contain values that have been influenced by the values of database items read since the savepoint was created. For example, after creating a savepoint, a transaction might read a database item, x, storing its value in local variable $X1$, then calculate a new value in local variable $X2$ and write it back to x. If the transaction subsequently rolls back to the savepoint, x is restored to its original value and $X2$ has a value that is no longer in the database. The value of $X2$ might influence the subsequent execution of the transaction. This means that rolling back to a savepoint does not create the illusion that execution between savepoint creation and rollback did not occur. Indeed, such an illusion would be inappropriate, since the transaction would then redo the rolled-back computation. The transaction needs to know that rollback has occurred so that a different execution path is taken afterward.

Note that the database state at a savepoint is not durable. If the transaction is aborted or the system crashes, the database is returned to the state it had when the transaction started. Although in one sense an abort can be viewed as a rollback to an (implicitly declared) initial savepoint, there is an important difference between abort and rollback to a savepoint. An aborted transaction does not continue after the abort is executed, whereas a transaction that has been rolled back to a savepoint does continue.

Also, note that after executing the rollback statement rollback(sp_i), all savepoints created after sp_i but before the rollback are inaccessible, since it makes no sense to roll back to them later in the computation.

19.2.2 Distributed Transactions

Many transaction processing applications have evolved in similar ways. Over the years an enterprise develops a number of dedicated transaction processing systems to automate individual activities, such as inventory, billing, and payroll. Such systems might have been developed independently, by different groups, at different times, in different locations, using different hardware and software platforms and different database management systems. Each system exports a set of transactions, T_i. These transactions might be stored procedures executed at a database server or applications programs to be executed at user sites. In the latter case the database server exports an SQL interface and the (sub)transaction at that site is the sequence of SQL statements that the application program executes. In many cases, these systems have been operational for years and are known to be reliable. Therefore, management will not allow them to be modified in any way.[1]

As the requirements for automation increase, the enterprise finds it necessary to integrate these systems in order to perform more complex activities. At this point the systems are referred to as **legacy systems** because they are presented to the application designer as complete, unmodifiable units that must be used in building a larger system. Similarly, their transactions are referred to as **legacy transactions**.

---

[1] In some extreme cases, the person who originally implemented a particular transaction has long since left the company, proper documentation does not exist, and no one else understands how the transaction works.

FIGURE 19.1 Distributed transaction invoking legacy transactions at several server sites.

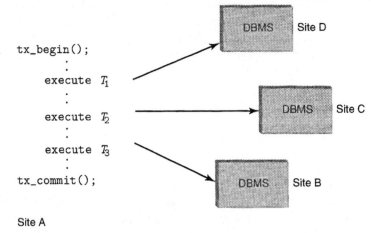

```
tx_begin();
    .
    .
    execute  T₁
    .
    execute  T₂
    .
    execute  T₃
    .
tx_commit();
```

Site A

Often the properties of legacy systems make integrating them into a larger system difficult.

For example, the inventory and billing systems might form components of a larger system for automating the sale of an item. Assuming that the servers are accessible through a network, a transaction in an integrated system is a program executed at some network site that invokes the legacy transactions that the servers export. Although it is possible that all of the individual systems reside on the same machine, this is generally not the case. We refer to such a transaction as a **distributed** or **global transaction**.

The situation is illustrated in Figure 19.1, which shows a distributed transaction that invokes three subtransactions. The execute statement can be viewed as a call either to a stored procedure at a server or to an application program provided by the legacy system and executed at site A. The figure shows a new syntax for managing the abstraction of a distributed transaction based on the X/Open standard, which we will discuss in Section 23.4. In contrast to begin_transaction(), tx_begin() is not a call to any particular database server. Instead, it is part of the API of the TP monitor, which controls the entire transaction processing system.

You should understand the advantage of constructing a distributed transaction in this way. The transaction sees billing and inventory as abstractions. Its logic can concentrate on integrating the results produced by the legacy transactions without concerning itself with the schema of the local databases, the details of the billing or inventory process, or issues such as atomicity, concurrency, and durability at each site.

For example, a company might have several warehouses at different sites. At each warehouse a transaction processing system maintains a local database for controlling inventory. The president of the company might want to execute a transaction at the main office (site A in Figure 19.1) that produces information based on the total inventory at all warehouses. That transaction causes legacy transactions (T_1, T_2, and T_3 in the figure) to be executed at each warehouse (sites B, C, and D in the figure) to gather the inventory information. Each legacy transaction communicates its result to the transaction at the main office, which integrates the information and produces a report.

More generally, a distributed transaction might consist of a program that invokes subtransactions at server sites as well as programs at other sites that are themselves distributed transactions (i.e., programs which invoke subtransactions). Hence, a distributed transaction can be viewed as a tree whose leaf nodes are subtransactions at server sites. Furthermore, servers might provide access to resources other than databases (such as files). Each subtransaction is a transaction at the server that it accesses and is therefore ACID. When these servers are database systems, we say that the distributed transaction executes in a multidatabase system. A **multidatabase** (sometimes called a **federated database**) is a loose confederation of databases that contain related information.

We assume that the database at each server, referred to as a local database, has **local integrity constraints**. Since each site maintains atomicity and isolation, these constraints are maintained despite the concurrent execution of the subtransactions of multiple distributed transactions at that site. In addition, the multidatabase, consisting of the combination of all local databases, might have **global integrity constraints** relating data at different sites. We assume that a distributed transaction is globally consistent and hence, when it executes in isolation, maintains those constraints as well.

As an example of a global integrity constraint, assume that a bank maintains local databases at all branch offices and that each database contains an item whose value is the assets of that branch. The bank also maintains a database at its central office that contains an item whose value is the total assets of the bank. A global integrity constraint might assert that the value of the total assets item at the central office is the sum of the values of the assets items at all of the local branches. Note that this constraint is not maintained by individual subtransactions. A deposit at a branch initiates a subtransaction at the branch's database that increments the branch's assets but not the total assets item at the central office. To maintain the global integrity constraint, the deposit subtransaction at the branch must be accompanied by a subtransaction at the central office to increment the total assets item by the same amount.

While it is the responsibility of the distributed transaction to maintain global consistency, the TP monitor might provide mechanisms to ensure that each distributed transaction (including all of its subtransactions) is atomic, isolated, and durable.

■ The atomicity of a distributed transaction implies that each subtransaction is atomic at the server it accesses and that either all subtransactions commit or all abort. Thus, when a subtransaction of a distributed transaction, T, completes, it cannot immediately commit because some other subtransaction of T might abort (in which case all of T's subtransactions must also abort). We refer to this all-or-nothing commitment as **global atomicity**.

- Isolation implies not only that each subtransaction is isolated from all other subtransactions executing at the same site (i.e., that each server serializes all the subtransactions that execute at that server) but also that each distributed transaction as a whole is isolated with respect to all others (i.e., that there is some global serialization order among all distributed transactions). Thus, **global serializability** implies that the subtransactions of two distributed transactions, T_1 and T_2, execute in such a way that at all servers it appears that T_1 preceded T_2 or that at all servers it appears that T_2 preceded T_1.

- The durability of a distributed transaction implies the durability of all of its subtransactions.

Global atomicity and isolation are sufficient to ensure that the concurrent execution of a set of distributed transactions has the same effect as if the distributed transactions had executed serially in some order. Since we assume that each distributed transaction taken as a whole is consistent, serializable execution implies that the concurrent schedule is correct. Later, we will discuss different models in which transactions are not necessarily globally atomic or isolated and in which correctness is not guaranteed.

Models of a distributed transaction.   A distributed transaction can be viewed as a tree. The root is the program that starts the transaction, and each descendant is a subtransaction that is initiated by the node which is its parent. The tree can be of arbitrary depth. Within that general structure are a number of options.

- The children of a particular subtransaction might or might not be able to execute concurrently.

- The parent of a set of subtransactions might or might not be able to execute concurrently with its children. In the case in which concurrent execution is possible, the parent might or might not be able to communicate with its children.

- In some models, only the root can request that the distributed transaction be committed. In other models, an arbitrary subtransaction can request that the transaction be committed, and it is the transaction designer's responsibility to ensure that only one subtransaction makes the request. In still other models, the right to request commit can be explicitly passed from one subtransaction to another.

A number of possible models exist within these options. Two particular variations predominate and can be viewed as extreme cases.

1. *Hierarchical model.* No concurrency is allowed within the transaction. Having initiated a subtransaction, the parent must wait until the subtransaction completes before proceeding. As a result, the parent can neither create additional subtransactions concurrent with the child nor communicate with it. The transaction is committed by the root. Procedure calling is a natural paradigm for communication within this model. TP monitors generally provide a special form of procedure calling known as **transactional remote procedure call (TRPC)**,

which, in addition to invoking a procedure, supports the abstraction of a distributed transaction. TRPC will be discussed in Section 23.5.3.

2. *Peer model.* Concurrency is permitted between a parent and its children and among the children. The hierarchical relationship between a parent and its children is minimized: once created, the child is coequal with, or a peer of, the parent. In particular, a parent and child can communicate symmetrically, and any participant can request that the transaction be committed. **Peer-to-peer communication** is the natural paradigm for communication within the peer model. A pair of subtransactions explicitly establishes a connection and then sends and receives messages over the connection. TP monitors generally support peer-to-peer communication, which we will discuss in Section 23.6.

19.2.3 Nested Transactions

Distributed transactions evolved out of a need to integrate, into a single transactional unit, transactions exported from legacy servers. Since each server supports the transaction abstraction, (sub)transactions separately control their commit/abort decision. As a result, the designer of the distributed transaction has little control over the structure of the distributed transaction. The function of each exported transaction is essentially fixed by the way data is distributed across the servers, and distribution might be controlled by such factors as where the data is generated or where it is accessed most often. This yields a bottom-up design, which might not reflect a clean functional decomposition of the application.

Because it was not conceived as a way of dealing with multiple servers or distributed data, the nested transaction model evolved differently. Its goal is to allow the transaction designer to design a complex transaction from the top down. The transaction is decomposed into subtransactions in a functionally appropriate way (not dictated by the distribution of data). Furthermore, although subtransactions still control their commit/abort decision, the handling of the decision is different. Instead of the all-or-nothing approach of the distributed model, individual subtransactions in the nested model can abort without aborting the entire transaction. Even so, the nested transaction as a whole remains globally isolated and atomic.

A number of concrete models for nested transactions have been proposed. We describe one such model, due to J. Eliot Moss [Moss 1985]. In that model, a transaction and all of its subtransactions can be viewed as a tree. The root of the tree is called the **top-level** transaction, and the terms "parent," "child," "ancestor," "descendent," and "sibling" have their usual meanings. Subtransactions that have no children are called **leaves**. Not all leaves need be at the same level. We assume that the transaction and all of its subtransactions execute at a single site. The semantics of the nested transaction model can be summarized as follows:

1. A parent can create children sequentially so that one child finishes before the next starts, or it can specify that a set of children execute concurrently. The parent does not execute concurrently with the children. It waits until all children in the set complete. Hence, it cannot communicate with its children while they

FIGURE 19.2 Structure of a travel planning transaction.

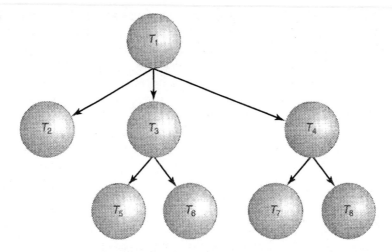

are executing. Once the children have completed, the parent resumes execution and can create additional children. Note that the tree structure depicting a nested transaction (Figure 19.2) does not distinguish children that execute concurrently from those that execute sequentially.

2. A subtransaction (and all of its descendents) appears to execute as a single isolated unit with respect to its concurrent siblings. For example, in Figure 19.2, if T_2 and T_3 execute concurrently, T_2 views the subtree (T_3, T_5, T_6) as a single isolated transaction. It does not see any internal structure. It follows that the effect of the concurrent execution of a set of siblings is the same as if they had executed sequentially in *some* serial order. Thus, the siblings are serializable with respect to each other.

    In some cases, the serialization order of the siblings affects the final state of the database. For example, in a banking application two concurrent siblings whose task is to write checks from the same account produce the same final balance independent of the actual order (assuming that the initial balance of the account was sufficient to cover both checks). However, the check numbers are dependent on the order. Thus, the nested transaction is not deterministic: the same transaction when run at different times can produce different results. If designed correctly, however, all possible results are acceptable to the application.

    We can view all nested transactions executing concurrently as being structured into a single tree with a (fictitious) "mother of all top-level transactions" as a root and all top-level transactions as its children. It then follows that a top-level transaction together with its descendents (taken as a single unit) is isolated with respect to each concurrently executing top-level transaction (and all its descendents). The hierarchical structure within a nested transaction is thus invisible outside of that transaction.

3. Subtransactions are atomic. Each subtransaction can abort or commit independently. The commitment of a subtransaction and its durability are conditional on the commitment of its parent. Hence, a subtransaction is finally committed

and made durable when all of its ancestors (including the top-level transaction) commit, at which point the entire nested transaction is said to have committed. If a subtransaction aborts, all of its children (even those that have committed) are aborted.

4. If a subtransaction aborts, it has the same effect as if it had not executed any database operations. Status is returned to the parent, and the parent can take appropriate action. An aborted subtransaction can thus alter the execution path of the parent transaction and, in this way, can have an impact on the database state. Contrast this to the situation with conventional (flat) transactions, in which an aborted transaction has no effect whatsoever. Also contrast this to distributed transaction, in which the abort of a subtransaction causes the entire transaction to abort.

5. A subtransaction is not necessarily consistent. However, the nested transaction as a whole is consistent.

The implementation of isolation for nested transactions is more complex than that for flat transactions, since concurrency is possible not only between nested transactions but within them as well. We will discuss this issue in Section 20.8.4.

We illustrate the nested transaction model using our travel-planning example. The nested structure of this transaction is shown in Figure 19.2.

Transaction T_1 makes airline reservations for a trip from London to Des Moines. It might first create a subtransaction, T_2, to make a reservation from London to New York and, when that completes, create a second subtransaction, T_3, to make a reservation from New York to Des Moines. T_3, in turn, might create an additional subtransaction, T_5, to make a reservation from New York to Chicago, and T_6, to make a reservation from Chicago to Des Moines. T_5 and T_6 might be specified to execute concurrently. They might access common data (e.g., the customer's bank account), but their execution is serializable.

If T_6 cannot make the reservation from Chicago to Des Moines, it can abort. When T_3 learns of the abort, it can abandon the plan to travel through Chicago and hence also abort (thus causing its other child, T_5, to abort and release the reservation from New York to Chicago). When T_1 learns of the abort, it can create a new subtransaction, T_4, to make reservations from New York to Des Moines through St. Louis (while still maintaining the reservation between London and New York). If T_4 commits, T_1 can commit and its effect on the database will be the sum of the effects of T_2, T_4, T_7, and T_8. The transaction as a whole is viewed as an isolated and atomic unit by other nested transactions.

19.3 Structuring an Application as Multiple Transactions

In a number of situations, it becomes necessary to decompose what might ordinarily be a single transaction into smaller transactions. For example, a long-running transaction might be decomposed so that locks it has acquired can be released at intermediate points, with the goal of improving performance. Or we might want to commit at intermediate points to avoid losing too much work in the event of a crash. In some situations, what might ordinarily be a single transaction involves subtasks that take place at different times. In this section, we discuss methods for providing such structure. We also discuss workflow management systems, which provide a way to view a complex business activity as a set of subtasks that must be executed in some application-dependent way.

19.3.1 Chained Transactions

Often, an application program consists of a sequence of transactions. For example, in a catalog-ordering application there might be a program that consists of a sequence of three transactions: order-entry, shipping, and billing. Between their execution, the program retains information in local variables about the items ordered and the person who ordered them, and it might perform some computations with this information.

A trivial optimization, called **chaining**, automatically starts a new transaction when the previous transaction in the sequence commits, thus avoiding the use of `begin_transaction()` (and the associated overhead of invoking the DBMS) for all but the first transaction in the sequence.[2] When chaining is enabled, an application program consisting of a sequence of transactions has the form

```
begin_transaction();
    S1;
commit();
    S2;
commit();
    . . .
    Sn-1;
commit();
    Sn;
commit();
```

where S_i is the body of the ith transaction, ST_i.

The execution of each commit statement makes the database changes caused by the prior transaction durable. Hence, if a crash occurs during the execution of ST_i, all changes made by $ST_1, \ldots, ST_{i-1}$ are preserved in the database when the system is restarted. Of course, information stored by the application in local variables is lost.

Chaining can be viewed from a different perspective when designing long-running transactions, such as the student billing transaction described earlier. Instead of the automatic start of a new transaction, our concern now is to avoid total rollback if a crash occurs. With chaining, a long-running transaction can be decomposed into a sequence of code fragments, $S_1, S_2, \ldots, S_n$, which are chained together

---

[2] Actually, `begin_transaction()` can be dispensed with there as well—the first interaction with the server can automatically start a transaction.

as shown above and in which each fragment is a subtransaction. For example, the transaction described earlier that posts interest to 10,000 bank accounts might be decomposed into 10 subtransactions, each of which posts interest to 1,000 accounts.

The following considerations arise when a long-running transaction is decomposed into a chain:

1. The good news is that if a crash occurs during a subtransaction, only the results of that subtransaction are lost since the results of prior subtransactions have already been made durable. (This behavior should be contrasted with that of a transaction using savepoints, where the work of the entire transaction is lost in a crash.) The bad news is that the transaction as a whole is no longer atomic. After recovery, the system assumes no responsibility for restarting the chain from the point at which the crash occurred.

2. Since the subtransactions were originally part of a single transaction, and so perform a single task, they generally need to communicate with each other. They share access to a common set of local variables, so communication can be easily accomplished. For example, if the interest-posting transaction is decomposed as described above, a local variable might contain the index of the last account updated. When a new subtransaction starts, it uses that variable to determine which account to process next. The problem with communication using local variables is that they do not survive a crash, and so, when resuming execution after a crash, a local variable cannot be used to identify the next account to be processed.

   As an alternative, the subtransactions might communicate through database variables. For example, the index of the last account updated by a subtransaction might be stored in a database item before the subtransaction commits. If a crash occurs during execution of the next subtransaction, that database item indicates where posting must resume. Note that in this case the database items used for communication are available to transactions executing in other (concurrent) applications. Care must be taken to ensure that the other applications do not tamper with this information.

3. The database context is not maintained between one subtransaction and the next in a chain. For example, if locks are used to implement isolation, all of the locks held by subtransaction ST_i are released when it commits. Thus, if ST_{i+1} is the next subtransaction in the chain and it accesses an item that ST_i has accessed, the value that ST_{i+1} sees might be different from the value the item had when ST_i committed (because some other transaction—not in the chain—modified the item and committed between the time ST_i committed and the time ST_{i+1} requested access to the item). The point here is that, in contrast to a single long-running transaction, each subtransaction in the chain is isolated but the chained transaction as a whole is not.

   Another component of the database context is the state of any cursor that the transaction has opened. Since commit closes cursors, any cursor that ST_i opens is not available to ST_{i+1}.

Although isolation is forfeited, chaining can yield a performance benefit. With locking, a long-running transaction can make the portions of the database that it accesses unavailable for long periods. This can create a performance bottleneck since concurrent transactions are made to wait until the transaction commits and releases the locks it has acquired. By breaking up the transaction into chained subtransactions, locks are released quickly and the bottleneck is eliminated.

4. Our initial view of chaining was one in which a sequence of individual transactions are processed and chaining automatically starts the next transaction in the sequence when the prior transaction completes. In that case, each individual transaction is consistent, so the database is in a consistent state between transactions. When we view chaining as a mechanism for decomposing a single long-running transaction, the situation is different. Although the entire long-running transaction is consistent, the individual subtransactions might not be. This creates a problem, since a subtransaction releases its database context when it commits, making it visible to other, concurrently executing transactions. If these transactions must see a consistent database state, we must require that the subtransactions be consistent. The issue of consistency does not arise with savepoints because the entire transaction is isolated and atomic in that case. Since the database context is not released at a savepoint, no concurrent transaction can see an inconsistent state.

The consistency of subtransactions is also required in order to deal with crashes. If a crash occurs, the chained transaction does not run to completion and its partial effects are visible to transactions in other applications when the system is restarted. Thus, just as the chained transaction is not isolated, it is also not atomic.

An alternate semantics for chained transactions. From a pedagogical point of view, it is interesting to consider an alternate semantics for chained transactions that deals with some of the issues raised by the conventional interpretation. To distinguish this new semantics from its more conventional counterpart, we use the function call chain(). A chained transaction now has the form

```
begin_transaction();
    S₁;
    chain();
    S₂;
    chain();
    ...
    Sₙ₋₁;
    chain();
    Sₙ;
commit();
```

`chain()` commits a subtransaction, ST_i (thus making it durable), and starts a new subtransaction, ST_{i+1}, hence the work lost in a crash is limited to the updates of the subtransaction being executed when the crash occurs. `chain`, however, does not release the database context, and it maintains cursors. When locks are used to implement isolation, any locks held by ST_i are not released but are instead passed on to ST_{i+1}. Thus, if ST_{i+1} accesses an item that ST_i accessed, the value it sees is the same as the value it had when ST_i committed. Since the modifications to the database caused by ST_i are not visible to concurrent transactions, the individual subtransactions need no longer be consistent, and ST_i can leave the database in an inconsistent state if ST_{i+1} has been designed to expect that state. Thus, the chained transaction as a whole is isolated, although performance suffers.

Crash recovery is complicated with this semantics. If recovery simply rolls back the subtransaction that was active at the time of the crash, isolation is not supported since transactions that start after recovery can see an inconsistent state. The chained transaction as a whole cannot be rolled back since earlier subtransactions in the chain have committed. This means that, with the new semantics, a chained transaction must be rolled forward once the first subtransaction has committed. If a crash occurs during the execution of ST_{i+1}, the recovery procedure restarts ST_{i+1} and delivers to ST_{i+1} the database context held by ST_i when it committed (i.e., the database context as it existed at that point, together with the locks held by ST_i). Restarting in this way provides both isolation and atomicity for the chain as a whole. Recall, however, that restarting a transaction is not normally the responsibility of a recovery procedure.

19.3.2 Sagas and Compensation

Suppose we use (the conventional notion of) chaining to decompose a single long-running transaction into a sequence of subtransactions, and, after some number of subtransactions have committed, we decide that all the work should be reversed. Unfortunately, atomicity cannot be achieved. Each committed subtransaction released the locks it held on the items it modified when it committed, so the new values were made visible to concurrent transactions, hence we can no longer guarantee that those subtransactions have had no effect.

But suppose we would like to forge ahead anyway and reverse the changes made by the committed subtransactions. We might think that one way to do this is to simply save the original value of each item at the time it was updated and restore that value to the item. We refer to this approach as physical restoration or *physical logging* (see Section 22.2.3). It works for flat or nested transactions since each updated item is locked until the entire transaction commits, hence each item's new value cannot have been accessed by any concurrent transaction.

Unfortunately, undoing changes made by a chained transaction is more complex. Suppose that transaction T_1 is decomposed into a chain of two subtransactions, $ST_{1,1}$, $ST_{1,2}$, and executed concurrently with transaction T_2. If the execution of T_2 is interleaved between the execution of $ST_{1,1}$ and $ST_{1,2}$, then T_2 can access an item, x, updated by $ST_{1,1}$. A problem arises if T_2 also updates x, and the decision to reverse

T_1 is made when $ST_{1,2}$ is executing. If T_2 commits, it would not be correct to simply restore the value x had before the update in $ST_{1,1}$ because the update made by T_2 would be lost. Hence, physical logging does not work in this situation.

A technique used to solve this problem is called **compensation**. Instead of restoring the value of an item updated by a transaction physically, we restore it *logically* by executing a **compensating transaction**. For example, in the student registration application, a *Deregistration* transaction logically reverses the effect of a successful *Registration* transaction. The *Registration* transaction increments the enrollment attribute of a course, and the compensating *Deregistration* transaction decrements the attribute. Compensation does the reversal correctly even if the execution of the *Registration* and *Deregistration* transactions for one student, A, are separated by the execution of one or both of these transactions for another student, B, although atomicity is not guaranteed. If A (temporarily) gets the last seat in the course, B will be denied entry before that seat reappears.

In some applications, the compensating transaction need not logically undo all database updates made by the transaction for which it compensates. For example, while a *Reservation* transaction might add a passenger's name to the mailing list the airline uses for advertising purposes, a *Cancellation* transaction might not remove it.

[Garcia-Molina and Salem 1987] proposed a transaction model, called a **Saga**, incorporating compensation and chaining. A compensating subtransaction is designed for each subtransaction in a chained transaction. If a chained transaction, T_i, consists of subtransactions $ST_{i,j}$, $1 \le j \le n$, and if $CT_{i,j}$ is a compensating subtransaction for $ST_{i,j}$, an execution of T_i can take two forms. If it completes successfully, the sequence of subtransactions executed is

$$ST_{i,1},\ ST_{i,2}, \ldots, ST_{i,n}$$

If a crash occurs during the execution of $ST_{i,j+1}$, that subtransaction is aborted and the following sequence is executed:

$$ST_{i,1},\ ST_{i,2}, \ldots, ST_{i,j},\ CT_{i,j}, \ldots, CT_{i,1}$$

In the absence of concurrency, all the updates made by T_i are reversed.

However, the atomicity and isolation of T_i is not guaranteed in a concurrent environment. As with chaining, intermediate states are visible to concurrent transactions, and this is true whether or not the Saga completes successfully. So Sagas are neither isolated nor atomic.

The Saga model assumes that all subtransactions are compensatable. Unfortunately, in some applications this is not true. For example, *Reset*(x) resets x to zero. It is not compensatable because the value of x at the time *Reset*(x) is executed has to be retained in order to do the reversal. The existence of noncompensatable subtransactions leads to more problems: compensatable subtransactions do not always work correctly in their presence. For example, a subtransaction that decrements x, *Dec*(x), compensates for a subtransaction that increments x, *Inc*(x). But if *Reset*(x), executed by one Saga, is interleaved between the execution of *Inc*(x) and *Dec*(x), executed by another Saga, compensation does not work. Nevertheless, compensation is a useful tool in several models that we discuss in this chapter and we will treat it in more depth in Chapter 20.

19.3.3 Declarative Transaction Demarcation

The primary goal of the nested and distributed transaction models is to provide rules for commitment when a single transaction is composed of multiple modules. In the case of nested transactions, modules commit conditionally based on their position in the calling hierarchy; in the case of distributed transactions, an all-or-nothing rule applies (either all the subtransactions commit or none do).

A second issue that arises is how the boundaries between transactions are to be specified when an application is constructed from multiple modules. This issue is referred to as **transaction demarcation**. Our assumption up to this point is that transaction demarcation is done explicitly. With chaining, the commit of one transaction in a chain initiates the next. Using the X/Open standard for distributed transactions, the application invokes tx_begin() to start a transaction and tx_commit() or tx_rollback() to end it. The term **programmatic demarcation** is used to describe this approach: the directives that set the boundaries are embedded within the application modules. This approach has an important limitation. By combining the application code with the directives that specify how the code is to be fit into a transaction, the transactional properties of the code, referred to as its **transaction context**, are fixed.

With **declarative demarcation**, the goal is to remove the specification of transaction boundaries from the modules making up the application. This allows the designer of the modules to concentrate on the business rules of the enterprise and not on the possible transactional contexts in which the module might execute. Each module—frequently referred to as a **component** in systems that use declarative demarcation—deals only with application-related issues, such as accessing a database and enforcing enterprise rules. The desired transactional context of each component is described in a separate module, sometimes called a **deployment descriptor**. Then at runtime, the system uses the information in the deployment descriptor to implement the desired transactional context.

Each application provides its own deployment descriptor to specify the transactional context appropriate for each module that executes in that application. For example, a particular component might be used in two different applications. In the first application, the deployment descriptor might specify that when that component is called, a new transaction is to be initiated. In the second application, the deployment descriptor might specify that if that component is called from within a transaction, it is to execute as part of that transaction; if not called from within a transaction, it is to execute without any transactional properties. Thus, with declarative demarcation, the same component can be used in different ways in different applications.

trans-attribute	Status of Calling Method	
	Not in a Transaction	In a Transaction
Required	Starts a New Transaction	Executes within the Transaction
RequiresNew	Starts a New Transaction	Starts a New Transaction
Mandatory	Exception Thrown	Executes within the Transaction
NotSupported	Transaction Not Started	Transaction Suspended
Supports	Transaction Not Started	Executes within the Transaction
Never	Transaction Not Started	Exception Thrown

FIGURE 19.3 The transactional context of a procedure based on the calling context and the `trans-attribute` value associated with the procedure.

Declarative demarcation is particularly relevant for legacy procedures that were created for a nontransactional context. Since no transactional directives are included in the code itself, the procedures can be used without change in a transactional context by providing an appropriate deployment descriptor.

Among the commercial systems that provide declarative demarcation are

- MTS (Microsoft Transaction Service): a TP monitor provided by Microsoft
- J2EE (Java 2 Enterprise Edition): a set of specifications for component-based applications provided by Sun Microsystems, which includes a TP monitor and which has been implemented in commercial products by a number of vendors, including IBM and BEA.

We discuss J2EE, but MTS provides virtually the same capabilities.

In J2EE the transactional context within which a procedure executes is based on the transactional context of the caller and on the value of an **attribute** of that procedure, called the `trans-attribute`, declared in a (separate) file associated with the procedure, called its **deployment descriptor**. The allowable values of the attribute are *Required*, *RequiresNew*, *Mandatory*, *NotSupported*, *Supports*, and *Never*. The possible combinations of the caller's transactional context and the callee's `trans-attribute` value, together with the resulting transactional context of the procedure when it is called are summarized in Figure 19.3.

- *Required*. The procedure must execute within a transaction. If it is called from outside a transaction, a transaction is started. If it is called from within a transaction, it executes within that transaction.
- *RequiresNew*. The procedure must execute within a new transaction. If it is called from outside a transaction, a transaction is started. If it is called from within a transaction, T, the transaction is suspended and a new transaction, T', is started. When the procedure completes, T' commits or aborts, and T resumes.

■ *Mandatory*. The procedure must execute within an existing transaction. If it is called from outside a transaction, an exception is thrown. If it is called from within a transaction, it executes within that transaction.

■ *NotSupported*. The procedure does not support transactions. If it is called from outside a transaction, a transaction is not started. If it is called from within a transaction, the transaction is suspended until the procedure completes, then the transaction resumes.

■ *Supports*. The procedure can execute either within a transaction or not within a transaction, but it cannot cause a new transaction to start. If it is called from outside a transaction, a transaction is not started. If it is called from within a transaction, it executes within that transaction.

■ *Never*. The procedure can never execute within a transaction. If it is called from outside a transaction, a transaction is not started. If it is called from within a transaction, an exception is thrown.

Interestingly neither J2EE nor MTS supports nested transactions in their current versions.

In most situations, procedures are specified to have attribute value *Required*. For example, the Deposit and Withdraw procedures in a banking application would most likely be specified to have attribute value *Required*. These procedures might be used in (at least) two transactional contexts for which the transactional behavior is slightly different.

1. A bank customer wants to perform a deposit to an account and executes a Deposit procedure. Since the trans-attribute value for the Deposit procedure is *Required*, it is executed as a transaction. The same reasoning applies for Withdraw.

2. A bank customer wants to perform a transfer of funds from one account to another and executes a Transfer procedure with attribute value *Required*. Transfer therefore executes as a transaction, *T*. The transaction calls the Withdraw procedure for one account and the Deposit procedure for the other. Because the trans-attribute values associated with Deposit and Withdraw are both *Required*, they automatically execute within *T* (as is appropriate for this application).

An example where the *RequiresNew* attribute might be appropriate is in a procedure that is provided by a business that wants to be paid for its services even if the transaction that called that procedure should subsequently abort.

An example where the *NotSupported* attribute might be appropriate is in a procedure that accesses some file system that does not support any transactional semantics.

In Section 23.10 we discuss J2EE in more detail and, in particular, how declarative transaction demarcation is implemented within J2EE.

19.3.4 Multilevel Transactions

Multilevel transactions are similar in some ways to distributed and nested transactions: a transaction is decomposed into a nested set of subtransactions. Unlike a nested transaction, however, the motivation for a multilevel transaction is increased performance. The goal is to allow more concurrency in the execution of independent transactions. To understand how this is achieved, it is necessary to look ahead a bit.

Isolation is often implemented using locks. When a transaction accesses an item, it locks it, forcing other transactions to wait until the lock is released before accessing the item. This prevents one transaction from seeing the intermediate results of another. If a transaction holds the locks it acquires until it commits, isolation is achieved, but only a limited amount of concurrency is allowed. The resulting performance enhancement, compared with serial execution, is thus limited.

The multilevel model improves on this situation by allowing the individual subtransactions of a multilevel transaction to (unconditionally) commit before the transaction as a whole commits, thus releasing locks and allowing concurrent multilevel transactions that are waiting to progress at an earlier time. This improves performance, but as a result one multilevel transaction can see the partial results produced by another. In contrast, in the nested transaction model the individual subtransactions can only conditionally commit, locks are not released to concurrent nested transactions, and one nested transaction cannot see the partial results of another. Nevertheless, the execution of multilevel transactions is atomic and isolated as we will see.

In this section, we discuss the multilevel transaction model based on the work of [Weikum 1991]. We will describe its implementation in Section 20.8.5, where the advantage of the model with respect to performance will become apparent. As with the nested transaction model, we assume that the subtransactions of a multilevel transaction execute at a single site.

The multilevel transaction model. A multilevel transaction accesses a database over which a sequence of abstractions has been defined. For example, at the lowest level the database might be viewed as a set of pages, which are accessed with read, *Rd*, and write, *Wr*, operations. At the next higher level, we might see the abstraction of tuples, which are accessed using SQL statements. (This is the level of abstraction generally presented by a DBMS.) A yet higher level might see a more application-oriented interface. For example, in the Student Registration System we might define a set of objects representing course sections and manipulate them with abstract operations for moving students between sections: a test and increment operation, *TestInc*, that conditionally adds another student to a section if there is enough room, and a decrement operation, *Dec*, that removes a student from a section.

Given these data abstraction levels, a transaction, *Move(sec$_1$, sec$_2$)*, that moves a student from section 1 of a large lecture class to section 2, can be structured as shown in Figure 19.4. The application level is the highest level in the figure. *Move* is a program that initiates a transaction by invoking begin_transaction, subsequently

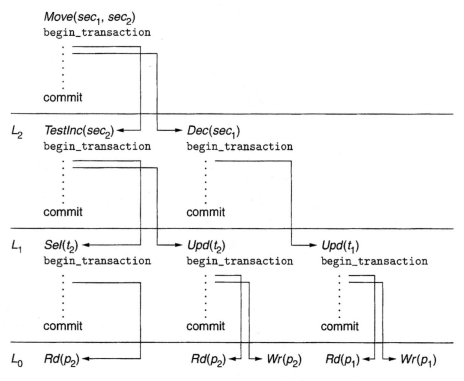

FIGURE 19.4 *Move* transaction viewed in the multilevel model.

invoking *TestInc* to test and increment the count of students in section 2 and, if successful, invoking *Dec* to decrement the count of students in section 1. At level L_2, *TestInc* is implemented by a program that uses a SELECT statement to determine if the student can be allowed in the section and an UPDATE statement that increments the count of students in the section if there is room. *Dec* is implemented by a program in L_2 that uses an UPDATE statement to unconditionally decrement the count of students in a section. We assume that section 1 and section 2 information is stored in tuples t_1 and t_2, respectively. At level L_1, these SQL statements are implemented in programs that read and write database pages. Tuple t_1 is stored in page p_1, and tuple t_2 is stored in page p_2. We ignore accesses to index pages in this example.

An operation invoked at some level can be viewed as a subtransaction at the level below. Thus, an invocation at L_2 of *Upd* causes the execution of a subtransaction at L_1. It, in turn, invokes *Rd* and *Wr*, each of which is implemented as a subtransaction at L_0. Similarly, the invocation of *TestInc* at the application level causes the execution of a subtransaction at L_2, which, in turn, invokes *Sel* and *Upd* at L_1. When a parent subtransaction creates a child subtransaction, it waits until the child completes. In contrast to the nested transaction model, we assume that each subtransaction is a sequential program, and hence children are created in sequence and do not execute concurrently. As a result, a multilevel transaction unfolds sequentially. Two other factors differentiate the multilevel model from the nested model.

1. All leaf subtransactions of the transaction tree are at the same level.
2. Only leaf subtransactions access the database.

Committing a multilevel transaction. The handling of commitment is a key difference between the nested and multilevel models and is one of the bases for the performance improvement that can be achieved with multilevel transactions. In contrast with the nested model, the commitment of a subtransaction is unconditional in the multilevel model. When a subtransaction, T, at any level of a multilevel transaction commits, the changes it has made to the data abstraction on which it operates become visible to other subtransactions at that level that are executing concurrently with T.

Unconditional commitment creates two new problems that must be solved to ensure that the multilevel transaction is isolated and atomic.

- *Isolation.* Intermediate database states produced by a subtransaction are visible to concurrent transactions before the entire multilevel transaction commits. For example, in Figure 19.4 the section count data item for section 2 is available to concurrent multilevel transactions as soon as *TestInc* commits (before *Dec* starts).

  While the transaction as a whole preserves integrity constraints, individual subtransactions might not. Hence, only when the last subtransaction of a multilevel transaction commits can we be sure that the database is in a consistent state. In Figure 19.4, between the execution of *TestInc* and *Dec*, the student who is being moved is counted in both sections. Thus we have to be concerned that concurrent transactions might see inconsistent states.

  Although it appears that multilevel transactions might not be isolated from one another, the implementation of the model, to be described in Section 20.8.5, does guarantee serializability. The transaction *is* isolated in the sense that a schedule produces the same effect as if the multilevel transactions had executed in some serial order.

- *Atomicity.* When a multilevel transaction is aborted, all of the updates it has made to the database must be reversed. However, as we discussed in connection with Sagas (Section 19.3.2), reversal cannot be performed physically: the individual subtransactions of a multilevel transaction commit when they are finished and give up any locks they have obtained, thus allowing concurrent subtransactions to read and write items they have updated.

  For example, consider two concurrent *Move* transactions, M_1 and M_2, executed from a state in which the count of the number of students in section 2 is initially c, as shown in Figure 19.5. The *TestInc* subtransaction of M_2 is executed between the execution of *TestInc* in M_1 and the time M_1 aborts. It is not possible to simply restore the count to c since the increment performed by M_2 (from $c + 1$ to $c + 2$) would be undone as well. Hence, physical logging does not work.

  As with Sagas, this problem is solved using **compensation**. Instead of restoring an old value physically, we reverse it *logically* using a **compensating subtransaction**. *Dec* logically reverses a successful *TestInc*, and hence is a compensating subtransaction. *Inc* (increment) logically reverses *Dec*.

In general, to reverse the effects of a subtransaction $ST_{i,j}$ at level L_i, at a point at which its L_{i-1} subtransactions, $ST_{i-1,1}, \ldots, ST_{i-1,k}$, have committed, we execute compensating subtransactions in reverse order: $CT_{i-1,k}, \ldots, CT_{i-1,1}$, where $CT_{i-1,j}$ compensates for $ST_{i-1,j}$. In Figure 19.4, if *TestInc(sec₂)* is aborted before *Upd(t₂)* is invoked, nothing need be done (because *Sel(t₂)* needs no compensation), but if it is aborted afterwards, a compensating update statement must be executed that decrements the count in t_2. If *Move* is aborted after *Dec(sec₁)* commits, compensating subtransactions for it and *TestInc(sec₂)* must be executed, in that order.

It might appear that compensation does not guarantee atomicity. For example, a subtransaction of T_2 might be interleaved between the execution of $ST_{i-1,j}$ and $CT_{i-1,j}$ of T_1, allowing it to access results computed in $ST_{i-1,j}$, which are subsequently compensated. However, when we discuss the implementation of multilevel transactions in Section 20.8.5, we will see that interleaving is restricted in a way that guarantees that compensation produces atomicity and serializability. This contrasts with the use of compensation in Sagas, where interleaving is not restricted and atomicity and serializability are not guaranteed. We will discuss other aspects of compensation in Section 20.6.

19.3.5 Transaction Scheduling with Recoverable Queues

With chaining, transactions are assembled in a sequence and are processed so that one starts as soon as the previous one completes. Sometimes, however, an application requires that transactions be executed in sequence but not that they be executed as a single unit. Instead, the requirement is that after one transaction completes, the next one will *eventually* be initiated and run to completion. So unlike chaining, a substantial interval might elapse between the completion of one transaction and the start of the next.

For example, a catalog ordering activity might involve three tasks—placing an order, shipping the order, and billing the customer. These tasks might be performed by three separate transactions. The work performed by the shipping and billing transaction can be executed at any convenient time after the order-entry transaction commits. However, it is important that these transactions be executed at some later time, even if the system crashes after the order is taken.

FIGURE 19.5 Schedule demonstrating that undoing the effect of a subtransaction using physical logging does not work.

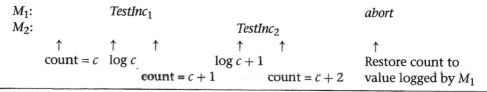

As another example, consider a distributed application in which a transaction, T, at a local site needs to cause some action at a remote site. If the remote action is incorporated into T, the network latency involved in invoking the action and receiving an acknowledgment becomes part of T's response time. If, however, it is not required that the remote action be performed as a single isolated unit together with T, but only that it ultimately be performed, then it can be designed as a separate transaction that T schedules for subsequent execution, and T's response time will not be degraded by network latency.

Applications such as these need some highly reliable mechanism to ensure that the transactions scheduled for future execution are in fact executed. One such mechanism is the **recoverable queue**. A recoverable queue has the semantics of an ordinary queue. Its Application Program Interface (API) allows a transaction to enqueue and dequeue entries. A transaction enqueues an entry describing some work that must be performed (at a later time) if the transaction commits. The information in the entry corresponds to the local state information that must be passed between successive transactions in a chain. At some later time, the entry is dequeued by another transaction that performs the work. This second transaction might be initiated by a server process that repeatedly dequeues entries from the queue and processes them.

To ensure that an entry enqueued by a committed transaction is eventually processed, the queue must be durable. Durability implies that the queue survives failures, so, as with the database itself, the queue must be stored redundantly on mass storage. Transaction atomicity demands that the *enqueue* and *dequeue* operations be coordinated with transaction commitment in the following ways:

- If a transaction enqueues an item and later aborts, the item is removed from the queue.
- If a transaction dequeues an item and later aborts, the item is replaced on the queue.
- An item enqueued by a transaction, T, that has not yet committed cannot be dequeued by another transaction (since we cannot be sure that T will commit).

Note that it would be possible to implement a queue with such properties directly in the database—a transaction wishing to enqueue an entry simply updates the tables used to implement the queue. The problem is that these tables are used heavily by many transactions, and if locking is used to implement isolation, they become a bottleneck, which degrades performance. Hence, it is desirable to implement a queue as a separate module that is treated differently from the point of view of isolation.

Recoverable queues can implement a variety of scheduling policies, including first-in/first-out (FIFO) and priority ordering. Or a process might be allowed to examine entries in the queue and select a particular entry for dequeueing. Note that, even when a queue has FIFO semantics, the entries might not be processed in FIFO order. For example, transaction T_1 might dequeue the head entry, E_1, from a FIFO queue, and at a later time transaction T_2 might dequeue the new head entry, E_2, from the queue. If T_1 subsequently aborts, E_1 is returned to the head of the queue. The

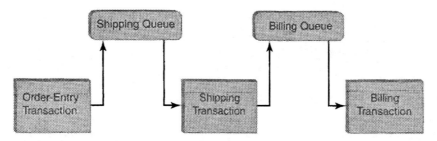

FIGURE 19.6 A system that uses recoverable queues in a pipeline organization.

FIGURE 19.7 A system that uses recoverable queues to achieve concurrency.

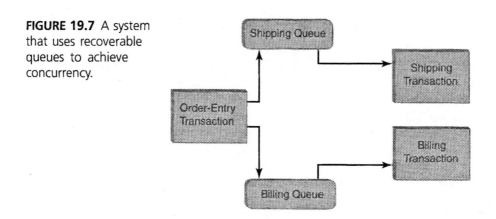

net effect will be that E_2 has been serviced, before E_1, thereby contradicting the requirements of a FIFO queue.

One way to organize the catalog ordering application is as a pipeline, as shown in Figure 19.6. The order-entry clerk initiates a transaction at the order-entry server, which enters the order, enqueues a shipping entry in a recoverable queue for a shipping transaction, and then commits. At a later time, the shipping server initiates a transaction that dequeues that entry, performs the required operations, enqueues a billing entry in a second recoverable queue for the billing server, and then commits. At a still later time, a billing server initiates a transaction that dequeues the entry, performs the required operations, and then commits. Such an organization is like a pipeline because an entry corresponding to a particular purchase progresses, in sequence, from one queue to the next.

Another way to organize this application is shown in Figure 19.7. An order-entry transaction enqueues entries in both a billing recoverable queue and a shipping recoverable queue and then commits. At a later time, a billing transaction can dequeue the entry from the billing queue and perform the appropriate operations, or a shipping transaction can dequeue the entry from the shipping queue and do its work. In this organization, the billing and shipping transactions for the same order can be executing concurrently. (Of course, the customer might be unhappy if he receives the bill before he receives the shipment.)

In the distributed system example, a transaction at central site A might enqueue an entry in a local recoverable queue describing an action that must be performed at remote site B. At a later time, a distributed transaction initiated at B might create a subtransaction at A to dequeue that entry and send it to B for execution.

Recoverable queues used to schedule real-world events. Another application of the recoverable queue is to achieve atomicity when a transaction is required to perform some real-world action, such as printing a receipt or dispensing cash at an ATM. In contrast to updating a database, real-world actions cannot be rolled back. Once performed by a transaction, they cannot be reversed by an abort (as a result of a system crash, for example). This means that transaction abort is not handled atomically. (What if a transaction in an ATM system dispenses cash and then the system crashes before the transaction commits? The database changes corresponding to the withdrawal are rolled back even though the customer is unlikely to return the cash.)

It might appear that the desired semantics—in which the real-world action occurs if and only if the transaction commits—can be achieved using a recoverable queue as follows. The transaction enqueues a request to perform the real-world action on a recoverable queue before committing. If the transaction aborts, the entry is deleted. If it commits, the entry is durably stored for servicing at a later time by a *real-world* transaction that performs the desired action.

Unfortunately, this "solution" only defers the problem to the real-world transaction. What happens if the system crashes while the real-world transaction is executing? We know that the entry will be preserved on the recoverable queue, but how can we tell whether or not the transaction performed the action before the crash? We need to know this to decide if the real-world transaction should be reexecuted when the system recovers.

One way to solve this problem requires assistance from the physical device that performs the real-world action. Suppose that the device maintains a counter that it increments each time it performs the action, and suppose that the increment and the real world action are done atomically: either both or neither happen. Furthermore, suppose that the counter is readable by the real-world transaction. After performing the action, the real-world transaction, T_{RW}, reads the counter and stores its updated value in the database before committing. When recovering after a crash, the system reads the counter and compares its value to the value stored in the database. If the two are the same, no additional real-world actions have been executed since the last real-world transaction committed. If not, the device counter must have a value that is one greater than the value stored in the database, indicating that a real-world action was performed but that the corresponding real-world transaction, T_{RW}, was aborted as a result of the crash. Hence, the entry that T_{RW} had dequeued was restored to the head of the queue and T_{RW} might or might not have stored the updated value of the counter in the database. Even if it had, that value was rolled back. The system can therefore deduce that the real-world *action* required by the entry at the head of the queue has been performed, but the corresponding real-world *transaction* did not commit. In this case the recovery procedure can simply delete the head entry before restarting the system.

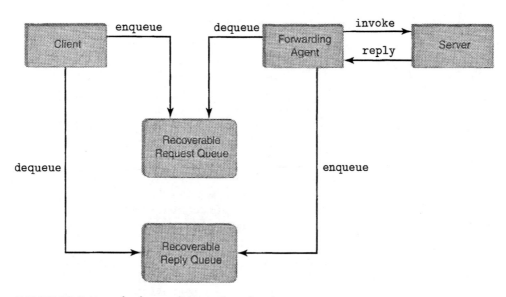

FIGURE 19.8 Use of a forwarding agent to invoke a server.

Recoverable queues used to support a forwarding agent. Another mechanism used in conjunction with recoverable queues is the **forwarding agent**. Consider a client that wants to invoke a service but determines that the target server is not operational. If the required service can be deferred, the client can enqueue the request for later servicing when the target server becomes available. A forwarding agent is a mechanism that can be used to invoke the target server at a later time. It periodically initiates a transaction that dequeues a request-for-service entry from the queue, invokes the target server, and awaits a response. If the transaction does not complete successfully (e.g., if the target server is still not available), it simply aborts and the entry is restored to the queue for later servicing. If the transaction commits, a response entry can be enqueued in a reply queue to be picked up at a later time by the client (see Figure 19.8). Note that the target server cannot (and need not) distinguish between the two circumstances under which it might have been invoked. The service that it performs is independent of whether it was invoked directly by the client or indirectly through the agent.

Recoverable queues as a communication mechanism. A recoverable queue can be viewed as a reliable communication mechanism by which modules communicate with each other. Unlike the communication methods discussed previously, in which the communication is *online* or immediate, communication using queues is *deferred*. This situation is analogous to leaving messages on a telephone answering machine. Since the queue is recoverable, the deferred communication can even take place across a crash of the system.

19.3.6 Workflows and Workflow Management Systems

A **workflow** is a model of a complex, long-running enterprise process generally performed in a highly distributed and heterogeneous environment. It is structured as a set of tasks that are executed in a specified partial order. A task in the workflow model need not be a subtransaction. For example, the catalog ordering system might include a task executed by a person (not a computer), whose purpose is to pack the merchandise before shipping. Other tasks might be database transactions. In the catalog-ordering example, shipping and billing transactions might be executed on different database systems at different locations.

A workflow is much less concerned with databases and ACID properties than are the models we have discussed. Isolating the execution of concurrent workflows or guaranteeing their atomicity are not major concerns. Individual tasks within a workflow can be database transactions, which are locally ACID, but the workflow does not distinguish such tasks from other, nontransactional tasks.

Each task in a workflow is performed by an **agent**, which can be a program, a hardware device, or a human. For keeping track of inventory, the agent might be a software system; for packing merchandise, the agent most likely is a human. A workflow might be performed by a number of agents over a significant period of time.

Each task has a physical status, such as executing, committed, or aborted. A task abort can be due to some system-related condition, for example, a server crash. Or the customer might decide to cancel the task during its execution. The failure of a workflow is not properly called an abort since some tasks might have completed and their results might have become visible.

In addition, the completion of a task might generate some logical status information indicating success or failure. For example, a billing transaction might discover that a customer has a bad credit rating. It completes in this case, but generates a logical failure status that is due to an application-related condition.

The tasks in a workflow have to be coordinated. For example, it might not be possible to schedule a particular task until two or more other tasks have completed (an *AND condition*), or perhaps several tasks can be executed concurrently.

Similarly, at a certain point in the execution of a workflow there might be several tasks that essentially accomplish the same goal, so only one of them should be executed (an *OR condition*). The choice of which to execute can depend on the logical or physical status or output generated by some prior task in the workflow or on the value of some external variable (e.g., the time of day).

A workflow describing the catalog ordering system is shown in Figure 19.9. Task T_1 takes the order. Task T_2 deletes the item from the inventory database and initiates tasks T_3 and T_4 concurrently. T_3 causes the item to be removed from the warehouse, while T_4 performs the billing function. Task T_5 packages the item when it has been removed. After billing and packaging, task T_6 arranges shipping, which can be by airmail (task T_7) or by land (task T_8)—only one of these alternatives is executed. Finally, when the customer signs the delivery papers the database is updated to indicate that the order has been fulfilled (task T_9).

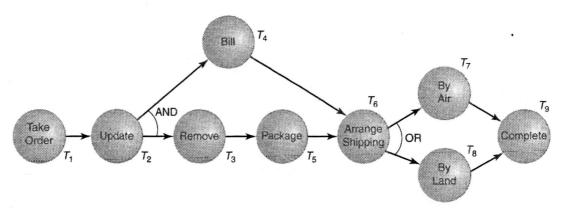

FIGURE 19.9 Workflow showing the execution precedence relationship between tasks of a catalog ordering system.

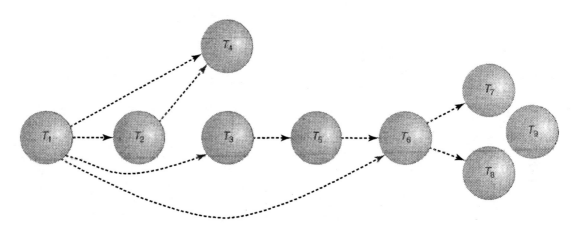

FIGURE 19.10 Flow of data in the catalog ordering system of Figure 19.9.

The results produced by one task frequently must be supplied as input to another, but this flow is not necessarily the same as the control flow. For example, in Figure 19.9 the customer's name and address, gathered during the execution of T_1, are sent to T_4 and T_6, while the identity of the item is sent to T_2 and T_3. T_2 then sends the item's cost to T_4. This flow of data and goods is shown in Figure 19.10. There is also a formatting issue—the data output by one task might have to be reformatted before it can be input to another task. Such issues come up frequently when information must be passed between legacy systems.

The generality of workflows follows partly from the fact that not all tasks are computational and not all agents are software systems. But even if all tasks are computational, the workflow model does not require the ACID properties. Consider isolation: as a workflow is executed, individual tasks might release resources they have accessed, making them available to tasks in other workflows. This means that intermediate states of one workflow might be visible to another that is concurrently executing. For example, tasks T_2 and T_4 update different databases. Consider two instances of the catalog ordering workflow, W_1 and W_2, which handle two distinct sales concurrently. If the complete execution of W_2 is carried out between the execution of T_2 and T_4 in W_1, then W_2 will see an intermediate state of the two databases that it could not have seen in any serial execution of the workflows. This might be an acceptable violation of isolation for this application.

As another example, consider that tasks in a business environment often collaborate: Human agents performing different tasks communicate data to each other during the course of execution. Such tasks are not isolated since data produced by one influences the execution of the other. Nevertheless, this form of communication might be appropriate for some applications.

Finally, it might be appropriate to weaken atomicity since some tasks might not be essential. The catalog-ordering workflow might include a task, T, that adds the customer's name to a mailing list. The failure of T (e.g., the mailing list database crashes) should not abort the entire workflow: the sale must be completed even if it is not possible to send an advertising brochure at a later time. Similarly, if T commits, it is not necessary to undo its effect if the workflow must be rolled back.

Workflow management systems. A **workflow management system (WfMS)** provides support for both specifying a workflow (at design time) and scheduling and monitoring its execution (at execution time). A workflow specification is generally not concerned with the details of a particular task but rather with the way the tasks are sequenced and the way data flows between them. A task can generally be thought of as a black box. It is a self-contained entity that can be used in the context of different types of workflows. For example, a credit-checking task might be used in the context of a mortgage application workflow, as well as a workflow that checks on an applicant applying for a job. Hence the sequencing of tasks in a particular workflow cannot be embedded in the task itself but must be specified externally. This is a major departure from the nested or distributed transaction model where the invocation of one subtransaction (task) is contained within another.

A WfMS might support a GUI that allows the application designer to specify the sequence of tasks in a graphical form as shown in Figure 19.9. Or it might provide a control flow language for this purpose, including the usual programming language constructs, such as conditional statements, while loops, and concurrent execution. In any case, the initiation of a task might be a function of the output or execution state of other tasks.

For example, the designer might specify

```
initiate T_j when T_k committed
```
19.1

where T_j and T_k are tasks. Here T_j starts only if T_k commits. If T_k aborts, T_j is not initiated at all. A specification of the form

```
initiate T_r, T_k when T_h committed
```

calls for the concurrent execution of tasks T_r and T_k when T_h commits. Another choice for the designer is

```
initiate T_q when T_k aborted
```

where T_q is a task that performs the same function as T_k in an alternate way. Using this technique, a number of paths leading to the successful completion of a workflow can be specified.

For example, T_k might be a transaction that books a New York-to-Washington air ticket, and T_q might be a transaction that books a New York-to-Washington rail ticket. Alternatively, the workflow might concurrently initiate T_k and T_q with the requirement that T_q commit only if T_k aborts.

The atomicity—or lack thereof—of a workflow is dependent on certain properties of its component tasks. A task can be **retriable**, meaning that, even if it initially aborts, it will eventually commit if retried a sufficient number of times. It is not necessary to specify an alternative path in case a retriable task aborts. It is only necessary to specify that the task be retried until it commits. For example, a deposit transaction is retriable, but a withdraw transaction is not (sufficient funds might never exist). If all tasks of a workflow are retriable, the workflow can always be completed.

The situation is more problematic if a nonretriable task, for which there is no alternate, aborts. The workflow cannot then successfully complete. The effects of tasks that have completed prior to that time must (generally) be reversed. For example, if the workflow has reserved hotels and transportation for a trip, the reservations must be canceled. We faced this problem with Sagas (and multilevel transactions) and saw that compensation, rather than physical restoration, is appropriate. As with Sagas (but in contrast with multilevel transactions), no guarantees are made as to the atomicity or serializability of the workflow when compensation is used.

If a compensating task exists for a task, T, then T is said to be **compensatable**. For example, a compensating task for T_2 in Figure 19.9 restores the item to the appropriate inventory record. If a failure happened during the execution of T_3 and T_4, these tasks are rolled back and compensating tasks are run first for T_2 and then for T_1. In general, compensating tasks are executed for each completed task in reverse order.

A workflow that consists only of compensatable tasks can always be reversed. However, some tasks are neither compensatable nor retriable. For example, a transaction that reserves and pays for a nonrefundable ticket is not compensatable (the ticket is nonrefundable) and not retriable (there is no guarantee that the ticket will ever become available). Such a transaction is often referred to as a **pivot**. (Note that this transaction is not compensatable because of a business rule of the enterprise: certain tickets are nonrefundable. By contrast, with Sagas [and multilevel transactions], we assumed that all subtransactions are compensatable.)

Reversing a workflow after a noncompensatable task has committed is not possible. Instead, atomicity requires that it must be possible to complete the execution at that point. All subsequently executed tasks must be retriable (or appropriate alternate paths must be provided). Hence, for a workflow to be atomic, its execution must consist of the execution of compensatable tasks followed by the execution of retriable tasks. A single pivot task can be executed between the two sets since if the need to undo the workflow occurs during its execution (prior to committing), it can be rolled back.

Workflow control involves automating the execution of a workflow by interpreting its specification. This interpretation can involve a number of issues.

- *Roles, agents, and worklists.* Each agent has an attribute indicating a set of **roles** it can assume, and each task has an associated role. Roles are used by the workflow controller to identify the agents that can perform a task that is ready to be executed. For example, a number of different sales representatives (agents) might be capable of performing task T_1 in Figure 19.9, but billing might be automated and performed by a software system (also an agent). The WfMS might select a particular agent to do the job using an algorithm that balances the load among agents. To facilitate such an assignment, each agent might be associated with a **worklist** enumerating the tasks (from different active workflows) currently assigned to it.

- *Task activation.* The WfMS monitors the physical and logical state of each task and, when a task changes its state (commits or aborts), the WfMS determines whether the initiation condition for a new task has been satisfied (Have all predecessor tasks completed? Is all input information for the task available?). It then selects and notifies the chosen agent and adds the task to its worklist. The WfMS evaluates logical and physical failure situations and initiates compensating tasks as needed.

- *State maintenance.* Assuming that the durability of the result produced by each task is provided by the server that implements the task, the only other issue related to durability concerns the state of the WfMS itself, which maintains the execution state of each active workflow. If this state and the inputs and outputs of the tasks are durable, the execution of the workflows can be resumed after a crash of the WfMS. This is referred to as **forward recovery**.

- *Filters.* Reformatting might be necessary when information from the output of one task is supplied as input to another. The WfMS might provide **filters** for this purpose. Note that the input to a task might be supplied by several prior tasks. The WfMS ensures that all input is present and properly formatted before a task is initiated. Furthermore, a filter might extract information used by the WfMS for the scheduling of subsequent tasks.

- *Recoverable queues.* Recoverable queues might be used by a WfMS as a mechanism for storing information about the tasks of an active workflow and for task sequencing.

The specification of an enterprise process as a workflow is particularly important when the process must satisfy a specific set of complex business rules. For example, management in the enterprise running the catalog-ordering system might have a rule that no merchandise can be shipped to any person who does not pass a credit check. Such rules can be incorporated into the workflow so that management can be sure that, even though many instances of the workflow are initiated in the course of a day (perhaps using human agents with minimum training), each instance is carried out according to the established policy.

Workflows are becoming increasingly important as a way to specify and implement the Web services that enterprises provide to each other and to their customers over the Internet. For example, a travel agency that plans vacations for their customers might utilize a workflow that involves Web services provided by airlines, hotels, tour guides, and credit card companies in various locations throughout the world. The workflow guarantees that all of these services are orchestrated in the way that is required by the travel agency. We discuss a particular workflow management system for Web services in Section 25.6.

BIBLIOGRAPHIC NOTES

The basic idea of a flat transaction has been around for a while. Early descriptions are contained in [Eswaran et al. 1976; Gray 1981; Gray et al. 1976] and an early implementation was presented in [Gray 1978]. A more recent and comprehensive description is found in [Gray and Reuter 1993; Lynch et al. 1994; Bernstein and Newcomer 1997]. Savepoints were introduced in [Astrahan et al. 1976]. A good overview of issues related to distributed transactions over a multidatabase can be found in [Breitbart et al. 1992]. Nested transactions were proposed in [Moss 1985]. Specific models of nested transactions were introduced in [Moss 1985; Beeri et al. 1989; Fekete et al. 1989; Weikum and Schek 1991; Garcia-Molina et al. 1991]. Nested transactions are implemented within the Encina TP monitor [Transarc 1996]. Multilevel transactions have been examined in a number of papers, including [Weikum 1991; Beeri et al. 1989; Beeri et al. 1983; Moss 1985]. A discussion of compensating transactions appears in [Korth et al. 1990]. Sagas were introduced in [Garcia-Molina and Salem 1987]. An excellent overview of a variety of more general transaction models (often referred to as extended transactions) is found in [Elmagarmid 1992] and [Jajodia and Kerschberg 1997]. Additional models are discussed in [Reuter and Wachter 1991; Chrysanthis and Ramaritham 1990; and Elmagarmid et al. 1990].

General overviews of workflow management can be found in [Georgakopoulos et al. 1995; Khoshafian and Buckiewicz 1995; Bukhres and Kueshn, Eds. 1995; Hsu 1995]. Two main issues have received considerable attention: development of the transaction models suitable for workflows and development of languages for workflow specification. Discussions of these issues can be found in [Rusinkiewicz and Sheth 1994; Alonso et al. 1996; Georgakopoulos et al. 1994; Alonso et al. 1997; Worah and Sheth 1997; Kamath and Ramamritham 1996]. If business rules are included as part of the workflow, many complex issues arise. First, the specification language must be rich enough to specify these rules. Second, the workflow must obey the rules, which is a nontrivial achievement. A number of research groups have been investigating formal approaches to workflow specification and algorithms for correct workflow execution. A partial list of this work includes [Orlowska et al. 1996; Attie et al. 1993; Wodtke and Weikum 1997; Singh 1996; Attie et al. 1996; Davulcu et al. 1998; Adam et al. 1998; Hull et al. 1999; Bonner 1999]. Another important issue—*interoperability* among workflows—has been taken up by the Workflow Management Coalition, which has published a number of standards in [Workflow Management Coalition 2000].

EXERCISES

19.1   The banking system described at the end of Section 22.1 can be structured either as a single transaction (with a savepoint after posting interest to each group of 1000 accounts) or as a chained transaction (with a commit point after posting interest to each group of 1000 accounts). Explain the differences in semantics between the two implementations. State when the printing of account statements takes place in each.

19.2   Explain the difference between each of the transaction models with respect to abort, commit, rollback, and isolation in the following cases:

a. A sequence of savepoints in a transaction and a chained transaction

b. A sequence of savepoints in a transaction and a nested transaction consisting of subtransactions that are executed serially

c. A sequence of savepoints in a transaction and a sequence of transactions linked by a recoverable queue

d. A sequence of chained transactions and a nested transaction consisting of subtransactions that are scheduled serially

e. A sequence of chained transactions and a sequence of transactions linked by a recoverable queue

f. A sequence of transactions linked by a recoverable queue and a nested transaction consisting of subtransactions that are executed serially

g. A nested transaction consisting of a set of concurrently executing siblings and a set of concurrently executing peer-related subtransactions of a distributed transaction

h. A nested transaction consisting of subtransactions that execute serially and a multilevel transaction

i. A nested transaction consisting of subtransactions that execute serially and a transaction using declarative demarcation consisting of modules specified with *RequiresNew*

19.3   Decompose the registration transaction in the Student Registration System design (given in Section C.7) into a concurrent nested transaction.

19.4   Redesign the registration transaction in the Student Registration System design (given in Section C.7) as a multilevel transaction.

19.5   Show how the withdraw transaction in an ATM system can be structured as a nested transaction with concurrent subtransactions.

19.6 a. Explain the difference in semantics between the two versions of chaining discussed in the text.

b. Which of these versions is implemented within SQL?

c. Give an example of an application where the second version would be preferable.

19.7 Explain how the Student Registration System could interface with a student billing system using a recoverable queue.

19.8 Give three examples of applications in which isolation is not required and a recoverable queue could be used.

19.9 Explain the difficulties in implementing a print operation in a transaction without the use of a recoverable queue. Assume that the transaction does not mind waiting until printing is complete before committing.

19.10 Consider the real-world transaction for dispensing cash discussed in Section 19.3.5. For each of the critical times—before, during, and after the execution of the real-world transaction—in which the system might crash, describe how the system (after it recovers from the crash) determines whether or not the cash has been dispensed. Discuss some ways in which the cash-dispensing mechanism itself might fail in such a way that the system cannot tell whether or not the cash has been dispensed.

19.11 Explain in what ways the execution of each individual SQL statement in a transaction is like a nested subtransaction.

19.12 Show how the credit card validation transaction described in the first paragraph of Chapter 1 can be structured as a distributed transaction.

19.13 The Student Registration System is to be integrated with an existing student billing system (which also bills for meal plans, dorm rooms, etc.). The databases for the two systems reside on different servers, so the integrated system is distributed. Using your imagination,

a. Give examples of two global integrity constraints that might exist for the global database of this system.

b. Give examples of two transactions that access both databases.

19.14 Describe the process that the admissions office of your university uses to admit new students as a workflow. Decompose the process into tasks, and describe the task interaction using a diagram similar to Figure 19.9.

19.15 Consider a transaction that transfers funds between two bank accounts. It can be structured into two subtransactions: one to debit the first account and the second to credit the second account. Describe how this can be done in (a) the hierarchical model and (b) the peer model.

19.16 Explain how nested transactions can be implemented using savepoints and procedure calls. Assume that the children of each subtransaction do not run concurrently.

19.17 In an application that uses declarative demarcation, one procedure that is called frequently from other procedures is a *logging* procedure that writes appropriate information about the state of the system into a log. What transaction attribute should be used for that procedure?

20

Implementing Isolation

Our university has over 10 thousand undergraduate students, and when the deadline for registration approaches, we might expect hundreds of students to be using the Student Registration System at the same time. The system must ensure that such a large number of concurrent users does not destroy the integrity of the database. Suppose, for example, that because of room size limitations, only 50 students are allowed to register for a particular course (that is one of the integrity constraints of the database), and suppose that 49 have already registered. If two additional students attempt to register concurrently, the system must ensure that no more than one of them succeeds.

One way to ensure the correctness of concurrent schedules is to run transactions serially, one at a time. Thus, when two students try to register for the last opening in a course, the transaction initiated by one of them will execute first, and that student will be registered. Once it has completed, the transaction initiated by the second will execute and that student will be told that the course is full. This type of execution is called **serial**, and the execution of each transaction is said to be **isolated**—the I in ACID.

The serial execution of a set of transactions has an important property. Recall that our assumption that transactions are consistent—the C in ACID—implies that if the database is in a consistent state and a transaction executes in isolation, it will execute correctly. Since the database has been returned to a consistent state, we can initiate the execution of a second transaction and, because it too is consistent, it will also execute correctly. Hence, if the initial database state is consistent, serial execution of a set of transactions—one transaction at a time—will be correct.

Unfortunately, serial execution is impractical. Databases are central to the operation of many applications and so must be accessed frequently. A system that requires that transactions be executed serially simply cannot keep up with the load. Furthermore, it is easy to see that, in many cases, serial execution is unnecessary. For example, if transaction T_1 accesses tables X and Y and if transaction T_2 accesses tables U and V, the operations of T_1 and T_2 can be arbitrarily interleaved and the end result—including the information returned by the DBMS to the transactions and the final database state—will be identical to the serial execution of T_1 followed by T_2

and also identical to the serial execution of T_2 followed by T_1. Since serial execution is known to be correct, this interleaved schedule must be correct as well.

The interleaved execution of a set of transactions is potentially far more efficient than serial execution of that set. Transaction execution requires the services of multiple system resources—primarily CPU and I/O devices—but a transaction frequently utilizes only one of these resources at a time. With concurrent execution of several transactions, we can potentially utilize a number of these resources simultaneously and hence improve system throughput. For example, while a CPU is doing some computation for one transaction, an I/O device might be providing I/O service for another.

Unfortunately, certain interleaved schedules can cause consistent transactions to behave incorrectly, returning the wrong result to the application and producing inconsistent database states. For that reason, we cannot allow arbitrary interleavings. The first question is how to decide which interleavings are good and which are bad. The next question is how to implement an algorithm that permits the good interleavings and prohibits the bad. We call such an algorithm a **concurrency control**. It schedules database operations requested by concurrently executing transactions in a way that ensures that each transaction is isolated from every other transaction. These are the questions we address in this chapter.

In most commercial transaction processing systems, concurrency control is done automatically and is invisible to the application programmer who designs each transaction as if it will execute in a nonconcurrent environment. Nevertheless, it is important to understand the concepts underlying the operation of concurrency controls because

1. Using a concurrency control to achieve isolation, in contrast to simply allowing arbitrary interleavings, can result in a significant increase in response time and a significant decrease in transaction throughput (measured in transactions per second). Hence, many commercial systems allow the option (sometimes as the default) of running transactions so that they are not completely isolated: various levels of reduced isolation are implemented. Since the designer might be tempted to use one of these options to increase system efficiency, it is important to understand how these reduced levels of isolation can lead to inconsistent databases and incorrect results.

2. Whether the designer chooses to achieve complete isolation or some reduced level of isolation, the overall efficiency of an application can be strongly influenced by the interaction between the concurrency control and the design of both the tables and the transactions within that application.

Isolation is a complex issue, so we break our discussion into two parts. In this chapter, we are primarily interested in isolation in an "abstract" database system. By "abstract" we mean a database in which each data item has a name, and read and write operations name the item that they access. Chapter 24 will be devoted to isolation in a relational database system, in which data is accessed using SQL statements that use conditions to identify rows to be addressed. Studying isolation in abstract databases helps us focus on key issues in concurrency control. The specifics of relational databases will lead to a refinement of the techniques developed for the abstract case.

20.1 Schedules and Schedule Equivalence

The concurrency controls we are interested in will work in any application. We do not discuss concurrency controls that are designed with a specific application in mind. In particular, we are not interested in controls that utilize information about the computation a particular transaction is carrying out. We are interested in controls that must separate good interleavings from bad ones without knowing what the transaction is doing. For example, a transaction might read the value of a variable in the database. If the concurrency control knows that the variable represents a bank account balance and that the transaction will request the read as a first step of a deposit operation, it might be able to use that information in choosing an acceptable interleaving. However, we assume that this information is not available to the concurrency control.

If we cannot use application-specific information, how do we decide which interleavings are correct? The answer lies in our basic assumption that each transaction is consistent and that therefore serial schedules must be correct. From this it follows that any interleaved schedule that has the same effect as that of a serial schedule must also be correct, and this is the correctness criterion we use. We will refine the notion of "has the same effect as that of a serial schedule" later, but you should understand that this is a conservative notion of correctness. As we shall see, for many applications, there will be executions that are correct even though they do not "have the same effect as that of a serial execution."

We assume that a transaction is a program whose data space includes the database and its local variables. While the local variables are accessible only by that transaction, the database is global and accessible by all transactions. The transaction uses different mechanisms to access the two parts of its data space. The local variables are directly accessible by the transaction (i.e., in its virtual memory), but the database is accessible only through calls to procedures provided by the database manager. For example, at a very low level of implementation detail, the transaction asks the database manager to copy a block of data from the database into its local variables— this is a **read request**; or it asks to overwrite a portion of the database with data stored in local variables—this is a **write request**. At this level, we view the database as a collection of data items and do not presume to know anything about the type of information stored in a data item. Also, we make no assumptions as to where the database is stored. Most likely, it is stored on a mass storage device, but in situations in which rapid response is required it can be stored in main memory.

A transaction, then, is a program in which computations made with the local variables are interspersed with requests for access to the database made to the database manager. Since the computation (on local variables) is invisible to the database manager, the manager's view of the execution of a transaction is a sequence

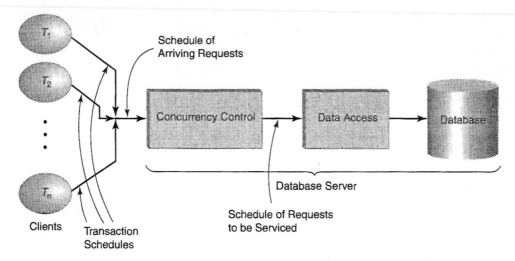

FIGURE 20.1 Role of a concurrency control in a database system.

of read and write requests, which we call a **transaction schedule**. If $p_{i,j}$ is the jth request made by transaction T_i, then

$$p_{i,1}, p_{i,2}, \ldots, p_{i,n}$$

is the transaction schedule of T_i, which consists of n requests to the database manager.

Since transactions execute concurrently, the database manager must deal with a merge of transaction schedules, which we refer to simply as a **schedule**. The database manager has the responsibility of servicing each arriving request. However, doing so in the order of arrival might lead to incorrect behavior. Hence, when a request arrives, a decision must be made as to whether to service it immediately. This decision is made by the manager's concurrency control. If the concurrency control decides that immediately servicing a request might lead to an incorrect schedule, it can delay servicing to a later time or it can abort the requesting transaction altogether.

Hence, the schedule serviced by the database manager might not be the same as the sequence of requests that arrives at the concurrency control. The concurrency control will, in general, reorder the requests. It cannot, of course, reorder the requests of a single transaction. Since we assume that a transaction is a sequential program, it will not submit a request until the previously submitted request has been serviced. The goal of the concurrency control is to reorder requests of *different* transactions in the arriving schedule so as to produce a correct schedule for servicing by the database manager. The system organization is shown in Figure 20.1.

Note that transforming the arriving schedule is not without its costs. A transaction might be either delayed or aborted. Delaying transactions reduces the overall concurrency level within the system and therefore can increase average response time and decrease throughput. Aborting a transaction is worse since it requires that the computation be repeated. Thus, it is important that the concurrency control does no unnecessary transformations, but should recognize as many correct arriving schedules as possible. Concurrency controls are generally incapable of recognizing *all* correct schedules and therefore sometimes perform unnecessary schedule transformations. The goal in designing a concurrency control is to minimize this waste.

We assume that *the execution of each database operation is atomic and isolated with respect to other database operations.* (This assumption might seem trivial for a simple read or write operation in an abstract database but is not so trivial for a complex SELECT operation in a relational database.) Although we have assumed that the concurrency control does not know the semantics of transactions (i.e., the nature of the computations), we assume that it does know the effect of each database operation, which we refer to as **operation semantics**. In this chapter, we are mainly concerned with read and write operations. In the next chapter, we will consider the operations performed on a relational database, such as SELECT and UPDATE.

Equivalence of schedules. Operation semantics is used to determine allowable schedules. To explain how, we must first explain what it means for two schedules to be equivalent. Recall that a schedule is correct if it is equivalent to a serial schedule. So what does it mean for two schedules to be equivalent?

We say that two database operations, p_1 and p_2, **commute** if, for all possible initial database states,

- p_1 returns the same value when executed in either the sequence p_1, p_2 or p_2, p_1
- p_2 returns the same value when executed in either the sequence p_1, p_2 or p_2, p_1
- The database state produced by both sequences is the same

Note that commutativity is symmetric: if p_1 commutes with p_2, then p_2 commutes with p_1.

Suppose that p_1 and p_2 are requests made by different transactions and are successive operations in a schedule, S_1. Then S_1 has the form

$$S_{1,1}, p_1, p_2, S_{1,2}$$

where $S_{1,1}$ is a prefix of S_1, and $S_{1,2}$ is a suffix of S_1. Suppose the two operations p_1 and p_2 commute. Then in schedule S_2,

$$S_{1,1}, p_2, p_1, S_{1,2}$$

all transactions perform the same computations as in schedule S_1 since the values returned to each transaction by read requests are the same in both schedules. Furthermore, both schedules leave the database in the same final state. Hence, we say that schedules S_1 and S_2 are **equivalent**. Operations that do not commute are said to **conflict**. Most important, two operations on different data items always commute. Commutativity is also possible between operations on the same item. For example, two read operations on the same item commute. However, a read and a write on the same item conflict because, although the final state of the item is the same independent of the order of execution, the value returned to the reader depends on the order of the operations. Similarly, two write operations on the same item conflict since the final state of the item depends on the order in which the writes occur.

In any schedule, successive operations that commute with each other and belong to different transactions can always be interchanged to form a new schedule that is equivalent to the original. Since equivalence is transitive we can demonstrate the equivalence of two schedules—both of which are merges of the same set of transaction schedules but which differ substantially in the way the merges are done—using a sequence of such simple interchanges. Unfortunately, demonstrating the equivalence of two schedules by performing such interchanges would be awkward for a concurrency control to do.

The design of most concurrency controls is based on the following theorem, which is an alternate way to demonstrate the equivalence of two schedules:

> **Theorem (schedule equivalence).** Two schedules of the same set of operations are equivalent if and only if conflicting operations are ordered in the same way in both schedules.

Note that we can prove this theorem if we can demonstrate that

> A schedule, S_2, can be derived from a schedule, S_1, by interchanging commuting operations if and only if conflicting operations are ordered in the same way in both schedules.

since we know that two schedules are equivalent if and only if one can be derived from the other by interchanging commuting operations.

The "only if" part of the theorem follows from the observation that the order of conflicting operations is preserved by the interchange procedure. Thus if conflicting operations were ordered differently in both schedules, S_2 could not have been obtained from S_1 using the interchange procedure.

The "if" part is a little more difficult. It can be demonstrated by showing that *any* schedule, S_2 (of the same set of operations as in S_1), in which conflicting operations are ordered the same way as in S_1, can be generated from S_1 using the interchange procedure. To show this, consider the schedule S_1:

$$\ldots, p_i, p_{i+1}, p_{i+2}, \ldots, p_{i+r}, \ldots$$

Suppose that S_2 is a schedule of the same set of operations, and in S_2 conflicting operations are ordered the same way as in S_1. Furthermore, suppose that there exists an i such that for all j satisfying $1 \leq j \leq r - 1$, p_i and p_{i+j} are ordered in the same way in both S_1 and S_2, but that p_i and p_{i+r} are ordered differently. Thus, p_{i+r} is the first operation following p_i in S_1 that is ordered differently in S_2, and so p_{i+r} precedes p_i in S_2. Operations p_i and p_{i+r} must commute since conflicting operations are ordered in the same way in S_1 and S_2.

Assume now that there is some k satisfying $1 \leq k \leq r - 1$ such that p_{i+r} does not commute with p_{i+k}. Then, in S_2, the operations must be ordered

$$\ldots, p_{i+k}, \ldots, p_{i+r}, \ldots, p_i, \ldots$$

since conflicting operations are ordered in the same way in both schedules. But this contradicts the assumption that p_{i+r} is the first operation following p_i in S_1 that is ordered differently in S_2.

For this reason, the assumption that there exists a k satisfying $1 \leq k \leq r - 1$, such that p_{i+r} does not commute with p_{i+k}, is false. Therefore, p_{i+r} commutes with all of the operations in $p_i, \ldots, p_{i+r-1}$, and a series of interchanges of adjacent operations can be used to create a schedule equivalent to S_1 that differs from S_1 only in that p_{i+r} precedes, rather than follows, p_i (as it does in S_2). The interchange procedure can be used repeatedly to reorder the operations that are ordered differently in S_1 and S_2 and thus to transform S_1 into S_2.

20.1.1 Serializability

We have shown that, if conflicting operations are ordered in the same way in two schedules, they are equivalent. Using this rule, we can specify interleaved schedules that are equivalent to serial schedules, and it is these schedules that the concurrency control is designed to permit. We refer to such schedules as serializable [Eswaran et al. 1976].

> A schedule is **serializable** if it is equivalent to a serial schedule in the sense that conflicting operations are ordered in the same way in both.

The notion of a serializable schedule provides the answer to our first question: How are we to decide which interleavings are correct?

> Since a serializable schedule is equivalent to a serial schedule and since we assume that all transactions are consistent, a serializable schedule of any application's transactions is correct.

Serializable schedules are correct for *any* application. However, for a particular application, serializability might be too strong a condition (some nonserializable schedules of that application's transactions might be correct) and can lead to an unnecessary performance penalty. Hence, concurrency controls generally implement a variety of isolation levels, the strongest of which produces serializable schedules. The application designer can choose a level appropriate for the particular application. In this chapter, we deal only with serializable schedules. We will discuss less stringent isolation levels in Chapter 21.

To illustrate serializability, suppose that $p_{1,1}$ and $p_{1,2}$ are two successive database operations requested by transaction T_1, and that $p_{2,1}$ and $p_{2,2}$ are two successive operations requested by transaction T_2. One sequence of interleaved operations is

$$p_{1,1}, p_{2,1}, p_{1,2}, p_{2,2}$$

If $p_{2,1}$ and $p_{1,2}$ commute, this interleaved sequence is equivalent to the serial schedule

$$p_{1,1}, p_{1,2}, p_{2,1}, p_{2,2}$$

and is thus correct.

FIGURE 20.2 (a) *Serializable* schedule; (b) Equivalent *serial* schedule.

$T_1:$ $r(x)$ $r(y)$ $w(y)$
$T_2:$ $r(x)$ $w(x)$

(a)

$T_1:$ $r(x)$ $r(y)$ $w(y)$
$T_2:$ $r(x)$ $w(x)$

(b)

Two transaction schedules are shown in Figure 20.2(a); each displayed on a different line. Time increases from left to right. The total schedule is a merge of the two transaction schedules, with the interleaving indicated spatially. The notation $r(x)$ indicates a read of the data item x; $w(x)$, a write. The value of a data item at any point in the schedule is the value written by the last preceding write or, if there is no preceding write, the initial value.

The schedule in part (a) of Figure 20.2 is interleaved (nonserial) because some of the operations of T_1 occur before those of T_2 and others occur after. The schedule in part (b) is serial, with T_1 completing before T_2 starts and we can denote it as $T_1 T_2$. The read and write operations on x executed by T_2 in Figure 20.2(a) commute with the read and write operations on y executed by T_1, and so that schedule can be transformed into the schedule in Figure 20.2(b) using a sequence of interchanges of adjacent commutative operations. Hence, the schedule of Figure 20.2(a) is serializable.

Now consider the two schedules from the point of view of the schedule equivalence theorem. The only conflicting operations in the two transactions are $r(x)$ in T_1 and $w(x)$ in T_2. Since they are ordered in the same way in both part (a) and part (b), the theorem tells us that the two schedules are equivalent.

Finally, note that although the schedule of Figure 20.2(a) is equivalent to the serial schedule $T_1 T_2$ in Figure 20.2(b), it is not equivalent to the serial schedule $T_2 T_1$.

As another example, the schedule shown in Figure 20.3 is not serializable. Since T_2 wrote x after T_1 read x, T_2 must follow T_1 in any equivalent serial order (because T_2's write does not commute with T_1's read and so cannot be interchanged with it). Similarly, since T_1 wrote y after T_2 read y, T_1 would have to follow T_2 in any equivalent serial order. Since T_1 cannot be both before and after T_2, there is no equivalent serial order.

Although the argument for equivalence between a serializable and a serial schedule is based on commutativity and the reordering of operations, the concurrency control does not necessarily reorder the operations of a serializable schedule before

FIGURE 20.3 Nonserializable schedule.

$$
\begin{array}{lllll}
T_1: & r(x) & & & w(y) \\
T_2: & & r(y) & w(x) &
\end{array}
$$

executing it. Since the effect of the serializable schedule is the same as that of the serial schedule, reordering is not required. If the concurrency control can determine that the (possibly interleaved) sequence of operations that has arrived is the prefix of a serializable schedule no matter what operations might be submitted later, it executes the operations as they arrive. If, however, it cannot be certain of this, some operations have to be delayed. Delay results in reordering. If p_2 arrives after p_1 and the execution of p_1 is delayed, then the order of execution will be p_2, p_1. The concurrency control uses this delaying tactic to produce a (possibly interleaved) schedule that it knows to be serializable. We describe later how this reordering is done.

20.1.2 Conflict Equivalence and View Equivalence

Two schedules are equivalent if conflicting operations are ordered in the same way in both. However, there are actually two different notions of equivalence: the one we have described, called **conflict equivalence** because of its defining property, and a second, called **view equivalence**. Two schedules of the same set of operations are **view equivalent** if they satisfy the following two conditions:

1. Corresponding read operations in each schedule return the same values (therefore, all transactions perform the same calculations and write the same values to the database in both schedules).

2. Both schedules yield the same final database state.

The first condition implies that the transactions in both schedules have the same view of the database—hence the name. The second condition is required since although transactions in both schedules write the same values to the database (since the first condition guarantees that transactions perform the same computations in both schedules), if the writes occur in different orders the two schedules might leave the database in different final states. The second condition restricts the ordering of write statements to the extent of requiring that the final states be the same: the last operation to write each data item must be the same in each schedule.[1]

The condition for conflict equivalence is *sufficient* to ensure view equivalence, but it is *not necessary*; that is, it is stronger than the condition for view equivalence.

---

[1] Another way to formulate the definition of view equivalence is first to say that there is a hypothetical transaction, T_f, that executes at the end of each schedule and reads all the items written by any transaction in that schedule. Then we can say that two schedules are view equivalent if corresponding read operations in each schedule (including the reads done by T_f) return the same values in both schedules.

FIGURE 20.4 Schedule demonstrating that view equivalence does not imply conflict equivalence.

T_1: $w(y)\ w(x)$
T_2: $r(y)$ $w(x)$
T_3: $w(x)$

Correspondingly, view equivalence is weaker than conflict equivalence. Although two conflict-equivalent schedules are also view equivalent (you are asked to prove this in Exercise 20.6), two view-equivalent schedules are not necessarily conflict equivalent. It might not be possible to derive one from the other by interchanging adjacent operations that commute (but see Exercise 20.39(a) for a special case in which two view-equivalent schedules are also conflict equivalent).

For example, the schedule shown in Figure 20.4 is not conflict equivalent to any serial schedule. The read and write operations on y by T_2 and T_1, respectively, do not commute; hence, if there were a conflict-equivalent serial schedule, T_2 must precede T_1. On the other hand, the two write operations on x by T_1 and T_2 do not commute either and imply that, in a conflict-equivalent serial schedule, T_1 must precede T_2, which is a contradiction. Note, however, that the serial schedule in which the transactions are executed in the order $T_2\ T_1\ T_3$ has the same effect as that of the schedule shown in Figure 20.4: x and y have the same final state, and the value returned to T_2 as a result of its read of y is the same in both. The schedule in Figure 20.4 is thus view equivalent to the serial schedule $T_2\ T_1\ T_3$ and so is serializable.

Although it might be possible to design concurrency controls based on view equivalence (and perhaps to gain additional concurrency because more serializable schedules are permitted), such controls are difficult to implement. For that reason, concurrency controls are generally based on conflict equivalence. In the remainder of the text, our use of the term "equivalence" will mean conflict equivalence unless we state otherwise.

20.1.3 Serialization Graphs

Another way to think about conflict serializability is based on serialization graphs. A **serialization graph** for a particular schedule, S, of committed transactions is a directed graph in which the nodes are the transactions participating in the schedule and there is a directed edge pointing from the node representing transaction T_i to the node representing transaction T_j,

$$T_i \rightarrow T_j$$

if, in S,

1. Some database operation, p_i, in T_i conflicts with some operation, p_j, in T_j
2. p_i appears before p_j in S

It follows that if a directed edge from T_i to T_j appears in a serialization graph for S, we can conclude that T_i must precede T_j in any schedule that is conflict equivalent to S.

For example, the serialization graph corresponding to the schedule in Figure 20.2(a) consists of the one edge,

$$T_1 \rightarrow T_2$$

because T_2 wrote x after T_1 read x.

The serialization graph for a particular schedule can be used to reason about the serializability of that schedule. For example, the serialization graph for the schedule in Figure 20.3 has two edges,

$$T_1 \rightarrow T_2$$

because T_2 wrote x after T_1 read x, and

$$T_2 \rightarrow T_1$$

because T_1 wrote y after T_2 read y. These two edges form a cycle:

$$T_1 \rightarrow T_2 \rightarrow T_1$$

Thus, we can conclude that, in any equivalent serial schedule, T_1 must precede T_2 and also T_2 must precede T_1. Clearly, this is impossible, so we can conclude that there is no equivalent serial schedule and thus that the schedule of Figure 20.3 is not serializable. More generally, we can state the following result:

Theorem (serialization graph). A schedule is conflict serializable if and only if its serialization graph is acyclic.

To prove this theorem, note that, if the serialization graph for a schedule, S, has a cycle, we can use the above reasoning to show that it is not serializable. Assume, on the other hand, that the graph is acyclic. Let $T_{i_1}, \ldots, T_{i_n}$ be a topological sort[2] of the transactions in the graph, and construct a serial schedule, S^{ser}, which corresponds to this ordering. The schedule S^{ser} is conflict equivalent to S because, if there is an edge from T_r to T_s in the serialization graph, there exists a conflict between an operation, p_r, of T_r and an operation, p_s, of T_s, and p_r precedes p_s in both S and S^{ser}. Since conflicting operations are ordered in the same way in both schedules, they are equivalent (according to the schedule equivalence theorem on page 818) and thus S is conflict serializable.

The serialization graph in Figure 20.5(a) is a somewhat larger example of a graph that has no cycles and hence corresponds to a serializable schedule. The graph

---

[2] A *topological sort* of an acyclic directed graph is any (total) ordering of the nodes in the graph that is consistent with the ordering implied by the edges in the graph. A given acyclic directed graph might have many topological sorts.

FIGURE 20.5 Two
serialization graphs.

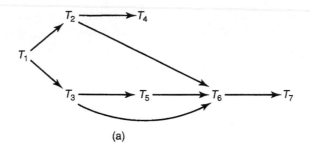

(a)

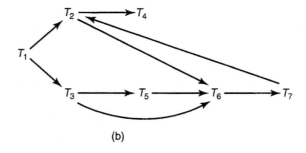

(b)

has many topological sorts, and hence there are many conflict-equivalent serial
schedules of its transactions. Two of these schedules are

$$T_1 \ T_2 \ T_3 \ T_4 \ T_5 \ T_6 \ T_7$$

and

$$T_1 \ T_3 \ T_5 \ T_2 \ T_6 \ T_7 \ T_4$$

The serialization graph in Figure 20.5(b) is obtained from the graph of Figure 20.5(a)
by adding the edge $T_7 \rightarrow T_2$. It corresponds to a nonserializable schedule because of
the cycle

$$T_2 \rightarrow T_6 \rightarrow T_7 \rightarrow T_2$$

20.2 Recoverability, Cascaded Aborts, and Strictness

Up to this point, our discussion has been motivated by serializability, and we
have assumed that all transactions commit. Life gets more complicated when we
consider the possibility that a transaction might abort. Additional restrictions must
be placed on schedules in that case to ensure atomicity. When a transaction commits,
durability requires that any changes it made to the database be made permanent.
When a transaction aborts, it must have the same effect as if it had never been
initiated. A transaction that has been initiated but has not yet committed or aborted
is said to be **active**.

FIGURE 20.6 (a) A nonrecoverable schedule; (b) Its recoverable counterpart.

T_1:$\qquad\qquad\quad$ $r(x)\ w(y)\ commit$
T_2: $\ w(x)$ $\qquad\qquad\qquad\qquad\qquad$ $abort$

(a)

T_1:$\qquad\qquad\quad$ $r(x)\ w(y)$ $\qquad\qquad\qquad\qquad\qquad$ $abort$
T_2: $\ w(x)$ $\qquad\qquad\qquad\qquad$ $abort$

(b)

When a transaction aborts, any changes it made to the database must be nullified. We say that the transaction must be **rolled back**. However, rolling back values the transaction has written to the database might not be sufficient to ensure that the aborted transaction has had no effect. Suppose that T_2 writes a new value to the variable x and that we allow x to be read by transaction T_1 before T_2 terminates, as shown in Figure 20.6(a). The read by T_1 is referred to as a **dirty read**, since T_2 has not committed. If we then allow the sequence of events "T_1 commits, T_2 aborts" to occur, T_2 will have had an effect on T_1 even though we roll x back to the value it had before it was written by T_2. Furthermore, since T_1 has committed, the information it has written to the database—in this case, a new value of y—has been made permanent. This creates a serious problem: that value might be a function of the value that T_1 read from T_2, and hence T_2 has (indirectly) affected the database state even though it has aborted. Thus the execution is not atomic.

Note that, if T_2 does not abort, the schedule in Figure 20.6(a) is serializable. Thus we see that dirty reads can occur in serializable schedules. Since we generally cannot prevent a transaction from aborting, we must design the concurrency control with additional restrictions so that the situation in Figure 20.6(a) cannot happen. Thus, in the above scenario, we cannot allow T_1 to commit until we know what T_2's outcome is. If T_1 had not committed, we could have aborted it when T_2 aborted, as in Figure 20.6(b).

A schedule is said to be **recoverable** [Hadzilacos 1983] if at the time when each transaction, T_1, commits, every other transaction, T_2, that wrote values read by T_1 has already committed. (Thus, if T_2 had aborted, T_1 could have been aborted as well.) A concurrency control is said to be recoverable if it produces only recoverable schedules. We require all concurrency controls to be recoverable. Note that dirty reads are possible in a recoverable schedule.

Dirty reads are undesirable even if transactions do not abort. A transaction, T_2, might update a data item several times, and a dirty read by a concurrent transaction, T_1, might see the intermediate value, as shown in Figure 20.7. Intuitively, we conclude that this cannot be a serializable schedule because intermediate values can never be read in a serial schedule (since the execution of transactions is not

FIGURE 20.7 A nonrecoverable schedule in which a transaction sees an intermediate state.

T_1: $r(x)$ *commit*
T_2: $w(x)$ $w(x)$ *commit*

FIGURE 20.8 Another nonrecoverable schedule.

T_1: $r(x)$ $r(y)$ *commit*
T_2: $w(x)$ $w(y)$ *commit*

FIGURE 20.9 A recoverable schedule that illustrates a cascaded abort. T_3 aborts, forcing T_2 to abort, which then forces T_1 to abort.

T_1: $r(y)$ $w(z)$ *abort*
T_2: $r(x)$ $w(y)$ *abort*
T_3: $w(x)$ *abort*

---

interleaved). The fact that the schedule in Figure 20.7 is not serializable follows from the fact that the read operation of T_1 conflicts with both writes of T_2.

Another example of a dirty read that leads to a nonrecoverable and nonserializable schedule is shown in Figure 20.8. This time, T_2 does not update the same data item twice, but the schedule is nevertheless not serializable because T_1 reads x after T_2 writes it and reads y before T_2 writes it.

Even though a schedule is recoverable, it might have another undesirable property: cascaded aborts. A schedule exhibits **cascaded aborts** if, in order to maintain recoverability, the abort of one transaction causes the abort of one or more other transactions.

Suppose that we allow values written to the database by transaction T_3 to be read by transaction T_2 before T_3 terminates, as shown in Figure 20.9. If T_3 now aborts, T_2 must also abort since it read a value that T_3 wrote. The abort of T_2 forces the abort of T_1 for similar reasons. In a more general case, an arbitrary number of transactions might have to be aborted—an undesirable situation. Thus, it is desirable to have concurrency controls that do not produce schedules containing cascaded aborts.

A concurrency control can eliminate cascaded aborts if it prohibits dirty reads. This condition is more stringent than that for recoverability, which allows T_1 to read a value written by an active transaction, T_2, but does not allow T_1 to commit until after T_2 commits.

However, we choose to require an even stronger condition than simply prohibiting dirty reads; that condition is strictness. A schedule is **strict** [Hadzilacos 1983] if no transaction reads *or writes* a data item written by an active transaction. A write of a data item written by an active transaction is called a **dirty write**. In Figure 20.10, T_2's write on x is dirty. Note that it is not necessary that T_2's write be the next op-

FIGURE 20.10 A schedule that illustrates the difficulty of handling rollback when dirty writes are allowed.

$$
\begin{array}{llll}
T_1: & w(x) & & abort \\
T_2: & & w(x) & & abort
\end{array}
$$

eration on x, only that the value overwritten by T_2 be uncommitted. Thus, in the schedule $w_1(x)\, r(x)\, w_2(x)$, the operation $w_2(x)$ is a dirty write even though the (dirty) read $r(x)$ (executed by any transaction) intervenes. A concurrency control is strict if it produces only strict schedules.

Clearly, a strict concurrency control is recoverable and does not exhibit cascaded aborts, but why have we imposed the additional condition on writing? The reason has to do with efficiency in implementing rollback in certain situations. Ordinarily, when we roll back the effect of a write of some data item, x, we expect to restore x to the value it had just before the write occurred. Suppose that we allow the value of x to be changed first by T_1 and then by T_2 (using a dirty write), as shown in Figure 20.10. If T_1 aborts, we do not have to restore the value of x at all since its value is the one written by T_2 and T_2 has not aborted. If T_2 now aborts as well, we have to restore x to the value it had just before T_1's write (not T_2's). Although we could design the system to perform correctly in all such situations, a strict system is much simpler to design since we can always roll back a write simply by restoring x to its value just before the write occurred. In nonstrict systems, the recovery algorithm is more complex, requiring an analysis of the writes made by a number of transactions and requiring the system to retain a sequence of overwritten values that corresponds to the sequence of dirty writes.

Thus if we require that schedules be both serializable and strict (or just serializable and recoverable), if a transaction in that schedule aborts and is rolled back, the resulting execution is atomic as well as serializable.

20.3 Models for Concurrency Control

In this section we give an overview of several ways in which a transaction can interact with a concurrency control and a database. There are two dimensions that can be used to describe this interaction. The first dimension characterizes it as either immediate update or deferred update.

- In an **immediate-update** system, if a transaction's request to write x is granted, the value of x is immediately updated in the database; if its request to read x is granted, the value of x in the database is returned. The situation is shown in Figure 20.11(a). It might appear that a read could return a value written by an as yet uncommitted transaction, which would mean that the concurrency control would not be strict, but we will see that this cannot happen.

- In a **deferred-update** system, if a transaction's request to write x is granted, the value of x in the database is not immediately updated. Instead, the new value

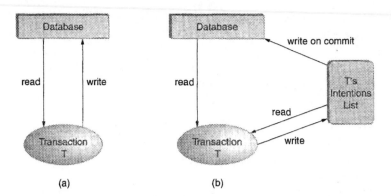

FIGURE 20.11 Dataflow in an (a) immediate-update and (b) a deferred-update concurrency control.

is saved in a buffer maintained by the system for the transaction and called its **intentions list**. If a transaction's request to read x is granted, the system returns the value of x in the database unless the transaction has previously written x, in which case the value x in its intentions list is returned. If and when the transaction commits, its intentions list is used to update the database. The situation is shown in Figure 20.11(b). Note that a value returned by a read is either a value the transaction itself has written or a value written by a committed transaction.

The second dimension deals with how the concurrency control decides whether or not to grant a transaction's request. As shown in Figure 20.1, the goal of a concurrency control is to transform the arriving sequence of requests into a strict, serializable schedule. When a transaction makes a request, the control must decide whether to grant it. The control knows the (partial) schedule of requests that have been granted but has no knowledge of requests that will be arriving in the future. Hence, it must be sure that, no matter what sequence of requests subsequently arrives, the total schedule will be serializable. The control's response to a specific request can be one of the following:

1. Grant the request.
2. Make the requestor wait until some other event occurs.
3. Deny the request (and abort the transaction).

Concurrency controls differ in the kinds of requests that are always granted (response [1] in the above list) and in the kinds of requests that might be delayed or denied. On this basis, concurrency controls can be characterized as either pessimistic or optimistic.

▦ In a **pessimistic** control, whenever a transaction attempts to perform any database operation, it must request permission. However, the transaction can commit at any time without requesting permission.

▧ In an **optimistic** control, a transaction can perform any database operation without requesting permission. However, the transaction must request permission to commit.

In both systems, a transaction can abort without requesting permission at any time before it commits.

The design of a pessimistic concurrency control is based on the philosophy that a bad thing is likely to happen: the accesses that transactions make to the database are likely to conflict. Hence, a pessimistic control grants a request only if the request does not cause the schedule to become nonserializable and it is certain that no subsequent request can possibly cause the schedule to become nonserializable as well. The control makes worst-case decisions and hence is called pessimistic. Since the resulting schedules are guaranteed to be serializable, a request to commit can always be granted.

The design of an optimistic control, on the other hand, is based on the philosophy that bad things are not likely to happen: the accesses that transactions make to the database are not likely to conflict. Hence, an optimistic control immediately grants each request for access. When a transaction requests to commit, however, the control must check to make sure that in fact no bad thing has happened—the requests granted to the transaction have caused the schedule to become nonserializable. In that case the transaction cannot be allowed to commit.

An optimistic algorithm might be appropriate for a large database in which transactions typically access only a few items, and those accesses are spread randomly over the database. The more such assumptions are violated, the more likely it is that conflicts will occur, and therefore, requests to commit will have to be denied. In particular, an optimistic algorithm is not appropriate for a database in which **hotspots** exist. These are data items that are heavily accessed in conflicting ways by many transactions.

Concurrency controls are generally characterized by the choices made in these two dimensions. The most commonly implemented concurrency control is the immediate-update pessimistic system, which we describe here in detail. We also discuss, briefly, the deferred-update optimistic system since it is useful in some situations. A deferred-update pessimistic system, which we do not discuss, is also possible.

20.4 A Strategy for Immediate-Update Pessimistic Concurrency Controls

We have required that concurrency controls be strict. A transaction must not be allowed to read or write an item in the database that has been written by another transaction that is still active. We justified this restriction as being necessary to ensure recoverability, to prevent cascaded aborts, and to enable efficient rollback. In this section, we discuss additional issues associated with immediate-update pessimistic systems and propose solutions.

FIGURE 20.12 A schedule that demonstrates that conflicting requests cannot be granted to active transactions if serializability is to be preserved.

T_1: $r(x)$ $w(y)$ *commit*
T_2: $w(x)$ request_$r(y)$

20.4.1 Conflict Avoidance

Suppose that transaction T_2 has written a new value to data item x and that transaction T_1 makes a conflicting request—for example, a request to read x—while T_2 is still active. This is a dirty read, and we have seen that to ensure strictness such a request cannot be granted, but let us ignore strictness for the moment and consider only the requirement of serializability. Since we are assuming an immediate-update system, if T_1's read request is granted, the value written by T_2 will be returned. Hence, if the concurrency control grants the request, it fixes an order between T_1 and T_2 in any serialization: T_1 must follow T_2. If T_1 and T_2 subsequently request access to another data item, y, the concurrency control will have to remember the order it had already fixed between them and ensure that the accesses to y do not contradict that order. Thus, if the accesses to y by T_1 and T_2 fix the order "T_2 must follow T_1 in any serialization," the two contradictory orders preclude any serial order equivalent to the resulting schedule.

The problem in the above scenario is actually more serious than it seems. Suppose that, after the accesses to x, T_1 writes a new value to y, then T_1 commits, and finally T_2 requests to read y, as shown in Figure 20.12. The concurrency control cannot grant the read, since the resulting schedule would not be serializable. Since T_2 cannot complete, it must be aborted, but unfortunately that too is impossible since T_1 has read a result (in x) that T_2 wrote and T_1 cannot be aborted (it has already committed).

The problem can be avoided by delaying T_1's commit, but this only leads to a cascaded abort. To avoid this problem and to ensure serializability, we require that the concurrency control adhere to the following rule:

> The concurrency control grants requests in such a way that each granted request does not determine an ordering among the active transactions.

To enforce this rule, the control will not grant a request to a transaction if it previously granted a conflicting request to another, still active, transaction. In Figure 20.12, T_1's request to read x is delayed until T_2 is no longer active. Keep in mind that, since transactions are sequential programs, delaying a request actually delays the entire transaction. If the rule is enforced, the schedule produced in this case is

$$w_2(x) \; r_2(y) \; commit_2 \; r_1(x) \; w_1(y) \; commit_1$$

Note that the rule precludes more than just dirty reads, as in Figure 20.12. Any request that conflicts with a previously granted request of a still active transaction

FIGURE 20.13 Another schedule demonstrating that conflicting requests cannot be granted to active transactions if serializability is to be preserved.

T_1: $w(x)$ $r(y)$ *commit*
T_2: $r(x)$ request_$w(y)$

	Granted Operation	
Requested Operation	read	write
read		X
write	X	X

FIGURE 20.14 The conflict table for an immediate-update pessimistic concurrency control. X denotes conflicting requests.

must be delayed, so the schedule shown in Figure 20.13 is as much a problem from the point of view of the rule as that shown in Figure 20.12.

If the requests made by T_1 and T_2 do not conflict, they can be granted. Requests do not conflict if one of the following conditions is true:

1. The requests refer to different data items.
2. The requests are both read requests.

Figure 20.14 displays the conflict relation in tabular form.

We need to show that a concurrency control based on conflicts produces schedules that are both strict and serializable. The following theorem states that result:

> **Theorem (commit order serialization).** Concurrency controls that do not grant a transaction's request if a conflicting request has already been granted to another still-active transaction produce schedules that are strict and serializable in the order in which the transactions commit (called the **commit order**).

Clearly, all schedules produced by such a concurrency control are strict since no transaction can read or write an item written by another still-active transaction. The more difficult part is to demonstrate serializability in commit order. To do this, we must first deal with the fact that schedules can contain operations of transactions that have not completed (previously we have restricted our discussion to schedules produced by completed transactions). When we say that such a schedule is serializable, we mean that it is equivalent to a schedule in which the operations of committed transactions are not interleaved and occur before those of uncommitted transactions. Henceforth, our notion of a serial schedule includes such schedules.

An inductive argument demonstrates the result. The induction is on the number, i, of committed transactions in a schedule. Consider the base case, $i = 1$. Only one transaction, T_1, has committed, and all others are active. Then the schedule looks as follows: *pre-commit commit$_1$ post-commit*, where *commit$_1$* is T_1's commit operation, *pre-commit* is the sequence of operations (of all transactions) that occur prior to that, and *post-commit* contains all operations that occur after. Neither *pre-commit* nor *post-commit* contain any commit operations. Since, prior to *commit*$_1$, all transactions are active, it follows from our assumptions about the concurrency control that no request in *pre-commit* conflicts with any other request in that part of the schedule. Hence, all operations in *pre-commit* commute. In particular, the operations of T_1 (which are all in *pre-commit*) can be interchanged with the operations of all the other transactions to produce an equivalent serial schedule in which all the operations of T_1 precede all the operations of all the other transactions. This demonstrates the base case.

Assume now that all schedules that contain exactly i committed transactions are serializable in commit order. Consider a schedule, S, containing $i + 1$ committed transactions, and let T be the last transaction to commit. Let $S = S_1 \, S_2$, where S_1 is the prefix of S up to (but not including) T's commit operation. Then S_1 contains i committed transactions and, from the induction hypothesis, is serializable in commit order. Let S_1^{ser} be the serial schedule equivalent to S_1. Thus, S is equivalent to the schedule $S_1^{ser} \, S_2$. S_1^{ser} has the form $S_{1,pre}^{ser} \, S_{1,post}^{ser}$, where $S_{1,pre}^{ser}$ is a serial schedule of the first i committed transactions and $S_{1,post}^{ser}$ is an interleaved schedule containing the operations of T, except its commit, as well as some operations of uncommitted transactions in S. The schedule $S_1^{ser} \, S_2$ has the property that all operations of T follow the ith commit. Furthermore, all operations of T must commute with all operations of any uncommitted transactions in S, so the operations of T can be interchanged in such a way that they follow those of all committed transactions and precede those of all uncommitted transactions. Once again, every pair so interchanged commutes, and thus the resulting schedule is serial and equivalent to S.

Because transactions that access only disjoint data items can be ordered arbitrarily, a serializable schedule can be equivalent to more than one serial schedule but, as we have just shown, one of these serial orders is the commit order.

Although all that we have required is that a schedule be serializable in some order, the user might expect transactions to be executed in commit order. For example, transactions frequently have external actions visible to the user (a deposit transaction outputs a receipt), and the user might expect the equivalent serial order to be consistent with these actions. Hence, a user who initiates T_2 after having observed the external actions of T_1 expects an equivalent serial order in which T_2 executes after T_1 (a withdraw transaction initiated after a receipt has been issued by a deposit transaction should see the result of that deposit in the database). One way to ensure that the order implied by these external actions is the same as the equivalent serial order is to serialize in commit order. Concurrency controls generally serialize transactions in commit order.

20.4.2 Deadlocks

When a transaction makes a request that conflicts with an operation that has been executed by another active transaction, serializability requires that the request not be granted at that time. The requesting transaction might be made to wait until

FIGURE 20.15 Schedule that exhibits deadlock.

T_1:	$w(x)$	request_$r(y)$	
T_2:		$w(y)$	request_$r(x)$

the conflict no longer exists (because the other transaction commits or aborts) and hence is no longer active. However, waiting can lead to a deadlock, as shown in Figure 20.15. When T_1 requests to read y, it is made to wait (until T_2 commits or aborts). When T_2 later requests to read x, it is made to wait (until T_1 commits or aborts). If no action is taken, both transactions will wait forever—a highly undesirable situation.

If you think that such a situation is unlikely to occur, consider the following schedule in which two transactions are each trying to update the same data item (perhaps they are both trying to make a deposit in the same bank account).

$$r_1(x)\ r_2(x)\ \texttt{request\_}w_1(x)\ \texttt{request\_}w_2(x)$$

Again, a deadlock results.

More generally, a **deadlock** is said to exist when there is a cycle of n transactions waiting for each other: T_2 is waiting for T_1, T_3 is waiting for T_2, ..., T_n is waiting for T_{n-1}, and T_1 is waiting for T_n.

Concurrency controls that make transactions wait must have some mechanism for dealing with deadlocks. A common one is for the control to construct a data structure representing the *waits_for* relation: If (T_1, T_2) is an element of *waits_for*, then T_1 is waiting for T_2. *waits_for* can be constructed when a conflict is detected. If T_1's request conflicts with an operation previously granted to an active transaction, T_2, (T_1, T_2) is inserted in *waits_for*. Whenever an element is inserted into *waits_for*, a check is made whether or not adding that element has produced a cycle, in which case a deadlock has been detected. If allowing T_1 to wait causes a deadlock, the concurrency control aborts one of the transactions in the cycle (often T_1).

A second mechanism for dealing with deadlock is **time out**. If the time a transaction waits to perform an operation exceeds some threshold, the control assumes that a deadlock has occurred. As a result, it aborts the transaction.

Finally, a timestamp technique [Rosenkrantz et al. 1978] can be employed to *prevent* (as contrasted with *detect*) deadlock. The concurrency control uses the current value of the clock as the timestamp of a transaction when it is initiated. Assuming that the clock advances more quickly than the rate at which transactions are initiated, each transaction's timestamp is guaranteed to be unique. If a conflict occurs, the concurrency control uses the timestamps of the two transactions involved to make a decision about waits or aborts. For example, it can adopt the policy that an older transaction never waits for a younger one (and can act on this policy by aborting the younger one).

20.5 Design of an Immediate-Update Pessimistic Concurrency Control

The standard technique for implementing an immediate-update pessimistic concurrency control uses **locking**. When a transaction makes a request to perform a database operation on a particular item, the system attempts to obtain an appropriate lock on the item for the transaction. For a read operation it attempts to obtain a **read lock**, and for a write operation it attempts to obtain a **write lock**. The transaction cannot perform the operation until the lock has been granted. A write lock is stronger than a read lock since, once a transaction holds a write lock on an item, it can both read and write the item.

In order to avoid placing an ordering among active transactions, the concurrency control observes the following rules when granting locks.

- ■ The concurrency control grants a read lock on a particular item only if no other active transaction has a write lock on that item. Since it will grant a read lock on an item even though another transaction already has a read lock on that item, a read lock is often referred to as a **shared lock**.

- ■ The concurrency control will grant a write lock on a particular item only if no other active transaction has a read or a write lock on that item. Hence a write lock is often referred to as an **exclusive lock**.

20.5.1 An Implementation Using Lock Sets and Wait Sets

To implement locking, we assume that the concurrency control associates each locked item, x, with a data structure called a **lock set**, $L(x)$, describing the locks held on x by currently active transactions. Given the above rules, it follows that if $L(x)$ is not empty, it can contain either multiple entries describing read locks on x or a single entry describing a write lock on x.

Similarly, we associate each locked item, x, with a data structure called a **wait set**, $W(x)$, which has an entry for each database operation on x that has been requested but for which a lock has not yet been granted. Because of the large number of items stored in a database, it is inefficient to maintain lock and wait sets for those items that are not being referenced. Hence, these sets are generally allocated dynamically for an item when it is first referenced, and the overhead of processing a lock request must include the time for managing the storage used to construct the sets. Generally a hash table is used. $L(x)$ and $W(x)$, if they exist, are found by hashing on x.

Finally we associate with each active transaction, T_i, a data structure called a **lock list**, $\mathcal{L}_i$, which is a list of all the entries the transaction has in lock and wait sets of different data items. Note that the lock list of T_i can have at most one item from a wait set because once a transaction's request is placed in a wait set, the transaction is suspended and it is not resumed until the entry in the wait set has been deleted.

A request by T_i to access x results in a call to a routine in the concurrency control that checks and grants locks. The routine manipulates $L(x)$, $W(x)$, and $\mathcal{L}_i$ by executing the following steps:

1. If T_i already holds a read lock on x and the request is a read, grant the request. If T_i already holds a write lock on x and the request is a read or a write, grant the request.

2. If T_i has not previously been granted an appropriate lock on x, search $L(x)$ for an entry that conflicts with the requested access. For example, if T_i requests to read x, a conflicting entry is a write lock held by T_j, $j \neq i$. If there are no conflicting entries, T_i's request can be granted, but one further situation must be considered.

    Suppose there is a conflicting request in $W(x)$. For example, $W(x)$ might contain an entry describing a request made by T_j to write x, and $L(x)$ might contain an entry describing a read lock held by another transaction, T_k. If T_i has made a read request, it can be serviced immediately since its request does not conflict with the existing lock held by T_k. However, if the scheduling algorithm allows T_j's request to be passed over in this way, it follows that a sequence of read requests can cause T_j to wait indefinitely. We refer to this situation as **starvation** and we say that the algorithm is **not fair**.

    Starvation does not result in nonserializable schedules, but it can be pretty annoying if your transaction is made to wait indefinitely, so concurrency controls are generally fair. One way to ensure fairness is to delay a transaction if its request conflicts with a request in $W(x)$ and to promote entries from $W(x)$ to $L(x)$ in a FIFO fashion (see step 4).

    With this in mind, if T_i's request conflicts with a request in $L(x)$ or $W(x)$, delay the request by inserting an entry identifying T_i and the requested lock type in $W(x)$, link it to $\mathcal{L}_i$, and block T_i. If there are no conflicting entries, grant T_i's request by inserting an entry identifying T_i and the requested lock type in $L(x)$, link the entry to $\mathcal{L}_i$, and resume T_i. We say that T_i *locks* x in this case.

3. A deadlock might result if T_i is made to wait. This would be the case if T_j is (transitively) waiting for T_i. This situation can be detected using the *waits_for* relation described in Section 20.4.2. If a deadlock is detected, abort and restart T_i (or some other transaction in the cycle).

4. When T_i commits or aborts, use $\mathcal{L}_i$ to locate and remove all of T_i's entries in lock sets (since T_i is no longer active). If a lock is removed from $L(x)$ and $W(x)$ is not empty, T_i's lock on x must have conflicted with at least one waiting request, and it might now be possible to grant that request. For example, if T_i held a write lock and there are transactions waiting to acquire read locks, all of their requests can be granted. On the other hand, if T_i held a read lock, and read locks are also held by other transactions, it will not be possible to grant requests in $W(x)$. Several strategies can be used to promote elements of $W(x)$ to $L(x)$ at this point. For example, a fair strategy is one in which requests in $W(x)$ are examined in *FIFO* (first-in-first-out) order. If a request can be granted, move it to $L(x)$ and examine the next request in $W(x)$. If not, examine no further requests. Alternatively, if the first request in the list is a read, grant all reads in the list. If the first request is a write, grant only that request. This algorithm departs from servicing requests in a FIFO order, but it does not result in starvation.

    When the promotion process is complete, $\mathcal{L}_i$ is destroyed.

This concurrency control guarantees that all schedules it permits are serializable since it grants only those requests that commute with requests previously granted to other active transactions.

The locking algorithm has the property that locks are obtained automatically. A transaction does not explicitly request a lock; it simply makes a request to access a data item, and, when the request is granted, the concurrency control automatically records that the transaction holds the appropriate lock. All locks are held until the transaction completes, at which point the control automatically unlocks all data items locked by the transaction. Since write locks are exclusive and held until termination, automatic locking guarantees strict schedules.

Locking to achieve statement-level atomicity and isolation. Whether or not a locking protocol is used to produce transaction isolation, the SQL standard requires that each SQL statement is executed atomically and that its execution is isolated with respect to other concurrently executing SQL statements. To achieve this the DBMS implements an *internal* locking protocol. When executing an SQL statement, in addition to obtaining read and write locks on database items, the DBMS obtains a number of short-duration locks, called **latches**, on various internal data structures, such as cache pages, index pages, lock tables, etc. The DBMS releases the latches when the execution of the SQL statement has completed.

20.5.2 Two-Phase Locking

While the automatic approach to locking is common, some systems allow manual locking and unlocking. In this case, a transaction *explicitly* makes a request to the concurrency control to grant a lock before making a separate request to access the item. As before, an access request is granted only if the concurrency control determines that the requesting transaction currently holds an appropriate lock on the item.

Unlocking can also be manual—except that all locks held by a transaction are released automatically when the transaction terminates. Manual unlocking seems to permit additional flexibility since, if a transaction releases locks prior to termination, concurrent transactions can access data items at an earlier time than that allowed by automatic unlocking. Unfortunately, however, to enforce strictness a transaction cannot release a write lock early. Hence, to enforce strictness early release applies only to read locks.

Furthermore, unless the early release of read locks is done properly, it can lead to nonserializable schedules. For example, consider the schedule shown in Figure 20.16, where $l(x)$ is a request to acquire an appropriate lock on x (read or write) and $u(x)$ is a request to release the lock held on x. T_1 reads x, unlocks it, and then reads y. Between the two accesses, T_2 makes conflicting accesses to both data items. The schedule is not serializable since each transaction must follow the other in any serial order. This situation could not have happened if locks were handled automatically by the concurrency control since locks are not released until

FIGURE 20.16 An example of a non-serializable schedule involving a transaction that is not two-phase.

T_1: $l(x)\ r(x)\ u(x)$ $l(y)\ r(y)\ u(y)$
T_2: $l(x)\ l(y)\ r(x)\ w(x)\ r(y)\ w(y)\ u(y)\ u(x)\ commit$

---

commit time. We next show that this situation can be avoided in a manual system by enforcing a protocol called two-phase locking.

A transaction is said to maintain a **two-phase locking** protocol [Eswaran et al. 1976] if it obtains all of its locks before performing any unlocks (it first goes through a locking phase, then an unlocking phase). The schedule of Figure 20.16 is not two-phase since T_1 locks y after unlocking x. Automatic locking is two phase.

> **Theorem (two-phase locking).** A concurrency control that uses a two-phase locking protocol produces only serializable schedules.

A proof of this theorem [Ullman 1982] uses the serialization graph theorem (Section 20.1.3) on page 823: a schedule is conflict serializable if and only if its serialization graph is acyclic. The proof is by contradiction. Assume that the serialization graph for a schedule produced by a two-phase locking concurrency control contains a cycle

$$T_1 \rightarrow T_2 \rightarrow \cdots \rightarrow T_n \rightarrow T_1$$

The edge $T_1 \rightarrow T_2$ implies that T_1 has an operation in the schedule that conflicts with and precedes an operation of T_2. Because the operations conflict, T_1 must have released a lock and T_2 must have acquired a lock between execution of the two operations. A similar situation must exist between T_2 and T_3, and the argument can be carried to the conclusion that T_1 released a lock before T_n acquired a lock. The edge $T_n \rightarrow T_1$ implies that T_n must have released a lock before T_1 acquired a lock. It therefore follows that T_1 acquired a lock after releasing a lock, in violation of the two-phase locking protocol. Hence, we have produced a contradiction, and we can conclude that the serialization graph for all schedules produced by a two-phase locking concurrency control must be acyclic and thus serializable.

When a two-phase locking protocol is used, one possible equivalent serial order is the order in which the transactions performed their first unlock operations. (You are asked to prove this result in Exercise 20.8.) Thus, if the schedule contains transactions T_1 and T_2 and if T_1's first unlock request occurs before T_2's first unlock request, T_1 precedes T_2 in one equivalent serial order. If the transactions hold all locks until commit time, the serialization is in commit order.

The two-phase requirement of the protocol does not distinguish between read and write locks. Serializability is guaranteed as long as locks are treated in a two-phase fashion. However, if write locks are released before commit time, strictness might be compromised and the resulting schedule might not be recoverable. Thus, when manual locking and unlocking are used (and the goal is to produce schedules that are both serializable and strict), write locks should be held until commit time, and read locks can be released early.

Two-phase concurrency controls that hold *all* locks until commit time (for example, automatic locking) are said to satisfy a **strict two-phase locking protocol**. Strict two-phase controls produce schedules that are serializable in commit order.

The word "strict" is (unfortunately) used in two different ways in the database and transaction processing literature. A two-phase locking concurrency control that releases read locks early is a strict concurrency control (because it does not release write locks early) but is not a strict two-phase locking concurrency control (as described in the previous paragraph).

Because the equivalent serial order is determined at run time, two-phase locking is referred to as a **dynamic protocol**, in contrast to **static protocols**, in which the order is determined when transactions are initiated. The timestamp-ordered concurrency control discussed in Section 20.9.1 is an example of a static protocol.

20.5.3 Lock Granularity

We have deliberately referred to the entity being locked as a data item without explaining what a data item is. We now define a **data item** to be any entity in the database that can be locked by a concurrency control algorithm—variable, record, row, table, file, etc. All locking algorithms in this chapter assume that an item has a name that uniquely identifies it. (In Chapter 21, we will see that this is not always the case.) This name is used to reference the item whenever it is accessed.

The size of the entity that is locked determines the **granularity** of the lock. Lock granularity is **fine** if the entity is small and **coarse** otherwise. The coarser the granularity, the more conservative the locking algorithm. Thus, in a DBMS that only supports table locks, an entire table is locked when only one row is accessed. Clearly, serializability is unaffected by lock granularity: as long as the items accessed are locked, a two-phase locking concurrency control produces serializable schedules even if some items are locked unnecessarily. Fine granularity locks have the advantage of allowing more concurrency since transactions need lock only the items they actually access. However, the overhead associated with fine-granularity locking is greater. Transactions generally hold more locks, and therefore more space is required to retain information about these locks. Furthermore, more time is expended in requesting locks for each individual item. Coarse-granularity locking solves these problems when transactions access multiple items in the same locked entity. For example, a transaction might access multiple rows in the same table. A single table lock makes this possible.

Many systems implement page locking as a compromise, locking the page in which the item is stored, not the item itself. The page address becomes the name of the entity that is locked. Page locking is conservative: not only is the item locked, but all other items stored on the same page are locked as well. But it is less conservative than table locking (assuming tables occupy more than one page).

20.6 Objects and Semantic Commutativity

The design of immediate-update pessimistic concurrency controls is based on the commutativity of database operations. In the simple systems we have been discussing, the only operations are read and write, and the only operations on a particular data item that commute are two reads.

If we allow more complex database operations and guarantee that the execution of each complex operation is isolated from the execution of every other complex operation (an important point that we will return to shortly), we can use the semantics of those operations to determine which operations commute and then use that information in the design of the concurrency control. In this section, we discuss object databases (Chapter 14), in which the database operations are methods defined on the objects stored in the database.

As an example of an object database, consider a banking application in which an account object has operations deposit(x) and withdraw(x) where x is the dollar amount. We assume that the account balance cannot be negative, so withdraw(x) returns the value OK if there are at least x dollars in the account and the withdraw is successful; it returns NO if there are fewer than x dollars in the account and the withdraw is unsuccessful.

The implementation of both of these operations involves a read of the database (to get the account balance) and a write to the database (to store the new value of the balance). A concurrency control operating at the read/write level declares a conflict between the read and write accesses of *any* pair of banking operations executed by different transactions on the same account. For example, if two deposit operations on the same account are executed concurrently, the read request of one will conflict with the write request of the other. Suppose, however, that a concurrency control is prepared to accept (higher-level) requests for method invocations. It can then use the fact that two deposit() operations on the same account commute—no matter the order in which they are executed, they return the same information (nothing) and leave the database in the same final state (the account has been incremented by the sum of the deposits). What is wrong with our analysis? Why is the commutativity apparent at the higher level and not at the lower level?

The answer is that, in deciding that two deposit operations commute, we used the fact that the program implementing deposit adds the amount deposited to the current balance, and that addition commutes. We refer to this information as the *semantics* of deposit. Read and write, however, carry very little semantic information. The concurrency control does not know how the information being read is used in the transaction's computation, or the relationship between the information read and the information written.

The lesson here is that more semantic information is available at higher levels, and hence the concurrency control can recognize more commutativity. This allows it to conclude that a larger set of interleaved schedules is equivalent to serial schedules and that less reordering needs to be done. Because reordering involves delays, the use of operation semantics can result in more concurrency and improved performance.

	Granted Mode	
Requested Mode	deposit()	withdraw()
deposit()		X
withdraw()	X	X

FIGURE 20.17 Conflict table for the account object. X denotes conflicts between lock modes.

While two deposit operations commute, `deposit(y)` and `withdraw(x)` on the same account conflict because `withdraw()` might return OK if executed after `deposit()` but NO if executed before (for example, if the balance was $x - y$ dollars before the operations started). Thus, we can construct the conflict table shown in Figure 20.17 and use that table as the basis of a concurrency control design. The rows and columns in the table correspond to the database operations, and for each such operation there is a corresponding lock that the control can grant. For example, when a transaction wants to invoke `deposit()` on some account, it requests a deposit lock on the account object. If no other transaction holds a withdraw lock on that object, the request is granted; otherwise, the transaction is made to wait. Note that this control achieves more concurrency than one based on read and write operations because the latter does not allow concurrent transactions to execute `deposit` operations on the same object whereas the control based on Figure 20.17 does.

Keep in mind that this analysis is based on the *important* assumption that the programs that implement the operations on an object are isolated—their execution is serializable. For example, the concurrent execution of the programs that implement read and write is serializable. It is not the case that if a (complex) item were concurrently read and written, the read might return the values of some subfields that had been updated by the write and the values of other subfields that had not yet been updated by the write. We will return to this assumption when we discuss the implementation of a multilevel concurrency control in Section 20.8.5.

20.6.1 Partial Operations and Backward-Commutativity

We can gain even more concurrency if we incorporate two additional concepts into the concurrency control design. First, we replace a single operation that can have several possible outcomes depending on the initial database state by several operations. For example, we can replace `withdraw(x)` with

- `withdrawOK(x)`, which can be executed when the balance in the account object is greater than or equal to x dollars

- `withdrawNO(x)`, which can be executed when the balance is less than x dollars

We assume that when a transaction submits a request to perform a withdraw operation, the concurrency control checks the balance in the account and determines whether to perform a `withdrawOK()` or a `withdrawNO()`. These new operations are said to be **partial operations** because each is defined only for a subset of initial states. For example, `withdrawNO(x)` is defined only in states in which the balance is less than x. Operations that are defined in all states are said to be **total operations**.

We will say that a schedule is defined in a particular initial state if, when executed starting in that state, all the partial operations it contains are defined. For example, the schedule

$$\texttt{withdrawOK}_1(x), \quad \texttt{deposit}_2(y) \qquad\qquad \textbf{20.1}$$

is defined if the initial account balance, z, satisfies $z \geq x$ and is not defined otherwise.

Second, we can extend the notion of commutativity to partial operations. For example, in all initial states in which (20.1) is defined, the schedule

$$\texttt{deposit}_2(y), \quad \texttt{withdrawOK}_1(x)$$

is also defined because, after the deposit operation, the balance is $z + y$, which is larger than x, and hence $\texttt{withdrawOK}_1(x)$ must be defined. Furthermore, the final account balance, $z - x + y$, is the same for both schedules. As a result, we say that `deposit()` backward-commutes through `withdrawOK()`.

More precisely, an operation, p, **backward-commutes** through an operation, q, [Weihl 1988] if, in all database states in which the schedule q, p is defined, the schedule p, q is also defined and in both schedules, q and p return the same values and the final state of the database is the same.[3] If p does not backward-commute through q, it is said to **conflict** with q. This definition differs from the definition of commutativity for total operations given in Section 20.1. In that definition, two operations commute if they perform equivalent actions when executed in either order starting from *any initial database state*. By contrast, an operation, p, backward-commutes through an operation, q, if they perform equivalent actions when executed in either order starting from *any initial database state in which the sequence q, p is defined*. Thus, the definition of backward-commute uses the definition of a partial operation.

Note that backward-commutativity is not a symmetric relation: p might backward-commute through q, but q might not backward-commute through p. For example, `deposit()` backward-commutes through `withdrawOK()`, but `withdrawOK()` does not backward-commute through `deposit()` because there might be states in which the schedule

$$\texttt{deposit}_2(y), \quad \texttt{withdrawOK}_1(x)$$

is defined, but the schedule

$$\texttt{withdrawOK}_1(x), \quad \texttt{deposit}_2(y)$$

is not. Some partial operations, however, do backward-commute through each other (e.g., two occurrences of `withdrawOK()`).

---

[3] A related concept, *forward-commutativity*, has also been defined; see Exercise 20.19.

	Granted Mode		
Requested Mode	deposit()	withdrawOK()	withdrawNO()
deposit()			X
withdrawOK()	X		
withdrawNO()		X	

FIGURE 20.18 Conflict table for an account object using partial operations and backward-commutativity. X indicates that the operation corresponding to the row does *not* backward-commute through the operation corresponding to the column.

A concurrency control can use the notion of backward-commutativity on partial operations in the same way it uses standard-commutativity on total operations. For example, if a transaction has a withdrawOK() lock on an account object, then a request for a deposit() lock on that object by another transaction can be granted because deposit() backward-commutes through withdrawOK().

More generally, if a transaction, T_1, has a q lock on an object, then a request by another transaction, T_2, for a p lock on the object can be granted if p backward-commutes through q. Note that since T_2's operation backward-commutes through T_1's operation, the two operations might have been performed in the opposite order and thus the control has not determined an ordering between T_1 and T_2.

On the basis of these ideas, we can expand the conflict table of Figure 20.17 into the conflict table of Figure 20.18. A space at the intersection of a row and column means that the operation corresponding to the row backward-commutes through the operation corresponding to the column, while an X indicates that it does not.

Although both tables exhibit the same number of conflicts, the table of Figure 20.18 allows more concurrency. For example, Figure 20.17 indicates that a withdraw request conflicts with both a prior deposit and a prior withdraw. However, Figure 20.18 indicates that a withdraw request conflicts with a prior deposit only if it is successful (withdrawOK) and conflicts with a prior withdraw only if the prior operation was successful and the request will fail (withdrawNO).

However, obtaining the additional concurrency involves additional run-time overhead. When a withdraw is invoked, the concurrency control must access the database to determine the value of the account balance so that it knows whether to request a withdrawOK() or a withdrawNO() lock. This additional overhead does not occur when the control is based on the table of Figure 20.17, which involves total, rather than partial, operations, since total operations commute in all states.

20.7 Atomicity, Recoverability, and Compensating Operations

Our concern up to this point has been with serializability, but we also have to consider the issue of recoverability (that is, we must guarantee that the execution is atomic if some transaction aborts). In a system in which the database is accessed with read and write operations, only the write modifies the database state. Since in such a system, a write to a data item, x, conflicts with all other operations on x, once a transaction, T, writes x, no other transaction can access x until T completes (assuming a strict two-phase concurrency control). Hence, if T aborts, it is only necessary to restore x to the value it had before T's write. We have referred to this as physical restoration.

Abort is more complicated in systems that support abstract operations since two abstract operations that modify the same data item (such as two deposit operations) might not conflict. Suppose that T_1 modifies x using operation $p(x)$, and then T_2 makes a request to modify x using a nonconflicting operation, $q(x)$. Since p and q do not conflict, the request can be granted, yielding the schedule $p(x)$, $q(x)$. But suppose T_1 later aborts. We cannot simply restore x to the value it had prior to the execution of p (physical restoration) since in reversing the effect of $p(x)$ we will in addition lose the effect of $q(x)$. We discussed this issue in connection with Sagas in Section 19.3.2 and concluded that compensation was the appropriate way to reverse the effects of a Saga that does not complete successfully.

Unfortunately, the use of compensation in Sagas is not sufficient to guarantee isolated and atomic schedules. However, we are now considering using compensation in a different model, one in which the interleaving of concurrent transactions is controlled using locks. We can do a better job here, but it will require a more precise definition of compensation and, in particular, how it interacts with the concurrency control. (The following analysis is particularly relevant to the implementation of multilevel transactions.)

To get a better understanding of compensation, we can view a database operation as a mapping from database states to database states. Thus, the operation that increments x by 1, $inc(x)$, maps the database state in which x has value 5 to the same state except that x has value 6 (the values of other variables are unaffected). If the mapping implemented by an operation is one-to-one, then there exists an inverse, or compensating, operation that implements a one-to-one mapping from the final state to the initial state. For example, the operation $dec(x)$ compensates for $inc(x)$. Note that the compensating operation has the same parameters as the operation for which it compensates (later we will examine a situation that does not have this property).

Returning to our earlier example, suppose that p has a compensating operation, p^{-1}. If T_1 is aborted using compensation we get the schedule $p(x)$, $q(x)$, $p^{-1}(x)$. How can we be sure that executing p^{-1} after q has modified x will correctly undo the effect of p? Fortunately, our concurrency control schedules q only if it commutes (perhaps backward-commutes) with p (i.e., a q-lock does not conflict with a p-lock), and therefore this schedule is equivalent to the schedule $q(x)$, $p(x)$, $p^{-1}(x)$. But this latter schedule is equivalent to just $q(x)$, and so compensation implemented abort correctly and produced atomicity. What we have demonstrated in this simple example is that recoverability can be achieved using compensation (Section 20.2). Thus, the requirement that nonconflicting operations commute is sufficient to guarantee both serializability and recoverability.

The general case. In the general case, consider a transaction, T, with transaction schedule

$$p_1, p_2, \ldots, p_n \qquad \textbf{20.2}$$

If T aborts after executing some operation, p_i, it is necessary to execute compensating operations for $p_1, p_2, \ldots, p_i$ in reverse order to abort the effects of T up to that point. The transaction schedule in that case is

$$p_1, p_2, \ldots, p_i, p_i^{-1}, p_{i-1}^{-1}, \ldots, p_1^{-1} \qquad \textbf{20.3}$$

Thus, there are n possible schedules for aborting T, one for each value of i (depending on when the decision to reverse T is made). All of these schedules have no net effect on the database. When we execute T, we cannot predict which of its $n + 1$ transaction schedules will occur.

When operations were restricted to read and write, an abort operation in a schedule denoted a complex action involving physically undoing all prior changes a transaction had made to the database. In contrast, schedule (20.3) explicitly describes the action of the abort. Our assumption is that when a transaction invokes abort, the concurrency control automatically introduces the appropriate compensating operations into the schedule. The transaction is aborted when its transaction schedule has completed. We refer to the use of compensation here, as well as in Sagas and workflows, as **logical rollback**.

A schedule is recoverable if each aborted transaction has no net effect on the database or on concurrently executing transactions. More precisely, a schedule S is recoverable if, for each aborted transaction, T, in S, S is equivalent to a schedule in which all of T's operations have been deleted.

Consider the following policy for a concurrency control that uses compensation.

1. The control grants compensating operations without checking for conflicts.[4]

2. The control grants forward operations only if they (backward-)commute with all forward operations that have been granted to active transactions (without considering possible conflicts with previously granted compensating operations of active transactions).

We now demonstrate that the policy is correct, in the sense that any schedule produced by the control is recoverable and that, after the recovery has taken place, the resulting schedule of transactions that have not aborted is serializable.

Consider an arbitrary schedule, S, that might have been produced by such a concurrency control and that is the merge of transaction schedules of both committed and aborted transactions (and thus contains both forward and compensating

---

[4] If the control were to delay a compensating operation because of a conflict, a deadlock might result. This is a possibility whenever a transaction is forced to wait. In such a case the abort could not be completed, causing a violation of the requirement that, in contrast to a request to commit, a request to abort is always granted.

operations). Consider the first compensating operation in S, p_i^{-1}. S has the form

$$S_{prefix}, p_i, S', p_i^{-1}, S_{suffix}$$

where S_{prefix} and S' have no compensating operations and S' is the sequence of operations that separates p_i from p_i^{-1}. Since the concurrency control would not have scheduled an operation in S' unless it commutes with p_i, this schedule is equivalent to the schedule

$$S_{prefix}, S', p_i, p_i^{-1}, S_{suffix}$$

which in turn is equivalent to the schedule

$$S_{prefix}, S', S_{suffix}$$

The transformation has in effect caused p_i and p_i^{-1} to annihilate each other and has thus reduced S to an equivalent schedule that is shorter.

The transformation can now be repeated to eliminate the second compensating operation in S and its matching forward operation. In this manner, all operations of aborted transactions (both forward and compensating) can be eliminated from S, producing an equivalent schedule of the transactions that have not aborted. Therefore, S is recoverable. Furthermore, the resulting schedule is conflict equivalent to a serial schedule. The fact that this type of transformation is always possible demonstrates the correctness of the concurrency control.

A schedule that can be reduced by such a transformation to a serializable schedule of transactions that have not aborted is said to be **reducible**. If a schedule of transactions, in which each transaction is represented by one of its transaction schedules, is reducible, then it is recoverable. All of the schedules produced by the concurrency control described in this section are reducible and hence recoverable.[5]

The undo operation. Unfortunately, not every operation, p, has a compensating operation because not every operation is one-to-one. For example, the operation *Reset(x)*, which sets the value of x to 0, does not have a compensating operation since the mapping is many-to-one. Since every value maps to 0, how can a compensating operation know what transformation was performed by the original operation (e.g., change 5 to 0) by just looking at the current state of the object? And if the transformation cannot be deduced, how can it be compensated for?

One way to handle this problem is to simply make a p-lock exclusive: assume that every operation conflicts with an operation, p, that is not compensatable. Then when T_1 gets a p-lock on x as a result of executing $p(x)$, no other transaction can execute an operation on x until T_1 commits or aborts. If T_1 aborts, the value of x can simply be physically restored to the value it had prior to the execution of p since no other transaction has accessed the dirty value.

---

[5] A more complete discussion of this subject can be found in [Schek et al. 1993].

OPTIONAL

We can think of physical restoration as being accomplished by an *undo* operation. Undoing an operation such as *Reset*(x) requires that we record some information about the state of x when the operation was executed. For example, if the value of x was 5 at the time *Reset*(x) was executed, we need to remember 5 so that we can return x to that value if the operation must be undone. We can define an undo operation, $p^{undo}(x, s)$, that undoes the execution of an operation $p(x)$. The parameter s contains sufficient information about the state of x at the time $p(x)$ was executed to perform the undo—the complete state does not necessarily have to be saved. *Set*(x, 5) is the undo operation for *Reset*(x) if x had value 5 when *Reset*(x) was executed. This resembles physical logging, an approach used to roll back a transaction that we will discuss in Section 22.2.

Thus an undo operation differs from a compensating operation in that its parameters include information about the database state when the operation it is undoing was executed, while the parameters of a compensating operation contain only the parameters of the operation being compensated.

Although an exclusive lock can be used to guarantee atomicity when p is not compensatable, the question is "Can we get more concurrency?" Stated another way, "If a transaction has a p-lock on x and p is not compensatable, are there *any* operations we can allow another transaction to perform on x"? The answer is "yes," but to understand this, we need to first understand why an undo operation cannot be used in the same way as a compensating operation.

Consider the schedule $p(x)$, $q(x)$. If s describes the state of x when p is executed in the schedule, then the undo operation for $p(x)$ is $p^{undo}(x, s)$. Unfortunately, the argument that we used earlier to show that compensation can be used to achieve recoverability does not work for the undo operation. Assume that $q(x)$ backward-commutes with $p(x)$, and that we want to undo the effect of $p(x)$. Why would it be incorrect to append $p^{undo}(x, s)$ to $p(x)$, $q(x)$? Since $q(x)$ backward-commutes through $p(x)$, the new schedule is equivalent to $q(x)$, $p(x)$, $p^{undo}(x, s)$. But in this schedule s might no longer describe the state of x when $p(x)$ is executed, so we cannot expect $p^{undo}(x, s)$ to work correctly.

For example, *Reset*(x) commutes with itself, but, assuming that the initial value of x is 5, the undo operation, *Set*(x, 5), does not work correctly in the schedule $Reset_1(x)$, $Reset_2(x)$, $Set_1(x, 5)$.

Thus, in order to guarantee recoverability, a stronger condition than simply commutativity is needed in deciding whether a request for a q-lock conflicts with a previously granted p-lock when p is not compensatable. In order to understand the most general form of that condition, we first need to point out that if p is a many-to-one operation, its range might be a proper subset of its domain. This is the case if the domain is finite, but it might also be the case if the domain is infinite. For example, *round* is a many-to-one operation that rounds each real number in its domain to the nearest whole number. Its range, the whole numbers, is a subset of the reals.

As a result, the domain of an undo operation can be a subset of the domain of the operation it undoes, and if that is the case, the undo is a partial operation. For example, the undo operation for *round*(x) is *restore*(x, s). Its domain is the set of whole numbers; it is undefined for other real numbers.

The state information, s, retained for use in *restore(x,s)* contains the sign of x when *round* was executed and the fractional change that was made at that time. The sign is required, since it might be changed by an interleaved execution of some other operation. Thus, if the value of x was -9.25 initially, s records the fact that *round* added .25 to a negative number. If x is still a negative number when *restore* is executed, then .25 has to be subtracted. If it is a positive number, .25 must be added.

Suppose *mag(x)* is the many-to-one operation that produces the magnitude of x. Its domain is the set of real numbers and its range is the set of positive real numbers. *mag(x)* commutes with *round(x)*. Under certain circumstances *mag(x)* also commutes with *restore(x,s)*. Thus, if the initial state of x is a whole number in the schedule $mag(x)$, $restore(x, s)$, the schedule is equivalent to $restore(x, s)$, $mag(x)$. If the initial state is not a whole number, *restore* is undefined. In the schedule $round_1(x)$, $mag_2(x)$, $restore_1(x, f)$, x is a whole number when $mag_2(x)$ is executed, and hence the schedule is equivalent to $round_1(x)$, $restore_1(x, s)$, $mag_2(x)$. As a result the undo operation performs correctly.

We can prove the following theorem.

> **Theorem (undo).** A locking concurrency control guarantees serializability and recoverability if the condition used by the control to determine that a request for a q-lock that does not conflict with a previously granted p-lock held by an active transaction is that
>
> 1. q backward-commutes through p and
> 2. Either p has a compensating operation, or when a p-lock is held, p^{undo} backward-commutes through q.

We have previously demonstrated the result when a compensating operation exists.[6] Suppose a compensating operation does not exist. To make the argument simple, assume that schedule S contains a single undo operation, $p_i^{undo}(x, s)$. Then it must also contain $p_i(x)$ and have the form

$$S_{prefix}, \; p_i(x), \; S', \; p_i^{undo}(x, s), \; S_{suffix}$$

T_i must hold a p-lock on x for the duration of S'. Hence, all the operations in S' commute with $p_i^{undo}(x, s)$, and it follows that S is equivalent to the schedule $\hat{S}$

$$S_{prefix}, \; p_i(x), \; p_i^{undo}(x, s), \; S', \; S_{suffix}$$

Since s describes the state of x when p_i is executed in S, it also describes the state when p_i is executed in $\hat{S}$. Since $p_i^{undo}(x, s)$ works correctly in $\hat{S}$ and the two schedules are equivalent, it also works correctly in S.

In some cases we can decompose an operation that has no compensating operation into two or more partial operations that do have compensating operations. Returning to the example in Section 20.6, the `withdraw(x)` operation does

---

[6] Note that when p has a compensating operation, it is always true that p^{-1} backward-commutes through q. See Exercise 20.41.

not have a compensating operation because it is many-to-one: for any value of x it has two possible results depending on whether the account balance covers the withdrawal. It does have an undo operation conditionalDeposit(x,y) where y was the account balance when withdraw(x) was executed. The semantics of conditionaldeposit(x,y) is that if $y \geq x$ (so that the withdrawal succeeded), it deposits x; otherwise it does nothing. However, if we decompose withdraw(x) into the two partial operations withdrawOK(x) and withdrawNO(x), then withdrawOK(x) has a compensating operation, deposit(x), and withdrawNO(x) does not need a compensating operation because it has no effect on the database. Note that even though withdraw(x) is not a one-to-one operation, its domain and range are identical: the set of all possible account balances.

20.8 Isolation in Structured Transaction Models

In Chapter 19, we introduced a number of transaction models. Having discussed serializability and locking, we can now show how to implement isolation within these models. We will devote all of Chapter 24 to showing how distributed transactions are implemented, so we do not discuss them here.

20.8.1 Savepoints

A savepoint (Section 19.2.1) is a mechanism used within a transaction, T, to achieve partial rollback. It should appear as if the database updates made by the portion of the transaction that were rolled back never happened. After the rollback completes, the items that have been restored can be unlocked and immediately made available (before the transaction completes) to concurrent transactions. Thus we have the following rules for handling savepoints in concurrency controls based on locks:

1. When a savepoint, s, is created, no change is made to any lock set. However, the concurrency control must remember the identity of all locks that T_i acquired prior to creating s, so that if T_i rolls back to s, it can release locks obtained subsequent to the creation. To accomplish this, the control places a marker in the lock list, $\mathcal{L}_i$, containing a number that represents the Id of the savepoint. Lock entries that follow this marker correspond to locks obtained after the creation of s.

2. When the transaction rolls back to s, the locks corresponding to all lock entries following the marker for s in $\mathcal{L}_i$ are released.

It would be a happy result if the above rules preserved isolation in a two-phase locking concurrency control, but this is sadly not the case. A transaction might read a data item, x, after creating a savepoint and then roll back, releasing the read lock. The effect is an early release of a read lock, which allows a non-two-phase schedule to be easily created. To preserve isolation, the second rule can be modified so that write locks are downgraded to read locks and read locks are not released.

20.8.2 Chained Transactions

Chaining can be used to decompose a transaction, T, into smaller subtransactions to avoid total rollback if a crash occurs. In Chapter 19, we discussed two different semantics for how chained transactions deal with the state of database items accessed by the transaction when control moves from one subtransaction in the chain to the next. Using `commit`, the state is not maintained between subtransactions, and, although the individual subtransactions are isolated and serializable, T as a whole is not. Using `chain`, the state is maintained between one subtransaction and the next, and T is isolated and serializable with respect to other transactions.

The `commit` operation is handled in the normal way: all locks are released. For the `chain` operation, locks are not released but are instead passed to the subsequent subtransaction in the chain. Durability is provided in both cases (as described in Chapter 22).

20.8.3 Recoverable Queues

A recoverable queue can be implemented as one or more tables within a database (since the database is durable), but performance suffers. The queue is a hotspot, accessed by many transactions, and, assuming the concurrency control is strict, locks on the queue would be held until commit time, creating bottlenecks.

For this reason, a recoverable queue is implemented as a separate module that uses locks but manages them in a manner suited to the needs of the queue. In one possible implementation, a separate lock is associated with each element on the queue and with the queue's head and tail pointers. A transaction wishing to enqueue or dequeue an element must first obtain a write lock on the tail or head pointer, respectively. A pointer is locked only for the duration of the enqueue or dequeue operation, whereas a lock on an element that is enqueued or dequeued is held until the transaction that performed the enqueue or dequeue operation commits or aborts. Thus, for example, a transaction, T, might dequeue an element from the queue and release the lock on the head pointer. Another transaction can then dequeue the next element before T commits or aborts.

Note that since the queue is implemented as a module separate from the database, the requirements of strictness and two-phase locking can be relaxed. The concurrency control is clearly not strict in the way it manipulates the lock on the pointer, and it need not be two-phase either. The queue is treated as an object with known semantics. Using the fact that it is used for scheduling work, concurrent operations that do not commute are allowed. For example, dequeue operations conflict: if their order is reversed, different elements are returned. However, by implementing the queue in a separate module, the conflict is not visible to the database and hence not taken into account by its concurrency control.

The purpose of the locks used to implement the queue is to guarantee the integrity of the individual enqueue and dequeue operations, not the serializability of the transactions that invoke them. As a result, concurrency is enhanced at the expense of isolation. Concurrent transactions might enqueue and dequeue elements on a set of queues in a variety of orders that would not be possible if serializable execution were enforced.

In contrast to its lock on the head or tail pointer, T always retains a write lock on the element it is accessing until it commits. This guarantees, for example, that after T enqueues an element, no other transaction, T', can dequeue that element until after T commits.

20.8.4 Nested Transactions

Nested transactions support concurrent execution of subtransactions. That is, several subtransactions of a top-level transaction can be executing concurrently and can request conflicting database operations. Hence, in addition to the rules governing the granting of locks to concurrent (nested) transactions, we must introduce new rules governing how locks are granted to the subtransactions of a single (nested) transaction.

The nested transaction model discussed in Section 19.2.3 adheres to the following rules:

1. Each nested transaction in its entirety must be isolated and hence serializable with respect to other nested transactions.

2. A parent subtransaction does not execute concurrently with its children.

3. Each child subtransaction (together with all of its descendants) must be isolated and hence serializable with respect to each of its siblings (together with all of that sibling's descendants).

To implement this we impose the following rules [Beeri et al. 1989]:

1. When a subtransaction of nested transaction, T, requests to read a data item, a read lock is granted if no other nested transaction holds a write lock on that item and all subtransactions of T holding a write lock on that item are its ancestors (and hence are not executing).

2. When a subtransaction of a nested transaction, T, requests to write a data item, a write lock is granted if no other nested transaction holds a read or write lock on that item and all subtransactions of T holding a read lock or a write lock on that item are its ancestors (and hence are not executing).

3. All locks obtained by a subtransaction are held until it aborts or commits. When a subtransaction commits, any locks it obtained that its parent does not hold are inherited by the parent. When a subtransaction aborts, any locks it obtained that its parent does not hold are released.

Since these rules are a superset of the rules that guarantee isolation among concurrent transactions, the schedules of concurrent nested transactions are serializable. To see that these rules enforce the desired semantics among siblings, observe that no lock held within the subtree rooted at one active subtransaction can conflict with a lock held within the subtree rooted at an active sibling. Thus, concurrently active siblings are not ordered by the database operations that have been performed within their subtrees. Therefore the siblings are isolated with respect to each other and hence serializable. They might be serializable in several possible orders, among which is always the order in which they commit (Section 20.4).

20.8.5 Multilevel Transactions

A concurrency control for multilevel transactions can be implemented by two rather elegant generalizations of the conventional, strict two-phase locking concurrency control described in Sections 20.4 and 20.5 [Weikum 1991]. The first generalization makes use of the semantics of the operations at each level; the second relies on the fact that multiple levels are involved.

Operation semantics and commutativity.   In Section 20.6, we discussed how the commutativity of operations on objects can be used in the design of conflict tables for immediate-update pessimistic concurrency controls. These ideas form a central part of the multilevel model.

Each level in a system that supports multilevel transactions produces its own (interleaved) schedule. Thus, for example, in Figure 19.4, on page 797, the schedule at level L_2 of the transaction $Move(sec_1, sec_2)$ is the sequence $TestInc(sec_2)$, $Dec(sec_1)$. (A reminder: $Move$ moves a student from one course section to another; $TestInc$ conditionally adds one student to a section; and Dec decrements the enrollment in a section.) A more interesting schedule is one that involves the concurrent execution of several multilevel transactions. For example, the L_2 schedule

$$TestInc_1(sec_2),\ TestInc_2(sec_2),\ Dec_2(sec_1),\ Dec_1(sec_1) \qquad \textbf{20.4}$$

involves the interleaved execution of two transactions, $Move_1(sec_1, sec_2)$ and $Move_2(sec_1, sec_2)$, each of which moves a student from section 1 to section 2. The interesting aspect of this schedule is that since the two decrement operations commute, (20.4) is equivalent to the schedule

$$TestInc_1(sec_2),\ Dec_1(sec_1),\ TestInc_2(sec_2),\ Dec_2(sec_1) \qquad \textbf{20.5}$$

and is thus serializable in the order $Move_1$, $Move_2$. Note that since two $TestInc$ operations on the same tuple do not commute, (20.4) is not serializable in the order $Move_2$, $Move_1$ (the initial state might be such that the first to execute succeeds in the increment while the second fails; thus, different results are returned to the caller if the order is reversed).

Suppose now that we examine the schedule (20.4) in terms of the operations that execute at L_1. We see the following:

$$Sel_1(t_2),\ Upd_1(t_2),\ Sel_2(t_2),\ Upd_2(t_2),\ Upd_2(t_1),\ Upd_1(t_1) \qquad \textbf{20.6}$$

As with the banking application discussed in Section 20.6, since update operations on the same tuple do not, *in general*, commute, this schedule is not serializable in either order. A higher-level view, however, shows that the updates implement Dec

| | **Granted Mode** | |
Requested Mode	TestInc	Dec
TestInc	X	X
Dec	X	

FIGURE 20.19 Conflict table for an L_2 concurrency control that schedules *TestInc* and *Dec* operations.

operations, and serializability becomes apparent. Once again, the more semantics available to the concurrency control, the more concurrency it can detect.

A concurrency control for L_2. To take advantage of semantics, we can construct a concurrency control for L_2 that uses a conflict table, C_2, shown in Figure 20.19. The rows and columns of C_2 correspond to operations supported at L_2. For example, a *Move* transaction is a program at the *application* level, L_3, containing invocations of *TestInc* and *Dec*, which are supported at L_2. The concurrency control at L_2 receives these invocations and decides whether they can be serviced using C_2. It grants *TestInc* and *Dec* locks for this purpose. Thus, if *Move* invokes $Dec(sec_2)$, the concurrency control grants a *Dec* lock on sec_2 if no other transaction has a *TestInc* lock on it; otherwise, the *Dec* request must wait. Once the lock has been granted, a program at L_2 can be executed that implements the *Dec* operation by invoking operations at L_1.

Now let us go back to the original example. Although the schedule of (20.4) is serializable in the order $Move_1$, $Move_2$, the two *TestInc* operations do not commute and so impose an ordering on the two transactions. Since the conventional, pessimistic concurrency control (described in Section 20.4) does not grant a request if it imposes an ordering among active transactions, the L_2 scheduler does not produce schedule (20.5). As with a conventional concurrency control, not all conflict-serializable schedules can be recognized. However, consider the following interleaved schedule of transactions $Move_1(sec_1,\ sec_2)$ and $Move_2(sec_1,\ sec_3)$:

$$TestInc_1(sec_2),\ \ TestInc_2(sec_3),\ \ Dec_2(sec_1),\ \ Dec_1(sec_1) \qquad \textbf{20.7}$$

This interleaving is allowed by the L_2 concurrency control since two decrement operations commute. To see that additional concurrency is gained, realize that we have not indicated when the transactions request to commit. Instead of committing immediately after completing $Dec_2(sec_1)$, $Move_2$ might continue to be active for an extended period of time. By recognizing the commutativity of decrement operations, the L_2 concurrency control can avoid delaying Dec_1 until $Move_2$ releases its Dec lock on sec_1.

Multilevel concurrency controls. It appears that the strategy for obtaining the best performance is to implement a concurrency control at the highest level, L_n, in the hierarchy (L_2 in Figure 19.4) in order to take advantage of the most semantics. But we have overlooked one important point. In the discussion in Section 20.4 of a conventional, pessimistic concurrency control, we implicitly assumed that the

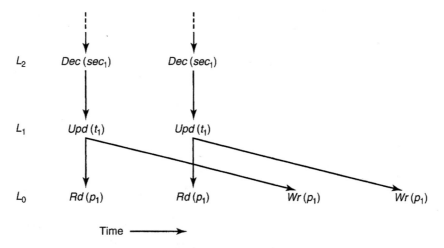

FIGURE 20.20 Decrement operations do not conflict at L_2, but arbitrary interleaving at lower levels can lead to problems.

read and write operations scheduled by the concurrency control were isolated with respect to each other. Thus, if the control scheduled a write operation after a read operation, it assumed that the read had completed before the write started. With a multilevel concurrency control, this is true when operations conflict but not necessarily true when they do not. Thus, if a transaction, T, executes $TestInc(sec_1)$ and a second transaction requests the same operation, it will be made to wait until T completes because two $TestInc$ operations on the same section conflict. Hence, the two operations will be totally ordered.

However, consider two operations that do not conflict and hence their concurrent execution is permitted by the concurrency control. In Figure 20.20, the L_2 concurrency control has scheduled the concurrent execution of two decrement operations invoked by transaction programs running at L_3. (The programs might invoke other operations as well, but we do not consider them here.) The decrement operation is implemented by a program (subtransaction) in L_2, and that program invokes operations supported by L_1. In this case, each instance of the decrement program makes only a single such invocation—of Upd. Each invocation of the Upd program in L_1 invokes read and write operations implemented in L_0.

As shown in the figure, each of the update statements reads the same value of the enrollment number stored in tuple t_1, decrements that value, and therefore stores the same value back in t_1. Thus, although two decrement operations have been performed, the enrollment has only been decremented by one. This is an example of the lost update problem introduced in Section 2.3, and the reason it has occurred is that the executions of the two instances of the program that implement the Upd operations are not isolated with respect to each other. This violates the assumption made by a concurrency control that each operation that it schedules is isolated (we

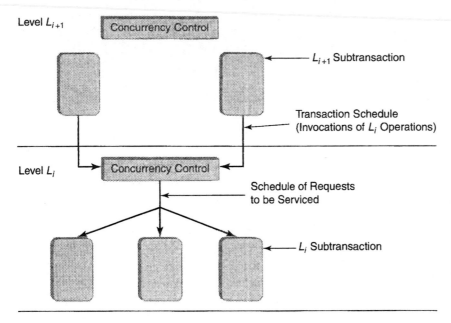

Level L_{i+1}

Concurrency Control

L_{i+1} Subtransaction

Transaction Schedule
(Invocations of L_i Operations)

Level L_i

Concurrency Control

Schedule of Requests
to be Serviced

L_i Subtransaction

FIGURE 20.21 Relationship between levels in a multilevel concurrency control.

discussed this issue on page 840). Operations are implemented by programs, and hence the programs must be serializable.

To overcome this problem, multilevel transactions use a multilevel concurrency control, which guarantees that the operations *at each level* are serializable and hence isolated with respect to each other. A **multilevel concurrency control** is composed of separate controls at each level. Thus, the control at L_i schedules the operation invocations it receives from subtransactions at L_{i+1} in accordance with a conflict table, C_i, which determines whether or not those operations can be executed concurrently. The control grants operation locks as described previously and releases them when the subtransaction at L_{i+1} commits. Figure 20.21 shows this organization.

A goal of a multilevel concurrency control is to guarantee that operations invoked by a program at any level are effectively isolated from each other. In other words, an operation invoked by a transaction at the application level is implemented by a program—think of it as a subtransaction—in L_n. That subtransaction then invokes a sequence of operations, each of which is implemented by a program in L_{n-1}. If the L_n concurrency control determines that op_1 and op_2, invoked by two application transactions, can be executed concurrently, then the subprograms, L_n, that implement these operations will be executed concurrently. These subprograms invoke lower-level operations and create an interleaved schedule at L_{n-1}. To guarantee that op_1 and op_2 are effectively isolated, this interleaved schedule at L_{n-1} must be serializable. That is, it must be equivalent to a serial schedule of the individual sequences. Note that the equivalent serial order is not important since op_1 and op_2

commute and therefore both orders produce the same result. The L_n concurrency control requires only that the schedule at L_{n-1} be equivalent to *some* serial schedule.

To guarantee the isolation of op_1 and op_2 we need a concurrency control at level L_{n-1} that guarantees that schedules at that level are serializable. The argument now repeats. The L_{n-1} control assumes that the operations it schedules are isolated units when in fact they are not. They are subtransactions that produce schedules at L_{n-2}. Hence, a concurrency control at L_{n-2} is needed to guarantee that these subtransactions are serializable.

Let us follow this reasoning, using Figure 20.20 as an example, and see why the L_0 schedule in that figure cannot be produced by a multilevel concurrency control. Two transactions at the application level (not shown in the figure) concurrently invoke $Dec(sec_1)$. The L_2 control sees that the two operations commute, so it grants Dec locks on sec_1 to both transactions, allowing two invocations of the L_2 subtransaction that implements Dec to run concurrently. Each subtransaction at L_2 is a program that invokes $Upd(t_1)$. Those invocations are passed to the L_1 control. The first L_2 subtransaction is granted an Upd lock on t_1, but the second must wait since Upd locks conflict. Thus, only a single invocation of the update subtransaction at L_1 is initiated. It invokes read and write operations on p_1. These are passed to the L_0 control, which grants the page locks on p_1 to the update subtransaction and schedules the operations. When the update subtransaction commits, it releases the page locks and returns to the Dec subtransaction that invoked it. When Dec commits, it releases the Upd lock, hence allowing the second invocation of the update subtransaction to commence, and returns to the application transaction that invoked it. In this way, a serializable L_0 schedule (not the schedule shown in Figure 20.20) is produced.

Using the same reasoning as in Section 20.6, we can show that all schedules produced by this concurrency control are recoverable (i.e., compensating operations work correctly and guarantee atomicity when transactions abort).

Using the multilevel model. The multilevel model (Section 20.8.5) of transactions is not widely available to application programmers since a concurrency control has to be provided at each level. If an application is decomposed into levels of abstraction, the application programmer will have to participate in building the concurrency controls for those levels. The model can be used, however, within a DBMS and its implementation utilizes the concept of latches.

Consider the example of granular locking on tuples and pages. An X lock must be acquired on a tuple and an IX lock on the page in which it is stored when the tuple is inserted. But the insert operation must, in addition, update other data structures in the page, for example, the structure that records information about storage allocation within the page. Maintaining locks on these additional items until the transaction completes would unnecessarily reduce concurrency since these locks would prevent other transactions from accessing the page in what might be totally nonconflicting ways.

To alleviate this problem, we can view the procedure that executes an SQL statement within the DBMS as a subtransaction of the transaction that submitted the statement. While the transaction sees the abstraction of tuples, the subtransaction sees the abstraction of page reads and writes. The subtransaction acquires latches on the pages it accesses and releases them when it commits. This ensures the isolation of the subtransaction with respect to concurrent subtransactions (or equivalently, the isolated execution of concurrently processed SQL statements within the DBMS). Since the latches need not be held until the transaction as a whole commits, access by concurrent transactions to other tuples and data structures within the page is possible. The transaction, in turn, retains higher-level locks on the tuples it accesses to ensure appropriate transaction isolation.

The tuple/page hierarchy within a DBMS is one example of an object hierarchy. In Section 20.6 we considered abstract operations on objects and assumed that they were isolated. However, an object in a hierarchy is implemented using lower-level objects, and isolation is not guaranteed. This is a context within which a multilevel control is useful. Using this model, each object implements a concurrency control using the semantics of the operations it supports and allows the concurrent execution of two operations on the object if they commute. The isolation of the procedures within the object that implement these operations is guaranteed by the concurrency controls at the objects that they, in turn, access.

20.9 Other Concurrency Controls

Locking forms the basis of most, but not all, of the concurrency control algorithms in commercial systems. We discuss two nonlocking algorithms in this section: timestamp-ordered concurrency controls and optimistic concurrency controls. The timestamp-ordered algorithm, one of the earliest concurrency control algorithms to be proposed, illustrates the use of timestamps to achieve synchronization. Optimistic concurrency controls are a more recent development and show promise in certain situations. In Section 21.5, we will discuss still another algorithm, multiversion concurrency control, which has been implemented in a number of commercial relational database systems.

20.9.1 Timestamp-Ordered Concurrency Controls

In a **timestamp-ordered concurrency control**, a unique timestamp, $TS(T)$, is assigned to a transaction, T, when it is initiated, and the concurrency control guarantees the existence of an equivalent serial schedule in which transactions are ordered by their timestamps. For this reason, timestamp-ordered controls are **static**; that is, the equivalent serial order is determined at the time they are initiated. Transactions are serialized in their initiation order, not necessarily their commit order.

Unique timestamps can be generated using a clock. The value of the clock at the time the transaction is initiated is taken as the timestamp. As long as the clock ticks faster than the rate at which transactions are initiated, each transaction will get a unique timestamp.[7] We describe an immediate-update version of a timestamp-ordered control; a deferred-update version is also possible.

A timestamp-ordered control stores with each data item, x, the following pieces of information:

- $rt(x)$, the largest timestamp of any transaction that has read x
- $wt(x)$, the largest timestamp of any transaction that has updated x
- $f(x)$, a flag that indicates whether the transaction that last wrote x has committed

The maintenance of this information implies additional overhead and hence is a disadvantage of this scheme. Additional space is required for each separately addressable item in the database. Furthermore, since this information is stored in the database, updates to it must be treated like updates to the data items themselves—they must be recorded on disk and they must be rolled back if the transaction aborts. This means that, in contrast to other controls, a read of a data item x causes a write of $rt(x)$. As a result of this large overhead, timestamp-ordered algorithms have not been widely used.

When a transaction, T_1, makes a request to read x, the concurrency control performs the following actions:

R1. If $TS(T_1) < wt(x)$, some transaction T_2, which must follow T_1 in the equivalent serial (timestamp) order, $(TS(T_2) > TS(T_1))$, has written a new value to x. T_1's read should return a value that x had prior to the write executed by T_2, but that value no longer exists in the database. Thus, T_1 is too old (has too small a timestamp) to read x. It is aborted and restarted (with a new timestamp).

R2. If $TS(T_1) > wt(x)$, there are two cases:

- If $f(x)$ indicates that the value of x is committed, the request is granted. If $TS(T_1) > rt(x)$, the value of $TS(T_1)$ is assigned to $rt(x)$.
- If $f(x)$ indicates that the value of x is not committed, T_1 must wait (to avoid a dirty read).

When T_1 makes a request to write x, the concurrency control performs the following actions:

W1. If $TS(T_1) < rt(x)$, some transaction T_2, which must follow T_1 in the equivalent serial (timestamp) order, has read an earlier value of x. If T_1 is allowed to commit, T_2 should have read the value that T_1 is requesting to write. Thus, T_1 is too old to write x. It is aborted and restarted (with a new timestamp).

---

[7] In a network in which each site generates its own timestamps using its own local clock, uniqueness is not guaranteed by this algorithm. To guarantee uniqueness, the algorithm is modified by assigning to each site at startup time a unique identifier. Each site appends its identifier to the value of its clock to form a timestamp. Thus, a timestamp at site i is (c_i, id_i), where c_i is the current value of its clock and id_i is i's unique identifier.

W2. If $rt(x) < TS(T_1) < wt(x)$, a transaction has stored a new value in x that, in a serial schedule ordered on timestamps, overwrites the value that T_1 is requesting to write (since $TS(T_1) < wt(x)$). Furthermore, no transaction with a timestamp between $TS(T_1)$ and $wt(x)$ previously requested to read x (since $rt(x) < TS(T_1)$).

- If $f(x)$ indicates that x is committed, any subsequent transaction with a timestamp between $TS(T_1)$ and $wt(x)$ that attempts to read x will be aborted (see $R1$). Hence, the value that T_1 is requesting to write will not be read by any transaction and will have no effect on the final database state. The request is thus granted, but the write is not actually performed. This action (not performing the write in this situation) is called the Thomas Write Rule [Thomas 1979].

- If $f(x)$ indicates that x is not a committed value, T_1 must wait (since the transaction that last wrote x might abort and the value that T_1 is requesting to write becomes the current value).

W3. If $wt(x), rt(x) < TS(T_1)$, there are two cases:

- If $f(x)$ indicates that the value of x is not a committed value, T_1 is made to wait since granting the request will complicate rollback (see the discussion in Section 20.2).

- If $f(x)$ indicates that the value of x has been committed, the request is granted. The value of $TS(T_1)$ is assigned to $wt(x)$, and the value of $f(x)$ is set to uncommitted. (Later, when T_1 commits, the value of $f(x)$ is set to committed.)

The sequence of requests shown in Figure 20.22 illustrates these rules. Assume that $TS(T_1) < TS(T_2)$, that at time t_0 the read and write timestamps of both x and y are less than $TS(T_1)$, and that both x and y have committed values. Then, at time t_1, rule $R2$ applies, the read request is granted, and $rt(y)$ is set to $TS(T_1)$. At t_2, using $W3$, the write request is granted, $wt(y)$ is set to $TS(T_2)$, and $f(y)$ is set to indicate that y is uncommitted. At t_3, $W3$ again applies, the write request is granted, $wt(x)$ is set to $TS(T_2)$, and since T_2 immediately commits, both $f(x)$ and $f(y)$ indicate committed values. At t_4, $W2$ applies since $rt(x)$ has not changed and $wt(x)$ is now $TS(T_2)$. The request is granted, although the write is not actually performed and $wt(x)$ is not updated.

The sequence is thus accepted by a timestamp-ordered control, but we do not refer to it as a schedule since the control does not submit the final write to the database. Note that the sequence is not conflict equivalent to a serial schedule and would not be accepted by a concurrency control based on conflict equivalence. (However, it is view equivalent to the serial schedule T_1, T_2.) This means that a timestamp-ordered control can accept sequences of requests that are not accepted by a control based on two-phase locking. Exercise 20.30 asks you to provide a schedule accepted by a two-phase locking concurrency control but not a timestamp-ordered control. It follows then that the two controls are incomparable: each can accept (serializable) schedules that will not be accepted by the other.

FIGURE 20.22 Sequence of requests accepted by a timestamp-ordered concurrency control. Assuming that $TS(T_1) < TS(T_2)$ and that the initial values of the read and write timestamps of x and y are smaller than both transactions' timestamps, T_1's final write is not performed.

$T_1:$		$r(y)$			$w(x)$ *commit*
$T_2:$			$w(y)$	$w(x)$ *commit*	
	t_0	t_1	t_2	t_3	t_4

20.9.2 Optimistic Concurrency Controls

In general, an optimistic algorithm consists of several steps. In the first, a task is executed under some (optimistic) assumption that simplifies the performance of the task. For example, in a security system the task might be a password check, and the assumption is made that the submitted password is correct. In a concurrency control the task is a transaction, and the assumption is made that conflicts with concurrent transactions will not occur. Hence, we need not be concerned with locking or waiting. Transactions read and write without requesting permission from the concurrency control and thus are never delayed. The second step validates the first step by checking to see if the assumption was actually true. If not, the task must be redone, which implies rollback in the concurrency control case. If the assumption is true, validation results in commitment.

This approach stands in contrast to the pessimistic approach, in which execution of the task is done cautiously. No simplifying assumptions are made in the first step, each request for database access is checked in advance, and appropriate actions are taken immediately if conflicts are detected. Hence, no second (validation) step is required in the pessimistic approach.

Since database accesses during the first step are unchecked and conflicts might actually occur, optimistic concurrency controls [Kung and Robinson 1981] generally use a deferred-update approach to avoid propagating the effects of an incorrectly executed transaction to the database. (If an immediate update approach were used, the updates performed by transactions that later roll back would be visible to concurrent transactions and would result in cascaded aborts.) The new values of the items written are stored in an intentions list and are not used to update the database immediately. Thus, a third step is needed for a transaction that modifies the database and is successfully validated: its intentions list is written to the database.

Since rollback is costly, an optimistic algorithm is appropriate only if conflicts are rare. Note that rollback is more costly with an optimistic algorithm than with a timestamp-ordered algorithm, since the rollback decision is made after the transaction completes. With a timestamp-ordered control a rollback decision is made while the transaction is still executing, which wastes less of the system resources. Rollback can also occur in a pessimistic algorithm because of deadlock. An important advantage of optimistic algorithms is that deadlocks cannot occur since one transaction never waits for another. In comparing the efficiency of optimistic and pessimistic algorithms, the costs of validation, managing the intentions list, locking, and rollback must be considered.

Because the database is not modified during the first step (writes might be requested but are not actually executed), this step is referred to as the **read phase**. The second step is referred to as the **validation phase**, and the third step, as the **write phase**. Thus, a transaction's writes are performed and appear in a schedule during its write phase (write requests during the read phase are not recorded in the schedule). For the sake of simplicity, we initially assume that the validation and write phases form a single critical section, and hence only one transaction can be executing its validation or write phase at a time (but a number of transactions can concurrently be executing their read phase while a single transaction is executing its validation or write phase). We will modify that assumption shortly. The three phases of a transaction are shown in Figure 20.23(a).

The validation phase ensures that S is equivalent to a schedule, S^{ser}, in which committed transactions are executed serially in the order in which they enter validation (i.e., the order in which they commit). The operations of uncommitted transactions follow those of committed transactions in S^{ser}.

There are two cases to consider when validating a transaction, T_1. In case 1 (the simple case), we consider a transaction T_2 that completes its write phase before T_1 starts its read phase, as shown in Figure 20.23(b). Since the two transactions are not concurrently active, all of T_1's operations follow all of T_2's in S. Hence the validation of T_1 against T_2 is always successful, and T_1 follows T_2 in S^{ser}.

Case 2 (the more interesting case) is shown in Figure 20.23(c). Here T_2 completed before T_1 entered validation but was still active when T_1 entered its read phase. If T_1 is successfully validated, then T_2 will precede T_1 in S^{ser}. Hence, validation of T_1 with respect to T_2 requires that if T_1 executes an operation, p, that conflicts with an operation, q, of T_2, p must follow q in S in order for S to be equivalent to S^{ser}.

Suppose that p is a read executed by T_1 during its read phase and that q is a write of the same item executed by T_2 during its write phase. Thus, the transactions have conflicting operations. As shown in Figure 20.23(c), the operations can occur in either order. If p precedes q, the order is contrary to the order in which the transactions enter validation, and hence, if T_1 were allowed to commit, the order would be contrary to the commit order in S^{ser}. Therefore, T_1 must not be successfully validated. It must be aborted. If the operations occurred in the opposite order, T_1 could be allowed to commit (since the order would be consistent with the commit order), but, unfortunately, optimistic controls do not generally record the order in which such operations occur. As a result, validation makes the worst-case assumption that the order is not consistent with the order of entry into validation.

Thus the condition for the validation of T_1 is that the set of items it has read must be disjoint from the set of items written by any transaction whose write phase overlaps T_1's read phase.

Note that when T_1 validates, the only check made concerns T_1's read operations. Validation does not check for conflicts involving T_1's write operations. Although a conflict also occurs if T_1 writes an item that T_2 reads or writes, it follows from Figure 20.23(c) (and the fact that only one transaction at a time can be in its validation or write phases) that if a write of T_1 (during its write phase) conflicts with a read or write of T_2 (during T_2's read or write phases), then the order of the

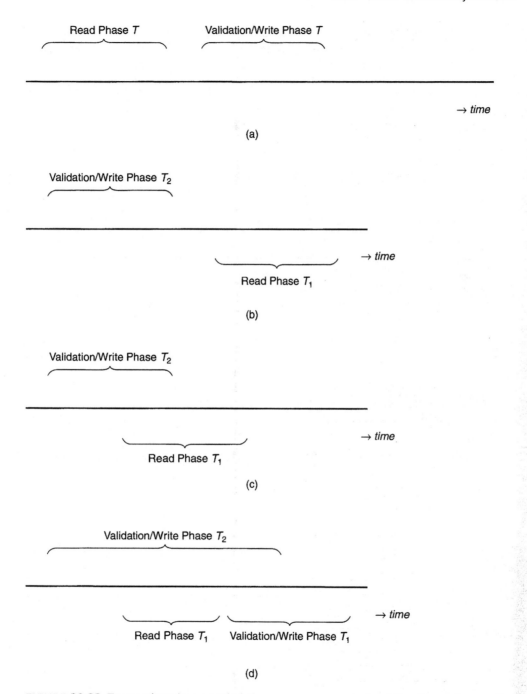

FIGURE 20.23 Transactions in an optimistic concurrency control: (a) the three phases of a transaction, (b) nonconcurrent transactions, (c) T_1 conflicts with T_2 if the set of items read by T_1 overlaps the set of items written by T_2, (d) T_1 conflicts with T_2 if the set of items read or written by T_1 overlaps the set of items written by T_2.

operations is consistent with the commit order. Thus, even though a read or write operation of T_2 conflicts with a write operation of T_1, T_1 can be successfully validated because these operations need not be interchanged in constructing S^{ser}.

A control implements the optimistic algorithm by recording, for each transaction, T, the set of items that were read, $R(T)$, and written, $W(T)$, by T. It eliminates case 1 by recording the set, L_1, of transactions that execute their validation or write phases concurrently with the read phase of T and validates T against only those transactions. Validation is successful if, for each transaction, T_i, in L_1, the condition

$$R(T) \bigcap W(T_i) = \Phi \qquad\qquad \textbf{20.8}$$

is satisfied. In other words, no transaction that executed concurrently with T and precedes it in the commit order wrote an item that T read. Alternatively, no transaction that committed during T's read phase wrote an item that T read.

We have made the assumption that only one transaction at a time is in its validation or write phase (this is called **serial validation**). Although this simplifies validation, it can create a bottleneck that restricts concurrency.

An alternative, **parallel validation**, avoids the bottleneck by allowing multiple transactions to execute their validation and/or write phases concurrently, as shown in Figure 20.23(d). As a result, conflicting write operations of two transactions must now be considered since they might occur in the wrong order. As with serial validation, the order in which transactions enter validation is the equivalent serial order. To accommodate the added concurrency, a transaction T must satisfy condition (20.8) for transactions in L_1, and in addition it must be validated against the set of all transactions, L_2, that entered validation before T entered validation and were still executing their validation or write phases at the time T entered validation. Any such transactions must precede T in the equivalent serial order. Therefore conflicts between the write operations of T and the read *or* write operations of a transaction, T_i, in L_2 must now be considered.

Thus, the parallel validation of a transaction, T, divides concurrently executing transactions into two sets. For transactions that completed their write phase before T entered its validation phase (L_1), the condition for validation is identical to the condition for serial validation in equation (20.8). For transactions that entered validation prior to T and are executing their validation or write phases when T enters validation (L_2), *two* conditions must be satisfied. In addition to equation (20.8), the set of items written by T must be disjoint from the set written by T_i in order for T to be successfully validated:

$$W(T) \bigcap W(T_i) = \Phi \qquad\qquad \textbf{20.9}$$

Note that a conflict between a write operation of T and a read operation of T_i is not a problem since the order of entry into validation implies that T's write must have followed T_i's read, and therefore the order of the operations in S is consistent with the commit order.

BIBLIOGRAPHIC NOTES

Two excellent books on concurrency controls are [Bernstein et al. 1987; Papadimitriou 1986]. A more theoretical discussion is given in [Lynch et al. 1994].

The concepts of serializability and two-phase locking were introduced in [Eswaran et al. 1976]. The result—that if a schedule is not serializable, there exists an integrity constraint that the schedule makes false—is proved in [Rosenkrantz et al. 1984]. The concepts of recoverability and strictness were introduced in [Hadzilacos 1983]. Backward and forward commutativity were introduced in [Weihl 1988] and are discussed in more detail in [Lynch et al. 1994]. Our implementation of nested transactions is taken from [Beeri et al. 1989] and the implementation of multilevel transactions is taken from [Weikum 1991]. One of the first timestamp-ordered concurrency controls is described in [Thomas 1979], which also introduced the Thomas Write Rule. Optimistic concurrency controls were introduced in [Kung and Robinson 1981]. Intentions lists were first suggested in [Lampson et al. 1981]. A different approach to designing concurrency controls based on the semantics of the application (as opposed to the semantics of the operations) is discussed in [Bernstein et al. 1999b; Bernstein et al. 1999a; Bernstein et al. 1998; Bernstein and Lewis 1996].

EXERCISES

20.1 State which of the following schedules are serializable.

    a. $r_1(x) \ r_2(y) \ r_1(z) \ r_3(z) \ r_2(x) \ r_1(y)$
    b. $r_1(x) \ w_2(y) \ r_1(z) \ r_3(z) \ w_2(x) \ r_1(y)$
    c. $r_1(x) \ w_2(y) \ r_1(z) \ r_3(z) \ w_1(x) \ r_2(y)$
    d. $r_1(x) \ r_2(y) \ r_1(z) \ r_3(z) \ w_1(x) \ w_2(y)$
    e. $r_1(x) \ r_2(y) \ w_2(x) \ w_3(x) \ w_3(y) \ r_1(y)$
    f. $w_1(x) \ r_2(y) \ r_1(z) \ r_3(z) \ r_1(x) \ w_2(y)$
    g. $r_1(z) \ w_2(x) \ r_2(z) \ r_2(y) \ w_1(x) \ w_3(z) \ w_1(y) \ r_3(x)$

20.2 Give all possible conflict-equivalent serial orderings corresponding to the serialization graph in Figure 20.5.

20.3 Use a serialization graph to demonstrate that the schedule shown in Figure 20.4 is not conflict serializable.

20.4 Suppose that we declare all of the database integrity constraints in the database schema so that the DBMS will not allow any transaction to commit if its updates violate any of the integrity constraints. Then, even if we do not use any concurrency control, the database always remains consistent. Explain why we must nevertheless use a concurrency control.

20.5 Give an example of a schedule of two transactions that preserves database consistency (the database satisfies its integrity constraints), but nevertheless yields a final database that does not reflect the effect of both transactions.

20.6 Prove that conflict equivalence implies view equivalence.

20.7 Give an example of a schedule in which transactions of the Student Registration System deadlock.

20.8 Prove that with a two-phase locking protocol, one possible equivalent serial order is the order in which the transactions perform their first unlock operation.

20.9 Give an example of a transaction processing system (other than a banking system) that you have interacted with, for which you had an intuitive expectation that the serial order was the commit order.

20.10 Give an example of a schedule that is serializable but not strict.

20.11 Give an example of a schedule that is strict but not serializable.

20.12 Give an example of a schedule produced by a nonstrict two-phase locking concurrency control that is not recoverable.

20.13 Give an example of a schedule produced by a recoverable but nonstrict concurrency control involving three transactions in which a deadlock occurs, causing a cascaded abort of all three.

20.14 Give an example of a schedule produced by a nonstrict two-phase locking concurrency control that is serializable but not in commit order.

20.15 Suppose that the account object, the conflict table for which is described in Figure 20.18, has an additional operation, balance, which returns the balance in the account. Design a new conflict table for this object, including the new operation.

20.16 Consider the following schedule of three transactions:

$$r_2(y) \; r_1(x) \; r_3(y) \; r_2(x) \; w_2(y) \; w_1(x) \; r_3(x)$$

a. Define a serialization between T_1 and T_2.
b. In what apparent order does T_3 see the database?
c. Is the schedule serializable?
d. Assuming that each transaction is consistent, does the final database state satisfy all integrity constraints?
e. Does the database state seen by T_3 satisfy all integrity constraints? Explain.

20.17

a. Assume that, in addition to the operations read(x) and write(x), a database has the operation copy(x,y), which (atomically) copies the value stored in record x into record y. Design a conflict table for these operations for use in an immediate-update pessimistic concurrency control.
b. Assume that, in addition to the operations read(x) and write(x), a database has the operation increment(x,C), which (atomically) increments the value stored in record x by the constant C, which might be positive or negative. Design a conflict table for these operations for use in an immediate-update pessimistic concurrency control.

20.18 Suppose that we have a queue object that implements an FCFS (first-come-first-served) discipline, with operations enqueue and dequeue. enqueue always succeeds and dequeue returns NO if the queue is empty and OK otherwise. Design a conflict table for this object using partial operations and backward commutativity.

20.19 A pair of (partial) database operations, p and q, are said to be **forward-commute** if, in every database state in which both p and q are defined, the sequences p, q and q, p are both defined and, in both sequences, p and q return the same values and the final database state is the same.

a. Describe how forward commutativity can be used in the design of a deferred-update pessimistic concurrency control.

b. Give a conflict table for such a control for the account object described in Figure 20.18.

20.20 In Section 20.7 we described a policy for a concurrency control that dealt with both forward and compensating operations and guaranteed that schedules were reducible. Generalize this policy to include undo operations using the conditions on the commutativity described in that section, and show that your generalization preserves reducibility.

20.21 Design a deferred-update pessimistic concurrency control.

20.22 Consider an implementation of chained transactions in which a subtransaction, when it commits, only releases locks on items that will not be accessed by subsequent subtransactions. Explain how this can affect the ACID properties of the overall chained transaction.

20.23 Give the conflict table for each level of the multilevel control described in Section 20.8.5. Each table indicates the conflicts for the operations used to implement the transaction Move(sec1, sec2). Assume that the operation TestInc is viewed as two partial operations TestIncOK and TestIncNO.

20.24 Give an example of a schedule in which a pessimistic concurrency control makes a transaction wait but later allows it to commit, while an optimistic concurrency control restarts the transaction.

20.25 Give an example of a schedule in which a pessimistic concurrency control makes a transaction wait but then allows it to commit, while an optimistic concurrency control allows the transaction to commit without waiting.

20.26 Give an example of a schedule that is acceptable (without any delays caused by locks) by an immediate-update pessimistic strict two-phase locking concurrency control, while an optimistic concurrency control restarts one of the transactions.

20.27 Can a deadlock occur in the timestamp-ordered control described in the text?

20.28 Give an example of a schedule produced by a timestamp-ordered concurrency control in which the serialization order is not the commit order.

20.29 Give an example of a schedule that is strict and serializable but not in commit order and that could have been produced by either a timestamp-ordered concurrency control or a two-phase locking concurrency control.

20.30 Give an example of a schedule that would be accepted by a two-phase locking concurrency control but not by a timestamp-ordered concurrency control.

20.31 Show that the following proposed protocol for a timestamp-ordered concurrency control is not recoverable.

Store with each data item the maximum timestamp of any (not necessarily committed) transaction that has read that item and the maximum timestamp of any (not necessarily committed) transaction that has written that item.

When a transaction makes a request to read (write) a data item, if the timestamp of the requesting transaction is smaller than the write (read) timestamp in the item, restart the transaction; otherwise, grant the request.

20.32 The *kill-wait* concurrency control combines the concepts of the immediate update concurrency control and the timestamp-ordered control. As in the timestamp-ordered system, when a transaction, T_1 is initiated, it is assigned a timestamp, $TS(T_1)$. However, the system uses the same conflict table as the immediate-update pessimistic control does and resolves conflicts using the rule

> If transaction T_1 makes a request that conflicts with an operation of active transaction, T_2
> > if $TS(T_1) < TS(T_2)$, **then** *abort* T_2, **else** *make T_1 wait until T_2 terminates*.

where *abort* T_2 is referred to as a *kill* because T_1 kills T_2.

a. Show that the kill-wait control serializes in commit order.
b. Give a schedule produced by a kill-wait control that is not serializable in timestamp order.
c. Explain why deadlock does not occur in a kill-wait control.

20.33 The *wait-die* concurrency control is another control that combines the concepts of the immediate-update concurrency control and the timestamp-ordered control.

> If transaction T_1 makes a request that conflicts with an operation of active transaction T_2
> > if $TS(T_1) < TS(T_2)$, **then** *make T_1 wait until T_2 terminates*, **else** *abort* T_1.

where *abort* T_1 is referred to as a *die* because T_1 kills itself.

a. Show that the wait-die control serializes in commit order and prevents deadlocks.
b. Compare the fairness of the execution of the kill-wait and wait-die controls.

20.34 Give a complete description of an algorithm for a parallel validation, optimistic concurrency control.

20.35 Describe a serial validation, optimistic concurrency control that uses backward validation and in addition uses timestamps to distinguish the order in which conflicting read and write operations occur. The validation condition in that case need not be conservative, and only conflicts that would violate commit order cause aborts.

20.36 Subroutines can be used in a flat transaction in an attempt to mimic the behavior of a subtransaction in the nested model: whenever a subtransaction aborts, the corresponding subroutine manually undoes any database updates it has performed and returns with status indicating failure. Explain why the nested model allows higher transaction throughput.

20.37 Suppose that transactions T_1 and T_2 can be decomposed into the subtransactions

$$T_1 : T_{1,1}, \; T_{1,2}$$

and

$$T_2 : T_{2,1}, \; T_{2,2}$$

such that the database items accessed by $T_{1,1}$ and $T_{2,1}$ are disjoint from the items accessed by $T_{1,2}$ and $T_{2,2}$. Instead of guaranteeing that all schedules involving T_1

and T_2 are serializable, suppose that a concurrency control guarantees that $T_{1,1}$ is always executed serializably with $T_{2,1}$ and that $T_{1,2}$ is always executed serializably with $T_{2,2}$.

a. Will T_1 always be serializable with T_2? Explain.

b. What minimal additional condition *on the subtransactions* guarantees that the effect of executing T_1 concurrently with T_2 is the same as a serial schedule?

c. Assuming that the condition of (b) holds, what advantage does the new concurrency control have over a concurrency control that guarantees serializability?

20.38 Suppose that transactions T_1 and T_2 can be decomposed into the subtransactions

$$T_1: T_{1,1}, T_{1,2}$$

and

$$T_2: T_{2,1}, T_{2,2}$$

such that each subtransaction individually maintains the consistency constraints of the database. Instead of guaranteeing that all schedules involving T_1 and T_2 are serializable, suppose that a concurrency control guarantees that all subtransactions are always executed serializably.

a. Will T_1 always be serializable with T_2? Explain.

b. Will integrity constraints be maintained by all possible schedules?

c. What possible problems might arise if the concurrency control schedules transactions in this way?

20.39 A **blind write** occurs when a transaction writes a database item it has not read. For example, in the Student Registration System a transaction might compute a student's GPA by reading her course grades, computing the average, and then (blindly) writing the result in the appropriate database item without first reading that item. Some applications have the property that no transactions perform blind writes. Show that for such applications

a. View equivalence is *equivalent* to conflict equivalence.

b. The timestamp-ordered concurrency control described in Section 20.9.1 never uses the Thomas Write Rule.

c. In the timestamp-ordered concurrency control described in the text, for each item, x, that a transaction, T, writes, when T commits, $rt(x) = wt(x) = TS(T)$.

20.40 State which of the following operations has a compensating operation.

a. Give all employees a 10% raise.

b. Give all employees making less than $10,000 a 10% raise.

c. Set the value of a particular item to 12.

d. Insert a new tuple with key 1111 into the database, and set the value of one of its attributes to 12.

e. Set the value of a particular item to the square of its original value.

20.41 Assume an operation p has a compensating operation p^{-1}. Show that if operation q commutes with p, then p^{-1} commutes with q.

20.42 Give an example of a schedule of consistent transactions that is not serializable but maintains the correctness of any integrity constraint that might conceivably be associated with the database.

21

Isolation in Relational Databases

In Chapter 20 we discussed isolation in the context of a simple database model in which data is accessed by read and write commands. We did this in order to concentrate on the problems of serializability and recovery. The simple model, however, is unrealistic. Most databases are relational and are accessed through SQL statements, and this introduces additional issues.

In this chapter we discuss concurrency controls that guarantee serializable schedules in relational databases. However, as we shall see, these concurrency controls often do not provide the performance characteristics required by heavily used systems. Hence, in the real world, less restrictive concurrency controls must often be used. These concurrency controls implement different *levels of isolation*, which do not guarantee serializable schedules. We explore the different isolation levels defined in SQL, how they are implemented, and how they can affect the correctness of transaction systems. We also discuss SNAPSHOT isolation, which is not one of the isolation levels defined in the SQL standard but which is important in the real world because it has been implemented by a number of vendors, including Oracle.

21.1 Conflicts in a Relational Database

Consider a table, ACCOUNTS, in a banking system that contains a tuple for each separate account. We might read all tuples in ACCOUNTS describing accounts controlled by depositor Mary using the SELECT statement

```
SELECT *
FROM ACCOUNTS A                                              21.1
WHERE A.Name = 'Mary'
```

The expression in the WHERE clause is referred to as the **read predicate** (attribute names are treated as variables in the predicate), and the statement returns all tuples that satisfy the predicate.

The SELECT statement is an operation that reads data in the relational model and corresponds to the read operation in the simple model discussed in Chapter 20.

Conflicts take a different form with such operations. For example, assume that ACCOUNTS has attributes AcctNumber (the key), Name, and Balance. Also assume that there is a table, DEPOSITORS, containing a tuple for each depositor, with attributes Name (the key) and TotalBalance, in which the value of the TotalBalance attribute is the sum of the balances of all that depositor's accounts. An audit transaction, T_1, for Mary might utilize the SELECT statement

```
SELECT SUM(Balance)
FROM ACCOUNTS A
WHERE A.Name = 'Mary'
```

to calculate the sum of the balances in Mary's accounts and then compare it with the result of executing

```
SELECT D.TotalBalance
FROM DEPOSITORS D
WHERE D.Name = 'Mary'
```

Mary should consider taking her business to another bank if the two numbers do not match.

A transaction, T_2, that creates a new account transaction for Mary with initial balance 100, inserts a tuple into ACCOUNTS using the statement

```
INSERT INTO ACCOUNTS                                      21.2
VALUES ('10021', 'Mary', 100)
```

and then updates TotalBalance by 100 in Mary's tuple in DEPOSITORS using

```
UPDATE DEPOSITORS
SET TotalBalance = TotalBalance + 100
WHERE Name = 'Mary'
```

The operations on ACCOUNTS performed by T_1 and T_2 conflict since INSERT does not commute with SELECT. If INSERT is executed before SELECT, the inserted tuple will be included in the sum; otherwise, it will not. Hence, if T_1 and T_2 are executed concurrently in such a way that T_2 is interleaved between the time T_1 reads ACCOUNTS and the time it reads DEPOSITORS, the audit transaction will fail. (The operations on DEPOSITORS also conflict.)

21.1.1 Phantoms

As with nonrelational databases, we can ensure serializability by using a locking algorithm. In designing such an algorithm, we must first decide what to lock. One approach is to lock tables. They have names, and those names are used in the SQL statements that access them. The SELECT statement can be treated as a read on the data item(s)—table(s)—named in the FROM clause, and DELETE, INSERT, and UPDATE can be treated as writes on the named tables. Therefore the concurrency control algorithms described in Chapter 20 can be used to achieve serializable schedules. As with page locking, table locking is conservative. The problem with this approach is the coarse granularity of the locks. A table might contain thousands (perhaps millions) of tuples. Locking an entire table because one of its tuples has been accessed might result in a serious loss of concurrency.

If, instead of locking tables, we associate a distinct lock with each tuple, lock granularity is fine, but the resulting schedules might not be serializable. For example, suppose that T_1 locks all tuples it has read in ACCOUNTS—those that satisfy the predicate Name = 'Mary'. The ability of a transaction to insert a new tuple into a table is not affected by locks held by other transactions on existing tuples in the table. As a result, T_2 can subsequently construct a tuple, t, that satisfies the predicate and describes a new account for Mary and insert it into ACCOUNTS. Hence, the following schedule is possible:

T_1 locks and reads all tuples describing Mary's accounts in ACCOUNTS.

T_2 adds t to ACCOUNTS and locks t.

T_2 locks and updates Mary's tuple in DEPOSITORS.

T_2 commits, releasing all locks that it holds.

T_1 locks and reads Mary's tuple in DEPOSITORS.

Here, T_2 has altered the contents of the set of tuples referred to by the predicate Name = 'Mary' by adding t. In this situation, t is referred to as a **phantom** because T_1 thinks it has locked all the tuples that satisfy the predicate but, unknown to T_1, a new tuple, t (that also satisfies the predicate), has been inserted by a concurrent transaction. A phantom can lead to nonserializable schedules and hence invalid results. In the example, the audit transaction finds that TotalBalance is not equal to the sum of the account balances.

The problem arises because the SELECT statement does not name a specific item. Instead, it specifies a condition, or predicate, that is satisfied by a number of tuples, some of which might be in a particular table and others of which, like t, might not. While we can set a lock on the tuples that already exist in a table, it is difficult to set a lock on those that do not. To eliminate the possibility of phantoms, we need a locking mechanism that prevents tuples that satisfy a predicate but are not present in the table (that is, phantoms) from being added to the table.

Although we have illustrated the phantom problem using a SELECT statement, the problem also exists with statements that update the database. For example, an UPDATE statement that updates all tuples in a table satisfying predicate P does not commute with an INSERT statement that inserts a tuple satisfying P into the table. Unfortunately, even if the transaction that does the update acquires locks on all updated tuples, a concurrent transaction can still perform the insert.

One approach to preventing phantoms is to lock the entire table—which will certainly prevent any new tuples, including phantoms, from being inserted. As we shall see in Section 21.3.1, however, table locking is not necessary since protocols exist that prevent phantoms but do not require that the entire table be locked. Hence, when commercial DBMSs use the term "tuple locking" (or "page locking") to describe a concurrency control algorithm, you should not assume that they have ignored the phantom problem. They might mean that tuple locks (or page locks) are used as a part of a more elaborate protocol that does guarantee serializability. As in all things, caution is in order—"When all else fails, read the manual." Still, there are many situations in which commercial DBMSs lock an entire table in order to prevent phantoms and achieve serializability.

21.1.2 Predicate Locking

One technique for dealing with phantoms is **predicate locking** [Eswaran et al. 1976]. A predicate, P, specifies a set of tuples. A tuple is in the set if and only if the tuples' attribute values make P true. For example, Name = 'Mary' is a predicate that specifies the set of all possible tuples that *might* exist in ACCOUNTS whose Name attribute has value Mary. This set is a subset of the set, D, of all possible tuples that could ever be stored in ACCOUNTS. Thus, a tuple in which Name has value Jane is an element D and might be in ACCOUNTS but is not in the subset specified by Name = 'Mary'. Note an important point: some of the elements of the subset specified by P might be in ACCOUNTS and some not. For example, the tuple, t, describing Mary's new account satisfies P but is not initially in ACCOUNTS.

Predicates and SQL statements.   An SQL statement associates a predicate with each table it accesses. The predicate is used by the statement to identify the tuples on which it operates. Thus, a SELECT statement that accesses a single table—named in its FROM clause—associates the predicate specified in its WHERE clause with that table. The predicate separates those tuples in the table that are in its result set from those that are not. Similarly, a DELETE statement associates the predicate specified in its WHERE with the table it accesses. The predicate identifies the tuples to be deleted.

Things can become more complicated if, for example, the WHERE clause contains a nested SELECT or the FROM clause names several tables. In these cases, several tables might be involved, each with an associated predicate. Although we could describe this more general case, we choose not to complicate the discussion since the goal here is only to present predicate locking as a concept.

The predicate associated with an INSERT statement describes the set of tuples to be inserted. In the simple case in which a single tuple is inserted, the predicate is

$$(A_1 = v_1) \wedge (A_2 = v_2) \wedge \ldots \wedge (A_n = v_n)$$

where A_i is the ith attribute name and v_i is the value of the attribute in the inserted tuple. The predicate specifies the set consisting of a single tuple that is to be inserted. For example, the predicate associated with the INSERT statement (21.2) is

$$(\text{AcctNumber}=\text{'10021'}) \wedge (\text{Name}= \text{'Mary'}) \wedge (\text{Balance}=\text{'100'}) \qquad \textbf{21.3}$$

More generally, the INSERT might contain a nested SELECT statement and refer to several tables.

```
INSERT INTO TABLE1, (... attribute list ...)
SELECT ... attribute list ...
FROM TABLE2
WHERE P
```

Clearly, P is associated with TABLE2, since the tuples read from that table satisfy P. The predicate associated with TABLE1, however, might be different since the two tables might have different schemas. For example, attributes named in P might not be included in TABLE1, and hence conjuncts referencing those attributes must be deleted. You are asked to investigate this issue in Exercise 21.2.

Finally, an UPDATE statement can be viewed as a DELETE statement followed by an INSERT statement, and hence it has two associated predicates. The first is the predicate P in the UPDATE statement's WHERE clause, which specifies the tuples to be deleted. The SET clause describes how those tuples are to be modified. The resulting set of tuples, described by a predicate, P', are then inserted. For example, the following UPDATE statement posts interest to all of Mary's accounts:

```
UPDATE ACCOUNTS
SET Balance = Balance * 1.05
WHERE Name = 'Mary'
```

In this case, the tuples deleted and the tuples inserted satisfy the same predicate, Name = 'Mary'. However, if Mary wants to add her middle initial to her name, we might execute the statement

```
UPDATE ACCOUNTS
SET Name = 'Mary S'
WHERE Name = 'Mary'
```

Now P is Name = 'Mary', but P' is Name = 'Mary S'. The predicate associated by the UPDATE with the table is $P \vee P'$.

Predicate locks. Having introduced the idea that an SQL statement associates a predicate with a table, we can now describe a locking technique that eliminates phantoms. When an SQL statement with predicate P accesses table R, it acquires a **predicate lock** on P. The lock is associated with R. You can think of the lock as locking the predicate or, alternatively, as locking *all* tuples satisfying P, whether or not they are in R. The situation is illustrated in Figure 21.1. All of the tuples in D

FIGURE 21.1 A SE-
LECT statement ac-
cesses table R with
predicate P. P speci-
fies a subset of D, the
set of all tuples that
could possibly be stored
in R. Some tuples in the
subset might be in R;
others might not.

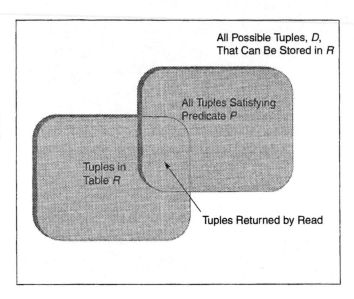

satisfying P are locked. If P appears in the WHERE clause of a SELECT statement, the
tuples in the result set are those in the intersection of the sets designated R and P
and the predicate lock is a read lock.

Similarly, for a DELETE statement, all tuples in D satisfying P are locked with a
predicate write lock, and the tuples in R satisfying P are deleted. In the case of INSERT,
the tuples inserted are predicate write locked. For example, when the new account
transaction inserts tuple t describing Mary's new account, it obtains a predicate write
lock on the predicate (21.3). With the UPDATE statement, the predicate $P \vee P'$ must
be write locked.

We now interpret the notion of a conflict somewhat more generally. Instead of
requiring that conflicting operations name the same data item, we specify that

> Two operations conflict if at least one is a write and the sets of tuples described by
> the predicates associated with the operations have non-null intersections.

For example, the SELECT (read) statement (21.1) that returns all tuples satisfying
the predicate Name='Mary' conflicts with the DELETE (write) statement

```
DELETE
FROM Accounts
WHERE Balance < 1
```

which deletes all accounts satisfying the predicate Balance < 1, since there exist
tuples in D satisfying both predicates—for example, the tuple satisfying

```
AcctNumber = '10000' ∧ Name = 'Mary' ∧ Balance = .5
```

Such a tuple *might* be in ACCOUNTS, and hence there exist states of ACCOUNTS for which the order of execution of the two statements yields different results. Thus, the SELECT conflicts with this DELETE. On the other hand, the SELECT does not conflict with

```
DELETE
FROM ACCOUNTS
WHERE Name = 'John'
```

since the predicates associated with the two statements have a null intersection and thus the statements commute. Finally, the statement

```
SELECT *
FROM ACCOUNTS
WHERE Name = 'Mary S'
```

conflicts with the UPDATE statement that adds Mary's middle initial to her Name attribute in ACCOUNTS.

Predicate locking solves the phantom problem we introduced earlier. When T_1 reads ACCOUNTS, it obtains a read lock on the predicate Name = 'Mary'. Later, when T_2 attempts to insert into ACCOUNTS the tuple t describing Mary's new account, it requests a write lock on predicate (21.3). Since the intersection of the two predicates is not null, a conflict exists and the write lock is not granted. The tuple t is a phantom (it does not exist in ACCOUNTS). Since the predicate lock on Name = 'Mary' includes t, it prevents t from being concurrently added.

In an implementation of predicate locking, we associate with each table, R, a lock set, $L(R)$, which contains the locks associated with all requests that have been granted to currently active transactions. Each element of $L(R)$ has a corresponding predicate. When a transaction requests a predicate lock for an operation that conflicts with an element of $L(R)$, the concurrency control makes the transaction wait.

With predicate locking, serializable schedules can be guaranteed at a finer granularity of locking than with table locks since we lock subsets of the set of tuples that might be in R rather than the entire table. Unfortunately, the conflict test—predicate intersection—is expensive to implement. This limits the usefulness of predicate locking and the technique is not used in commercial DBMSs. However, as we discuss in Section 21.3.1, most DBMSs do implement a restricted form of predicate locking that locks indices.

21.2 Locking and the SQL Isolation Levels

Although most commercial DBMSs implement techniques (which we will describe shortly) that guarantee serializability, the resulting performance is inadequate for some applications. Hence, there is considerable incentive to release locks earlier than would be required to guarantee serializability. Early release is possible when

Level	Dirty Reads	Nonrepeatable Reads	Phantoms
READ UNCOMMITTED	Yes	Yes	Yes
READ COMMITTED	No	Yes	Yes
REPEATABLE READ	No	No	Yes
SERIALIZABLE	No	No	No

FIGURE 21.2 Anomalies allowed and disallowed at each isolation level.

weaker levels of isolation [Gray et al. 1976] are used. The SQL standard defines four isolation levels and, as we saw in Section 8.2.3, each transaction can individually choose one of the four. In order of decreasing strength, they are

SERIALIZABLE

REPEATABLE READ

READ COMMITTED

READ UNCOMMITTED

A given DBMS will not necessarily support all isolation levels. It usually provides a particular level as the default and has mechanisms for requesting one of the other supported levels.

SERIALIZABLE corresponds to the notion of serializable execution discussed in this text and is the only level that guarantees correctness for *all* applications. The enhanced performance that can be achieved with weaker levels is obtained at the risk of incorrect execution.

With the exception of SERIALIZABLE, the SQL standard [SQL 1992] specifies the isolation levels in terms of certain undesirable anomalies (sometimes called phenomena) that are to be prevented at each level. An anomaly that is prevented at one level is also prevented at each higher level.

▪ At READ UNCOMMITTED, dirty reads (see Section 20.2) are possible.

▪ At READ COMMITTED, dirty reads are not permitted, but successive reads of the same tuple by a particular transaction might yield different values.

▪ At REPEATABLE READ, successive reads of the same tuple executed by a particular transaction do not yield different values, but phantoms are possible.

▪ At SERIALIZABLE, phantoms are not permitted. Transaction execution must be serializable.

The anomalies allowed and disallowed are summarized in Figure 21.2.

One might think from the definition of the isolation levels that schedules that do not exhibit dirty reads, nonrepeatable reads, and phantoms are serializable. As we shall see, this is not the case.

SQL isolation levels do not deal with dirty writes, which, as we saw in Section 20.2, are undesirable for several reasons. For example, the schedule in Figure 20.10, page 827, which illustrates a dirty write, does not involve dirty reads, nonrepeatable reads, or phantoms and is, in fact, serializable; hence it does not violate the requirements of any of the isolation levels.

The SQL standard specifies that different transactions in the same application can execute at different levels and each such transaction sees or does not see the anomalies corresponding to its level. For example, when a transaction executing at REPEATABLE READ reads a tuple several times, the same value is always returned even though concurrent transactions are executing at other levels. Similarly, a transaction executing at SERIALIZABLE must see a view of the database that is serialized with respect to the changes made by all other transactions, regardless of their levels.

Independent of the isolation level, the SQL standard requires that a DBMS guarantee that each SQL statement is executed atomically and that its execution is isolated from the execution of other statements.

Locking implementation of the isolation levels.   By defining isolation levels in terms of behavior, the SQL standard does not constrain the implementation of a concurrency control. In particular, the definition does not imply that the concurrency control must be implemented using locks. Locks, however, form the basis of most concurrency controls, and hence it is useful to consider how the levels can be supported in a lock-based system. We describe a hypothetical implementation proposed in [Berenson et al. 1995].

Each level is implemented using locks in different ways. Thus, at a particular level, a lock can be conventional (locking an item such as a tuple, page, or table) or a predicate lock. For pedagogical reasons, we will allow predicate locks in our hypothetical implementation even though they are generally not used in practical implementations. This allows us to be more precise about what needs to be locked. A practical implementation would replace predicate locks with table locks or it would use other techniques (see Section 21.3.1).

A lock can be held until commit time—we refer to such a lock as being of **long duration**—or it can be released after the statement that has accessed the item or predicate has been completed, in which case it is of **short duration**. Short-duration locks are not sufficient to guarantee serializability. However, by requiring a transaction to request such a lock, the concurrency control can check whether conflicting locks are held by other transactions and force the requestor to wait in that case. If a lock is not requested (as in READ UNCOMMITTED), the existence of a conflicting lock in a lock set is ignored.

All isolation levels use write locks in the same way. Long-duration write locks are obtained on the predicates associated with UPDATE, INSERT, and DELETE statements.

The implementation of a particular level not only rules out the appropriate undesirable anomalies but possibly other undesirable anomalies as well. Thus, since write locks are of long duration at all levels, dirty writes are ruled out at all levels. Read locks obtained by a SELECT statement are handled differently at each level.

Level	Read Locks
READ UNCOMMITTED	None
READ COMMITTED	Short-duration on tuples returned
REPEATABLE READ	Long-duration on tuples returned
SERIALIZABLE	Long-duration on predicate specified in statement

FIGURE 21.3 Read locks used in the locking implementation of each isolation level. All levels use long-duration write locks on predicates.

- **READ UNCOMMITTED.** A read is performed without obtaining a read lock. Since reading does not involve the locking mechanism, one transaction might hold a write lock on some item or predicate while another reads it. Thus, a transaction might read uncommitted (dirty) data.

- **READ COMMITTED.** Short-duration read locks are obtained on each tuple, t, returned by a SELECT. As a result, conflicts with write locks are detected and, since write locks are of long duration, dirty reads are impossible. However, since the read lock on t is released when the read is completed, two successive SELECT statements in a particular transaction that both return t might be separated by the execution of another transaction that updates t and then commits. Hence, the value of t returned by the two statements might be different.

- **REPEATABLE READ.** Long-duration read locks are obtained on each tuple, t, returned by a SELECT. As a result, a nonrepeatable read of t is not possible. Since the predicate associated with the SELECT is not locked, however, phantoms can occur.

- **SERIALIZABLE.** All read (and write) locks are long-duration predicate locks, and thus phantoms are not possible. All transactions are serializable.

The use of read locks at each level is summarized in Figure 21.3. Note that, since all write locks are long duration and all levels other than READ UNCOMMITTED acquire read locks before reading an item, a schedule in which all transactions run at levels higher than READ UNCOMMITTED will be strict.

The read locks acquired at the lower isolation levels are weaker than the long-duration predicate read locks used at SERIALIZABLE. This is the source of the performance improvement that these levels can achieve. The management of read locks at a particular level eliminates the anomalies prohibited at that level, independent of whether or not concurrent transactions execute at different levels.

Since all transactions use long-duration predicate write locks, their write operations are serializable. Since, in addition, a transaction, T, running at SERIALIZABLE uses long-duration read predicate locks, *all* of its operations are serializable with respect to the write operations of all other transactions, independent of their isolation level. Hence, T either sees all or none of the updates performed by a concurrent transaction. Transactions executing at lower levels, however, might see the partial results of concurrent transactions and hence do not necessarily see a consistent state. There-

FIGURE 21.4 Schedule involving a read of uncommitted data. T_2 executes at READ UNCOMMITTED.

T_1: $r(t_1:1000)$ $w(t_1:900)$ $\qquad\qquad\qquad\qquad$ $r(t_2:500)$ $w(t_2:600)$ *commit*
T_2: $\qquad\qquad\qquad\qquad$ $r(t_1:900)$ $r(t_2:500)$ *commit*

fore their updates might cause inconsistencies. SERIALIZABLE transactions might see those inconsistencies, and their computations might be affected as a result.

The dangers of executing at lower isolation levels. By allowing transactions to run at isolation levels weaker than SERIALIZABLE, nonserializable schedules can be produced. Thus, a transaction might see inconsistent data and, as a result, might write inconsistent data into the database. To see how this can happen at each of the lower levels, consider the following examples.

- READ UNCOMMITTED. A transaction, T_2, executing at READ UNCOMMITTED might read dirty values produced by another active transaction, T_1. Such values might never be committed and so are meaningless. For example, T_1 might write a value, v, to a data item and later abort. T_2 might read the data item before T_1 aborts and return v to the user. Or T_2 might compute a new value based on v and store it in a different data item, thus corrupting the database since the transaction that produced v aborted.[1] Or T_1 might write v to the data item and then overwrite v with a second value. In this case, v is an intermediate value not meant for external consumption.

  Even if T_1 writes only final values, if T_2 reads them before T_1 commits, problems can arise. For example, in the schedule of Figure 21.4, T_1 is a transaction that transfers $100 from an account whose balance is stored in tuple t_1 (initially $1,000) to an account whose balance is stored in tuple t_2 (initially $500). T_2 is a read-only transaction executing at READ UNCOMMITTED that prints out the balance of all accounts. In Figure 21.4, T_2 reads an uncommitted value of t_1 and hence does not report the $100 being transferred in either account.

- READ COMMITTED. A transaction, T_1, executing at READ COMMITTED uses short-duration read locks on individual tuples. Hence, as shown in Figure 21.5, it is possible for T_2 to update tuple t and then commit between successive reads in T_1. One might not think that this is too serious an issue since it is unlikely that a transaction will read the same tuple twice. However, incorrect results can occur even when the transaction does not attempt a second read. Figure 21.6 shows a schedule in which T_1 and T_2 are both deposit transactions executing at READ COMMITTED that operate on an account whose balance is stored in tuple t. Since T_1 uses short-duration read locks, it is possible for T_2 to update t and then commit. As a result, the effect of T_2's update is lost. Note that both transactions

---

[1] To protect against database corruption, transactions running at READ UNCOMMITTED are often required to be read-only.

FIGURE 21.5 Schedule involving a nonrepeatable read. T_1 executes at READ COMMITTED.

T_1: $r(t:1000)$ $r(t:2000)$ *commit*
T_2: $w(t:2000)$ *commit*

FIGURE 21.6 Schedule illustrating the lost-update problem at READ COMMITTED.

T_1: $r(t:1000)$ $w(t:1100)$ *commit*
T_2: $r(t:1000)$ $w(t:2000)$ *commit*

FIGURE 21.7 Schedule illustrating that a transaction executing at READ COMMITTED might see an inconsistent view of the database.

T_1: $r(x:10)$ $r(y:15)$ ... *commit*
T_2: $w(x:20)$ $w(y:15)$ *commit*

read committed data. This is an example of the lost-update problem introduced in Chapter 2.

Figure 21.7 shows an example of a transaction, T_1, whose view of the database is inconsistent as a result of being executed at READ COMMITTED. Suppose an integrity constraint states that the values of x and y must satisfy $x \geq y$, but between the reads (after T_1 has released the read lock on x), T_2 changes both values (such that the new values satisfy the integrity constraint) and then commits. T_1 reads the value of x before T_2's update and the value of y afterwards—a view of the database that does not satisfy the constraint ($x = 10$, $y = 15$). Since transactions are guaranteed to execute correctly only when they see a consistent view of the database, T_1 might subsequently execute in an unpredictable manner and write erroneous data into the database. Even if T_2's writes were such that the two values read by T_1 happened to satisfy the constraint, the fact that they came from two different versions of the database could cause T_1 to execute incorrectly.

▪   REPEATABLE READ. Since tuples, but not predicates, have long-duration locks, phantoms can occur. We saw in Section 21.1.1 that this can cause incorrect behavior. Note that the example there also involved a transaction seeing an inconsistent view of the database.

21.2.1 Lost Updates, Cursor Stability, and Update Locks

Figure 21.6 shows a lost update that occurs because short-duration read locks are used at READ COMMITTED. A special case of the lost update problem—when reading is done through a cursor—can be prevented by an isolation level called CURSOR STABILITY, which is provided instead of READ COMMITTED in some implementations of SQL.

When a transaction, T_1, opens an INSENSITIVE cursor over a table, R, a copy of the result set is made and all subsequent FETCH statements through the cursor are done to the copy. Therefore, no matter at which isolation level T_1 is executing, the FETCH statements do not see any subsequent updates to R made by a concurrent transaction, T_2 (or even updates made directly to R by T_1 itself).

However, if T_1 opens a cursor that is not declared INSENSITIVE (for example, if it is KEYSET_DRIVEN), pointers to the tuples in R that are in the result set are returned and all subsequent FETCHs are done through the pointers. If T_1 is executed at READ COMMITTED, it acquires only a short-duration read lock on each tuple fetched. If T_1 and T_2 run concurrently, T_1 might fetch some tuples through the cursor before they are updated by T_2 and others after T_2 has updated them and committed.[2]

An even more troublesome situation might arise if T_1 first reads a tuple and later updates it before moving the cursor. In that case, T_2 might read and update the tuple and commit between T_1's read and write while the cursor is pointing at it. As a result, T_2's update will be lost. The CURSOR STABILITY isolation level prevents such lost updates.

CURSOR STABILITY is an extension of READ COMMITTED. Hence, it provides a level of isolation whose strength lies between READ COMMITTED and REPEATABLE READ. With CURSOR STABILITY, as long as a cursor opened by transaction T_1 points to a particular tuple, that tuple cannot be modified or deleted by another transaction, T_2. Once T_1 moves or closes the cursor, however, T_2 can modify or delete the tuple.

As with the other isolation levels, CURSOR STABILITY can be implemented using long-duration write predicate locks. Read locks are handled as follows:

> CURSOR STABILITY. Short-duration read locks are obtained for each tuple read, except if the tuple is accessed through a cursor. In that case a **medium-duration** read lock is acquired. The lock is retained while the cursor points to the tuple and released when the cursor is moved or closed.

The schedule shown in Figure 21.6 can occur if CURSOR STABILITY is used because we have implicitly assumed that neither T_1 nor T_2 refers to t through a cursor. Suppose, however, that T_1 is posting interest to all accounts in a bank. It accesses each tuple successively through a cursor, first reading the balance in t and then updating t with a new balance. With CURSOR STABILITY, the read lock that T_1 acquires on t is maintained until it requests to update t, at which point the lock is upgraded to a write lock, which is held until T_1 commits (since write locks are of long duration). Hence, it is not possible for another transaction, T_2, to update t between T_1's read and update.

Consider the situation shown in Figure 21.8. Suppose that T_2 is a deposit transaction that accesses t directly through an index and that it executes at READ COMMITTED or CURSOR STABILITY (it makes no difference in this case since it does not use a cursor). T_2 reads t after T_1 has read it. When T_1 requests to update t, its

---

[2] There might be some confusion here because of the requirement in the SQL standard that each SQL statement is executed in an atomic and isolated fashion. In the case of a cursor, execution of OPEN and FETCH are individually atomic and isolated.

FIGURE 21.8 Schedule illustrating that CURSOR STABILITY is not a panacea.

T_1:	$r(t)$	$w(t)$	commit
	(through cursor)	(through cursor)	
T_2:	$r(t)$	$w(t)$	commit
	(through index)	(through index)	

read lock can be upgraded to a write lock since T_2's read lock is short duration. Unfortunately, the lost-update problem is not solved. The value T_2 writes (after T_1 commits) is based on the value returned by its previous read, not on the new value written by T_1, so T_1's update is lost.

Before we describe how this problem can be solved, consider another case based on the same sequence of reads and writes as shown in Figure 21.8, only now both transactions execute at CURSOR STABILITY and access t through a cursor. Once again, the situation is not a happy one as both T_1 and T_2 hold their (medium-duration) read locks after reading and a deadlock results when both try to upgrade to write locks. Clearly, CURSOR STABILITY offers only a partial solution to the lost-update problem.

Some commercial DBMSs provide additional mechanisms to deal with these problems.

▪ In some systems, a transaction, T, can request a write lock on an item at the time it reads the item so that it can update the item later. This avoids the need to upgrade the read lock (and hence avoids the deadlock), but it suffers from the need to lock out all other transactions starting from T's first access, even if the other transactions only want to read the item.

▪ Some systems provide a new type of lock, called an **update lock**, which can be used by transactions that initially want to read an item but later might want to update it.[3] It allows a transaction to read but not write the item and indicates that the lock is likely to be upgraded to a write lock at a later time. Update locks conflict with one another and with write locks, but not with read locks. For that reason, if T_1 and T_2 both attempt the same sequence of operations as shown in Figure 21.8 and both initially request update locks, the first request will be granted and the other will wait. In this way, both lost updates and deadlocks are avoided. Since update and read locks do not conflict, however, if T_2 wants only to read t, it can acquire a read lock between T_1's read and write since T_1 holds only an update lock in that interval. T_1 must upgrade its update lock to a write lock before it writes the item.

▪ Some systems provide a version of READ COMMITTED called OPTIMISTIC READ COMMITTED. If T_1 executes at this level, it obtains the same short-duration read lock that would be obtained at READ COMMITTED. However, if T_1 later tries to

---

[3] An update lock is sometimes called a *read-with-intention-to-write* lock.

write a tuple, t, that it has previously read, it is aborted if some other transaction has modified t and committed between the time T_1 read t and the time it tries to write t. This approach is called "optimistic" because each transaction optimistically assumes that it need not retain read locks on tuples to prevent lost updates.[4] As with other optimistic algorithms, the transaction is aborted if that assumption turns out to be false. Although OPTIMISTIC READ COMMITTED prevents lost updates, problems can still arise (see Exercise 21.13).

21.2.2 Case Study: Correctness and NonSERIALIZABLE Schedules—The Student Registration System

We have shown examples of transactions that behave incorrectly when executed at each isolation level lower than SERIALIZABLE. However, the news is not all bad. The semantics of an application can often be used to demonstrate that when a particular transaction is executed at an isolation level lower than SERIALIZABLE, all of the resulting schedules produce acceptable results. Such transactions can take advantage of the increased concurrency and resulting performance gains that follow from using a lower isolation level.

For example, we might be concerned that some nonserializable schedules allowed by a weak isolation level will result in the violation of an integrity constraint. Recall, however, that many integrity constraints can be declared in the database schema and are automatically checked by the DBMS. Thus, a violation will be detected, and the transaction that caused the violation will be aborted when it requests to commit. Assuming that such schedules do not occur frequently, a net performance gain may result by executing the application at the weaker level.

In addition to schedules that cause violations of schema constraints, we must also be concerned with schedules that

- Produce database states that violate integrity constraints not declared in the schema

- Produce database states that are consistent but incorrect because they do not reflect the desired result of the transaction—for example, a database state resulting from a lost update

- Return data to the user based on a view of the database that is not obtained from a consistent snapshot—for example, by a read-only transaction executing at READ UNCOMMITTED

When we consider whether or not a specific transaction in some application can be executed at a weaker isolation level, we must investigate its interaction with all the other transactions in the same application. Consider the Registration transaction of the Student Registration System, whose requirements and schema were given in Sections B.2 and 4.8. Can it execute correctly at READ COMMITTED? To answer this

---

[4] This approach is sometimes called *first-committer-wins* because the first transaction to write a tuple is allowed to commit—*wins*—and the second transaction that attempts to write the tuple is aborted—*loses*. We discuss first-committer-wins further in Section 21.5.3.

question, we must investigate how each instance of a Registration transaction can interact with other instances of the Registration transaction and with instances of all the other transaction types in the system.

Do not expect the discussion to contain theorems or general principles. This is an area in which experience and creativity count as well as the ability to consider a large number of boring details. That is one reason why people who do this for a living get the big bucks.

To make the discussion concrete, we will assume that the DBMS uses the locking implementation of each isolation level described earlier in this section. Suppose a particular instance of the Registration transaction, T_1, attempts to register a student, s, for a course, c. To do this, it performs the following sequence of steps (some steps have been omitted):

1. Determine c's prerequisites by reading the table REQUIRES, which has a row for each prerequisite of each course.

2. Check that s has satisfied each of c's prerequisites by reading TRANSCRIPT to determine if s has taken each prerequisite and received a grade of at least C.

3. Check that the total number of credits that will be taken by s will not exceed 20 by reading TRANSCRIPT to determine all the courses in which s is already registered.

4. Check that there is enough room in c and, if so, increment the current enrollment. To do this, T_1 executes

```
UPDATE CLASS
SET Enrollment = Enrollment + 1
WHERE CrsCode = :courseId AND Enrollment < MaxEnrollment
```

where the course code of class c is stored in the host variable courseId, and we assume that CLASS has attributes MaxEnrollment, which contains the maximum allowable enrollment in c, and Enrollment, which contains the number of students currently registered for next semester. (Note that the condition Enrollment < MaxEnrollment is actually unnecessary since [as shown in Section 4.8] a constraint that eliminates overenrollment is incorporated in the schema of CLASS. However, we can expect that many students will attempt to enroll in classes that are full, and it is more efficient to check the constraint in the UPDATE statement and abort the transaction immediately.)

5. Insert a row in TRANSCRIPT indicating that s is registered for c.

Suppose that T_1 is executed at READ COMMITTED. We need to consider the following situations.

■ While T_1 is reading REQUIRES in step 1 (using short-duration read locks on rows), a concurrent Course Information transaction, T_2, might update REQUIRES by inserting new rows corresponding to new prerequisites for c (together with the enforcement dates for these prerequisites) and then commit.

To make the example more interesting, assume that T_1 reads REQUIRES using a DYNAMIC cursor. If T_1 and T_2 execute concurrently, T_1 might see some but not all of the rows that T_2 has inserted. Hence, T_1 is not serializable with respect to T_2.

However, in this situation nonserializability does not cause a problem because it was specified in Section B.3 that new prerequisites do not apply to current registrants. Therefore, in determining c's prerequisites in step 1, T_1 ignores any prerequisites that have been added during the current semester (using the date attribute of each prerequisite row). Thus it makes no difference if T_1 misses some of the prerequisites added by T_2 because it ignores any it does read. For this reason, T_1 executes correctly at READ COMMITTED. Thus this schedule is nonserializable, but nevertheless correct.

Execution is also correct at READ COMMITTED if T_1 uses a KEYSET_DRIVEN cursor because it does not see *any* of the inserted rows and hence it appears as if the transactions are executed serially with T_2 following T_1.

■ After T_1 reads TRANSCRIPT in step 2 and gives up the short-duration read locks on the rows it has read, a concurrent Student Grade transaction, T_2, might update TRANSCRIPT by changing a grade in a course s has taken. The change might affect a course that is a prerequisite to c.

First we observe that if T_2 changes the grade after T_1 gives up its read locks, T_1 will not see the change. Therefore the effect of the execution of T_2 is the same as if it was serialized after T_1. So far, so good.

But before we can say that T_2 is serializable after T_1, we must consider how T_1 and T_2 might interact with other transactions in a more complex schedule. For example, after T_2 changes the grade and commits, another transaction, T_3, might read the new grade and then write some item, x, and commit. Then T_1 might read x.

$$
\begin{array}{lll}
T_1: & r(\text{grade}) & \qquad\qquad r(x)\ \textit{commit} \\
T_2: & \quad w(\text{grade})\ \textit{commit} & \\
T_3: & \qquad\qquad r(\text{grade})\ w(x)\ \textit{commit}
\end{array}
$$

This schedule is nonserializable since there is a cycle in the serialization graph:

$$T_1 \rightarrow T_2 \rightarrow T_3 \rightarrow T_1$$

To see if such an interaction can take place, we must analyze all of the possible interactions between T_1 (the Registration transaction), T_2 (the Student Grade transaction), and all of the other transactions in the application—a tedious and error-prone task. If such an interaction can occur, we must analyze its effect on the application.

■ It might appear that, as the result of a lost update, the concurrent execution of two Registration transactions attempting to enroll two different students in c can cause the MaxEnrollment to be exceeded. This would be possible if each transaction gave up its read locks between the check and increment of Enrollment. However, this situation cannot occur because the check and increment are performed in step 4 as part of the isolated execution of a single SQL statement (note that it is not necessary to rely on the protection afforded by long-duration write locks to ensure this).

■ Two instances of the Registration transaction are executed concurrently for the same student, s (attempting to register for two different courses). In step 3 each instance reads TRANSCRIPT to determine the number of credits for which s has already registered. If each executes that step before the other executes step 5 they will both calculate the same number, and in step 5 each will insert a phantom row not seen by the other. If s has room for only one additional course, the credit limit will be exceeded.

The designer of the system might conclude, however, that it is extremely unlikely that a particular student, with room for only one more course, will execute two Registration transactions at the same time and that this particular interleaving of the transactions will occur. Hence the Registration transaction can be safely executed at READ COMMITTED. (If such a conclusion cannot be justified, the Registration transaction would have to be executed at SERIALIZABLE to eliminate the phantoms.)

Another alternative would be to include the integrity constraint "a student cannot be registered for more than 20 credits in any given semester" in the database schema instead of having it checked within the Registration transaction. Then the system would check that this integrity constraint was not violated, and if the above interleaving occurred, one of the transactions would be aborted. Thus the Registration transaction could be safely executed at READ COMMITTED.

Thus we might decide that the Registration transaction can run correctly at READ COMMITTED. Hence, the read locks acquired in steps 1, 2, and 3 will be released early, improving performance.

We have given an example of an application involving a transaction that can be executed correctly at an isolation level lower than SERIALIZABLE. The cautious designer should, however, assume that lower levels of isolation can produce incorrect results unless it can be demonstrated, using the semantics of the application, that such results are not possible.

Furthermore, note that the errors resulting from choosing an isolation level that is too weak are very difficult to track down. They occur in a schedule in which transactions happen to be interleaved in a particular way. This might happen rarely if the transactions involved are infrequently invoked,[5] and the effects might not become apparent until long after the execution has taken place. For that reason, the system might appear to work correctly for long periods of time until an inconsistent state is suddenly detected. It might be extremely difficult to determine the sequence of events that caused the error.

---

[5] But note that in a high-performance transaction processing application, a situation that occurs only once in a million transaction executions might occur several times a day.

There is an additional caution from a software-engineering viewpoint. Even though the semantics of the initial version of an application might guarantee only correct schedules at lower isolation levels, the semantics of later versions, in which new transactions are added or older transactions are changed, might not. Thus, the reasoning that leads to the choice of isolation levels should be carefully documented (perhaps in the Design Document) so that the system maintainers can determine whether or not it is still valid for later versions.

21.2.3 Serializable, SERIALIZABLE, and Correct

We have used three terms in describing schedules produced by a concurrency control:

- *Serializable.* Equivalent to a serial schedule.
- SERIALIZABLE. An SQL isolation level. Dirty reads, unrepeatable reads, and phantoms are not allowed, and schedules must be serializable (as stated in the ANSI specifications [SQL 1992]).
- *Correct.* Leaves the database in a state that is consistent, that correctly models the real world, and that satisfies the business rules of the enterprise (as stated in the Specification Document).

These definitions are related as follows (assuming that each transaction is consistent):

- If a schedule is serializable, it is correct.
- If a schedule has been produced by a set of transactions executing at the SERIALIZABLE isolation level, it is serializable (and hence correct).

However, these implications do not go both ways.

- A schedule might be correct, even though it is not serializable.
- A schedule might be serializable, even though it has been produced by transactions executing at isolation levels lower than SERIALIZABLE.

Thus correctness can often be obtained without using the stringent locking protocols required to *guarantee* serializable schedules.

21.3 Granular Locking: Intention Locks and Index Locks

In the previous section, we discussed how the performance of a transaction processing system can be improved through the use of isolation levels weaker than SERIALIZABLE. Performance can also be affected by lock granularity. The good news here, however, is that the choice of granularity *only* affects performance; the choice does not affect correctness. In this section we consider locking algorithms that allow granularity to be adjusted to the needs of the transactions.

The designer of a locking system faces a trade-off between concurrency and overhead in choosing lock granularity. Hence, when implementing a concurrency control for an application that involves some transactions that access large blocks of data (e.g., an entire table) and others that access very small blocks (e.g., a few tuples), it is desirable to use a locking mechanism that allows different granularities.

Granular locking [Gray et al. 1976] is designed to meet this need. A transaction requiring access to a large block of data can lock the block with a single request. A transaction requiring access to small amounts of data within a block can lock each piece individually. In the latter case, several transactions can simultaneously hold locks on small items within the same block.

Managing locks at different levels of granularity presents a new problem. Suppose, for example, a system allows a transaction to lock a record and also to lock specific fields within a record—two locks with different granularity. If transaction T_1 has obtained a write lock on field F within record R, then a request by T_2 for a write lock on the entire record should be denied since it permits T_2 to access F. The problem is to design an efficient mechanism that the concurrency control can use to recognize the lock on F when a lock on R is requested.

The solution is to organize locks hierarchically. Before obtaining a lock on F, T_1 must first obtain a lock on R. The two locks must be acquired in the specified order. Then, when T_2 requests a lock on R, the concurrency control will recognize that a potential conflict exists because T_1 holds a lock on R. But what kind of a lock does T_1 get? Clearly, it would not be a read or write lock since in that case there would be no point in acquiring an additional fine-granularity lock on F, and the effective lock granularity would be coarse.

DBMSs therefore provide a new type of lock, the **intention lock**. Before a transaction can obtain a shared or exclusive lock on an item, it must obtain appropriate intention locks on all containing items in the hierarchy of granularity. Thus, before T_1 can obtain a lock on F, it must first obtain an intention lock on R. Intention locks come in three flavors.

1. If T_1 wants to read a field in R, it must first get an **intention shared** (IS) lock on R. It can then request a shared (S) lock on that field.

2. If T_1 wants to update a field in R, it must first get an **intention exclusive** (IX) lock on R. It can then request an exclusive (X) lock on that field.

3. If T_1 wants to update some fields in R but needs to read all of the fields to determine which ones to update (for example, it wants to change all fields with values less than 100), it must first obtain a **shared intention exclusive** (SIX) lock on R. It can then read all fields in R and request an X lock on the fields it updates. (A SIX lock is a combination of a shared (S) lock and an IX lock on R.)

Although transactions now must acquire additional locks, performance gains are possible since intention locks commute with many other lock types. The conflict table for granular locks is given in Figure 21.9. It indicates, for example, that a request for an IX lock on an item is denied if the item is already S-locked. The justification for this is that the S lock allows all contained items to be read whereas the IX lock allows a transaction to request write locks on some of those items. In contrast, a request for an IX lock is granted if the item is already IS-locked. The justification

Requested Mode	Granted Mode				
	IS	IX	SIX	S	X
IS					X
IX		X		X	X
SIX		X	X	X	X
S		X	X		X
X	X	X	X	X	X

FIGURE 21.9 Conflict table for intention locks. X indicates conflicts between lock modes.

for this is that the IS lock allows some subset of the contained items to be S-locked while the IX lock allows some subset of the contained items to be X-locked. These subsets might be disjoint, and if so there is no conflict. If they are not disjoint, the conflict will be detected at the lower level since the transactions will have to obtain S and X locks on the individual contained items.

In the previous example, T_1 wants to access only F and hence uses fine-grained locking. It acquires an IX lock on R and an X lock on F. T_2 wants to access all fields in R and hence uses course-grained locking. It requests an exclusive lock on R. The lock conflict at R will be detected by the concurrency control using the conflict table of Figure 21.9.

In the general case, the items to be locked are organized in a hierarchy that can be represented as a tree, where the item represented by a node in the tree is contained within the item represented by its parent. Thus, locking an item in the tree implicitly locks all of its descendents. (Locking a record implicitly locks all of its fields.) The general rule is that, before a lock can be obtained on a particular item (which need not be a leaf), an appropriate intention lock must be obtained on all of the containing items (ancestors) in the hierarchy. Thus, in order to lock a particular item in S mode, a transaction must first acquire IS locks on all items on the path to the item from the root, in the order they are encountered. The S lock is acquired last to ensure that the transaction cannot actually access the target object until all locks are in place. Locks are released in the opposite order. Similarly, to obtain an X lock on an item, IX locks must first be obtained on all items on the path from the root to the item.

We intentionally based our example on a system using records and fields, rather than tables and tuples, so that phantoms would not be an issue. In the next section we discuss phantoms in more detail. But consider the following example, which gives a preview of what is to come. A SELECT and an UPDATE statement access a table. In the absence of predicate or granular locks, the UPDATE statement gets a long-duration X lock on the entire table. This prevents the SELECT statement from accessing the table. If the DBMS supports granular locking at the table and row level, the UPDATE statement might acquire a SIX lock on the table and X locks on the rows that satisfy its WHERE clause. These locks prevent concurrent transactions from reading those rows, from changing any rows in the table, and from inserting new rows, but they allow the SELECT statement to read other rows. Thus, granular locking prevents phantoms at the SERIALIZABLE level and uses weaker locks at all isolation levels than nongranular locking. Hence, granular locking has the potential for increasing concurrency.

21.3.1 Index Locks: Granular Locking without Phantoms

We discussed two methods for guaranteeing serializable schedules in a relational database—predicate locking and table locking. We pointed out the deficiencies of each: the computational complexity of predicate locking and the coarse granularity of table locking. The coarse granularity of table locking can be overcome by locking individual tuples, but this can lead to phantoms and nonserializable behavior. Locking the pages on which the tuples are stored (instead of the tuples themselves) is in some ways more efficient but can also lead to phantoms.

A number of DBMSs eliminate phantoms and guarantee serializable schedules by using an enhanced method of granular locking. Recall that the essential requirement for preventing phantoms is that, after a transaction, T_1, has accessed a table, R, using a predicate, P, no concurrently executing transaction, T_2, can insert into R a (phantom) tuple that also satisfies P, until after T_1 terminates. The method depends heavily on whether the access path to R involves an index. If not, all pages have to be scanned and the entire table has to be locked with an S or X lock. If an index is available, however, finer granularity locking is possible.

Assume that the DBMS uses page locking (the method works for tuple locking as well). If no index is available and

- If T_1 has executed a SELECT statement on R, the DBMS must search every page in R to locate the tuples that satisfy P. To perform the search, T_1 acquires an S lock on R. If that lock is held until T_1 commits, T_2 cannot insert a phantom since it would need to acquire a (conflicting) IX lock on R.

- If T_1 has executed a DELETE statement on R, the DBMS must search every page in R to locate the tuples that satisfy P. To perform the search, T_1 first acquires a SIX lock on R and then X locks on the pages containing tuples satisfying P. If these locks are held until T_1 commits, T_2 cannot insert a phantom since it would first need to acquire a (conflicting) IX lock on R.

We consider an UPDATE statement later. Hence, when no index is used, granular locking prevents phantoms.

The situation is more involved if T_1 accesses R through an index. In that case, an entire scan of R is not required. If T_1 executes a SELECT statement on R using predicate P, it acquires only an IS lock on R and S locks on the pages of R containing tuples satisfying P. It locates these pages using the index. Similarly, if T_1 executes a DELETE statement on R using predicate P, it acquires only an IX lock on R and X locks on the pages of R containing tuples satisfying P, which it locates through the index.

Unfortunately, this locking protocol does not prevent phantoms. If T_2 attempts to insert a phantom into R, it can obtain an IX lock on R since an IX lock does not conflict with either the IS or the IX locks obtained by T_1. Hence, there is no conflict at the table level. And if the phantom is stored on a page that is different than the pages locked by T_1, there will be no conflict at the page level either. Thus it will be possible for T_2 to insert the phantom. Some mechanism is needed to prevent this.

For example, the table STUDENT in the schema for the Student Registration System on page 116 has an attribute Address (for simplicity we assume that the address simply designates the town), and T_1 might execute the SELECT statement

```
SELECT *
FROM STUDENT S
WHERE S.Address = 'Stony Brook'
```
21.4

If there is an index, ADDRIDX, on Address for the relation STUDENT, it will be used to find the students living in Stony Brook. An IS lock will be acquired on STUDENT, and an S lock will be acquired on all pages containing tuples describing students living in Stony Brook. However, these locks will not prevent T_2 from inserting a tuple, t, describing a new student living in Stony Brook, since T_2 needs to obtain only an IX lock on STUDENT and an X lock on the page in which t is to be inserted (this page might be different from all of the pages in which tuples for students living in Stony Brook are currently stored).

To prevent phantoms in this case, in addition to an appropriate intention lock on the table and page locks on the data pages accessed, a transaction acquires locks on pages of the index structure itself. To understand this, we need to consider the storage structure used for the table. Structures fall into two categories. The first constrains the page(s) into which a tuple, describing a student who lives in Stony Brook, can possibly be stored.[6] A storage structure organized around a clustered index is of this type: the location of a row is controlled by the value its attributes assign to the search key of the index. For example, if ADDRIDX is a clustered B^+ tree with search key Address, then the row must be placed in sorted order based on the value "Stony Brook". A clustered hash index, in which all rows that hash to a particular bucket are placed in the same page, is another example.

If STUDENT is organized in accordance with the second type of storage structure, there is no unique page into which all tuples that describe students living in Stony Brook must be placed. For example, if STUDENT has a clustered index with search key Id, then the row for a student living in Stony Brook might be placed in any page.

The strategy for preventing phantoms depends on the type of the storage structure. If it is of the first type, T_1 can delay T_2 by obtaining a long-duration lock (S or X, depending on whether T_1 is reading or writing) on the page(s) of STUDENT in which all rows that describe students who live in Stony Brook must be stored. Since this is the page into which t must be inserted, T_2 is delayed until T_1 completes. For example, if STUDENT has a clustered hash index with search key Address, and T_1

---

[6] We have ignored overflow pages. More generally we can consider an overflow page to be an extension of the page to which it is attached.

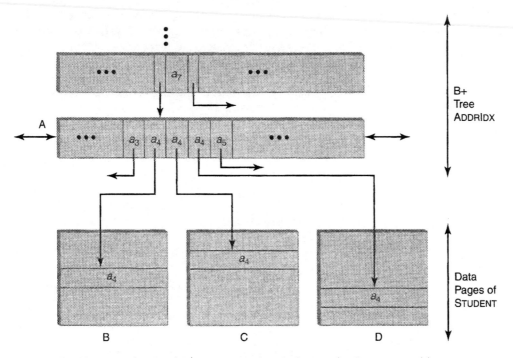

FIGURE 21.10 An unclustered B$^+$ tree secondary index on the STUDENT table.

executes the statement (21.4), it will acquire an S lock on the bucket to which Stony Brook is hashed.

If the storage structure is of the second type, T_1 acquires long-duration read locks on pages of the index it uses in its access path. Figure 21.10 illustrates the case in which a B$^+$ tree with search key Address is used as a secondary, unclustered index on STUDENT. Address values are denoted a_i, such that $a_i < a_{i+1}$. We have assumed that $a_4 =$ "StonyBrook" and that pages B, C, and D in the STUDENT storage structure contain the tuples describing the students who live there. It is important to note that, since the index is unclustered, pages B, C, and D need not be consecutive in the storage structure. In executing the SELECT statement (21.4), T_1 obtains a long-duration S lock on the leaf page, A, of the index,[7] which contains pointers to pages B, C, and D.

An attempt by T_2 at a later time to insert a new tuple describing a student who lives in Stony Brook requires that a pointer to the data page that will contain the tuple be inserted in every index on STUDENT. In the case of ADDRIDX, the pointer must be inserted in index page A since address values are sorted at the leaf level. Inserting the pointer requires an X lock on A, which generates a conflict with T_1, and so T_2 is forced to wait. The new tuple is thus prevented from becoming a phantom despite the fact that it might ultimately be stored in a data page other than B, C, or D and

---

[7] More generally, there might be several such leaf pages, but the algorithm is unchanged.

the fact that T_1 and T_2 acquire compatible locks (IS and IX) on STUDENT. The lock on A must be retained by T_1 until it commits.

By locking the index in this fashion, a transaction effectively obtains a predicate lock on a simple predicate: one that specifies a search-key value (such as *key = value*) or one that specifies a search key by range (such as *low ≤ value ≤ high*). A nice feature of this policy, as compared with predicate locking, is that the entire range need not be locked initially. Index leaf pages and data pages are locked as the scan proceeds. Thus, only the first index leaf page is locked for the duration of the scan, whereas a lock on the last one is not acquired until the scan nears completion. If a predicate-locking policy were implemented, the lock on the predicate would be obtained initially and would restrict access to the entire range. We discuss a more efficient way to effectively obtain predicate locks on ranges of search-key values later in this section on page 894.

Although this method eliminates phantoms caused by INSERT statements, several other issues arise with UPDATE statements. Since an UPDATE can be treated as if it were a DELETE (which deletes the tuples to be updated), followed by an INSERT (which inserts the updated tuples), it has the interesting property that it is both subject to phantoms, because of the DELETE part, and the cause of phantoms, because of the INSERT part. If a storage structure of the first type is used, a tuple, t, updated by T_1 might have to be moved to a new page. For example, with hashing, if an attribute of t contained in the hash key is changed, t must be moved to a new bucket. In this case, in order to prevent T_2 from inserting a phantom tuple satisfying the WHERE clause of the UPDATE statement, T_1 must retain a lock on the bucket that originally contained t. In addition, T_1 obtains a lock on the bucket to which t is moved. If a storage structure of the second type based on a clustered index is used and an attribute of t in the search key is changed, the pointer to t must be moved to a new position. T_1 must retain a lock on the index page that originally contained the pointer to prevent a pointer to a phantom tuple from being inserted later. In addition, T_1 obtains a lock on the index page to which the pointer to t is moved. (Since both index pages are modified, these would be X locks.)

We summarize the protocol when no index is used and when a B$^+$ tree index is used.

Granular locking protocol for relational databases.

▦ If no index can be used in the execution of an SQL statement
  - A SELECT statement obtains an S lock on the table.
  - An UPDATE or DELETE statement obtains a SIX lock on the table and an X lock on the page(s) containing the tuples to be updated or deleted.
  - An INSERT statement obtains an IX lock on the table and an X lock on the page(s) containing the tuples to be inserted.
▦ If a B$^+$ tree index is used on the access path
  - A SELECT statement obtains an IS lock on the table and an S lock on the page(s) containing tuples satisfying the statement's WHERE clause.

- An INSERT, UPDATE, or DELETE statement obtains an IX lock on the table and an X lock on the page(s) containing the tuples to be inserted, updated, or deleted.
- A SELECT, INSERT, UPDATE, or DELETE statement obtains an S lock on the leaf pages of the B$^+$ tree that were read during the search and X locks on any pages of the B$^+$ tree that were updated.

If the locks are long duration, the protocol has the property that when an attempt is made to insert a phantom, a lock conflict occurs

- At the table level when indices are not involved
- Along the indexing path when indices are involved

As a result, it does not allow phantoms and produces serializable schedules.

Even when indices are not used, this protocol allows more concurrency than an implementation that eliminates phantoms by using table locks. In this protocol, a transaction, T_1, that executes a write statement that does not use indices requires only an SIX lock on the table (instead of an X lock) and X locks on the pages containing rows that are updated, inserted, or deleted. These locks prevent concurrent transactions from reading those rows and from changing any rows in the table. However, a concurrent transaction, T_2, that uses an index to read rows need only acquire an IS lock on the table, and the IS lock does not conflict with T_1's SIX lock. If the rows to be read by T_2 are not stored in pages that are X-locked by T_1, its access is not delayed (as it would be if the entire table had been X-locked by T_1). Thus, this protocol prevents phantoms with less locking (hence increasing concurrency). If indices are used by the write statement, the protocol achieves even more concurrency.

Granular locking can be used at isolation levels lower than SERIALIZABLE, where phantoms are not an issue. For example, a SELECT statement executing at REPEATABLE READ obtains an IS lock on the table and an S lock on the pages containing tuples satisfying the statement's WHERE clause. In contrast to SERIALIZABLE, however, it does not require long-duration read locks on the leaf pages of indices used by the statement.

Key-range locking. Key-range locking is essentially a refinement of the index locking scheme just described that allows ranges of search-key values to be locked. Instead of locking leaf index pages, it locks index entries at the leaf level. The problem is that an index entry specifies a unique key value. How can we interpret a lock on an entry as a range?

Consider the following example. Suppose the domain of an indexed attribute is the letters from A to Z and, at some particular instant, the index contains keys C, G, P, R, and X. A lock on a leaf index entry can be interpreted as a lock on the half-open interval that starts with the value in the entry and ranges up to, but not including, the value in the next entry. For example, a lock on the entry containing G is interpreted as a lock on all keys in the half-open interval, $[G, P)$, which includes G but not P. We refer to this as a **key-range lock**.

There are two intervals within the range of all key values that need special attention.

- A lock on the last key pointer, X, is interpreted as a lock on X and all larger keys, which we will denote $[X, \infty)$.

- The interval, $[A, C)$, consisting of all keys less than C cannot be specified in this way since A is not present in the index. Hence, an extra lock must be allocated for the initial range if A is not present in the index.

With the additional lock, and in the above example, key-range locking allows the following intervals (which cover the entire range) to be locked:

$$[A, C), \ [C, G), \ [G, P), \ [P, R), \ [R, X), \ [X, \infty)$$

While the lockable intervals are determined by the state of the index, the predicate in an SQL statement specifies an arbitrary interval. To obtain a key-range lock on an arbitrary interval, we lock the minimum set of leaf index entries such that the union of their lock intervals includes the target range. In the example,

- To obtain a lock on all keys, k, such that $H \le k \le Q$, we would lock G and P.
- To obtain a lock on all keys, k, such that $H \le k \le R$, we would lock G, P, and R.
- To obtain a lock on all keys, k, such that $H \le k \le Y$, we would lock G, P, R, and X.

To see how this locking protocol prevents phantoms, we first show how the protocol is used to INSERT a new key, J.

- Obtain a write lock on the key G, thus locking the key range $[G, P)$ that includes J.
- Insert J, thus splitting the interval into two, $[G, J)$ and $[J, P)$.
- Obtain a long-duration write lock on J, thus locking the interval $[J, P)$.
- Release the lock on G.

If as a result of executing a SELECT statement, a transaction holds a key-range lock on any interval that contains J, it would have obtained a long-duration read lock on G. Since the INSERT statement requires a write lock on G, it must wait. Hence phantoms are prevented.

An interesting situation arises if a transaction, T_1, requesting access to an interval, is delayed until another transaction, T_2, that has executed an INSERT statement, has completed. For example, suppose a SELECT statement in T_1 requests to read all entries between U and W. At the time the statement is executed, this requires a lock on R (which locks the interval $[R, X)$). If T_2 is inserting S, it holds a lock on R and T_1 must wait. Since the INSERT splits the interval $[R, X)$ into $[R, S)$ and $[S, X)$, T_1 no longer requires a lock on R when T_2 completes. Instead T_1 needs a lock on S since the interval $[U, W]$ is now included in $[S, X)$. To deal with such situations, a transaction that waits for a key-range lock must reevaluate the entry it is attempting to lock when the leaf level changes. This problem also occurs with index locking. For example, while a transaction waits for a lock on an index page, the page might be split because another transaction has done an INSERT.

Key-range locking has the potential to provide more concurrency than index locking because it operates at a finer granularity. Instead of locking an entire index page, and thus locking the interval implied by all index entries in the page, key-range locking locks only the index entries that cover the interval to be locked. It can be viewed as a special form of predicate locking in which the predicate corresponding to a key range is locked.

Lock escalation.   The overhead of granular locking becomes excessive when a transaction accumulates too many fine-grain locks. This overhead takes two forms: the space overhead within the DBMS for recording information about each lock acquired and the time overhead necessary to process each lock request. When a transaction begins acquiring a large number of page (or tuple) locks on a table, it will likely continue to do so. Therefore, it is beneficial to trade in those locks for a single lock on the entire table.

This technique is known as **lock escalation**. A threshold is set in the concurrency control that limits the number of page locks a transaction can obtain on a particular table. When the transaction reaches that limit, the concurrency control attempts to lock the entire table (in the same mode as the page locks). When the table lock is granted, the page locks and the intention lock on the table can be released. Note the danger of deadlock in this scheme. If two transactions are acquiring page locks, at least one of them is a writer, and both reach their threshold, a deadlock results since neither can escalate their locks to a table lock.

Locking protocol for B$^+$ trees.   When locks were introduced in Chapter 20, we associated them with data items. In the previous section we saw that by associating locks with index leaf pages we could solve the phantom problem in a neat way. But now you should be suspicious. An index can be regarded as a special table that is implicitly accessed in the course of executing an SQL statement. What about locking the rest of the index?

For example, chaos would result if one transaction was updating (perhaps splitting) a page of a B$^+$ tree while another was reading it. Figure 21.11(a) is copied from Figure 9.19, and Figure 21.11(b) shows the first stage of the process of splitting index page B to accommodate the insertion of vera. A concurrent search for vince initiated in this state would yield a negative result. So it appears that index structures must be locked. This is unfortunate from a performance point of view since an index is a heavily used data structure. Although transactions might access the rows of a table in a random way, they all have to traverse the same index, starting from its root, to get there. Hence, locking the index can easily create a bottleneck. What is an application to do?

Clearly, we would like to minimize the amount of locking. Our initial proposal would simply be to associate a lock with each index page and require that a transaction accessing a page hold the lock for the duration of the access. But that does not eliminate the problem illustrated in Figure 21.11(b). If the lock on B is released immediately after the page has been modified, a search for vince will still fail.

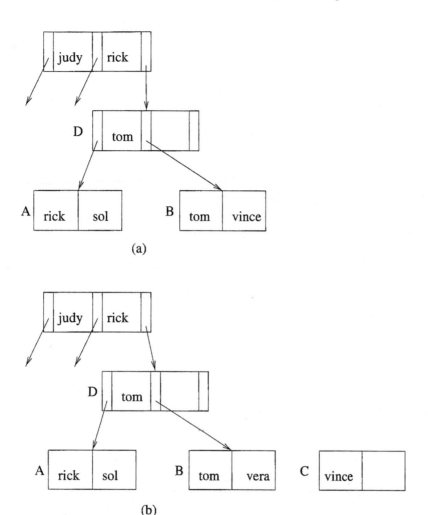

FIGURE 21.11 Two successive intermediate states in the insertion of **vera** into the B$^+$ tree of Figure 9.19.

Fortunately, there is a way out of this dilemma. Since the information in an index is not directly accessible to the application, the serializability of transactions does not have to include the operations they (implicitly) invoke on indexes. It is sufficient to require only that these operations perform as specified when executed concurrently. We can guarantee this by requiring that the individual operations are serializable. That is, the concurrent execution of a set of index operations is equivalent to a serial execution of the same operations.

A limited set of operations are defined on an index: search, insert, and delete. DBMSs control their interleaving by considering how they might be interleaved and then use latches, and a special protocol for managing the latches, to guarantee that damaging interleavings are prevented. The protocol need not be two phase because the pages and entries of an index are not accessed in an arbitrary way. The protocol used for a B^+ tree has some interesting features that we briefly discuss here.

The goal in using latches to synchronize access to a B^+ tree is to guarantee that operations on the tree (not necessarily the transactions that invoke them) are serializable. These operations all follow the same pattern: they start at the root and traverse a path to the leaf. If all operations were searches (i.e., they were read-only) there would be no problem. Concurrent searches could be arbitrarily interleaved—that is, they could overtake one another—as they travel down the tree, and we would be guaranteed that they would be serializable. It is only when we introduce operations that modify the tree that we must be vigilant. We must deal with interactions between searches and modifying operations, and among modifying operations.

The simplest protocol we could adopt is to require that (1) searches obtain read latches on all index pages they access, (2) inserts and deletes obtain write latches on all index pages they access (since those pages might have to be split, merged, or modified), and (3) these latches are acquired in a two-phase fashion (and are released when the operation completes). This protocol would guarantee that operations are serializable. In addition, of course, it might be necessary that latches on leaf level index pages be held until commit time (as described earlier) if phantoms are to be prevented. Unfortunately, we have seen that a two-phase protocol leads to performance problems, and so we need a protocol that releases latches earlier.

An improvement on this protocol is called **lock coupling**. When we apply coupling to searches, a read latch on a parent node can be released as soon as a read latch on a child node has been acquired since the parent is never revisited. In Figure 21.11(a) a search for vince can release the latch on D as soon as the latch on B has been acquired. For the moment we will continue to require that insert and delete operations obtain write latches in a two-phase fashion. The algorithm violates the two-phase condition since a search can acquire a read latch after releasing a read latch. However, we can take advantage of our knowledge of the kinds of operations that are performed on the tree to demonstrate that, despite the violation, they are serializable (see Exercise 21.19). Lock coupling is sometimes called **crabbing** because it "walks" down the tree in a crab-like fashion.

Coupling provides additional concurrency since a modifying operation that is initiated after a search does not have to wait at the root for the search to finish. It can follow the search down a path and can actually complete if it branches off to a different leaf index page. Thus, in Figure 21.11(a), once a search for vince has released the latch on D, an operation that inserts rob can move on to A. A search, of course, will be delayed at the root by a modifying operation, so we have to look for a better solution. For example, an insert holds a write latch on the root until the insertion completes.

An obvious improvement would be to apply lock coupling to write latches, but unfortunately, that does not work. Modifying operations have the unpleasant property that they might have to retrace their steps and go back up the tree after descending to a leaf if pages have to be split or merged. With lock coupling this would imply that they would have to reacquire latches that they had previously released.

Reacquisition violates serializability: when a modifying operation reacquires a latch on a page it might find that the page has been changed by a concurrent modifying operation.

We can improve concurrency, however, by requiring a modifying operation to acquire update latches instead of write latches as it descends the tree. The update latch could be converted to write latches at a later time (without violating the two-phase requirement) if the operation had to retrace its steps. A search operation can now progress down the same path as a modifying operation and even overtake it since read and update latches do not conflict.

There are still several problems to this approach. For one thing, modifying operations still block each other at the root since update latches conflict. Furthermore, deadlock is now possible. For example, in Figure 21.11(a) the operation that inserts[8] vera might hold an update latch on D and a write latch on B. It might then request to upgrade the update latch on D to a write latch in order to insert the pointer to C. A concurrent search for vince might hold a read latch on D and request a read latch on B, yielding a deadlock. Despite this problem, update latches appear to be a good idea, since the splits and merges that require modifying operations to retrace their steps back up the tree occur infrequently.

But we are not quite finished. We can alleviate both of these problems by noticing that a modifying operation, as it descends down a path, can place a limit on how far back up the tree it can possibly go. Consider an insert operation, $ins1$. Suppose it traverses a node, n, that is not full (such as D in Figure 21.11(a)). It can conclude that it will not need to split n, and hence it will not need to modify n's parent. Note that a concurrent insert, $ins2$, cannot fill n while $ins1$ is executing further down the tree since $ins1$ holds an update latch on n that stops $ins2$ on its descent. This limits the amount of backing up that $ins1$ might have to do. We can take advantage of this observation by modifying the protocol for insert operations. When, on its descent, an insert operation acquires an update latch on a node that is not full, it can release the update latches it holds on *all* ancestor nodes. A similar optimization applies to delete operations.

Table partitioning. Table partitioning is a useful technique related to granular locking. Consider again the table STUDENT. An application wishing to extract information about students living in Stony Brook might execute the statement

```
SELECT *
FROM STUDENT S
WHERE S.Address = 'Stony Brook'
```

In an alternative organization of the data, STUDENT is partitioned into separate tables, called **partitions**, one for each town. For example, we might put all of the tuples satisfying the predicate Address = 'Stony Brook' in one table, STUD_SB and

---

[8] See Exercise 21.20 for a treatment of deletes.

all tuples satisfying the predicate Address = 'Smithtown' in another, STUD_SM, and so forth. A transaction wishing to retrieve information about students living in Stony Brook now executes

```
SELECT *
FROM STUD_SB
```

Thus, a table lock on the partition is equivalent to a predicate lock on the predicate used to perform the partitioning. This eliminates the need for index locking as a substitute for predicate locking when the predicate is Address = *some town*. Since the original table no longer exists, we are not implementing two different granularities of locking. Therefore, a transaction requesting a table lock on a partition need not get an intention lock at a higher level. Partitioning was discussed in more detail in Chapter 16. Its advantage is that since the granularity of partitions is finer than the granularity of the original table, a higher degree of concurrency can be obtained without the overhead of managing intention locks. The disadvantage is that queries that span multiple partitions become more difficult to process. For example, a query that retrieves the tuples of all students living in Stony Brook or Smithtown, or a query that uses a predicate that does not involve the attribute Address, must access multiple tables.

21.3.2 Granular Locking in an Object Database

Many of the ideas in granular locking for relational databases also apply to object databases. Consider a bank account application. A relational database might have a table ACCOUNTS with tuples representing individual accounts. Similarly an object database might have a class ACCOUNTSCLASS in which individual accounts are represented by object instances of the class. Just as a tuple is contained in a table, we can view an object as being contained in a class. Furthermore, we can use the same lock modes (shared and exclusive and the corresponding intentions modes) and interpret them in an object database in the same way as they are interpreted in a relational database:

- In a relational database, locking a table implicitly locks all the tuples in it.
- In an object database, locking a class implicitly locks all the objects in it.

Thus, in the bank's object database, a granular locking protocol requires that we get the appropriate intention lock on ACCOUNTSCLASS before we can get a lock on a particular account object.

Object databases also support inheritance. Thus, in the bank application, the class hierarchy might include the fact that SAVINGSACCOUNTSCLASS and CHECKING-ACCOUNTSCLASS are subclasses of ACCOUNTSCLASS and that ECONOMYCHECKING-ACCOUNTSCLASS is a subclass of CHECKINGACCOUNTSCLASS. Since an object in the class ECONOMYCHECKINGACCOUNTSCLASS is also an object of the parent classes

CHECKINGACCOUNTSCLASS and ACCOUNTSCLASS, a lock on ACCOUNTSCLASS implicitly locks all the objects in CHECKINGACCOUNTSCLASS and ECONOMYCHECKING-ACCOUNTSCLASS. Similarly, before we can get a lock on the ECONOMYCHECKING-ACCOUNTSCLASS class, we must get the appropriate intention locks on both the CHECKINGACCOUNTSCLASS class and the ACCOUNTSCLASS class. Thus, locking a class implicitly also locks

- All of its objects
- All of its descendant classes (and hence all the objects in those classes)

We now summarize our discussion with a (somewhat simplified)[9] protocol for granular locking of object databases.

Granular locking protocol for object databases.

- Before obtaining a lock on an object, the system must get the appropriate intention locks on the class of that object and on all parent classes of that class.
- Before obtaining a lock on a class, the system must get the appropriate intention locks on all parent classes of that class.

With these ideas in mind, we see that much of this discussion on isolation and granular locking for relational databases also applies to object databases.

21.4 Tuning Transactions

Performance is a key issue in the design of systems. In Chapter 12 we described techniques for improving the performance of individual SQL statements. In this section, we list additional techniques that can be used to improve performance at the transaction level.

- Transactions should execute at the lowest level of isolation consistent with the requirements of the application.
- The trade-off between including integrity constraints in the schema, so that the DBMS enforces them, and encoding enforcement in the transactions should be examined carefully. For example, a transaction that modifies a data item named in a constraint might change the item in a way that cannot possibly cause a violation, but if the constraint is part of the schema it will be (unnecessarily) checked when the transaction commits. If such transactions are frequently executed, it might be better to restrict constraint checking to the code of transactions that might cause a violation. On the other hand, such a decision should be weighed

---

[9] Some DBMSs might allow different granularities—for example, attribute level (individual attributes of an object), or database level. In some DBMSs, a write lock on a class allows the program to change the class declaration, including its methods. Other DBMSs might distinguish between a lock on the class instances, which refers to all of the objects currently in the class (similar to a table lock) and a lock on the class itself, which allows changes to the class definition (similar to a schema lock).

against the potential maintenance overhead. If, at a later time, we need to modify the constraint, the code of all transactions that check this constraint must also be changed and recompiled. This would not be necessary if the constraint were part of the schema.

- By declaring certain integrity constraints in the database schema so that they are automatically checked by the DBMS, it may be possible to execute a transaction at an isolation level lower than that consistent with the requirements of the application. (The transaction would not execute correctly at that isolation level if those integrity constraints were not checked by the DBMS.) This is essentially an optimistic approach in that it assumes that certain interleavings that cause a database to become inconsistent are unlikely. In the (rare) case in which such interleavings occur, the DBMS aborts the transaction when it detects the violation. Keep in mind, however, that errors that do not result in integrity constraint violations will not be detected.

- Transactions should be as short as possible in order to limit the time that locks must be held. It is particularly important to gather all the needed information interactively from the user before initiating the transaction. Since user interactions take a long time, locks should not be held while they are in progress. It is also desirable to decompose a long transaction into a sequence of shorter ones (assuming that this can be done while maintaining consistency). In the extreme case, each SQL statement becomes a single transaction.

- Indices can be used to increase concurrency (because they allow the DBMS to use index locks) as well as to decrease the execution time of certain operations.

- The database should be designed so that the transactions invoked most frequently can be efficiently executed. This might involve *denormalization* (see Section 6.13) to avoid expensive joins.

- Lock escalation is inefficient if the escalation threshold will likely be reached and a table lock will ultimately be acquired. Some databases permit a transaction to explicitly request a table lock before accessing a table (manual locking). Alternatively, if the number of required page (or tuple) locks can be estimated, and it is not too large, the threshold can be set above that value.

- Lock granularity can often be decreased and hence concurrency increased by partitioning one or more of the tables.

- In systems that use page locking, lock conflicts can occur if two transactions access different tuples that happen to be stored on the same page. Putting these tuples on separate pages reduces such conflicts. Similarly, if a single transaction accesses a number of tuples, lock conflicts with other transactions can be reduced if all of those tuples are clustered on a small number of pages.

- A deadlock can occur if one transaction accesses two tables in one order and another transaction accesses them in the opposite order. If possible, transactions that access common resources should all acquire locks on those resources in the same order.

21.5 Multiversion Concurrency Controls

By a **version** or **snapshot** of a database we mean an assignment of values to each database item, x, such that x's value in the version is the value assigned by the last committed transaction that wrote to x. Thus, the value of an item that has been updated by an uncommitted transaction does not appear in the version. Many versions of a database are produced during the execution of a particular schedule of transactions. In a multiversion DBMS, different versions are retained, and the concurrency control need not use the most recent version to satisfy a request to read an item.

In this section, we discuss three multiversion concurrency controls. The advantage of these algorithms is that (in most cases) readers are not required to set read locks. Therefore, a request to read a data item does not have to wait, and a request to write a data item does not have to wait for a reader. This is an important advantage, particularly in the many applications where reading occurs far more frequently than writing. These advantages come at the expense of the additional system complexity required to maintain multiple versions of the database.

Of the three algorithms we discuss, only the first always produces serializable schedules. The other two can produce nonserializable schedules and hence incorrect database states.

Transaction-level read consistency. The first question that must be addressed in specifying a multiversion concurrency control is "What value is returned to a transaction that requests to read an item in the database?" As with the READ COMMITTED isolation level, multiversion algorithms guarantee that only committed data is returned (because, by definition, a version contains only committed data). Recall, however, that at READ COMMITTED nonrepeatable reads can occur. Similarly, with a multiversion control, successive reads by the same transaction might return data from different versions. Thus, the transaction might see an inconsistent view of data. To deal with this situation, some multiversion algorithms guarantee a stronger condition called **transaction-level read consistency**: the data returned by *all* of the SQL statements executed in a transaction comes from the same version of the database. Transaction-level read consistency, however, does not necessarily guarantee serializability.

The next question that must be addressed is "What version of the database is accessed by an SQL statement?" A multiversion control might satisfy a read request with the value of an item obtained from an arbitrary version. For example, assume that transactions T_1 and T_2 are active in a conventional (single-version) immediate-update pessimistic system. If T_1 has written an item and T_2 makes a request to read the item, a conflict exists and T_2 waits. In a multiversion system, T_2's request might be satisfied immediately using a version that was created before T_1's write (note that this need not be the most recently committed version). T_2 then precedes T_1 in any equivalent serial order.

These ideas are illustrated in the following schedule:

$$w_0(y) \; commit_0 \; r_2(x) \; w_1(x) \; w_1(y) \; commit_1 \; r_2(y) \qquad \textbf{21.5}$$

Assuming transaction T_2 starts after T_0 commits, a control that implements transaction level read consistency might satisfy all read requests submitted by T_2 using the version created by T_0. In that case, the value returned by operation $r_2(y)$ is the value written by $w_0(y)$, which is not the value in the last committed version at the time the read is executed.

21.5.1 Read-Only Multiversion Concurrency Control

In the general case, the design of a multiversion concurrency control that ensures serializable schedules can be quite complex. However, there is a special case called a **Read-Only multiversion concurrency control** that is easier to implement and produces serializable schedules.

A Read-Only multiversion concurrency control distinguishes in advance between two kinds of transactions: **read-only** transactions, which contain no write operations, and **read/write** transactions, which contain both read and write operations.

- Read/write transactions use a conventional, immediate-update, pessimistic concurrency control with a strict two-phase locking protocol for all (read and write) operations. Transactions access the most current version of the item read or written. Hence read/write transactions are provided with transaction-level read consistency and are serializable in commit order.

- All the read operations of a read-only transaction, T_{RO}, are satisfied using the most recent version of the database that existed when T_{RO} made its first read request. Hence, read-only transactions are provided with transaction-level read consistency.

The combined schedule of read-only and read/write transactions is serializable. The equivalent serial order is the commit order of the read/write transactions, with each read-only transaction inserted immediately after the read/write transaction that created the version it read. For example, in schedule (21.5) the equivalent serial order of read/write transactions is T_0, T_1 and the serial order of the complete schedule is T_0, T_2, T_1 since the read-only transaction T_1 read the version produced by T_0. Note that the equivalent serial order is not necessarily the commit order.

To implement this control, the DBMS maintains older versions of each item for use by read-only transactions. We will see in Chapter 22 that DBMSs generally keep version information in their log for recovery purposes, so the maintenance of this information is not unique to multiversion systems. Multiversion systems, however, have the additional requirement of being able to make earlier versions accessible to read-only transactions in an efficient manner. Read/write transactions lock an item as a whole and read the most recent version when it is unlocked.

Read-only transactions do not observe locks, and the only issue is how to provide the appropriate value to satisfy a particular read request. To do this, the system stores with each value of an item a **version number**, which is assigned when the read/write

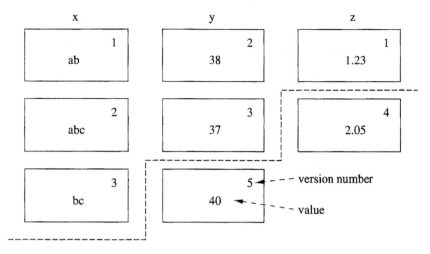

FIGURE 21.12 Satisfying a read request in a multiversion database.

transaction, $T_{R/W}$, that wrote the value commits. To determine what version number to assign, the system maintains a **version counter** (**VC**) which is incremented when $T_{R/W}$ commits. At that time, the (incremented) value of VC is assigned as the version number of all the items written by $T_{R/W}$. Older versions of the item are retained (perhaps in the log). $T_{R/W}$ has created a new version of the database consisting of the new versions of the items it has updated and the most recent versions (at the time $T_{R/W}$ commits) of all other items. A version contains only **committed** values.

Each read-only transaction is assigned a **snapshot number**, which is the value of VC that existed when it made its first read request. All subsequent read requests are satisfied using values drawn from the version with that snapshot number.

The situation is illustrated in Figure 21.12. The database consists of three items, x, y, and z. The successive values of each item are tagged with version numbers. For example, there are two versions of z, the first created by the first transaction to commit and the second created by the fourth transaction to commit. Assume that a read-only transaction, T_{RO}, makes its first read request when VC has the value 3. Hence, its snapshot number is 3 and it gets the values of x, y, and z that lie immediately above the dotted line. Versions 4 and 5 of the database might be created while T_{RO} is executing, but it does not see those versions.

Overhead is involved in storing the version numbers. Furthermore, as a practical matter the number of accessible earlier versions might be limited, and hence a (long-running) read-only transaction that draws its information from a very old version might have to be aborted if that version is no longer available.

This control has the highly desirable property that read-only transactions do not have to obtain any locks. For that reason, read-only transactions never have to wait, and read/write transactions never have to wait for read-only transactions. The cost of this property is a more complex concurrency control, the additional storage required to maintain multiple versions tagged with version numbers, and some possible nonintuitive behavior due to the serialization of read-only transactions in an order different than commit order. For example, a read-only transaction that reports bank balances might commit at a later time than a bank deposit transaction but not report the result of the deposit because it executed its first read before the deposit transaction started.

21.5.2 Read-Consistency Multiversion Concurrency Controls

For applications that can tolerate nonrepeatable reads, some commercial DBMSs, such as Oracle, use an algorithm called the **Read-Consistency** concurrency control, which extends the Read-Only control to deal with read/write transactions.

- Read-Only transactions are treated as in the Read-Only control and therefore are provided with transaction-level read consistency.

- Write statements in read/write transactions use long-duration write locks applied to the most current version of the item being written. A transaction attempting to write an item that is write-locked by another transaction must wait.

- Read statements in read/write transactions do not request read locks (read locks are not implemented in this control). Instead, each read request is provided with the value of the most recent version of the requested item (the version that was current when that read request was made).

The Read-Consistency control provides a stronger version of the standard READ COMMITTED isolation level described in Section 21.2 (and is the implementation of READ COMMITTED provided by Oracle). As with the locking implementation of READ COMMITTED, write locks are long duration and reads return committed values. However, the Read-Consistency control provides transaction-level read consistency for read-only transactions, which is not provided by the locking implementation of READ COMMITTED (nor is it required by the ANSI definition of READ COMMITTED).

A nice property of the Read-Consistency control is that no transaction needs to acquire a lock for a read operation. Hence, reads never wait for writes, and writes never wait for reads. As with READ COMMITTED, reads performed by read/write transactions are not repeatable, and so schedules can be nonserializable. For example, the schedule shown in Figure 21.6, which exhibits a lost update, can be produced by this control.

21.5.3 Case Study: SNAPSHOT Isolation

Still another variation on the same idea is called SNAPSHOT isolation [Berenson et al. 1995]. Variants of SNAPSHOT isolation have been implemented by a number of database vendors, including Oracle. In fact SNAPSHOT isolation is Oracle's implementation of SET TRANSACTION LEVEL SERIALIZABLE (although the resulting schedules are not necessarily serializable).

SNAPSHOT isolation does not distinguish between read-only and read/write transactions. It is defined as follows:

- All read operations of a transaction are satisfied using the version of the database that was current when the transaction made its first read request. Thus, all transactions are provided with transaction-level read consistency.

■ If two transactions, T_1 and T_2, are concurrent (their execution overlaps in time), the set of data items written by T_1 must be disjoint from the set written by T_2. This is called the **disjoint-write property**. If the two transactions attempt to write the same data item, one of them will be aborted. In this definition, a data item can be considered to be either a row or a table (or even an individual attribute within a row), but since tables provide a coarse granularity, which negatively affects performance, we will henceforth assume that a data item is a row.

The disjoint-write property has the important effect of eliminating lost updates. Consider, for example, the lost update shown in Figure 21.6 on page 880. Since T_1 and T_2 are concurrent and their write sets are not disjoint, only one will be allowed to commit.

We describe two implementations of the disjoint-write property, both based on the use of a version counter, VC, that is incremented whenever a transaction that has written an item commits. As before, the incremented value is the version number of the new version created by the transaction. In both implementations, each transaction is assigned a snapshot number (which is the value of VC when it made its first read request). Note that the version number of the version created by T is greater than T's snapshot number.

First-committer-wins implementation. One way to ensure the disjoint-write property is by using a **first-committer-wins** strategy. A transaction, T_1, is allowed to commit only if there is no other transaction that (1) committed between the time T_1 made its first read request and the time it requested to commit, and (2) updated a data item that T_1 also updated. If this is not the case, T_1 aborts. Clearly a concurrency control that implements first-committer-wins ensures the disjoint-write property.

The first-committer-wins property can be implemented without write locks using a deferred-update system. While executing, T_1's updates are stored in an intentions list. When it has completed, it is validated (as in an optimistic concurrency control but with a different validation criterion). Validation is successful if T_1's snapshot number is greater than or equal to the version number of each item that it has updated.

■ Suppose that when T_1 requests to commit, the version number of some item that T_1 has updated is greater than T_1's snapshot number. This means that some other transaction, T_2, wrote that item and committed while T_1 was executing. In this case, T_1 must be aborted since T_2 is the first committer—and it wins.

■ Suppose that at the time T_1 requests to commit, the version number of all items that T_1 has updated is less than or equal to T_1's snapshot number. Then T_1's intentions list is used to create a new version of the database by appending a new value to each database item named in the list, tagged with the incremented version counter. ·

As illustrated in Figure 21.12, if T_1's snapshot number is 3, and T_1 has written to x and y, then T_1's request to commit will be denied. Although there are no newer versions of x, a newer version of y was created by a different (committed) transaction while T_1 was executing.

As with the optimistic concurrency control algorithm, this control has the property that no locks are needed; hence, neither reads nor writes ever wait, but transactions might be aborted when they complete.

A locking implementation. The disjoint-write property can also be implemented using an immediate-update locking protocol involving only write locks. This is the implementation provided by Oracle. When a transaction, T_1, requests to write a data item, x

- If no other transaction has a write lock on x,
    - If the version number of x is greater than T_1's snapshot number, T_1 is aborted since a concurrent transaction wrote x and committed before the request (and the first committer wins).
    - If the version number of x is less than or equal to T_1's snapshot number, T_1 is granted a write lock on x and allowed to write it. The lock is retained until T_1 commits or aborts.
- If another transaction, T_2, has a write lock on x, T_1 waits until T_2 terminates.
    - If T_2 commits, T_1 is aborted (T_2 is the first committer and wins).
    - If T_2 aborts, T_1 is granted the lock and allowed to write x (assuming no other transaction is also waiting for that lock).

This control has the property that no read locks are needed. Hence, reads never wait and writes never wait for reads, but transactions might be aborted while waiting for write locks (either because the transaction holding that lock commits or because of a deadlock).

Non-serializable schedules and SNAPSHOT isolation. Although SNAPSHOT isolation eliminates many anomalies, it does not guarantee that all schedules will be serializable, hence transactions can perform incorrectly. For example, in Figure 21.13, T_1 and T_2 are two bank withdrawal transactions that are withdrawing funds from different accounts, with balances a_1 and a_2, owned by the same depositor, d. The bank has a business rule that an individual account balance can be negative, but the sum of the balances in all accounts owned by each depositor must be nonnegative. Thus, if d has only two accounts, the constraint is $a_1 + a_2 \geq 0$. Both T_1 and T_2 are consistent: they read the balances in both accounts before making withdrawals, and thus, when executed in isolation, each maintains the constraint. In the example, each account has $10 initially and each transaction concludes that it is safe to withdraw $15 because the combined balance is $20. However, in the schedule shown, which is allowable in SNAPSHOT isolation (because T_1 and T_2 write to different data items), the final values of a_1 and a_2 are both $-$5, thus violating the constraint. Note that this schedule is not serializable because T_2 must be after T_1 (T_2 wrote a_1 after T_1 read it) and T_1 must be after T_2 (T_1 wrote a_2 after T_2 read it). (For a continuation of this example, see Exercise 21.25.)

FIGURE **21.13** SNAPSHOT-isolated schedule that is not serializable and leads to an inconsistent database.

$$T_1 : r(a_1 : 10)\ r(a_2 : 10) \qquad\qquad\qquad\qquad w(a_2 : -5)\ commit$$
$$T_2 : \qquad\qquad\qquad r(a_1 : 10)\ r(a_2 : 10)\ w(a_1 : -5)\ commit$$

SNAPSHOT isolation and the isolation-level anomalies. Even though the example of Figure 21.13 demonstrates that SNAPSHOT isolation can produce nonserializable schedules, note that these schedules do not exhibit any of the anomalies associated with the lower isolation levels—dirty reads, nonrepeatable reads, and phantoms (as well as dirty writes and lost updates, which are not part of the definitions of the isolation levels).

We need to clarify the statement that SNAPSHOT isolation does not allow phantoms. In a SNAPSHOT-isolated schedule, a transaction, T, might execute a SELECT statement based on a predicate, P, and a concurrent transaction might later insert a tuple, t, that satisfies P (seemingly a phantom). However, t will not be returned in a subsequent execution by T of the same SELECT statement since its result set will be calculated from the same version of the database used by the first execution. On this basis, one might say that t is not a phantom. We give two examples, one where the insertion does not cause an incorrect schedule and one where it does.

- In the example in Section 21.1.1 involving a single-version database and Mary's accounts, the audit transaction, T_1, saw inconsistent data because a phantom was inserted between its two SELECT statements, changing the state of that version. In a multiversion database, a version, once created, never changes. With SNAPSHOT isolation, the result sets for both statements are calculated using one of those versions, hence T_1 does not see the updated value of TotalBalance. Therefore, it executes correctly.

- Suppose that the bank database has an integrity constraint stating that no depositor can have more than 10 accounts. To enforce this, an add_new_account transaction first executes a SELECT statement using the predicate Name = 'Mary' to determine the number of Mary's accounts. If the number is nine or less, it inserts a tuple corresponding to a new account for Mary. If two instances of add_new_account execute concurrently, and both have the same snapshot number indicating a version in which Mary has nine accounts, they will both insert a tuple corresponding to a new account. Mary now has 11 accounts, in violation of the constraint. The schedule is nonserializable and incorrect.

There is no agreed-upon definition in the literature of what constitutes a phantom. Some sources say that an isolation level permits phantoms if, when a transaction executes the same SELECT statement twice, the second execution can return a result set containing a (phantom) tuple not contained in the first. Using this definition, phantoms are permitted at REPEATABLE READ but not at SNAPSHOT isolation.

FIGURE 21.14 SNAPSHOT-isolated schedule that is not serializable and does not exhibit any of the named anomalies.

$T_1:$	$r(x)$		$w(x)$ commit			
$T_2:$		$r(x)$ $r(y)$			$w(y)$ commit	
$T_3:$				$r(x)$ $r(y)$ $w(z)$ commit		

However, the second example illustrates that the effect of phantoms still exists with SNAPSHOT isolation even though, according to the above definition, the insertions do not constitute phantoms. If we had executed the transactions in that example at REPEATABLE READ, the same (nonserializable) schedule would be permitted and we would say that phantoms did occur.

Using the definition of phantoms based on the successive execution of SELECT statements, it follows that SNAPSHOT isolation does not exhibit any of the bad anomalies that define the lower isolation levels. Nevertheless, it does not meet the ANSI definition of SERIALIZABLE [SQL 1992], which states that (in addition to not allowing any of the three anomalies) SERIALIZABLE must provide what is "commonly known as fully serializable execution." This is certainly not the case for SNAPSHOT isolation. Schedules that do not contain the three anomalies of dirty reads, nonrepeatable reads, and phantoms are sometimes called **anomaly serializable**. Thus, SNAPSHOT-isolated schedules are anomaly serializable, but might not be serializable.

This again shows that correctness should not be defined by the absence of certain specific anomalies. Some authors use the term **write skew** to describe the anomaly exemplified by Figure 21.13. But even adding that anomaly to the list should not give you much confidence that the list is complete. For example, the schedule shown in Figure 21.14, which is allowable in SNAPSHOT isolation, is not serializable because its serialization graph has a cycle

$$T_3 \rightarrow T_2 \rightarrow T_1 \rightarrow T_3$$

However, it does not exhibit any of the named anomalies, including write skew.

Figure 21.15 shows another schedule [Fekete et al. 2000] permitted at SNAPSHOT isolation that is not serializable because its serialization graph has the cycle

$$T_3 \rightarrow T_2 \rightarrow T_1 \rightarrow T_3$$

The interesting thing about this example is that it involves a read-only transaction, T_3. The read/write transactions, T_1 and T_2, by themselves, are serializable (T_2 precedes T_1). However T_3 sees a snapshot of the database that never existed. Specifically, T_3 sees the effect of T_1, but not the effect of T_2, even though T_2 precedes T_1 in the (only possible) equivalent serial order.

Correct execution at SNAPSHOT isolation. Even though SNAPSHOT isolation does not guarantee serializable executions, many applications do run serializably at SNAPSHOT isolation. For example, the TPC-C Benchmark (*http://www.tpc.org/tpcc*), which is an application that is used to compare the performance of different vendors'

FIGURE 21.15 Another schedule permitted at SNAPSHOT isolation that is not serializable and does not exhibit any of the named anomalies. This one involves a read-only transaction.

T_1: $r(x)$ $w(x)$ *commit*
T_2: $r(x)$ $r(y)$ $w(y)$ *commit*
T_3: $r(x)$ $r(y)$ *commit*

FIGURE 21.16 SNAPSHOT-isolated schedule for a ticket-reservation application. The schedule exhibits write skew and is not serializable but is nevertheless correct.

$T_1: r(s_1:U)\ r(s_2:U)$ $w(s_2:R)$ *commit*
T_2: $r(s_1:U)\ r(s_2:U)\ w(s_1:R)$ *commit*

DBMSs, has been shown to execute serializably at SNAPSHOT isolation [Fekete et al. 2000].

Many other applications run correctly at SNAPSHOT isolation even though some of their schedules exhibit write skew and are nonserializable. For example, consider an application containing a transaction that reserves a seat for a concert. The transaction examines the status of a number of seats and reserves one. An integrity constraint asserts that the same seat cannot be reserved by more than one person. Suppose that two ticket-reservation transactions execute concurrently and produce the schedule shown in Figure 21.16 (which is virtually identical to the schedule shown in Figure 21.13). Each reads the tuples corresponding to seats s_1 and s_2 and determines that they are both unreserved (U). Then T_1 reserves s_1 by updating its status (to R) in the database; similarly, T_2 reserves s_2. The schedule is correct for this application, even though it exhibits write skew (and hence the schedule is not serializable). Furthermore, if both transactions try to reserve seat s_1, only one will commit because of the disjoint-write property, preserving the integrity constraint. Hence, any schedule of ticket-reservation transactions will execute correctly at SNAPSHOT isolation.

Because of the multiversion aspect of SNAPSHOT isolation, serializable SNAPSHOT-isolated schedules can sometimes yield nonintuitive behavior. For example, the schedule of Figure 21.17 is serializable in the order

$$T_3 \rightarrow T_2 \rightarrow T_1$$

where T_3 precedes T_1 even though it started after T_1 committed.

FIGURE 21.17 SNAPSHOT-isolated schedule that is serializable but in which T_3 precedes T_1 in the equivalent serial order even though it started after T_1 committed.

T_1: $r(x)$ $w(x)$ *commit*
T_2: $r(x)$ $r(y)$ $w(y)$ *commit*
T_3: $r(y)$ $w(z)$ *commit*

In practice, many applications run correctly under SNAPSHOT isolation, particularly if most of the integrity constraints are encoded into the database schema (see Exercise 21.25). However, the cautious designer will perform a careful analysis of the application before making that design decision.

BIBLIOGRAPHIC NOTES

Phantoms and the use of predicate locks to eliminate them were introduced in [Eswaran et al. 1976]. The definition of the SQL isolation levels can be found in [Gray et al. 1976] and in the ANSI SQL standard [SQL 1992]. The locking implementation of the isolation levels is discussed in [Berenson et al. 1995]. [Gray et al. 1976] contains a good discussion of granular locking. Multiversion concurrency controls are discussed in [Bernstein and Goodman 1983; Hadzilacos and Papadimitriou 1985]. The design of a multiversion, optimistic concurrency control is described in [Agrawal et al. 1987]. SNAPSHOT isolation was first discussed in [Berenson et al. 1995]. [Fekete et al. 2000] discusses the conflict aspects of SNAPSHOT isolation and gives a sufficient condition for a SNAPSHOT-isolated schedule to be serializable. They also prove that the TPC-C Benchmark application executes serializably at SNAPSHOT isolation, and they provide the example of nonserializable execution with a read-only transaction. [Bernstein et al. 2000] discusses an approach to proving correctness of schedules at lower isolation levels based on the semantics of the transactions. [Bernstein et al. 1987] contains an excellent summary of many concurrency control algorithms, including index locking. An early version of lock coupling was described in [Shoshani and Bernstein 1969]. Concurrency control in an object database is discussed in [Cattell 1994].

EXERCISES

21.1 Suppose that the transaction processing system of your university contains a table in which there is one tuple for each currently registered student.

a. Estimate how much disk storage is required to store this table.

b. Give examples of transactions that must lock this entire table if a table-locking concurrency control is used.

21.2 Consider an INSERT statement that inserts tuples into table T and that contains a nested SELECT statement having predicate P in its WHERE clause. Assume P is a simple predicate that does not contain a nested SELECT statement and consists of a conjunction of clauses of the form (`Attribute` *op* `constant`). Describe the predicate associated with T.

21.3 Choose a set of transactions for an application of your choice (other than a banking or student registration system). For each isolation level weaker than SERIALIZABLE, give an example of a schedule that produces an erroneous situation.

21.4 Assume that transactions are executed at REPEATABLE READ. Give an example in which a phantom occurs when a transaction executes a SELECT statement that specifies the value of the primary key in the WHERE clause.

21.5 Assume that transactions are executed at REPEATABLE READ. Give an example in which a phantom occurs when a transaction executes a DELETE statement to delete a set of tuples satisfying some predicate, P.

21.6 Assume that transactions are executed at REPEATABLE READ. Give an example in which an UPDATE statement executed by one transaction causes a phantom in an UPDATE statement executed in another.

21.7 Consider a schema with two tables, TABLE1 and TABLE2, each having three attributes, attr1, attr2, and attr3, and consider the statement

```
SELECT T1.attr1, T2.attr1
FROM TABLE1 T1, TABLE2 T2
WHERE T1.attr2 = T2.attr2 AND T1.attr3 = 5
       AND T2.attr3 = 7
```

Give an INSERT statement that might cause a phantom.

21.8 Explain the difference between a nonrepeatable read and a phantom. Specifically, give an example of a schedule of the SQL statements of two transactions that illustrate the two cases. Specify an isolation level in each case.

21.9 For each of the locking implementations of the isolation levels, state whether IS locks are required and when they can be released.

21.10 The following procedure has been proposed for obtaining read locks.

Whenever an SQL statement reads a set of rows that satisfies some predicate in a table, the system first gets an IS lock on the table containing the rows and then gets an S lock on each of the rows.

Explain why this procedure allows phantoms.

21.11 Give an example of a schedule produced by a read-only multiversion concurrency control in which the read/write transactions serialize in commit order while the read-only transactions serialize in a different order.

21.12 Give an example of a schedule of read/write requests that is accepted by a multiversion concurrency control in which transaction T_1 starts after transaction T_2 commits, yet T_1 precedes T_2 in the serial order. Such a schedule can have the following nonintuitive behavior (even though it is serializable): you deposit money in your bank account; your transaction commits; later you start a new transaction that reads the amount in your account and finds that the amount you deposited is not there. (*Hint:* The schedule is allowed to contain additional transactions.)

21.13 Show that the schedule shown in Figure 21.13 for incorrect execution at SNAPSHOT isolation can also occur when executing at OPTIMISTIC READ COMMITTED (Section 21.2.1) and will also be incorrect.

21.14 Give examples of schedules that would be accepted at

a. SNAPSHOT isolation but not REPEATABLE READ
b. SERIALIZABLE but not SNAPSHOT isolation

21.15 A particular read-only transaction reads data that was entered into the database during the previous month and uses that data to prepare a report. What is the weakest isolation level at which this transaction can execute? Explain.

21.16 Explain why a read-only transaction consisting of a single SELECT statement that uses an INSENSITIVE cursor can always execute correctly at READ COMMITTED.

21.17 Suppose that a locking implementation of REPEATABLE READ requires that a transaction obtain an X lock on a table when a write is requested. When a read is requested, a transaction is required to obtain an IS lock on the table and an S lock on the tuples returned. Show that phantoms cannot occur.

21.18 Consider an isolation level implemented using long-duration granular locks on rows and tables. Under what conditions can phantoms occur?

21.19 Show that the algorithm for concurrently accessing a B$^+$tree in which operations that only search the tree use lock coupling and operations that modify the tree handle write latches in a two-phase fashion guarantees that all operations are carried out successfully.

21.20 In Section 21.3.1 we described an algorithm that allowed the concurrent execution of a search for a unique key and an insert of a row in a B$^+$ tree. Extend the algorithm to range searches and deletes.

21.21 a. Give an example of a schedule of two transactions in which a two-phase locking concurrency control causes one of the transactions to wait but a SNAPSHOT isolation control aborts one of the transactions.
b. Give an example of a schedule of two transactions in which a two-phase locking concurrency control aborts one of the transactions (because of a deadlock) but a SNAPSHOT isolation control allows both transactions to commit.

21.22 Explain why SNAPSHOT-isolated schedules do not exhibit dirty reads, dirty writes, lost updates, nonrepeatable reads, and phantoms.

21.23 Consider an application consisting of transactions that are assigned different isolation levels. Prove that if transaction T is executed at SERIALIZABLE and transaction T' is any other transaction, then T either sees all changes made by T' or it sees none.

21.24 All of the transactions in some particular application write all of the data items they read. Show that if that application executes under SNAPSHOT isolation, all schedules of committed transactions will be serializable.

21.25 Consider the schedule of two bank withdrawal transactions shown in Figure 21.13 for which SNAPSHOT isolation leads to an inconsistent database. Suppose that the bank encodes, as an integrity constraint in the database schema, the business rule "The sum of the balances in all accounts owned by the same depositor must be nonnegative." Then that particular schedule cannot occur.

Although the integrity constraint is now maintained, the specification of a particular transaction might assert that when the transaction commits, the database state satisfies a stronger condition. Give an example of a stronger condition that a withdrawal transaction might attempt to impose when it terminates and a schedule of two such transactions at SNAPSHOT isolation that causes them to behave incorrectly.

21.26 The following multiversion concurrency control has been proposed.

> Reads are satisfied using the (committed) version of the database that existed when the transaction made its first read request. Writes are controlled by long-duration write locks on tables.

Does the control always produce serializable schedules? If not, give a nonserializable schedule it might produce.

21.27 We have given two different implementations of the READ COMMITTED isolation level: the locking implementation in Section 21.2 and the read-consistency implementation in Section 21.5. Give an example of a schedule in which the two implementations produce different results.

21.28 The granular locking protocol can exhibit a deadlock between two transactions, one of which executes a single SELECT statement and the other a single UPDATE statement. For example, suppose that one transaction contains the single SELECT statement

```
SELECT COUNT (P.Id)
FROM EMPLOYEE P
WHERE P.Age = '27'
```

which returns the number of employees whose age is 27, and the other contains the single UPDATE statement

```
UPDATE EMPLOYEE
SET Salary = Salary * 1.1
WHERE Department = 'Adm'
```

which gives all employees in the administration a 10% raise. Assume that there are indices on both Department and Age and that the tuples corresponding to the department Adm are stored in more than one page as are those corresponding to age 27. Show how a deadlock might occur at isolation levels other than READ UNCOMMITTED.

21.29 Give an example of a schedule executing at SNAPSHOT isolation in which two transactions each introduce a phantom that is not seen by the other transaction, resulting in incorrect behavior. Assume that the data items referred to in the description of SNAPSHOT isolation are rows.

21.30 In an Internet election system, each voter is sent a PIN in the mail. When that voter wants to vote at the election web site, she enters her PIN and her vote, and then a voting transaction is executed.

In the voting transaction, first the PIN is checked to verify that it is valid and has not been used already, and then the vote tally for the appropriate candidate is incremented. Two tables are used: One contains the valid PINs together with an indication of whether or not each PIN has been used and the other contains the names of the candidates and the vote tally for each. Discuss the issues involved in selecting an appropriate isolation level for the voting transaction. Discuss the issues involved in selecting appropriate isolation levels if a new (read-only) transaction is introduced that outputs the entire vote tally table.

21.31 An airlines database has two tables: FLIGHTS, with attributes flt_num, plane_id, num_reserv; and PLANES, with attributes plane_id, and num_seats.

The attributes have the obvious semantics. A reservation transaction contains the following steps:

```
        SELECT F.plane_id, F.num_reserv
        INTO :p, :n
        FROM FLIGHTS F
        WHERE F.flt_num = :f
A.      SELECT P.num_seats
        INTO :s
        FROM PLANES P
        WHERE P.plane_id = :p
B.      . . . check that n < s . . .
C.      UPDATE FLIGHTS F
        SET F.num_reserv = :n + 1
        WHERE F.flt_num = :f
D.      COMMIT
```

Assume that each individual SQL statement is executed in isolation, that the DBMS uses intention locking and sets locks on tables and rows, and that host variable f contains the number of the flight to be booked. The transaction should not overbook the flight.

a. Assuming that the transaction is run at READ COMMITTED, what locks are held at points A, B, and D?
b. The database can be left in an incorrect state if concurrently executing reservation transactions that are running at READ COMMITTED are interleaved in such a way that one transaction is completely executed at point B in the execution of another. Describe the problem.
c. In an attempt to avoid the problem described in (b), the SET clause of the UPDATE statement is changed to F.num_reserv = F.num_reserv + 1. Can reservation transactions now be run correctly at READ COMMITTED? Explain.
d. Assuming that the transaction is run at REPEATABLE READ and that the tables are accessed through indices, what table locks are held at points A, B, and D?
e. What problem does the interleaving of (b) cause at REPEATABLE READ? Explain.
f. Does the interleaving of (b) cause an incorrect state if the transaction (either version) is run using SNAPSHOT isolation? Explain.
g. To keep track of each passenger, a new table, PASSENGER, is introduced that has a row describing each passenger on each flight with attributes name, flt_num, seat_id. SQL statements are appended to the end of the transaction (1) to read the seat_id's assigned to each passenger on the flight specified in f and (2) to insert a row for the new passenger that assigns an empty seat to that passenger.

What is the weakest ANSI isolation level at which the transaction can be run without producing an incorrect state (i.e., two passengers in the same seat)? Explain.

21.32 Two transactions run concurrently, and each might either commit or abort. The transactions are chosen from the following:

$$T_1: \ r_1(x) \ w_1(y)$$
$$T_2: \ w_2(x)$$
$$T_3: \ r_3(y) \ w_3(x)$$
$$T_4: \ r_4(x) \ w_4(x) \ w_4(y)$$

In each of the following cases, state (yes or no) whether the resulting schedule is always serializable and recoverable. If the answer is no, give an example of a schedule that is either not serializable or not recoverable.

a. T_1 and T_2 both running at READ UNCOMMITTED
b. T_2 and T_2 both running at READ UNCOMMITTED
c. T_1 and T_2 both running at READ COMMITTED
d. T_1 and T_3 both running at READ COMMITTED
e. T_1 and T_3 both running at SNAPSHOT isolation
f. T_1 and T_4 both running at SNAPSHOT isolation

21.33 Give an example of a schedule that could be produced at SNAPSHOT isolation in which there are two transactions that execute concurrently but do not have the same snapshot number and do not see the same snapshot of the database. (*Hint:* the schedule can contain more than two transactions.)

21.34 A database has two tables:

STUDENT(Id, Name, $\cdots$)—Id and Name are both unique
REGISTERED(Id, CrsCode, Credit, $\cdots$)—contains one row for each course each student is taking this semester

A transaction type, *T*, has two SQL statements, *S*1 followed by *S*2 (with local computations between them):

```
S1    SELECT   SUM(R.Credits), S.Id
      INTO     :sum, :id
      FROM     STUDENT S, REGISTERED R
      WHERE    S.Name = 'Joe' AND S.Id = R.Id
      GROUP BY S.Name, S.Id
```

```
S2    UPDATE   Registered
      SET      Credits = Credits + 1
      WHERE    Id = :id AND CrsCode = :crs
```

*S*1 returns the total number of credits for which Joe is registered, together with his Id. *T* maintains the integrity constraint "no student shall register for more than 20 credits." If Joe has less than 20 credits, *T* executes *S*2 to increment the number of credits for which Joe has registered in a particular course. Suppose Joe executes two instances of T concurrently at the following isolation levels. In each case say whether or not the named violation of the constraint can occur and, if the answer is yes, explain how (e.g., what locks are or are not held).

a. READ COMMITTED

      lost update

      violation of the integrity constraint

      deadlock

b. REPEATABLE READ

      lost update

      violation of the integrity constraint

      deadlock

c. SNAPSHOT

      lost update

      violation of the integrity constraint

      deadlock

22

Atomicity and Durability

In previous chapters we made the unrealistic assumptions that transactions commit and that the system never malfunctions. The reality is quite different. Transactions can be aborted for a variety of reasons, and hardware and software can fail. Such events must be carefully handled to ensure transaction atomicity. Furthermore, a failure might occur on a mass storage device, causing the loss of information written to the database by committed transactions, thus threatening durability.

In this chapter, we discuss the basic problems that must be solved to achieve atomicity and durability and some techniques to do so. Our description is not meant to reflect the design of any particular failure recovery system. Instead, we emphasize principles that underlie the design of a number of such systems.

22.1 Crash, Abort, and Media Failure

Although the reliability of computer systems has increased dramatically over the years, the probability of a failure is still very real. A failure might be caused by a problem in the processor or in the main memory units (for example, a power loss) or by a bug in the software. Such failures cause the processor to behave unpredictably, perhaps writing spurious information in arbitrary locations in main memory, before finally performing some action that causes it to shut down. We refer to such a failure as a **crash**, and we assume that when a crash occurs, the contents of main memory are lost. For this reason, main memory is referred to as **volatile storage**. It is possible that a failing processor might initiate a spurious write to the mass storage device, but such an event is so unlikely that we assume that the contents of mass storage survive a crash.

In general, a number of transactions will be active when a transaction processing system crashes, which means that the database will be in an inconsistent state. When the system is restarted after a crash, service is not resumed until after a **recovery procedure** is executed to restore the database to a consistent state. The major issue in the design of a recovery procedure is how to deal with a transaction, T, that was active at the time the crash occurred. Atomicity requires either that the recovery procedure cause T to resume execution so that it can complete successfully—called

rollforward—or that any effects that T had prior to the crash be undone—called **rollback**.

Rollforward is often difficult, if not impossible. If T is an interactive transaction, resumption requires the cooperation of the user at the terminal. The user must know which of the updates she requested prior to the crash had actually been recorded in the database, and resume submitting requests from that point. Rolling forward a programmed transaction is further complicated by the fact that the local state (the state of T's local variables) might have been in volatile memory at the time of the crash and hence might be lost. T cannot be resumed from the point at which the crash occurred unless its local state is restored. Thus, in order to roll T forward after a crash, special measures must be taken to periodically save T's local state on a mass storage device during transaction execution.

For these reasons, transactions active at the time of a crash are usually rolled back during recovery in order to achieve atomicity. Note that our primary concern here is with the changes T made to the database before the crash. A transaction might have had other, external, effects such as printing a message on the screen or actuating a controller in a factory. External actions are difficult to reverse, although we discussed one technique for handling them in Section 19.3.5.

The rollback mechanism is required to deal not only with crashes but with transaction aborts as well. A transaction might be aborted for a number of reasons.

- A transaction might be aborted by the user—for example, because he entered incorrect input data.

- A transaction might abort itself—for example, because it encountered some unexpected information in the database.

- A transaction might be aborted by the system—for example, because the transaction has become deadlocked with other transactions, the system does not have sufficient resources to complete it, or allowing it to commit would result in the violation of some integrity constraint.

Media failure.   Durability requires that the effects of a transaction on a database not be lost once the transaction has committed. Databases are stored on mass storage devices—usually disks. Since crashes typically do not affect these devices, mass storage is referred to as **nonvolatile** storage. However, mass storage devices are subject to their own forms of failure, which are referred to as **media failures**. A media failure might affect all or some of the data stored on the device. The redundant storage of data is used to ensure a measure of durability in spite of such a failure. The more redundant copies that are kept, the more media failures that can be tolerated. Thus, durability is not absolute. It is related to the value of the data and the amount of money the enterprise is willing to spend on protecting it. A media failure might occur while transactions are executing, so the recovery procedures for media failure must also provide rollback capabilities.

22.2 Immediate-Update Systems and Write-Ahead Logs

The mechanism for rollback is different in immediate- and deferred-update systems. Since immediate-update systems are more common, we deal with them first. Our description of such a system proceeds in stages. In this section, we describe a simple, but impractical system to introduce the major ideas. In later sections we discuss some of the complexities that must be dealt with in commercial systems and describe some of the changes that must be made to the simple system to handle them.

Immediate-update systems maintain a **log**, which is a sequence of records. Records are appended to the log as transactions execute and are never changed or deleted. The log is consulted by the system to achieve both atomicity and durability. For durability, the log is used to restore the database after a failure of the mass storage device on which the database is stored. Hence, the log must be stored on a nonvolatile device. Typically, a log is a sequential file on disk. It is often duplexed (and the copies stored on different devices) so that it survives any single media failure. Some DBMSs maintain a single log while others allocate a separate log for each database.

The organization of memory is shown in Figure 22.1. For efficiency, the unit of transfer between the database on mass store and main memory is the page. Recently accessed pages are kept in a cache in main memory. Moreover, information that will eventually be stored in the log is usually first put into a log buffer in main memory. The existence of the cache and log buffer complicates the processing required for rollback and commitment. In this section, we assume that neither a cache nor a log buffer is used but that information is directly read from and written to the database and directly written to the log. We will consider the effect of the log buffer and cache in Section 22.2.1.

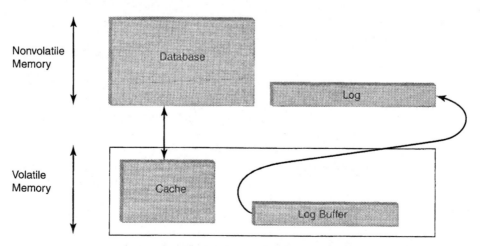

FIGURE 22.1 Organization of memory.

When a transaction executes a database operation that changes the state of the database, the system appends an **update record** to the log (no record need be appended if the operation merely reads the database). An update record describes the change that has been made and, in particular, contains enough information to permit the system to undo that change if the transaction is later aborted. Since the records are appended when the changes are made, the log contains the merge of the update records of all transactions.

In its simplest form, an update record contains the **before-image** of the database item that has been modified—that is, a physical copy of the item before the change was made. If the transaction aborts, the update record is used to restore the item to its original value—hence, the before-image is sometimes referred to as an **undo record**. If the concurrency control enforces serializable execution (i.e., the item was exclusively locked when it was changed) and the concurrency control is strict, the new value could not have been viewed by concurrent transactions, and therefore the aborted transaction will have had no effect on other transactions, and after restoration it will have had no effect on the database either. In addition to the before-image, the update record identifies the transaction that made the change—using a **transaction Id**—and the database item that was changed. We introduce other information contained in the update record as our discussion proceeds.

Because the update record contains a physical copy of the item, this form of logging is referred to as **physical logging**.

If the system aborts a transaction, T, or T aborts itself, rollback using the log is straightforward. The log is scanned backwards starting from the last record appended, and, as T's update records are encountered, the before-images are written to the database, undoing the change.

Since the log might be exceedingly long, it is impractical to search back to the beginning to make sure that all of T's update records are processed. To avoid a complete backward scan, when T is initiated a **begin record** containing its transaction Id is appended to the log. The backward scan can be stopped when T's begin record is encountered. (For easier access, the log records of a transaction can be linked together, with the most recent record at the head of the list.)

Savepoints can be implemented by generalizing this technique. Each time a transaction declares a savepoint, a **savepoint record** is written to the log. The record not only contains the transaction Id and the identity of the savepoint but might contain information about any cursors open at the time the savepoint was declared. To roll back to a specific savepoint, the log is scanned backward to the specified savepoint's record. The before-image in each of the transaction's update records that are encountered during the scan is applied to the database. Any cursor information in the record is used to reestablish the cursor's position at the time the savepoint was declared.

Rollback because of a crash is more complex than the abort of a single transaction since, on recovery, the system must first identify the transactions to be aborted. In particular, the system must distinguish between transactions that completed (committed or aborted) and those that were active at the time the crash occurred. All of the active transactions must be aborted.

When a transaction commits, it writes a **commit record** to the log. If it aborts, it rolls back its updates and then writes an **abort record** to the log. Both records contain the transaction's Id. After writing a commit or abort record, the transaction can release any locks it holds.

Using these records, the identity of the transactions active at the time of the crash can be determined by the recovery procedure. It scans the log backward starting from the last record appended before the crash occurred. If the first record relating to T is an update record, T was active when the crash occurred and must be aborted. If the first record is a commit or abort record, the transaction completed and its update records can be ignored as they are subsequently encountered.

Note that, for durability, it is important to write a commit record to the log when T commits. Because our simplified view assumes that the database is immediately updated when T makes a write request, all database modifications requested by T will be recorded in nonvolatile memory when it requests to commit. However, the commit request itself does not guarantee durability. If a crash occurs after a transaction makes the request, but before the commit record is written to the log, the transaction will be aborted by the recovery procedure and the system will not provide durability. Hence, a transaction has not actually committed until the commit record has been appended to the log on mass storage.

> Appending a commit record to the log is an atomic action (either the record is in the log or it is not in the log), and the transaction is committed if and only if the action has completed.

Checkpoints. One last issue must be addressed with respect to crashes. Some mechanism must be included to avoid a complete backward scan of the log during recovery. Without such a mechanism, the recovery process has no way of knowing when to stop the search for a transaction that was active at the time of the crash since such a transaction might have appended an update record at an early point in the log and then made no further database updates. The recovery process will find no evidence of the transaction's existence unless it scans back to that record. To deal with this situation, the system periodically writes a **checkpoint record** to the log listing the identities of currently active transactions. The recovery process must (at least) scan backward to the most recent checkpoint record. If T is named in that record and the recovery process did not encounter a completion record for T between the checkpoint record and the end of the log, then T was still active when the system crashed. The backward scan must continue until the begin record for T is reached. It terminates when all such transactions are accounted for. Only the most recent checkpoint record is used (a checkpoint record supersedes the one preceding it). The frequency with which these records are written to the log affects the speed of recovery since frequent checkpointing implies that less of the log has to be scanned.

An example of a log is shown in Figure 22.2. As the recovery process scans backward, it discovers that T_6 and T_1 were active at the time of the crash because the last records appended for them are update records. It uses the before-images in these update records (in the sequence they are encountered in the backward scan) to

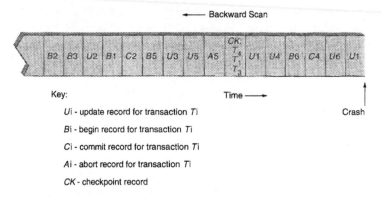

FIGURE 22.2 Log example.

roll back the database items to which they refer. Since the first record it encounters for T_4 is a commit record, it learns that T_4 was not active at the time of the crash and therefore ignores T_4's update records. When it reaches the checkpoint record, it learns that at the time the checkpoint was taken, T_1, T_3, and T_4 were active (T_6 is not mentioned in the checkpoint record since, as indicated by its begin record, it began after the checkpoint was taken). Thus, it concludes that, in addition to T_1 and T_6, T_3 was active at the time of the crash (since it has seen no completion record for T_3). No other transaction could have been active and hence these are the transactions that must be aborted. The recovery process must now continue the backward scan, processing all update records for T_1 and T_3 (there will be no update records for T_6 since its begin record has already been encountered) in the order they are encountered. The scan ends when the begin records for these transactions have been reached.

Write-ahead logging. We have assumed that an update record for a database item, x, is written to the log at the time x is updated in the database. In fact, the update of x and the append of the update record must occur in some order. Does it make a difference in which order these operations are performed? Consider the possibility that a crash occurs at the time the operations are performed. If it happens before either operation is completed, there is no problem. The update record does not appear in the log, but there is nothing for the recovery process to undo since x has not been updated. If the crash happens after both operations are performed, recovery proceeds correctly, as described above. Suppose, however, that x is updated first and that the crash occurs before the update record is appended to the log. Then the recovery process has no way of rolling the transaction back because there is no before-image in the log that the recovery process can use. Recovery thus cannot return the database to a consistent state—an unacceptable situation.

If, on the other hand, the update record is appended first, this problem is avoided. On restart, the recovery process simply uses the update record to restore x. As shown in Figure 22.3, it makes no difference whether the crash occurred before or

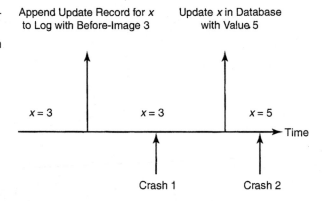

FIGURE 22.3 The recovery procedure can handle database restoration correctly with a write-ahead log.

after the transaction wrote the new value of x to the database. The original value of x was 3, a transaction updated it to 5, and the crash occurred before the transaction committed. If the crash occurred after the update record was appended but before x was updated (Crash 1 in the figure), when the system is restarted the value of x in the database and the before-image in the update record will both be 3. The recovery process uses the before-image to overwrite x—which does not change its value—but the final state after recovery has completed is correct. If the crash occurred after x was updated (Crash 2 in the figure), recovery restores x to 3.

Hence, the update record must always be appended to the log before the database is updated. This is referred to as the write-ahead feature, and the log is referred to as a **write-ahead log**.

22.2.1 Performance and Write-Ahead Logging

While write-ahead logging works correctly, it is unacceptable from a performance point of view since it doubles the number of I/O operations needed to update the database. A log append must now be performed with every database update. To avoid this overhead, database systems generally use a log buffer in volatile memory as temporary storage for log records. The log buffer can be viewed as an extension of the log on mass storage. Log records are appended to the buffer, and periodically it is appended, or **flushed**, to the log, as shown in Figure 22.1. With a log buffer, the cost of writing to the log is prorated over all log records contained in the buffer.

From the point of view of crash recovery, the difference between the log buffer in volatile memory and the log on mass storage is crucial: the log buffer is lost when the system crashes.

Furthermore, our description has ignored the fact that, to improve performance, most database systems support a cache in volatile storage of recently accessed database pages. Thus, when a transaction accesses a database item, x, the database system brings the database page(s) on mass storage containing x into the cache and then copies the value of x into the transaction's local variables. The page is kept in the cache under the assumption that there is a high probability that the transaction will later update x or read another item in the same page. If so, a page transfer will have been avoided since the page will be directly accessible (no I/O required) in the cache. We discuss caches in detail in Section 12.1.[1]

Use of the log buffer and the cache complicates write-ahead logging because they affect the time at which the database and the log on mass storage are actually updated. Two properties of the simple scheme described previously must be preserved: the write-ahead feature and the durability of commitment.

The write-ahead feature is preserved by ensuring that a dirty page in the cache is not written to the database until the log buffer containing the corresponding update record has been appended to the log. Two mechanisms are generally provided for this purpose. First, database systems generally support two operations for appending a record to the log: one that simply adds the record to the log buffer (and relies on the fact that the buffer will ultimately be flushed to the log) and one that adds the record to the buffer and then immediately writes the buffer to the log. The latter operation is referred to as a **forced** operation.

Whereas a normal (unforced) write simply registers a request to write a page to mass storage (the I/O operation is done at a later time), a forced write does not return control to the invoker until the write is complete. Since the log is sequential, when a routine requests a forced write of an update record, of necessity it forces all prior records into the log as well. When the routine resumes execution, it is guaranteed that these records are stored on mass storage. A request can then be safely made to write the corresponding dirty cache page to the database.

The second mechanism involves numbering all log records sequentially with a **log sequence number (LSN)**, which is stored in the log record. In addition, for each database page, the LSN of the update record corresponding to the most recent update of an item in the page is stored in that page. Thus, if a database page contains database items x, y, and z, and if the item updated most recently is y, the value of the LSN stored in the page is the LSN of the last update record for y.

With the forced write and the LSN, we are in a position to ensure the write-ahead feature. When space is needed in the cache and a dirty page, P, is selected to be written to mass store, the system determines if the log buffer still contains the update record whose LSN is equal to the LSN stored in P. If so, the LSN of P must be greater than the LSN of the last record in the log *on mass storage*. Therefore, the log buffer must be forced to mass storage before the page is written to the database. If not, the update record corresponding to the most recent update to an item in the page has already been appended to the log on mass storage and the page can be written from the cache immediately.

---

[1] Operating systems often maintain their own cache (e.g., Unix). This can cause problems for DBMSs since not only does the additional caching impact performance (a page brought in from the disk has to be copied from the operating system's cache to the DBMS's cache), but when the DBMS wants to write a page to disk, the page may get no further then the operating system's cache for an indeterminate period of time. We will see shortly that this is a major issue. As a result, DBMSs often use a *raw partition*: a raw disk that can be accessed directly without going through the operating system's file system.

Thus we see that to achieve the write-ahead feature, we must sometimes delay the writing of a cache page containing the new value of an item until the log buffer containing the corresponding update record (which contains the old value of the item) has been written to the log. In addition, to achieve durability, we must ensure that the *new* values of all items updated by T are in mass store before T's commit record is appended to the log on mass store. Otherwise, if a crash occurs after the commit record has been appended but before the new values are in mass store, the transaction will have been committed but the new values will have been lost, and hence durability in spite of system crashes has not been achieved.

There are two ways to ensure durability: a **force** policy and a **no-force** policy. With a force policy the force operation is also used for writing pages in the cache. Database pages in the cache that have been updated by T are forced out to the database before T's commit record is appended to the log on mass storage. The sequence of events when a transaction is ready to commit is as follows:

1. If the transaction's last update record is still in the log buffer, force it to the log on mass store. This ensures that all old values are durable.

2. If any dirty pages that have been updated by the transaction remain in the cache, force them to the database. This ensures that all new values are durable.

3. Append the commit record to the log buffer. When it is written to the log on mass store (see below) the transaction will be durable.

Figure 22.4 illustrates the sequence of events for a transaction, T, that has updated an item, x. The update record, with LSN j and before-image x_{old}, is in the log buffer, and the updated page, with the new value, x_{new}, and the LSN of the update record, is in the cache. The page is dirty: it has not yet been written to mass storage. Its original version, with value x_{old} and LSN s, $s < j$, is still on mass storage. The update record must be on mass storage (step 1 in the figure) before the dirty page can be written (step 2) to satisfy the write-ahead property. It might be necessary to force the log buffer to ensure this. Similarly, the dirty page must already be on mass storage before the commit record, with *LSN k, $k > j$*, can be appended to the log buffer, to ensure that the dirty page gets to mass storage before the commit record does (step 3). It is necessary to force the dirty page to ensure this.

Note that it is not necessary to force the commit record. However, the transaction is not committed until the commit record has been written to the log on mass storage. In some systems, the log buffer is forced when a commit record is appended to the buffer, thus causing the commit to take effect immediately. Other systems do not force the buffer at this time, so a write to the log is avoided, but the commit does not take effect until a later time when the log buffer is flushed. This protocol is referred to as **group commit** since the group of transactions whose commit records are in the log buffer when the next write occurs all commit at once.

A major drawback of the force policy for ensuring durability is that the writing of dirty cache pages and commit are synchronous. The pages modified by a transaction must be written to the database before the transaction can commit. Since page writes are slow, transaction commit is delayed and response time suffers.

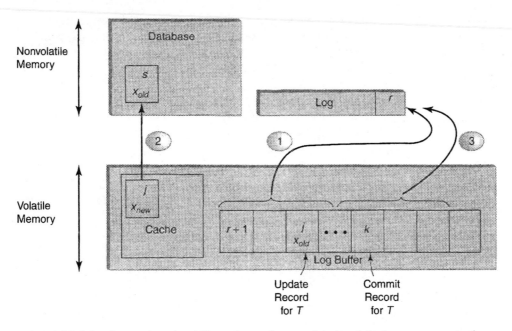

FIGURE 22.4 Implementing durability using a force policy. It might be necessary to force the pages that a transaction has updated out of the cache before the transaction's commit record is written to the log. Before the dirty page updated by T, with LSN value j, can overwrite the earlier version of the page, with LSN s, $s < j$, in the database, it might be necessary to force the log buffer (1) so that the update record with LSN equal to j is on mass storage. After the dirty page has been written, (2) the commit record for T can be appended to the log buffer (3). The log buffer can be written to the log at a later time.

Another disadvantage of the force policy has to do with hotspots—pages that are frequently modified by different transactions (for example, those holding system-related information). An LRU page replacement algorithm might choose not to write such a page out of the cache, but with a force policy the page will be written each time a transaction that has modified the page commits. Thus the force policy conflicts with the efficiency that is being sought by the LRU strategy. The advantage of a force policy, on the other hand, is that no action need be taken to recover a committed transaction after a crash. At the time the transaction's commit record is written to the log on mass store, all of the new values that it has created have been copied to the database on mass storage as well. With a no-force policy, which we describe in the next section, this is not necessarily the case.

22.2.2 Checkpoints and Recovery

In the previous section, we pointed out that the new value of an item, x, updated by a transaction, T, might still be in a dirty page in the cache in volatile memory when T requests to commit. To make T durable, the system must record the new value of x

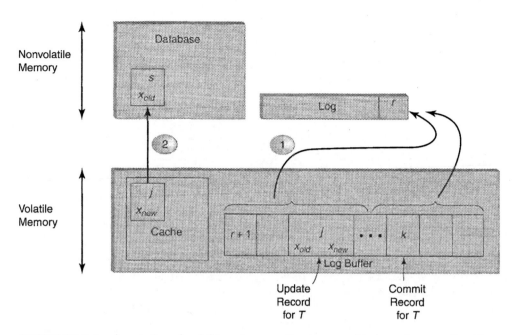

FIGURE 22.5 Implementing durability using an after-image with a no-force policy. The write-ahead feature requires that before a dirty page with LSN j updated by T can overwrite the earlier version of the page, with LSN s, $s < j$, in the database (2), the corresponding update record must be written to the log on mass storage (1). Although the commit record cannot be written before the update record, the relationship between the time the commit record is written and the time the dirty page is written is not constrained.

in nonvolatile memory before T's commit record is made durable by transferring it from the log buffer to the log. A common way of guaranteeing that the new value is in nonvolatile memory is to store after-images (in addition to before-images) in update records in the log.

In its simplest form, an **after-image**—sometimes called a **redo record**—of an updated item is a physical copy of the item's new value. Because all of T's update records precede its commit record in the log, when T's commit record is written to the log on mass storage, the new values of all database items it has created will be on mass storage as well. Then, even if the database page containing x has not been updated on mass storage at commit time and the system crashes after T commits, the new value of x can be installed in the database page on recovery using the after-image as shown in Figure 22.5. The write-ahead feature still requires that the update record be written to the log on mass storage before the dirty page is written to the database, but there is no longer any ordering specified between writing the commit record and writing the dirty page. In particular, the commit record can be written out to the log in durable storage before all the cached pages modified by T have been written.

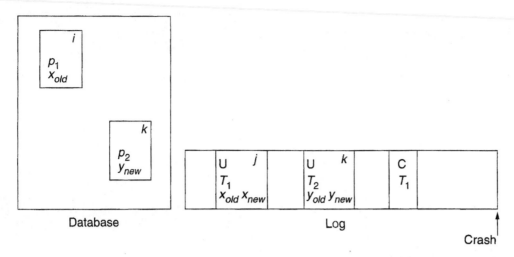

FIGURE 22.6 The state of mass storage seen by the recovery procedure after a crash has occurred and a no-force policy is used for implementing durability. Page p_1 was modified by committed transaction T_1 but was not written from the cache prior to the crash. This is indicated by the fact that the LSN in the page, i, satisfies $i < j$. Page p_2 was modified by transaction T_2, which was active at the time of the crash and was written prior to the crash.

The obvious advantage of a no-force policy is that a transaction can commit without having to wait until all of the pages it has updated have been forced from the cache. The disadvantage is that, when a crash occurs, recovery is complicated by the following possible situations:

- Some pages in the database might contain updates written by uncommitted transactions. These pages must be *rolled back* using the before-images in the log. This problem exists with either a force or a no-force policy.

- Some pages in the database might not yet contain updates made by committed transactions. These pages must be *rolled forward* using the after-images in the log. This problem exists only with a no-force policy.

The situation is shown in Figure 22.6.

We have already dealt with the rollback problem. The question now is how to identify those database pages that must be rolled forward.

One way of doing this is to use a **sharp checkpoint**. Before writing a checkpoint record, *CK*, to the log buffer, processing is halted and all dirty pages in the cache are written to the database. As a result, a recovery process scanning *CK* can conclude that all updates described by updated records in the log prior to *CK* were written to the database before the crash. If *CK* is the most recent checkpoint record, only updates recorded after it in the log *might* not have been written to the database. Using this information, recovery can proceed in three passes.

Pass 1. The log is scanned backward to the most recent checkpoint to determine which transactions were active at the time of the crash (and must be rolled back).

Pass 2. The log is scanned forward (replayed) from the checkpoint. The after-images in all update records (of committed, aborted, *and* active transactions) are used to update the corresponding items in the database. At the end of this pass, the database has been brought up to date with respect to all changes made by all transactions prior to the crash.

Pass 3. The log is scanned backward to roll back all transactions active at the time of the crash. The before-image in each update record of these transactions is used to reverse the corresponding update in the database. This pass completes when the begin records of all the transactions to be rolled back have been reached. The effect is the same as if all active transactions have aborted.

DO-UNDO-REDO is the name given to this general form of recovery. DO refers to the original action of the transaction in updating a data item, UNDO refers to the rollback that occurs in pass 3 if the transaction does not commit, and REDO refers to the rollforward that occurs in pass 2.

There are three things to consider in using this technique.

1. Transactions that update items and abort after the checkpoint pose a special problem. Their updates were rolled back before the abort record was appended to the log (before the crash), and, unfortunately, these updates will be restored to the database during pass 2. To ensure that the recovery process handles these transactions properly, a rollback operation should be treated as an ordinary database update performed by the transaction. An aborted transaction that had updated an item, x, will thus have two records in the log for that item, as shown in Figure 22.7:

   • An update record associated with the update it performed before aborting, with before-image x_{old} and after-image x_{new}
   • A **compensation log record** associated with the reversal of that update during abort processing, with before-image x_{new} and after-image x_{old}

   The compensation log record follows the update record in the log, and the abort record for the transaction follows the last compensation log record. The pass 2 scan first processes the update record and writes its after-image to the database; it then processes the compensation log record and writes its after-image to the database. The final value of x in the database is x_{old}. Since the transaction was not active at the time of the crash, its update and compensation log records are ignored during pass 3. Because compensation log records can be viewed as update records, this technique has the nice property of allowing committed and aborted transactions to be treated in the same way.

2. Some cache pages updated after the last checkpoint record was written might have been written to the database. Hence, in pass 2 some of the update records

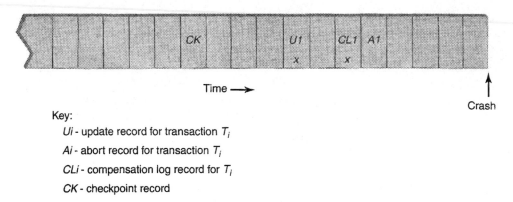

Key:

    Ui - update record for transaction T_i

    Ai - abort record for transaction T_i

    CLi - compensation log record for T_i

    CK - checkpoint record

FIGURE 22.7 Log showing records for an aborted transaction that has updated database variable *x*. The log contains both an update record and a compensation log record for *x*.

encountered describe updates already transferred to the database. Using the after-images in these records to update the database is unnecessary but not incorrect. In this case, the value of the item in the database and the after-image in the update record are identical, so the use of the after-image has no effect.[2]

3. There is a possibility that the system will crash (again) during recovery, in which case the recovery procedure will be reinitiated. Depending on the pass during which the second crash occurs, a before- or after-image might be applied to a database item a second time. An update using this image, however, is **idempotent**—that is, updating a database item with a particular after-image several times has the same effect as that of a single update. A crash during recovery (or, in fact, several crashes) therefore does not affect the outcome. When recovery finally completes, uncommitted transactions have been aborted and updates made by committed transactions have been recorded in the database.

    Idempotency is an essential feature of physical logging. We have seen its role in several places. It is assumed in the design of the write-ahead log since the application of the before-image to a page that had not yet been updated prior to the crash caused no problem. It is also assumed in the previous bullet, where in pass 2 the application of the after-image to a page that had been updated prior to the crash caused no problem.

Fuzzy checkpoints. The use of sharp checkpoints has one major disadvantage. The system must be halted to write dirty pages from the cache before the checkpoint record is written to the log buffer, and such an interruption of service is unacceptable in many applications. The procedure can be modified slightly to deal with this

---

[2] Note that several updates of the same database item might have been made after the checkpoint record is written. In that case, the after-image and the item would not be identical. However, after the most recent update record is processed in pass 2, the item will have been brought to the value it had before the crash.

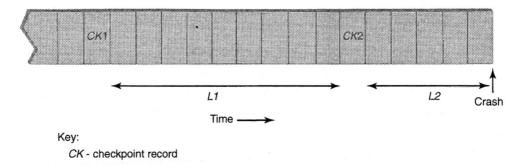

Key:
CK - checkpoint record

FIGURE 22.8 Use of fuzzy checkpoints.

problem by using **fuzzy checkpoints**. The dirty pages are not written from the cache when a checkpoint record is written to the log; instead, their identity is simply noted (in volatile memory), and they are subsequently written to the database (in the background) during normal processing. The only restriction is that the next checkpoint not be taken until all dirty pages noted at the previous checkpoint have been written.

Fuzzy checkpoints are illustrated in Figure 22.8. At the time *CK2* is appended to the log buffer, all dirty pages that were in the cache when *CK1* was appended have been written to the database. The modifications to these pages correspond to update records that appeared in the log prior to *CK1*. A database update corresponding to an update record in region *L1* of the log creates a dirty page, *P*, that might be in the cache when *CK2* is appended to the log buffer (*P* might also have been written by that time, but we cannot be sure). If *P* is still in the cache when *CK2* is appended to the log buffer, its identity is noted. We cannot guarantee that it has been written to the database until the next checkpoint record is appended. Since in the figure the system crashes before that happens, we must make the worst-case assumption that update records in regions *L1* and *L2* are not reflected in the database.

In order to bring the database to a state that contains all updates done prior to the crash, pass 2 of the recovery procedure must be modified so that the forward scan starts at *CK1* instead of *CK2*. Pass 1 still completes at *CK2* since its purpose is to identify transactions active at the time of the crash. Recovery is now slower than with sharp checkpoints. The trade-off between the speed of recovery and availability during normal operation must now be evaluated to decide whether sharp or fuzzy checkpoints are appropriate for a particular installation.

Archiving the log. We must deal with one other problem so that our description of logging and recovery is (relatively) complete. We have said that log records are appended to the log and never deleted. What happens when mass storage fills with log records? You might think that initial portions of the log can simply be discarded, but log records are often held for substantial periods of time for several reasons.

For one, the log contains information that might be useful for purposes other than recovery. For example, it contains the sequence of updates that brought each data item to its current state. This is useful if the enterprise is called upon to explain the state of an item. For example, an inventory database might record the number of widgets in stock, but the log records how frequently widgets have been sold and resupplied, an item of information that might be useful in streamlining business policy. The log can also be used to analyze performance. For example, if each record contains a timestamp, the response time of each transaction can be calculated. Another reason for not discarding log records is connected with media failure, which we discuss in Section 22.4.

If the log cannot be discarded, an initial portion of it must be moved offline, to tertiary storage (e.g., tape). This is referred to as **archiving**. Only recent log records need to be retained online, and the question now reduces to deciding at what point a portion of the log can be moved. Certainly, records of active transactions must be maintained online in order to handle abort and recovery quickly, so portions of the log containing records whose LSN is less than the LSN of the begin record of the oldest active transaction can be archived. However, the need to recover from media failure introduces other constraints, which we discuss in Section 22.4.

22.2.3 Logical and Physiological Logging

Physical logging has an important disadvantage, particularly when it is used in support of relational databases. A simple update might result in changes to a large number of pages in the database. In that case, the before- and after-images can be large and difficult to manage. For example, the insertion of a row into a table might require a complete reorganization of the page to which it is added. In addition to storing the row, the page's header information (which locates the items and the free space within the page) must be updated. Furthermore, similar changes must be made to each index referring to the table. If the index is a B^+ tree, page splitting might occur. All regions affected have to be recorded in the before- and after-images, making the update record large and increasing the I/O overhead necessary to manage the log. *Logical logging* is a technique for overcoming this problem.

With **logical logging**, instead of storing a snapshot of the updated item in the update record, the operation itself and its compensating operation are recorded. For example, the INSERT operation that inserts row r into table T has a compensating operation that deletes that record. Thus the undo record is *<delete, r, T>* and the redo record is *<insert, r, T>*. Rollback and rollforward now consist of applying the appropriate operation instead of simply overwriting the affected area as in physical logging. In this way, logical logging has the potential of reducing the overhead of log maintenance.

Undo operations (Section 20.7) can be used in the same way. For example, the UPDATE operation

```
UPDATE   T
SET      Grade = 'A'
WHERE    StudId= '1234567' AND CRSCODE = 'CS305'
```

does not have a compensating operation (since it is not one to one), but it has an undo operation that updates the value of Grade to what it was before the UPDATE was executed. Thus, if the grade was originally *I*, the undo is an identical update statement except that the set clause is SET Grade = 'I'.

Crash recovery is complicated by the fact that logical operations are not necessarily idempotent. For example, the result of executing the statement

```
UPDATE   T
SET      x = x+5
```

once is not the same as the result of executing it twice. So, in this case, the UPDATE operation is not idempotent. It is thus important to know, when processing an update or compensation log record during pass 2, whether or not the updated database page was flushed before the crash. If so, applying the redo operation in pass 2 can produce an incorrect state. In the above example, if the page on which *x* is stored was written to the database immediately prior to a crash, the logical redo during recovery will cause *x* to be incremented twice.

Fortunately, the problem is easily overcome using the LSN in the page. If during pass 2 it is found that the LSN in a page is greater than or equal to the LSN of an update record for an item in that page (indicating that the page already contains the result of applying the update operation), then the redo operation is not performed.

Unfortunately there is another, more serious, problem. We have implicitly assumed that logical operations are done atomically—for example, either tuple *t* has been inserted in a table or it has not. However, several pages might have to be modified in order to do an insertion, and hence the logical operation is not atomic with respect to failure: the system might crash after some, but not all, pages have been written. Hence, the data might be in an inconsistent state on recovery. Inconsistency here takes a different form. For example, the data page containing *t* might have been written to mass storage, but not the index page that should contain a pointer to *t*. This is different from the state that might be produced by an inconsistent transaction since in this case it is not the data values that are inconsistent but the way they are stored.

The application of a logical operation to an inconsistent state is likely to fail. With the insert example, the application of a logical redo record in pass 2 might result in two copies of *t* in the table. Furthermore, how do we even know whether the logical redo should be applied since the LSN of the data page is greater than or equal to the LSN of the update record for the insert, while the LSN of the index page is smaller? Idempotency guarantees that this is not a problem when physical logging is used. It is also not a problem for logical logging if the logical operation affects only a single page since then execution of the operation is atomic and the LSN in the page indicates whether or not it has happened.

To overcome this problem, **physiological logging** can be used. This technique is a compromise between physical and logical logging (the name is an abbreviation of the more descriptive *physical-to-a-page, logical-within-a-page*). A logical operation that involves multiple page updates is decomposed into multiple, logical, mini-operations in such a way that each mini-operation is confined to a single page (this is the physical dimension to physiological logging) and preserves page consistency. Hence, mini-operations can always be performed on pages, no matter when a failure occurs. The logical operation "Insert t into table T" might be decomposed into the mini-operation "Insert t into a particular page of the file containing T," which is followed by one or more mini-operations such as "Insert a pointer to t into a particular page of an index for T." Each mini-operation gets a separate log record, so recovery will work correctly even if a crash occurs while it is taking place. Since logical mini-operations are not necessarily idempotent, LSNs can be used (as described above) to determine which mini-operations have been applied to a page during pass 2.

In the example above, a mini-operation is a logical operation that is confined to a single page. An update record is created for each of these operations, containing the nature of the mini-operation (e.g., insert), its arguments (e.g., t), and the identity of the page affected. If the mini-operation or its inverse cannot be conveniently represented logically, a physical log record can be used. Thus, physiological logging involves a combination of both physical and logical logging.

22.3 Recovery in Deferred-Update Systems

In a deferred-update system, a transaction's write operation does not update the corresponding data item in the database. Instead, the information to be written is saved in a special area of memory called the transaction's intentions list. The intentions list is *not* stored durably. If the transaction commits, its intentions list is used to update the database. If the transaction aborts, its intentions list is simply discarded. Similarly, if the system crashes, no special action need be taken to abort active transactions since they have made no changes to the database.

To make committed transactions durable, the log and log buffer architecture is used. We assume physical logging for simplicity in the following discussion. When a transaction updates a data item, in addition to saving the new value in the intentions list, the system appends an update record containing an after-image to the log buffer. A before-image is not required in this case since the database item is not updated until after the transaction commits. At that time the transaction must be durable and the changes that it has made will not be undone; hence no before-image is needed. Since there is no before-image, the write-ahead policy does not apply.

At commit time, the system appends a commit record to the log buffer, which it then forces to the log in nonvolatile memory. Since the update records precede the commit record in the log, the force of the commit record guarantees that all update records are also on nonvolatile storage. After the commit operation has completed, the system updates the database from the transaction's intentions list. This corresponds to the write phase in an optimistic concurrency control. It then releases the transaction's locks and writes a **completion record** to the log.

The system might crash between the time the transaction has committed and the time the new values in its intentions list have been written to the database. Since the intentions list is lost, recovery must use the log to complete the installation of the transaction's updates. To speed this process, the system uses a variant of the checkpoint procedure described previously for a pessimistic system. The system periodically appends to the log a checkpoint record that now contains the identities of committed transactions whose intentions lists are currently being used to update the database.

On restart, the recovery process determines the identities of committed transactions whose intentions lists might not have been processed completely when the crash occurred. It does this in pass 1 by scanning the log backward until it gets to the first checkpoint. If the first record it finds for a transaction is a commit record, it knows that the intentions list for that transaction might not have been processed completely. If the first record for a transaction is a completion record, it knows that the intentions list had been processed completely. When the backward scan gets to the first checkpoint, it finds the names of the remaining transactions whose intentions lists had not been processed completely when that checkpoint record had been appended. Then, in pass 2, it uses the update records of the transactions it found in pass 1 to update the database. Recovery is no longer concerned with rolling back database updates performed by transactions that were active at the time of the crash since active transactions do not update the database. Hence, pass 3 is not required.

22.4 Recovery from Media Failure

Durability requires that no information written by a committed transaction be lost. A simple approach to achieving this is to maintain two separate copies of the database on two different nonvolatile devices (perhaps supported by different power supplies) such that simultaneous failure of both devices is unlikely. Mirrored disks are one way to implement this approach. A mirrored disk is a mass storage system in which, whenever a request to write a record is made, the same record is written on two different disks. Thus one disk is an exact copy, a mirror image, of the other. Furthermore, the double write is transparent to the requestor.

A database stored on a mirrored disk will be durable if a single media failure occurs. In addition, the system will remain available if one of the mirrored disks fails since it can continue to operate using the other. When the failed disk is replaced, the system must resynchronize the two. By contrast, when durability is achieved using a log (as described next), recovery from a disk failure might take a significant period of time, during which the system is unavailable to its users.

Even when an immediate update system uses a mirrored disk, it must still use a write-ahead log to achieve atomicity. Thus (in an immediate-update system), before-images are still needed to roll back database items when a transaction aborts, and after-images are still needed to roll forward database items when a transaction commits.

A second approach to achieving durability involves restoring the database from the log when a media failure occurs. One way to do this is to play the log forward *from the beginning* using the after-images in the update records. However, this is impractical because of the size of the log. It will take an enormous amount of time, during which the system is unavailable. A solution is to make an archive copy, or **dump**, of the database periodically.

Recovery using the dump depends on how it was taken. For some applications, the dump can be produced offline. The system is shut down at some convenient time by not allowing new transactions to be initiated and waiting until all active transactions have terminated. A dump is then taken, and when it has been completed, an **end dump** record is written to the log and new transactions can be accepted. To restore the database after a media failure, the system starts with the most recent dump file and then makes two passes through the log records that were appended after the most recent end dump record:

1. A backward pass in which it makes a list of all the transactions that committed after the dump was taken.

2. A forward pass in which it copies into the database the redo records of all of the transactions on the list.

Fuzzy dumps. With many applications, the system cannot be shut down. This calls for a **fuzzy dump**, taken while the system is operating. The fuzzy dump sequentially reads all records in the database, ignoring locks. Thus, transactions can be executing during the dump and can update records and later commit or abort. The dump program can read those records before or after they are written.

Consider an immediate-update system using physical logging. If the two-pass recovery procedure described above were used with a fuzzy dump, the second (forward) pass restores (using after-images in the log) the value of each database item written by a transaction that committed after the dump started, whether or not the dump had in fact read that value. As shown in Figure 22.9(a), the value of x recorded in the dump reflects the effect of T, but the value of y does not. Since T commits after the dump starts, however, the after-images of all changes it has made will be used in reconstructing the database starting from the dump. This is unnecessary for x, but rolls y forward to its proper value. The procedure also handles the case shown in Figure 22.9(b), in which a transaction starts after the dump has completed and later aborts since its update records are ignored in pass 2.

However, the two-pass procedure does not handle two situations correctly:

- The database pages written by a transaction, T, that commits before the dump starts might not be written to the database until after the dump completes. In that case, the dump does not contain the new value written by T, but T is not included in the list of committed transactions, obtained in pass 1, whose update records are used to roll the database forward in pass 2. This happens because the commit record of T precedes the dump record and the forward scan begins with the dump record.

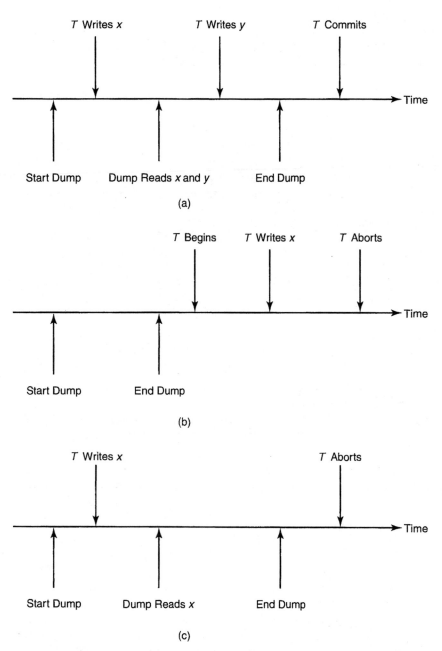

FIGURE 22.9 Effect of transactions being active while a dump is taken.

- The dump might read a value written by a transaction that is active during the dump but later aborts. In that case, the value recorded in the dump will not be rolled back. This situation is shown in Figure 22.9(c).

To overcome these problems, a fuzzy dump uses the same strategy employed for fuzzy checkpoints.

1. Before starting the dump, the checkpoint record *CK2*, shown in Figure 22.8, is appended to the log, followed by a **begin dump** record. As described in connection with that figure, the presence of *CK2* in the log ensures that all dirty pages in the cache when *CK1* was appended have been written to the database and so are recorded in the dump.
2. Compensation log records are used to record the reversal of updates during abort processing.

To restore the database, the system first reloads the dump file. Then it makes three passes through the log.

Pass 1. This is a backward pass starting at the end of the log and continuing to the most recent checkpoint record. During this pass, the system makes a list, *L*, of all transactions that were active when the failure occurred.

Pass 2. This is a forward pass starting at the second most recent checkpoint record preceding the begin dump record (corresponding to *CK1* in Figure 22.8) and continuing to the end of the log. During this pass, the system uses the redo records of all transactions to roll the database forward from the state recorded in the dump.

Pass 3. This is a backward pass starting at the end of the log and continuing to the earliest begin record of a transaction in *L*. During this pass, the system uses the undo records of all transactions in *L* to roll back their effect.

All redo records (including compensation log records) for updates that might not be included in the dump are replayed in pass 2. Thus, when pass 2 completes, the database will be rolled forward from the state recorded in the dump to the state it had when the failure occurred. Only the effects of transactions that were active when the media failed need to be reversed, and they are dealt with in pass 3.

In summary, media recovery requires the most recent dump of the database and that portion of the log containing all update records of all updates that might not be in the dump. Note that the required portion of the log will generally be greater than the portion required for crash recovery. Both portions must include the begin record of the oldest active transaction. However, crash recovery additionally requires that the log contain the two most recent checkpoint records, while media recovery requires the two checkpoint records preceding the start of the dump. Furthermore, if the most recent archived copy of the database is damaged, the same algorithm can be used to restore an earlier copy.

With physiological logging, instead of unconditionally applying before- and after-images during passes 2 and 3, the LSN is used, as described in Section 22.2.3, to determine whether or not an operation should be applied.

BIBLIOGRAPHIC NOTES

One of the first discussions on logging and recovery technology is in [Gray 1978]. Much of the current technology is based on the implementations of System R [Gray et al. 1981] and Aries (Algorithm for Recovery and Isolation Exploiting Semantics) [Mohan et al. 1992]. Excellent summaries of the technology are in [Haerder and Reuter 1983; Bernstein and Newcomer 1997; Gray and Reuter 1993]. A more abstract view of failures, in which recovery and serializability are integrated into a single model, is described in [Schek et al. 1993].

EXERCISES

22.1 Describe the contents of each of the following log records and how that record is used (if at all) in rollback and in recovery from crashes and media failure.

    a. Abort record
    b. Begin record
    c. Begin dump record
    d. Checkpoint record
    e. Commit record
    f. Compensation log record
    g. Completion record
    h. Redo record
    i. Savepoint record
    j. Undo record

22.2 Suppose that the concurrency control uses table locks and that a transaction performs an operation that updates the value of one attribute of one tuple in one table. Does the update record have to contain images of the entire table or just the one tuple?

22.3 Suppose that a dirty page in the cache has been written by two active transactions and that one of the transactions commits. Describe how the caching procedure works in this case.

22.4 Suppose that the database system crashes between the time a transaction commits (by appending a commit record to the log) and the time it releases its locks. Describe how the system recovers from this situation.

22.5 Explain why the log buffer need not be flushed when an abort record is appended to it.

22.6 Explain why the LSN need not be included in pages stored in the database when physical logging is used together with a cache and log buffer.

22.7 Suppose that each database page contained the LSN of the commit record of the last transaction that has committed and written a database item in the page, and suppose that the system uses the policy that it does not flush the page from the cache until the LSN of the oldest record in the log buffer is greater than the LSN of the page. Will the write-ahead policy be enforced?

22.8 The second step of the sharp checkpoint recovery procedure is as follows: The log is scanned forward from the checkpoint. The after-images in all update records are used to update the corresponding items in the database. Assuming a locking concurrency control in which locks are held until commit time, show that the updates can be performed in either of the following orders:

a. As each update record is encountered in the forward scan, the corresponding database update is performed (even though the update records for different transactions are interleaved in the log).

b. During the forward scan, the update records for each transaction are saved in volatile memory, and the database updates for each transaction are all done at once when the commit record for that transaction is encountered during the forward scan.

22.9 In the sharp checkpoint recovery procedure, explain whether or not the system needs to obtain locks when it is using the after-images in the log to update the database.

22.10 Consider the following two-pass strategy for crash recovery using a sharp checkpoint and physical logging: (1) The first pass is a backward pass in which active transactions are rolled back. Active transactions are identified as described in Section 22.2. The pass extends at least as far as the begin record of the oldest active transaction or the most recent checkpoint record, whichever is earlier in the log. As update records for these transactions are encountered in the scan, their before-images are applied to the database. (2) The second pass is a forward pass from the most recent checkpoint record to roll forward, using after-images, all changes made by transactions that completed since the checkpoint record was written (compensation log records are processed in the same way as ordinary update records so that aborted transactions are handled properly). Does the procedure work?

22.11 In order for logical logging to work, a logical database operation must have a logical inverse operation. Give an example of a database operation that has no inverse. Suggest a procedure involving logical logging that can handle this case.

22.12 Consider using the crash recovery procedure described in Section 22.2 (intended for physical logging) when logical logging is used. Explain how the procedure has to be modified to handle crashes that occur during recovery. Assume that the effect of each update is confined to a single page.

22.13 Explain why, in a deferred-update system, the write-ahead feature that is a part of immediate-update systems is not used when a database item is updated.

22.14 Explain why in a deferred-update system, the system does not first copy the intentions list into the database and then append the commit record to the log.

22.15 Assume that the system supports SNAPSHOT isolation. Describe how a sharp (nonfuzzy) dump could be taken without shutting down the system.

22.16 a. Explain how the log is implemented in your local DBMS.

b. Estimate the time in milliseconds to commit a transaction in your local DBMS.

22.17 The LSN stored in a page of the database refers to an update record in the log describing the most recent update to the page. Suppose that a transaction has performed the last update to a page and later aborts. Since its update to the page is reversed, the LSN in the page no longer refers to the appropriate update record. Why is this not a problem in the description of logging in the text?

22.18 An airlines reservation system has demanding performance and availability standards. Do the following play a role in enhancing performance? Do they enhance availability? Explain your answers.

    a. Page cache
    b. Log buffer
    c. Checkpoint record
    d. Physiological logging
    e. Mirrored disk

PART SIX

Distributed Applications and the Web

In this part we will discuss some of the newest and most exciting applications of databases and transaction processing systems: systems that operate in distributed environments and, in particular, on the Internet.

In Chapter 23 we will discuss the back-end implementations of transaction processing systems: the various architectures used in the implementation, including two- and three-tiered systems and the TP monitor. Then we will describe how these architectures can be implemented on the Internet and how Web applications servers are built using J2EE.

In Chapter 24 we will discuss how the ACID properties are (or are not) implemented in a distributed environment. The chapter also contains a description of protocols that support data replication.

In Chapter 25 we will describe the emerging front-end standards for business-to-business interactions over the Internet: the XML based interfaces that enable servers to interact smoothly over the Web without human intervention. The role of transactions in these standards is highlighted.

In Chapter 26 we will introduce encryption techniques and describe how they are used in the implementation of security in Internet interactions, including SSL and certificates. We will then discuss a number of XML-based encryption protocols.

23

Architecture of Transaction Processing Systems

Transaction processing systems are among the largest software systems in existence. They must be built to respond to a wide spectrum of applications, so the demands on them vary greatly. At one extreme are single-user systems accessing a local database. At the other extreme are multiuser systems in which a single transaction can access a heterogeneous set of resource managers that are distributed across a network, and in which thousands of transactions can be executing each second. Many such systems have critical performance requirements and are the foundation of vital enterprises.

To create and maintain such a complex system, a functional decomposition into modules that perform distinct tasks is essential. In this chapter, we discuss the modular structure of these systems, taking a historical perspective. We start with the earliest and simplest systems and then move forward in time and complexity, introducing new elements one step at a time. We describe the various tasks that must be performed, show how they are mapped into modules, and explain how these modules communicate in each organization.

Some of the largest and most sophisticated transaction processing systems are on the Internet. At the end of the chapter, we describe how the architectures described earlier in the chapter are implemented in this context.

23.1 Transaction Processing in a Centralized System

Due to hardware limitations, the earliest transaction processing systems were centralized. All modules resided on a single computer—for example, a single PC or workstation servicing a single user, or a mainframe computer with many connected terminals servicing multiple users concurrently. We consider these two cases separately.

23.1.1 Organization of a Single-User System

Figure 23.1 shows how a single-user transaction processing system might be organized on a PC or workstation. The user module performs **presentation and application services**. Presentation services displays forms on the screen, and it handles the flow of information from and to the user through the forms. A typical cycle of

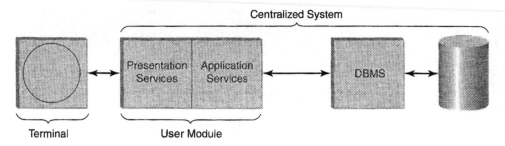

FIGURE 23.1 Single-user transaction processing system.

activity might start with presentation services displaying a form on which the user enters information in textboxes and then submits a request for service by making an appropriate click. Presentation services recognizes the click, and it calls application services to satisfy the request, passing to it the information that has been input. Application services checks the integrity constraints not specified in the schema and executes a sequence of steps in accordance with the rules of the enterprise.

Application services must communicate with the database server. For example, the application service that registers a student for a course in the Student Registration System has to make sure that the student has taken the prerequisite courses and must add the student's name to the class roster. Its requests to access the database might be implemented in embedded SQL statements that are sent to the database server.

Note that the user does not interact directly with the database server. Instead the user invokes programs that act as intermediaries. To allow a user direct access to the database server—for example, by specifying the SQL statements to be executed directly from the terminal—is dangerous since a careless or malicious user could easily destroy the integrity of the database by writing erroneous data. Even allowing the user read-only access to the data has drawbacks. For one thing, it is generally not a simple matter to formulate an SQL query to return the information a user might want to see. For another, there might be information in the database that some users are not allowed to see. Grade information for a particular student that must not be given to any other student but can be made available to a faculty member is one example.

These problems can be solved by requiring that the user access the database indirectly through application services. Since the application services is implemented by the application programmer, one can hope that its accesses to the server are correct and appropriate.

Although a program within application services can be viewed as a transaction, the full power of a transaction processing system is not required in this case. For example, with a single-user system only one transaction is invoked at a time, so isolation is automatic. Mechanisms might still be needed to implement atomicity and durability, but they can be relatively simple for the same reason.

Although one can argue that single-user systems are too simple to be included in the category of transaction processing systems, they illustrate two of the essential services that must be provided in all of the systems we will be discussing: presentation services and application services. In particular, one advantage of separating presentation services from application services is that the designers of one need not be concerned with the details of the other. Thus the designers of application services can concentrate on the business rules of the enterprise and do not have to be concerned with the details of dealing with the presentation of the input and output. In fact the hardware or software drivers involved with presentation services can be changed without having any effect on the application services software (assuming the interface between the two services remains the same).

23.1.2 Organization of a Centralized Multiuser System

Transaction processing systems supporting an enterprise of any size must permit multiple users to have access to them from multiple locations. Early versions of such systems involved the use of terminals connected to a central computer. In situations in which the terminals and the computer were confined to a small area (for example a single building), communication could be supported over hard-wired connections. More frequently, however, the terminals were located at remote sites and communicated with the computer over telephone lines. In either case, a major difference between these early systems and current multiuser systems is that the terminals were "dumb." They had no computing capability. They served as I/O devices that presented a simple, generally textual interface to the user. In terms of Figure 23.1, presentation services (beyond those built into the terminal hardware) were minimal and had to be executed at the central site. While such systems could be spread over a substantial geographical area, they were not considered distributed since all of the computing and intelligence resided at a single site.

The introduction of multiuser transaction processing systems motivated the development of transactions and the need for the ACID properties. Since multiple users interact with the system concurrently, there must be a way to isolate one user's interaction from another. Because the system is now supporting a major enterprise, as contrasted with an individual's database, issues of atomicity and durability become important.

Figure 23.2 shows the organization of early multiuser transaction processing systems. A user module, containing both presentation and application services, is associated with each user and runs at the central site. Since a number of users execute concurrently, each user module is executed in a separate process. These processes run asynchronously and can submit requests for service to the database server at any time. For example, while the server is servicing a request from one application to execute an SQL statement, a different application might submit a request to execute another SQL statement. Sophisticated database servers are capable of servicing many such requests simultaneously, with the guarantee that each SQL statement will be executed as an isolated and atomic unit.

As we have seen, however, such a guarantee is not sufficient to ensure that the interactions of different users are appropriately isolated. To provide isolation, the application program needs the abstraction of a transaction. A transaction support

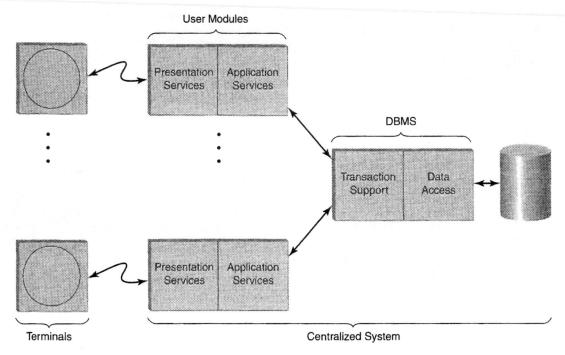

FIGURE 23.2 Multiuser centralized transaction processing system.

module is therefore provided within the database server to implement commands such as begin_transaction, commit, and rollback and to provide atomicity, isolation, and durability. This module includes the concurrency control and the log. Since presentation, application, and database services are all supplied at the same site, this organization is referred to as a **single-tiered model**.

23.2 Transaction Processing in a Distributed System

Modern transaction processing systems are generally implemented on distributed hardware involving multiple independent computers at geographically distinct sites. The ATM machine is separate from the bank's computer, and a computer at a ticket agent's site is separate from the airline's main reservation system. In some cases, an application might communicate with several databases, each stored on a different computer. The computers are connected in a network, and modules located at any site can exchange messages in a uniform way.

The architecture of these systems is based on the client/server model. With distributed hardware, the client and server modules need not reside at the same site. The location of the database servers might depend on a number of factors, including

■ *Minimization of communication costs or response time.* For example, in an industrial system consisting of a central office, warehouses, and manufacturing facilities, if most of the transactions accessing employee records are initiated at the central office, these records might be kept at that location and the inventory records kept at the warehouses.

■ *Ownership and security of data.* For example, in a distributed banking system with a computer at each branch office, a branch might insist that the information about its accounts be kept locally in its own computer.

■ *Availability of computational and storage facilities.* For example, a sophisticated database server can reside only at a site that includes extensive mass storage facilities.

When a transaction processing system is distributed, its *database portion* might still be *centralized;* that is, it might utilize a single database server residing on a single computer. Alternatively, the database might be *distributed;* that is, it might utilize multiple database servers residing on the same or different computers. Thus, a transaction processing system can be distributed but have a centralized database.

23.2.1 Organization of a Distributed System

The organization of a distributed transaction processing system evolved from the multiuser system shown in Figure 23.2. As a first step, terminals are replaced by client computers, so the user module, responsible for presentation and application services, now resides on a client computer and communicates with the database server. This is referred to as a **two-tiered model**. Figure 23.3 shows the organization of a distributed transaction processing system with a centralized database. Application programs on client machines initiate transactions, which, as shown in Figure 23.2, are handled by the transaction support module on the database server to ensure atomicity and isolation.

The database server might export an SQL interface so that an application program on the client computer can send a request to the database server to execute a particular SQL statement. However, several important problems arise when client machines directly use such an interface. One problem has to do with the integrity of the database. As with a single-user system, our concern is that the client machines, which reside at client sites, might not be secure and hence might not be trustworthy. An erroneous or malicious application program, for example, can destroy database integrity by submitting an improper update statement.

Another significant problem relates to network traffic and the ability of the system to handle a large number of clients. A user wishing to scan a table might execute SQL statements that cause all of the rows of the table to be transferred from the database server to the client machine. Since these machines can be widely separated, considerable network traffic might be required even though the result of the transaction might involve only a few of the rows transferred. Unfortunately, the network can support only a small number of clients if such requests have to be processed in this way.

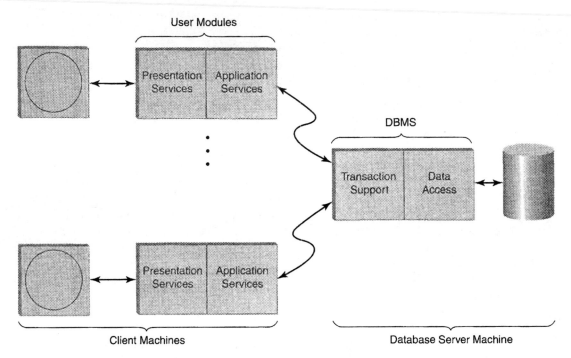

FIGURE 23.3 Two-tiered multiuser distributed transaction processing system.

Stored procedures.   One way to address this problem is through stored procedures. Instead of submitting individual SQL statements, the application program on the client computer requests that a particular stored procedure be executed by the database server. In effect, the application program is now provided with a high-level, or more abstract, database interface. For example, a database server for a bank might make `deposit()` and `withdraw()` stored procedures available to application programs.

Stored procedures have several important advantages.

■ They are assumed to be correct and their integrity can be maintained at the database server. Application programs executed on client computers are prohibited from submitting individual SQL statements. Since the only way the client computer can access the database is through the stored procedures, the consistency of the database is protected.

■ The designer of the application program does not have to know the schema of the database in order to design and build the application programs. And if, at some later time, the schema of the database has to be changed for some reason, the stored procedures that access the database might have to be recoded, but none of the application programs that call those procedures need to be changed.

■ The SQL statements of a stored procedure can be compiled and prepared in advance and therefore can be executed more efficiently than interpreted code.

■   The service provider can more easily authorize users to perform particular application-specific functions. For example, only a bank teller, not a customer, can issue a certified check. Managing authorization at the level of individual SQL statements is difficult. A withdraw transaction might use the same SQL statements and access the same tables as a transaction that produces a certified check. The authorization problem can be solved by denying the customer direct access to the database and instead allowing him permission to execute the withdraw stored procedure, but not the certified check stored procedure.

■   By offering a more abstract service, the amount of information that must be communicated through the network is reduced. Instead of transmitting the intermediate results of individual SQL statements between the application program on the client machine and the database server, all processing of intermediate results is now done by the stored procedure at the database server, and only the initial arguments and final results pass through the network. This is how the table scan described above can be performed. Data communication is thus reduced, and a larger number of clients can be served. However, the database server must be powerful enough to handle the additional work that the execution of stored procedures entails.

The three-tiered model.   The idea of providing higher-level services to the client computer can be carried one step further. Figure 23.4 shows a **three-tiered model** of a distributed transaction processing system, which contrasts with the two-tiered system of Figure 23.3. The user module has been divided into a presentation server and an application server that execute on different computers. Presentation services, at the client site, assembles the information input by the user, makes certain validity checks on the information (e.g., type checking), and then sends a request message to the application server, executing elsewhere in the network.

The application server executes the application program corresponding to the requested service. As before, this program implements the rules of the enterprise, checking conditions that have to be satisfied in order for the request to be executed and invoking the appropriate stored procedures at the database server to carry it out. The application program views the servicing of a user request as a sequence of tasks. Thus, in the design of the Student Registration System given in Section C.7.2, the registration transaction performs (among others) the tasks of checking that the course is offered, that the student has taken all of the course prerequisites, and that the student has not registered for too many courses, before finally performing the task of registering the student.

Each task might require the execution of a complex program, and each program might be a distinct stored procedure on the database server. The application program controls transaction boundaries by invoking begin_transaction and commit and hence can cause the procedures to be executed within a single transaction. Moreover, it encourages task reuse. If tasks are chosen to perform generally useful functions, they can be invoked as components of different application programs. In the general case, the transaction is distributed, having the application program as a root, and the

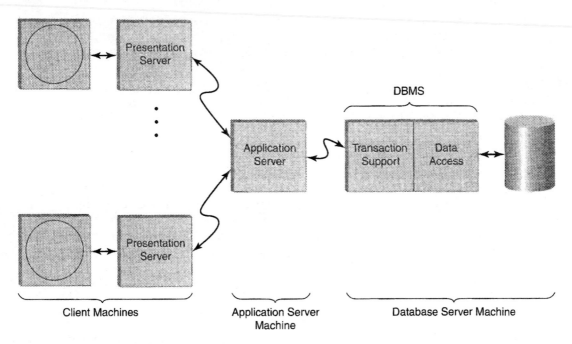

FIGURE 23.4 Three-tiered distributed transaction processing system.

stored procedures are the component subtransactions executing on different servers. In this case, more elaborate transaction support, which we discuss in Section 23.4, is required.

The application can be thought of as a workflow (Section 19.3.6), consisting of a set of tasks that must be performed in some specified order (although all tasks in this case are computational). The application server can be thought of as a workflow controller, controlling the flow of tasks required to implement the user's request.

Figure 23.4 shows a single application server with multiple clients. Since the servicing of a single client request might take a substantial amount of time, a number of client requests might be pending at the same time. Hence, the application server must handle requests concurrently in order to maintain an adequate level of performance. It might do this by allocating a process for each user. Unfortunately, processes carry substantial overhead, and thus the number of processes that can be used in this way is limited. Hence, application servers are often constructed using a multithreaded process (instead of multiple processes), with each user assigned to a different thread. Overhead is reduced since thread switching is much more efficient than process switching. Furthermore, since the information needed to describe each thread within a multithreaded process is much less than the information needed to describe a process, the total amount of information that must be maintained is greatly reduced. The application server can maintain a pool of threads to avoid dynamic thread creation, and it can allocate a thread to a user as needed.

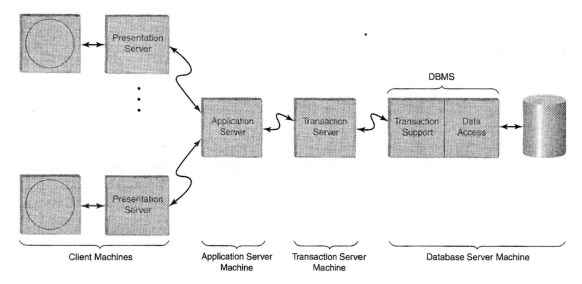

FIGURE 23.5 Three-tiered distributed transaction processing system with tasks executed in a transaction server.

Multiple instances of the application server might exist—particularly if there are many clients. Each instance might reside on a separate computer, and each computer might be connected to a distinct subset of the clients. For example, an application server and the clients it services might be geographically close to one another. Alternatively, a client might connect to any application server.

In some organizations, the stored procedures, which implement the tasks invoked by the application program, are moved out of the database server and executed in a separate module called a **transaction server**, as shown in Figure 23.5. The transaction server is generally located on a computer physically close to the database server in order to minimize network traffic, whereas the application server is located near or at the user site. The transaction server now does the bulk of the work since it submits the SQL statements to the database server and processes the data returned. The application server is primarily responsible for sending requests to the transaction servers.

Although not shown in Figure 23.5, there might be multiple instantiations of the transaction server. This is an example of a **server class**, which is used when it is expected that the server will be heavily loaded. Instances of the class might run on different computers connected to the database server in order to share the transaction load arising from concurrently executing workflows. More generally, there might be multiple database server machines storing different portions of the enterprise's database—for example, a billing database on one server and a registration database on another. A particular transaction server might then be capable of executing only a subset of the tasks and be connected to a subset of the database servers. In that case, the application server must invoke the appropriate

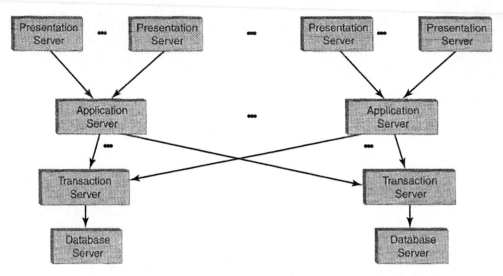

FIGURE 23.6 Interconnection of presentation, application, and transaction servers in a three-tiered architecture.

transaction server to get a particular task done. This selective invocation is frequently referred to as **routing**. An application program acting as a distributed transaction routes requests to multiple transaction servers, as shown in Figure 23.6.

Separating the transaction server from the database server is useful in the following situations:

1. Different components of an enterprise use different sets of procedures to access a common database. Separating these sets on different transaction servers allows each component to more easily control its own procedures. For example, the accounting system and the personnel system of a large corporation might use completely different procedures that access the same data.

2. A single procedure must access several different databases on different server machines.

3. The database server must handle requests arising from a large user population and hence can become a bottleneck. Moving stored procedures off the database machine eases this load.

Among the advantages of separating the client machines from the application server machine are these:

1. The client computers can be smaller (and hence cheaper). This is particularly important in applications involving hundreds, and perhaps thousands, of client machines.

2. System maintenance is easier since changes in enterprise rules (causing changes to the workflow program) can be localized to the application server computer instead of to all client computers.

3. The security of the system is enhanced since individual users do not have physical access to the application server computer and so cannot easily change the application programs.

Case Study: The three-tiered architecture and levels of software abstraction.
From a software-engineering viewpoint, one approach to designing a complex application is to structure it hierarchically, as a sequence of levels of abstraction. Each level is built using the abstractions implemented in the level preceding it. In terms of our implementation of the Student Registration System, the lowest level is the conceptual level supported by the DBMS, which supplies the abstraction of individual SQL statements. The middle level consists of the methods checkCourseOffering(), checkCourseTaken(), checkTimeConflict(), checkPrerequisites(), and add-RegisterInfo() (described in Section C.7.3), which uses the SQL statements. The next level of abstraction is the complete transactions, such as Register(). Note that by using the middle level, transactions are shielded from database-related concerns (i.e., the actual SQL queries). The top level of abstraction includes the modules for interacting with the user, for instance, a GUI that allows the student to fill out the forms required for course registration.

We now see that a correspondence can be established between the levels of abstraction in the application design and the three-tiered architecture. In the Student Registration System, presentation services software sees the abstraction of the total registration interaction provided by the application server. The application server, in turn, sees the abstraction of the individual checking tasks provided by the transaction server, which in turn uses the conceptual level abstraction provided by the DBMSs.

23.2.2 Sessions and Context

Each of the architectures we have discussed involves **sessions** between clients and servers. A session exists between two entities if they are communicating with one another to perform some job and each maintains some state information, or **context**, concerning its role in that job. Two types of sessions are particularly important in the context of transaction processing systems: communication sessions and client/server sessions. We discuss them next.

Communication sessions. In the two-tiered model, presentation/application servers communicate with database servers; in the three-tiered model, presentation servers communicate with application servers, which in turn communicate with database (or transaction) servers. The handling of a client request often involves the efficient and reliable exchange of multiple messages between communicating modules. In this case, communication sessions are generally established. A communication session requires that each communicating entity maintains context information, such as the sequence numbers of the messages transmitted in each direction (for reliably transmitting messages), addressing information, encryption keys, and the current direction of communication. Context information is stored in a data structure called a **context block**.

Messages must be exchanged just to set up and take down a communication session, which makes the cost of these activities nontrivial. As a result, it is wasteful for the presentation server to create a communication session each time a client makes a request or for the application server to create a session each time it has to get service from a database server. Instead, long-term communication sessions are created between servers. Each session is **multiplexed**: it carries messages for many concurrently executing clients.

One advantage of using a three-tiered model is made apparent by Figure 23.6. A large transaction processing system might involve thousands of client machines and multiple database servers. In the worst case, each client in a two-tiered model would have a (long-term) connection to each database server and the total number of connections would be the product of these two numbers—a potentially large number. The overhead of establishing these connections and the storage costs for context blocks within each database server would become excessive.

By introducing the application level, each client now needs to establish a single connection to an application server and the application server needs to establish connections to the database servers. However, a connection between an application server and a database server can be shared—multiplexed—by multiple transactions running on behalf of multiple users on that application server. In the best case only a single connection exists between an application server and a database server. Then, if there are n_1 client machines, n_2 application servers, and n_3 database servers, the worst-case number of connections in a two-tiered architecture is $n_1 * n_3$, whereas the number of connections in a three-tiered architecture is $n_1 + (n_2 * n_3)$. Since n_2 is much less than n_1, a substantial reduction in the number of connections results. Hence, a three-tiered architecture scales better as the system grows to handle a large client population.

Client/server sessions.   A server may need to maintain context information about each client for which it provides a service. Consider a database server servicing a client that accesses a table through a cursor. The client executes a sequence of SQL statements (OPEN, FETCH) to create a result set and retrieve its rows. Context has to be maintained by the server so that it can process these statements. Thus, for a FETCH statement, the server must know which row was returned last. Alternatively, the server managing a store's Web site maintains shopping-cart context for each client. A typical client interaction involves a sequence of requests that update the state of the cart. Furthermore, the server does not want to have to authenticate the client and determine what it is authorized to do each time a request is made. Hence, authentication and authorization information can also be stored in the context.

The context used by the server for a particular client/server session can be maintained in a number of different ways.

- *Stored locally at the server.* The server can maintain its client context locally. Each time the client makes a request, the server looks up the client's context and interprets the request using that context. Notice that this approach works well if the client always calls the same server, but care must be taken if the requested service is provided by an arbitrary instance of a class of servers. In that case, successive requests might be serviced by different instances, and context stored locally by one will not be available to another. Furthermore, if the number of clients is large and sessions are long, the server will be maintaining context for many clients simultaneously and session maintenance may be a serious burden.

- *Context stored in a database.* The server can store each client's context in a database. This approach can avoid the problem of server classes, if all instances of the class can access the same database.

- *Context stored at the client.* The context can be passed back and forth between client and server. The server returns its context to the client after servicing a request. The client does not attempt to interpret the context but simply saves it and passes it back to the server when it makes its next request. This approach relieves the server of the need to store the context and also avoids the problem of server classes. Sensitive information in the context that should not be accessible to the client can be encrypted.

When context information is stored on the server or in a database, the server has the problem of locating a client's context when a request from that client arrives. Frequently this problem is solved using a **context handle**, which is a pointer to where the server has stored the client's context. The handle is passed by the server to the client with each server response and is returned by the client to the server in the next request. The interpretation of the handle is totally under the control of the server. The client should not modify it in any way. One example of a context handle is the **cookie** used for client/server applications over the Internet. Sometimes cookies contain some context information as well as a pointer to additional information stored at the server site.

We have so far focused only on the context associated with a sequence of requests made by a client to a particular server and have overlooked the important issue that context must also be associated with a transaction as a whole (which can include multiple requests to *different* servers and hence might encompass multiple sessions). The need for this is illustrated in Figure 23.7, in which a client has set up one session with server $S1$ and another session with server $S2$; both servers have used server $S3$ to fulfill the client's requests. The problem is that issues such as isolation and atomicity are associated with the transaction as a whole and not with any particular session. For example, locks (discussed in Chapter 20) are used to implement isolation. $S3$ must use transaction context to determine that a lock acquired in handling a request from $S1$ for a particular transaction can be used in servicing a request from $S2$ for the same transaction.

When a user logs on at a client machine, a client/server session, with associated context, is established between the client and the application server to handle the user. A thread in the application server (a multithreaded process) is allocated to support the server's end of the session. Client context can be stored in the thread's private stack, and the process's global data, data shared among all threads, can store

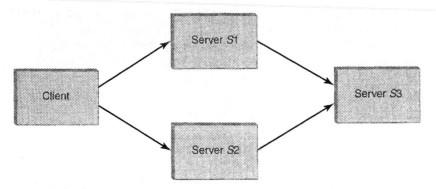

FIGURE 23.7 Transaction context must be maintained when two servers access the same server on behalf of a single transaction.

the state of any resources maintained by the server for use by all clients. Multiplexed communication sessions between the application server and transaction servers are an example of such a resource.

23.2.3 Queued Transaction Processing

The two-tiered model shown in Figure 23.3 is referred to as **data centered**, whereas the three-tiered model shown in Figure 23.5 is referred to as **service centered**. In both, the client and server engage in **direct transaction processing**. The client invokes a server and then waits for the result. The service is provided as quickly as possible and a result is returned. The client and server are thus synchronized.

With **queued transaction processing**, the client enqueues a request on a queue of pending requests to the server and then performs other tasks. The request is dequeued when the server is ready to provide the service. A request from a presentation server, for example, is often enqueued in front of an application server until an application server thread can be assigned to handle the requests. Later, when the service is completed, the server can enqueue the result on a separate result queue. The result is dequeued still later by the client. The client and server are thus unsynchronized.

With recoverable queues, queue operations are transactional. The handling of a request in a queued transaction processing system might involve three transactions, as shown in Figure 23.8. The client executes transaction T_1 to enqueue the request prior to service; the server then executes transaction T_2, which dequeues the request, services it, and enqueues the result on the reply queue; and the client finally executes transaction T_3 to dequeue the result from the reply queue. Figure 23.8 should be compared with Figure 19.8 on page 803. The main difference is that in Figure 19.8 a forwarding agent is used to dequeue the request from the request queue and invoke a (passive) server whereas in Figure 23.8 the server (actively) dequeues the request.

Queued transaction processing offers a number of advantages. The client can input a request at times when the server is busy or down. Similarly, the server can return results even if the client is unprepared to accept them. Furthermore, if the

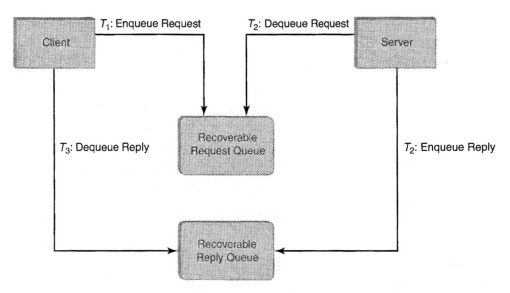

FIGURE 23.8 Queued transaction processing involves two queues and three transactions.

server crashes while the request is being serviced, the service transaction is aborted and the request is restored to the request queue. It is serviced when the server is restarted, without any intervention by the client. Finally, when multiple servers become available, the queue can be integrated into an algorithm that balances the load on all servers.

23.3 The TP Monitor: An Overview

A TP monitor is a collection of software modules that augment the services provided by an operating system. An operating system creates the abstraction of concurrently executing *processes* that can communicate with one another using a message-passing facility, and provides them with shared access to the physical resources of the computer system. The TP monitor extends this to create the abstraction of *transactions* that execute concurrently in a distributed environment. As shown in Figure 23.9, a TP monitor can be viewed as a layer of software between the operating system and the application routines.

Examples of the services provided by a TP monitor are

- Communication protocols of various kinds
- Security of distributed applications, including authentication and encryption
- Atomicity, isolation, and durability of distributed transactions

These services can be provided in an application-independent way; they have general utility and hence can be used in many different distributed applications.

FIGURE 23.9 Layered structure of a transaction processing system.

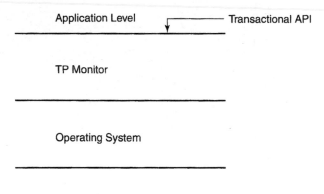

A number of TP monitors exist. Tuxedo and Encina are early examples. Microsoft Transaction Server (MTS) is a more recent entry into the field, and Java Transaction Service (JTS) is a specification of a Java-based TP monitor. All of them include or specify a set of application-independent services that, though needed in a transaction processing system, are not usually provided by an operating system.

Homogeneous and heterogeneous transaction processing systems.   Early transaction processing systems were **homogeneous**, involving the hardware and software of a single vendor. Such systems utilized interfaces designed by the vendor—**proprietary interfaces**—that enabled its products to be interconnected in a variety of ways. Even when these interfaces were published, it was difficult to incorporate products from other vendors into the system because different vendors used different interfaces.

Many current transaction processing systems are **heterogeneous**, involving the products of multiple vendors: hardware platforms, operating systems, database managers, and communication protocols. Homogeneous systems have evolved into heterogeneous systems for the following reasons:

- Newer applications often require the interconnection of older, legacy systems produced by different vendors that had previously operated independently. For example, over the years each department in a company might have developed its own purchasing system. Now the company requires a company-wide purchasing system that interconnects all local systems.

- There are more vendors supplying hardware and software components, and users demand the ability to incorporate the best components available regardless of the supplier.

The implementation of heterogeneous systems requires vendors to agree on (1) standardized, nonproprietary interfaces—**open interfaces**—that define the content and format of the information that must be exchanged in an interaction and (2) communications software to transmit that information. If a legacy system that uses a nonstandard, proprietary interface is to be included, a **wrapper** program can be written as a bridge between interfaces.

Homogeneous transaction processing systems are frequently referred to as **TP-Lite**. Heterogeneous transaction processing systems tend to be more complex since there is more emphasis on strict boundaries between the various functions, and are referred to as **TP-Heavy**. We will be discussing TP-Heavy systems in what follows.

TP monitors are particularly important in the architectures of heterogeneous systems, where the abstraction of a transaction must be implemented and maintained in the context of the interconnection of a number of different systems, possibly from different vendors.

Middleware. To promote the development of open distributed systems in general—and transaction processing systems in particular—various software products have been developed that are frequently referred to as middleware. **Middleware** is software that supports the interaction of clients and servers, often in heterogeneous systems. Many of the modules provided by a TP monitor fall under the general heading of middleware.

JDBC and ODBC (Sections 8.5 and 8.6) are two examples of middleware that allow an application to interact with database servers from a variety of vendors. CORBA (Section 14.6), another example, allows applications to access objects distributed through a network.

23.3.1 The Services Provided by a TP Monitor

The following services are generally provided by a TP monitor.

Communication. The TP monitor supports the abstractions used by application program modules to communicate with one another. The application views these abstractions as an API. The abstractions are implemented within the TP monitor using the lower-level message-passing facility provided by the operating system. Two abstractions often provided are remote procedure call and peer-to-peer communication. Remote procedure call is commonly used by application programs due to its simplicity and its natural relationship to the client/server model. Peer-to-peer communication is more complex, but more flexible. System level modules tend to communicate in this way in order to use the flexibility to optimize performance. Communication with most DBMSs is done through peer-to-peer connections. We discuss communication in Section 23.5.

Global atomicity and isolation. One goal of a TP monitor is to guarantee global atomicity and isolation. The subtransactions of a distributed transaction might execute at a variety of different resource managers. Frequently these are database managers that implement atomicity and isolation locally for individual subtransactions. Unfortunately, local isolation and local atomicity do not guarantee global isolation and global atomicity. To guarantee these properties globally, the actions of the resource managers must be coordinated.

The TP monitor is responsible for providing this coordination. In a TP-Lite system, coordination might be integrated into the vendor's resource managers, while in a TP-Heavy system coordination is generally the responsibility of a separate, off-the-shelf module called a **transaction manager**. When a distributed transaction requests to commit, the transaction manager engages in an exchange of messages with the resource managers, called an **atomic commit protocol**, to ensure that they either all commit their subtransactions or all abort them. We discuss transaction managers in more detail in Section 23.4.

In order for a transaction manager to coordinate the individual resource managers participating in a distributed transaction, it must be informed whenever the transaction invokes a new resource manager. Thus, each time the application initiates a new subtransaction (by communicating with a resource manager for the first time), the transaction manager must be informed. Hence, the transaction manager's role is tied in with the communication abstraction used by the application. Support for global atomicity thus involves both the transaction manager and the communication facility. This is a complex issue, which we will discuss separately in Section 23.5.3.

In contrast to database managers, some resource managers might provide no local support for isolation and atomicity. For example, a transaction might access files maintained by a file server. Access to them should be isolated and atomic. Thus, if the transaction updates two files, no concurrent transaction should see one update and not the other. If the file server does not support isolation, a transaction might use a lock manager provided by the TP monitor. The manager implements general purpose locks. An application can associate a lock in the lock manager with a file in the file server. A transaction that accesses a file should set the corresponding lock (by calling the lock manager) before calling the file server to do the access. This corresponds to the manual locking discussed in Section 20.5. If all transactions follow this protocol, accesses to the file can be synchronized in the same way as accesses to data items in a database server that provides a concurrency control.

Similarly, if the file server does not log before-images, it does not support atomicity. In that case the TP monitor might provide a log manager that the transaction can explicitly use to durably store the images so that changes made by an aborted transaction can be rolled back.

Load balancing and routing. Large transaction processing systems use server classes. If the servers in a class are distributed across a network, availability increases and, since they can execute concurrently, performance is improved. When a client invokes a service supported by a server class, the TP monitor can route the call to any of the servers in the class. Some TP monitors use load balancing as a criterion in this choice. They might use a round robin or randomizing algorithm to distribute the load across the servers, or they might keep information on the number of sessions (perhaps as measured by the number of peer-to-peer connections) that each server in the class is handling and choose the one whose load is the smallest. Load balancing can be integrated with queueing when queued transaction processing is provided.

Recoverable queues. In addition to supporting queued transaction processing, recoverable queues are generally useful for asynchronous communication between application modules and are provided by many TP monitors.

Security services. The information used in a transaction processing system often needs to be protected. Encryption, authentication, and authorization are the foundation of protection and for that reason are often supported by TP monitors. We will discuss these services in Chapter 26.

Threading. We have seen (for example, in connection with an application server) that threads reduce the overhead of handling a large number of clients in a transaction processing system. Unfortunately, not all operating systems support multithreaded processes. Some TP monitors provide their own threading to deal with this. In such cases, the operating system schedules a process for execution, unaware that the process contains monitor code to support threads internally. The code selects the particular thread to be executed next.

Supporting servers. TP monitors provide a variety of servers that are useful in a transaction processing system. For example, a timing server might keep clocks on different computers synchronized; a file server might be provided as a general utility.

Nested transactions. Some TP monitors provide support for nested transactions.

Since we have introduced a number of terms in this chapter that are often confused, we will review their definitions at this point in our discussion.

- A **transaction server** executes the application subroutines that implement the basic units of work from which an application program is built.

- A **transaction manager** is a resource manager that supports the atomic execution of distributed transactions.

- A **TP monitor** includes the transaction manager, transaction servers, and the underlying middleware necessary to tie together the modules of the transaction processing system.

- A **transaction processing system** includes the TP monitor as well as the application code and the various resource managers, such as DBMSs, that make up the total system.

23.4 The TP Monitor: Global Atomicity and the Transaction Manager

A major issue in the implementation of distributed transactions is global atomicity. While atomicity at any particular server can be implemented by that server, global atomicity requires the cooperation of all servers involved in the transaction: either they all agree to commit their subtransactions or they all agree to abort them. Cooperation is achieved through the use of a protocol.

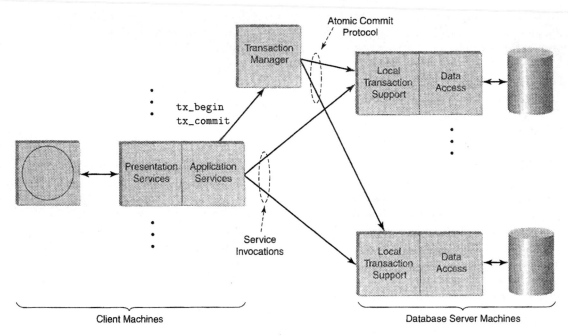

FIGURE 23.10 Two-tiered multidatabase transaction processing system in which a transaction can access several database servers.

The algorithm for implementing global atomicity can be integrated into the individual servers in a TP-Lite system. In TP-Heavy systems, the algorithm is often implemented in a separate middleware module, shown in Figure 23.10, called a transaction manager. For simplicity, the figure shows a two-tiered system, but three tiers are frequently involved.

In both cases, the module for supporting global atomicity responds to commands from the application program (perhaps an application server) that set the boundaries of a distributed transaction, and coordinates the commitment of its subtransactions. To do this, it must know when the transaction as a whole and each of its subtransactions are initiated. Here we describe the process as it works in TP-Heavy systems, which, because of their heterogeneity, rely on interface standards. One such standard is the X/Open standard API.

X/Open was defined by X/Open Company Limited, an independent worldwide organization supported by many of the largest information systems suppliers and software companies. Part of this API is the tx interface, which supports the transaction abstraction and includes tx_begin(), tx_commit(), and tx_rollback(). These procedures are called from the application and implemented in the transaction manager. To be specific in describing concepts related to distributed transactions, we base our discussion on this standard.

The application calls tx_begin when it wants the transaction manager to know that it is starting a distributed transaction. The transaction manager records the existence of a new distributed transaction and returns an identifier that uniquely names it. Hence, the transaction manager can be regarded as a resource manager in which the resource managed is the set of transaction identifiers. Later, when the application requests service from a server the transaction manager is informed of the existence of the new subtransaction at the server's site.

The application calls `tx_commit` to inform the transaction manager of the distributed transaction's successful completion. The transaction manager then communicates with each server hosting a subtransaction in such a way that either all subtransactions commit or all abort, thus making the distributed transaction globally atomic. An atomic commit protocol controls the exchange of messages for this purpose. In this role, the transaction manager is frequently referred to as the **coordinator**. (We will discuss the most commonly used atomic commit protocol in Section 24.2.)

Each of the `tx` procedures is a function that returns a value that indicates the success or failure of the requested action. In particular, the return value of `tx_commit()` indicates whether the distributed transaction actually committed or aborted and the reason for an abort. For example, the distributed transaction might be aborted if the transaction manager discovers that one of the database servers has crashed or that communication to that server has been interrupted.

23.5 The TP Monitor: Remote Procedure Call

The general distributed transaction model presented in Section 19.2.2 involves a set of related computations performed by a number of modules, which might be located at different sites in a network and which communicate with one another. For example, an application module might request service from a database server, or the application itself might be distributed and one application module might call for the services of another.

Consider a course-registration application program, $A1$ (perhaps executing in the context of a transaction on an application server), that invokes a stored procedure on a database server, $D1$, to register a student in a course, and then invokes a procedure in a remote application program, $A2$, to bill that student. $A2$ might in turn invoke a stored procedure on a different database server, $D2$, to record the charge. Both $D1$ and $A2$ are viewed as servers by $A1$ (and $D2$ is viewed as a server by $A2$), but only $D1$ and $D2$ are resource managers in the sense that they control resources whose state must be made durable. Hence, only $D1$ and $D2$ need participate in the atomic commit protocol. If $A1$ is executing in the context of a transaction, T, we say that T **propagates** from $A1$ to $A2$ and $D1$[1] as a result of the invocations made in $A1$.

Although message passing underlies all communication, a TP monitor generally offers an application several higher-level communication abstractions. The one

---

[1] Some TP monitors permit violations of this general rule. For example, $A1$ can specify that $A2$ not be included in T. Similarly, $A2$ can itself specify that it not be included in T. In addition, commands have been defined that permit a routine to temporarily exclude itself from the current transaction and then resume its participation at a later time.

chosen might depend on the structure of the application. In some cases there is a strict hierarchical relationship between the modules. For example, a client module might request service from a server module and then wait for a reply. In this case, a procedure-calling mechanism is particularly convenient. In other applications a module might treat the other modules it interacts with as peers. In that case, the peer-to-peer communication paradigm is appropriate. Often legacy modules are involved, and their mode of communication is fixed.

In this section, we discuss communication using remote procedure call, and in Section 23.6 we discuss peer-to-peer communication. In Section 23.7 we discuss event communication, which is particularly appropriate for handling exceptional situations.

A network-wide message-passing facility can support communication between modules, but it suffers from the deficiency that the interface it presents to the modules is not convenient to use. Invoking operating system primitives for sending and receiving a message is neither elegant nor simple. Users prefer the procedural interface of a high-level language and benefit from the type checking automatically provided by a compiler. For these reasons, it is desirable to create a procedure-calling facility that makes invoking a procedure in a possibly remote module similar to calling a local procedure (one linked into the caller's code). Such a facility supports **remote procedure call**, or RPC [Birrell and Nelson 1984, 1990].

Using RPC, a distributed computation takes on a tree structure since a called procedure in one module can in turn invoke a procedure in another. The procedure that initiates the computation as a whole is referred to as the **root**.

The execution of a remote procedure is handled by a thread in the target module. Local variables are allocated in the thread's stack. When the procedure returns, the stack is deallocated and hence cannot be used to store the context of the distributed computation in anticipation of future calls. For this reason, RPC communication is referred to as **stateless**. If context must be maintained over several calls, the called procedure must store it globally or it must be passed back and forth using a context handle (see Section 23.2.2).

23.5.1 Implementation of Remote Procedure Call

RPC is implemented using **stubs**. A client stub is a routine linked to a client. A server stub is a routine linked to a server. The routines serve as intermediaries between the client and server as shown in Figure 23.11. A client calls a server procedure using that procedure's globally unique name. The name is a character string known to the users of the system. The call does not invoke the procedure directly, however. Instead, it invokes the client stub, which locates the server (using directory services, which we will describe shortly) and sets up a connection to it. The stub generally converts the arguments from the format used by the client to the format expected by the server and then packs them, together with the name of the called procedure, into an invocation message, a process called **marshaling of arguments**, and uses the message-passing facility provided by the operating system to send the message

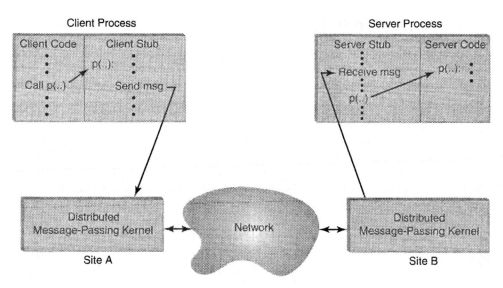

FIGURE 23.11 Use of stubs to support remote procedure call.

to the server. In its message-passing role, the operating system is often referred to as a **distributed message-passing kernel**.

In the figure, the server happens to be on a different machine. The server stub receives invocation messages from all clients. It extracts the arguments in a particular message and invokes the appropriate procedure using a standard (local) procedure call. The result of the call is returned to the server stub, which sends it back to the client stub using the message-passing facility, and the client stub returns it to the client (recall that the client stub was invoked by the client application using a conventional procedure call). Thus, RPC is a high-level communication facility implemented by the procedure call mechanism coupled with the operating systems' message-passing facility.

The stub mechanism has several advantages. Only the stubs interface to the operating system. It appears to the client and to the server that they are communicating with each other directly through a conventional procedure call. Furthermore, the stub mechanism makes a call to a server on a local machine and a call to a server on a remote machine appear identical to the client: in both cases it appears as an invocation of a local procedure linked into the client code. Hence, the client code need not be aware of the physical location of the server. It uses the same mechanism to communicate with a local server as with a remote server. Finally, if modules are moved, the client and server code need not be changed. This feature is generally referred to as **location transparency**.

In connecting clients to servers, stubs must deal with the possibility of failure. Failure in a single-site system is relatively infrequent and generally comes in the form of a crash. Failures in a distributed system can include not only the crash of a particular computer but also a communication failure. Such a failure might be relatively permanent (a communication line can be down for an extended period) or transient (a message can be lost but subsequent messages might be transmitted correctly). With hundreds, and possibly thousands, of connected computers, communication lines, routers, and so forth, the probability that all are functioning correctly is significantly smaller than the probability of a single site functioning correctly. Since RPC requires the services of a number of these units, failure handling plays a more prominent role.

Failure is not necessarily total. Large parts of the system might still be functioning, and the application might be required to remain operational despite the failure of some of its components. Stubs can play a role in this. For example, if a stub times out because a response to a prior invocation message is not received, it might resend the message to the same server, or perhaps to a different server in the same class, or abort the client. Unfortunately, there might be a number of reasons why a response is not received—message loss, server crash—and an action appropriate in one case might not be appropriate in another. A number of sophisticated algorithms have been formulated to respond to failures, and these can add considerable complexity to the stub.

In addition to adding to the complexity of the stub, network failures can compromise location transparency since the nature of the failure might be visible to the application through the RPC interface. For example, if the caller is informed that the server is unavailable, it is apparent that the called procedure is remote. Other issues that affect location transparency are the absence of global variables and the fact that parameters are not passed by reference. Finally, since multiple machines are now involved, new security issues might arise. We discuss some of these security issues in Section 26.4.1.

23.5.2 Directory Services

A server is known to its clients by its interface. The interface is published and contains the information a client needs to invoke the server's procedures: procedure names and descriptions of parameters. As discussed in Sections 14.5.1 and 14.6, an interface definition language (IDL) is a high-level language that is used to describe the interface. An IDL compiler compiles the interface description into a header file and server-specific client and server stubs. The header file must be included with the application program when it is compiled, and the client stub is linked to the client code in the resulting module. The use of an IDL file to describe the server interface encourages the development of open systems. The client and server can be built by different vendors as long as they agree on the interface through which they communicate.

The server interface, however, does not specify the identity and location of a server process that will actually execute the procedure. The location might not be known at compile time, or it might change dynamically. Furthermore, the server might be implemented as a class, with instances executing on different nodes in a network. The system must therefore provide a run-time mechanism to bind a client to a server dynamically.

Binding can be achieved by requiring that a server, S, when it is ready to provide service to clients, register with some central naming service available to all clients. Such a service is often provided by a separate **name**, or **directory**, **server**.

To register, S supplies to the directory server its globally unique name (the character string used by clients) and network address, the interfaces it supports, and the communication protocol(s) it uses to exchange messages with clients (these are the messages used to implement RPC communication). For example, S might accept messages requesting service only over a TCP connection. This is an example of a server (S) acting as a client with respect to another server (the directory server).

The client stub submits a server name or the identification of a particular interface to the directory server and requests the network address and communication protocol to be used to communicate with a server having that name or supporting that interface. Once this information has been provided, the client stub can communicate directly with the server.

Although the directory server is itself a server, it must have some special status since clients and servers have to be able to connect to it without having to use another directory server (to avoid the chicken-and-egg problem). Hence, it should reside at a well-known network address that can be determined without using a directory server.

A directory server can be a complex entity. One source of that complexity is a result of the central role it plays in distributed computing. If the directory server fails (perhaps because the host on which it resides crashes), clients can no longer locate servers and new distributed computations cannot be established. To avoid such a catastrophe, directory service itself might be distributed and/or replicated across the network. However, this raises new problems: making sure that replicas are up to date and that a client anywhere in the network can locate a directory server that has the information it requires.

The **Distributed Computing Environment** (DCE) [Rosenberry et al. 1992] is an example of middleware that supports distributed systems such as TP monitors.[2] Among the services it provides are RPC between modules running on different operating system platforms. Directory services are provided in connection with this as well as other basic features, such as the security services that we will discuss in Chapter 26.

23.5.3 The Transaction Manager and Transactional RPC

The transaction manager's role in implementing global atomicity is illustrated in Figures 23.12 and 23.13. The X/Open system calls `tx_begin()`, `tx_commit()`, and `tx_rollback()` to invoke procedures within the transaction manager (*TM*) that initiate and terminate transactions. When an application initiates a transaction, T, it invokes `tx_begin()`. As shown in Figure 23.12, *TM* returns a transaction identifier, *tid*, that uniquely identifies T. The transaction identifier is retained in the client stub.

---

[2] The TP monitor Encina is based on DCE.

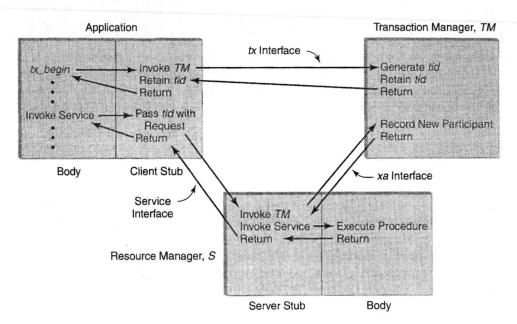

FIGURE 23.12 Communication with the transaction manager to implement transactional remote procedure call.

Subsequently, whenever the client invokes a resource manager, S, the client stub appends *tid* to the call message to identify the calling transaction to S. If this is the first request by T to S, the server stub at S notifies *TM* that it is now performing work for T by calling *TM*'s procedure xa_reg() and passing *tid*. Thus, *TM* can record the identities of all resource managers that participate in T. S is referred to as a **cohort** of T. xa_reg() is part of X/Open's xa interface between a transaction manager and a resource manager. When a transaction manager and a resource manager both support the xa interface, they can be connected in support of distributed transactions even though they are the products of different vendors.

Note that the standard defines both the tx interface, between an application and a transaction manager, and the xa interface, between a transaction manager and a resource manager, but it does not define an interface between an application and a resource manager. That interface is defined by the resource manager itself.

Since procedure calling is a synchronous communication mechanism (the caller waits until the callee has completed), when a subtransaction completes its computation, all subtransactions it has invoked have also completed. Hence, when the root of the transaction tree finishes its computation, the entire distributed transaction is complete and the root can request that the transaction be committed by calling the transaction manager procedure tx_commit(), as shown in Figure 23.13. (If the client wishes to abort T, it calls tx_rollback().) The transaction manager must then make sure that termination is globally atomic—either all servers invoked by T commit or all abort. It does this by engaging in an atomic commit protocol in which

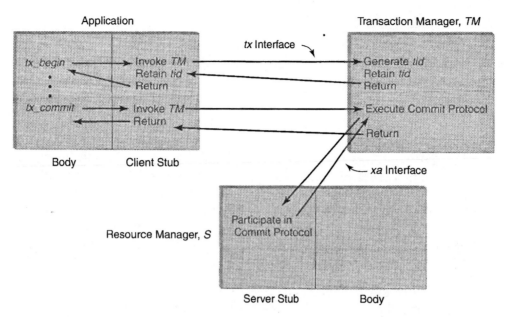

FIGURE 23.13 Communication with the transaction manager to perform an atomic commit protocol.

it serves as coordinator and the resource managers serve as cohorts. The most widely used atomic commit protocol, *two-phase commit*, will be described in Section 24.2.

To execute a commit protocol, the transaction manager must communicate with all cohorts (e.g., *S*), as shown in Figure 23.13. It does this by using callbacks that the resource managers have registered with it. In addition to the normal service interface that a resource manager presents to an application, it offers a set of **callbacks** to the transaction manager. These are resource manager procedures that the transaction manager can use for a variety of purposes. Each resource manager might offer different callbacks depending upon the services it is capable of performing. Those that can engage in an atomic commit protocol register callbacks for that purpose.[3] If a cohort does not register such callbacks, it cannot participate in the protocol and global atomicity cannot be guaranteed.

The procedure-calling mechanism we have just discussed (involving the use of *tid* and the xa interface) is thus an enhanced version of the RPC mechanism and is one ingredient used to implement global atomicity. This mechanism is provided by the TP monitor and referred to as a **transactional remote procedure call**, or **TRPC**.[4]

Global atomicity is implemented by the stubs and the transaction manager. It involves the following:

---

[3] Callbacks to support distributed savepoints are another example.

[4] TRPC can be implemented as an enhancement of the authenticated RPC to be discussed in Section 26.6.

- Establishing an identity for T with the transaction manager when T is initiated
- Including T's identity as an argument in procedure call messages
- Notifying the transaction manager whenever a new resource manager is invoked
- Executing the atomic commit protocol when the transaction completes (Section 24.2)

An additional obstacle that must be overcome to achieve global atomicity (and that must be handled by TRPC) is caused by failures in the network. We saw in Section 23.5 that a number of failure situations might prevent the client stub from receiving a reply to an invocation message sent by it to a server, S, and that these situations are indistinguishable to the client stub. The actions a stub might take can lead to several different outcomes. In particular, if the stub re-sends the invocation message, the service might be performed twice. Furthermore, if the invocation message is not re-sent, the stub cannot assume that the service was not performed since the message might have been received and processed at S, but the reply message might have been lost.

The actions of the stub when a failure occurs must ensure that the requested service is performed exactly once at S, allowing the transaction to continue, or that the requested service is not performed at all and (assuming that the service cannot be provided at a different server) the transaction is aborted. Thus, the stub ensures what is called **exactly once semantics**.

The situation is further complicated by the fact that S might have invoked another server, S', in performing the requested service. If the site at which S executes has crashed, and S' executes elsewhere in the network, an **orphan** results: The task at S' has no parent process (i.e., S) to which it reports. The stub has the nontrivial job of guaranteeing exactly once semantics under these circumstances.

23.6 The TP Monitor: Peer-to-Peer Communication

With remote procedure call, a client sends a request message to a server to invoke a procedure and waits for a reply. Hence, communication is synchronous. The subtransaction is performed at the server and a reply message is sent when service is completed. The request/reply pattern of communication is asymmetric, and the client and server do not execute concurrently.

In contrast, **peer-to-peer communication** is symmetric. Once a connection is established, both parties use the same send and receive commands to converse. It is also more flexible since any pattern of messages between peers can be supported. The send is an asynchronous operation, meaning that the system buffers the message that has been sent and then returns control to the sender. Unlike RPC, the sender can thus execute concurrently with the receiver. The sender might perform some computation or send additional messages, and thus a stream of messages might flow from the sender to the receiver before the receiver replies. As with RPC, peer-to-peer communication is supported by a lower-level message-passing protocol (such as TCP/IP or SNA).

As usual, flexibility comes at the price of added complexity. Each party must be prepared to deal with the pattern of messages used by the other, which means that there is now more room for error. For example, if each process is in a state in which it is expecting a message from the other before it can continue, deadlock results. Peer-to-peer communication is often supported by TP monitors not only because of its added flexibility, but also because many database servers (often running on mainframes) use this mode of communication.

23.6.1 Establishing a Connection

A variety of peer-to-peer protocols exist. Our discussion in this section is based on IBM's commonly used SNA protocol LU6.2 [IBM 1991] and an API that interfaces to it.

To begin a conversation, a module must first set up a connection to the program with which it wishes to communicate. This is done with an `allocate()` command that has as an argument the target program's name. A new instance of the program is created to handle the other end of the conversation. In contrast to RPC, location transparency is not a goal: the requester explicitly provides the address of the receiving program.

Returning to the example of a distributed computation in Section 23.5, $A1$ might set up a peer-to-peer connection to $A2$. A new instance of the billing program is initiated to receive the messages sent by $A1$ over the connection.

While connections in LU6.2 are half duplex, connections generally might be half or full duplex. With **half duplex**, messages can flow in either direction over the connection, but at any given time one module, A, is the sender (the connection is currently in **send mode** for A) and the other module, B, is the receiver (the connection is currently in **receive mode** for B). A sends an arbitrary number of messages to B and then passes send permission to B. This makes B the sender and A the receiver. When B finishes sending messages, it passes send permission back to A and the process repeats. This contrasts with a **full duplex** connection, in which either party can send at any time. With half duplex, the current direction of the connection is a part of its context.

When a program in module A, executing as part of a transaction, sets up a connection to a program instance in module B, the transaction propagates from A to B. Once the connection has been established, A and B are equal partners and all messages over the connection pertain to that transaction. Client/server context can be conveniently stored at each end of the connection in local variables, allowing each arriving message to be interpreted by the receiving program with respect to the context. For this reason, protocols built using peer-to-peer interactions are often **stateful**.

A module can engage in an arbitrary number of different peer-to-peer connections concurrently. Because any module participating in the transaction can set up a new connection to any other module, the general structure of a distributed transaction is typically that of an acyclic graph, as shown in Figure 23.14, in which nodes represent the transaction's participants and links represent connections. The graph

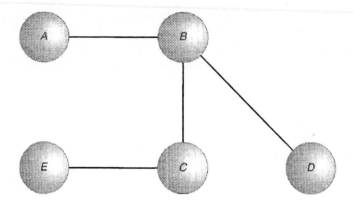

is acyclic because a new instance of a program is created whenever a connection is set up. Hence, nodes in the graph represent program instances, and it is not possible for a program to set up a connection to an existing instance. In the figure, for example, C and D might represent different instances of the same program. No node occupies a unique position analogous to the root node of a procedure-calling hierarchy.

23.6.2 Distributed Commitment

The rules governing commitment are consistent with the equal status of the participants in a transaction that uses peer-to-peer connections: any node can request to commit the transaction. In contrast to the hierarchical model of distributed transactions, where only the root module can request to commit (and therefore, since communication is synchronous, all subtransactions must have completed at that time) transactional peers are not synchronized. When a participant decides to commit, its transactional peers might still be executing and not yet ready to commit. Hence, an integral part of committing a transaction in the peer-to-peer model is ensuring that all participants have completed. As a result, the atomic commit protocol must both guarantee that all participants have completed and that they either all commit or all abort. The following description is based on [Maslak et al. 1991].

In a properly organized transaction, a single module, A, initiates the commit. All of A's connections must be in send mode at this time. A initiates the commit by declaring a **syncpoint**, which causes a **syncpoint message** to be sent over each of A's connections. A then waits until the commit protocol completes.

Participant B, connected to A, might not have completed its portion of the transaction when it receives the syncpoint message. When B has completed and all of its connections (other than the connection to A) are in send mode, it also declares a syncpoint, which causes a syncpoint message to be sent over all of its connections (other than the connection to A). In this way, syncpoint messages spread through the transaction graph. A node having only one connection is a leaf node in the tree (e.g., E in the figure). After receiving a syncpoint message, it also declares a syncpoint when it completes, although no additional syncpoint messages result.

Eventually, each peer has declared a syncpoint, and all are synchronized at their syncpoint declarations. When a leaf node declares a syncpoint, a response message is sent back up the tree to the root. When all leaves have responded, the root can conclude that the entire transaction has completed. A description of the atomic commit protocol in the context of peer-to-peer communication is provided in Section 24.2.3.

The syncpoint protocol requires that only one module initiate it and that a module declare a syncpoint only if (1) all of its connections are in send mode and it has not yet received a syncpoint message, or (2) all but one of its connections are in send mode and it has received one syncpoint message over the connection in receive mode. If the protocol is not used correctly, the transaction is aborted. For example, if two participants initiate the protocol by declaring a syncpoint, syncpoint messages converge on some intermediate node over two connections. This violates the protocol and causes the transaction to abort.

The implementation of global atomicity uses a module similar to the transaction manager, called a **syncpoint manager**. In a manner similar to the technique used with RPC, each time A invokes a resource manager for the first time, the syncpoint manager is informed of a new participant in the transaction. Similarly, if A sets up a connection to B, the syncpoint manager is informed. The syncpoint manager must direct the atomic commit protocol among the participants of the transaction (in this case, A is included as a participant).

23.7 The TP Monitor: Event Communication

When modules communicate using RPC, the callee, or server, is structured to accept service requests. It exports procedures that clients can call and whose purpose is to service the requests. When no request is being processed, the server is idle, waiting for the next invocation. The situation is similar when peer-to-peer communication is used. In this case, the server accepts a connection and executes a receive command. Once again, however, when no service has been requested, the server is idle.

Both procedural and peer-to-peer communication are useful in designing modules whose primary purpose is to service requests from other modules. However, these modes of communication are often inappropriate for a module that must deal with an exceptional situation but cannot simply wait for that situation to occur because it has other things to do.

For example, suppose that a module, M_1, repeatedly reads and records the temperature in a furnace. A second module, M_2, which controls the flow of fuel to the furnace (and perhaps executes on a different computer), might want to be informed of the exceptional case in which the temperature reaches a certain limit. (Perhaps M_2 shuts down the furnace in that case.) Since M_2 must function as a controller, it needs a way to find out when the exceptional case occurs. One way to implement this requirement is for M_2 to periodically call on M_1, using procedural communication, and request that it return the current recorded temperature. Another is for M_2, using a peer-to-peer connection, to periodically send a message to M_1 requesting the temperature. These approaches are referred to as **polling**. If it is unlikely that the value will ever reach the limit, polling is wasteful of resources since M_2 is constantly making requests but the replies indicate that no action need be taken. If M_2 must respond quickly when the value reaches the limit, polling is even more wasteful since in this case more-frequent communication is required.

As a second example, consider a point-of-sale system in which an application module, M, on a sales terminal responds to service requests from customers input at the keyboard. If the system is about to be taken offline temporarily, an out-of-service message must be printed on the terminal. Unfortunately, if M is designed to respond only to inputs from the keyboard, it will not recognize communication coming from the central site and cannot be notified to print the message. Once again, a convenient mechanism for responding to exceptional situations is needed.

In the point-of-sale system, it might be possible to redesign M, using a standard client/server paradigm, to respond to a request from the central site (in addition to requests coming from the keyboard). However, this might not be sufficient if the response to the central site is time critical. If the required response time is less than the time allotted to service a keyboard request, the central site might be forced to wait for a time that exceeds the maximum response time. Hence, an interrupt mechanism is necessary.

Exceptional situations are referred to as **events**. Some TP monitors provide an **event communication** mechanism with which one module that recognizes an event can conveniently notify another module, M, to handle that event. Notification might take the form of an interrupt, causing M to execute an event-handling routine.[5]

The module that agrees to be interrupted uses the event-handling API of the TP monitor to **register** an **event handler** (or callback) that it wishes to execute when notified of an event. In Figure 23.15, M has registered the handler foo with the TP monitor. Since M does not wait for the event to occur but continues to engage in its usual activities, event notification is said to be **unsolicited**.

The system interrupts M when an event it is to handle occurs. It saves M's current state and passes control to foo. When foo exits, the system, using the saved state, returns control to the point at which M was interrupted. M can thus respond immediately when the event occurs. This response is asynchronous because it cannot be determined in advance when the event will occur and thus at what point during M's execution (i.e., between which pair of instructions) foo will be executed. While fast response is often important, careful design is required to ensure that the execution of the handler does not interfere with the interrupted computation.

As depicted in Figure 23.15, the event-generating module, N, invokes **notify** of the event API to indicate to the system that an event has occurred and that the module M is to be interrupted. This process is often called **notification**. Assuming

---

[5] Our discussion is based on event communication in the Tuxedo transaction processing system [Andrade et al. 1996].

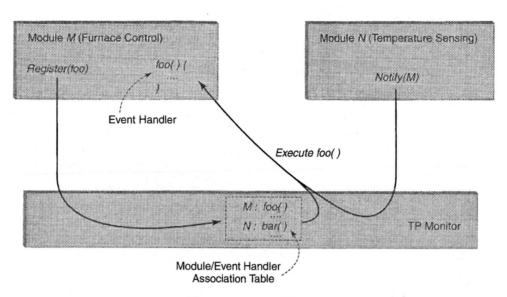

FIGURE 23.15 Event processing that links an event-generating module with an event-handling module.

that a handler has been registered by M, the TP monitor causes it to be executed. The API might allow a message to be passed to M by the event-generating module as an argument.

23.7.1 Event Broker

While the event communication described in the previous section is useful, it has one important drawback. The event-generating module must know the identity of the modules to be notified (there can be more than one). In an application in which the modules that respond to events might change, it is desirable to make the target event-handling modules transparent to the event-generating module. This can be done with an event broker.

An **event broker** is a server provided by a TP monitor, which functions as an intermediary between event-generating and event-handling modules. When an event broker is used, each event is given a name. An event-handling module, M, after registering an event-handling routine, *foo*, with the TP monitor, **subscribes** to an event, E, by calling the broker using the event API. The name of the event is supplied as an argument. The broker then records the association between the named event and M. An event can have more than one subscriber, in which case a list of event-handling modules is associated with it. When the event occurs, the event-generating module, N, **posts** the event with the broker (again using the broker's API and passing the name of the event an argument). The broker then notifies all modules that previously subscribed to the event. The situation just described

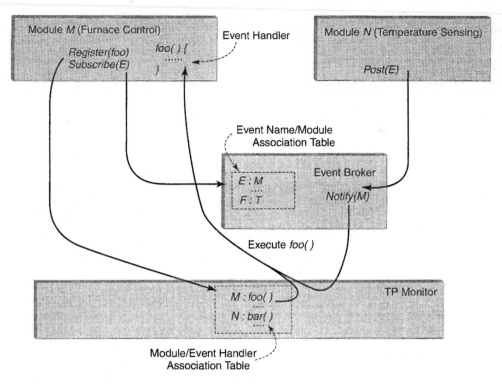

FIGURE 23.16 Use of an event broker to process event postings.

is shown in Figure 23.16. Although the figure looks similar to Figure 23.15, notice that the broker keeps an association between named events and event-handling modules, and uses notify to communicate with an event-handling module. The association between the event-handling module and the event-handling routine is kept in the TP monitor, as before.

As with other forms of communication, communication through events can cause a transaction to propagate from one module to another. For example, if the action post(Event) was performed as part of a transaction in the event-generating module, the resulting handler execution can become part of that transaction as well. In some situations, however, the handler's execution should not be part of the transaction that posted the event. For example, a transaction performing some database activities might find an uncorrectable database error, which requires it to abort. Before aborting, the transaction might want to post an event to notify the database administrator of the error. The event handler should not be a part of the transaction. If it were, it would be aborted when the transaction aborts and the database administrator would not be notified. The rules governing when transactions propagate as a result of event postings are a part of the protocol implemented by the transaction processing system.

23.8 Storage Architectures

One of the goals of the various architectures we have been discussing is to increase transaction throughput. Many large systems require a throughput of thousands of transactions per second. There is one bottleneck to achieving such throughput that we have not yet discussed: disk I/O. Although processor and memory speeds continue to increase significantly every year, disk-access speeds increase much less rapidly and are still measured in milliseconds. It is hard to achieve a throughput of a thousand transactions per second when each disk access takes a time measured in thousandths of a second.

Disk caches.   One approach to increasing throughput involves the use of the disk cache maintained by the DBMS. A disk cache is a region in main memory in which recently accessed database pages are stored. If at some later time, a transaction either reads or updates an item on a page that is stored in the cache, a disk access will have been avoided and a hit will be said to have occurred.

We discussed disc caches in detail in Section 12.1. Here we just note that to obtain a high throughput, many designers consider it mandatory to obtain a hit rate of over 90% (90% of the accesses can be satisfied from the cache). To achieve such a hit rate, the cache size must often be a significant percentage of the size of the database. In some large applications, the cache size is measured in tens of gigabytes.

RAID systems and disk striping.   Even if a 95% cache hit rate can be achieved, the remaining 5% of accesses that require disk I/O can considerably slow down the system. Another way to increase throughput is through the use of RAID systems with disk striping. A **Redundant Array of Independent Disks (RAID)** system consists of a set of disks configured to appear to the operating system to be a single disk with increased throughput and reliability compared to the throughput and reliability of the individual disks making up the RAID. The increased throughput is obtained by partitioning—or striping—each file across several disks, and the increased reliability is obtained using some form of redundant storage.

We discussed RAID systems in detail in Section 9.1.1. Here we just remind you that (1) a number of different levels of RAID systems have been defined, depending on the type of data striping and redundancy they provide; and (2) the levels usually recommended for high performance transaction processing applications are Level 5 with a write cache (block-level striping of both data and parity information) and Level 10 (a striped array of mirrored disks).

Direct attached storage.   It is often the case that the database is spread over several disks or RAID systems, directly connected to a DBMS. This might be done because the database is too large to fit on a single disk or because the system can achieve higher throughput if it can access several disks concurrently. For example, different tables might be stored on different disks. When several transactions access the tables, or when one transaction wants to perform a join on the tables, the accesses can be done concurrently. Alternatively, a single table might be explicitly partitioned (in the schema) into several tables, each of which is stored on a different disk (a subset of the rows or columns is stored on each disk). Then, for example, operations that require a complete table scan can be done concurrently. We discussed partitioning as a way to do database tuning in Sections 12.2.4 and 12.5 and as a way to distribute data in a distributed database system in Section 16.2.

Network attached storage and storage area networks. Instead of having the disks, RAID systems, or other storage devices connected directly to the DBMS, they might be put on a network connected to the DBMS. We discuss two different architectures of this type.

- In **network attached storage** (NAS), the storage devices are directly connected to a file server—sometimes called an **appliance**—instead of to the DBMS. The file server is a resource manager that provides a general-purpose storage facility. It offers its services to clients and other servers (e.g., DBMSs) through a network. Thus, the files stored on the appliance can be shared among all the applications and servers on the network.

- In a **storage area network** (SAN), a DBMS or file server communicates with its storage devices through a separate, high-speed network. The network operates at about the speed of the bus on which a storage device might be directly connected to the server. The server accesses the devices using the same commands (and at the same speed) as if it were connected directly to them. Clients and other servers communicate with the server through a separate (conventional) network similar to the one on which a NAS might be connected.

Both NAS and SAN networks can scale to a much larger number of storage devices than if those devices were directly connected to a server. Scaling with NAS involves adding additional file servers. Scaling with SAN, in addition, involves adding more storage devices on the high-speed network.

SANs are generally thought to be preferable for high-performance transaction processing applications because they allow the DBMS to manage the storage devices directly instead of accessing files indirectly through a file server.

A NAS might be more appropriate for an application that requires a large amount of file sharing among different servers. One example might be the Web site for a national newspaper with an archiving service, in which a number of servers need to share access to a large set of Web pages that might be requested by clients.

23.9 Transaction Processing on the Internet

The growth of the Internet has stimulated the development of many Internet services involving distributed transactions and heterogeneous systems. These services are provided by servers, called Web servers, that are capable of communicating over the Web. Often Web servers have throughput requirements of thousands of transactions per second. The systems generally fall into two categories: **customer-to-business** (C2B) and **business-to-business** (B2B). You are probably familiar with C2B systems.

These are the ones which you, as a customer, interact with over the Internet. For example, you might buy a book at *Amazon.com*. Your interaction involves fetching pages from Amazon's Web site that are displayed by your Web browser, entering data in input boxes, and clicking on links and buttons.

B2B systems are more complex since they are fully automated. A program on one business's Web site communicates with a program on another business's Web site with no human intervention (and without the use of a browser). Instead of simply purchasing a few items, a B2B system might involve complex agreement protocols and substantial commercial transactions.

Internet services can be decomposed into two parts. Front-end systems deal with the interface that the system offers to customers and businesses. How is the system described to users? How is it invoked? Back-end systems deal with implementing the application that actually provides the service.

In the next subsection we discuss the architecture of C2B systems in which the front end is provided by a Web browser and the back end is provided using the architecture discussed earlier in this chapter. Section 23.10 then describes how the back end of C2B systems can be implemented using commercial Web application servers. The same back-end implementation can be used for B2B systems, but with a different front end. B2B front-ends are discussed extensively in Chapter 25.

23.9.1 Architectures for C2B Transaction Processing Systems on the Internet

Web transaction processing systems often make use of two Java constructs: the applet and the servlet. When a Web server supporting C2B interactions sends a page to a customer's browser, it can include with the page one or more programs, called **applets**, written in Java.[6] Applets execute in a programming environment supplied with the browser. They can animate the page, respond to certain events (such as mouse clicks), and interact with the user and the network in other ways.

The browser displays the page when it is received and possibly executes specified applets. The page might include buttons, text boxes, and the like, to be filled in by the user. Associated with the page, but usually hidden from the user, is (1) the URL of a Web server (perhaps different from the one that sent the page) to which the user-supplied information is to be transmitted, and (2) the name of an application on that server to process the information.

While applets are client-side applications, a **servlet** is a Java program on the server that makes use of standard Java servlet API that supports many of the activities needed by server-side applications. For example, methods are provided for reading and writing the information on an HTML page. A servlet has a lifetime that extends beyond the interactions of any single user. When a servlet is started, it creates a number of threads. The threads are allocated dynamically to serve requests for service as they arrive. Requests are generally submitted using the HTTP protocol

---

[6] Or they might include Microsoft's ActiveX Controls, which are typically written in Visual Basic.

(discussed in Section 25.3) and might be sent by a browser or by another application on the Web. The servlet can concurrently handle as many requests as there are threads.

Servlets are not the only way used to interact with Web servers. An older mechanism involves **CGI scripts**. CGI is technically inferior to servlets but has the advantage that scripts can be written in any language, while servlets must be written in Java. Another mechanism that is quickly gaining momentum is .NET. Like CGI, applications can be written in any language, but for the moment the .NET infrastructure is available only for the Windows platform. Java servlets, on the other hand, can be made platform independent.

We discuss three possible ways in which a transaction processing system can be organized to provide C2B service over the Internet.

1. *Two-tiered.* The browser acts as both a presentation and an application server, and the database server resides at the Internet site containing the Web server. The servlet thread at the Web server responds to a request from a browser with an HTML page (with which the user interacts), together with the application program written as a Java applet. After the user fills in the appropriate fields on the page, the applet, which implements the enterprise rules, executes from within the browser. The applet might initiate a transaction and then submit SQL statements or call stored procedures for processing by the database server. The applet communicates with the database server using JDBC (see Section 8.5). This model is similar to that of Figure 8.9, page 295. The JDBC driver might be downloaded from the Web server with the Java applet, in which case it sets up a network connection to the database server. Or the driver might reside on the Web server and receive commands from the browser as data through the servlet thread.

2. *Three-tiered.* The browser acts as the presentation server, and the servlet thread on the Web server acts as the application server. When the Web server is contacted, a servlet thread sends the browser an HTML page with which the user interacts. When the user fills in the page and submits it to the server, a servlet thread, which implements the enterprise rules, is assigned to that interaction. Now the servlet thread, instead of the applet, might initiate a transaction on the database server, as in Figure 23.4. When the servlet thread completes, it can return an HTML page to the browser.

3. *Four-tiered.* Most high-throughput applications use the architecture shown in Figure 23.17 in which there are three tiers at the server site (these, in fact, can be three different sites) and one tier at the browser site. The browser connects to the servlet thread on the Web server, which then processes the information returned by the browser. The Web server might respond to the browser with a new page, or it might invoke an appropriate program on the application server to process the user's request. The application server executes on a different computer, which might be separated from the Web server by a **firewall** to protect it from receiving spurious messages from other sources. The application program might initiate transactions involving data on the database server, which might

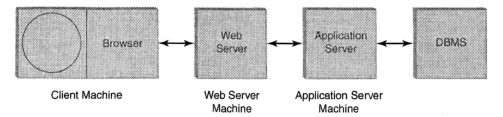

FIGURE 23.17 An Internet-based client connected to a four-tiered transaction processing system.

be separated from the application server computer by a (different) firewall.[7] When the application program completes and returns information to the servlet thread, the thread prepares the appropriate HTML page and returns it to the browser. The application server views the browser and the Web server together as its presentation server.

This architecture is particularly appropriate for high-throughput applications because it allows multiple application servers. The Web server might include a load-balancing module that selects a particular application server to support a user session. An application server might access multiple database servers throughout the enterprise (for example, inventory, shipping, and billing databases) and in other enterprises (for example, for credit card approval). For really high-throughput applications, there might also be multiple Web servers, with an extra layer of HTTP routers that are connected directly to the Internet, whose job is to relay an HTTP request to a particular Web server.

To further increase throughput, systems using this architecture might cache appropriate information on all tiers. For example, the Web server might cache commonly used HTML pages, and the application server might cache commonly used entity beans (see below).

23.10 Web Application Servers—J2EE

A number of vendors provide products called **Web application servers**, which include modules that can be used to build transaction processing systems for the Web. Web application servers provide similar functionality to TP monitors and include services that are particularly oriented toward Web applications. Unfortunately, the terminology is confusing since Web application servers are frequently called simply "application servers" and we have been using that term to describe only the middle tier of a transaction processing system. To avoid any confusion, we will continue to use the term "Web application server" to refer to the commercial products.

Most commercial Web application servers are built using the technology of Java 2 Enterprise Edition (J2EE). Only Microsoft's Web application server is based on .NET technology. J2EE includes a set of Java classes, called *beans*, that can be adapted to

---

[7] Firewalls can also be used in three-tiered and other Web architectures.

support the business methods of an application. J2EE supports Java servlets and in addition provides a number of transaction-oriented services especially designed for Web applications.

23.10.1 Enterprise Java Beans

Enterprise Java beans are Java classes that can be used to encapsulate the business methods of an enterprise. They are generally invoked by a servlet and execute within an infrastructure of services provided by J2EE. The infrastructure supports transactions, persistence, concurrency, authorization, etc. In particular, it implements the declarative model of transaction demarcation discussed in Section 19.3.3. This allows the bean programmer to focus on the business rules and methods of the enterprise rather than on the system-level aspects of the application.

There are three types of enterprise Java Beans: *entity beans*, *session beans*, and *message-driven beans*. We discuss them in the following paragraphs.

Entity beans. Each **entity bean** represents a persistent business object whose state is stored in a database. Typically, each entity bean corresponds to a database table, and each instance of that bean corresponds to a row in the table. For example, in a banking application, there might be an entity bean called ACCOUNT, with fields that include `accountId`, `ownerName`, `socSecNum`, and `balance` and with methods that include `Deposit` and `Withdraw`. The ACCOUNT bean might correspond to a database table called ACCOUNT with attributes `accountId`, `ownerName`, `socSecNum`, and `balance`. Each instance of the ACCOUNT bean corresponds to a row in the ACCOUNT table. Each entity bean must have a primary key. For the ACCOUNT bean, the primary key might be `accountId`.

Entity beans can be used in an application program just like any other object. However, any changes made to an entity bean by the program are *persistent* in that they are propagated to the corresponding item in the database. Thus, in the banking application, any changes to the `balance` field of an instance of the ACCOUNT bean are propagated to the `balance` attribute in the corresponding row in the ACCOUNT table.

Persistence can be managed either by the bean itself, using SQL code written by the application programmer, or automatically by the system. Every entity bean must execute within the context of a transaction, and that transaction must be managed by the system. We will discuss these issues later in this section. Because the state of an entity bean is saved in a database, its lifetime extends beyond any one interaction and even survives system crashes.

Session beans. A **session bean** is instantiated when a client initiates an interaction with the system. It maintains the context, or state, of the client's session and supplies the methods that implement client requests. An example of a session bean is SHOPPINGCART, which provides the services of adding items to a "shopping cart" as the customer scans a catalog and then of purchasing the selected items. Each such service is provided by one or more business methods of the bean. Examples of such methods might be `AddItemToShoppingCart` and `CheckOut`. The context maintained

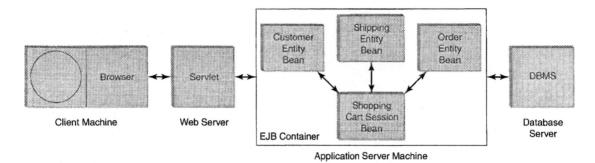

FIGURE 23.18 A four-tiered Internet-based architecture for the shopping-cart transaction.

by an instance of SHOPPINGCART would identify the items in the client's shopping cart.

Session beans can also be stateless, in which case they do not maintain context between requests. An example of a stateless session bean is STOCKQUOTE, an instance of which responds to a sequence of individual requests from a client for stock quotations. In this case no context is needed. All the information required to satisfy a request is contained in the parameters of the method call.

The lifetime of a session bean is just one session. The state of the bean is not persistent beyond that session and does not survive system crashes. In the shopping cart application, we might say that customers get their own shopping carts, which are returned after they leave the store.

Session beans can use the services of entity beans. When the customer wants to complete an order by purchasing the items in the shopping cart, the Check-Out method is called. It, in turn, calls methods in the appropriate entity beans, CUSTOMER, ORDER, and SHIPPING, to record the purchase in the corresponding database tables.

A session bean can also call other session beans, perhaps on other J2EE servers, if it needs to use their services. For example, to transfer funds between accounts at different banks, the session bean at the first bank might need to use the services of a session bean at the second bank.

A method in a session bean can be transactional. For example, the CheckOut method in SHOPPINGCART might execute as a transaction. Transactions can be managed either by the bean itself using standard JDBC code or automatically by the system as described later in this section.

An architecture for a four-tiered implementation of the shopping application is shown in Figure 23.18. The browser accesses a servlet on the Web server. The servlet calls the appropriate method in the SHOPPINGCART session bean on the application server. The method in SHOPPINGCART calls appropriate methods in the entity beans, which then make their state persistent in the database on the database server. Each instance of a purchase is executed as a transaction.

Message-driven beans. All of the communication we have discussed so far involves invoking methods in session or entity beans and is therefore synchronous.

For example, in the shopping cart application, the servlet invokes a method in the session bean and waits for a response. Similarly, the session bean calls a method in an entity bean and waits for a response before proceeding. Sometimes, however, the invoker does not need to wait. In that case communication can be asynchronous, with the potential for increasing throughput. **Message-driven beans** are provided for this purpose.

A message-driven bean is similar to a stateless session bean in that it implements the business rules of some enterprise but does not maintain its state between invocations of its methods. The caller, which might be a session bean, an entity bean, another message-driven bean, or any system or component that uses **Java Message Service** (JMS), invokes the message-driven bean by sending it a message. The message is buffered on a JMS message queue. When a message arrives on a message queue, the system calls an appropriate message-driven bean to process that message. Thus a message-driven bean acts as a message **listener**, waiting for the arrival of a message. JMS message queues have the same semantics as the recoverable queues discussed in Section 23.2.3. The sender does not wait, and the message-driven bean does not return a result when it completes. Thus, message-driven beans provide a mechanism that allows applications to operate asynchronously.

For example, a method in the session bean for the shopping-cart application might send an asynchronous message to the shipping-department application telling it to ship the purchased items. The session bean method can then terminate. The shipping department might have a message queue, ShippingMessageQueue, on which it receives such messages and a message-driven bean, SHIPPINGMESSAGE-QUEUELISTENER, which processes messages according to the business rules of the enterprise. Each message-driven bean must have an onMessage method that is invoked automatically when a message is received. The method performs the service requested in the message and can call methods in other beans for this purpose.

A message-driven bean is stateless: after an instance of the bean has completed processing one message, its state is deallocated and the bean can be immediately reused to process another message on the queue from the same or a different application. As with a session bean, methods in a message-driven bean can be transactional, and that transaction can be managed either by the bean itself or by the system.

Structure of an enterprise Java bean.   Every enterprise Java bean has an ejb-name. For example, the name of the shopping-cart session bean might be SHOPPINGCART. An entity or session bean consists of a number of parts: (1) the bean class, which contains the implementation of the business methods of the enterprise; (2) a deployment descriptor, which contains metadata describing the bean; and (3) various interfaces. As described in more detail below, clients access the bean only through these interfaces. The interfaces contain the signatures of the business methods, whose implementations are in the bean class, and signatures of other methods, whose purpose is to control various life-cycle issues (e.g., creation and destruction of the bean). In contrast to the methods in the bean class, the system provides the implementation of the methods whose declaration is given in the interfaces. A

FIGURE 23.19 A portion of a deployment descriptor describing authorization properties.

```
<method-permission>
    <role-name>teller</role-name>
    <method>
        <ejb-name>Account</ejb-name>
        <method-name>Withdraw</method-name>
    </method>
</method-permission>
```

message-driven bean consists of only a bean class and a deployment descriptor (no interfaces) since clients can access it only through its message queue.

- The **bean class** contains the business methods of an enterprise. For example, the bean class of SHOPPINGCART might be called SHOPPINGCARTBEAN and might contain business methods AddItemToShoppingCart and CheckOut. The bean programmer must provide application code for these business methods.

- The **deployment descriptor** contains declarative metadata describing the bean. For an entity bean, the descriptor can specify persistence information (i.e., how it relates to a database table), transactional information (i.e., what is the transactional semantics when a method is called), and authorization information (i.e., who is allowed to invoke a method). For a session or message-driven bean, the deployment descriptor can describe its transactional and authorization properties. For example, the deployment descriptor for the Withdraw method of an ACCOUNT entity bean must specify that it is to be executed as a transaction, and it might specify that it can be invoked on behalf of either the owner of the account or a teller. It might also specify that its persistence is to be managed by the bean programmer (rather than automatically).

  Deployment descriptors are written in XML and can be quite complex. Fortunately, most Web application servers provide graphic tools that can be used to build deployment descriptors by filling in various forms on the screen. Figure 23.19 shows part of a deployment descriptor that specifies that the Withdraw method in the ACCOUNT bean can be executed by a teller. We discuss how persistence and transactional properties are specified later in this section.

- The **remote interface** is used by clients to access an entity or session bean that is executing on the server. Remote access is provided by Java's RMI (Remote Method Interface), which has facilities similar to RPC. For each method in the bean class, the signature of a corresponding method is declared in the remote interface. The client calls the interface method rather than directly calling the bean method. Hence, the interface method acts as a proxy for the associated bean method. The interface method executes on the server along with the corresponding bean method. It implements the semantics specified in the deployment descriptor and then calls the bean method. For example, if the deployment descriptor specifies that a bean method is to be executed as a transaction, the corresponding interface method initiates a transaction and then calls the bean method. When the call returns, the interface method commits or aborts the transaction. The remote interface for the SHOPPINGCART session bean might also be called SHOPPINGCART. It contains methods AddItemToShoppingCart and CheckOut. The bean programmer must supply declarations for these interface methods, but the system provides the implementation based on information in the deployment descriptor.

■ The (optional) **local interface** is used by local components (i.e., components in the same container—see below) to access methods within an entity or session bean without the overhead of RMI. For example, beans local to the ACCOUNT entity bean might want to use its Deposit and Withdraw methods, so signatures corresponding to these methods would be included in the local interface. The local interface for the ACCOUNT entity bean might be called LOCALACCOUNT. As with the remote interface, the methods in the local interface act as proxies for the methods in the bean class. When a local interface method is called, it implements the semantics specified in the deployment descriptor and then calls the corresponding bean method. The bean programmer must supply declarations for these interface methods, but the system provides the implementation.

The semantics of local and remote interfaces are not identical. For remote interfaces, parameters are passed by value/result; for local interfaces, they are passed by reference.

■ A **home interface** declares the signatures of methods that control the life cycle of a bean. Methods for creating and removing beans fall in this category. In this context, the home interface is often referred to as a **factory** since it produces new instances of the bean. Any remote client of the bean can call these home interface methods.

For example, the home interface for the SHOPPINGCART session bean class might be called SHOPPINGCARTHOME. A client that wants to establish a new shopping session calls the create() method of SHOPPINGCART to create a new instance of the bean to use in the session. Create is a static method. That is, it operates on the class as a whole, not on an individual instance. The client later calls a remove() method to remove the instance when the session is completed.

The home interface for the ACCOUNT entity bean class might be called ACCOUNTHOME. A client that wants to establish a new account calls the create method of ACCOUNTHOME to create a new instance of the bean (a new row in the table) corresponding to the new account.

The home interface for an entity bean also declares signatures of finder methods that can be used to locate one or more instances of a particular bean and return references to them. A finder method is also a static method. For example, a client that wants to deposit money in a particular account might first use the method findByPrimaryKey() to obtain a reference to the particular instance of the entity bean corresponding to the primary key supplied as an argument. It can then use the reference to invoke the methods of that instance. The bean

FIGURE 23.20 A portion of a deployment descriptor for a session bean showing how the various interfaces of the bean are named and declaring that the bean is stateful and executes container-managed transactions.

```
<enterprise-beans>
    <session>
        <ejb-name>ShoppingCart</ejb-name>
        <remote>ShoppingCart</remote>
        <local>LocalShoppingCart</local>
        <home>ShoppingCartHome</home>
        <local-home>LocalShoppingCartHome</local-home>
        <ejb-class>ShoppingCartBean</ejb-class>
        <session-type>stateful</session-type>
        <transaction-type>container</transaction-type>
        ......
    </session>
......
</enterprise-beans>
```

programmer can declare other finder methods as well, for example, to find all the accounts corresponding to a particular `ownerName`.

■ The (optional) **local home interface** is used by local clients (within the same container) to access life-cycle (and finder) bean methods. The home interface for the Account entity bean class might be called LocalAccountHome.

Figure 23.20 shows a portion of a deployment descriptor of the ShoppingCart session bean that specifies the names of the various interfaces of the bean. Note that `ejb-name` specifies the name of the bean, while `ejb-class` is the bean class that contains the implementation of the business methods implemented by the bean. The deployment descriptor also specifies that the session bean is stateful and that the transactions it executes are container-managed (as discussed later).

By contrast, Figure 23.21 shows a similar portion of a deployment descriptor of the ShippingMessageQueueListener message-driven bean. Note that a message-driven bean has no remote, local, or home interfaces, but instead the descriptor contains information about the bean's message queue. The EJB 2.1 specification allows message-driven beans to accept messages from messaging services other than JMS. In the figure, the `<messaging-type>` attribute states that the bean is using JMS, the `<message-destination-type>` attribute states that the bean uses a JMS Queue (corresponding to point-to-point JMS messaging) rather than a Topic (corresponding to publish/subscribe messaging), and the `<message-destination-link>` is a link to the name of the queue. Later, in Figure 23.23, we show a portion of a deployment descriptor of an entity bean.

FIGURE **23.21** A portion of a deployment descriptor for a message-driven bean.

```
<enterprise-beans>
  <message-driven>
    <ejb-name>ShippingMessageQueueListener</ejb-name>
    <ejb-class>ShippingMessageQueueListenerBean</ejb-class>
    <messaging-type>javax.jms.MessageListener</messaging-type>
    <transaction-type>container</transaction-type>
    <message-destination-type>javax.jms.Queue</message-destination-type>
    <message-destination-link>ShippingMessageQueue</message-destination-link>
    ......
  </message-driven>
......
</enterprise-beans>
```

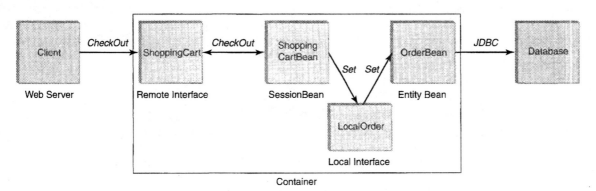

FIGURE **23.22** The remote and local interfaces within the container for one interaction in the SHOPPINGCART session bean.

23.10.2 The EJB Container

Enterprise Java beans execute in a special environment called an **EJB container**, which is provided by the Web application server. An EJB container can support multiple beans. The container provides system-level support for the beans, based partly on the metadata in their deployment descriptors.

The interface methods, together with the methods of the beans, execute in the context of the container. The client invokes an interface method instead of directly invoking the corresponding bean method. The interface method implements the semantics specified in the deployment descriptor when the call is made and then calls the bean method. The situation is shown in Figure 23.22. The methods of the home interface also execute in the context of the container.

Persistence of entity beans: container-managed persistence.   The persistence of an entity bean can be managed either by the bean itself, using JDBC code written by the bean programmer—**bean-managed persistence**—or automatically by the EJB container based on information in the bean's deployment descriptor—**container-managed persistence**. We discuss container-managed persistence (CMP) in what follows and deal with bean-managed persistence later in the section.

With CMP, the container explicitly creates and maintains connections to the database, relieving the client of this responsibility. The deployment descriptor is used to specify the connection protocol to connect to that database. However, deployment descriptor formats for these purposes are vendor specific, and we do not discuss them here.

With CMP, the container handles all the database accesses; the bean contains no code to access the database. The programmer must declaratively specify the persistent fields within the bean's deployment descriptor. The default assumption is that the name of the entity bean is the same as the name of the corresponding table and that the fields of an entity bean and the attributes in the corresponding database table have the same names. The bean name and field names (together with relationships, which we discuss later) are part of the **abstract schema** of the bean.

The term "abstract" is used to distinguish the schema of the bean from the physical schema of the underlying database. Since the bean methods are written in terms of the abstract schema and do not contain the code to connect to or access the database, the bean becomes portable: it can be connected to a different database by appropriately modifying the deployment descriptor. However, J2EE only describes the default mapping of the abstract schema of the bean to the physical schema of the database, one which is based on the identity of the names. It does not say how such a mapping should be described in the deployment descriptor when the names in the abstract and the physical schemas differ. Each vendor can provide a proprietary method to describe such mappings.

The deployment descriptor specifies the fields that are to be persistent and managed by the container. For example, Figure 23.23 shows a portion of a deployment descriptor for the ACCOUNT entity bean showing that the `balance` and `accountId` fields are container managed and that the `accountId` field is the primary key.

With CMP, the bean programmer must declare in the entity bean a `get` method and a `set` method for each persistent field. For example, the methods for the `balance` field of the ACCOUNT entity bean are

```
public abstract float getBalance( );
public abstract void setBalance(float Balance);
```

The name of an access method must start with `get` or `set` followed by the capitalized name of the persistent field. When the bean is deployed in the EJB container, the container generates the appropriate code for these methods. In a similar fashion, the signatures of the methods in the home interface must be provided by the bean programmer, but the bodies are provided automatically when the bean is deployed.

`get` and `set` methods can be included in the local and remote interface of the bean so that fields can be manipulated by bean clients. Thus, when a client wants to make a withdrawal from the bank, the client's session bean can either call the

FIGURE **23.23** A portion of a deployment descriptor for an entity bean showing how fields are specified as container managed and which field represents the primary key.

```
<enterprise-beans>
    <entity>
        <ejb-name>Account</ejb-name>
        <remote>Account</remote>
        <local>LocalAccount</local>
        <home>AccountHome</home>
        <local-home>LocalAccountHome</local-home>
        <ejb-class>AccountBean</ejb-class>
        <persistence-type>Container</persistence-type>
        <cmp-field>
            <field-name>balance</field-name>
        </cmp-field>
        <cmp-field>
            <field-name>accountId</field-name>
        </cmp-field>
        <primkey-field>accountId</primkey-field>
        ......
    </entity>
......
</enterprise-beans>
```

Withdraw method in the entity bean (assuming such a method exists) or it might directly call the getBalance and setBalance methods of the entity bean to do the same thing. Of course, this second alternative reveals to the session bean information about the internal organization of the database (an attribute name) that might better be kept concealed. Note that, if the session bean calls the Withdraw method in the entity bean, the Withdraw method will call the same getBalance and setBalance methods since that is the only way to access the balance field of the bean: with CMP, the fields cannot be accessed directly using SQL statements.

The set method does not immediately cause the database to be updated. The method that actually updates the database is called ejbStore. The implementation of ejbStore is also generated by the container. Recall that an entity bean can be used only in the context of a transaction. When that transaction commits, ebStore is automatically called by the container to perform the appropriate updates.

Container-managed relationships.   For entity beans that have CMP, the container can also provide a **container-managed relationship** (CMR). In addition to fields that represent data items, such as balance, entity beans can have fields that represent relationships between entity beans. These are the relationships we first introduced in Section 4.3. They can be one-to-one, one-to-many, or many-to-many, and they can be unidirectional or bidirectional.

For example, the entity beans ACCOUNT and BANKCUSTOMER might be related through a relationship called ACCOUNTSIGNERS. The relationship might be implemented in ACCOUNT using a relationship field `signers`. The value of `signers` in a particular instance of ACCOUNT contains references to the instances of BANK-CUSTOMER corresponding to customers who can sign checks for the account. If the relationship is bidirectional, BANKCUSTOMER will also have a relationship field, perhaps named `canSignFor`. Its value, in a particular instance of BANKCUSTOMER, contains references to the instances of ACCOUNT corresponding to accounts for which that customer can sign. ACCOUNTSIGNERS is a many-to-many relationship since multiple customers can sign for a single account and multiple accounts can be signed for by a single customer. The relationship allows an application to locate related entities starting from either a customer or an account.

If a relationship is declared to be container managed in the deployment descriptor, the container will implement the relationship in the tables of the database. Figure 23.24 shows a portion of the deployment descriptor for the relationship ACCOUNTSIGNERS. Note that a relationship has an `ejb-relation-name`, and each participant in the relationship has an `ejb-relationship-role-name`. A new field is declared in both ACCOUNT and BANKCUSTOMER indicating the bidirectionality. The field types are Java collections, indicating that the relationship is many-to-many. If the relationship had been unidirectional, only one new field would have been declared.

The container will create a new table to store a many-to-many relationship such as `signers`. For a one-to-one relationship, it will create an appropriate foreign key in both tables participating in the relationship.

The bean programmer must declare within both entity beans participating in the relationship the appropriate get and set methods for the relationship fields. For example, for ACCOUNT

```
public abstract Collection getSigners( );
public abstract void setSigners(Collection BankCustomers):
```

Note the use of collections to handle the "many" part of the relationship. Thus the getSigners method returns the collection of references to the entity beans corresponding to BANKCUSTOMERS who can sign checks for the account. The setSigners method sets the `signers` relationship field in the ACCOUNT entity bean to be the collection of references to the BANKCUSTOMER entity beans specified in the method's parameter. Similarly, a getCanSignFor and setCanSignFor method would be provided for BANKCUSTOMER.

The container generates the code for the get and set methods, including code to maintain the referential integrity of the relationship (Section 3.2.2) as specified in the deployment descriptor.

CMRs can be specified only among entity beans that are in the same container. The get and set methods for relationships are invoked through the local interface of the bean, not the remote interface.

FIGURE 23.24 A portion of a deployment descriptor describing a relationship.

```
<ejb-relation>
    <ejb-relation-name>AccountSigners</ejb-relation-name>
    <ejb-relationship-role>
        <ejb-relationship-role-name>account-has-signers
            </ejb-relationship-role-name>
        <multiplicity>many</multiplicity>
        <relationship-role-source>
            <ejb-name>Account</ejb-name>
        </relationship-role-source>
        <cmr-field>
            <cmr-field-name>signers</cmr-field-name>
            <cmr-field-type>java.util.Collection</cmr-field-type>
        </cmr-field>
    </ejb-relationship-role>
    <ejb-relationship-role>
        <ejb-relationship-role-name>customers-sign-accounts
            </ejb-relationship-role-name>
        <multiplicity>many</multiplicity>
        <relationship-role-source>
            <ejb-name>BankCustomer</ejb-name>
        </relationship-role-source>
        <cmr-field>
            <cmr-field-name>canSignFor</cmr-field-name>
            <cmr-field-type>java.util.Collection</cmr-field-type>
        </cmr-field>
    </ejb-relationship-role>
</ejb-relation>
```

EJB Query Language: finder methods and select methods. For CMP, the code for the method findByPrimaryKey() is automatically generated by the container, based on the entry in the deployment descriptor giving the name of the primary key. The container will also generate the code for other finder methods declared in the home interface, based on queries specified in the deployment descriptor using a query language, **EJB QL** (EJB Query Language). EJB QL is based on SQL but is embedded in XML.

Figure 23.25 shows a portion of a deployment descriptor for a finder method findByName that might be included in either or both the remote and the local home interface of ACCOUNT. It contains a query to be used as the basis of the method. ownerName is one of the fields of ACCOUNT. The query returns a collection, each element of which maps to the remote or local interface (depending on whether the finder method is declared in the remote home interface or the local home interface of the bean) of an instance of ACCOUNT. Hence, a client can use the result of the query

FIGURE 23.25 A portion of a deployment descriptor describing an EJB QL query.

```
<query>
    <query-method>
        <method-name>findByName</method-name>
        <method-params>
            <method-param>string</method-param>
        </method-params>
    </query method>
    <ejb-ql>
        select object(A) from Account A where A.ownerName = ?1
    </ejb-ql>
</query>
```

to invoke the methods of any entity bean referred to in the collection. The name of the owner of each bean in the collection is the value of the positional parameter denoted ?1. The keyword OBJECT denotes the fact that its argument, the variable A, ranges over instances of a class.

EJB QL can also be used to specify queries for select methods. A **select method** is more general than a get (which can return only the value of a field of a particular instance of a bean) and finder methods (which can return only collections of references to instances of the bean that contains the finder method). In addition to mimicking a finder method, a select method can return a collection of field values (this corresponds to a result set) or an aggregation over field values. For example, a bank might enforce a business rule that allows the balance in a depositor's account to be negative, as long as the sum of the balances in all accounts owned by that depositor is positive. Hence, the withdraw method, in addition to updating the balance field of a particular account, needs to sum up the balance fields of other accounts having the same social security number. It does this using a select method based on the query

```
SELECT SUM S.balance
    FROM ACCOUNT A
    WHERE A.socSecNum = ?1
```

Note that the keyword OBJECT is not used in the SELECT clause since S.balance is not a range variable.

In addition, a select method can return a collection of references to instances of related entity beans using a relationship field of the bean containing the select method. This requires the use of path expressions, and we do not discuss it here.

Select methods are static methods (since they must access all instances). They can be invoked only from within a method of the entity bean itself, and hence they are not declared in any interface. Furthermore, they implement only a subset of the semantics of SQL's SELECT statements. For example, the current version of the

EJB specifications (version 2.1) does not allow select methods to perform joins, but later versions might allow them. As with finder methods, with CMP, the container generates the code for a select method.

Persistence of entity beans: bean-managed persistence. With bean-managed persistence (BMP), the bean programmer must provide the JDBC statements to access the database. One reason why a system designer might decide to use BMP is to map an entity bean to a view involving several tables instead of mapping the bean to a single table. CMP could not automatically deal with such a mapping.

Whether persistence is bean managed or container managed, clients of the bean must use the life-cycle methods in the bean's home interface: for example, the create, remove, and finder methods. For BMP, the container does not automatically generate the code for these methods. Code must be provided by the bean designer that uses SQL explicitly. Thus, the user-defined create method might involve an SQL INSERT statement, a remove method might involve an SQL DELETE statement, and finder methods might involve an SQL SELECT statement.

Even when designers choose BMP, they might build beans using get and set methods. But in this case the container does not automatically generate the code for these methods, and the designer must manually generate the programs for these methods using JDBC calls. Or the designer can choose not to use get and set at all and directly access the bean fields using JDBC.

As with CMP, the container automatically calls ejbStore when a transaction involving a bean commits. However, with BMP, the container does not automatically generate the code for ejbStore. The bean programmer can provide a program for ejbStore to perform the necessary updates or can provide a null program for ejbStore and perform the updates with standard JDBC calls within the bean methods.

Setting transaction boundaries. Two issues have to be dealt with if bean execution is to be transactional: transaction boundaries have to be set (this is primarily an issue of atomicity), and concurrency has to be managed (this is primarily an issue of isolation). We will deal with boundaries in this subsection and concurrency in the next.

A session or message-driven bean can initiate a transaction by explicitly executing an appropriate command, in which case we refer to the transaction as having **bean-managed demarcation**. Alternatively, transaction initiation for such beans can be automatically done by the EJB container when a bean method is called based on information in the bean's deployment descriptor. Such a transaction is referred to as having **container-managed demarcation**. Container-managed demarcation is an example of the use of declarative transaction demarcation, as described in Section 19.3.3.

An entity bean, on the other hand, cannot start a transaction explicitly (i.e., it cannot be specified to have bean-managed demarcation): transaction demarcation is required and must be container managed.

With bean-managed demarcation, the bean programmer must explicitly specify within the bean the appropriate JDBC or JTA statements to start and commit (or abort) the transaction. An interesting aspect of the J2EE specification asserts that if a method in a stateful session bean with bean-managed demarcation initiates a transaction but does not commit or abort it, the transaction persists so that execution of the next method of the bean that is invoked becomes part of the same transaction. This continues until some method commits or aborts the transaction.

With container-managed demarcation, the programmer must declaratively specify in the deployment descriptor the circumstances under which a transaction is to be initiated (see below). This can be done for each individual method of the bean separately or for the bean as a whole.[8] The proxy routines in the remote and local interface are automatically generated in conformance with this information and execute within the container. Assuming a transaction is to be initiated, the interface method creates a transaction and then calls the corresponding bean method. When the method returns, the interface method can request that the transaction be committed or aborted.

In the case of container-managed demarcation for a message-driven bean, the transaction is initiated by the container *before* the onMessage method is called. As a result, the transaction includes the step of removing the message from the queue. Hence, if the transaction aborts, the message is returned to the queue and will be serviced later by another instance of the bean. By contrast, with bean-managed demarcation, the transaction is initiated explicitly during the execution of the onMessage method *after* the message has been removed from the queue. Thus if the transaction should abort, the message that initiated the transaction will not be put back on the queue, and hence the transaction will not be reexecuted.

The designer can specify in the deployment descriptor how the bean is to participate in a transaction. The possibilities (*Required*, *RequiresNew*, *Mandatory*, *NotSupported*, *Supports*, and *Never*) are described in detail in Section 19.3.3 and are summarized in Figure 19.3 on page 794. Certain restrictions exist on their use.

- For message-driven beans, only *Required* and *NotSupported* are allowed. If the method in the calling module (the module that sent the message) is part of a transaction then, based on the semantics of JMS, the message will not actually be placed (i.e., be visible) on the message queue until that transaction commits (see Section 23.2.3). Thus a message-driven bean is never called by a client from within a transaction that is active when the bean is started. This explains why only *Required* and *NotSupported* are allowed with message-driven beans.

- For stateless session beans, *Mandatory* is *not* allowed. If it were, and the bean was called from a client that is not in a transaction, the bean would throw an exception; hence the restriction.

---

[8] This type of declarative demarcation of transactions is also provided by the Microsoft MTS (Microsoft Transaction Service), which is part of .NET.

■ For entity beans, only *Required*, *RequiresNew*, and *Mandatory* are allowed (since an entity bean must always execute within a transaction).

For example, a session bean might explicitly start a transaction (hence bean-managed demarcation) and then call an entity bean whose deployment descriptor specifies container-managed demarcation with attribute value *Required*. As a result, the method executed in the entity bean would be part of the same transaction, and the transaction as a whole would be characterized as having bean-managed demarcation. If the attribute value in the entity bean were *RequiresNew*, a new transaction having container-managed demarcation would be initiated when the entity bean is called and would commit on return.

The following element is a portion of a deployment descriptor stating that the Checkout method of the SHOPPINGCART session bean is to utilize container-managed transaction demarcation with attribute *Required*.

```
<container-transaction>
    <method>
        <ejb-name>ShoppingCart</ejb-name>
        <method-name>Checkout</method-name>
    </method>
    <trans-attribute>Required</trans-attribute>
</container-transaction>
```

Whether the demarcation is bean managed or container managed, the container includes a transaction manager, which acts as a coordinator for a two-phase commit protocol. For example, a single session bean might access several entity beans associated with multiple databases in the same container. The container's transaction manager would coordinate the beans at commit time. Alternatively, a session bean might call methods of other session beans, which might execute in different containers, and all of these session beans might access entity beans associated with different databases. In this case, the transaction managers of the set of containers involved would participate in the protocol as shown in Figure 24.4.

A transaction with container-managed demarcation is aborted and rolled back if a system exception is thrown or if a session or entity bean aborts itself by calling the setRollbackOnly method. A transaction with bean-managed demarcation aborts itself by explicitly calling the appropriate JDBC or JTA statements.

Managing transactional concurrency. By its nature, an instance of a message-driven bean is executed on behalf of only one client at a time: the client that sent the message. Furthermore, whenever a session or entity bean is called, the caller gets its own instance of that bean. Hence, beans are not multithreaded, and access to variables local to a bean does not require synchronization.

Concurrently executing instances of entity beans, however, can conflict with one another since a number of such beans might refer to the same row in a database table. Database accesses are handled in the normal way by the DBMS's concurrency control. The programmer might be satisfied with the default level of concurrency provided by the DBMS, or he can specify the level explicitly in the deployment descriptor or—for bean-managed demarcation—using the appropriate JDBC commands.

The J2EE standard does not say when the changes made by a transaction are to be propagated to the database. In most implementations, the changes are propagated when the transaction commits by ejbStore. However, this can lead to deadlocks (if a transaction first obtains a read lock when a get is executed and, at commit time, requests write locks to do the propagation). Some vendors of Web Application Servers allow the descriptor to specify that propagation is to occur at an earlier time. For example, propagation might be done at set time.

Some vendors offer alternatives to the J2EE approach to concurrency just discussed, which make use of delayed propagation. In one such alternative the container plays a role in controlling the isolation level. An optimistic algorithm is implemented. The container sets the isolation level at the DBMS to READ COMMITTED so that a transaction does not obtain any long-term read locks. When a get occurs, the value is read from the database into the entity bean, and when a set occurs the value is saved in the entity bean (and not written into the database). The entity bean is thus being used as an element of an intentions list (Section 20.9.2). When the transaction completes, the container performs a validation check to ensure that no item that the transaction read was written *since the read took place*. If the transaction passes the validation check, the updated items are then copied from the entity bean into the database. For example, the check might be performed as part of ejbStore.

Note that this is not the same validation check made in the optimistic concurrency control discussed in Section 20.9.2. In that control, when a transaction completes, a validation check is made to determine whether an item it read was changed by a concurrent transaction *any time within its read phase*. Both validation methods produce serializable schedules.

If instead, the validation checked only that the items that had been read *and then written* by the transaction had not been changed after the read took place, that would have been an implementation of OPTIMISTIC READ COMMITTED (Section 21.2.1) and would not necessarily yield serializable schedules.

23.10.3 Using Java Beans

Part of the vision underlying enterprise Java beans is that they could be reused. For example, Sam's Software Company might be in the business of supplying components to enterprises that want to build Internet business applications. Sam's might be selling a set of beans for shopping-cart applications, including a SHOPPING-CART session bean. Henry's Hardware Store, which wants to implement an Internet shopping-cart application, might purchase those beans from Sam's. Henry's system might use all the beans they purchased from Sam's, except that, instead of using SHOPPINGCART exactly, the system creates a child session bean, HENRYSSHOPPING-CART. Some of the methods in SHOPPINGCART have been changed to reflect Henry's business rules. Henry's programmers might also edit the deployment descriptors of some of the beans to make them conform to Henry's needs and map them to Henry's database.

The job of implementing Henry's system has been drastically reduced. Henry's programmers need be concerned mainly with Henry's business rules, not with the technical details of the operational environment in which the system will run. After obtaining, and perhaps modifying, the beans, the major remaining job is to assemble the beans and deploy them within a Web application server.

Once Henry's system is complete, it can run on any computer using any Web application server that supports J2EE. Note, however, that while all commercial Web application servers that support J2EE provide all the features of the current J2EE standard, they each also provide a number of additional proprietary features. Any application that uses those features might not be portable between Web application servers.

Web application servers usually supply graphical tools for creating skeleton versions of servlets, and enterprise Java beans for specifying their properties, for assembling these components, and for deploying them in an application. Among the other services provided by Web application servers are

- *Transaction oriented services.* These services include Java Transaction API (JTA), Java Transaction Services (JTS), Java Messaging Service (JMS), Java Database Connectivity (JDBC), and so on.

- *Services usually offered by TP monitors.* These services include access to a transaction manager, load balancing, multithreading, security services, communication protocols, and so on.

- **Support for business-to-business XML-based Web services.** These services include support for XML, SOAP, UDDI, WSDL, etc. We discuss these services in Chapter 25.

Our goal here is not to make you an expert in J2EE or any particular commercial Web application server, but to make you aware that such tools can considerably simplify the implementation of Web-based transaction processing systems. Understanding the principles described in this text will make it easier to understand and correctly use the detailed information provided in technical manuals.

BIBLIOGRAPHIC NOTES

Much of the material on transaction processing systems in this chapter was drawn from two books. [Gray 1978] is encyclopedic in its coverage of transaction processing systems, and the student is urged to go to this excellent source for additional information. Another excellent source is [Bernstein and Newcomer 1997]. [Gray 1978] gets down to implementation details, but Bernstein and Newcomer focus on a higher level of coverage of much of the same material. Their work includes a very useful discussion of the two-tiered and three-tiered models and a description of several TP monitors. Additional information on Tuxedo can be found in [Andrade et al. 1996]. Material on Encina can be found in [Transarc 1996]. RPCs were introduced by [Birrell and Nelson 1984]. A description of IBM's LU6.2, the most commonly used peer-to-peer protocol, can be found in [IBM 1991]. A general discussion of communication techniques, including RPC, can be found in [Peterson and Davies 2000]. The discussion of the handling of exceptional situations is based on the model used in the Tuxedo system [Andrade et al. 1996]. Description of the X/Open model for distributed transaction processing can be found in [*X/Open CAE Specification Structured Transaction Definition Language (STDL)* 1996] and [*X/Open Guide Distributed Transaction Processing: Reference Model*, Version 3 1996b].

Vast literature exists on programming Web applications (including database applications) using Java servlets. A few recent titles include [Hall 2000; Hunter and Crawford 1998; Sebesta 2001; Berg and Virginia 2000].

Documentation for J2EE version 1.4 can be found at *http://java.sun.com/j2ee /download.html*. Documentation on Enterprise Java Beans version 2.1 is at *http://java .sun.com/products/ejb/docs.html*.

EXERCISES

23.1 Explain the advantages to a bank in providing access to its accounts database only through stored procedures such as deposit() and withdraw().

23.2 Explain why the three-level organization of a transaction processing system (including transaction servers) is said to be scalable to large enterprise-wide systems. Discuss issues of cost, security, maintainability, authentication, and authorization.

23.3 Explain what happens in a three-level architecture for a transaction processing system if the presentation server crashes while the transaction is executing.

23.4 Explain why the *cancel* button on an ATM does not work after the *submit* button has been pressed.

23.5 Explain the advantages of including a transaction server in the architecture of a transaction processing system.

23.6 Give an example of a transaction processing system you use that is implemented as a distributed system with a centralized database.

23.7 Give an example in which a transaction in a distributed database system does not commit atomically (one database manager it accessed commits, and another aborts) and leaves the database in an inconsistent state.

23.8 Explain whether the system you are using for your project can be characterized as TP-Lite or TP-Heavy.

23.9 List five issues that arise in the design of heterogeneous distributed transaction processing systems that do not arise in homogeneous distributed systems.

23.10 Explain the difference between a TP monitor and a transaction manager.

23.11 Give three examples of servers, other than transaction servers, database servers, and file servers, that might be called by an application server in a distributed transaction processing system.

23.12 Describe the architecture of the student registration system used by your school.

23.13 State two ways in which transactional remote procedure calls differ from ordinary remote procedure calls.

23.14 Suppose that a transaction uses TRPC to update some data from a database at a remote site and that the call successfully returns. Before the transaction completes, the remote site crashes. Describe informally what should happen when the transaction requests to commit.

23.15 Explain the difference between the `tx_commit()` command used in the X/Open API and the COMMIT statement in embedded SQL.

23.16 Propose an implementation of distributed savepoints using the `tx` and `xa` interfaces to the transaction manager. Assume that each subtransaction (including the transaction as a whole) can declare a savepoint, and that when it does so, it forces its children to create corresponding savepoints. When a (sub)transaction rolls back to a savepoint, its children are rolled back to their corresponding savepoints.

23.17 Give three advantages of using an application server architecture in a client server system.

23.18 Give an example of an event, different from that given in the text, in which the callback function should not be part of the transaction.

23.19 Explain how peer-to-peer communication can be used to implement remote procedure calling.

23.20 Explain some of the authentication issues involved in using your credit card to order merchandise over the Internet.

23.21 Implement a Web tic-tac-toe game in which the display is prepared by a presentation server on your browser and the logic of the game is implemented within a servlet on the server.

23.22 Print out the file of cookies for your local Web browser.

23.23 Consider a three-tiered system interfacing to a centralized DBMS, in which $n1$ presentation servers are connected to $n2$ application servers, which in turn are connected to $n3$ transaction servers. Assume that for each transaction, the application server, on average, invokes k procedures, each of which is executed on an arbitrary transaction server, and that each procedure, on average, executes s SQL statements that must be processed by the DBMS. If, on average, a presentation server handles r requests per second (each request produces exactly one transaction at the application server), how many SQL statements per second are processed by the DBMS and how many messages flow over each communication line?

23.24 In Section 23.10 we discuss an optimistic concurrency control that uses a different validation check than the concurrency control described in Section 20.9.2. Give an example of a schedule that would be allowed by the validation check of Section 23.10 but not by the validation check of Section 20.9.2.

24

Implementing Distributed Transactions

Many transaction processing applications must access databases at multiple sites, perhaps scattered throughout the world. For example, in our university, much of the information about the research contracts obtained by our faculty is maintained in a database located in the state capital, several hundred miles away. We discussed the database and query design issues related to distributed database systems in Chapter 16. In this chapter, we discuss transaction-related issues. In particular, we might require that transactions that access such distributed databases maintain the same correctness conditions as the local transactions we have been discussing—namely the ACID properties.

24.1 Implementing the ACID Properties

A **distributed transaction**, T, is a transaction that accesses databases at multiple sites in a network. The portion of a distributed transaction that executes at a particular site is called a **subtransaction**. For example, a database manager might export stored procedures that T can invoke as subtransactions. Or T might submit individual SQL statements to be executed by the database manager, in which case the sequence of SQL statements submitted by T becomes T's subtransaction at that manager. T might invoke subtransactions so that they execute in sequence (one completes before another starts) or concurrently (several can execute at the same time and perhaps communicate with one another while they are executing).

Distributed database systems are useful when the organizations they support are themselves distributed and each component maintains its own portion of the data. Communication costs can be minimized by placing data at the site at which it is most frequently accessed, and system availability can be increased since the failure of a single site need not prevent continued operation at other sites. For example, the Student Registration System might be implemented as a distributed system. Student information might be stored on one computer and course information on a different computer. The two computers might be located in different buildings on campus.

We refer to the individual database managers that execute subtransactions of a distributed transaction as **cohorts** of that transaction. A database manager is a

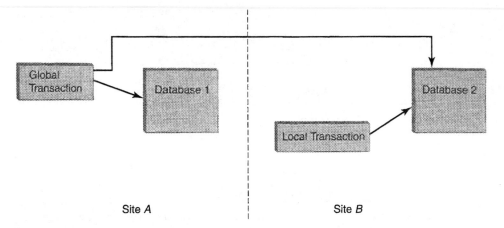

FIGURE 24.1 Data access paths for a distributed transaction.

cohort of each distributed transaction for which it is executing a subtransaction and might be a cohort of a number of distributed transactions simultaneously.

We would like each distributed transaction to satisfy the ACID properties. The module responsible for doing much of the work necessary to implement these properties is called the **coordinator**. In most systems, the transaction manager is the coordinator.

In addition to serving as a cohort of a distributed transaction, a database manager might execute a stored procedure or a series of SQL statements for an application that does not require the services of any other database manager. Such an application is invoking a (single-site) transaction rather than a subtransaction of a distributed transaction. Since the database manager does not distinguish between these two cases, we frequently refer to a subtransaction as simply a transaction. The data access paths for a distributed transaction are shown in Figure 24.1.

Consider the nationwide distribution system of a hardware manufacturing company. The company maintains a network of warehouses at different sites throughout the country, and each site has its own local database, which stores information about that site's inventory. A customer at some site might initiate a transaction requesting 100 dozen widgets. The transaction might read the data item containing the number of widgets currently in the local warehouse and find that there are only 10 dozen, which it (tentatively) reserves, and then access data at one or more of the other warehouses to reserve the additional 90 dozen widgets. After all 100 dozen have been located and reserved, the data items at each of the sites are decremented and appropriate shipping orders generated. If 100 dozen cannot be located, the transaction releases all reserved widgets and commits, returning failure status to the customer. In this way, either all sites at which widgets have been reserved decrement their local databases or none do.

Physical failures are more complex when transactions are distributed. We saw in Chapter 22 that a crash is a common type of failure. In a centralized system, all the modules involved in the transaction fail when the computer crashes. With distributed transactions, the crash of some computer in the network can cause some subset of modules to fail while the rest continue to execute. Special protocols must be designed to handle this new failure mode.

A similar situation arises when a communication failure causes the network to become **partitioned**. In this case, operational sites cannot communicate with one another. We discuss how to deal with such failures in Section 24.2.2. We assume that a distributed transaction can abort (and hence must be recoverable) and that once it commits, the system must ensure that all database changes it has made (at all sites) are durable.

If we assume that each site supports the ACID properties locally and ensures that there are no local deadlocks, then the distributed transaction processing system also must ensure the following:

■ *Atomic termination.* Either all cohorts of a distributed transaction must commit or all must abort.

■ *No global deadlocks.* There must be no global (distributed) deadlocks involving multiple sites.

■ *Global serialization.* There must be a (global) serialization of all transactions (distributed and otherwise).

We discuss each of these issues in this chapter (Sections 24.2, 24.4, and 24.5). We also consider data replication and issues related to the distribution of data in a network (Sections 24.7 and 24.8).

24.2 Atomic Termination

To ensure global atomicity, a distributed transaction can commit only if all of its subtransactions commit. Even though a subtransaction has successfully completed all of its operations and is ready to commit, it cannot unilaterally decide to do so because some other subtransaction of the same distributed transaction might abort (or might already have aborted). In that case, the entire distributed transaction must be aborted. Thus, when a subtransaction has completed successfully, it must wait for all others to complete successfully before it can commit.

The coordinator executes an **atomic commit protocol** to guarantee global atomicity. The communication paths related to the protocol are shown in Figure 24.2. When an application program initiates a distributed transaction, T, it notifies the coordinator, thus setting the initial transaction boundary. Each time T invokes the services of a resource manager for the first time, that manager informs the coordinator that it has joined the transaction. When T completes, the application informs the coordinator, thus setting the final transaction boundary. The coordinator then initiates the atomic commit protocol.

Atomicity requires that, when T completes, either all cohorts must commit their changes or all must abort. In processing T's request to commit, therefore, the

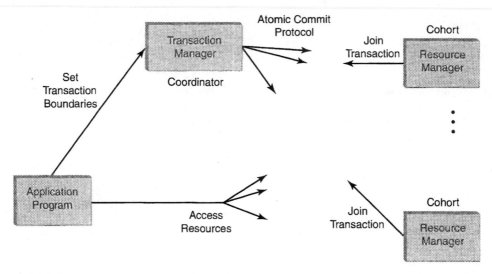

FIGURE 24.2 Communication paths in an atomic commit protocol.

coordinator must first determine if all cohorts agree to do so. Some of the reasons a cohort might be unable to commit are

- The schema at a cohort site might specify deferred constraint checking (see Section 8.3). When the subtransaction at the site completes, the database manager might determine that a constraint is violated and abort the subtransaction.

- The database manager at a cohort site might use an optimistic concurrency control. When the subtransaction at the site completes, the manager performs the validation procedure. If validation fails, the manager aborts the subtransaction.

- A subtransaction at a site, S, might have been aborted by the concurrency control at S or because of a (local) deadlock or a (local) conflict with other subtransactions at S.

- The cohort site might have crashed and so is unable to respond to the protocol messages sent by the coordinator.

- Some communication lines might have failed, preventing the cohort from responding to the protocol messages sent by the coordinator.

24.2.1 The Two-Phase Commit Protocol

A number of atomic commit protocols have been proposed, but the one that is in common use is called the **two-phase commit protocol** [Gray 1978; Lampson and Sturgis 1979] (in Exercise 24.8 we describe another atomic commit protocol). The protocol is initiated by the coordinator when the transaction requests to commit. To perform the protocol, the coordinator needs to know the identities of all the cohorts of the transaction. Therefore, when the transaction is initiated, the coordinator allocates a **transaction record** for the transaction in volatile memory. Furthermore, each time a resource manager joins the transaction, its identification is appended to that transaction record. We discussed this situation in Section 23.5.3 for RPC communication and in Section 23.6 for peer-to-peer communication. Thus, when the transaction requests to commit, the transaction record contains a list of all its cohorts.

We describe the protocol as a series of messages exchanged between the coordinator and the cohorts. When the transaction requests to commit, the coordinator starts the first phase of the two-phase commit protocol by sending a **prepare message** to each cohort. The purpose of this message is to determine whether the cohort is willing to commit and, if so, to request that it prepare to commit by storing all of the subtransaction's update records on nonvolatile storage.[1] Having the update records in nonvolatile storage guarantees that if the coordinator subsequently decides that the transaction should be committed, the cohort will be able to do so, even if it crashes after responding positively to the *prepare message*.

If the cohort is willing to commit, it ensures that its update records are on nonvolatile storage by forcing a **prepared record** to its log. It is then said to be in the **prepared state** and can reply to the *prepare message* with a **vote message**.

The vote is **ready** if the cohort is willing to commit and **aborting** if it had aborted at an earlier time or is unable to commit for one of the reasons cited previously. Once a cohort votes "ready," it cannot change its mind since the coordinator uses the vote to decide whether the transaction as a whole is to be committed. The cohort is said to have entered an **uncertain period** because it does not know whether the subtransaction will ultimately be committed or aborted by the coordinator. It must await the coordinator's decision, and during that waiting period it is blocked in the sense that it cannot release locks and the concurrency control at the cohort database cannot abort the subtransaction. This is an unfortunate situation that we will return to in Section 24.6. If the cohort votes "aborting," it aborts the subtransaction immediately and exits the protocol. Phase 1 of the protocol is now complete.

The coordinator receives, and records in the transaction record, each cohort's vote. If all votes are "ready," it decides that T can be committed globally, records the fact that the transaction has committed in the transaction record, and forces a **commit record**—containing a copy of the transaction record—to its log.

As with single-resource transactions, T is committed once that commit record is safely stored in nonvolatile memory. All update records for all cohorts are in nonvolatile memory at that time because each cohort forced a prepare record before voting. Note that we are assuming that the transaction manager and each of the cohort database managers have their own independent logs.

The coordinator then sends each cohort a **commit message** telling it to commit. It is now apparent why the coordinator's commit record must be forced. If a *commit message* were sent to a cohort before the commit record was durable, the coordinator might crash in a state in which the message had been sent but the record was not

---

[1] A cohort site where only reads have been performed can implement a simplified version of the protocol. See Exercise 24.12.

durable. Since each cohort commits its subtransaction when the *commit message* is received, this would result in an inconsistent state: the distributed transaction is uncommitted, but the cohort's subtransaction is committed. Commit processing at the cohort is carried out as described in Section 22.2 and involves the forcing of a commit record to the database manager's log (to indicate that the subtransaction is committed), lock release, and local cleanup. After a cohort performs these actions, it sends a **done message** back to the coordinator indicating that it has completed the protocol.

When the coordinator receives a *done message* from each cohort, it appends a **completion record** to the log and deletes the transaction record from volatile memory. The protocol is then complete. For a committed transaction, the coordinator executes two writes to its log, only one of which is forced. The cohort forces two records in the commit case: the prepare record and the commit record. The number of forced writes is a factor in evaluating the efficiency of a protocol since each time a routing forces an I/O operation it must wait until the operation completes.

If the coordinator receives any "aborting" votes, it deallocates *T*'s record in volatile storage and sends an **abort message** to each cohort that voted to commit (cohorts that voted to abort have already aborted and exited from the protocol). The coordinator does not record the abort in its log because this protocol has the presumed abort property, which we discuss in Section 24.2.2. On receiving the *abort message*, the database manager aborts the cohort and writes an **abort record** in its log. The arrival of the *commit* or *abort message* at the cohort ends its uncertain period.

The sequence of messages exchanged between the application, the coordinator (transaction manager), and cohort (resource manager) is shown in Figure 24.3.

Summary of the two-phase commit protocol.   We summarize the two-phase commit protocol here:

Phase 1

1.   The coordinator sends a *prepare message* to all cohorts.

2.   Each cohort waits until it receives a *prepare message* from the coordinator. If it is prepared to commit, it forces a prepared record to its log, enters a state in which it cannot be aborted by its local control, and sends "ready" in the *vote message* to the coordinator.

     If it cannot commit, it appends an abort record to its log. Or it might already have aborted. In either case, it sends "aborting" in the *vote message* to the coordinator, rolls back any changes the subtransaction has made to the database, releases the subtransaction's locks, and terminates its participation in the protocol.

Phase 2

1.   The coordinator waits until it receives votes from all cohorts. If it receives at least one "aborting" vote, it decides to abort, sends an *abort message* to all cohorts

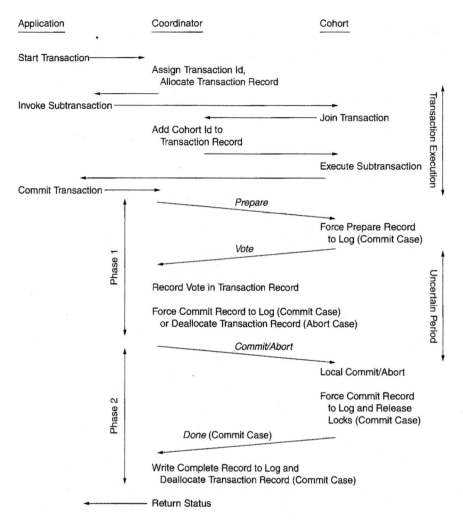

FIGURE 24.3 Exchange of messages in a two-phase commit protocol.

that voted "ready," deallocates the transaction record in volatile memory, and terminates its participation in the protocol.

If all votes are "ready," the coordinator decides to commit (and stores that fact in the transaction record), forces a commit record (which includes a copy of the transaction record) to its log, and sends a *commit message* to each cohort.

2. Each cohort that voted "ready" waits to receive a message from the coordinator. If a cohort receives an *abort message*, it rolls back any changes the subtransaction has made to the database, appends an abort record to its log, releases the subtransaction's locks, and terminates its participation in the protocol.

If the cohort receives a *commit message*, it forces a commit record to its log, releases all locks, sends a *done message* to the coordinator, and terminates its participation in the protocol.

3. If the coordinator committed the transaction, it waits until it receives *done messages* from all cohorts. Then it appends a completion record to its log, deletes the transaction record from volatile memory, and terminates its participation in the protocol.

The atomic commit protocol across multiple domains.   Up to this point, we have assumed that the commit protocol for the entire distributed transaction is directed by a single transaction manager. In actuality, a transaction manager's responsibility is often limited to a **domain**, which typically includes all of the resource managers at the site at which the transaction manager executes (although other organizations are possible). When an application program in one domain, D_A, invokes a resource manager in another, D_B, the transaction managers in both domains, TM_A and TM_B, are informed. TM_A is regarded as the parent of TM_B in this case. The protocol then involves multiple transaction managers controlling multiple domains.

With multiple domains, the messages of the atomic commit protocol travel over the edges of a tree, as shown in Figure 24.4. Leaf nodes are the (cohort) resource managers that participated in the transaction, and the root, TM_A, is the transaction manager that controls the domain, D_A, containing the application program, *App*, that initiated the transaction. Note that application modules are not part of the tree since only resource and transaction managers (coordinators) participate in the protocol. An interior node in the tree represents a transaction manager that coordinates resource managers in its domain and acts as a cohort with respect to its parent transaction manager. In the figure, *App* has, directly or indirectly (through other application programs), invoked resource managers in domains *B* and *C*.

App sends its request to commit to TM_A, which initiates phase 1 of the protocol among its children by sending each a *prepare message*. Thus, TM_A sends a *prepare message* to both local resource managers (e.g., RM_A) and both remote transaction managers (e.g., TM_B). When a transaction manager receives a *prepare message*, it initiates phase 1 of the protocol among its children by sending each a *prepare message*. For example, when TM_C receives the *prepare message* from TM_A, it sends a *prepare message* to each of its two (resource manager) children.

On the basis of the votes TM_C receives from its children, it responds with an appropriate vote to TM_A. Thus, if it receives "ready" votes from both resource managers, it forces a prepared record (including the transaction record containing information about its direct descendents) to its log and responds with a "ready" vote. If TM_A commits, TM_B will be able to commit its descendents in the tree, even if it should crash during the uncertain period and be restarted later.

If TM_A also receives "ready" votes from TM_B and the two resource managers in D_A, it enters phase 2 of the protocol by committing the transaction and sending a *commit message* to each of its children. TM_B and TM_C then initiate phase 2 of the protocol by relaying the *commit message* to their children. While the figure shows a

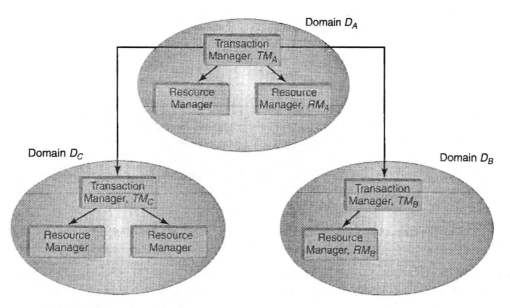

FIGURE 24.4 Distributed transaction structured as a tree.

tree with only two coordinator levels, a general distributed transaction might have an arbitrary number of levels.

TM_B acts as the representative of the resource managers in D_B with respect to TM_A and thus is a cohort with respect to (coordinator) TM_A. Hence, TM_A must be informed that TM_B is one of its cohorts, and TM_B must be informed of its dual role with respect to RM_B and TM_A. In the X/Open model of distributed transactions, the responsibility for spreading this information is placed on a server called the **communication resource manager**, and the interface between a transaction manager and the communication resource manager in its domain is called the **xa+ interface**.

24.2.2 Dealing with Failures in the Two-Phase Commit Protocol

The two-phase commit protocol includes measures for dealing with various kinds of failures that might occur in a distributed system.

- A **timeout protocol** is executed if a site times out while waiting for a message. (A timeout might occur either because the sending site has crashed, the message is lost, or the message delivery system is slow.)
- A **restart protocol** is executed by a site recovering from a crash.

If a site cannot complete the commit protocol until some failure is repaired, we say that the site is **blocked**. When a site blocks, the decision to commit or abort is delayed for an arbitrary period of time. This delay is particularly undesirable at a cohort site that uses a locking concurrency control since items that the subtransaction has locked remain unavailable to other transactions at that site. For this reason, it is important to understand the circumstances under which the two-phase commit protocol results in blocking. We consider the various failure situations next. We describe these situations as if the protocol tree contains exactly two levels. However, the same decisions are made between a parent and its children at any pair of adjacent levels in a tree with multiple levels.

The cohort times out while waiting for a prepare message. The cohort can be certain that no decision to commit has yet been taken at any site (since it has not yet voted). It can therefore decide to abort. If a *prepare message* subsequently arrives, the cohort can simply respond with an "aborting" vote, which will prevent any site from reaching a commit decision (since such a decision requires "commit" votes from all sites). In this way, global atomicity is preserved.

The coordinator times out while waiting for a vote message. This situation is similar to the one above. The coordinator can decide to abort and send an *abort message* to all cohorts. Note that all sites might have sent *commit messages*, but one of the messages might not have been delivered during the timeout period. In this case, the coordinator aborts the transaction, even though all of the cohorts are operational and voted to commit—a counterintuitive situation.

The cohort times out while waiting for a commit or abort message. This situation is more serious since the cohort has voted "ready" and is in its uncertain period. It is blocked until it can determine if the coordinator has made a decision and, if so, what that decision is. The cohort cannot unilaterally choose to commit or abort since the coordinator might have made a different choice, thus violating unanimity.

The cohort can attempt to communicate with the coordinator, requesting the transaction's status. If this is not possible (the coordinator has crashed or the network is partitioned), the cohort can try to communicate with other cohorts. (To facilitate such communication, the coordinator can provide a list of all cohorts in the *prepare message*, which the cohort can store in the prepare record that it writes to the log.) If the cohort finds a cohort that has not yet voted, both decide to abort. This is safe since the coordinator cannot have decided to commit if any cohort has not yet voted. If it finds a cohort that has aborted or committed, it makes the same decision. If all other cohorts it finds are also in their uncertain period, it remains blocked until communication can be established with the coordinator or a cohort that has committed or aborted.

The coordinator times out while waiting for a done message. The coordinator communicates with the cohort requesting the *done message*. When a *done message* has been received from each cohort, it deallocates the transaction record.

The coordinator crashes. When the coordinator restarts after a crash, it searches its log. If, for some transaction, T, it finds a commit record but no completion record, it must be in phase 2 of the protocol for T. The coordinator restores T's transaction record (found in *T*'s commit record) to volatile memory and resumes the protocol by sending a *commit message* to each cohort since the crash might have occurred before the *commit messages* were sent. If the coordinator does not find a commit record for some transaction, two possibilities exist.

1. The protocol was still in phase 1 when the crash occurred.
2. The coordinator has aborted the transaction.

The coordinator cannot distinguish between these two cases since in both it has not written any records to its log. Fortunately, it does not need to distinguish between them since in the first case the transaction is aborted and hence the two cases can be treated identically: the coordinator takes no action with respect to *T*. If the first case has occurred, and a cohort queries the coordinator concerning the status of *T*, the coordinator will reply with an *abort message* since it will not find a transaction record for *T* in volatile memory. This is allowable because the transaction was in phase 1 of the protocol when the coordinator crashed, and hence the coordinator had not made any decision before the crash. The second case is also handled correctly since no action is the correct course if *T* had previously aborted. This reasoning is part of the presumed abort protocol described next.

The cohort crashes or times out while in the prepared state—the presumed abort property. When a cohort restarts after a crash, it searches its log. If it finds a prepared record but no commit or abort record, it knows that it was in the prepared state at the time of the crash. It requests the transaction's status from the coordinator. The coordinator might also have been restarted (see above), or the cohort might have crashed while the coordinator remained active. If the coordinator finds the transaction record for the transaction in volatile memory, the coordinator can immediately respond to the request. However, if it does not find a transaction record, it presumes (without checking its log) that the transaction has aborted and reports that to the cohort. This feature of the protocol is referred to as **presumed abort**[2] [Mohan et al. 1986].

The presumed abort feature works because the absence of a transaction record indicates that one of the following is true:

- The coordinator has committed the transaction, received *done messages* from all cohorts, and deleted the transaction record from volatile memory.
- The coordinator has crashed, and its restart protocol found commit and completion records for the transaction in its log.
- The coordinator has aborted the transaction and deleted the transaction record.

---

[2] One dictionary definition of the word *presume* is "to expect or assume, to regard as probably true as in 'innocence is presumed until guilt is proven.'" However, in this case the coordinator knows that the transaction has aborted.

- The coordinator has crashed, and its restart protocol did not find any records for the transaction in its log (it aborted the transaction or was in phase 1 of the protocol when it crashed).

Since the cohort is still in the prepared state (and hence has not sent a *done message*), the first and second possibilities are ruled out. Therefore the coordinator can report that the transaction has aborted. This same reasoning applies if the cohort times out in its prepared state and requests the transaction's status from the coordinator. (Note that, when the commit protocol is used across multiple domains, each coordinator in the protocol tree can use the presumed abort property to respond to requests from its cohorts.)

Note that we have implicitly taken advantage of the fact that the cohort forces the commit record to the log before it sends the *done message*. If the record were not forced, it would be possible for the cohort to crash after sending the message but before the commit record is appended to its log. In that case (assuming all other cohorts send *done messages*), the coordinator will have committed the transaction and deleted the transaction record. But when the cohort is restarted, it believes it is in the prepared state (since there is no commit record in its log), and the coordinator will respond "abort" to the cohort's query, causing a violation of global atomicity.

Timeout Protocol for the Two-Phase Commit Protocol.

- *TO1. Cohort times out while waiting for a prepare message.* The cohort decides to abort.

- *TO2. Coordinator times out while waiting for a vote message.* The coordinator decides to abort, sends an *abort message* to each cohort from which it received a "ready" vote, deletes the transaction record from volatile memory, and terminates its participation in the protocol.

- *TO3. Cohort times out while waiting for a commit/abort message.* The cohort attempts to communicate with the coordinator to determine the outcome of the transaction. If it can communicate with the coordinator, the coordinator can use the presumed abort property to formulate its answer. If the cohort cannot communicate with the coordinator, it attempts to communicate with another cohort. If it finds one that has committed or aborted, it makes the same decision. If it finds one that has not yet voted, they both decide to abort. Otherwise the cohort blocks.

- *TO4. Coordinator times out while waiting for a done message.* The coordinator sends a message to the cohort requesting that the *done message* be sent. It maintains the transaction record in its volatile memory until it has received a *done message* from each cohort.

Restart protocol for the two-phase commit protocol.   The protocol for restarting a coordinator or cohort site after a crash can be built on the crash recovery procedure described in Section 22.2.

- *RES*1. If the restarted site is a cohort site and, for some transaction, the site's crash recovery procedure finds a commit or abort record in its log, that transaction has completed, and the procedure takes no additional actions beyond those discussed in Section 22.2.

- *RES*2. If the restarted site is a cohort and, for some transaction, the site's crash recovery procedure finds a begin transaction record in its log but does not find a prepared record (and hence the cohort has not yet voted), the procedure takes no additional actions beyond those discussed in Section 22.2 (i.e., it aborts the subtransaction).

- *RES*3. If the restarted site is a cohort and, for some transaction, the site's crash recovery procedure finds a prepared record but no commit or abort record in its log (and hence the cohort might have sent a ready vote before the crash), the crash occurred during the cohort's uncertain period. The crash recovery procedure acquires locks on all items that the transaction updated (these items are named in the update records in the log) so that when the system is restarted, the items are inaccessible to other transactions, and then it restores the updates. The cohort then follows the protocol TO3.

- *RES*4. If the restarted site is the coordinator and, for some transaction, it finds a commit record but no completion record in its log, the crash occurred after the coordinator had committed the transaction but before it had received a *done message* from each cohort. When the coordinator is restarted, the transaction record is restored to volatile memory from the commit record. The coordinator then follows the protocol TO4.

The presumed commit property. Although the two-phase commit protocol with the presumed abort property has been chosen as the X/Open standard, it is not the only protocol for implementing global atomicity. In particular, it is interesting to consider a protocol that implements a **presumed commit** property.

The goal of the protocol with presumed commit is to eliminate the *done messages* that committed cohorts send with presumed abort after they have completed commit processing. Recall that after the coordinator sends *commit messages*, it keeps the transaction record in its volatile memory until it has received a *done message* from each cohort. The coordinator knows that after it receives a *done message* from a cohort, that cohort will never again request status, so when it receives *done messages* from all cohorts, it can delete the transaction record. If, on the other hand, the coordinator aborts the transaction, it sends *abort messages* to the cohorts and immediately deletes the transaction record, so there is no need for a cohort to reply with a *done message*. If a cohort queries the coordinator and no transaction record is found, the coordinator presumes that the transaction has aborted and sends an *abort message*.

Our plan is to reverse this situation. When the coordinator commits a transaction and sends a *commit message* to each cohort, it immediately deletes the transaction record from volatile memory, and thus a cohort does not have to reply with a *done message*. When the coordinator aborts a transaction and sends an *abort message* to each cohort, it retains the transaction record until each replies with a *done message*. Since most transactions commit, fewer *done messages* will be sent. This is an advantage that presumed commit has over presumed abort.

With this strategy, when a cohort times out or restarts in the prepared state and queries the coordinator concerning the status of the transaction, if the coordinator finds no transaction record in its volatile memory, it can presume that the transaction has committed. If the transaction had aborted, the transaction record would be present (since not all cohorts have responded with *done messages*). In either case the coordinator can report the transaction's status to the cohort.

We need to argue that the strategy works. The argument rests on the requirement that the only times at which the transaction record can be deleted from the coordinator's volatile memory are when the transaction commits or when, in the abort case, all *done messages* have been received. However, there is a problem. If the coordinator crashes before it has made a decision to commit or abort, the contents of volatile memory will be lost. Since no information about the transaction exists in the coordinator's log, it will not be able to reconstruct the transaction record when it recovers. If one of the cohorts then queries the coordinator, it will incorrectly report that the transaction has committed.

To fix this problem, the coordinator forces a **start record**, including a copy of the transaction record, to its log at the beginning of the first phase of the protocol. Now if the coordinator crashes before deciding commit or abort, its restart procedure will find the start record, but no commit or abort record, in the log. The procedure can then deduce that a decision has not yet been made and choose to abort the transaction and restore the transaction record, indicating the abort, to volatile memory. The start record must be forced to ensure that before any cohort can enter the prepared state (and perhaps send a query message) the transaction record can be restored to volatile memory if the coordinator crashes.

To understand how the coordinator's actions relate to the cohort's actions, consider the following cases:

- *The coordinator crashes before deciding.* If the coordinator crashed before sending a *prepare message*, the cohort will timeout and abort. This is consistent with the fact that the coordinator has chosen to abort the transaction. If the coordinator crashed after sending a *prepare message* but before deciding, the cohort will respond with a *vote message* and will timeout waiting for a *commit* or *abort message*. It will then send a query to the coordinator. The coordinator's restart procedure will have reconstructed the transaction record in volatile memory and, when the query is processed, will reply that the transaction has aborted.

- *The coordinator crashes after deciding to abort.* In this case the coordinator might have sent one or more *abort messages*, and hence, instead of a query, the coordinator might receive *done messages*. The coordinator then waits to receive *done messages* from all cohorts before deleting the transaction record. If it times out waiting for a particular cohort's *done message*, it requests that that cohort send a *done message* when the cohort completes abort processing. Note that it is not necessary for the coordinator to force an abort record if it decides to abort. If the coordinator crashes before the abort record is appended to its log, its restart procedure will find a start record, but no commit or abort record, in the log and correctly consider the transaction to be aborted.

■ *The coordinator crashes after deciding to commit.* We still require that the coordinator force a commit record when it decides to commit the transaction in order to ensure that the transaction is committed before *commit messages* are sent. If the coordinator subsequently crashes, its restart procedure will conclude that the transaction has committed and will not reconstruct the transaction record.

We must also consider the forcing question on the cohort side. If the transaction aborts, the cohort must force an abort record to its log before sending the *done message*. If it were not forced, the cohort might crash after the *done message* was sent but before the abort record was appended. Thus, the cohort will appear to be in the prepared state when it recovers. Unfortunately, if the coordinator received *done messages* from all cohorts, it would have deleted the transaction record. A subsequent query by the cohort would elicit an incorrect (presumed) commit response from the coordinator.

A protocol with the presumed commit property has the advantage that when a transaction commits (the usual situation), no *done* messages are sent. This can speed up the protocol. However, it has the disadvantage that in both the commit and the abort cases, the coordinator is required to force a start record. This can slow the protocol.

In summary, when a transaction commits using the presumed abort protocol

■ The coordinator makes one forced log write (the commit record) and sends two messages to the cohorts (*prepare* and *commit*).

■ A cohort makes two forced log writes (a prepared record and a commit record) and sends two message (*ready* and *done*).

By contrast, when a transaction commits using the presumed commit protocol

■ The coordinator makes two forced log writes (the start record and the commit record) and sends two messages to the cohorts (*prepare* and *commit*).

■ A cohort makes two forced log writes (a prepared record and a commit record) and sends one message (*ready*).

Although it appears that the costs and benefits of the two protocols are similar, there is a substantial difference if the transaction is structured as a tree as in Figure 24.4. With presumed commit, each local transaction manager in the tree must force a start record to its log when it enters the first phase of the protocol. If the tree is deep, a large number of forced writes must be done in sequence (as the tree is descended). These forced writes can incur a substantial amount of execution time. This is one reason why the presumed abort protocol was selected as the X/Open standard.

Formats and protocols: the X/Open standard. The two-phase commit protocol ties together software modules, such as DBMSs and a transaction manager, that might have been provided by different vendors. If these modules are to communicate effectively, and if application programs are to communicate with them, they must agree on communication conventions, sometimes called the **format and protocols** (**FAP**). Standardization of the FAP promotes **interoperability** among products of different vendors.

The X/Open standard permits interoperability by defining a set of function calls for exchanging protocol messages and the formats of those messages. With X/Open, the names of functions called by applications and implemented in the transaction manager (coordinator) are prefixed with `tx`—for example, `tx_begin()` is the function called to start a transaction and `tx_commit()` to commit it. Similarly, X/Open function calls from the transaction manager to resource managers and vice versa are prefixed with `xa`. Thus, when a resource manager (cohort) wants to join a transaction, it calls `xa_reg()`. When the transaction manager wants to send a *prepare message* to a resource manager it calls `xa_prepare()`, and the value returned is a "ready" or "aborting" vote. If all votes are "ready," the transaction manager sets the return value of the application program's call of `tx_commit()` to commit and calls each of the resource managers with `xa_commit()`. If one or more of the return values of `xa_prepare()` is "aborting," the transaction manager sets the return value of the application's call of `tx_commit()` to "abort" and calls each of the resource managers with `xa_abort()`.

24.2.3 The Peer-to-Peer Atomic Commit Protocol

A variation of the two-phase commit protocol achieves the atomic commitment of transactions that use peer-to-peer communication.[3]

In Section 23.6 we introduced the syncpoint manager as the module that coordinated the atomic commit protocol in a manner analogous to the way the transaction manager coordinates the atomic commit protocol when RPC communication is used. We assumed that all participants in a distributed transaction resided in the same domain, and hence a single syncpoint manager sufficed. In general, however, multiple domains, and hence multiple syncpoint managers, will be involved.

A syncpoint manager, SM_A, associated with an application program, A, keeps a record of all application programs and resource managers in its domain, D_A, with which A has directly communicated. Similarly, if A sets up a connection to B in its domain, D_B, SM_A is informed of the fact that SM_B is participating in the transaction.

Assuming that A initiates the commit protocol by declaring a syncpoint, all of its connections must be in send mode. SM_A assumes the root position in a tree similar to the one pictured in Figure 24.4 and starts phase 1 of the protocol by sending a *prepare message* to each resource manager that A has invoked and a *syncpoint message* over each of its connections to other application programs. Then A waits until the protocol completes. When the *syncpoint message* arrives at some other application program, B, that program might not have completed its portion of the transaction. When it does and all of its connections (other than the connection to A) are in send

---

[3] This description is based on [Maslak et al. 1991].

mode, it also declares a syncpoint. This causes SM_B to send a *prepare message* to each resource manager that B has invoked and a *syncpoint message* to each program (other than A) with which B has communicated. Then B waits until the protocol completes. In this way, *syncpoint message* spreads to all modules that have participated in the transaction.

Assuming that all peers want to commit, each eventually declares a syncpoint, all are synchronized at their syncpoint declarations, and the associated resource managers are in a prepared state. "Ready" *vote messages* propagate up the tree, and phase 1 of the two-phase commit protocol completes. Then phase 2 starts, and the transaction is committed by the tree of syncpoint managers. Commit status is also returned to each program, which can then continue its execution by starting a new transaction.

If a peer decides to abort, local rollback is initiated and abort status is sent to all resource managers, causing them to roll back as well. Abort status is also returned to each program, which can then continue executing by starting a new transaction.

24.3 Transfer of Coordination

Generally, the transaction manager associated with the site at which the transaction is initiated becomes the coordinator. It communicates with the cohorts to carry out the atomic commit protocol. The cohorts might be resource managers, but more generally they are transaction managers in a distributed transaction tree.

There are several reasons why basing coordination at the initiator site might not be an optimal arrangement. For one thing, the initiator site might not be the most reliable site involved in the transaction. For example, the transaction might be initiated as the result of some action at a point-of-sales terminal and involve servers in the store's main office and at the customer's bank. It might be safer to have coordination located at one of these servers. In order to allow this, the protocol can be modified so that coordinator status is transferred from one participant to another.

A second reason for transferring coordination has to do with optimizing the number of messages to be exchanged during the protocol. The two-phase commit protocol (with the presumed abort property) involves the exchange of four messages between the coordinator and each cohort. It is possible to improve on this. For example, the following modified protocol involves two participants, P_1 and P_2, that can be thought of either as transaction managers (each of which controls a set of cohort resource managers) or servers.

1. P_1 initiates the protocol by entering the prepared state (if P_1 is a transaction manager, its cohorts are all in their prepared states). It then sends a message to P_2, which simultaneously says that P_1 is prepared to commit and requests that P_2 both prepare and commit the transaction as a whole. Thus, the message is a combination of a "ready" vote and a *prepare message* and has the effect of transferring the coordinator role to P_2.

2. P_2 receives the message and, assuming it is willing to commit, enters the prepared state. Since it knows that P_1 is prepared, P_2 can decide to commit the

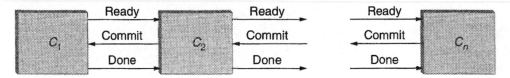

FIGURE 24.5 The linear commit protocol.

transaction as a whole and take the actions necessary to commit the transaction locally. It responds to P_1 with a *commit message*.

3. P_1 receives the message, commits locally, and responds with a *done message* to P_2.

The *done message* is required because of the presumed abort property: P_2, acting as the new coordinator, must remember the transaction's outcome in case the *commit message* it sent to P_1 is not received. It can then respond to a query from P_1 asking about the transaction's outcome. The *done message* indicates to P_2 that it can delete the transaction record from volatile memory. The fact that the protocol has completed with an exchange of only three messages (instead of four) shows that the number of messages exchanged can be optimized.

24.3.1 The Linear Commit Protocol

The **linear commit protocol** is a variation of the two-phase commit protocol that uses transfer of coordination. The cohorts are assumed to be interconnected in a (linear) chain as shown in Figure 24.5. Assume that the leftmost cohort, C_1, initiates the protocol. When it is ready to commit, it goes into the prepared state and sends a *ready message* to the cohort on its right, C_2, indicating that it is ready to commit and transferring coordination to C_2. After the message is received, if C_2 is willing to commit, it also goes into the prepared state and relays the message to the cohort on its right, again transferring coordination. The process continues until the message reaches the rightmost cohort, C_n. If C_n agrees to commit, it commits and sends a *commit message* to C_{n-1}, which commits and propagates the message down the chain until it reaches C_1, which then commits. Finally, a *done message* is propagated up the chain from C_1 to C_n to complete the protocol. The *done message* is required to allow C_{i+1}, acting as coordinator for C_i, to delete the transaction record from its volatile memory.

If, after receiving the first protocol message, a cohort wants to abort the transaction, it aborts and sends *abort messages* to the cohorts on its left and right. Those cohorts abort and forward the *abort message* further along the chain until it reaches both ends. The logging, timeout, and recovery protocols used to achieve atomicity for various types of failure are similar to those for the two-phase commit protocol (see Exercise 24.9).

The linear commit protocol involves fewer messages than the two-phase commit protocol and hence saves on communication costs. If n is the number of cohorts, the linear commit requires $3(n-1)$ messages, whereas the two-phase commit requires $4n$ messages (a separate coordinator is involved). On the other hand, the two-phase commit completes after a sequence of four message exchanges (independent of the number of cohorts) since the coordinator communicates with all cohorts in parallel. The linear commit requires a sequence of $3(n-1)$ exchanges because messages are sent serially.

24.3.2 Two-Phase Commit without a Prepared State

The basic idea in transfer of coordination can be used to adapt the two-phase commit protocol to situations in which (exactly) one of the cohorts, C, does not support the two-phase commit protocol (for example, if C does not understand the *prepare message* and does not have a prepared state, which might be the case if C is an older legacy system). In this case the coordinator executes phase 1 of the protocol with the cohorts that do support a prepared state in the normal way. If all of these cohorts agree to commit, the coordinator requests that C commit its subtransaction (this is not the *commit message*, which is part of the two-phase commit protocol). This effectively allows C to decide whether the transaction as a whole will be committed, but C is not smart enough to realize this. If C responds to the coordinator that it has committed, the coordinator sends *commit messages* to the other cohorts and completes phase 2 of the protocol. If C responds that it has aborted, the coordinator sends abort messages to the other cohorts.

Note that C does not actually function as a coordinator since it does not take the steps necessary to handle failures: it does not maintain a transaction record for the distributed transaction, nor does it understand a *done message*. Thus, it cannot respond to queries from other cohorts if a failure occurs. Hence, coordination is not completely transferred.

24.4 Distributed Deadlock

Pessimistic concurrency controls that employ waiting are subject to deadlock. Assuming that the concurrency control at each site does not permit a deadlock locally, we want to ensure that the overall system is not subject to distributed deadlock. For example, a simple distributed deadlock between two distributed transactions, T_1 and T_2, both of which have cohorts (subtransactions) at sites A and B, will result if the concurrency control at site A makes T_1's cohort, T_{1A}, wait for T_2's cohort, T_{2A}, while the concurrency control at site B makes T_2's cohort, T_{2B}, wait for T_1's cohort, T_{1B}.

Note that in the general model of a distributed transaction, the cohorts can run concurrently, whereas a transaction accessing a single database is purely sequential. Hence, in the above example, T_{2A} not only holds some resource for which T_{1A} is waiting but can actually progress since it is not delayed by the fact that T_{2B} is waiting. Deadlock still occurs, however, since T_2 cannot release its locks until it commits globally, which will not happen if T_{2B} is waiting. Ultimately, in such a situation, all progress in the deadlocked transactions stops.

In general, a distributed deadlock cannot be eliminated by aborting and restarting a single cohort. The statements executed by a cohort are really a subsequence of the statements executed by the transaction as a whole. They cannot be reexecuted because other cohorts might already have executed statements that logically follow them. For example, T_{1A} might have sent a message to T_{1B} containing some results that it had computed before the deadlock occurred. Restarting T_{1A} without restarting T_{1B} makes no sense since the message will be resent, so the entire distributed transaction must be restarted.

The techniques to detect a distributed deadlock are simple extensions of those discussed in Section 20.4.2. In one, the system constructs a distributed *waits_for* relation and searches for cycles whenever a cohort is made to wait. For example, a cohort of T_1 informs its coordinator that it is waiting for a cohort of T_2. T_1's coordinator then sends a **probe** message to T_2's coordinator. If T_2's coordinator has also been informed by one of its cohorts that it is waiting for a cohort of T_3, the probe message is relayed by the coordinator of T_2 to the coordinator of T_3. A deadlock is detected if the probe returns to T_1's coordinator.

Another technique uses timeout: whenever the wait time experienced by a cohort at some site exceeds some threshold, the concurrency control at that site assumes that a deadlock exists and aborts the cohort.

Finally, the timestamp technique [Rosenkrantz et al. 1978] described in Section 20.4.2 can be used for distributed transactions with one small generalization. To ensure that timestamps created at one site are different from timestamps created at all other sites, each site is assigned a unique identifier. A coordinator at site A creates a timestamp for a distributed transaction, T, by concatenating A's site identifier to the right of the value obtained from A's clock. When T creates a cohort at some site, it sends along the value of its timestamp. With a single, unique timestamp associated with all of T's cohorts, the strategy of never allowing an older transaction to wait for a younger transaction eliminates distributed deadlocks.

24.5 Global Serialization

In a centralized system, the goal of a concurrency control is to respond to requests to access items in the database so as to produce a specified level of isolation. With a distributed transaction, multiple DBMSs are involved, each of which might be supporting a different isolation level. Under such circumstances, the isolation between concurrent distributed transactions is poorly defined. Suppose, however, that we consider the problem of implementing globally serializable schedules. A simple (albeit impractical) approach is to provide a single control at some central site. All requests (at any site) are sent to this site, which maintains the data structures for implementing the locks for data items at all sites.

Such a system is just a centralized concurrency control in which the data is distributed. Unfortunately, this approach has significant drawbacks: it requires excessive communication (with the delays that this implies), the central site is a bottleneck, and the entire system is vulnerable to the failure of that site.

A better approach, and the one generally followed, is for each site to maintain its own concurrency control. Whenever a (sub)transaction makes a request to perform an operation at some site, the concurrency control at that site makes a decision based only on local information available to it, without communicating with any other site. Each concurrency control separately uses the techniques previously described to ensure that the schedule it produces is equivalent to at least one serial schedule of transactions and subtransactions of distributed transactions at its site. The overall design of the system must then ensure that distributed transactions are serialized globally—that is, that there is at least one equivalent serial ordering on which all sites agree.

Our concern, since the sites operate independently and might even employ different concurrency control algorithms, is that there might be no ordering on which all sites agree. Consider distributed transactions T_1 and T_2 that might have subtransactions at sites A and B. At site A, T_{1A} and T_{2A} might have conflicting operations and be serialized in the order T_{1A}, T_{2A}, while at site B, conflicting subtransactions of the same two transactions might be serialized T_{2B}, T_{1B}. In that case, there is no equivalent serial schedule of T_1 and T_2 as a whole.

We can ensure that local serializability at each site implies global serializability using nothing more than the individual concurrency controls and the two-phase commit protocol. Specifically it can be shown that

> If the concurrency controls at each site independently use either a strict two-phase locking or an optimistic algorithm, and the system uses a two-phase commit protocol, every global schedule is serializable (in the order in which their coordinators have committed them). [Weihl 1984]

While we do not prove that result here, it is not hard to see the basic argument that can be generalized into a proof. Suppose that sites A and B use strict two-phase locking concurrency controls, that a two-phase commit algorithm is used to ensure global atomicity, and that transactions T_1 and T_2 are as described above. We argue by contradiction. Suppose that the conflicts described above occur (so that the transactions are not serializable) and that both transactions commit. T_{1A} and T_{2A} conflict on some data item at site A, so T_{2A} cannot complete until T_{1A} releases the lock on that item. Since the concurrency control is strict and a two-phase commit algorithm is used, T_{1A} does not release the lock until after T_1 has committed. Since T_2 cannot commit until after T_{2A} completes, T_1 must commit before T_2. But if we use the same reasoning at site B, we conclude that T_2 must commit before T_1. Hence, we have derived a contradiction, and it follows that both transactions cannot have committed. In fact, the conflicts we have assumed at sites A and B yield a deadlock, and one of the transactions will have to be aborted.

You might think that virtually all systems use one of the specified concurrency control algorithms and thus satisfy the theorem. But many applications execute at isolation levels lower than SERIALIZABLE and hence do not satisfy the theorem.

24.6 When Global Atomicity Cannot Be Guaranteed

In practice, there are a number of situations in which an atomic commit protocol cannot be completed and hence global atomicity cannot be guaranteed.

- *A cohort site does not participate in two-phase commit.* A particular site might not support the protocol. For example, a resource manager might be a legacy system that does not support a prepared state. Alternatively, a site might elect not to participate to avoid the degradation of performance that can occur with blocking. A transaction is blocked during the uncertain period and holds locks that prevent other transactions from accessing the locked items. Since the site cannot control the length of the uncertain period, it is no longer independent: factors that control access to locked resources are controlled elsewhere. For example, the length of the uncertain period depends on the speed with which other cohorts respond to *prepare messages* and the efficiency of the message-passing system. If the coordinator crashes or the network becomes partitioned, a cohort might remain blocked for a substantial period of time.

  Cohort sites that elect to participate in the protocol often deal with this problem by unilaterally deciding to commit or abort a blocked subtransaction in order to release locks. Such a decision is referred to as a **heuristic decision**. Unfortunately, assigning a technical name does not change the fact that global atomicity might be compromised as a result of such an action. A heuristic decision might cause global inconsistency in the database (a subtransaction that updated a data item at one site might commit, but a subtransaction of the same distributed transaction at a different site that updated a related data item might abort). Such inconsistencies can sometimes be resolved in an ad hoc manner by communication among the database administrators at the different sites. Although heuristic decisions do not preserve global atomicity, they are the only way to resolve an important practical problem.

  A cohort site might not participate for reasons unrelated to performance. For example, the site might charge a fee to execute a subtransaction and, when the subtransaction completes and returns a result, might demand the fee even if the overall distributed transaction subsequently aborts. Therefore, the site administrator might insist that the subtransaction commit as soon as it completes, without waiting for the distributed transaction to commit or abort globally.

- *The language does not support two-phase commit.* On the application side, some database query languages allow a transaction to connect to multiple DBMSs but do not support two-phase commit. When a transaction completes, it sends individual (independent) commit commands to each DBMS. Thus, the all-or-none commit provided by a two-phase commit protocol is not enforced, and so the transaction is not guaranteed to be globally atomic. For example, most versions of embedded SQL do not support two-phase commit. However, JDBC and ODBC both provide APIs for implementing two-phase commit: JTS (Java Transaction service) for JDBC and MTS (Microsoft Transaction Server) for ODBC.

■ *The system does not support two-phase commit.* Support of the two-phase commit protocol requires that the system middleware include a coordinator (transaction manager) and that the application, coordinator, and servers agree on conventions for exchanging protocol messages. For example, the X/Open standard specifies APIs for this purpose (e.g., the tx and xa interfaces). For many applications, such system support is not available, and so the two-phase commit cannot be implemented.

24.6.1 Weaker Commit Protocols

If sites do not participate in a two-phase commit protocol (or some other atomic commit protocol), the execution of distributed transactions is not guaranteed to be isolated or atomic. Nevertheless, systems might have to be designed under this constraint. In such cases, the application designer must carefully assess how this affects the correctness of the database and the ultimate utility of the application to its clients.

When the two-phase commit is not supported, or for some other reason is not used, one of the following weaker commit protocols might be used.

■ In the **one-phase commit protocol**, the application program does not send commit commands to any site until all subtransactions have completed. If any abort, the distributed transaction is aborted. If all complete successfully, it sends a separate commit command to each site. Some sites might commit, and some might abort. A distributed transaction implemented with embedded SQL might operate in this fashion.

■ In the **zero-phase commit protocol**, each subtransaction commits as soon as it completes. Hence, some sites might commit and some might abort.

■ In the **autocommit protocol**, a commit operation is performed immediately (automatically by the system) after each SQL statement. Autocommit is the default in ODBC and JDBC.

None of these protocols guarantees global atomicity since subtransactions (or operations) might commit at some sites and abort at others. However, we can say that if (1) the concurrency control at each site uses either a strict two-phase locking or an optimistic algorithm, (2) the application program uses a one-phase commit protocol, and (3) the subtransactions at all sites commit, then all global schedules are serializable (in the order in which the application programs have committed them) and all global and local integrity constraints are maintained.

The same reasoning that justifies a similar result for the two-phase commit applies here—with the added restriction that the subtransactions at all sites must commit. If some subtransactions abort (so that distributed transactions are not necessarily atomic) the parts of the transactions that do commit are serializable.

With the zero-phase commit protocol, a subtransaction might commit and release locks at one site before another subtransaction is initiated and acquires locks at another site. Hence, from a global perspective, locking is not two-phase. As a result, global serializability is not guaranteed, even if the subtransactions at all sites commit. Transactions might be serializable in different orders at different sites. Each subtransaction maintains the local integrity constraint at the site at which it executes, but the schedule of distributed transactions does not necessarily maintain global integrity constraints.

The zero-phase commit protocol holds locks for a shorter period of time than does the one-phase commit protocol, and hence can provide better performance. Zero-phase commit might therefore be appropriate for applications in which there are no global integrity constraints and so global serializability is not an issue.

An example where zero-phase commit might be used is the Internet grocer application described in Section 16.2.3. The company has a headquarters site that registers customers and accepts purchase orders, and a number of warehouse sites throughout the country from which the groceries are delivered to the customers. Information about each customer is stored both at the headquarters site and the local warehouse site from which that customer's grocery orders will be delivered.

A customer registration transaction might consist of two subtransactions, executed in sequence: the first creates a customer record at the headquarters site, and the second creates a corresponding record at the appropriate warehouse site. The transaction can be viewed as having a zero-phase commit protocol since the first subtransaction is allowed to commit before the second is initiated. The reason for this design is to allow rapid response to the customer who is registering online. Although a global integrity constraint asserts that a customer recorded at a warehouse site is also recorded at headquarters, the fact that it is temporarily violated is viewed as acceptable because the record at the warehouse site is not needed until the customer makes an order, presumably at a later time. Note also that the (sub)transaction at the warehouse site is retriable: even if it should abort the first time it is executed, it will eventually commit if retried. Thus, the integrity constraint will ultimately be satisfied. We return to this example in Section 24.7.2 on asynchronous replication (the customer record is replicated in two databases).

The autocommit protocol holds locks for the shortest possible time and hence yields the best performance, but it does not guarantee even local serializability at each site. For this reason, it is not guaranteed to maintain either global or local integrity constraints.

In the one-phase and zero-phase commit protocols, if the application program requests that a subtransaction at some site be committed and it is aborted instead, the program is notified of the abort and might be able to take alternate action—perhaps retrying the subtransaction or initiating a new subtransaction at a different site. For some applications, this feature can be a significant advantage compared with the two-phase commit protocol in which, when a subtransaction at any site aborts, the entire distributed transaction aborts.

24.7 Replicated Databases

A common technique for dealing with failures is to replicate portions of a database at different sites in the network. Then if a site crashes or becomes separated from the network because of a partition, the portion of the database being maintained by that site can still be accessed by contacting a different site that holds a replica. We say that the **availability** of the data has been increased.

Replication can also improve the efficiency of access to data (hence increasing transaction throughput and decreasing response time) since a transaction can access the nearest replica, perhaps one that exists at the site at which the transaction is executing. For example, in the Internet grocer application discussed in Section 16.2.3, the company has a table describing its customers that is replicated at its headquarters site and at the local warehouse from which a customer's orders are delivered. Transactions involving the delivery of merchandise execute at the warehouse site and use the replica stored there, while transactions involving monthly mailings to all customers execute at headquarters and use the replica stored there.

Of course, replication has its costs. First, more storage is required. Second, the system becomes more complex since we must properly manage access to replicated data. For example, if we allow two transactions to access and perhaps to update different replicas of the same item, each might be unaware of the effects of the other, resulting in a problem similar to the lost update problem. Thus, a replicated system must ensure that the replicas of a data item are properly updated and that an appropriate value is supplied to a transaction that requests to read an item. In the Internet grocer application, the replicated customer information needs to be updated only when the customer information changes—for example, a change of address, which occurs infrequently.

An item is said to be **totally replicated** if a replica exists at every site. It is said to be **partially replicated** if replicas exist at some, but not all, sites.

If the DBMS itself does not support replication, the application itself can replicate data items. The DBMS is then unaware of the fact that distinct items at different sites are replicas of one another. If $x1$ and $x2$ are replicas of a data item, each transaction must explicitly maintain the integrity constraint $x1 = x2$. A transaction that accesses a replicated data item must specify which replica it wants by addressing a specific DBMS. A transaction that updates a replicated item must explicitly initiate subtransactions to update each replica.

Instead of requiring transactions to manage replication, most commercial DBMSs provide a special subsystem for this purpose—a **replica control**—which makes replication invisible to the application. The replica control knows where all replicas of a data item are located. When a transaction requests to read or write an item, it does not specify a particular replica. The request is processed by the replica control, which automatically translates it into a request to access the appropriate replica(s) and passes the request to the local concurrency control (if the replica is local) and/or to the remote site(s) at which the replica resides. We assume that concurrency controls implement a locking protocol, so when replicas are accessed they are locked in the same way as are ordinary data items: a shared lock for read access; an exclusive lock for write access. The concurrency control is unaware that a data item might actually be a copy of another data item at a different site. The relationship between the replica control and the concurrency control is shown in Figure 24.6.

FIGURE 24.6 Relationship between replica control and concurrency control in a replicated database.

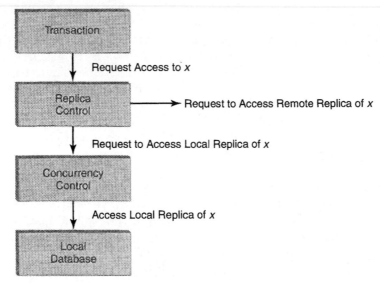

Replica controls in commercial DBMSs attempt to maintain some form of **mutual consistency**. With **strong mutual consistency**, every committed replica of an item always has the same value as every other committed replica. Unfortunately, performance considerations often make this goal impractical to achieve, and so most replica controls maintain the more modest goal, **weak mutual consistency**: all committed replicas of an item *eventually* have the same value, although, at any particular time, some might have different values. A variety of algorithms are used to maintain these goals.

The simplest replica control system is referred to as a **read-one/write-all** system. When a transaction requests to read a data item, the replica control can return the value of any one—presumably the nearest—of its replicas. With a fully replicated system, transactions that do not update replicated data items need not make any remote accesses and hence can respond rapidly to the user. When, however, a transaction requests to update a data item, the replica control must execute an algorithm that (eventually) causes all replicas of the item to be updated. This is the difficult case, and different algorithms have different characteristics. Generally speaking, read-one/write-all systems yield an improvement in performance over nonreplicated systems (where reads might have to access distant data items) if reads occur substantially more frequently than updates.

When a transaction requests to read a data item, the replica read is locked and the lock is held to commit time. Write locks are also held to commit time. The only issue is: what replicas are write locked and when? Read-one/write-all systems come in two varieties in this regard: synchronous update and asynchronous update. We discuss synchronous-update systems in Section 24.7.1 and asynchronous-update systems in Section 24.7.2.

24.7.1 Synchronous-Update Replication Systems

In a **synchronous-update system**, when a transaction updates a data item, the replica control locks and updates all of the replicas before the transaction commits. As a result, strong mutual consistency is maintained, transactions execute serializably, and database consistency is preserved. Synchronous replication is also referred to as **eager** replication since replicas are updated immediately.

Locking can be done in one of two ways.

1. *Pessimistically.* All necessary locks are acquired before the transaction proceeds beyond the statement that requested the access.

2. *Optimistically.* Only a single replica is locked and updated when the statement is executed. The other replicas are locked and updated later but before the transaction commits.

In either form, a new type of deadlock, **one-item deadlock**, is possible. This occurs if two updaters of the same item run concurrently and each succeeds in locking a subset of the item's replicas. Such deadlocks can be resolved with the usual protocols.

When a transaction commits, we must guarantee that each updated replica of an item is durable. It is not sufficient to simply commit the transaction at the site at which it was initiated (and release its locks) and send commit messages to replica sites since a replica site might crash before receiving the message. In that case, if the replica is not updated when the site recovers, a read request for the item by another transaction that uses that replica will not return the correct value.

The two-phase commit protocol can be used to overcome this problem. The cohorts are the replica sites that the transaction has accessed.[4] The prepared state is necessary to guarantee that all updates are durable before the transaction actually commits.

Unfortunately, eager replication has the effect of requiring the transaction to acquire additional locks, which increases the probability of deadlock. Furthermore, the response time is greatly increased due to the time required to handle lock requests for remote replicas and the fact that the transaction cannot complete until durability at all replica sites is ensured. These factors negatively impact performance, and for this reason synchronous replication has limited applicability.

The quorum consensus protocol. Although synchronous-update read-one/write-all replication can increase availability for readers, it does not help updaters. Because of the write-all requirement, the update cannot be completed if any site has crashed. We now describe a variant of synchronous replication in which no operation need access all replicas, so a data item might still be available even though some replica is inaccessible. To achieve this goal, we no longer insist on maintaining (even weak) mutual consistency. As a result, replica values are no longer identical. Despite this, the goal is the same as for read-one/write-all replication: all schedules resulting

---

[4] A replica site at which only reads have been performed can give up its read locks as soon as it receives the *prepare message*. See Exercise 24.12.

from the use of a quorum consensus replica control should be equivalent to serial schedules in which there is only one copy of each data item.

The basic idea of the **quorum consensus** protocol [Gifford 1979] is that when a transaction makes a request to read or write a replicated item, the concurrency control first locks some subset of the replicas, called a **read quorum** or a **write quorum** respectively, before granting the request. In the read case, the value returned to the transaction is then constructed from the values of the replicas in the read quorum. In the write case, all the replicas in the write quorum are then updated with the value to be written.

If the number of replicas in a read quorum is p and the number of replicas in a write quorum is q, we require that $p + q > n$ and $q > n/2$, where n is the total number of replicas. This ensures that there is a nonempty intersection between any read quorum and any write quorum and between any two write quorums of a particular item. As a result, whenever concurrent transactions execute conflicting operations on a replicated item, a lock request made by one of them will not be granted at the site of at least one replica, and one of the operations will be forced to wait. Note that the read-one/write-all system can be viewed as a quorum consensus protocol in which the number of replicas in a read quorum is one and in a write quorum is n.

With a quorum consensus algorithm it is possible to trade off the availability and the cost of the operations on an item. The smaller the value of p, the more available an item for reading and the lower the cost of a read. Similarly, the smaller the value of q, the more available an item is for writing and the lower the cost of a write. The availabilities of read and write are related, however. The more available and efficient read is, the less available and efficient write is and vice versa.

When a write request is granted, only the items in the write quorum are updated. Mutual consistency is not maintained since replicas not in the write quorum are not updated. As a result, replicas of an item will generally have different values, only some of which are current. We assume that, when each transaction commits, it is assigned a unique timestamp and that each replica of an item has the timestamp of the (committed) transaction that last wrote it. Since each read quorum intersects each write quorum, each read quorum intersects the write quorum assembled by the most recent writer. Therefore, at least one replica in each read quorum has the current value.

The problem is: how can the replica control identify such a replica? If the clocks at each site are exactly synchronized, this is not hard to do. Suppose that transactions T_1 and T_2 both update the same item, and T_1's update is first. Since their write quorums intersect, T_2's update must occur after T_1 commits (if T_1 and T_2 were concurrent, T_2 would have been forced to wait). Thus, since timestamps are assigned at commit time, T_2's timestamp must be greater than T_1's timestamp, and it follows that in any read quorum a replica with the largest timestamp in the quorum has the current value of the item.

Unfortunately, clocks at different sites are not exactly synchronized, and the consensus algorithm must take this into account. A technique for doing this is the subject of Exercise 24.21.

We can now summarize the quorum consensus protocol. We assume that an item, R, is stored as a set of replicas in the system and that each replica contains a value and a timestamp. We also assume an immediate-update pessimistic concurrency control and a strict two-phase commit protocol. Finally, we require that the timestamps of transactions are consistent with their commit order.

Quorum Consensus Replica Control Protocol.

1. When a transaction executing at site A makes a request to read or write a particular item, the replica control at A sends the request to a read or write quorum of sites containing the replica. If the concurrency control at all quorum sites can grant the appropriate lock on the replica, the requested operation is performed and a reply is returned to the replica control at A. If the request is a read, the reply contains the value of the replica and its timestamp.

2. When replies have been received by the replica control at A from a quorum of sites, the transaction can proceed. If the request was a read, the replica control at A returns to the transaction the value of the replica in the quorum with the largest timestamp.

3. A transaction commits using the two-phase commit protocol, where the cohorts are all of the sites at which it holds a read or write lock.[5] The coordinator obtains a timestamp for the transaction using its local clock and sends it with the prepare message. If the transaction commits, each cohort at which a write occurred updates its replica with the value of the timestamp before unlocking it.

As long as the control can assemble the necessary quorums for all operations, the protocol can proceed even when failures have occurred. When a site fails and is subsequently restarted, some of its replicas might have very old timestamps. The site need take no special recovery action, however, since the values contained in these replicas will not be used by any transaction until after they have been overwritten by some later transaction, at which time they will be current.

We have described the quorum consensus algorithm because it is an elegant solution to the replication problem. It has not, however, received wide acceptance among vendors of database systems.

24.7.2 Asynchronous-Update Replication Systems

In an **asynchronous-update system**, when a transaction updates a data item, the replica control updates some but not all of the replicas before the transaction commits. Most often, only a single replica is updated. The other replicas are updated after the transaction commits, and hence only weak mutual consistency is maintained. These later updates might be triggered by the commit operation or perhaps executed periodically at fixed time intervals. Asynchronous replication is referred to as **lazy** since replicas are not updated immediately. The updates are not done as a

---

[5] As before, a replica site at which only reads have been performed can release its read locks as soon as it receives the *prepare message*.

FIGURE 24.7 Schedule illustrating the possibility of inconsistent views with lazy replication. T_1 updates x and y at sites A and B. T_{ru} propagates the updates after T_1 commits. Because propagation is asynchronous, T_2 sees the new value of y but the old value of x.

T_1: $w(x_A)$	$w(y_B)$	*commit*				
T_2:		$r(x_C)$	$r(y_B)$	*commit*		
T_{ru}:					$w(x_C)$	*commit*

part of the transaction itself so that, in contrast to synchronous-update replication, *the system as a whole might not be serializable and transactions might see an inconsistent state.*

For example, Figure 24.7 shows a schedule in which transaction T_1 updates x_A—the copy of x at site A, and y_B—the copy of y at site B. After T_1 commits, transaction T_2 reads y_B—hence getting the new value of y—and the replica of x at site C, x_C, that has not yet been updated. Thus, T_2 sees a (possibly) inconsistent view of the database. Later, a replica update transaction, T_{ru}, that updates all replicas of x and y, including x_C, is executed.

In the context of replication, **capture** refers to the process by which the replica control recognizes that an update of a data item by an application has occurred and that the new value must be propagated to all replicas whose value has not been updated. Capture can take two forms: the log can be monitored and updates to replicated items noted for later propagation; or triggers can be set in the database to record the changes. **Apply** refers to the process by which replica sites are informed of the updates they must perform to keep their replicas current.

Different applications are best served by different forms of asynchronous replication. In some cases, the emphasis is on keeping the replicas as tightly synchronized as possible. Although serializability is not ensured, the goal is to minimize the interval between the time one replica is updated and the time the update is applied to the other replicas. A distributed application that maintains account or customer service records might fall in this category, which is variously referred to as **group**, **peer-to-peer**, or **multimaster** replication. In other cases, tight synchronization is not crucial. For example, an organization might have a large sales force in the field that periodically logs in to a central site and downloads a reasonably up-to-date view of the data. The form of replication that is frequently used in this case is **primary copy** replication. A third form of replication is referred to as **procedural** and applies when large blocks of data must be updated.

Primary copy replication. In this approach to replication, a particular replica of a data item is designated the **primary copy** [Stonebraker 1979], and other replicas are **secondary copies**. Secondary copies are created by **subscribing** to the changes made at the primary copy. Although a transaction can read any copy, it can update only the primary. In one approach, if transaction T at site A wants to update data item x, it must obtain an exclusive lock on the primary copy of x, x_p, and update it. Even if there is a secondary copy at A, x_A, the secondary is not updated immediately. As a result, if two transactions want to update x, the first must commit before the lock on x_p can be granted to the second. Thus, the write operations of transactions are serialized, but read operations are not. In another approach, the application simply transmits updates to the primary copy to be processed later.

T's updates are asynchronously and nonserializably propagated to secondary copies (including x_A) after it commits. Since T and the apply step do not constitute a single isolated unit, replicas are updated in a nonserializable fashion. Since reads can be satisfied using arbitrary replicas, concurrent transactions might see an inconsistent view of the database (as shown in Figure 24.7) and function incorrectly as a result.

With primary copy replication, all updates are funneled through the primary copy. If T updates x, the site at which x_p exists executes replica-update transaction(s) to implement the apply step after T commits. A single update transaction might update all replicas (as in Figure 24.7), or an individual update transaction for each replica might be used. If the update transactions at each replica site are executed in the same order as that in which the primary copy is updated, the replica control system guarantees weak mutual consistency.

In a variant of primary copy replication, if T at site A requests to update x, and x_A is not the primary copy, it locks both the primary copy of x and x_A and updates them as part of the transaction. Other secondary copies are updated as previously described after T commits. In this way, the user at A can execute subsequent transactions that read x_A without having to wait for the update to propagate back from the primary to A.

In an alternate approach to the apply step, instead of propagating updates from the primary copy when a transaction commits, the replica control system at a site periodically broadcasts the current values of primary copies at its site to other sites. The broadcast should be transactionally consistent, containing all of the updates performed by committed transactions on primary copies of data items at the site since the last broadcast.

In some implementations, each secondary site can declare a view of the primary item, and only that view is transmitted. This is particularly useful if the secondary sites communicate with the primary site through a low-bandwidth (e.g., telephone) connection and it is therefore important that only relevant data be replicated at each site.

In still another approach to the apply step, updates are not automatically propagated from the primary site, and replica sites explicitly request that their view be refreshed. This is referred to as a **pull strategy** since the secondary sites pull the data from the primary sites. In contrast, in the **push strategy** of the algorithms we have described up to this point, the primary site pushes data out to the secondary. Push strategies reduce the interval in which replica values are outdated. In either case, all replicas of an item will eventually contain the same value, so weak mutual consistency is supported.

A pull strategy might be appropriate when secondary sites are mobile computers (perhaps hand-held) used by a large sales force in the field. A salesperson might update his replica when he connects to the network. Since bandwidth is small,

FIGURE 24.8 With group replication, updates might reach replicas in different orders, leading to violation of mutual consistency.

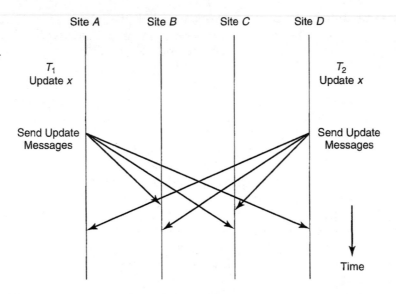

he defines a view that includes only information pertaining to his sales region. In this application, the replicas can be slightly (for example, minutes or hours) old. Read accesses predominate. A write occurs only when a new contract is signed, and the new information is sent to the primary first and broadcast to (or pulled by) all secondaries later. If the update occurs while the secondary is disconnected, it must be saved until a connection is established.

Group replication. In contrast to primary copy replication, with group replication an update can be made to any replica—presumably the nearest one. (Thus, if a database is totally replicated, read/write as well as read-only transactions can be completed using only data at the local site.) The updates made by a transaction, T, are later propagated to the other replicas. Since propagation is asynchronous, global serializability cannot be guaranteed.

As with primary copy replication, group replication can lead to nonserializable, and hence incorrect, schedules. For example, a schedule similar to the one shown in Figure 24.7 is possible. In addition, without further refinement, it might not even support weak mutual consistency. Figure 24.8 illustrates a situation in which two concurrent transactions, T_1 and T_2, executing at sites A and D, respectively, update replicas of data item x locally. As shown, the order of arrival of the messages that propagate those updates might be different at different replica sites. Since the final value of a replica is the value in the last message received, mutual consistency might not be preserved. In the terminology of replication, a **conflict** has occurred and the replica control system must employ a **conflict resolution** strategy to guarantee **convergence** and preserve mutual consistency.

One algorithm that guarantees weak mutual consistency associates a unique timestamp with each update and with each replica. An update's timestamp is the time at which the update was requested, and a replica's timestamp is the timestamp of the last update applied to it. Weak mutual consistency can be ensured if a replica site simply discards an arriving update when its timestamp is less than that of the replica's timestamp. This is an example of the Thomas Write Rule [Thomas 1979] we discussed in Section 20.9.1. With this algorithm, the value of each replica eventually converges to the value contained in the update with the largest (most recent) timestamp. Although the rule guarantees weak mutual consistency, lost updates are possible: two transactions read and update different replicas, but only the result of one survives. For this reason, the algorithm might not be appropriate for some applications.

Unfortunately, no algorithm exists that correctly merges the effects of different transactions in such situations for all applications. In some applications, the appropriate conflict resolution strategy is obvious. For example, if a directory is replicated and concurrent transactions append distinct entries to different replicas, the final value of all of the directory's replicas should contain both entries. Thus, a conflict-resolution strategy for a particular application can often be devised. In the general case, a replica control system can notify the user when it detects a conflict and allow the user to resolve it. Since there is no conflict-resolution strategy that is guaranteed to be correct, some commercial systems provide several alternative ad hoc strategies, including "Oldest update wins," "Youngest update wins," "Update from the highest priority site wins," and "User provides a procedure for conflict resolution."

Procedural replication. This form of replication is useful when updates need to be applied to many items in a batch-oriented fashion—for example, if interest has to be posted to each bank account and bank records are replicated at several sites. If each update were separately transmitted over a network, communication costs would be high. An alternative is to replicate a stored procedure at each secondary site and invoke that procedure at all replicas when the data is to be updated.

Summary. *The trade-off between synchronous- and asynchronous-update systems is one of correctness versus performance.* Many commercial DBMSs provide both types of replication. The designer should be aware that asynchronous updates can produce nonserializable schedules that might be incorrect and yield an inconsistent database.

In some applications, however, asynchronous updates are acceptable. For example, in Section 24.6.1 we described an Internet grocer application in which information about a customer was stored at both the headquarters site and at a warehouse site. We did not assume that a customer's record was identical at the two sites and treated the registration transaction as two separate subtransactions using a zero-phase commit. If, however, the records were identical, the database could be viewed as replicated and an asynchronous-update algorithm would produce the same result: the record would be created by a transaction at headquarters site, and, after the transaction had committed, it would be propagated to the warehouse site. As with the zero-phase commit, the response time seen by the user is minimized.

24.8 Distributed Transactions in the Real World

Although the theory underlying distributed transaction processing systems might seem complex, its final results are surprisingly simple and practical. If the concurrency control at each site is either a strict two-phase locking (pessimistic) control or an optimistic control (hence schedules are locally serializable), a two-phase commit protocol is used (hence transactions are globally atomic), and synchronous-update replication is used (hence, strong mutual consistency is maintained), distributed transactions will be globally serializable. Global deadlocks, which might arise as the result of waits imposed by pessimistic controls, can be resolved using timestamps, waits-for graphs, or timeout.

Atomicity and isolation are the properties of a transaction processing system that guarantee that if the transactions of an application are consistent, the application will run correctly. We have now seen that, in order to improve performance, distributed transaction processing systems frequently do not support atomicity and isolation completely. Transactions at a site might not run at the SERIALIZABLE isolation level, the two-phase commit protocol might not be used in committing distributed transactions, or an asynchronous-update technique might be used to support replication. Whether these compromises cause incorrect behavior is very much dependent on the semantics of the application. For this reason, in building a particular transaction processing system, these issues must be considered carefully.

BIBLIOGRAPHIC NOTES

A comprehensive discussion of distributed transactions can be found in [Gray and Reuter 1993]. [Ceri and Pelagatti 1984] is more theoretical in its orientation.

The two-phase commit protocol was introduced in [Gray 1978; Lampson and Sturgis 1979]. The presumed abort property for the two-phase commit protocol was discussed in [Mohan et al. 1986]. A more powerful commit protocol, called three-phase commit, was introduced in [Skeen 1981]. The wound-wait and kill-wait systems, which use a timestamp technique to avoid deadlocks, were introduced in [Rosenkrantz et al. 1978]. A proof that the two-phase commit protocol, together with two-phase locking local concurrency controls, guarantees global serializability was given in [Weihl 1984]. The quorum consensus protocol was introduced in [Gifford 1979]. Primary copy replication was introduced in [Stonebraker 1979], and the Thomas Write Rule is from [Thomas 1979].

EXERCISES

24.1 Describe the recovery procedure if a cohort or coordinator crashes at the following states within the two-phase commit protocol:

a. Before the coordinator sends the *prepare message*

b. After a cohort has voted but before the coordinator has decided commit or abort

c. After the coordinator has decided to commit but before the cohort has received the *commit message*

d. After the cohort has committed, but before the coordinator has entered the completion record in the log

24.2 Explain why a cohort does not have to force an abort record to the log during the two-phase commit protocol.

24.3 Explain how the fuzzy dump recovery procedure must be expanded to deal with prepared records in the log (assuming the site engages in the two-phase commit protocol).

24.4 Describe the two-phase commit protocol when one or more of the database managers is using an optimistic concurrency control.

24.5 Describe the presumed abort feature in the case in which multiple domains are involved.

24.6 Describe how the two-phase commit protocol can be expanded to deal with a cohort site that uses a timestamp-ordered concurrency control.

24.7 Give schedules of distributed transactions executing at two different sites such that the commit order is different at each site but the global schedule is serializable.

24.8 Phase 1 of the *Extended Two-Phase Commit Protocol* is identical to Phase 1 of the two-phase commit protocol we have described. Phase 2 of the extended protocol is as follows:

> *Phase Two.* If the coordinator received at least one "aborting" vote during Phase 1, it decides to abort, deallocates the transaction record from its volatile memory, sends an *abort message* to all cohorts that voted "ready," and terminates the protocol. If all votes are "ready," the coordinator enters its uncertain period, forces a *willing_to_commit record* (which contains a copy of the transaction record) to its log, and sends a *commit message* to each cohort. Note that the transaction is not yet committed.
>
> If a cohort receives an *abort message*, it decides to abort, rolls back any changes it made to the database, appends an abort record to its log, releases all locks, and terminates. If a cohort receives a *commit message*, it decides to commit, forces a commit record to its log, releases all locks, sends a *done message* to the coordinator, and terminates the protocol.
>
> The coordinator waits until it receives the first *done message* from a cohort. Then it decides to commit, forces a commit record to its log, and waits until it receives a *done message* from all cohorts. Then it writes a completion record to its log, deletes the transaction record from its volatile memory, and terminates.

Describe timeout and restart procedures for this protocol. Show that this protocol blocks only when the coordinator and at least one cohort crash (or a partition occurs) or when all cohorts crash. Give an example where the transaction aborts even though all cohorts voted "ready."

24.9 Design a logging, timeout, and restart procedure for the linear commit protocol. Do not assume the existence of a separate coordinator module. Assume that all communication between cohorts is carried on along the chain.

24.10 Consider a distributed transaction processing system that uses a serial validation optimistic concurrency control at each site and a two-phase commit protocol. Show that deadlocks are possible under these conditions.

24.11 Prove that if all sites use optimistic concurrency controls and if a two-phase commit protocol is used, distributed transactions are globally serializable.

24.12 If a cohort in a distributed transaction has performed only read operations, the two-phase commit protocol can be simplified. When the cohort receives the *prepare message*, it gives up its locks and terminates its participation in the protocol. Explain why this simplification of the protocol works correctly.

24.13 Consider the following atomic commit protocol that attempts to eliminate the blocking that occurs in the two-phase commit protocol. The coordinator sends a *prepare message* to each cohort containing the addresses of all cohorts. Each cohort sends its vote directly to all other cohorts. When a cohort receives the votes of all other cohorts it decides to commit or abort in the usual way.

a. Assuming no failures, compare the number of messages sent in this protocol and in the two-phase commit protocol. Assuming that all messages take the same fixed amount of time to deliver, which protocol would you expect to run faster? Explain.

b. Does the protocol exhibit blocking when failures occur?

24.14 The *kill-wait* concurrency control of Exercise 20.32 is based on locking. When it is used in a distributed system, it is referred to as the *wound-wait* protocol. We assume that a distributed transaction uses RPC to communicate among cohorts so that when the two-phase commit protocol starts, all cohorts have completed. The *kill* primitive is replaced by a *wound* primitive.

If the cohort of transaction, T_1, at some site makes a request that conflicts with an operation of the cohort of an active transaction, T_2, at that site, then

$$\text{if } TS(T_1) < TS(T_2) \text{ then } wound\ T_2 \text{ else } make\ T_1\ wait$$

where *wound* T_2 means that T_2 is aborted (as in the *kill-wait* protocol), unless T_2 has entered the two-phase commit protocol, in which case T_1 waits until T_2 completes the protocol.

Explain why this protocol prevents a global deadlock among transactions.

24.15 Suppose the nested transaction model were extended so that subtransactions were distributed over different sites in a network. At what point in the execution of a distributed nested transaction would a cohort enter the prepared state? Explain your reasoning.

24.16 In the text we state that if, in a distributed database system, each site uses a strict two-phase locking concurrency control (all locks are held until commit time) and the system uses a two-phase commit protocol, transactions will be globally serializable. Does the result also hold if the concurrency controls are not strict—read locks are released early—but are two phase?

24.17 Explain how to implement synchronous-update replication using triggers.

24.18 Design a quorum consensus protocol in which, instead of a timestamp field, each item has a version number field, which is updated whenever the item is written.

24.19 Consider a quorum consensus protocol in which an item is stored as five replicas and the size of each read and write quorum is three. Give a schedule that satisfies the following conditions:

> Three different transactions write to the item. Then two of the replica sites fail, leaving only three copies—*all of which contain different values*.

Explain why the protocol continues to execute correctly.

24.20 Consider a quorum consensus protocol in which an item is stored as n replicas, and the size of read and write quorums are p and q respectively.

a. What is the maximum number of replica sites that can fail and still have the protocol work correctly?

b. What is the minimum value that p and q can have such that $p = q$?

c. Select p and q so that the maximum number of replica sites can fail and still have the protocol work correctly. For this selection, how many sites can fail?

24.21 The quorum consensus replication algorithm requires that the timestamps of transactions be consistent with their commit order. In the absence of synchronized clocks, this requirement is not easily met. Propose an alternate algorithm for tagging replicas that can be used with quorum consensus. (*Hint:* Instead of assigning timestamps to transactions, assign version numbers to individual replicas.)

24.22 Describe an application of replicated data items in which serializability is not needed.

24.23 In what way is the checkbook you keep at home for your checking account like an asynchronous-update replication system?

24.24 Give an example of a nonserializable schedule produced by a primary copy asynchronous-update replication system.

24.25 The following variant of the primary copy asynchronous-update replication protocol has been proposed for totally replicated systems.

a. A transaction executing at site A updates only the replicas at A before it commits (it needed to access no other site since replication is total).

b. After the transaction commits, a second transaction is initiated to update the primary copies of all items updated at A.

c. After the transaction in step (b) has completed, each primary site propagates the update made at that site to all secondaries (including the one at site A). Updates made to a primary copy by several transactions are propagated to secondaries in the order in which the primary was updated.

Explain why, in step (b), all primaries must be updated in a single transaction and, in step (c), the update is propagated to site A.

24.26 Explain how triggers can be used to implement primary copy replication.

24.27 Describe a design of a logging protocol for distributed savepoints.

24.28 In the presumed commit version of the two-phase commit protocol described in the text, when the protocol starts, the coordinator forces a start record to its log. Describe a situation in which, if the coordinator had not forced this record to its log, the protocol would not work correctly.

25

Web Services

25.1 The Basic Idea

Web services are one of the most exciting new application areas on the Internet. On hearing this, you might ask

What's all the fuss about? It's easy to obtain a Web service. For example, if I want to make a reservation on an airline flight, I first go to Google to find the Web addresses of the airline. Then I go to their Web site, make a few clicks to read their schedule, a few more clicks to find the flight I want, and a final click to charge the reservation I want to my credit card. Done!

All well and good, but now consider another scenario in which that approach does not work so well:

You are a travel agent, and you want to schedule a trip for a client. First you want to get quotes on fares from a number of airlines for that date and time. Then you want to make the airline reservation on the cheapest airline. After that, you want to perform similar activities to make hotel reservations and reserve a car. Actually, you are performing these services for about twenty-five clients at the same time.

You certainly do not want to do all this by making individual clicks on a Web page. You want the services to be performed by a program that reads a local file to determine the required activities and then sends messages over the Internet to other programs at the sites of the airlines, the hotels, and the car rental agencies.

This is the type of scenario for which Web services are oriented. They are, in general, business-to-business (B2B) systems, in contrast to the customer-to-business (C2B) systems with which you might be more familiar.

B2B systems are widely viewed as one of the fastest-growing areas of Web applications with a huge market potential. They open up exciting opportunities for businesses to

- Provide their services to an expanding world-wide market
- Outsource nonessential functions to other businesses and concentrate on core services

- Obtain services they need for their business from a world-wide network of possible service providers

- Establish partnerships with businesses from around the world to provide combined services that are better and less expensive than any one business could provide

And, most importantly, the costs of obtaining or providing these services, the so-called *transaction costs*, are sharply reduced compared with conventional methods. Thus, in the travel agency example, the transaction costs of obtaining the airline and hotel reservations by computer-to-computer communication are essentially zero compared with the costs of a human obtaining those reservations using the telephone or sitting at a computer terminal.

Web services can be regarded as the next step in several trends related to software integration. In Chapter 19 we discussed distributed transactions as a mechanism for integrating independent functions within the same enterprise. While Web services provide a model for doing the same thing, the ultimate goal is to provide integration beyond enterprise boundaries, where the modules being integrated have been developed by completely independent organizations. This type of integration should be possible as the field matures and standards take hold. Furthermore, whereas standards like CORBA (see Section 14.6) are oriented toward fine-grained integration at the level of objects, Web services are oriented toward coarse-grained integration at the level of entire services.

In this section, we briefly discuss some of the issues that arise in providing a service of this type.

- How can a company that wants to provide a particular service describe it to potential users? Such a description must include the format of the messages required to invoke the service and the address of the site at which the service is provided. The description must be understandable by both people and programs.

- How can a company that wants to obtain a particular service discover what companies provide it and, for each provider, find the information necessary to invoke that service? The service description must be discoverable by both people and programs.

- How can we ensure that an invocation message sent by the service requester will be understood by the service provider since the programs might be written in different languages, and the data types recognized by the languages might not be consistent? Furthermore, the programs might be executing under different operating systems on computers produced by different vendors. This issue is called **interoperability**.

The following technologies characterize and support Web services. But we want to caution you that this field is changing very rapidly. By the time you read this, many details of the proposed standards that we discuss might change. We are presenting a snapshot of a rapidly changing field.

- **XML** (Extensible Markup Language). Web services are described using XML, and the bodies of the various messages exchanged between services are XML documents. The use of XML allows the description to be independent of the hardware or software platforms involved and hence addresses the interoperability issue. For example, when a C++ program invokes a Web service, the arguments are converted into an XML format before they are passed to the service. When the invocation message reaches the service site, the arguments are converted to the format expected by the service, which might be implemented in Java. Thus the Java program can understand the data sent by the C++ program. We discussed XML in Chapter 15.

- **SOAP.**[1] The messages used by Web services are generally sent using the SOAP protocol. SOAP messages are XML documents and are exchanged using both synchronous, *request/response*, and asynchronous, *one-way*, communication. The original emphasis of SOAP was to support RPC and the transfer of parameter values with a request/response message pattern, but the protocol is increasingly used simply to support the exchange of arbitrary XML documents using both message patterns. It is anticipated that such document transmission will ultimately be its dominant use. This use of SOAP to transmit XML documents is often referred to as a **document-centric** approach. SOAP messages are frequently carried as the data portion of HTTP messages. We briefly discuss HTTP (Section 28.3) before giving a more complete discussion of SOAP (Section 28.4).

- **WSDL** (Web Services Description Language). A Web service can be described by the operations it makes available to other services and the information it exchanges when those operations are invoked. WSDL is used for such descriptions and hence provides the functionality of an Interface Definition Language, IDL (see Section 23.5.2). For example, an operation that provides fare quotes for an airline receives a request from a travel agent. The request contains an XML document listing flight numbers and dates. The service responds with an XML document containing the requested fares. The WSDL description of the operation includes the name of the operation, the messages exchanged during the operation, and an itemization of the data contained in each message.

  In addition, the WSDL description specifies a message transport that can be used to carry the information, how the data items are mapped to the format of the messages used by that transport, and the address of the service. This information is generally referred to as a **binding** and hence WSDL can be thought of as "IDL with binding." Frequently, the transport is SOAP over HTTP.

  We sometimes say that the service *exposes* or *exports* a WSDL interface. By that we mean that the implementation of the service is hidden from its users, while its interface is published so that potential users can access it. The WSDL description itself is in the form of an XML document.

---

[1] Although the term SOAP started out as an acronym for Simple Object Access Protocol, it is now simply accepted as a name with no further meaning. Whatever the original intention, invoking object methods is now the least important use of the protocol

Although WSDL allows the specification of request/response message exchanges, the emphasis in the Web services community is moving toward loosely coupled, one-way, asynchronous interactions that allow more flexibility. Message delays, failures, and the uncertainty of linking up with a module whose implementation is under the control of an unrelated organization make this form of coupling more appropriate. This philosophy differentiates Web services from the more tightly coupled, synchronous, RPC-oriented approach taken by CORBA (see Section 14.6).

■ **BPEL** (Business Process Execution Language). The implementation of a complex Web service will generally involve synchronous and/or asynchronous interactions with the client and with other Web services. For example, the travel service might receive a client request, obtain price quotes from a number of airlines services, order tickets from one of them, interact with the client's credit card company, and finally send the tickets to the client. Hence, the service can be viewed as a workflow that communicates with other services. We discussed workflows in Section 19.3.6. The individual messages exchanged with these services are described in the WSDL documents they export, and the sequence in which these interactions (think tasks) take place amounts to a workflow. BPEL describes that workflow. It is a full-blown programming language with an emphasis on communication. A BPEL description of a workflow is in the form of an XML document.

■ **UDDI** (Universal Description, Discovery, and Integration). UDDI addresses the problem of publishing and discovering Web services. It provides a registry (database) in which both of the following are included:

  • Companies that want to provide Web services can publish information about their services (including a WSDL description of how the service can be invoked).

  • Companies that want to utilize services available on the Web can search the database to discover companies that provide such services.

  The information stored in the UDDI registry is contained in XML documents.

■ **WS-Coordination.** Complex Web services might require some aspects of transactional atomicity. WS-Coordination provides a framework for coordinating the termination of a set of Web services.

Security is important when interacting with Web services. Messages might have to be encrypted, and the various principals involved in requesting and supplying Web services might have to be authenticated. We discuss security for Web services in Section 26.14.

Front-end systems, back-end systems, and transaction processing. Many enterprises doing business over the Web implement the services they provide with transaction processing systems such as those we discussed in Chapter 23. For example, the implementation of an operation getFareOp that provides price quotes for airline reservations might involve the execution of a transaction that accesses a database that stores fares. In the context of Web services, such a transaction processing system is called a **back-end system**. By contrast, the systems we will discuss in this chapter are called **front-end systems**. Front-end systems describe how services are described and invoked, while back-end systems describe how they are implemented.

A back-end system can be exposed on the Web by equipping it with a WSDL interface. We can think of that interface as a simple front-end system and the combination of the front end and the back end as an extension of the transaction processing systems we discussed in Chapter 23.

In the C2B systems described in Section 23.9, the front-end systems cause Web pages to be displayed by the client's browser, and HTTP is used for communication. If the system is implemented in J2EE (Section 23.10), an HTTP message is received by a servlet, which interprets it and then calls a session bean in the back end to implement the service. Similarly, a B2B system is invoked by a SOAP message. The message is received by a SOAP-processing module that interprets it and then (again assuming J2EE) calls a session bean in the back end that implements the service.

Frequently, the implementation of an operation exported by a Web service involves the use of operations exported by other services. Hence, one service integrates the functionality of other services. This integration can be expressed as a BPEL program that invokes the other services. A system that performs this integration is also referred to as a front-end system, but in this case the front-end system is not directly connected to a back-end system. Instead, it invokes back-end systems and other front-end systems through their WSDL interfaces. Hence, to expand on our comparison of front-end and back-end systems, front-end systems are concerned with how Web services are exposed on the Web, how they are invoked, and how they integrate other services. Back-end systems are concerned with how the basic functionality (e.g., database transactions) are implemented.

Thus, Web services are provided by systems that combine front ends and back ends in a variety of ways. Such systems can be viewed as extensions of the transaction processing systems we discussed in Chapter 23. Furthermore, just as an invocation of a back-end system might require transactional properties, the invocation of a front-end system that integrates the operations of other Web services might also require transactional properties. WS-Coordination is designed for this purpose. Thus the material in this chapter also extends the discussion of workflows, distributed transactions, and atomic commit protocols in Chapters 19 and 24.

25.2 Web Basics

Before starting a discussion of Web services it is useful to set the stage by reviewing a few relevant facts about the Internet that supports these services. The Internet is a collection of interconnected computers that communicate by exchanging messages. Each computer is directly connected to a subset of neighboring machines through network links. A message is passed using a store-and-forward technique in which it moves from machine to neighboring machine as it travels from source to destination.

A hierarchical set of protocols supports communication, with each level in the hierarchy implementing a communication abstraction based on the services provided by lower levels. The physical level provides the abstraction of sending bits over the communication devices. The link level transmits packets between neighboring nodes using the services of the physical level. The network level implements an end-to-end abstraction by moving an entire message from source to destination using the services of the link level.

Our story starts at the next level, called the **transport level**, which provides the basic end-to-end service of moving data from source to destination in a way that insulates higher levels from having to deal with the idiosyncrasies of the intervening networks and provides certain quality-of-service guarantees. Such guarantees might be concerned with reliability, throughput, and delay.

A **connection-oriented** transport level is one in which a connection between two endpoints is set up before any data is transmitted and then removed when communication has completed. The connection is established by reserving resources at the endpoints, and perhaps at intermediate nodes as well, so that data can be moved in a way that is consistent with the guarantees. Data structures are set up at the endpoints to store the state of the connection: who is entitled to send data next, what is the sequence number to be used, etc. In some implementations, a path between the endpoints, consisting of a sequence of intermediate nodes, might be determined at the network level and physical resources along the path are reserved: bandwidth on communication lines and buffer space in nodes.

By maintaining state information, the connection-oriented approach is in a position to provide such features as reliability (lost data can be detected), sequencing (data segments are received in the same order as they are sent), and flow control (the rate at which data is sent can be controlled). For example, the sequence number stored at an endpoint enables the receiver to detect missing or out-of-order data. On the other hand, the connection set-up and take-down costs are not trivial. Hence, the connection-oriented approach is most suitable in situations in which large amounts of data must be transferred.

Our interest in this issue arises from the fact that Web communication is generally based on the **Transmission Control Protocol** (TCP), which is a transport level connection-oriented protocol. The **Hypertext Transfer Protocol** (HTTP) is built on top of TCP and is designed specifically for Web communication. HTTP messages are contained in TCP data that travels over TCP connections. Indeed, you can think of the Web as a set of clients and servers on the Internet that communicate using HTTP. Hence, before we start discussing Web services, we need to spend a little time discussing HTTP.

25.3 Hypertext Transfer Protocol

HTTP is a connection-oriented protocol that supports the exchange of messages with arbitrary content (not just HTML pages) between a source and a destination. It has a request/response structure and was originally designed to support simple interactions between a client (browser) and a Web server. The client sends a request message containing a Uniform Resource Locator (URL), more generally, a Uniform Resource Identifier (URI) that identifies a page to a Web server, and the server responds with a response message containing the page.

Request and response messages have different formats. The first line of a request message, referred to as the **request line**, has the form

method   URL   HTTP_version

The *URL* field identifies an item in the network and consists of three parts: the protocol, the host name, and the local name of an item at that host. For example, in the URL http://www.yourbusiness.com/pages/display, the prefix http identifies the protocol used to access an item, www.yourbusiness.com identifies the machine hosting the item, and /pages/display names an item at that machine.

The *method* field names the method to be invoked at the server that receives the message. Some commonly used methods are

- GET—requests the page identified by the URL
- HEAD—requests information *about* the page identified by the URL (the page is not transmitted)
- POST—contains information to be used at the server, which can include much more than just a URL. (We describe an important use of this below.)

The request line can be followed by one or more **header lines** having the form

field_name : *value*

Each header line supplies a different type of information to the server as identified by the field name. For example, a From field provides the sender's e-mail address, a Content-Type field describes the format of the data being sent, an Accept field specifies an acceptable response format, and an If-Modified-Since field (which might be used when a GET method is invoked) instructs the server to respond with the page identified in the URL only if it has been modified since the time (value) supplied. A SOAPAction header line is used if the data carried by the HTTP message is a SOAP message. It identifies the SOAP processor at the server that is to receive the message. The last header line is followed by an empty line, and any data follows that.

A simple client/server interaction starts when the user clicks on a link on a page displayed by a browser. The browser, using the services of a directory server (Chapter 23), translates the host name in the URL associated with the link into an Internet host address. The complete address consists of the host address followed by a TCP port number, which is an internal address within the host. The default port number for HTTP messages is 80, which identifies a process at the server, frequently referred to as an HTTP processor, that processes HTTP messages. The browser then sets up a TCP connection to the server and sends an HTTP message specifying the GET method to request the page identified in the URL.

The response message begins with a status line having the form

HTTP_version   status_code   reason

The *reason* is a human readable explanation of the three-digit *status code* that encodes the outcome of the request. As with the request message, it can be followed by one or more header lines. For example, an Expires header gives the time at which the accompanying page should be considered stale, and a Last-Modified header gives the time the page was last modified. If a page has been requested, it follows the header fields.

Returning to our example and assuming the server can locate the requested page, the server sends a response message containing the page, and the browser displays the page, completing the interaction. In Version 1.0 of the protocol, the server then disconnects. This might seem wasteful since the user is likely to request additional pages but is done because the server can maintain a limited number of connections and has no idea of whether, or when, the user will send another message. The implication is that each client/server interaction has to pay the price of connection setup and takedown. This is described as the "stateless" aspect of the protocol, meaning that no connection information is maintained at either end between interactions. Version 1.1 of HTTP improves on this by allowing the TCP connection to stay in place for possible future interactions. The problem, however, is to decide how long to keep the connection open, since the user might go to lunch at that point. A timeout mechanism can be used for this purpose, with the result that a new connection might have to be set up if another interaction does not occur soon enough.

One of the powerful features of HTTP is that it allows the user to do more than simply follow links from one Web page to another. More generally, the user can invoke programs on the server (although this is not the technique generally used for Web services). In this case the HTML page displayed by the browser contains a form element. For example, the form might be opened by the tag

```
<FORM  action="http://www.yourbusiness.com/servlets/placeorder"
       method="POST">
```

and have input boxes that the browser displays and into which the user enters data, which serve as parameters to the program to be invoked at the server. The action and method attributes are used for this purpose. The value of action specifies where the parameters are to be submitted: in this case the program which handles the data has the local name /servlets/placeorder on the destination server www.yourbusiness.com. Note that the destination might be different from the server that supplied the page. If the appropriate TCP connection does not exist, the client must set it up prior to sending the message. The value of method specifies the method field in the request line of the HTTP message used to invoke the program. The convention for transmitting the parameters depends on the method. If it is POST, the parameters are encoded in the data part of the request message; if it is GET, they are encoded as a suffix to the URL in the request line. The URL in this case might be

```
http://www.yourbusiness.com/servlets/placeorder?box1="12"&box2="Nov"
```

where 12 and Nov are the data supplied by the user in input fields number 1 and 2.

25.4 SOAP: Message Passing

Web services are based on XML, and SOAP has been generally accepted by Web service implementors as the communication protocol for transmitting information in XML format between SOAP-enabled clients (as opposed to ordinary browsers). The information might be an arbitrary XML document, in which case it is referred to as **document-style SOAP.** Alternatively, the information might describe the invocation of a remote procedure, in which case it is referred to as **RPC-style SOAP.** SOAP itself, however, is simply a protocol for transmitting a single message, so the invocation of a remote procedure will involve the use of two RPC-style SOAP messages. In this case, SOAP prescribes a particular XML format for the messages.

XML is the essential ingredient here since it supports interoperability. In addition to being a simple mechanism for transmitting XML data, SOAP provides for extensibility, error handling, and flexible data encoding. The World Wide Web Consortium (W3C) sets the standards in the Web services area. At the time that this chapter was written, Version 1.2 of SOAP had achieved the status of a recommendation by W3C. A protocol recommended by W3C is essentially a standard. We will discuss that version here.

SOAP describes how a message is to be formatted but does not specify how it is to be delivered. The message must be embedded in a transport level protocol for this purpose, and HTTP is commonly used: the SOAP message becomes the body of an HTTP message and is sent to the destination. At the next lower level in the protocol hierarchy, the HTTP message becomes data in a TCP stream sent over a connection. Assuming that the destination is **SOAP enabled**, an HTTP listener (at port 80) passes the body of the HTTP message on to the SOAP processor—a program that understands SOAP and is capable of processing the message.

An embedding of a SOAP message in HTTP is shown in Figure 25.1. Our example concerns an airline, SlowHawk, and will be used throughout the chapter. In this case, the SOAP message is carried in the data part of an HTTP message invoking the POST method. The destination URL has been split between the request line, which contains the argument /fareService/getFareOp (identifying a procedure to be invoked), and the Host header line that provides the host address, www.SlowHawk.com, of the service. Since a SOAP message is being sent, the Content-Type field is set to application/soap+xml (as opposed to text/html, which is appropriate for a browser). The SOAPAction header contains a URI that identifies the operation that the message is intended to invoke. It can be used in message routing or by a firewall

FIGURE 25.1 SOAP embedded in HTTP.

```
POST /fareService/getFareOp HTTP/1.1
Host: www.SlowHawk.com
Content-Type: application/soap+xml
Content-Length: 1000
SOAPAction: http://www.SlowHawk.com/fareService/getFareOp
```

. . . A SOAP message, such as the one in Figure 25.2, goes here . . .
. . . The Content-Length *header assumes that the message length is 1000. . . .*

FIGURE 25.2 The structure of a SOAP message.

```
<s:Envelope xmlns:s="http://www.w3.org/2003/05/soap-envelope">
  <s:Header>
    <!-- The header element is optional -->
    <!-- If present, header blocks go here -->
  </s:Header>
  <s:Body>
    <!-- An XML document goes here -->
  </s:Body>
</s:Envelope>
```

for message filtering. The SOAPAction header is required when the HTTP message contains a SOAP message.

While HTTP is a common way to transmit SOAP messages, the messages can also be transmitted in other ways. For example, the message can be sent as the body of an e-mail message using the Simple Mail Transfer Protocol (SMTP). The technique used to transmit SOAP messages is referred to as a **binding**. It was a goal of the SOAP developers to allow for flexible binding. For example, a particular Web service might provide two bindings: a customer can submit a SOAP request using HTTP or e-mail. The design of the SOAP message format is not dependent on the choice of binding.

The structure of a SOAP message is shown in Figure 25.2. It consists of an optional header element and a mandatory body element wrapped in an Envelope element. The name space describing the Envelope tag, *http://www.w3.org/2003/05 /soap-envelope*, not only identifies the XML document as a SOAP message but also identifies the version. Different versions use different namespaces. A receiving SOAP processor can decide, based on the namespace URI, whether it is capable of processing the message. The tags Envelope, Header, and Body are defined in that namespace. The header element supports extensibility, which we will discuss later.

SOAP specifies a structure for a single message. Often Web services will need to exchange multiple messages. They may do this in a conversational mode in which there is no fixed pattern. The decision as to who sends a message next might be dynamically determined based on the XML documents exchanged. The XML documents form the body of the SOAP messages.

Alternatively, there might be a predetermined pattern. For example, having sent a particular message, the sender expects to get two responses back. The simplest pattern is the request/response pattern, which is natural for procedure invocation and is referred to as RPC-style SOAP. We discuss it next. It is important to note that remote procedures do not have to be invoked using this format and that request/response communication is not restricted to the invocation of remote procedures. A request/response exchange might simply be transmitting XML documents.

25.4.1 SOAP and Remote Procedure Call

Suppose the GoSlow Travel Agency uses a service provided by the SlowHawk airline to obtain quotes on airline fares. SlowHawk offers a method getFareOp that returns the quote and makes a reservation that will be held for a short period of time while the client decides whether or not to use it. GoSlow invokes getFareOp using the RPC-style SOAP request message shown in Figure 25.3. The response message from the method is shown in Figure 25.4. Request and response information is contained in the Body of the messages. A complete description of this information might be provided using an Interface Definition Language, but this is not part of SOAP.

FIGURE 25.3 The RPC-style SOAP request message for getFareOp.

```
<s:Envelope xmlns:s="http://www.w3.org/2003/05/soap-envelope"
    xmlns:xs="http://www.w3.org/2001/XMLSchema"
    xmlns:xsi="http://www.w3.org/2001/XMLSchema-instance">
  <s:Body>
    <n:getFareOp xmlns:n="http://www.goslow.com/wsdl/trips"
      s:encodingStyle="http://schemas.xmlsoap.org/soap/encoding">
      <n:custId xsi:type="xs:string">
        xyz123
      </n:custId>
      <n:destination xsi:type="xs:string">
        Chicago
      </n:destination>
      <n:departureDate xsi:type="xs:date">
        2004-12-27
      </n:departureDate>
      <n:returnDate xsi:type="xs:date">
        2005-1-04
      </n:retur
    </n:get
  </s:Body
</s:Envelope
```

FIGURE 25.4 The RPC-style SOAP response message from getFareOp.

```
<s:Envelope xmlns:s="http://www.w3.org/2003/05/soap-envelope"
    xmlns:xs="http://www.w3.org/2001/XMLSchema"
    xmlns:xsi="http://www.w3.org/2001/XMLSchema-instance">
  <s:Body>
    <n:getFareOpResponse xmlns:n="http://www.goslow.com/wsdl/trips"
      s:encodingStyle="http://schemas.xmlsoap.org/soap/encoding">
      <n:custId xsi:type="xs:string">
        xyz123
      </n:custId>
      <n:tripNo xsi:type="xs:float">
        10997890
      </n:tripNO>
      <n:cost xsi:type="xs:float">
        327.98
      </n:cost>
    </n:getFareOpResponse>
  </s:Body>
</s:Envelope>
```

The organization of the information is self-evident. The name of the element in the request body is the same as the method name (getFareOp), and the name of the element in the response body is (by convention) the method name with Response appended to the end (e.g., getFareOpResponse). The names of the child elements in the request message must be the same as the names of the input parameters of the method, and they appear in the same order. The names of the child elements in the response message are the same as the names of the output parameters of the method, and they appear in the same order. All of these names are drawn from the namespace http://www.goslow.com/wsdl/trips, which we will see in Figure 25.21 when we discuss WSDL. If a child element appears in both the request and response structures, it is an in/out parameter. An additional child element, with tag result, is used in the response message if the method returns a value, but that is not needed here. We will discuss the encodingStyle attribute at the end of this section.

In this example the arguments involve only the simple data types float, date, and string. Since these correspond to types in XML Schema, the arguments are easy to send. The sender transforms the arguments from the binary representation used by the client's host language to the ASCII strings required in the XML representation within SOAP.

In general, however, a structured type, such as an array or record, might be passed as an argument. The sender and the receiver must agree on the XML format to be used in the SOAP messages to describe that type. For example, are the elements of an array to be sent as a sequence of rows or a sequence of columns? What tags will be used? The sender then must convert its internal data into the ASCII string corresponding to that format when sending the message, and the receiver must convert from that format into its internal format after receiving the message. The conversion at the sender is called **serialization**, and at the receiver it is called **deserialization**.

Serialization/deserialization is not so easily done—since the client and server might be implemented in different languages on different platforms, and as a result there is no guarantee that the deserialization tool at the server will understand how the serialization was done at the client. There are several techniques for dealing with this problem. We describe one here and return to this issue in Section 25.5.2.

SOAP defines a data model that can be used to represent arbitrary data structures and then specifies rules for transforming instances of that model into the serialized ASCII strings contained in SOAP messages. For example, an instance of the model might represent a particular array of values, and the SOAP data model specifies how it should be represented as an ACSII string. It is up to the client and server to map an instance of a type specified in the client's or server's language into an instance of the model. Since the rules specify the serialization of each model instance, each client's and server's type instance is, as a result, mapped to a serialized string. The client and server must provide serialization and deserialization programs that implement that mapping.

The fact that SOAP rules have been used to serialize the request message of Figure 25.3 is indicated by the value of the encodingStyle attribute of the getFareOp element. In order to be completely flexible, however, SOAP allows applications to define their own set of rules to perform this function. Thus, with one set of rules an array might be serialized as a sequence of rows using one set of tags, while in another it might be serialized as a sequence of columns using a different set of tags. The set of rules that have been used are identified by the encodingStyle attribute. In most cases the standard SOAP encoding rules are indicated.

There must be a serializer and a deserializer program for every data type in the request and response messages. Many vendors supply programs that implement the SOAP encoding rules for the simple and structured types defined in the SOAP standard for languages such as Java and C++ (that is, they serialize and deserialize the data types in Java or C++ into the ASCII corresponding to the types defined in the SOAP standard). The encodingStyle attribute can be attached to any element other than the Envelope, Header, and Body elements, and its value specifies the style the sender used to serialize the data in that element. RPC-style messages in which data is encoded using the rule set named in the most local encodingStyle attribute are referred to as **RPC/encoded**.

25.4.2 SOAP Extensibility

The designers of SOAP were keenly aware that in the rapidly developing Web environment new infrastructure facilities would constantly be emerging. Thus, although today we might invoke the getFareOp method by simply supplying the method name and arguments as shown in Figure 25.3, later we might introduce security and require that the requester be authenticated before the method is invoked, or we might want to charge for the service and require that a billing routine be executed first. Encryption and logging are other examples. The key thing to note is that the information required to invoke the method does not change. However, additional information might be required by the new infrastructure service that is essentially orthogonal to the invocation information. Thus, the name and password necessary for authentication and the credit card number necessary for billing are unrelated to the method name and arguments required for invocation.

Extensibility refers to the fact that the information that must be supplied to an infrastructure service can be added without making any change to the body of the message that contains the information for the ultimate destination (e.g., the invocation information). SOAP provides the Header element for this purpose. A header can contain any number of child elements called **header blocks**, each of which carries information for a particular infrastructure service. Since XML allows an element to declare its own namespace, a development group can design the structure of a block for a particular service without worrying about interference from other groups developing blocks for other services. This not only illustrates the utility of the namespace concept, but also shows the advantage of being able to associate a namespace with an individual element (and its associated scope).

Figure 25.5 shows the request message of Figure 25.3 with the addition of a header block to accommodate an authentication service. The block uses the name-space www.SlowHawk.com/authentication/ in which the tags authinfo, name, and password are defined.

Having inserted the authentication information into the message, we next have to describe how the authentication server gets to perform its function before getFareOp is invoked. This issue is complicated by the fact that the authentication server might reside at a node, referred to as an **intermediary**, that is different from the node at which getFareOp is executed. The off-loading of infrastructure services is helpful when a Web service is heavily used. In this case the message must be routed through the intermediary, which accesses the header block on its way through, performs the infrastructure service, and then relays the message to the next (perhaps final) destination. Hence, the client must send the message to the intermediary, not to the destination server.

For example, SlowHawk might receive requests through a proxy machine that acts as an intermediary by performing authentication. The proxy scans the header looking for blocks that it should process. Each block is identified by its tag and namespace and can optionally have an attribute, role, that identifies the purpose of the block. The block should be processed by an intermediary designed to fulfill that purpose. Correspondingly, each SOAP node assumes certain roles and processes those blocks whose role attribute matches one of its functions.

A role value of next in a header block acts as a wild card: all intermediaries assume this role. Hence, a header block with role next should be processed by any intermediary that receives the message. Blocks that do not have a role specified are intended for the final destination.

The processing of a header block is mediated by the block's mustUnderstand attribute, which indicates whether or not an intermediary that assumes the role

FIGURE 25.5 A SOAP message for invoking `getFareOp` that uses an intermediate authentication server.

```
<s:Envelope xmlns:s="http://www.w3.org/2003/05/soap-envelope"
      xmlns:xs="http://www.w3.org/2001/XMLSchema"
      xmlns:xsi="http://www.w3.org/2001/XMLSchema-instance">
  <s:Header>
    <auth:authinfo xmlns:auth="www.SlowHawk.com/authentication/"
        s:role="SlowHawk.proxy.com"
        s:mustUnderstand="true">
      <auth:name> John Smith </auth:name>
      <auth:password> doggie </auth:password>
    </auth:authinfo>
    <!-- Other header blocks go here -->
  </s:Header>
  <s:Body>
    <n:getFareOp xmlns:n="http://www.goslow.com/wsdl/trips"
        s:encodingStyle="http://schemas.xmlsoap.org/soap/encoding">
      <n:custId xsi:type="xs:string">
        xyz123
      </n:custId>
      <n:destination xsi:type="xs:string">
        Chicago
      </n:destination>
      <n:departureDate xsi:type="date">
        2004-12-27
      </n:departureDate>
      <n:returnDate xsi:type="xs:date">
        2005-01-04
      </n:returnDate>
    </n:getFareOp>
  </s:Body>
</s:Envelope>
```

stated in the block is required to process the block. If it has value `true` and an intermediary that assumes the role is unwilling to process the block (perhaps because of its contents), the message is aborted and a fault message is returned to the sender. Header blocks that do not contain `mustUnderstand="true"` (i.e., the value is `false` or the attribute is not present) are regarded as optional. In that case, if an intermediary that assumes the role does not process the block, the block is simply ignored. A header block dealing with priority might be treated in this way.

A message might travel through a number of intermediaries on its way to its final destination. At each node the header is scanned and the appropriate blocks are processed. After processing a block, the intermediary might delete it and send

FIGURE 25.6 The SOAP message that the intermediary sends to the final destination.

```
<s:Envelope xmlns:s="http://www.w3.org/2003/05/soap-envelope"
        xmlns:xs="http://www.w3.org/2001/XMLSchema"
        xmlns:xsi="http://www.w3.org/2001/XMLSchema-instance">
  <s:Header>
        <ident:userId xmlns:ident="www.SlowHawk.com/authentication/">
          <ident:Id> 123456789 </ident:Id>
        </ident:userId>
  </s:Header>
  <s:Body>
      <n:getFareOp xmlns:n="http://www.goslow.com/wsdl/trips"
        s:encodingStyle="http://schemas.xmlsoap.org/soap/encoding">
        <n:custId xsi:type="xs:string">
          xyz123
        </n:custId>
        <n:destination xsi:type="xs:string">
          Chicago
        </n:destination>
        <n:departureDate xsi:type="date">
          2004-12-27
        </n:departureDate>
        <n:returnDate xsi:type="xs:date">
          2005-01-04
        </n:returnDate>
      </n:getFareOp>
  </s:Body>
</s:Envelope>
```

the message forward. The intermediary can also reinsert the header block (perhaps with new contents) or add new header blocks intended for nodes further down the chain. The final destination processes all headers with unspecified roles, as well as the message body. Notice that the destination need not be aware that any processing by intermediaries has taken place.

The message that the intermediary sends to the destination is shown in Figure 25.6. The authentication header block shown in Figure 25.5 has been deleted, and a new block has been added containing the (authenticated) Id determined by the proxy. In this case the destination uses Id to determine if the client is authorized to invoke getFareOp. Since the new block will be processed by the destination, it does not contain a role attribute.

WS-Addressing. As we have described it up to this point, a SOAP message does not contain the address of the intended receiver. The address must be provided separately by the program that constructs the SOAP message to the program that

FIGURE **25.7** WS-Addressing header blocks for the message of Figure 25.3.

```
<wsa:Action>http://www.SlowHawk.com/wsdl/trips/getFarePT/itineraryMsg
</wsa:Action>
<wsa:To> ··· URI identifying final destination ··· </wsa:To>
<wsa:MessageId> ··· unique message identifier ··· </wsa:MessageId>
```

implements the transport protocol that will carry the message and is included in the transport header. For example, the address is contained in the HTTP header in Figure 25.1. Furthermore, it might also be necessary to separately specify to the transport protocol the identity of the particular processor at the destination address that should receive the message. With HTTP this is the value in the SOAPAction header line. Providing this information separately is awkward since it makes the sending of a SOAP message dependent on the particular transport protocol in use: the information has to be provided in different ways to different protocols. This runs counter to a fundamental goal of the Web services architecture: it should be transport-neutral.

Furthermore, when security is an issue, spreading the message-relevant data over two protocols means that two different security mechanisms must be used. Techniques for securing a SOAP message, which we will discuss in Chapter 26, do not secure information provided outside the message.

For these reasons, it is desirable to make SOAP transport-neutral. All the information needed to send a SOAP message should be contained in the message itself. In this way, the message can be constructed in a uniform way by the sender and delivered to any transport protocol, which can then use the information in a transport-specific way.

WS-Addressing makes this possible by introducing header blocks into the SOAP message containing the missing information.[2] Additional blocks to be inserted in the header of the message of Figure 25.3 are shown in Figure 25.7. The prefix wsa identifies the WS-Addressing namespace, *http://schemas.xmlsoap.org/ws/2004/08 /addressing*. The address of the destination is provided by the To element. The Action element identifies the purpose of the message for the receiving SOAP processor. The purpose is determined by the application semantics. For example, the message might be a request to invoke a particular operation. The *recommended* way to identify the purpose of a message is to provide a URI that refers to the WSDL declaration of the information it carries—more precisely, that identifies the declaration of the WSDL message carried by the SOAP message. This is done by concatenating the target namespace of the WSDL document with the port type and the message name (details that will be clarified when we discuss Figure 25.22.) The value of the Action

---

[2] This discussion is based on the specification document submitted to W3C for approval entitled "Web Services Addressing (WS-Addressing)," August 10, 2004.

element should be identical to the value in the SOAPAction header line when the SOAP message is carried by HTTP.

While these two elements are required, a number of optional elements are also defined. The MessageId element provides a unique identifier for the message. In some situations it is useful to relate one message to another—for example a response to a prior request might want to identify that request. A RelatesTo header element is defined for this purpose, and in this case it would contain the identifier of the request.

Finally, WS-Addressing introduces the complex type EndpointReferenceType. An instance of the type contains all the information needed to address a message to an endpoint. For example, a sender might pass to a receiver an endpoint reference for an endpoint to which the receiver should send a reply (or a fault) message. (The endpoint might have a different address than the sender's.) The sender might use a ReplyTo header block, which takes an endpoint reference as its value.

The following is an example of an endpoint reference:

```
<wsa:EndpointReference
        xmlns:wsa="http://schemas.xmlsoap.org/ws/2004/08/addressing"
        xmlns:gs="http://www.goslow.com/wsdl/trips">
    <wsa:Address> <!-- a URI goes here --> </wsa:address>
    <wsa:PortType> gs:tripPT </wsa:PortType>
    <wsa:ReferenceProperties>
        <gs:Id> 16022875 </gs:Id>
    </wsa:ReferenceProperties>
</wsa:EndpointReference>
```

The value of the Address attribute is the URI of the destination and is the only required item. Information about the WSDL description of the endpoint can be provided. The portType element is an example of this (the service and port can also be named).

The ReferenceProperties element has child elements that are used to provide further identification of the message's target (beyond just the URI) at the destination (e.g., a shopping cart identifier). For example, a transaction might send a message to a receiver containing an endpoint reference to be used for a reply. It might include its Id in the reference. The Id will simply be copied by the receiver into a SOAP header block when a reply message is constructed (its value is not used by the receiver). The header block will be used when the reply arrives back at the sender to identify the transaction. Thus an endpoint identifies a target at some level of granularity. In some contexts this identification can be done with just a URL. In others, more is involved.

The endpoint reference might also supply policy information (e.g., should the message be encrypted, and if so, how).

After all this discussion, we can finally discuss how a process knows how to address a SOAP message. If the destination is known in advance, the information needed in the two SOAP header blocks that must be included in the message, To and Action, can be stored statically in the sending process. Or it can be retrieved from a WSDL specification (which we will discuss in Section 25.5). But suppose this is not the case? Suppose the process receives in a message an endpoint reference that it wants to use to address another message? The Address element of the reference is copied to the To header block in the new message. The value of the Action header block is obtained from the WSDL specification (see page 1066). The children of ReferenceProperties are copied verbatim as header blocks in the message and are used at the destination site to further direct the message.

This leaves open the question of how a node on the message path knows whether to relay the message on to an intermediary or send it to the final destination and, if it is to be sent to an intermediary, which one? The current approach to this is referred to as **next hop** routing: each node on the path makes this decision based on the destination address, information in header blocks, and information stored locally.

25.4.3 SOAP Faults

SOAP explicitly provides a mechanism for communicating information back to the sender about faults that arise while an intermediary or the final destination is processing the message. Faults are divided into categories. For example, a Version-Mismatch fault indicates that the namespace identifying the Envelope tag is not understood by the receiver (the receiver does not understand the version of SOAP used by the sender). A MustUnderstand fault indicates that an intermediary was not prepared to process a block addressed to it in which the value of the mustUnderstand attribute was true. A Sender fault indicates that there is a problem with the contents of the message, and a Receiver fault indicates that the problem is not with the message.

Although a SOAP body can contain an arbitrary XML document, we have seen that when a message is used to invoke a remote procedure, the body takes on a particular format. Similarly, SOAP provides an explicit format for a fault message. It contains a fault code, which places the fault in an appropriate category, a human-readable explanation of the fault, the identity of the node at which the fault occurred, and an optional element in which application-specific information can be provided.

25.4.4 SOAP Binding

A SOAP message is transmitted between two sites using a transport protocol. Since the transport is typically HTTP, we will say a few words about that particular binding. But keep in mind that other transport protocols can be used. SOAP does not require any particular transport.

When bound to HTTP, SOAP messages can be sent using either GET or POST. With POST, the SOAP envelope becomes the data part of an HTTP request message. When RPC-style SOAP is used to format the SOAP message (for example the message in Figure 25.3), a procedure is being invoked and results are generated which are returned in a SOAP response message. The SOAP response (for example the message in Figure 25.4) is carried in the data part of the HTTP response.

With document-style SOAP, communication can be one-way or request/response. In the latter case the sender transmits an XML document and the receiver responds with an XML document. However, the response is not built into the SOAP protocol as with RPC-style SOAP: two separate messages are involved, and each is carried in an HTTP request message. Keep in mind, that whenever an HTTP request message is transmitted, an HTTP (not a SOAP) response is generated automatically. This can serve as an acknowledgment that the XML document contained in the request has been received.

A nice feature of the HTTP binding when RPC-style SOAP is being transmitted, is that it provides a way to automatically associate the response with the corresponding request. This is important if an application is concurrently communicating with multiple servers and is referred to as **correlation**. In that case the application might have several requests outstanding. When a response arrives, it is necessary to associate it with the corresponding request. Since HTTP uses TCP, correlation follows from the fact that the response arrives in the HTTP response message on the same connection over which the request was sent.

With other transports (for example, email), correlation might not be automatic and it might be necessary to include a `MessageId` header block in the request message and a `RelatesTo` header block in the associated response message containing the same unique Id so that the two messages can be matched. The use of such header blocks is particularly appropriate if the application is communicating with several other services in conversational mode.

SOAP utilizes the HTTP GET method in the special case in which the application simply wants to retrieve a resource, that is, the server is accessed in read-only mode. This usage is a SOAP-level version of the interaction that occurs when a browser requests an HTML page: the browser sends an HTTP request message invoking the GET method, and the page is returned in the HTTP response message. A SOAP interaction of this sort is essentially the same except that a SOAP message is returned in the HTTP response instead of an HTML page. Since a SOAP message can contain an arbitrary XML document, this is appropriate when the application wants to process the information instead of displaying it. Since the interaction simply retrieves a SOAP message (XML document) identified by a URI—the only information that has to be sent to the target server in the request is that URI.

The HTTP binding supports this type of SOAP interaction by using an HTTP GET request that identifies the desired SOAP message (XML document) in the URI field and has an `Accept` field with value `application/soap+xml` to indicate that a SOAP message is expected in the response. The request message has no SOAP content. For example, a request to fetch SlowHawk's schedule for flights to Boston might have the form

```
GET /fareService/schedules?destination="Boston"  HTTP/1.1
Host: www.SlowHawk.com
Accept: application/soap+xml
```

Note that when GET is used, only the HTTP response message contains a SOAP message, while with POST, SOAP messages might be contained in both the HTTP request and in the response.

25.5 WSDL: Specifying Web Services

We have seen how SOAP can be used to encapsulate XML data exchanged by Web services, but how does one *describe* that service and how the data is exchanged? That is the problem addressed by WSDL (Web Services Description Language), which is under active development. At the time that this chapter was written, Version 1.1 was a W3C working draft and Version 2.0 was already under consideration. Since BPEL, which we discuss in Section 25.6, is based on Version 1.1, we will primarily be concerned with that version. Version 2.0 has some interesting features, which we will point out at the end of Section 25.5.

WSDL describes message exchange at two levels:

- The **abstract level** describes the (abstract) interface supported by a Web service. It gives the names of *operations* supported by the Web service, the *messages* used to invoke them, and the data types of the different items in the messages. It groups related operations into what it calls a *port type*. The abstract level can be viewed as an Interface Definition Language.

- The **concrete level** specifies how the abstract level is implemented. It gives a Web address at which the operations of a port type can be invoked and specifies how the messages that are exchanged through that address are *bound* to a specific transport protocol (for example, HTTP). It also groups Web addresses (and hence bindings of port types) together into something it refers to as a *service*.

25.5.1 The Abstract Level

In many respects describing a service at the abstract level is like describing an object in an object-oriented language. The abstract level defines the following elements:

- Optional **type** definitions in the XML Schema format. These types are used to specify message parts, as described below. See Section 15.3 for a detailed exposition of schema documents in XML.

- **Port types**. A port type provides an abstract description of a collection of operations. This description is analogous to an object interface.

- **Operations**. An operation is analogous to a method of an object. A description of an operation includes a set of messages that the operation expects as input and returns as output. An operation can also return a *fault* message if an execution of the operation ends abnormally.

■ **Messages**. Messages are used to invoke operations and return results. Messages are described independently of operations, and each operation refers to messages that describe its input, output, and faults. A message can have multiple **parts**. Each part is described by a type and is an input or output parameter of an operation.

An operation together with its messages and their parts corresponds to the signature of a method.

The overall structure of a WSDL specification at the abstract level is depicted in Figure 25.8. The italicized symbols are names of types, messages, port types, and operations, which are chosen by the user. Nonitalicized symbols are part of the WSDL syntax. The template shows the main components of an abstract level WSDL specification, how the namespaces are defined and used to identify the types and messages introduced by a WSDL document, and how user-defined types are used to give structure to messages. For instance, the template shows a two-part message where the structure of the first part is defined by a complex type defined in the same WSDL document, and the second part's type is a standard XML Schema type. We discuss each component of an abstract WSDL specification below.

Message descriptions.   Operations are invoked by messages. An example of a message description used in getFareOp is given in Figure 25.9. Each message can contain a number of parts. By decomposing the (abstract) message into parts it is possible to place different items of data in different positions within the (concrete) message of the transport protocol that carries the data. Thus, one part might be mapped to a SOAP header block while another might be stored in the body of a SOAP message. Each part has a type. We have assumed that all the declarations in this example appear in an XML document whose default namespace is *http://schemas.xmlsoap.org/wsdl/*, which declares tags such as part, message, etc.

The types in the getFareOp example are simple, but other applications might require complex types, which can be declared in the WSDL document or in an application-specific schema document.

Note that the message in Figure 25.9 is the WSDL declaration of the contents of the SOAP message in Figure 25.3 even though the names do not correspond. The name in Figure 25.3, getFareOp, is the name of the procedure being called, as required in RPC-style messages. The name in Figure 25.9, itineraryMsg, can be arbitrarily chosen. It would be a mistake to call it getFareOp, since that name is used for the operation that uses the message, as shown in Figure 25.10.

Operations.   An operation is described by the messages it exchanges and the pattern in which the exchange takes place. An operation used in the GoSlow example is shown in Figure 25.10. Different patterns are appropriate for different operations. Version 1.1 of WSDL supports two patterns. Version 2.0 provides more flexibility (see Section 25.5.4).

FIGURE 25.8 Skeleton of an abstract level WSDL description.

```
<definitions targetNameSpace="myNamespace"
        xmlns="http://www.w3.org/2003/06/wsdl"
        xmlns:xs="http://www.w3.org/2001/XMLSchema"
        xmlns:myPrefix="myNamespace">
    <types>
        <schema xmlns="http://www.w3.org/2001/XMLSchema"
                xmlns:myPrefix="myNamespace"
                targetNameSpace="myNamespace">
            <complexType name="myType1"> ... </complexType>
                ...
        </schema>
    </types>
        ...
    <message name="myMessage1">
        <part name="part1" type="myPrefix:myType1"/>
        <part name="part2" type="xs:string"/>
    </message>
    <message name="myMessage2">
        <part name="anotherPart1" type="..."/>
    </message>
        ...
    <portType name="myPortType">
        <operation name="myOperation">
            <input message="myPrefix:myMessage1"/>
            <output message="myPrefix:myMessage2"/>
            <fault message="..."/>
        </operation>
    </portType>
        ...
    <!-- Concrete level declarations go here -->
</definitions>
```

FIGURE 25.9 An abstract description of a WSDL message.

```
<message name="itineraryMsg">
    <part name="custId" type="xs:string"/>
    <part name="destination" type="xs:string"/>
    <part name="departureDate" type="xs:date"/>
    <part name="returnDate" type="xs:date"/>
</message>
```

FIGURE 25.10 The operation getFareOp.

```
<operation name="getFareOp">
  <input message="gs:itineraryMsg"
    wsa:Action="http://www.SlowHawk.com/wsdl/trips/getFarePT
    /itineraryMsg"/>
  <output message="gs:itineraryRespMsg"
    wsa:Action="http://www.SlowHawk.com/wsdl/trips/getFarePT
    /itineraryRespMsg"/>
  <fault name="invalidArgFault"
    wsa:Action="http://www.SlowHawk.com/wsdl/trips/getFarePT
    /invalidArgFaultMsg"
    message="gs:invalidArgFaultMsg"/>
</operation>
```

■ *Request/response*. An input message (of the type specified by the operation's input child element) is sent by the requester, and an output message (of the type specified by the operation's output child element) is returned by the provider. WSDL does not specify whether the communication is synchronous (the requester waits until it receives the output message) or asynchronous (the requester does not wait but continues its execution after sending the message and separately receives the output message at a later time). Thus, the request/response pattern might be used synchronously to implement an RPC interaction, or it might be used asynchronously to implement an interchange of e-mail messages.

The (optional) fault element identifies the declaration of a message that is returned to the invoker if a fault occurs. The provider responds to an input message with either the output message or a message of the type specified in the fault element (but not both).

Figure 25.10 gives an example of an RPC operation, getFareOp, supported by SlowHawk. The fact that both input and output messages are specified indicates that the operation uses a request/response message-exchange pattern. For simplicity we have assumed that the WSDL declarations for both GoSlow and SlowHawk are combined in the same document (more realistically, each organization would publish its own WSDL document). The document is shown in Figures 25.21–25.23. We have assumed that the target namespace of the document containing all these declarations is http://www.goslow.com/wsdl/trips and that this namespace is denoted with the prefix gs. Hence, the operation declaration is referencing message declarations that appear elsewhere in the same document.

The wsa:Action attribute in the message element is the WS-Addressing extension of WSDL that was referred to on page 1060. Its value, a URI, identifies the purpose of the message and is used as the value of the Action header block of the SOAP message that carries the WSDL message. The attribute is optional: it can be explicitly specified for a message of the port type (as is done in the

FIGURE 25.11 The getFarePT port type.

```
<portType name="getFarePT">
    <operation name="getFareOp">
        . . .
    </operation>
    <!--other operations, if implemented, would be declared here  -->
</portType>
```

figure), or a WS-Addressing default procedure can be used to construct a value. In the figure the value shown is actually the default value. Keep in mind that WSDL is transport-neutral. We have described how the value of Action is used by SOAP. It might be used differently if SOAP is not used, or it might be ignored.

Messages are defined separately from operations because a particular message might be used in different operations. For example, we have used the name itineraryMsg (rather than getFareOpMsg) for the input message type of the operation getFareOp because we will be using this type of message in several different operations.

■ *One-way.* An input message (of the type specified by the input child) is sent by the requester, and no response is returned by the provider. (Recall, however, that if HTTP is used to transport the message, an HTTP acknowledgment will be received by the HTTP processor at the requester's site.) Hence, the operation specifies only an input message. No fault messages are allowed with this pattern. This style is often used to invoke a Web service asynchronously. The requester does not wait for a response. However the provider might respond at a later time with a message directed to an operation supported by the requester. We will see examples of such services in Sections 25.6.

Port types. A port type groups together related operations. For example, SlowHawk might support the port type, getFarePT, shown in Figure 25.11. In this case there is only one operation, but the figure indicates where other operations would be declared if they were present.

25.5.2 The Concrete Level
The concrete level describes how port types and their operations are bound to transport protocols and Web locations. The concrete level defines the following elements:

■ A **binding** describes how the abstract messages used by the operations of a port type are mapped to concrete messages that are transmitted by a particular transport protocol. For example, if the message is to be sent using SOAP over HTTP, the binding describes how the message parts are mapped to elements in the SOAP body and header and what the values of the attributes are. In addition, the binding describes how values are to be serialized within a message.

FIGURE 25.12 Outline of a complete WSDL document.

```
<definitions targetNamespace=" . . . "
                <!-- specification of other namespaces -->
                xmlns="http://www.w3.org/2003/06/wsdl/">
    <!-- Abstract level specification -->
        <types>
            <!-- XML Schema types used in this document -->
        </types>
        <message>  . . . </message>
            <!-- other messages are specified here -->
        <portType> . . . </portType>
            <!-- other port types are specified here -->
    <!-- End of the abstract level -->
    <!-- Concrete level specification -->
        <binding> . . . </binding>
            <!-- other bindings are specified here -->
        <service>
            <port> . . . </port>
            <!-- other ports are specified here -->
        </service>
            <!-- other services are specified here -->
    <!-- End of the concrete level -->
</definitions>
```

■ A **port** maps a binding to a Web address. In the context of WSDL, an endpoint corresponds to a port. A port specifies the address at which the operations of a port type, using a particular transport protocol, can be invoked.

■ A **service** is a collection of related ports.

The overall structure of a WSDL document, which includes both the abstract and concrete levels, is shown in Figure 25.12. We next discuss the components of the concrete WSDL specification in more detail.

Services.   A service gives a name to a set of ports. Each port specifies the address at which the operations of a particular port type can be invoked together with the binding to be used. Since, as we shall see shortly, the binding specifies a port type, the port effectively ties the port type to an address. Taken together, the ports of a service host a set of related operations that are offered to customers.

Consider the following declaration:

```
<service name="getFareService">
    <port name="getFareRPCPort"
            binding="gs:GetFareRPCBinding">
```

```
        <soap:address location=
            "http://www.SlowHawk.com/fareservice1"/>
    </port>
    <!-- other ports go here -->
</service>
```

The port getFareRPCPort identifies a particular binding—getFareRPCBinding—and the Web address at which messages that use that binding are to be sent. The service getFareService groups getFareRPCPort with other related ports. The prefix gs indicates that the service is declared in the same WSDL document as the abstract elements.

A service supported by a server might contain several ports for the same port type—but provided through different bindings. This allows a requester to choose the most convenient way to communicate with that server. Alternatively, different implementations of the same port type might be referenced by ports of different services supported by different servers. For example, the travel industry might specify a standard port type for making airplane reservations, and different airlines might provide different reservation services, each of which implements the port type. In this case the implementations of the port types at the different servers should provide semantically equivalent behavior.

RPC-style binding.   A binding element is the most complex aspect of a WSDL document. Its structure must be flexible enough to accommodate the message formats used by a variety of different transports. We will describe three different bindings for getFarePT. We first consider SOAP over HTTP since it is widely used and it illustrates many features of a binding element.

Suppose we want the operations of getFarePT to be invoked with RPC-style SOAP messages sent using HTTP. Then we might declare the binding getFareRPC-Binding, shown in Figure 25.13, for that purpose. The name of the port type being bound is indicated by the type attribute of the outer binding element.

The child soap:binding is an example of an extension of WSDL that provides information specific to a SOAP binding. We assume that the prefix soap is associated with *http://schemas.xmlsoap.org/wsdl/soap/*—the namespace used by all SOAP-related elements and attributes of WSDL. In our discussions they all will be identified with the soap prefix.

It is important to keep in mind that the elements input and output inside a binding element, such as the one in Figure 25.13, are *not* in themselves SOAP messages and neither are the similarly named elements in an abstract level description of an operation, as in Figure 25.10. Instead, these are descriptions from which the actual SOAP messages are *constructed*. We will explain how this is done shortly.

The soap:binding element specifies the message format (via the style attribute) and transport (via the transport attribute) to use. In Figure 25.13, the transport is SOAP over HTTP, and the format is rpc. Hence, we expect a message that looks like Figure 25.3. If, instead, the style attribute had value document, the message body would have a different structure, which we will discuss later in this

FIGURE 25.13 An RPC/encoded SOAP binding for getFarePT.

```
<binding name="getFareRPCBinding" type="gs:getFarePT">
  <soap:binding style="rpc"
    transport="http://schemas.xmlsoap.org/soap/http/"/>
  <operation name="gs:getFareOp">
    <input>
      <soap:body
        use="encoded"
        namespace="http://www.goslow.com/wsdl/trips"
        encodingStyle="http://schemas.xmlsoap.org/soap/encoding/"/>
    </input>
    <output>
      <soap:body
        use="encoded"
        namespace="http://www.goslow.com/wsdl/trips"
        encodingStyle="http://schemas.xmlsoap.org/soap/encoding/"/>
    </output>
  </operation>
</binding>
```

section. Another possible transport is SOAP over SMTP. It can be used to deliver SOAP messages by email and will also be discussed later in this section.

Binding-related details of each operation of a port type are described in the operation child element of binding. (This use of the word "operation" should be contrasted with the signature of an operation, which is described at the abstract level of WSDL using the operation child element of portType.) getFarePT contains only one operation, getFareOp. The name attribute gives the name of the operation. The operation element contains a description of each of the messages the operation can send or receive. Thus, the input child element describes the input message and the output child describes the output message. A fault child would describe the fault message, but it is omitted in our example.

RPC-style binding and SOAP messages.   We have seen that the binding uses the elements input, output, and fault to describe messages at the concrete level, but these elements do not actually name any messages. The question therefore is, Which messages do these elements refer to? The answer is that descriptions at the concrete level are related to the descriptions at the abstract level through the operation that they both describe. For instance, in Figure 25.13 the input and output elements describe the operation getFareOp. The abstract level description of this operation appears in Figure 25.10, from which we know that the input element refers to the message itineraryMsg and the output element to itineraryRespMsg.

Since the binding style in this case is rpc, RPC-style SOAP messages will be constructed (similar to the messages in Figures 25.3 and 25.4). Thus, each part of itineraryMsg is a parameter of the operation getFareOp, and the information returned is stored in the body of the message itineraryRespMsg. Since all of this information is stored in the SOAP body, the input and output elements in Figure 25.13 contain only a soap:body child—another SOAP-related element of WSDL. With other types of bindings, some information might be carried in a SOAP header, and a soap:header child would be included to describe this.

We are now ready to explain how an actual SOAP message is constructed from a WSDL binding and an abstract message description—in the example, how the SOAP message in Figure 25.3 is obtained. Let N be the element tagged getFareOp in Figure 25.3. It is the child of the Body element in the envelope of the SOAP message being constructed. N's tag is obtained from the name attribute of the operation element of the binding element. The namespace attribute of soap:body provides the value for the xmlns attribute in N's opening tag. It designates the target namespace of the WSDL document in which the message is declared (see Figures 25.3 and 25.21). Similarly, the encodingStyle attribute of soap:body provides the value for the encodingStyle attribute in N's opening tag.

Next, the abstract WSDL message is identified as explained earlier. In our case, it is the message itineraryMsg described in Figure 25.9. Finally, each part of itineraryMsg describes a parameter of the operation and yields a child element of N. The part's name, specified in the WSDL (abstract level) message declaration, becomes the child's tag.

RPC-style binding and parameter serialization. The next question is how the values of the parameters to an operation are serialized in the SOAP message being constructed. In the WSDL message declaration, each part has an associated type, which might be complex. In that case the type declaration, which we will refer to as an **abstract type** declaration, will be an element of some WSDL schema. (Figure 25.8 on page 1065 shows a skeleton of abstract level type declarations.)

Earlier (page 1055), we pointed out that if the SOAP communication is specified as RPC/encoded, the serialization of a parameter in a SOAP message is generated by a serializer program at the client. How can we be sure that the string generated by the client's SOAP serializer corresponds to the abstract type declaration in the WSDL file? In fact, it might not! And if it does not, does that mean that it is incorrect? Again, the answer is no! Then how can a receiver determine that a received message is correct? The use attribute is provided for this purpose. It has two possible values: encoded and literal.

■ If the use attribute of the soap:body element in the binding has the value encoded, then the values of the parameters are serialized using the encoding mechanism specified in the encodingStyle attribute of the element (which becomes the encoding style attribute used in the SOAP message). This situation is depicted in Figure 25.13. An **RPC/encoded** binding specifies that the parameters of an RPC-style message are to be serialized through the set of rules specified in the encodingStyle attribute. Note that in Figure 25.3 (which is an RPC/encoded SOAP message) each parameter child has a type attribute. Using this attribute

FIGURE **25.14** An RPC/literal SOAP binding for the `getFarePT`.

```
<service name="GetFareService">
  <port name="GetFareDocPort" binding="gs:GetFareDocBinding">
    <soap:address location="http://www.SlowHawk.com/fareservice2/"/>
  </port>
</service>

<binding name="GetFareDocBinding" type="gs:GetFarePT">
  <soap:binding style="rpc"
        transport="http://schemas.xmlsoap.org/soap/http"/>
  <operation name="gs:getFareOp">
    <input>
      <soap:body
        use="literal"
        namespace="http://www.goslow.com/wsdl/trips"/>
    </input>
    <output>
      <soap:body
        use="literal"
        namespace="http://www.goslow.com/wsdl/trips"/>
    </output>
  </operation>
</binding>
```

the receiver can determine the specific encoding rule that was used to serialize the argument.[3]

■   If the use attribute of the soap:body element in the binding has the value literal, the parameter element in the SOAP message body is an ASCII string that is a literal instance of the part's type as specified in the message declaration. This binding is referred to as **RPC/literal** and is illustrated in Figure 25.14.

In some cases the instance is directly available. For example, if the value of the parameter is XML data, it will already be an instance of the type. In other cases it might be necessary to explicitly construct an instance of the type. For example, the arguments produced by a procedure call in a Java program must be converted from binary to the ASCII strings that corresponds to the type definitions. We addressed this issue earlier (page 1054) when we introduced the

---

[3] The specification of the type attribute is useful in cases in which subtypes of a parameter's base type have been declared (perhaps using XML's type extension feature) to carry additional information for particular argument values. For example, if the destination is a city with multiple airports, the destination part might have to include an additional element identifying a specific airport. Although the message declaration specifies that the parameter is of the base type, a specific invocation might pass a value of the subtype.

use of rules to serialize data. In this case we are also serializing data, with the difference that instead of using rules in accordance with some encoding style, the serialization constructs an instance of the type.

Although with RPC/literal the serialized arguments are literal instances of schema types, the SOAP Body *as a whole* is not described by a (single) schema. Instead it is constructed as described in connection with Figure 25.3: the procedure name is the tag of the child of the Body element, and it has child elements for each parameter tagged with that parameter's name. Thus, with both RPC/literal and RPC/encoded, the Body is not an instance of a schema (even though with RPC/literal the parameter values are instances of schema types).

As an example of where RPC/encoded and RPC/literal bindings give different strings for particular parameters, suppose a procedure has n parameters, all of the same abstract type. The body of an RPC-style SOAP request message produced by a serializer will generally contain n child elements, each of which is an instance of the type. Each instance is the value of a parameter and, correspondingly, the value of a part of the request message.

But suppose in a particular invocation the values of all the parameters are the same. Then the serializer might be smart enough to encode the request message differently. The message will still contain a child element for each parameter. But instead of a child being an instance of the abstract type, it is a pointer to a single instance of the type stored as a separate element elsewhere in the message. That instance contains the value being passed to all parameters. Clearly the request message contains the proper information to invoke the procedure *if it is interpreted correctly*. However, if the deserializer is expecting parts that conform to the abstract type declaration, it will be greatly disappointed.

The problem, then, boils down to this. In some cases each argument is an exact, or *literal*, instance of the parameter type specified in the WSDL message declaration. In other cases, each argument is produced by a serializer that *encodes* data in accordance with some rules, and hence the argument is not necessarily an instance of the schema type specified for the parameter in the message declaration. There might be several forms that the argument can take, all semantically correct. RPC-style SOAP often uses the encoding approach. The deserializer can validate the message if it knows (1) that it has been encoded, (2) the encoding style rules that were used (since it will then know all the forms the parameter might take), and (3) the type of the argument.

Document-style binding. With an RPC-style binding, the information transmitted between a client and a server consists of the parameters of a procedure call. However, Web services are becoming increasingly document-centric, and the information transmitted consists of XML documents rather than procedure parameters.

For example, an operation, sendInvoiceOp, of port type invoicePT might send an invoice using a one-way pattern. The message, sendInvoiceMsg, that carries the invoice might have one part, named invoice (which is the actual document to be sent) whose type describes instances of invoices. The appropriate WSDL declarations could be

```
<types>
    <schema xmlns="http://www.w3.org/2001/XMLSchema"
            xmlns:inv="http://www.invoicesource.com/invoice"
            targetNameSpace="http://www.invoicesource.com/invoice">
            ...
        <complexType name="invoiceType"> ... </complexType>
    </schema>
</types>
    ...
<message name="sendInvoiceMsg">
    <part name="invoice" type="inv:invoiceType"/>
</message>
    ...
<portType name="invoicePT">
    <operation name="sendInvoiceOp">
        <input message="inv:sendInvoiceMsg"/>
    </operation>
</portType>
```

The binding in this case is shown in Figure 25.15. Document-style communication is indicated in the soap:binding element, and the value of the use attribute of the input element is set to literal, which indicates that no encoding is involved. Hence this binding is referred to as a **document/literal** binding.

In this example, the WSDL message declaration has a single part and the Body of the corresponding SOAP message contains an invoice—an XML document whose

FIGURE 25.15 A document/literal SOAP binding for the invoicePT.

```
<binding name="sendInvBinding" type="inv:invoicePT">
    <soap:binding style="document"
        transport="http://schemas.xmlsoap.org/soap/http"/>
    <operation name="inv:sendInvoiceOp">
        <input>
            <soap:body
                use="literal"
                namespace=
                    "http://www.invoicesource.com/invoice"/>
        </input>
    </operation>
</binding>
```

schema is given by the part's type, invoiceType, and is specified in the message declaration.

```
<s:Envelope xmlns:s="http://www.w3.org/2003/05/soap-envelope">
    <s:Body>
        <!-- an instance of invoiceType goes here -->
    </s:Body>
</s:Envelope>
```

To ensure compatibility with older specifications (and not for technical reasons), WSDL constructs a message using a document-style binding differently than it does using an RPC-style binding. The difference is that with a document-style binding, the part's name (invoice) does not appear as a tag in the SOAP message. In contrast, with RPC-style binding, each message part gives a name to a child element in the message body. But with both document/literal and RPC/literal, the part itself is an instance of the schema that describes the part's type.

Document-style binding generalized. The document/literal binding can also be used with multipart messages. But, again, in order to ensure backward compatibility, a new strategy is used to specify the types of the parts. Although we did not discuss it before, types for message parts can be specified indirectly: the part child of the message element can use an element attribute (instead of a type attribute) whose value is the name of an element declared elsewhere. In this case, the type of the part is the type of that element. For example, if you want to send two invoices, the relevant WSDL declarations would be

```
<types>
    <schema ... >
        <element name="firstInvoice" type="inv:invoiceType"/>
        <element name="secondInvoice" type="inv:invoiceType"/>
        <complexType name="invoiceType">
            <!-- the complex type definition goes here -->
        </complexType>
    </schema>
</types>
    ...
<message name="sendInvoiceMsg">
    <part name="invoice1" element="inv:firstInvoice"/>
    <part name="invoice2" element="inv:secondInvoice"/>
</message>
```

Now the Body element of the SOAP envelope will contain two child elements:

```
<s:Envelope xmlns:s="http://www.w3.org/2003/05/soap-envelope">
    <s:Body>
```

```
            <firstInvoice ··· >
                <!-- an instance of invoiceType goes here -->
            </firstInvoice>
            <secondInvoice ··· >
                <!-- an instance of invoiceType goes here -->
            </secondInvoice>
        </s:Body>
    </s:Envelope>
```

The children are instances of the schema elements firstInvoice and second-Invoice, and the tag names come from the names of the elements rather than the parts (as would be the case with RPC-style messages).

With RPC-style binding, part types can be specified with either a type or an element attribute, and, in fact, the same message can contain some parts with one specification and some with the other. Not so with the document-style binding: it can specify a multipart message *only* if all of its parts use the element attribute.

So far we have seen only bindings that use the HTTP transport. As an alternative, Figure 25.16 shows a document/literal binding of getFarePT to SOAP over SMTP. In this figure, the port GetFareSMTPPort can be used to communicate with the service by email. The address to which the email is to be sent is specified in

FIGURE 25.16 A document/literal SMTP binding for getFarePT.

```
<service name="GetFareService">
    <port name="GetFareSMTPPort" binding="gs:GetFareSMTPBinding">
        <soap:address location="mailto:fareservice@SlowHawk.com"/>
    </port>
</service>

<binding name="GetFareSMTPBinding" type="gs:GetFarePT">
    <soap:binding style="document"
        transport="http://schemas.xmlsoap.org/soap/smtp"/>
    <operation name="gs:getFareOp">
        <input>
            <soap:body
                use="literal"
                namespace="http://www.goslow.com/wsdl/trips"/>
        </input>
        <output>
            <soap:body
                use="literal"
                namespace="http://www.goslow.com/wsdl/trips"/>
        </output>
    </operation>
</binding>
```

FIGURE 25.17 Description of the `GetFareService`.

```
<service name="GetFareService">
    <port name="GetFareRPCPort" binding="gs:"GetFareRPCBinding">
        <soap:address location=
            "http://www.SlowHawk.com/fareservice1/"/>
    </port>
    <port name="GetFareDocPort" binding="gs:GetFareDocBinding">
        <soap:address location=
            "http://www.SlowHawk.com/fareService2/"/>
    </port>
    <port name="GetFareSMTPPort" binding="gs:GetFareSMTPBinding">
        <soap:address location=
            "mailto:fareservice@SlowHawk.com"/>
    </port>
    <port name="GetFareGETPort" binding="gs:GetFareGETBinding">
        <soap:address location=
            "http://www.SlowHawk.com/fareservice3/"/>
    </port>
    <port name="GetFarePOSTPort" binding="gs:GetFarePOSTBinding">
        <soap:address location=
            "http://www.Fare.com/fareservice4/"/>
    </port>
</service>
```

the `location` attribute of the `soap:address` element of the port. The fact that the binding describes both an input and an output element shows that, although document/literal is a natural way to bind one-way communication, there is no reason why it cannot be used for request/response communication as well.

A Web service can provide ports with the same functionality but different bindings. Some might use HTTP and some SMTP; some might use the RPC-style and some the document-style messages. For instance, SlowHawk Airline might make the port type `GetFarePT` available through a number of different bindings with the corresponding ports gathered together under a single service. This is shown in Figure 25.17.

As Web services become more document-centric, the document/literal binding is likely to become the prevalent form of messaging. One might wonder if document/encoded is possible as a binding style. The Web services community has not yet figured out what this might mean, so it is not likely to make an appearance any time soon.

25.5.3 Putting It All Together

A WSDL description of a Web service has as its root a `definitions` element. Its children are the various elements we have discussed. An outline of a WSDL document is

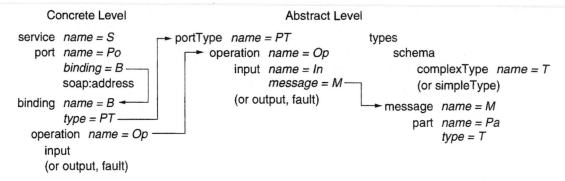

FIGURE 25.18 An overview of the relationships among the WSDL components. Attributes are italicized to distinguish them from elements.

shown in Figure 25.12. An example of such a document for GoSlow is given in Figures 25.21, 25.22 and 25.23. In this example, declarations for distinct Web services are lumped together in a single WSDL document to avoid complexity. In real life, each service would supply a *separate* WSDL document describing the operations it exports.

Figure 25.18 is an overview of some of the main elements of WSDL and the connections among them. The top-level elements are service, binding, message, type, and portType. The indented items denote information represented by child elements. The level of indentation denotes the level of nesting of the various elements and attributes.

25.5.4 WSDL Version 2.0

A number of changes are being considered in WSDL Version 2.0.[4] Some names will likely be different. A portType will be called an interface, and a port will be called an endpoint. Messages have been eliminated. An operation will describe a message by referring directly to a type declaration in the types component of the WSDL document.

An interface now takes the form shown in Figure 25.19. Two interesting new features are shown in the figure. The first is the pattern attribute of the operation element. It permits a variety of **message exchange patterns** (MEPs) to be specified for the operation. We have seen two patterns in WSDL Version 1.1: request/response and one-way. The pattern attribute allows an arbitrary number of patterns to be specified. A message exchange pattern is denoted by a URI.

An MEP is not a part of the WSDL document. Instead, it is described separately in terms of placeholders (think formal parameters) such as In and Out to denote a message sent to or received from the server and assigned a URI. Each of the actual

---

[4] This description is based on the working draft entitled "Web Services Description Language (WSDL) Version 2.0 Part 1: Core Language," August 3, 2004, *http://www.w3.org/TR/wsdl20*.

FIGURE 25.19 A getFareIF interface that inherits operations from another interface (WSDL Version 2.0).

```
<interface name="getFareIF" extends="reservationIF">
    <fault name="invalidArgFault"
        element="invalidArgFaultElem"/>
    <operation name="getFareOp"
        pattern="http://www.w3.org/2004/03/wsdl/in-out">
        <input messageLabel="In"
            element="gs:itineraryElem"/>
        <output messageLabel="Out"
            element="gs:itineraryRespElem"/>
        <outfault ref="invalidArgFault"
            messageLabel="Out"/>
    </operation>
    <!-- other operations are specified here -->
</interface>
```

messages exchanged by the operation—the input and output children of the operation element in the port type declaration—have a corresponding messageLabel attribute that identifies its placeholder in the description of the MEP.

A set of patterns has been predefined. In-Out, which is used in Figure 25.19, is one of them. It corresponds to the standard request/response pattern. The messageLabel attribute of input indicates that it corresponds to the In placeholder Some of the other patterns are In-Only (corresponding to one-way), Robust In-Only (In-Only with the possibility that the server responds with a fault message), and In-Optional-Out (which is like In-Out except that the response from the service is optional).

The structure of the input (or output) message (described by message and part elements in Version 1.1) is determined by the element in some schema document referred to by the element attribute. Faults are treated a little differently. A fault child of interface (there may be several) identifies, with its element attribute, the message that will be sent when a particular fault occurs. To allow for the fact that several operations within a particular interface might raise the same fault, fault is not local to an operation. Instead, any operation that raises the fault has an outfault child element that references fault. Its messageLabel attribute identifies the placeholder of the message in the MEP that the fault message is associated with. The fault message might be associated with the output message and *replace* that message if a fault occurs (as in the In-Out pattern). Alternatively, the fault might be associated with the input message and be *triggered by* that message if a fault occurs (as in the Robust In-Only pattern).

The second feature, indicated by the extends attribute of the interface element, allows an interface to inherit operations from other interfaces in an inheritance hierarchy based on the IsA relationship (Sections 4.4, 4.6.3, and 14.3.1). In the example, getFareIF extends the interface reservationIF in the sense that getFareIF contains getFareOp and, in addition, all the operations of reservationIF. For example, reservationIF might include a getScheduleOp operation, which returns the schedule of flights.

25.6 BPEL: Specifying Business Processes

In Section 25.5 we discussed how WSDL can be used to specify an interface that a server can present to the world. For example, SlowHawk's interface exposed the operation getFareOp that a client can invoke to obtain the airfare for a particular flight.

However, B2B interactions are generally more complex than this simple example. They do not consist of just a single operation invocation. Instead, there might be a lengthy exchange of information involving a sequence of operation invocations between a client and a server. Furthermore, the server might invoke other servers—hence becoming a client itself—in order to satisfy the initial request. In addition, the server has to maintain state during the processing of the interaction. The contents of a message received has to be interpreted in the context of events that have occurred up to that point, for example messages that were previously received. The state will, in general, determine the future behavior of the server.

We illustrate this situation with an example that expands on the getFarePT discussed earlier. Suppose our goal is to implement a full-blown travel agency service, GoSlow. GoSlow exports a port type containing three operations:

1. makeTripOp that takes a customer Id, a destination, a departure date, and a return date as input parameters and returns a trip number and a cost

2. acceptTripOp that takes a customer Id, a trip number and credit card information as input and returns a complete itinerary

3. cancelTripOp that takes a customer Id and a trip number as input parameters and returns an acknowledgement

When a client invokes makeTripOp, GoSlow's job is to make air and hotel reservations. To do this, GoSlow invokes getFareOp at the airline server, SlowHawk, to reserve a flight and gets back a reservation number and the cost. It also invokes getRoomOp at the hotel server, RoachHeaven, to reserve a room and gets back a reservation number and the cost. GoSlow then computes the total cost, assigns a trip number, and then returns both to the client. The state maintained by GoSlow at this point would include the client identification, reservation numbers, and cost. The client then invokes either acceptTripOp or cancelTripOp to confirm the reservations and pay for or cancel the reservations.

You can think of GoSlow as implementing a workflow. It receives a client request, makes reservations, responds to the client, then waits for either a confirmation or cancellation, and so forth. It is also an example of what has come to be called a **business process**, since it represents the way GoSlow does one aspect of its business. We will refer to it here as simply a process. GoSlow publishes its WSDL interface and interacts with other processes (for example, SlowHawk) through their WSDL interfaces. Interactions might use request/response (perhaps implementing RPC) or one-way messaging.

What is new here? First, there is a protocol that the client must follow. After invoking makeTripOp, the client must invoke either acceptTripOp or cancelTripOp. Unfortunately, WSDL does not provide GoSlow with a way of describing this protocol to the client. WSDL can only describe the individual exported operations in isolation.

One way to describe a protocol for a business process such as GoSlow is to publish GoSlow's program. But the client does not need or want all the details. A skeletal program that shows that GoSlow first accepts an invocation of makeTripOp and then accepts an invocation of either acceptTripOp or cancelTripOp is sufficient.

This approach has another important advantage. A skeletal program can show how GoSlow manipulates some of its local variables, and the values of these variables can be used to describe data-dependent protocols. For example, if a client accepts a trip made by GoSlow by invoking acceptTripOp, it must specify whether it will pay using a credit or a debit card. GoSlow's future actions, including the services it subsequently invokes, might depend on this information, which is a part of GoSlow's state. Therefore, the sequence of interactions followed by GoSlow is data dependent.

Thus, the program description goes well beyond the information presented through WSDL in that it shows the sequence in which operations are invoked and accepted and how that sequence is affected by the state of the process. The process is said to **orchestrate**[5] the use of the operations published in WSDL files.

Languages for describing business processes are currently a hot topic in the Web services community. In this section we present one such language, Business Process Execution Language for Web Services Version 1.1 (BPEL4WS, or simply BPEL). BPEL is undergoing standardization at the time of the writing of this text, but it is a leading contender and illustrates the issues that are addressed in an orchestration language. Version 1.1 of BPEL is based on Version 1.1 of WSDL.

Before getting into the details of the BPEL language, we need to distinguish between two levels of process[6] description. At one level we have what is called an **executable process** that contains all the details of the process, including a full description of the process state and how it is manipulated. At the other extreme we have what is called an **abstract process** that (should) contain only those aspects of the process that are necessary to describe its interface to other processes and is therefore not executable. You can think of an abstract process as (roughly) a projection of the corresponding executable process.

An abstract process differs from an executable process in two important ways. First, it is concerned with the protocol-relevant parts of the state. For example, the type of meal that you order on the flight is probably not protocol-relevant since the sequence of messages exchanged is not likely to depend on whether or not you are

---

[5] A buzz word in the Web services community that refers to the way the conductor of an orchestra organizes the services provided by the musicians into a coherent product.
[6] A better word would be program, but we will stay with BPEL terminology.

a vegetarian. Hence, your choice of meal ought not to be accessed by the abstract version of GoSlow. However, the protocol might be sensitive to whether you are paying with a credit card or a debit card: the sequence of messages exchanged might depend on the mode of payment. So this item must be accessible to the abstract process. Thus, if a client process has requested credit card payment, it can tell from the abstract process the sequence of messages that will follow.

A protocol-relevant item of data is referred to as a **property**. BPEL effectively prevents abstract processes from using data other than properties to affect the flow of control of the protocol. We discuss this restriction on page 1093.

Secondly, although the price of a ticket might be protocol-relevant (a ticket costing more than $1000 might require a special method of payment), the algorithm used to calculate the price might be complex, embarrassing to the airline, and have no impact on the flow of messages. Hence, the algorithm is coded into the executable version of the process but need not appear in the abstract version. BPEL uses what it calls **opaque assignment** to gloss over such details. Opaque assignment is permitted only in abstract processes, and it will be explained in more detail on page 1091. Its use implies a difference in the data manipulation techniques available to the two kinds of processes.

BPEL can be used to describe both an abstract and an executable version of the same business process. While the designers do not claim that the executable version of BPEL is a complete language for the purposes of implementing a business process on a particular platform, they do assert that it "defines a portable execution format for business processes that rely exclusively on Web service resources and XML data."[7]

25.6.1 Communication

Communication is central to Web services, so it is a good place to start our discussion of BPEL. In Section 25.5.1 we described several patterns of communication. BPEL provides three activities (the BPEL terminology for statements) for controlling communication.

1. An **invoke** activity names a particular operation and one or two variables. If a single variable is named, the operation specifies one-way communication, whereas if two variables are named the operation specifies request/response communication. In both cases the activity causes the value of the first variable to be sent in the operation's input message. If two variables are named, the invoker waits until the output message is returned and assigned to the second variable and then resumes execution. Waiting is appropriate if a procedure is being invoked. Hence, BPEL imposes a synchronous programming style on the use of the operation. If only a single variable is named in the activity, the invoker resumes as soon as the input message is sent.

---

[7] See *Business Process Execution Language for Web Services* Version 1.1, March 31, 2003, *http://www.106 .ibm.com/developerworks/webservices/library/ws-bpel*.

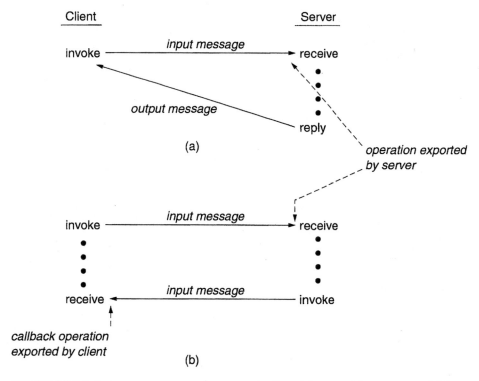

FIGURE 25.20 Common patterns of communication: (a) request/response and (b) one-way.

2. A **receive** activity is used to receive a message that has been sent either synchronously or asynchronously by an `invoke`. The process waits until the message arrives.

3. A **reply** activity is used to send a response to a request/response-style invocation that was previously received. The process resumes execution immediately.

The two common patterns of communication—request/response and one-way—are shown in Figure 25.20. Figure 25.20(a) illustrates synchronous request/response communication. In Figure 25.20(b) the client invokes an operation but does not wait for a response. Hence, if a response is forthcoming, it is sent asynchronously by the server to a port type exported by the client. This response is often referred to as a **callback**.

Having described communication in general terms we are now in a position to get more specific. A listing of a portion of the WSDL file for the GoSlow example is shown in Figures 25.21 to 25.23. For simplicity we have assumed that the declarations for all the Web services involved in the example are contained in a single file. More realistically, the declarations for each service would be provided in a separate file provided by that service.

FIGURE 25.21 A portion of the WSDL file showing messages used in the GoSlow example.

```
<definitions targetNamespace="http://www.goslow.com/wsdl/trips"
  xmlns="http://www.w3.org/2003/06/wsdl/"
  xmlns:xs="http://www.w3.org/2001/XMLSchema"
  xmlns:gs="http://www.goslow.com/wsdl/trips"
  xmlns:plnk="http://schemas.xmlsoap.org/ws/2003/05/partner-link/"
  xmlns:bpws="http://schemas.xmlsoap.org/ws/2003/03/business-process/">

<!-- This message type is used for the following interactions:
  customer to travel agent: quote request
  travel agent to airline: quote request
  travel agent to hotel: quote request  -->
<message name="itineraryMsg">
  <part name="custId" type="xs:string"/>
  <part name="destination" type="xs:string"/>
  <part name="departureDate" type="xs:date"/>
  <part name="returnDate" type="xs:date"/>
</message>

<!-- This message is used for the travel-agent-to-customer and
  airline-to-travel-agent interactions  -->
<message name="itineraryRespMsg">
  <part name="custId" type="xs:string"/>
  <part name="tripNo" type="xs:string"/>
  <part name="cost" type="xs:float"/>
</message>


<!-- A message for the customer to travel agent interaction: OK  -->
<message name="acceptTripMsg">
  <part name="custId" type="xs:string"/>
  <part name="cardNo" type="xs:string"/>
  <part name="credDeb" type="xs:string"/>
  <part name="tripNo" type="xs:string"/>
</message>

<!-- A fault message used in the travel agent to airline interaction  -->
<message name="invalidArgFaultMsg">
  <part name="custId" type="xs:string"/>
  <part name="faultString" type="xs:string"/>
</message>

<!-- Omitted messages: cancelTripOp, invalidCustFaultMsg,
  badPayFaultMsg, etc. -->
```

FIGURE **25.22** A continuation of the WSDL file shown in Figure 25.21 containing port types used in the GoSlow example.

```
<portType name="tripPT">              <!-- provided by GoSlow -->
  <operation name="makeTripOp">
    <input message="gs:itineraryMsg"/>
    <output message="gs:itineraryRespMsg"/>
    <fault name="invalidCustFault"
      message="gs:invalidCustFaultMsg"/>
  </operation>
  <operation name="acceptTripOp">
    <input message="gs:acceptTripMsg"/>
    <output message="gs:acceptTripRespMsg"/>
    <fault name="badPayFault"
        message="gs:badPayFaultMsg"/>
  </operation>
  <operation name="cancelTripOp">
    <input message="gs:cancelTripMsg"/>
    <output message="gs:cancelTripRespMsg"/>
  </operation>
</portType>

<portType name="hotelCallbackPT">      <!-- provided by GoSlow -->
  <!-- hotel calls back to confirm or deny -->
  <operation name="receiveResOp">
    <input message="gs:receiveResMsg"/>
  </operation>
</portType>

<portType name="getFarePT">         <!-- provided by SlowHawk -->
  <operation name="getFareOp">
    <input message="gs:itineraryMsg"
      wsa:Action="http://www.SlowHawk.com/wsdl/trips/getFarePT
      /itineraryMsg"/>
    <output message="itineraryRespMsg"
      wsa:Action="http://www.SlowHawk.com/wsdl/trips/getFarePT
      /itineraryRespMsg"/>
    <fault name="invalidArgFault"
      message="gs:invalidArgFaultMsg"
      wsa:Action="http://www.SlowHawk.com/wsdl/trips/getFarePT
      /invalidArgFaultMsg"/>
  </operation>
</portType>
```

FIGURE 25.22 (continued)

```
<portType name="roomResPT">        <!-- provided by RoachHeaven -->
    <operation name="getRoomOp">
        <input message="gs:itineraryMsg"/>
    </operation>
    <operation name="cancelRoomOp"
        <input message="gs:cancelRoomMsg"/>
    </operation>
</portType>
```

We have omitted some elements at the abstract level of WSDL to avoid excess detail. We have also omitted all elements at the concrete level since they are not directly accessible to a BPEL process. For example, BPEL does not provide mechanisms to directly access a binding. The fact that binding information is not accessible ensures that the same process description can be reused with different transports. However, even though the concrete declarations are not accessible, lower-level modules of the executable version of a process use bindings when the process communicates with other processes. The bindings provide the information needed to format and address messages that are sent and to process messages that are received.

Partner link types.   Each process uses WSDL declarations at the abstract level to describe the elementary communication activities in which it is willing to engage. But to specify the activities precisely, we need, in addition, a way to describe the connections between processes. For example, GoSlow is a process that requests a hotel reservation by invoking an operation on the port type `roomResPT`, which is provided by some other process. It expects that that process will respond by invoking an operation on the port type `hotelCallbackPT`, which GoSlow provides. Similarly, RoachHeaven provides a port type `roomResPT` to receive a reservation request from another process and expects to respond using a port type `hotelCallbackPT` provided by that process. Clearly, GoSlow and RoachHeaven satisfy a necessary condition to do business since they each provide the port types needed by the other. (On the other hand, the condition is not sufficient since it says nothing about the sequence in which operations over these port types are invoked and accepted.)

WSDL has been extended to enforce this condition through the introduction of partner link types. The fact that the tag `partnerLinkType` comes from a namespace (prefixed `plnk`) different from the WSDL namespace is an indication that an extension of WSDL is involved. A `partnerLinkType` has a name and one or two roles. Each role is named and describes one end of a possible connection by specifying one port type that must be provided by the process at that end. For example, the partner link type `GoSlowRoachLT` in Figure 25.23 has been declared to support a room reservation interaction and specifies that the process providing the hotel service must provide the `roomResPT` port type, and the process requesting a reservation must provide the `hotelCallbackPT` port type.

FIGURE 25.23 A continuation of the WSDL file shown in Figures 25.21 and 25.22 containing properties, property aliases, and partner link types used in the GoSlow example.

```
<bpws:property name="Id" type="xs:string"/>      <!-- properties -->
<bpws:property name="payType" type="xs:string"/>

<bpws:propertyAlias propertyName="gs:Id"        <!-- property aliases -->
    messageType="gs:itineraryMsg" part="custId"/>

<bpws:propertyAlias propertyName="gs:Id"
    messageType="gs:itineraryRespMsg" part="custId"/>

<bpws:propertyAlias propertyName="gs:payType"
    messageType="gs:acceptTripMsg" part="credDeb"/>

<plnk:partnerLinkType name="custGoSlowLT">      <!-- partner Link Types -->
    <!-- link between customer and travel agency  -->
    <plnk:role name="travelService">
        <plnk:portType name="gs:tripPT"/>
    </plnk:role>
</plnk:partnerLinkType>

<plnk:partnerLinkType name="GoSlowHawkLT">
    <!-- link between travel agency and airline  -->
    <plnk:role name="airline">
        <plnk:portType name="gs:getFarePT"/>
    </plnk:role>
</plnk:partnerLinkType>

<plnk:partnerLinkType name="GoSlowRoachLT">
    <!-- link between travel agency and hotel  -->
    <plnk:role name="hotel">
        <plnk:portType name="gs:roomResPT"/>
    </plnk:role>
    <plnk:role name="roomReq">
        <plnk:portType name="gs:hotelCallbackPT"/>
    </plnk:role>
</plnk:partnerLinkType>
<!-- declarations of bindings, ports and services would go here -->
</definitions>
```

As a special case, if only one end of the connection needs to supply a port type for the interaction, only one role needs to be specified in the partner link. In this case any process can communicate with the process that assumes that role. For example, any process can be a customer of GoSlow. A customer does not need to provide a port type if it does not expect a response or if the operation it invokes uses a request/response pattern of communication.

Properties.   An abstract process is concerned with the protocol-relevant items in a message. For example, the part credDeb of the acceptTripMsg message indicates whether the customer intends to pay with a credit card or a debit card. This information is protocol-relevant since GoSlow communicates differently with its partners depending on the mode of payment. BPEL insists that any protocol-related item— an item used by an abstract process—be specified using a property declaration. This restriction on abstract processes guarantees that their control flow, and hence the protocol that they implement, is based on properties (we will return to this point on page 1094).

A **property declaration** introduces a global property name and an associated XML Schema type. The property is associated with a data item of the same type using a **property alias**. In Figure 25.23, a property declaration introduces the global property name payType, and a propertyAlias declaration associates that name with the credDeb part of the acceptTripMsg message. More generally, a property alias can be used to associate a property with any element or attribute *within* a message part using XPath expressions.

We will see shortly that a customer Id is also protocol-relevant. It might be contained in several messages, and it might be given different part names in each, but it always has the same significance with respect to application logic. For example, the message itineraryMsg associated with GoSlow's port type tripPT has the part custId that is used to convey the customer's Id. Since GoSlow and SlowHawk would normally create separate WSDL files to describe their services and would design their messages separately, SlowHawk might use a part named clientId to convey the same information (we do not do this here to keep the example simple). By aliasing both these parts to the property name Id, GoSlow (and particularly its abstract version) can be written entirely in terms of Id. This makes it easier to understand and highlights the semantics of the protocol.

Thus, properties serve two functions. They are used to limit the access of abstract processes to protocol-relevant data, and they also provide a uniform way to refer to protocol-relevant data.

25.6.2 Processes

Our first version of (a fragment of) the GoSlow process is shown in Figure 25.24. We are interested primarily in communication, so an abstract process is shown, as indicated by the abstractProcess attribute of the process element. GoSlow communicates with three processes—the customer, SlowHawk, and RoachHeaven—

FIGURE 25.24 An elementary version of the GoSlow process expressed in BPEL.

```
<process name="GoSlowProcess"
  targetNamespace="http://www.goslow.com/wsdl/trips-bp"
  xmlns="http://schemas.xmlsoap.org/ws/2003/03/business-process/"
  xmlns:gs="http://www.goslow.com/wsdl/trips"
  abstractProcess="yes">

<partnerLinks>
  <partnerLink name="customer" partnerLinkType="gs:custGoSlowLT"
    myRole="travelService"/>
  <partnerLink name="airProvider" partnerLinkType="gs:GoSlowHawkLT"
    partnerRole="airline"/>
  <partnerLink name="hotelProvider" partnerLinkType="gs:GoSlowRoachLT"
    myRole="roomReq" partnerRole="hotel"/>
</partnerLinks>

<variables>
  <variable name="itineraryVar" messageType="gs:itineraryMsg"/>
  <variable name="itineraryRespVar" messageType="gs:itineraryRespMsg"/>
  <variable name="getFareVar" messageType="gs:itineraryMsg"/>
  <variable name="acceptTripVar" messageType="gs:acceptTripMsg"/>
  <variable name="invalidArgFaultVar"
      messageType="gs:invalidArgFaultMsg"/>
</variables>
<sequence>
  <receive partnerLink="customer" portType="gs:tripPT"
    operation="makeTripOp" variable="itineraryVar"/>
  <assign>
    <copy>
      <from variable="itineraryVar"/>
      <to variable="getFareVar"/>
    </copy>
  </assign>
  <invoke partnerLink="airProvider" portType="gs:getFarePT"
    operation="getFareOp" inputVariable="getFareVar"
    outputVariable="itineraryRespVar"/>
  <assign>
    <copy>
      <from opaque="yes"/>
      <to variable="itineraryRespVar" part="cost"/>
    </copy>
  </assign>
  <reply partnerLink="customer" portType="gs:TripPT"
    operation="makeTripOp" variable="itineraryRespVar"/>
  <!-- Second half of protocol goes here (Figure 25.26) -->
</sequence>

</process>
```

which are referred to as **partners**, and for this communication, partner links are needed.

Partner links. A partner link type describes a requirement on the port types supported by two processes that interact, but it does not identify the processes. Many pairs of processes might meet that requirement. There is a need for a mechanism that can be used by a process to claim one end of such a connection. The partner link is used for that purpose. Partner link declarations are part of BPEL rather than WSDL since they are specific to a particular process's participation in an interaction.

Each `partnerLink` element in Figure 25.24 specifies a partner link type, the role (of that partner link type) played by GoSlow, `myRole`, and the role played by the process at the other end of the link, `partnerRole`. The individual communication activities within the process refer to a `partnerLink` in order to specify the source or target of a message.

It might be necessary for one or both of a pair of processes to support several port types in order to interact. Since a partner link type names a single port type at each end, several partner links must be used. In that case, the language supports a `partners` element that allows partner links to be grouped together with the effect that a suitable partner has to support all the partner links in the group.

Variables. Variables are defined next. They are used for storing messages that have been received or sent, as well as arbitrary data. Their values form a part of the state of the process. The type of each variable can be a message type, an XML simple type, or an XML schema element. They are declared, respectively, using statements of the form

```
<variable name="..." messageType="..."/>
<variable name="..." type="..."/>
<variable name="..." element="..."/>
```

A variable of message type has the part structure of the named type, and each part can be an arbitrary XML document. Hence, a data item in the variable is identified with the variable name, the part name, and an XPath query that returns a single node.

Basic activities. The `sequence` tag introduces the main body of the process and says that the enclosed activities are to be executed sequentially (sequence is actually a structured rather than a basic activity, but we need it here). In order to discuss communication concepts in an orderly way, we have ignored the hotel reservation in this version of the process and we will also assume that only one customer at a time invokes `makeTripOp`. Here we illustrate request/response-style communication both between the customer and GoSlow and between GoSlow and SlowHawk. One-way communication will be discussed in Section 25.6.3.

The first activity in the `sequence` receives an invocation by specifying the desired partner link, port type, and operation, and the local variable into which the input message is to be placed. Simply specifying the port type is not sufficient. An operation must be specified since a port type can include several operations. A partner link must also be specified since a particular port type might be used by several other processes through different partner links. For example, port type *PT* might occupy a role in two distinct partner link types, *PLT*1 and *PLT*2. A process might declare two partner links, one based on *PLT*1 and the other based on *PLT*2, and in each claim the role corresponding to *PT* as myrole. Hence the process must specify in the receive activity over which partner link it wants to receive a message.

Note that several partner links might be based on the *same* partner link type. For example, GoSlow might communicate with two different airlines, each of which provides a port of type getFarePT. It would have a different partner link for each, but each link would be based on the same partner link type.

The data sent by the customer is received by GoSlow in itineraryVar, and we could have used this variable in the invoke statement that follows (as inputVariable="itineraryVar"). We choose not to do this so we can illustrate the **assign** activity. A simple form of assign appears next. It copies the contents of one variable, itineraryVar, to another variable, getFareVar, of the same message type.

Next GoSlow invokes getFareOp and waits for a response. Note that the activity specifies variables to accommodate the message sent (getFareVar) and the response message (itineraryRespVar).

Finally, GoSlow performs an *opaque* initialization of the variable itinerary-RespVar (explained below) and then replies to the customer.

Note that Figure 25.24 is only a fragment of the GoSlow process. We will add some missing pieces soon.

Opaque assignment.   Processes (abstract and executable) can engage in arbitrarily complex computations that result in the assignment of a value to an item. In order to omit from an abstract process the details of a computation that appears in a corresponding executable process, BPEL allows an abstract process (but not an executable process) to execute opaque assignments. An opaque assignment statement assigns to an item a nondeterministically chosen value from the item's domain. The value chosen is an example of a result that might be produced by the computation. Thus the computation in the executable process can be replaced by opaque assignment in the corresponding abstract process.

An example of opaque assignment is shown in the assign statement following the invocation of getFareOp in Figure 25.24. To keep the example short we have assumed that the response to the invocation of getFareOp received by GoSlow from SlowHawk and the response to makeTripOp sent by GoSlow to the customer utilize the same variable, itineraryRespVar. However, the value of cost in the two processes differ. GoSlow presumably adds to the airfare reported by SlowHawk the cost of the hotel (we have not considered the hotel yet) and its commission. The computation for doing this is hidden in the abstract process using opaque assignment.

It might be argued that since an abstract process is not executable, opaque assignment serves no purpose. Why not simply omit the computation of the executable process without replacing it with an opaque assignment? You can do this (and we have omitted without replacement other computations), but replacement preserves the structure of the executable process. Furthermore, replacement of computations that assign new values to properties allows us to check that protocol-relevant data is properly initialized (cost is not protocol-relevant, but it illustrates opaque assignment). Finally, by nondeterministically choosing the value to be assigned from the domain of the target variable, it is possible to use an abstract process to emulate the message sequences that an executable business process might produce. For example, a property whose value has been assigned opaquely can be used in the condition of a switch construct (Section 25.6.3), which determines the flow of control of the business process.

Other types of the assign activity are available to both abstract and executable processes, but since their purpose is to support computation, their use in abstract processes is discouraged (but not prohibited). Hence, although an abstract process can utilize all of the variants of the assign activity allowed to executable processes and more (i.e., opaque assignment), the intent is that most of the computation that appears in an executable process is omitted from its abstract counterpart.

25.6.3 Structured Activities

BPEL is a complex language, and it is not our intention to cover all of its features. However, it's interesting to see a few of the structured activities that are used to control the flow of execution. We have already discussed the sequence activity.

Flow.   Concurrency is provided with the flow activity. Figure 25.25 shows a reimplementation of the GoSlow fragment corresponding to Figure 25.24, except we have now introduced the hotel service. The flow activity causes all the activities nested within it to be executed concurrently. In this case there are two activities, invoke (for obtaining an airline reservation) and sequence (for obtaining a hotel reservation). Hence, requests for air and hotel reservations are processed at the same time. Control exits from flow when all nested activities terminate.

The protocol for reserving a room, shown in Figure 25.25, is different from the protocol for reserving a flight since RoachHeaven expects to communicate with its clients asynchronously. The declaration of the operation getRoomOp in the WSDL file specifies only an input variable, and the corresponding invocation of the operation by GoSlow does not wait for a response. Instead, RoachHeaven responds by asynchronously invoking a callback operation provided by GoSlow on port type hotelCallbackPT. GoSlow must explicitly execute a receive activity to get this response.

Note that we do not show the assignment activities in Figure 25.25. Full assignments (assignment to all parts) must be included in the corresponding executable process, but in many cases even assignment to properties can be omitted in abstract processes. Furthermore, mention of the variables used by communication activities (e.g., receive, reply, invoke) can also be omitted in abstract processes. We will not cover the rules that govern all the possibilities.

FIGURE 25.25 Introducing concurrency into the GoSlow process.

```
<sequence>
  <receive partnerLink="customer" portType="gs:tripPT"
    operation="makeTripOp"/>
  <flow>
    <invoke partnerLink="airProvider" portType="gs:getFarePT"
      operation="getFareOp"/>
    <sequence>
      <invoke partnerLink="hotelProvider" portType="gs:roomResPT"
        operation="getRoomOp"/>
      <receive partnerLink="hotelProvider" portType="gs:hotelCallbackPT"
        operation="receiveResOp"/>
    </sequence>
  </flow>
  <reply partnerLink="customer" portType="gs:tripPT"
    operation="makeTripOp"/>
  <!-- Second half of protocol goes here (Figure 25.26) -->
</sequence>
```

Pick. GoSlow operates in an asynchronous environment that does not allow it to predict the sequence of events to which it must respond. For example, GoSlow has no way of knowing if, after the customer receives GoSlow's reply to its invocation of makeTripOp, the customer will invoke acceptTripOp or cancelTripOp. Hence, GoSlow must be prepared to receive both invocation messages (although only one will arrive). The pick control construct is provided for this purpose, and its use is illustrated in Figure 25.26. The fragment shown is meant to be inserted after the reply statement in Figures 25.24 or 25.25.

The pick control construct contains a set of nested clauses, each of which corresponds to an event that might occur. At run time, the clause corresponding to the first event to occur is executed, and the pick is then exited. Hence, in contrast to flow, only one clause gets executed. An event is either the arrival of a message, accepted by an onMessage clause, or a timeout, accepted by an onAlarm clause. At least one onMessage clause is required. In the example, GoSlow is willing to accept an invocation of either acceptTripOp or cancelTripOp and times out if neither arrives within a specified time interval. Note the similarity between onMessage and receive.

Switch. Figure 25.26 elaborates on the first onMessage clause to illustrate the switch activity. This activity consists of a list of case clauses followed by an optional otherwise clause.

The value of the condition attribute of a case clause is a Boolean expression conforming to XPath 1.0 syntax. Compliant implementations of the current version of

FIGURE 25.26 The second half of the GoSlow process.

```
<pick>
  <onMessage partnerLink="customer" portType="gs:tripPT"
         operation="acceptTripOp" variable="acceptTripVar">
    <switch>
      <case condition=
           "getVariableProperty('acceptTripVar','gs:payType')=credit">
        <sequence>
          <!-- handle credit payment -->
        </sequence>
      </case>
      <case condition=
           "getVariableProperty('acceptTripVar','gs:payType')=debit">
        <sequence>
          <!-- handle debit payment -->
        </sequence>
      </case>
      <otherwise>
        <throw faultName="payFault"/>
      </otherwise>
    </switch>
  </onMessage>

  <onMessage partnerLink="customer" portType="gs:tripPT"
       operation="cancelTripOp" variable="cancelTripVar">
    <!-- handle cancellation -->
  </onMessage>

  <onAlarm for="timeout interval">
    <!-- handle time out -->
  </onAlarm>
</pick>
```

BPEL are required to support the XPath language. How does an XPath expression access data in a BPEL process? The answer to this question has important implications concerning the difference between an abstract and an executable process.

BPEL introduces two extension functions to XPath that can be used in an XPath expression to enable it to access BPEL data: getVariableProperty and getVariableData. getVariableProperty returns the value of a property. Recall that a property is aliased to an item embedded in an XML document that forms a message part. getVariableData returns the value of an *arbitrary* item embedded in a message part (not just one that is pointed to by a property). Abstract processes are not permitted to use getVariableData, while executable processes can use both.

Since these functions are the only way to access data from within conditions, the control flow of an abstract process, and hence the sequence with which it executes communication activities, can be dependent only on properties. Thus, if an abstract process gives a complete description of a process's protocol, that protocol must be entirely dependent on properties.[8]

The conditions in switch clauses are evaluated in order, and the first clause whose condition has value true is executed, and then the switch activity is exited. If all conditions are false, the otherwise clause is executed. If no otherwise clause is present, the switch is exited normally.

Since the protocol depends on the payment type, the switch activity in Figure 25.26 tests the property payType (using getVariableProperty) when accept-TripOp is invoked. If payType (which actually refers to the part credDeb in accept-TripMsg—see Figure 25.23) has a value other than credit or debit, a fault is thrown. We deal with faults in Section 25.6.6.

While. For brevity we omit a discussion of the while activity. As you might expect, it has a body that is repeatedly executed until an XPath condition becomes false.

25.6.4 Links

The design of BPEL has been influenced from two different directions. Influence from the programming languages community is shown in the traditional structured control constructs that we have discussed and that are provided in the language. A second influence comes from the workflow community, since a BPEL process can be thought of as a workflow. In this community a workflow is traditionally viewed as a graph that can take an arbitrary (not necessarily structured) form. The graph consists of nodes representing tasks (perhaps representing the invocation or execution of an operation) and edges representing precedence relations describing the order in which tasks are to be executed. The link construct is introduced into BPEL to accommodate this view.

A precedence relationship is implicit in the sequence activity. It specifies that the nested activities are to be executed in the order given. In contrast, the flow activity does not specify any constraints on the order in which activities in different branches are to be executed. Thus, in Figure 25.25 the invocation of getFareOp in the first branch can be arbitrarily interleaved between the asynchronous invocation of getRoomOp and the callback response in the second branch. This is acceptable in this application since there is no relationship between making an airline reservation and a hotel reservation.

However, in a more complex application, a precedence relationship might exist between tasks on different sequential branches. For example, making a hotel

---

[8] Note that an abstract process can access an arbitrary part of a variable (whether or not it contains properties) using assignment, so it would not be accurate to say that an abstract process can access only properties. But an assignment to an item that is not a property does not affect control flow due to this restriction.

reservation might involve getting price quotes from several hotels and then choosing the hotel based on how much money is left in the travel budget after the cost of the airline ticket has been deducted. In that case, while price quotes can be obtained in the second branch concurrently with the invocation of getFareOp in the first, the choice of hotel and the confirmation of the hotel reservation in the second depends on the completion of getFareOp in the first.

A **link** provides a means to introduce a precedence relationship that restricts the unconstrained concurrency of activity execution in different branches of a flow activity. Each link has a name and is declared local to the flow. It synchronizes the execution of exactly one source activity and one target activity within the flow. The source activity is identified by a source element within the activity that names the link. The target activity is identified by a target element within the activity naming the same link. The implication of a link between a source activity and a target activity is that the source must complete before execution of the target starts. A typical situation is shown in Figure 25.27. Although activities A and B are in different branches of the flow, B cannot be started until A has completed.

While the basic concept of a link is simple, the situation gets dramatically more involved when we consider this type of synchronization in more detail.

■ Source and target activities need not be at the same level of nesting. For example a target activity might constitute one branch of the flow while the corresponding source might be nested arbitrarily deeply within control constructs in another branch. But certain restrictions—which we do not discuss—apply.

FIGURE 25.27 The use of a link to synchronize activities within a flow.

```
<flow>
    <link name="AtoB"/>
    <sequence>
        <invoke ··· />
        <invoke name="A" ··· >
            <source linkName="AtoB"/>
        </invoke>
        <invoke ··· />
    </sequence>
    <sequence>
        <invoke ··· />
        <invoke name="B" ··· >
            <target linkName="AtoB"/>
        </invoke>
        <invoke ··· />
    </sequence>
</flow>
```

■ In some cases even though execution of the activity that is the source of a link completes, it might not be appropriate to initiate the target activity. To introduce this flexibility, a source activity can have an associated `transitionCondition`, which is a function of variables accessible to the source activity and produces a positive or negative **link status**. This status is used in conjunction with the `joinCondition` discussed next.

■ An activity can be the target of several links. Such an activity can have a `joinCondition` attribute, which is a Boolean expression over the status of those links. It specifies the condition that must be satisfied in order for the activity to be initiated, and it is evaluated when the status of all the incoming links has been determined. For example, the activity might be initiated if the status of any one of the incoming links is positive. Alternatively, the condition might stipulate that the status of all incoming links must be positive.

■ What happens if the activity that is the source of a link is not executed? For example, the activity might be on a branch of a `switch` statement that is not chosen in a particular execution of the process. Since the `joinCondition` at the target activity cannot be evaluated until the status of all the target's incoming links have been determined, this causes a problem. To deal with this situation, if an activity will not be executed, the switch statement sets the status of all its outgoing links to negative.

■ If the `joinCondition` of an activity evaluates to false, the activity will not be executed and a `joinFailure` fault is thrown. In applications where this situation is not considered abnormal, the fault can simply be suppressed. In this case the status of all of the activity's outgoing links is set to negative, and as a result the fact that the activity is not executed is propagated to other activities that are targets of its outgoing links. This is referred to as **dead-path-elimination**.

Links provide an alternate way of controlling the sequencing of activities in a workflow. In fact one could envision a workflow in which each activity constitutes a different branch of an enormous `flow` and the activities are interconnected by a network of links that specify the order in which they are to execute. This is essentially the graphical view of a workflow in which control constructs, which also specify the precedence of task execution, are not used. Hence, BPEL provides the designer with two distinct ways of specifying precedence, which can be used in conjunction with one another.

25.6.5 BPEL and WS-Addressing

Each communication statement in a BPEL process explicitly names the port type and operation that is to be invoked at the destination. Hence, we say that a BPEL process is *statically dependent* on the abstract WSDL interface. Each communication statement also names a partner link, but it does not identify the process at the other end of the link. In the GoSlow example our assumption has been that GoSlow deals with only a single airline, SlowHawk. Hence, the partner role, `airline`, of its partner link, `airProvider`, can be initialized at deployment time to refer to SlowHawk.

More generally, the port type getFarePT might be supported by a number of airlines, and GoSlow must determine the airline appropriate for a particular trip dynamically. Thus, there is a need to provide a mechanism in BPEL to specify at run time the process referred to by a partner link.

BPEL relies on WS-Addressing and the endpoint reference type (which contains all the information necessary to address a message) to provide this mechanism. If, as in the GoSlow example, the endpoint reference corresponding to the partner role of a partner link is known in advance, it can be associated with that role at deployment time.[9] If this is not the case, the appropriate endpoint reference can be assigned to the role at run time.

For example, a dynamic version of GoSlow might maintain a database listing all the airlines supporting getFareOp, their endpoint references, and the destination cities that they reach. When a customer requests a trip to a particular destination, GoSlow can access the database to select an appropriate airline. Assuming that the endpoint reference of the selected airline is stored in part airEPR of variable airInfo, GoSlow can assign the reference to the partnerRole of airProvider using the following form of the assignment activity designed to manipulate partner links

```
<assign>
    <copy>
        <from variable="airInfo" part="airEPR"/>
        <to partnerLink="airProvider"/>
    </copy>
</assign>
```

The to child need not specify which role of airProvider is the target of the assignment, since myRole cannot be changed. (This is the subject of Exercise 25.11.) Similarly, the endpoint reference associated with either role of a partner link can be assigned to a variable.

Having initialized airProvider to refer to the selected airline, GoSlow can invoke getFareOp using the invoke statement shown in Figure 25.24. Thus, the target address is determined (dynamically) at run time, but the operation and port type are determined (statically) at design time.

Endpoint references are manipulated opaquely by BPEL: their contents cannot be accessed using the BPEL language itself. However, in the executable version of BPEL, lower-level modules that manipulate messages sent by a BPEL program use endpoint references to determine message destinations (and, in some situations, bindings as well).

---

[9] It might seem that an endpoint reference, whose main component is a URI, would be associated with a port rather than a partner link. Recall, however, that BPEL is independent of the concrete level of WSDL where ports are defined. As a result BPEL does not deal with ports.

25.6.6 Handling Errors

Web services interactions typically involve a number of processes, implemented by different organizations, executing at independent sites spread across the Internet. Hence, the interaction generally takes a significant amount of time, and failures are not uncommon. In addition to the other failure modes one would expect in a conventional distributed application, the fact that components are developed by different organizations makes it more likely that messages contain unexpected and/or undesired data. These are the problems that one would expect in a loosely coupled environment, and BPEL provides a flexible structure for dealing with them.

Fault and compensation handlers are used to reverse the effects of partially completed interactions. The execution of these handlers is tied in with the concept of scopes. A **scope** is a feature of most programming languages (think `begin/end` blocks) and serves to define the execution context of an activity. A scope can have a name and local declarations and encloses a (possibly complex) activity to be executed. Declarations include, among other items, local variables, fault handlers, and a compensation handler. (Note, however, that properties do not have scope—they are always global to the entire process.) Scopes can be nested in the usual way to create a global/local execution environment for the activity.

Compensation.   A process invokes the services of other processes in the course of performing an interaction. Even if the computation performed by each process is a transaction, it is unlikely that the interaction will use a two-phase commit protocol to ensure global atomicity since the organizations involved are independent, and interactions are lengthy. Using a two-phase commit causes locks to be held for long periods and sites to lose control over when locks are released (see Section 24.6). If two-phase commit is not used, individual sites might commit during an interaction that ultimately fails. We saw in Section 20.7 that compensation is a technique for recovering in such a case.

A compensation handler can be declared local to a scope. The implication is that, in BPEL's view, a scope encapsulates a basic unit of work that either completes successfully or fails, and that compensation can be used to reverse the effects of a successfully completed scope at a later time. Furthermore, at most one compensation handler can be declared. The implication is that, in BPEL's view, how success is achieved is a detail hidden within the scope. There is only one kind of success, and the details of how it is to be reversed are hidden within the compensation handler.

A simple scenario that illustrates the use of compensation is shown in Figure 25.28. Scope *B* is nested immediately within scope *A*. It is an activity in the sequence of activities that constitute scope *A*. Scope *B* contains the invocation of a Web service, *reserveOp*. Suppose that after exiting from scope *B* normally (*reserveOp* has completed successfully), a fault occurs in *activities-2* that requires the reversal of *reserveOp*. When the fault is raised, control will be passed to a fault handler (we will discuss fault handlers in the next subsection) local to scope *A* (assuming that such a handler has been declared). Reversal can be done by invoking—from within that handler—the compensation handler local to scope *B*.

FIGURE 25.28 A simple process fragment illustrating compensation.

```
<scope name="A">
    <sequence>
        <!-- activities-1 -->
        <scope name="B">
            <compensationHandler>
                <invoke ..cancelOp.. >
            </compensationHandler>
            <invoke ..reserveOp.. >
        </scope>
        <!-- activities-2 -->
    </sequence>
</scope>
```

Compensation is not automatic. The application programmer must explicitly code the body of the handler. Thus, more generally, scope B might invoke several operations, not all of which require compensation. Identifying those that require compensation, determining the correct compensating operation for each, and deciding on the order in which compensating operations are invoked are all decisions that the application programmer must make and encode in the body of the handler.

A handler is invoked using the `compensate` activity, which names the scope to which the handler is local (the scope to be compensated for). For example, the compensation handler local to scope B is invoked from scope A using `<compensate scope="B"/>`. Compensation can only be invoked if execution of scope B has terminated normally—that is, the unit of work has been successfully completed. In BPEL terminology, the compensation handler local to a scope is **installed** when normal exit from the scope has occurred. Uninstalled handlers cannot be invoked.

Scope B terminates abnormally if a fault occurs during its execution. The nature of the fault and the point at which it was raised within the scope determine the actions to be taken to reverse the partial execution. Hence, in contrast to compensation, reversal after a fault depends on the specific details of the event. We will discuss faults shortly.

Compensation applies only to the scope's external effects—the effects of the operations it has invoked at other sites. On entry, a scope's compensation handler is given a snapshot of the process's state at the time control exited (normally) from the scope. Since it can access only the snapshot and not the variables themselves, compensation cannot affect the state of the process and applies only to external activities.

When the compensation handler completes, control returns to the point following the `compensate` activity that called it. That still leaves open one question. Where in the process can a `compensate` activity be placed? In BPEL, compensation handles failure, and failure is detected when a fault occurs. Hence, a `compensate` activity can appear only within a fault handler or a compensation handler. (The execution of compensation handlers can be nested if nested scopes have to be reversed. You will see an example of this shortly.)

Faults. Faults signal failure and start the process of reversing the effects of an interaction. A fault might be raised in a process if it gets a fault response to an operation that it has invoked synchronously. Alternatively, a process might explicitly execute a throw activity if it recognizes that an anomalous situation has arisen. An example of this is shown in Figure 25.26. Finally, a **standard** fault—a fault recognized by the BPEL processor such as joinFailure—might occur.

When a fault, f, is raised in a scope, S, all activities within S are immediately terminated. Since S might enclose a flow, terminating an activity might imply cutting off a concurrent activity at an arbitrary point. For example, one branch of a flow might execute a synchronous invoke while another faults. Although the invoke is terminated, the invoked server might still be servicing the request.

When termination is complete and if S has declared a fault handler for f, control is passed to it. Based on the nature of f, the handler can invoke compensation handlers for scopes immediately enclosed in S that have completed normally and clean up after other, immediately enclosed, activities (this is complicated by the fact that the handler might not know how far S had progressed when f occurred). While processing f, the fault handler might throw a fault (possibly f), which will be raised in the immediately enclosing scope.

If S has not declared a handler for f locally, f is raised in the immediately enclosing scope and on up the line until a handler is found or the process is terminated abnormally. Assuming that some handler, F, processes f without throwing another fault, control ultimately exits from F. If F is local to scope S' (which might be S), control resumes in the scope that immediately encloses S', at the activity immediately following S'.

Whether a fault handler local to scope S throws a fault or simply exits from that handler, S is said to have exited abnormally. Hence, if a compensation handler has been declared local to S it is *not* installed—compensation cannot be invoked for a scope that has not terminated normally. This makes sense since compensation applies to a unit of work that has completed successfully.

To illustrate these points, consider the interaction between GoSlow and SlowHawk. The reply activity that SlowHawk might use to respond to a faulty invocation of getFareOp by GoSlow is

```
<reply partnerLink="myCustomer" portType="mygs:getFarePT"
    operation="getFareOp" variable="myFaultVar"
    faultName="invalidArgFault"/>
```

This version of the reply activity is different from the one used in Figure 25.24. In this case the fault named in the faultName attribute is being reported. Furthermore, the value returned is of type invalidArgFaultMsg (see Figure 25.22) instead of itineraryRespMsg, which is the type used for a normal return. (Note that the

FIGURE 25.29 Catching a fault in GoSlow.

```
<invoke partnerLink="airProvider" portType="gs:getFarePT"
        operation="getFareOp" inputVariable="itineraryVar"
        outputVariable="itineraryRespVar"/>
    <catch faultName="gs:invalidArgFault"
        faultVariable="invalidArgFaultVar">
        <sequence>
            <invoke partnerLink="hotelProvider"
                portType="gs:roomResPT"
                operation="cancelRoomOp"/>
            <reply partnerLink="customer"
                portType="gs:tripPT"
                operation="makeTripOp"
                faultName="invalidCustFault"/>
            <!-- other activities -->
        </sequence>
    </catch>
</invoke>
```

variable, partner link, and prefix mygs are declared locally to SlowHawk, but that mygs refers to the WSDL definitions of Figures 25.21–25.23.)

The reply raises an invalidArgFault at the point in GoSlow where getFare is invoked. In general, a fault handler is declared local to a scope using a catch element, but in this case it is convenient to attach the catch directly to the invocation (i.e., the invoke activity implicitly defines a scope). As a result, the invocation of getFareOp in Figure 25.24 is modified, as shown in Figure 25.29, in order to handle invalidArgFault. When the fault is raised in GoSlow, the value of myFaultVar is assigned to invalidArgFaultVar, and the handler code is the sequence within the catch. If a room reservation was made prior to the fault, cancelRoomOp is invoked. After replying to the customer, the handler might raise a fault that causes GoSlow to terminate.

If there were several invocations of getFareOp within GoSlow, it might be better to declare a single catch element local to a scope that contains all the invocations rather than declaring catch elements local to each invoke. A fault thrown by any invocation winds up in this handler. In either case, the handler cancels the room reservation and returns a fault to the customer.

The throw activity is illustrated in Figure 25.26. GoSlow raises the fault payFault if the customer has supplied a value of payType other than credit or debit as a parameter of acceptTripOp. We can expect that GoSlow would declare a handler for payFault in a scope that contains the throw. The handler would execute a reply to return a badPayFault to the customer (see Figure 25.22).

In general, several fault handlers (including possibly a <catchAll> handler) can be declared local to a scope to handle different faults. All are children of a single

<faultHandlers> element. The rules for determining the appropriate handler for a specific case are detailed and uninteresting.

Typically, the body of the fault handler invokes a compensation handler for each immediately enclosed scope, S, that has completed normally. One possible situation is shown in Figure 25.30. Fault $f2$ occurs in $scope_2$ and is handled by the catch element local to that scope. The handler cleans up locally, compensates for $scope_3$ and $scope_4$ (which have completed normally), and then throws the fault $f1$.

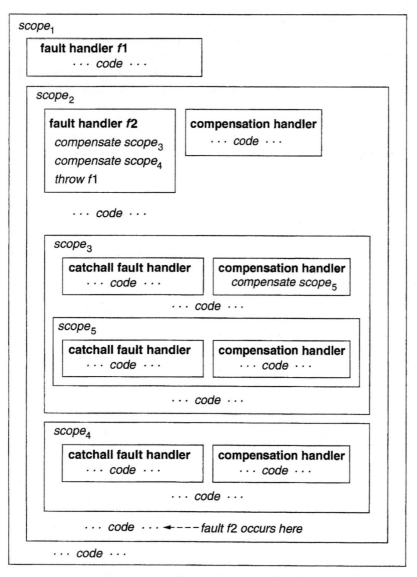

FIGURE 25.30 Example of the interaction between fault and compensation handlers.

$scope_2$ exits abnormally and $f1$ is handled in $scope_1$. The compensation handler for $scope_3$ compensates for $scope_5$.

Default handlers.   If a business process contains an activity throw f, it is clear that the application programmer should provide a handler for f. Similarly, a fault response to an invocation, such as invalidArgFault, should be anticipated by the invoker and provided for. But what about a standard fault (for example, join-Failure)? The programmer might be excused for not providing handlers for all standard faults in a particular scope and simply allow them to be passed up and handled in a global scope (perhaps by a catchall handler). But there is a subtle problem here. A scope, S, which does not handle a fault, and hence allows it to be raised in the immediately enclosing scope, does not exit normally. As a result, a compensation handler declared in S will not be installed and cannot subsequently be invoked from a global location. This can be a serious problem if S or a scope nested within S has invoked external services that need to be reversed.

For example, if in Figure 25.30 the catchall fault handler in $scope_3$ had not been declared and fault $f2$ had been raised in $scope_3$, the handler for $f2$ in $scope_2$ would get control but would not be able to invoke the compensation handler local to $scope_3$.

BPEL deals with this problem by providing a default fault handler for unhandled faults in each scope. Its purpose is to invoke all compensation handlers for immediately enclosed scopes that have completed normally (in the reverse order of completion of the corresponding scopes) and then to reraise the fault globally. With this feature, before $f2$—which we are now assuming was raised in a scope ($scope_3$) that has no fault handler—is reraised in $scope_2$, the default fault handler for $scope_3$ will get control and invoke the compensation handler for $scope_5$.

Unfortunately, this is not a complete solution to the problem since no compensation will be performed for an external activity occurring immediately within $scope_3$. A fault handler in $scope_3$ is needed in that case, and it must first determine that such an activity has completed.

Default fault handlers provide a partial solution to the problem of reversing the effects of abnormally exited scopes as a fault is propagated up the line. But that is not the whole story. What if a compensation handler for a scope is not declared? For example, suppose that the compensation handler for $scope_3$ had not been declared and $f2$ is raised in $scope_2$, as shown in the figure. It would not be possible for the fault handler for $f2$ in $scope_2$ to invoke an installed compensation handler for $scope_5$ since the latter is not visible from the former. BPEL deals with this problem by providing a default compensation handler for each scope in which a compensation handler has not been declared. It invokes compensation handlers in all immediately nested scopes. In the example, the handler for $f2$ in $scope_2$ can invoke the (default) compensation handler in $scope_3$, which will invoke the (explicitly declared) compensation handler for $scope_5$.

Thus, default fault handlers support compensation when faults are propagated up the line, while default compensation handlers support the propagation of compensation down the line.

25.6.7 Handling Multiple Requests

There is a major deficiency in the way GoSlow has been implemented in the previous sections. It can handle only one customer interaction. Of course, we could modify it to handle multiple requests, one at a time, by simply placing the process in a while loop. However, we would like it to handle interactions concurrently, as a multithreaded server. BPEL provides two features to support this goal.

Multiple customer interactions can be handled concurrently by creating multiple instances of the process, one for each interaction. Ordinarily, the first activity of such a process is a receive that receives a request from a customer, as in Figure 25.24. In BPEL the receive can contain a createInstance attribute. If its value is set to yes, the reception of a message creates a new instance of the process to handle the arriving message. The default value is no. This is the only way a new instance of a process can be created.

For example, if the initial receive statement in GoSlow is replaced by

```
<receive partnerLink="customer" portType="gs:tripPT"
        operation="makeTripOp" variable="itineraryVar"
        createInstance="yes"/>
```

then each customer request will be handled by a separate instance of GoSlow and these instances can execute concurrently.

There are a few restrictions on the use of this feature. The receive must be the initial activity in the process. This makes sense since the activity that is enabled when the new instance is created is the activity following the receive. If an activity preceded the receive, it would not be executed in the new instance.

The restriction is not meant to exclude the possibility that there are several initial activities. This might be necessary in the case in which there are several distinct requests that a customer might submit. For example, in addition to tripPT, GoSlow might support a port type containing operations that allow customers to query a database of possible destinations. We want a new instance of GoSlow to be created for either type of request, but we cannot know in advance which type will arrive next. One way to handle this is to have pick be the initial activity and to set the createInstance attribute to yes in each of its onMessage clauses. Thus the restriction is relaxed to allow either a pick or a receive to be the first activity.

Creating process instances to provide concurrency introduces a new problem. How does a customer address the correct instance? This is not a problem if the customer's interaction consists of a single, synchronous invocation of an operation on a server, and the server does not invoke other servers in the process of handling the request. In that case, the customer's invocation message creates the new instance of the server, and when the instance replies, the interaction is over. The customer does not have to send a subsequent message.

Consider, however, a customer's interaction with GoSlow. Assuming the customer books the trip, this involves two invocations: first makeTripOp and then acceptTripOp. If two customers concurrently book a trip, a distinct instance of

GoSlow will be created for each. The problem is to decide to which instance an invocation message for `acceptTripOp` sent by one of the customers should be delivered.

The solution to this problem relies on the likelihood that there is some identifying item of information contained in the messages that are exchanged in a particular interaction. For example, the customer's Id is contained in all the messages of a trip interaction. If the run-time infrastructure hosting the business processes associates a process instance with an Id value, it can identify the target instance of a particular message by examining the Id value the message carries. An order number and social security number are other examples of identifying items of data.

Unfortunately, the infrastructure has no way of knowing which parts of a message are identifying items. Hence, in order to implement this solution, BPEL provides the application programmer with a construct to specify those parts.

In a more general situation, the messages of an interaction might be identified by several such items. For example, if GoSlow had to allow for the possibility that a single customer might run several trip-booking interactions concurrently, the messages of an interaction would have to be identified by both a trip number and a customer Id. Finally, it might be the case that different identifying items are used in different messages of the same interaction. For example, the messages in GoSlow's conversation with SlowHawk might all contain a purchase order number, not the customer's Id, while the messages in GoSlow's conversation with the customer might all contain the customer's Id but not the purchase order number—but all these messages belong to the same interaction.

Clearly, handling all these situations is a complex business. Let us look at a simple case. BPEL allows a process to declare a **correlation set** local to a scope. This is a set of properties such that all messages having the same values of all the properties in the set are part of the same interaction and hence are handled by the same instance. Thus, a correlation set identifies a particular instance of a process among a set of instances of that process, and a correlation set and a port together uniquely identify a process instance among all process instances at a host machine.

For example, in the case of GoSlow, we might include the following correlation set in the declarations of Figure 25.24:

```
<correlationSets>
    <correlationSet name="custCorr"
          properties="gs:Id"/>
</correlationSets>
```

In the general case, the value of the `properties` attribute might be a list of properties (e.g., trip number, customer Id), but in this case, the value of the property Id is sufficient to distinguish the messages of one interaction from the messages of another.

Having defined a correlation set we can use it in a communication activity. For example, in order to adapt GoSlow to concurrently handle customers, we modify the `receive` activity in Figure 25.24 as follows:

```
<receive partnerLink="customer" portType="gs:tripPT"
        operation="makeTripOp" variable="itineraryVar"
        createInstance="yes">
    <correlations>
        <correlation set="custCorr" initiate="yes"/>
    </correlations>
</receive>
```

The value yes assigned to the `createInstance` attribute of the `receive` indicates that a new instance of GoSlow is to be created when a message is received. The `correlations` child lists the correlation set(s) that should be used to match an arriving message to an instance. The value yes assigned to the `initiate` attribute of the `correlation` element (its default value is no) indicates, in addition, that values in the received message should be used to initialize the properties of the correlation set associated with the instance. Thus, the new version of the `receive` activity creates a new instance of GoSlow. It associates with it a new instance of the correlation set `custCorr` when a message arrives, and it initializes the correlation set instance with the value of Id in the arriving message.

Instance creation and correlation set initialization do not necessarily go hand in hand. A single instance might sequentially engage in several conversations (one conversation ends before the next starts) using the same correlation set. In this case a new conversation starts with a `receive` activity that initializes the correlation set, but the `receive` does not create a new instance. However, BPEL imposes the restriction that a set can be initialized only once. Hence, the instance of the process would have to exit the scope (and deallocate the set) and then reenter the scope in which the set is declared, and the correlation set will be initialized anew.

In general, the `<correlations>` element introduces one or more correlation sets. Each set is a list of properties, and each property in the set identifies (through a `propertyAlias` association) an item in the arriving message. Once a correlation set has been initialized, other `receive` activities in the instance that name the same correlation set will accept only messages containing that value.

In the GoSlow example, in addition to modifying the `receive` that accepts the invocation of `makeTripOp` to create a new instance and initialize a correlation set, the `onMessage` clause of the `pick` in Figure 25.26 (which is effectively a `receive` activity) must be modified in a corresponding way:

```
<onMessage partnerLink="customer" portType="tripPT"
        operation="acceptTripOp" variable="acceptTripVar">
    <correlations>
        <correlation set="custCorr"/>
```

```
        </correlations>
        <!-- the switch activity goes here -->
    </onMessage>
```

Here it is not appropriate to create a new instance, so the createInstance attribute of onMessage has the value no (by default). Furthermore, it is not appropriate to initialize the correlation set, so the initiate attribute of the correlation element also has the value no (by default). Hence, the activity only accepts invocations of acceptTrip carrying a value of Id equal to the value associated with the instance when the instance was created by the receive statement.

Having introduced correlation sets it is now possible to state two fairly intuitive rules that relate to it. First, it should never be the case that (at execution time) a process has two receive type statements (a receive statement or an onMessage clause of a pick) enabled at the same time with the same partner link, port type, operation, and correlation set(s). For example, this might happen (in an erroneous process) if the statements were embedded in two branches of a flow. Such a situation would imply that an arbitrary decision would have to be made at run time to choose the statement that accepts a particular arriving message. The semantics of a process that violates this restriction are not defined.

The second rule states that it should never be the case that a process has accepted more than one outstanding synchronous request from a particular partner link, port type, operation, and correlation set(s). If this rule were violated—perhaps by executing identical receive statements on different branches of a flow—the target of a subsequently executed reply would not be uniquely specified.

25.6.8 Front-End and Back-End Systems

Now that we have seen some of the details of BPEL and WSDL, we can return to our discussion of front-end and back-end systems. Figure 25.31 shows how these systems might communicate in the course of a B2B interaction. A front-end system (for example, the one at the right of the figure) might be implemented in BPEL (or another language that mimics a BPEL specification). In providing service, it might invoke other front-end systems (for example, the one at the top of the figure) and back-end systems (for example, the one at the bottom of the figure). The back-end system might be a transaction processing system implemented as described in Chapter 23. Both the front-end and the back-end systems expose WSDL interfaces and are invoked using SOAP messages.

For example, GoSlow and SlowHawk might be implemented in BPEL in two front-end systems. An invocation of makeTripOp at GoSlow results in a nested invocation of getFareOp at SlowHawk to obtain the required fare. Although we did not discuss getFareOp, it might, in turn, invoke a transaction exported by a back-end transaction processing system. GoSlow's operation acceptTripOp accepts credit or debit card information and performs the processing necessary to complete a reservation. This might involve invoking an operation approveOp at the card company's site, which might involve the services of banking and database systems

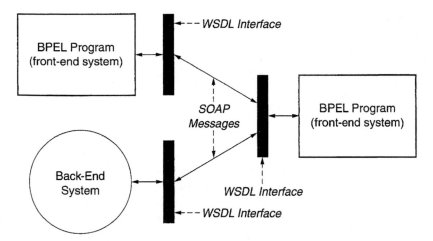

FIGURE 25.31 An example of interconnected Web services.

elsewhere. Hence, approveOp is implemented in a front-end system at the card company, which invokes these other, back-end, systems. Finally, acceptTripOp invokes a (local) back-end transaction processing system on the GoSlow server to record information about the reservation.

25.6.9 Interacting with a Web Service: Projection of a BPEL Process

Suppose you are a potential client of GoSlow and want to find out how to interact with it to plan a trip. Unfortunately, GoSlow's WSDL interface is not sufficient for that purpose since it contains only the operations and messages you must use but says nothing about how you must sequence the messages in order to complete an interaction. In this case the sequencing is trivial (makeTripOp followed by either acceptTripOp or cancelTripOp), but in a more realistic situation a more complex interaction might be required.

The information you want can be found in the executable BPEL process in GoSlow's front-end, but that contains more information than you need. An abstract version of the process is sufficient, but even that contains more information than necessary since, for example, you do not care how GoSlow interacts with other services (e.g., SlowHawk) to provide the service you requested, what properties GoSlow uses, how GoSlow processes fault conditions, how GoSlow maintains your state, and so on.

The information you need can be provided by a **projection** of the abstract process that contains only the communication with the customer, together with the control structures pertinent to that communication. Such a projection, or view, of the abstract GoSlow process (Figures 25.24 and 25.26) is shown in Figure 25.32. From this you can easily see what messages you must interchange and in what order.

FIGURE 25.32 A projection of the GoSlow process for use by a client.

```
<process name="GoSlowProcess"
      targetNamespace="http://www.goslow.com/wsdl/trips-bp"
      xmlns="http://schemas.xmlsoap.org/ws/2003/03/business-process/"
      xmlns:gs="http://www.goslow.com/wsdl/trips"
      abstractProcess="yes">
<sequence>
      <receive portType="gs:tripPT"
            operation="makeTripOp"/>
      <reply portType="gs:TripPT"
            operation="makeTripOp"/>
      <pick>
            <onMessage portType="gs:tripPT"
                    operation="acceptTripOp">
                       . . .
            </onMessage>
            <onMessage portType="gs:tripPT"
                    operation="cancelTripOp">
                       . . .
            </onMessage>
      </pick>
</sequence>
</process>
```

Projections can also be made for the various partners that provide the services used by GoSlow, for example the SlowHawk airline. The partners can use such projections, together with the corresponding projections of their own BPEL processes, to ensure that the processes are compatible (that they send and receive matching messages at the appropriate times). Projections might become an important use case for BPEL as an increasing number of enterprises seek to develop business processes that interact smoothly with each other.

25.7 UDDI: Publishing and Discovering Information about Services

Now that we have explained how a business, for example, Company A, can use WSDL to describe the services it is willing to perform, there remains the problem of how another business, Company B, that might want to use that service can discover that Company A provides the service and then obtain its WSDL description. This is the problem addressed by UDDI (Universal Description, Discovery, and Integration). As with the other protocols we have discussed, UDDI is still under active development. We give a brief overview of version 3.0, which at the time this book was written was a technical committee specification.

UDDI provides a means by which service providers can publish information about the services they provide and requesters can find information about which providers provide the services they want and how to obtain those services. More specifically UDDI provides

- A *Registry* (*database*) that contains information about
  - Business entities
  - Informal descriptions of the services provided by those entities
  - Various categorizations of those entities and services that can be used as the basis for searches in the registry
  - WSDL descriptions of those services
- *Inquiry and Publisher Interfaces* (*query and update languages*) that
  - Requestors can use to find and retrieve information from the registry
  - Providers can use to enter information into the registry

In some respects, a UDDI registry can be viewed as a telephone book, and the information stored in it can be characterized the same way telephone book information is characterized (except that the last characterization is new).

- *White page information.* Name, Address, Contact Person, Web site, etc.
- *Yellow page information.* Type of Business, Locations, Products, Services, Categorizations
- *Green page information.* Technical information about business services, including pointers to WSDL descriptions of the services

25.7.1 Data Structures in the UDDI Registry

A UDDI registry is a database, and so we start with a diagram that helps describe the data structures in a registry. Figure 25.33 shows an overview of the data structures that appear in a UDDI registry that is being used to describe a service.

There are four "top-level" data structures in the registry: businessEntity, businessService, bindingTemplate, and tModel. Each top-level structure has a unique key called its **universal unique identifier** (uuid).[10] For example in Figure 25.34, we show a businessEntity whose businessKey is denoted as uuid:123BZK. (publisherAssertion is not a top-level data structure and does not have a uuid. We will discuss its use later in this section.)

For simplicity, we have omitted some of the optional elements within the data structures. The businessEntity and businessService structures can contain optional categorization elements that describe the business entity and its services.

---

[10] The system assigns the uuid to ensure uniqueness. Version 3 of UDDI allows services to propose their own keys, which do not have to be in the form of uuids and which the system checks for uniqueness. We do not discuss this possibility any further.

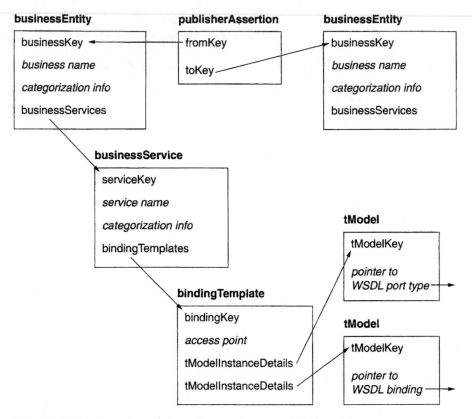

FIGURE 25.33 Overview of the data structures in a UDDI registry.

Using these elements, the registry can be searched for specific businesses or services based on international or industry categorization standards. Examples of such standards are the U.S. government's NAICS (National American Industry Classification System) and the International Standards Organization's ISO 3166 geographic categorization. Individual industries can also publish their own standard categories, which can be included in these optional elements.

The UDDI registry structures are:

- **businessEntity.** The businessEntity is the highest-level data structure in the registry. It contains white page information about the business (for example, a travel agency)
    - The name of the business, address, contact persons, etc.
    - Optional categorization information that can be used in searches to find the business
    - One or more businessService data structures, each of which describes a different service the business provides

FIGURE **25.34** A simple example of a businessEntity data structure.

```
<businessEntity businessKey="uuid:123BZK">
    <name> SlowHawk </name>
    <description> Airline </description>
    <contacts> . . . </contacts>
    <businessServices>
        <businessService> . . . </businessService>
    </businessServices>
    <categoryBag>
        <!-- We expand this example later -->
    </categoryBag>
</businessEntity>
```

FIGURE **25.35** A simple example of a businessService data structure.

```
<businessService serviceKey="uuid:123SRK">
    <name> Fare Service </name>
    <description> Provides fares for specific flights </description>
    <bindingTemplates>
        <bindingTemplate> . . . </bindingTemplate>
    </bindingTemplates>
    <categoryBag> . . . </categoryBag>
</businessService>
```

Figure 25.34 shows a simple example of a businessEntity data structure. The businessKey is a unique identifier for the business. The businessServices element contains one or more businessService data structures that describe the services provided by that business. This example does not have any of the optional categorization elements. Figure 25.38, which we discuss later, is an expansion of this figure that does contain such categorization elements.

▪ **businessService.** A businessService data structure contains yellow page information about one specific service a particular business provides

- The name, unique identifier, and informal description of that service
- One or more bindingTemplate data structures, each of which describes a different binding for that service
- Optional categorization information that can be used in searches to find the service

Figure 25.35 shows a simple example of a businessService data structure. Again, this example does not have any of the optional categorization elements.

FIGURE 25.36 A simple example of a `bindingTemplate` data structure.

```
<bindingTemplate bindingKey="uuid:123BNK"/>
  <description> GetFare SOAP binding </description>
  <accessPoint useType="endPoint"/>
    http://www.SlowHawk.com
  </accessPoint>
  <tModelInstanceDetails>
    <tModelInstanceInfo tModelKey="uuid:3456TMK">
      <description> WSDL port type of GetFare </description>
    </tModelInstanceInfo>
    <tModelInstanceInfo tModelKey="uuid: . . . ">
      <description> WSDL RPC/encoded binding of getFare </description>
    </tModelInstanceInfo>
  </tModelInstanceDetails>
</bindingTemplate>
```

- ■ **bindingTemplate.** A `bindingTemplate` data structure contains green page information about one specific binding of one specific service a particular business provides.[11]

  - The unique identifier and informal description of the binding
  - The Web address at which that binding can be accessed (provided in the port declaration local to the WSDL description of the service)
  - One or more `tModelKeys` that point to `tModel` data structures, which provide technical details about that binding for that service. (We explain why there are often two such keys when we discuss `tModels` in the next bullet.)

  Thus, the `bindingTemplate` data structure relates a service to a binding of that service. Figure 25.36 shows a simple example of a `bindingTemplate` data structure.

- ■ **tModel (technical model).** A `tModel` data structure contains green page information describing the technical details of a service. In particular a `tModel` contains (within `overviewDoc`) a pointer to a file containing the WSDL description of the service. Specifically, a `tModel` data structure contains

  - The name and informal description of the technical information represented by the `tModel`
  - A pointer to the location of the WSDL information represented by the `tModel`

---

[11] We have used the word "binding" in several contexts in this chapter. A SOAP binding maps a SOAP message to a particular transport protocol. A WSDL binding maps an abstract message described in a port type to a concrete message sent using a particular transport protocol to a particular port. A UDDI `bindingTemplate` maps the name of a service to its WSDL description.

FIGURE 25.37 A simple example of a tModel data structure.

```
<tModel tModelKey="uuid:3456TMK">
    <name> getFarePT </name>
    <description> WSDL port type of getFare Service </description>
    <overviewDoc>
        <overviewURL>
            http://www.SlowHawk.com/GetFarePTDescription
        </overviewURL>
    </overviewDoc>
</tModel>
```

Figure 25.37 shows a simple example of a tModel data structure.

According to the published "best practices" for using a UDDI registry to store information about WSDL services, a bindingTemplate should contain two different tModelKeys that point to two different tModels for a specific service. One tModel points to a file containing the WSDL description of the port type of that service, and the other points to a file containing the WSDL description of the binding.

One reason for having two tModels for the same service is that the port type might be shared by many businesses that provide the same service. For example, the airline industry might define a standard getFare service described by a generic port type, and many individual airlines might provide that service, each with its own binding. Thus the bindingTemplates of each of the services provided by the different airlines would point to the same tModel for the port type and different tModels for their individual bindings. The services of all the airlines would be semantically equivalent, but would be implemented differently.

Another reason for having two tModels is that a single provider might support two or more different bindings of the same service, each described by a different bindingTemplate. Each of these bindingTemplates would point to the same tModel that describes the port type of that service and different tModels that correspond to the different bindings.

Actually, tModel data structures have a number of different uses in UDDI registries in addition to pointing to WSDL files.

- They are used to point to files containing categorization information. Such tModels might be referenced by businessEntity, businessService, or publisherAssertion data structures.
- They are used to point to files containing complex search criteria that can be used by the find methods in the query language, which are discussed in Section 25.7.2.

Figure 25.38 is an expansion of Figure 25.34 that includes categorization information involving a tModel. The categoryBag items can contain one or

FIGURE 25.38 An example of a `businessEntity` data structure that includes a `categoryBag` that refers to a `tModel`.

```
<businessEntity businessKey="uuid:123BZK">
    <name> SlowHawk </name>
    <description> Airline </description>
    <contacts> . . . </contacts>
    <businessServices>
        <businessService> . . . </businessService>
    </businessServices>
    <categoryBag>
        <keyedReference
            keyName="Scheduled Passenger Air Transportation"
            keyValue="481111"
            tModelKey="uuid:C0B9FE13-179F-413D-8A5B-5004DB8E5BB2"/>
    </categoryBag>
</businessEntity>
```

more `keyedReference` elements. Within each `keyedReference` element is a `tModelKey`, whose uuid points to a `tModel` that contains information about a particular categorization. The `keyValue` gives a particular key within that categorization, and the `keyName` is an informal human-readable name for the meaning of that key. This key can then be used in a search for that business entity, as shown later in Figure 25.41.

In Figure 25.38, the uuid C0B9FE13-179F-413D-8A5B-5004DB8E5BB2 in the `tModelKey` corresponds to the North American Industry Classification System (NAICS), and the `keyValue` 481111 corresponds to "Scheduled Passenger Air Transportation Industry" within that classification.

■ **publisherAssertion.** A `publisherAssertion` data structure represents relationships between pairs of `businessEntity` structures. For example, one businessEntity might be a subsidiary or a partner of the other. The data structure contains

- A `fromKey` and a `toKey`, which are `businessKeys` that point to the two `businessEntity` data structures for which a relationship is being defined
- A description of the relationship (within the `keyedReference`)

Figure 25.39 shows a simple example of a `publisherAssertion` data structure. It states that the business entity with the key uuid:123BZK (which according to Figure 25.38 is SlowHawk) is a parent business of the entity with the key uuid:123SUB.

Using these data structures, a requester can find all of the WSDL services provided by a business, and for each of these services all of the bindings for that service, and for each binding the detailed WSDL description of that binding. To actually find this information, the requester can use the *Inquiry Interface*, discussed next.

FIGURE 25.39 A simple example of a `publisherAssertion` data structure.

```
<publisherAssertion>
    <fromKey> uuid:123BZK </fromKey>
    <toKey> uuid:123SUB </toKey>
    <keyedReference
        tModelReference="uuid: . . . "
        keyName="subsidiary"
        keyValue="parent-child" />
</publisherAssertion>
```

25.7.2 The Inquiry Interface (Query Language)

The **Inquiry Interface** can be used by requesters to obtain information from a UDDI registry. The messages in the Inquiry Interface are shown in Figure 25.40. There are two kinds of messages: get messages and find messages.

The get messages take as input the key value of a data structure and return as output a copy of the data structure. Thus, if the requester knows the value of the key of a particular data structure (the businessKey, serviceKey, bindingKey or tModelKey), he can obtain a copy of that data structure with the appropriate get message.

If the requester does not know the appropriate key value, he can retrieve information about the different data structures using the appropriate find message based on various search criteria. Included with this retrieved information are key values, which can be used in subsequent get messages.

We discuss the find_business message in some detail. The others are similar. A simple example of find_business message is

```
<find_business xmlns="urn:uddi-org:api_v3">
    <name>SlowHawk</name>
</find_business>
```

This example uses a simple search criterion—the name of the business. UDDI offers a large and expandable set of search criteria, including name, identifier, key, category, etc. and a large number of search qualifiers including, exact match, approximate match, case-sensitive match, etc.

A slightly more complex example of a find_business message is shown in Figure 25.41. Here, we are searching for businesses based on a key value of 481111 as specified by the categorization corresponding to the uuid in the tModel (C0B9FE13–179F–413D–8A5B–5004DB8E5BB2), which we have already noted is the North American Industry Classification System. The results of the find operation are sorted alphabetically by name in descending order. We assume the businessEntitys are described with categoryBags as in Figure 25.38. Note that in order to formulate this query, the requester had to know both the keyValue for the passenger airline

FIGURE 25.40 The messages in the Inquiry Interface.

get_businessDetail
> *Returns a* businessDetailMessage *containing information about all the* businessEntities *that satisfy the specified* businessKeys

get_serviceDetail
> *Returns a* serviceDetailMessage *containing information about all the* businessServices *that satisfy the specified* serviceKeys

get_bindingDetail
> *Returns a* bindingDetailMessage *containing information about all the* bindingTemplates *that satisfy the specified* bindingKeys

get_tModelDetail
> *Returns a* tModelListDetailMessage *containing information about all the* tModels *that satisfy the specified* tModelKeys

find_business
> *Returns a* businessListMessage *containing information about all the* businessEntities *that satisfy a particular criterion*

find_service
> *Returns a* serviceListMessage *containing information about all the* businessServices *that satisfy a particular criterion*

find_tModel
> *Returns a* tModelListMessage *containing information about all the* tModels *that satisfy a particular criterion*

find_binding
> *Returns a* bindingDetailMessage *containing information about all the* bindingTemplates *that satisfy a particular criterion*

find_relatedBusiness
> *Returns a* relatedBusinessesListMessage *containing information about all the* businessEntities *related to a given* businessEntity *based on a particular criterion*

FIGURE 25.41 An example of `find_business` message based on a search key.

```
<find_business xmlns="urn:uddi-org:api_v3">
    <findQualifiers>
        <findQualifier>sortByNameDesc</findQualifier>
    </findQualifiers>
    <categoryBag>
        <keyedReference
            keyName="Scheduled Passenger Air Transportation"
            keyValue="481111"
            tModelKey="uuid:C0B9FE13-179F-413D-8A5B-5004DB8E5BB2"/>
    </categoryBag>
</find_business>
```

FIGURE 25.42 A simple example of a `businessList`.

```
<businessList  . . . />
    <businessInfos>
        <businessInfo businessKey="uuid:123BZK"/>
            <name>SlowHawk</name>
            <serviceInfos>
                <serviceInfo serviceKey="uuid:123SRK"/>
                    <name> Fare Service </name>
                </serviceInfo>
                <serviceInfo serviceKey= . . . />
                    <name>  . . . </name>
                </serviceInfo>
            </serviceInfos>
        </businessInfo>
    </businessInfos>
</businessList>
```

industry (481111) and the `tModelKey` for the NAICS (uuid:C0B9FE13-179F-413D-8A5B-5004DB8E5BB2). Such information might be separately available in published sources or over the Internet.

Figure 25.42 shows a simple example of the `businessList` returned by a call to `find_business`. It includes the `businessKey` of SlowHawk and the `name` and `serviceKey` of its services (assuming SlowHawk provides only two services).

WSDL services have been defined for the inquiry and publisher interfaces InquireSoap and PublishSoap. We give an example of InquireSoap here and one of PublishSoap in Section 28.7.3. Figure 25.43 shows the InquireSoap port type definition for `find_business`, and Figure 25.44 shows the message definitions. The

FIGURE 25.43 The WSDL port type definition for find_business.

```
<portType name="InquireSoap">
    <operation name="find_business"
        <input message="tns:find_business"/>
        <output message="tns:businessList"/>
        <fault name="error"
            message="tns:dispositionReport"/>
    </operation>
</portType>
```

FIGURE 25.44 The message definitions for find_business.

```
<message name="find_business">
    <part name="body"
        element="uddi:find_business"/>
</message>

<message name="businessList">
    <part name="body"
        element="uddi:businessList"/>
</message>
```

bodies of the messages are just the corresponding UDDI structures for the messages, as described in the element attribute of the part child in the message definition.

We do not discuss the get messages. They are basically quite simple. An example of a get_businessDetail message is

```
<get_businessDetail>
    <businessKey> uuid:123BZK </businessKey>
</get_businessDetail>
```

This query returns a businessEntity data structure corresponding to the businessKey that was supplied as input.

25.7.3 The Publisher Interface (Update Language)

The **Publisher Interface** can be used by businesses to store and update information in a UDDI registry. The messages in the Publisher Interface are shown in Figure 25.45. (The last three messages are retrieval, not update, messages.)

One part of each message is an authentication token so that only the appropriate party can access the registry through this interface. Furthermore, the Publisher

FIGURE 25.45 The messages in the Publisher Interface.

```
save_business
     Creates or updates businessEntity

delete_business
     Deletes businessEntity

save_service, delete_service

save_binding, delete_binding

save_tModel, delete_tModel

set_publisherAssertions
     Sets all the assertions for a publisher

add_publishersAssertions
     Adds one or more assertions to a publisher's collection

delete_publisherAssertions
     Deletes one or more assertions from a publisher's collection
get_publisherAssertions
     Returns the set of publisherAssertions for a publisher

get_assertionStatusReport
     Returns status of current and outstanding publisherAssertions
     for a publisher

get_registeredInfo
     Returns list of all businessEntity and tModel data
     controlled by a publisher
```

Interface requires that the messages be sent in encrypted form so that no other parties can read or alter the messages that are sent.

The PublishSoap port type for save_business is shown in Figure 25.46. Figure 25.47 shows the definition of the messages, and Figure 25.48 shows the XML schema for the save_business element included in these messages.

One part of the save_business element is a businessEntity element (or a subset of such an element). If this is a new businessEntity (not an updating of an old one), the registry assigns some elements to it, for example, a unique businessKey and authorizedName, which cannot be included in the input message,

FIGURE 25.46 The PublishSoap port type for `save_business`.

```
<portType name="PublishSoap">
    <operation name="save_business"
        <input message="tns:save_business"/>
        <output message="tns:businessDetail"/>
        <fault name="error"
                    method="tns:dispositionReport"/>
    </operation>
</portType>
```

FIGURE 25.47 The message definitions for `save_business`.

```
<message name="save_business">
    <part name="body"
        element="uddi:save_business"/>
</message>

<message name="business_detail">
    <part name="body"
        element="uddi:business_detail"/>
</message>
```

FIGURE 25.48 The schema for `save_business`.

```
<complexType name="save_business">
    <sequence>
        <element ref="uddi:authInfo"/>
        <element maxOccurs="unbounded" minOccurs="0"
        ref="uddi:businessEntity"/>
        <element maxOccurs="unbounded" minOccurs="0"
        ref="uddi:uploadRegister"/>
    </sequence>
    <attribute name="generic" type="string" use="required"/>
</complexType>
```

but which will appear in the output message.[12] If it is an update of an existing element, it might be only a subset of that element, in which case only the elements in the subset are changed. The output message is the updated `businessEntity`. The

---

[12] As we have noted, version 3.0 of UDDI allows the service to propose its own key, which the system then checks for uniqueness.

remaining `save` messages are defined similarly. The `delete` messages take as inputs authentication information and the key to the structure to be deleted.

25.7.4 Some Final Observations about UDDI

One feature of UDDI that we have not discussed is a *subscription service* by which businesses that are service requesters can be notified whenever the information about a particular service is changed in the registry. This information would obviously be useful for requesters who use the same service on a periodic basis.

A related feature, which was added in version 3, is a new data structure, `operationalInfo`, that contains historical information about each publishing operation, such as when information about some service was added or modified. Then there is a new operation, `get-operationalInfo`, to retrieve that information.

Many companies offer a variety of tools for inquiry and publishing in UDDI registries. Some offer GUIs that involve filling in various fields on a form and submitting that form. Others offer Java APIs for querying and updating a UDDI registry. These APIs involve defining an object corresponding to the query or update, filling in certain attributes in that object, and then calling the appropriate procedure.

25.8 WS-Coordination: Transactional Web Services

Coordination refers to the act of organizing a number of independent entities to achieve some goal. The goal might be related to security, replication, etc., but our interest is in organizing the termination of transactions and workflows. An example of this is the two-phase commit protocol: the coordinator supervises the cohorts, and the goal is atomic termination.

Termination control is a concern in the Web services area. For example, it might be appropriate for an operation (or some portion of an operation) exported by a Web service to be atomic. This is easy to do if the operation does not invoke other Web services since atomicity can be implemented by a back-end server. However, if the operation does invoke other services—for example, GoSlow's operation `makeTripOp` invokes SlowHawk and RoachHeaven (Figure 25.25 on page 1093)—it will be more difficult to achieve atomicity. Coordination will be required, and complete atomicity might not be possible.

The first thing to note is that BPEL does not support transactions. It does provide for compensation, but this is only a tool that is useful in *implementing* transactional support. Second, the transaction manager that is supplied by a TP monitor is not oriented to the Web services environment. The X/Open standard is not based on XML or SOAP. Furthermore, X/Open assumes a more integrated environment. For example, with RPC communication it is assumed that stubs exist at server sites to automatically register a subtransaction when it is invoked.

WS-Coordination fills this gap. It provides a general framework for supporting coordination among Web services for a variety of purposes. Although it has not yet been accepted as a standard, we discuss it here since its initial application will be to support termination protocols. We also discuss two protocols that can be executed within the WS-Coordination framework: WS-AtomicTransaction and WS-BusinessActivity.[13]

WS-Coordination can be viewed as an XML-based tool for organizing a number of independent applications into a coordinated activity. It allows an application to activate a coordination context that describes the coordination type it wants to impose on an activity and to pass the context to the participating applications. It allows each application to register for a protocol that controls its role in that coordination type. Finally, it provides a framework within which the execution of the protocol is supported. These terms will be made clear in the following discussion.

WS-Coordination.   WS-Coordination assumes the existence of coordinator sites on the Web. An application, App_1 (for example, GoSlow), that wants to initiate a coordinated activity first uses the **activation service** of a coordinator, C_1, to create a **coordination context** for a particular type of activity. For example, App_1 might create an activity with coordination-type atomic transaction in order to provide for the all-or-nothing termination of a distributed interaction. A coordination type is identified by a URI, and WS-Coordination is extensible in the sense that as new coordination types are needed, they can easily be added. Nothing in WS-Coordination depends on the characteristics of a particular coordination type.

The context returned by the activation service to the application describes the activity and can be sent in a message to another application that might join the activity. It contains a unique identifier for the activity (the equivalent of a transaction identifier—see page 972), the coordination type, and an endpoint reference (see the discussion of WS-Addressing on page 1058) of a **registration service** within C_1.

App_1 can then invoke C_1's registration service through the endpoint reference, passing the context as an argument and specifying a protocol that it wishes to use in participating in the activity. Each activity type has an associated set of protocols. Each participant can choose a protocol that it will use to participate in the activity. For example, a module participating in an activity being coordinated as an atomic transaction might register for a two-phase commit protocol (we will see other possibilities shortly). The registration service responds by returning an endpoint reference for a **protocol service** that implements the requested protocol and that is used for exchanging protocol messages with the application at execution time. This is the endpoint that a participant in an atomic transaction protocol would use to send *prepared* or *committed* messages.

The role of WS-Coordination as a framework for coordination is now apparent. The protocol to be executed is controlled by the protocol service. Each protocol service has its own specification. Its goal, and the details of the messages exchanged to achieve that goal, are protocol dependent and are separately specified. Thus, creating an atomic transaction involves using WS-Coordination together with a protocol service that supports WS-AtomicTransaction. WS-Coordination's responsibility is

---

[13] This section is based on the version of WS-Coordination, WS-AtomicTransaction, and WS-BusinessActivity dated November, 2004.

simply to create a coordination context for the activity, register the participants in the activity, and distribute endpoint references to the protocol service.

For example, App_1 might create an activity with coordination type atomic transaction. This establishes C_1 as the root coordinator of the activity. App_1 might then use the registration endpoint reference in the coordination context returned by C_1 to register for a particular protocol, p_1, associated with atomic transactions. It also sends the context, as a SOAP header element, in an application message to App_2, inviting it to join the activity. App_1 might be GoSlow, and App_2 might be SlowHawk. App_2 joins by registering with C_1 or with a different coordinator, C_2, for a protocol, p_2, passing the activity's context as an argument. In the latter case, C_2 communicates with C_1 (using the endpoint reference in the context). As a result, it becomes a subordinate coordinator as in Figure 24.4 and acts as an intermediary between C_1 and App_2.

Similarly, if App_1 (or App_2) invokes a server, R_1 (such as a DBMS), it sends the context to R_1. R_1 registers with C_1 or with a different coordinator. It is important to relate WS-Coordination to the implementation of the two-phase commit protocol described in Section 24.2.1. There registration is implicit: when a server is invoked, the coordinator is automatically notified through the *xa* interface, and there is only one protocol available. WS-Coordination offers more flexibility in activity types and protocols but requires more involvement of the participants. Participants must explicitly pass contexts in application messages and register for protocols.

WS-AtomicTransaction. An atomic transaction is appropriate for a short-lived activity involving participants who trust one another and who operate within a tightly coupled organization. The activity should be short-lived since atomicity requires that participants keep resources locked until termination completes. Trust is required since an untrustworthy participant can cause the entire transaction to abort, wasting the efforts of the other participants.

The AtomicTransaction activity type offers three protocols. Different participants in the same activity can register for different protocols. The protocol service must keep track of the identities of the participants and the protocols for which they have registered.

- *Completion protocol.* One participant, usually the application that creates the activity (App_1 in our example), registers for this protocol and becomes the application that initiates the commit protocol by sending a commit message to the coordinator. When the protocol completes, this participant will be notified by the coordinator of the outcome.

- *Durable2PC protocol.* This is the standard two-phase commit protocol with presumed abort that was discussed in Section 24.2. A module that registers for this protocol exchanges *prepare, vote, commit,* and *done* messages with its coordinator as described there.

- *Volatile2PC protocol.* This is identical to Durable2PC, but its implementation satisfies the following condition. The coordinator sends *prepare* messages to participants registered for Volatile2PC first, before sending them to those registered for Durable2PC. Only when *vote* messages have been returned from all Volatile2PC participants are *prepare* messages sent to participants registered for Durable2PC.

Why are both Volatile2PC and Durable2PC needed? The protocols address an issue caused by the presence of caching servers on the Web. These servers act as intermediaries between content servers and clients that access the content. Performance is enhanced and bottlenecks avoided by storing recently accessed content on a caching server. A client transaction reads and updates content in the cache, greatly reducing the need to access the content server. However, a problem arises when the transaction completes but the updated content in the cache has not yet been transferred back to the content server. The updated content must be transferred back to the content server before the transaction is allowed to commit.

There is nothing new here. This is exactly the problem discussed in Section 22.2.1, but the context is different. In that case the DBMS managed both the cache and durable storage and could arrange to delay the commit until all of the dirty pages created by a transaction had been flushed from the cache to the database. In the Web case, the cache and the database are managed by different Web servers. If all prepare messages were sent at the same time, the content server might vote commit without being in the prepared state: it might not be aware that a dirty page created by the transaction is present in the cache. Since a cache server does not support durability, a crash might result in the loss of a dirty page.

Delaying prepare messages to participants registered for Durable2PC solves this problem. The cache server registers for Volatile2PC and does not send a vote message to the coordinator until all of an activity's dirty content has been sent to the content server. Then when the content server receives a prepare message, it is aware of all of the activity's dirty content and can make it durable before voting.

A participant can register for multiple protocols. For example, it might register for both Completion and Durable2PC if it wants to both initiate termination and participate in the termination decision.

The atomic commit protocol is virtually identical to the one described in Chapter 24. The protocol service acts as the coordinator. If the participant that registered for the Completion protocol requests to rollback, the coordinator simply sends `rollback` messages to all the cohorts (cohorts do not reply to this message). If the request is to commit, the following steps are taken:

1. The coordinator sends *prepare* messages to all the cohorts who registered for the Volatile2PC protocol, and each cohort can reply with either a *prepared* message,[14] an *aborted* message, or a *readOnly* message (the standard implements the read-only optimization discussed in Section 24.2.1).

---

[14] In Chapter 24 this was referred to as a *ready* message. We will follow the terminology used in the WS-AtomicTransaction specification.

2. If all the Volatile2PC cohorts respond with either *prepared* or *readOnly* messages, the coordinator sends *prepare* messages to all the cohorts who registered for the Durable2PC protocol. Each such cohort can reply with either a *prepared*, *aborted*, or *readOnly* message.

3. If all the cohorts respond with either *prepared* or *readOnly* messages, the coordinator decides to commit and sends a *commit* message to all the cohorts that responded with prepared messages. The cohorts reply with *committed* messages[15]. The coordinator can forget about the activity when all *committed* messages have been received. If any cohort responded with an *aborted* message, the coordinator decides to abort and sends *rollback* messages to all the cohorts that responded prepared. The cohorts do not reply (as explained in the presumed abort protocol).

To deal with timeout and recovery issues, the specification uses the presumed abort protocol (Section 24.2.2), and the coordinator and cohorts must perform the logging described in that protocol. The specification provides a *replay* message that a cohort can send to the coordinator during a recovery or timeout protocol to determine the status of the activity.

The protocol illustrates the use of some of the WS-Addressing header elements discussed on page 1060. For example, a register message must contain a MessageId and ReplyTo header, while a response to the message must contain a RelatesTo header.

WS-BusinessActivity. The concept of an atomic transaction is well established, and while WS-AtomicTransaction has not been accepted as a standard, Its specification is fairly stable. The concept of a business activity, on the other hand, is a subject of considerable debate, and its specification is still undergoing change. Despite this, we include a description of the latest business activity proposal because it sheds light on the issues involved in relaxing the ACID requirements of a transaction.

The general Web environment encompasses a number of features that render the atomic transaction model inappropriate for many activities.

■ Message delays and communication with humans can lengthen the execution time of an interaction.

■ Since a server might be providing service to a wide variety of clients, server loading is unpredictable, making the time it takes for a server to respond to an invocation unpredictable.

■ Servers are controlled by different organizations that might not trust one another. An untrustworthy participant can abort an entire transaction or cause unreasonable delays.

■ Site and communication failures are more likely.

---

[15] In Chapter 24 these were referred to as *done* messages.

■ It might be necessary to allow a participant to withdraw from an activity before the activity completes. For example, a server might not be willing to participate in the two-phase commit protocol. It might simply execute an operation and withdraw from the activity, making its state visible to subsequently invoked operations and making the implementation of isolation impossible. Thus, the set of participants is dynamic.

For all of these reasons, a more flexible and less ambitious termination protocol is required for many activities.

The concept of a business activity, specified in WS-BusinessActivity, has been proposed to deal with such issues. It is instructive to think of a business activity as composed of a nested set of subtransactions, each of which might be implemented using WS-AtomicTransaction. A subtransaction is generally confined to a single, tightly-coupled organizational domain and moves the business activity from one "consistent" state to another.

The termination of a business activity is more complex than an atomic transaction. With atomic transactions, atomicity dictates an all-or-nothing discipline: if a participant fails for any reason, the entire transaction is aborted. The sequence of messages in the two-phase commit protocol that does the termination is completely defined and can be separated from application logic. As a result, a protocol service for an atomic transaction can be provided by an off-the-shelf coordinator.

Business activities are different. For one thing, compensation can be used to undo the effect of a committed participant. Secondly, the failure of one participant does not necessarily imply that all others must compensate their effects. Furthermore, a variety of application-level failure conditions might arise, and the activity might need to respond differently to each. As a result, separating application logic from the protocol service does not always work in this situation. For example, the decision as to whether compensation is required when a particular participant faults might depend on the semantics of the application. Hence the application must explicitly deal with the fault. Furthermore, if one participant aborts, the application might decide to invoke a different participant to accomplish the same or a related task. This is similar to the nested transaction model (Section 19.2.3) in which if one subtransaction aborts, the parent transaction can use application logic to decide to invoke a different subtransaction to accomplish the task.

As a result, in some situations the protocol service must be integrated into the application code. This allows the application to decide how coordination should be accomplished. The mechanism for making this happen is readily available: the endpoint returned when a participant registers can target an application module.

WS-BusinessActivity defines two coordination types. The `AtomicOutcome` coordination type requires that all participants must either complete successfully or all must compensate their effects. With the `MixedOutcome` coordination type, some participants might complete successfully while others might compensate.

Within each coordination type, two termination protocols are supported. Participants in the same activity can register for different protocols.

■ *BusinessAgreementWithParticipantCompletion*. The participant notifies the coordinator when it has completed its participation. For example the participant might have been asked to provide some specific service. The participant notifies the coordinator when that service has been completed.

■ *BusinessAgreementWithCoordinatorCompletion*. The coordinator notifies the participant when its services are no longer required. For example, the participant might be providing a sequence of services for a particular business activity (e.g., a sequence of stock quotes), and the participant does not know and hence needs to be notified when no further quotes will be requested.

Suppose a participant in an activity with coordination type MixedOutcome registers for the *BusinessAgreementWithParticipantCompletion* protocol. The participant might notify the coordinator that it has completed by sending a *Completed* protocol message. This indicates that it has completed successfully, and effectively tells the coordinator that it is in the prepared state. Alternatively, the participant might send an *Exit* protocol message (indicating that it is withdrawing from the protocol) or a *Fault* protocol message (indicating that it has failed). The protocol service can respond to a *Completed* message with either *Close* (indicating that the participant should commit) or *Compensate* (indicating that the participant should reverse its action). The choice might depend on an arbitrary application-related condition in which case the coordination logic must be integrated with the application.

Alternatively, a rule for how the choice is to be made might be specified in the coordination context (using an extension element). For example, a majority rule would specify that a *Close* message should be sent if a majority of the participants complete successfully. In this case integration is not required and an off-the-shelf protocol service can be used.

The coordinator can also initiate termination of a participant using the *cancel* message.

The following example illustrates a typical situation. A buyer service might invoke the activation service of a coordinator to create a coordination context for a business activity having the MixedOutcome coordination type. The service might then pass the context on to three suppliers (participants) in application messages that request quotes. The suppliers register for the *BusinessAgreementWithParticipantCompletion* protocol and might use the coordinator's registration service for this purpose.

We assume that the buyer implements the protocol service and hence coordinates the termination protocol for the three participants. A state diagram that describes all possible message sequences between the coordinator and one particular participant in the *BusinessAgreementWithParticipantCompletion* protocol is shown in Figure 25.49. Protocol states are shown in ovals, solid arrows are messages sent by the coordinator, and dashed arrows are messages sent by the participant.

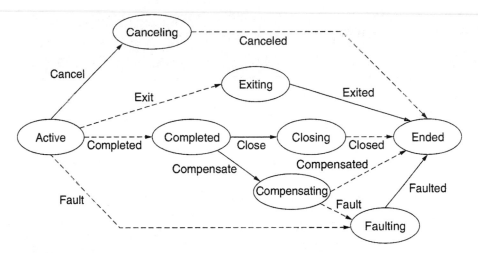

FIGURE 25.49 State diagram for the BusinessAgreementWithParticipantCompletion protocol. Protocol states are shown in ovals, solid arrows are messages sent by the coordinator, and dashed arrows are messages sent by the participant.

Supplier *A* might suffer some failure and declare its completion with a *Fault* protocol message. Suppliers *B* and *C* might perform some computation, update their databases, and declare their completion with *Completed* protocol messages containing quotes. The buyer decides to select the quote from *B*. Hence, acting as coordinator and executing the protocol service described in the figure, the buyer sends a *Compensate* protocol message to *C* and a *Close* protocol message to *B*. *C* responds with a *Compensated* message, and *B* responds with a *Closed* message. These sequences of messages correspond to paths shown in the figure.

The sequence of messages described in this example represent one possible sequence allowed in the protocol. There are a number of other possible sequences between the buyer and *A*, *B*, and *C*. The choice of the sequence depends on the application logic. For example, *B* detects a fault, and the buyer decides to do business with *A* and not *C*, etc. Hence, in contrast to WS-AtomicTransaction, application logic has been combined with coordination. The integration of the protocol service with the buyer's application code in the example allows this to happen. However, combining the protocol service with the application is not mandatory. With a different application, an endpoint reference to a protocol service implemented by an off-the-shelf coordinator could be returned to the participants.

The state diagram for the *BusinessAgreementWithCoordinatorCompletion*, shown in Figure 25.50, is almost identical to that in Figure 25.49 except for the *Complete* message and the *Completing* state. The coordinator sends this message when it needs to notify a participant that its services are no longer required. This corresponds to asking the participant to enter the prepared state.

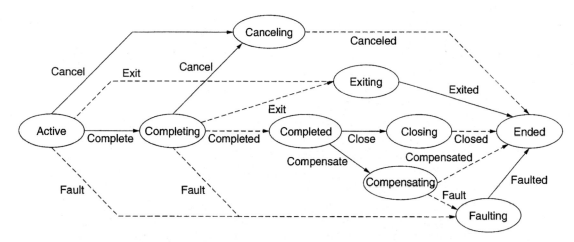

FIGURE 25.50 State diagram for the BusinessAgreementWithCoordinatorCompletion protocol. Protocol states are shown in ovals, solid arrows are messages sent by the coordinator, and dashed arrows are messages sent by the participant.

BIBLIOGRAPHIC NOTES

Material on the protocols discussed in this chapter can be found at the Web sites of the appropriate standardization organizations or the companies developing them.

- *HTTP http://www.w3.org/Protocols/#Specs*
- *SOAP http://www.w3.org/TR/SOAP/*
- *WS-Addressing http://www.w3.org/Submission/2004/SUBM-ws-addressing-20040810/*
- *WSDL http://www.w3.org/TR/wsdl/*
- *BPEL http://www.ibm.com/developerworks/library/ws-bpel/*
- *UDDI http://uddi.org/pubs/uddi-v3.00-published-20020719.htm*
- *WS-Coordination http://xmlcoverpages.org/WS-Coordination200411.pdf*
- *WS-AtomicTransaction http://xmlcoverpages.org/WS-AtomicTransaction200411.pdf*
- *WS-BusinessActivity http://xmlcoverpages.org/WS-BusinessActivity200411.pdf*

EXERCISES

25.1 SOAP extensibility relates to the use of intermediaries and SOAP headers to add features to a Web service that is invoked using SOAP messaging. Give an example of an extension and how an intermediary and header would be used to implement it.

25.2 Give the declaration of a Java method that corresponds to the RPC SOAP messages in Figures 25.3 and 25.4.

25.3 Give an example of a Java object that can be serialized into the parts of the messages in the WSDLgetFareOperation.

25.4 Propose a declaration for receiveResMsg, and give RPC/literal and document/literal bindings for hotelCallbackPT.

25.5 SlowHawk wants to provide an asynchronous version of its service to give fare information. One asynchronous message requests fare information, and a second asynchronous message provides the fare information. Design WSDL specifications for these two services, and then design a BPEL specification for the business process consisting of these two services.

25.6 SlowHawk provides versions of the getFarePT (Section 25.5) that use the HTTP GET and POST protocols. Show a possible binding for each of these protocols. (You might have to look on the Web to get additional information not in the text.)

25.7 A stock brokerage company offers a getQuote service in which a requester sends a getQuoteRequest message containing a stock symbol and the brokerage company responds with a GetQuoteResponse message containing the current quotation for that stock. Suppose all that is known is the name of the brokerage company? Describe informally the sequence of UDDI queries you would use to find out the details of the RPC SOAP messages needed to invoke that service.

25.8 Two BPEL processes are said to be **compatible** if there are no communication deadlocks: every send in one process is received by the other, and every receive in one process has a corresponding send in the other. Give an example of two noncompatible processes for which every receive in one of the processes has a corresponding send in the other, but there is a communication deadlock.

25.9 Design the outline of a BPEL process that the vendor can use to describe the following business process:

> When you buy something over the Internet, you send the vendor the name, catalog number, and price of the item you want. Then the vendor sends you a form to fill out, containing the name, catalog number, and price of the item and requesting your name, address, credit card number, and expiration date. You return the form to the vendor. The vendor then sends your name, credit card number, and the price of the item to the credit card company to be approved. After it is approved, the vendor sends you a confirmation message. Then it sends a message to the warehouse to ship the item.

25.10 Explain which parts of the business process in the previous example should be part of an ACID transaction (Section 25.8).

25.11 Design the outlines of BPEL processes for two sites that are performing the following bidding workflow:

> Site 1 decides to offer an item for sale at some offering price and sends that offer in a message to site 2. When site 2 receives that message, it decides whether it wants to accept that offer or make a new bid (at some lower price). It sends that information, either new bid or accept, in a message to site 1. When

site 1 receives that message, it decides whether it wants to accept that bid or make a new offer (at a higher offering price). It then sends that information in a message to site 2. The bidding continues, sending messages back and forth, until one of the sites, s_a decides to accept a bid or offer and sends that information in a message to the other site, s_b. After sending that accept message, s_a exits the process, and after receiving the accept message, s_b also exits the process.

25.12 Explain why an assignment of an endpoint reference to `myRole` of a `partnerLink` makes no sense.

25.13 Show the changes to GoSlow that will be required if customers invoke `makeTripOp` using a one-way pattern and pass an endpoint reference for a callback.

25.14 Give an example of a business activity (Section 25.8) involving a travel agency in which a `compensate` message will be sent after an activity has completed.

25.15 Scope $S3$ is nested in scope $S2$ which is nested in scope $S1$. Assume that fault handlers for fault f exist in each scope and that compensation handlers $C2$ and $C3$ have been declared in $S2$ and $S3$. In each of the following cases, either explain how the specified sequence of events might happen or why the sequence is impossible

a. Suppose f is raised in $S2$ after $S3$ has exited normally and $C2$ is entered before $C3$.

b. Suppose f is raised in $S2$ after $S3$ has exited normally and $C3$ is entered.

c. Suppose f is raised in $S1$ after $S2$ has exited normally and $C2$ is entered before $C3$.

d. Suppose f is raised in $S1$ after $S2$ has exited normally and $C3$ is entered before $C2$.

e. Suppose f is raised in $S1$ after $S2$ has exited normally, no handler for f has been declared in $S1$. Describe the sequence of events that occurs.

f. Suppose f is raised in $S1$ after $S2$ has exited normally, no handler for f has been declared in $S1$, and no compensation handler has been declared in $S2$. Describe the sequence of events that occurs.

g. Suppose f is raised in $S1$ after $S2$ has exited normally, no handler for f has been declared in $S1$, and no compensation handler has been declared in $S2$. Describe the sequence of events that occurs.

25.16 Correlation sets can be associated with `invoke` statements (as well as `receive` statements) using

```
<invoke partnerLink="···" portType="···"
     operation="···" inputVariable="···">
     <correlations>
          <correlation set="···" initiate="yes/no"/>
     <\monocorrelations>
</invoke>
```

Give a circumstance under which it might be useful to do this.

26

Security and Electronic Commerce

Security is a major issue in the design of applications that deal with privileged information or that support systems on which life and property depend. In most applications the participants in a transaction must identify each other, with a high degree of certainty, and they might want to ensure that no third party is observing or modifying the information being exchanged.

Security issues are particularly important for transactions executed over the Internet because it is relatively easy for imposters to pretend to be other than who they actually are and for eavesdroppers to listen in on the exchanges between participants. And with the increasing amount of electonic commerce (both customer-to-business and business-to-business), server sites want to be able to reassure their users that interactions are secure.

26.1 Authentication, Authorization, and Encryption

Authentication refers to the process by which the identity of a participant is established. When you perform a transaction at an automated teller machine (ATM), the system establishes your identity using the information on your ATM card and your personal identification number (PIN). Furthermore, you may want to establish that you are talking to a real ATM and not a machine that looks like an ATM but is actually a "Trojan horse" designed to obtain your PIN. Similarly, when you are considering executing an Internet transaction with Macy's and you have to supply your credit card number to the server, you want to make certain that you are actually talking to that server and not to three students in a dorm room pretending to be Macy's.

Authorization refers to the process that determines the mode in which a particular client is allowed to access a specific resource controlled by a server. The client is assumed to have been previously authenticated. Authorization can be individual (*you* are allowed to withdraw money from your bank account) or group-wide (*all tellers* are allowed to write certified checks), and it is specified in terms of the services that the server offers. For example, "withdraw money from a specified account," or "write a certified check."

Encryption is used to protect information stored at a particular site or transmitted between sites from being accessed by unauthorized users. A variety of highly sophisticated algorithms exist to transform this information into a bit stream that is intelligible only to selected users.

Since encryption plays an important role in authentication and authorization, we quickly review its general structure first. Then we discuss authentication and authorization and how all three concepts are applied in electronic commerce transactions. Finally we discuss how these concepts are incorporated into XML.

26.2 Encryption

The general model of an encryption system is shown in Figure 26.1. The information to be sent is generally a string of characters referred to as **plaintext**. It is encrypted by a program (or device) that transforms it into **ciphertext**, and it is the ciphertext that is actually transmitted. At the receiving end, the ciphertext is decrypted by another program (or device) that transforms it back into the original plaintext.

The goal of an encryption system is to protect information from an **intruder**. Intrusion is generally assumed to take two forms: **passive**, in which an intruder can only copy information in transit; and **active**, in which an intruder can, in addition, modify information in transit, resend previously sent messages that it has copied, or send new messages. While no practical encryption system can completely defend against an intruder with unlimited computational resources (which can be used to analyze the ciphertext), the goal is to make intrusion so difficult that it becomes extremely unlikely that an intruder will succeed.

There are a variety of encryption algorithms, and it is generally assumed that the intruder knows the particular algorithm used in the system under attack. However, each algorithm is parameterized by one or more **keys**, which control the encryption and decryption process. Recovery of the plaintext from the ciphertext without the

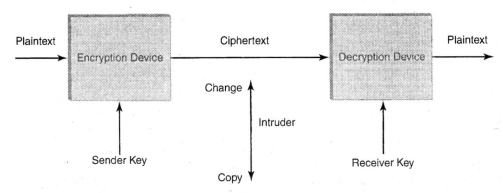

FIGURE 26.1 Model of an encryption system.

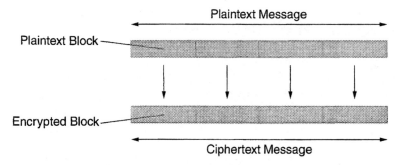

FIGURE 26.2 Encryption using a block cipher.

decryption key is exceedingly difficult. Hence, the strength of the technique depends on keeping the decryption key secret.[1]

We use the notation

$$ciphertext = K_{sender}[plaintext]$$

to denote that the ciphertext is the plaintext encrypted by the sender with the key K_{sender}. The complete encryption system, including encryption and decryption, can be represented with the notation

$$plaintext = K_{receiver}[K_{sender}[plaintext]]$$

which states that, if the plaintext is first encrypted with K_{sender} and then decrypted with $K_{receiver}$, the result will be the original plaintext.

Symmetric cryptography. With **symmetric cryptography**, the same key is used for both encryption and decryption ($K_{sender} = K_{receiver}$). The key is known only to the two communicating processes (since it can be used to decrypt the ciphertext) and is used by both to encrypt and decrypt a back-and-forth exchange of messages referred to as a **session**. In this context, the key is often referred to as a **session key**. Generally, each session gets a new session key.

Several common techniques are used in symmetric cryptography. With a **block cipher**, the plaintext is divided into fixed-size blocks, which are then mapped in a one-to-one fashion into ciphertext blocks as shown in Figure 26.2. The particular mapping is a function of the encryption algorithm and key. The sequence of cipher-text blocks is the encrypted message. Since the mapping is one to one, the plaintext can be recovered.

A **substitution cipher** is one type of block cipher. A variety of substitution ci-phers have been proposed for mapping plaintext blocks. For example, a **monoalpha-betic** (sometimes called *simple*) substitution cipher has a block size of one character,

---

[1] A truly unbreakable encryption system is the **one-time pad** [Stallings 1999; Schneier 1995], which uses a randomly generated key that is as long as the message and is used for one message and then discarded.

and a one-to-one mapping from the set of characters onto itself is used to construct the ciphertext. Thus, if *a* is mapped to *c*, each occurrence of *a* in the plaintext is replaced by *c* in the cipher text.

A **polyalphabetic** substitution cipher is made up of multiple monoalphabetical substitution ciphers. For example, there might be ten different monoalphabetical ciphers. The first character is encrypted with the first cipher, the second with the second cipher, and so on, until the tenth character, after which the sequence starts over with the eleventh character being encrypted with the first cipher. For example, the plaintext message *aa* . . . would be mapped to *cr* . . . if *a* were mapped to *c* by the first cipher and *a* were mapped to *r* by the second.

A **polygram** substitution cipher is one in which the block size is more than one. For example, if the block size is three, the block *cde* might be encrypted as *zyy*, *cxy* as *rst*, and *dce* as *dtr*. Then the plaintext message *cdecxy* would be mapped to *zyyrst*.

A **transposition** cipher is also a block cipher, but in contrast to a substitution cipher, the order of the characters in each plaintext block is altered to produce the ciphertext block—the reordering is the same on each plaintext block and is described by the key. For example, with a block size of three, the key "312" indicates that the characters in each block are to be reordered such that the first character in the ciphertext block is to be the third character in the plaintext block, the second character in the ciphertext block is to be the first character in the plaintext block, and the third character in the ciphertext block is to be the second character in the plaintext block. Then the plaintext message *cdecxy* would be mapped to *ecdycx*.

Ciphers that map plaintext blocks into ciphertext blocks are subject to a frequency analysis attack. It is assumed that the intruder knows the block size and can measure the frequency with which each plaintext block is used in normal (unencrypted) communication. The intruder can then compare that with the frequency with which ciphertext blocks appear in an encrypted stream. By matching ciphertext and plaintext blocks with similar frequency characteristics, the intruder can greatly reduce the number of alternatives that must be tested to determine which plaintext block maps into a particular ciphertext block. The longer the encrypted stream the intruder can monitor, the more accurate the frequency estimate of the ciphertext blocks and the greater the reduction in computation that will result. The frequency analysis attack renders many substitution ciphers with small block sizes of little use since accurate frequency profiles for small plaintext blocks are available.

ANSI's **Data Encryption Standard** (DES) is a symmetric encryption technique that uses a sequence of stages to encrypt a block of plaintext. As shown in Figure 26.3, each stage encrypts the output of the previous stage. All stages use a 64-bit block size, and each uses either a substitution or a transposition cipher. The result of combining these two cipher techniques is sometimes referred to as a **product cipher**. DES uses a 56-bit key as input to a key generator to produce a different 48-bit subkey for each of the stages.[2] The standard is in wide use, for example, within the banking and financial services industry.

---

[2] The key has been criticized by cryptographic experts as being too small.

64-bit Plaintext Block

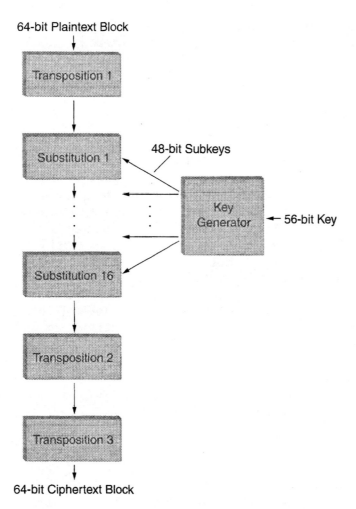

64-bit Ciphertext Block

FIGURE 26.3 The processing of a plaintext block using DES.

A **bit stream cipher**, is an example of an encryption technique that is not based on blocks. The ciphertext stream is the result of taking the bit-by-bit exclusive OR of the plaintext stream and a pseudorandom sequence of bits produced by a random number generator. The key in this case is the initial seed supplied to the generator. By using the key with the same generator at the receiving end, the same pseudorandom sequence can be produced to decrypt the ciphertext, once again using a bit-by-bit exclusive OR.

Asymmetric cryptography.   In contrast to symmetric cryptography, **asymmetric cryptography** associates with each user an encryption key and a decryption key. The encryption key is not a secret. A user distributes her encryption key openly to anyone who might want to send her a message. It is therefore referred to as a public key, and it is known to potential intruders. The user, however, keeps her decryption key private: it is known only to herself. If sender S wants to communicate plaintext message M to user C and K_C^{pub} is C's public key, then S sends the ciphertext message $K_C^{pub}[M]$. Furthermore, if K_C^{priv} is C's private key, asymmetric cryptography implements the relationship

$$M = K_C^{priv}[K_C^{pub}[M]]$$

which asserts that C can recover the plaintext by decrypting a message encrypted with K_C^{pub} using K_C^{priv}.

If, as is generally the case, information must be transferred in both directions between two processes, each process uses the other's encryption key to encrypt messages it sends. Because the encryption key can be made public, asymmetric cryptography is referred to as **public-key cryptography**. (Symmetric cryptography, in which the key is known only to the communicating processes, is referred to as **secret-key cryptography**.) The concept of public-key cryptography was proposed in [Diffie and Hellman 1976], but almost all public-key cryptography systems are based on the RSA algorithm [Rivest et al. 1978]. An excellent description of the mathematics underlying the RSA algorithm and of many other cryptographic algorithms and protocols is given in [Schneier 1995].

We briefly describe the RSA algorithm. To design an encryption/decryption key pair, two large prime numbers, p and q, are selected, and an integer, d, is chosen that is relatively prime to $(p - 1) * (q - 1)$ (d and $(p - 1) * (q - 1)$ have no common factors other than 1). Finally, an integer e is computed such that

$$e * d \equiv 1 \ (mod \ (p - 1) * (q - 1))$$

The encryption key is (e, N), and the decryption key is (d, N), where $N = p * q$ and is referred to as the modulus.

For example, (using small prime numbers) we might select p and q to be 7 and 13. Then N is 91, and $(p - 1) * (q - 1)$ is 72. We can choose d to be 5 (which is relatively prime to 72) and e to be 29 because $e * d$ equals 145 and

$$145 \equiv 1 \ (mod \ 72)$$

Then the encryption key is $(29, 91)$, and the decryption key is $(5, 91)$.

The message to be encrypted is broken into blocks such that each block, M, can be treated as an integer between 0 and $(N - 1)$. To encrypt M into the ciphertext block, B, we perform the calculation

$$B = M^e \ (mod \ N)$$

To decrypt B, we perform

$$M = B^d \ (mod \ N)$$

The protocol works correctly because

$$M = (M^e \ (mod \ N))^d \ (mod \ N) \ = \ M^{e*d} \ (mod \ N) \qquad\qquad \textbf{26.1}$$

More information on public key cryptography is provided in [Schneier 1995].

Returning to the example, assume M is 2. Then to encrypt M, we compute

$$2^{29} \ (mod \ 91) = 32$$

Thus the encrypted message, B, is 32. To decrypt B, we compute

$$32^5 \ (mod \ 91) = 2$$

which is the plaintext message M.

Although d and e are mathematically related, factoring N (a large integer) to obtain p and q (and ultimately d and e) is extremely difficult. Hence, only the receiver can decrypt messages sent to it.

Public-key encryption is a very powerful technique, but it is more computationally intensive than symmetric cryptography (exponentiation of large numbers to large powers is expensive, although not nearly as expensive as factoring a large number, which would be necessary to break the encryption). For that reason, it is generally used to encrypt a few small blocks of information, exchanged as part of a protocol, rather than large blocks of data, which are generally encrypted using symmetric techniques.

26.3 Digital Signatures

One very important use of asymmetric cryptography is to implement **digital signatures**. As with a conventional signature attached to a document, a digital signature works in two ways. It can be used by the sender, C, of a document to prove that he authored the document, and it can be used by the receiver of the document as evidence that C authored it. The latter case is referred to as **nonrepudiation**: once you send a signed check, you cannot, at a later time, deny that you authorized a money transfer. A digital signature also serves a third, very important purpose. Once a document is signed, it cannot be modified without invalidating the signature. Hence, a digital signature guarantees data integrity.

As with public-key cryptography, the concept was first described in [Diffie and Hellman 1976], but, like public-key systems, most digital signature systems are based on the RSA algorithm [Rivest et al. 1978] or on other algorithms developed specifically for signatures.

Digital signatures based on encryption algorithms utilize a property of many asymmetric encryption algorithms—the roles of the public and private keys can be reversed: the private key can be used to encrypt plaintext, and the resulting ciphertext can be decrypted using the corresponding public key

$$M = K_C^{pub}[K_C^{priv}[M]] = K_C^{priv}[K_C^{pub}[M]] \qquad\qquad \textbf{26.2}$$

Assuming (26.2), a simple-minded signature algorithm is one in which C signs a document, M, by encrypting it with her private key, K_C^{priv}. If the receiver can recover meaningful information (e.g., an ASCII string) by decrypting a message using K_C^{pub}, the receiver can conclude that the message could have been generated only by C since only C knows K_C^{priv}. (Someone else might actually have sent the message, but only C could have generated it.) This technique assumes that the receiver knows C's public key, K_C^{pub}. The process of distributing public keys and related issues are discussed in Sections 26.4 and 26.8.

Note that since anyone can decrypt the message with the public key, the message is not hidden. Message hiding is not the purpose of a digital signature protocol.

A problem with this technique is that encrypting and decrypting an entire message using a public-key algorithm can be computationally intensive and time consuming. To reduce this time, some function, f, of M is computed—generally a hash—that produces a result that is considerably smaller than M itself. $f(M)$ is sometimes called a **message digest** of M. f effectively divides the set of all messages into equivalence classes: all the messages that are mapped to a particular digest value are in the same class. f is assumed to be known to intruders as well as to the communicants. $f(M)$ is encrypted with K_C^{priv} and referred to as a digital signature, which is transmitted along with M.

Thus, C sends two items, $K_C^{priv}[f(M)]$ and M, to the receiver. The receiver decrypts the first item using K_C^{pub} and then compares the outcome with the result of applying f to the second item. If the two are the same, the receiver should be able to conclude that M could have been generated only by C. To safely allow such a conclusion, however, we must deal with some other issues.

Consider an intruder that listens to and copies a signed transmission, $(K_C^{priv}[f(M)], M)$, from C.

1. The intruder might use the signature $K_C^{priv}[f(M)]$ to sign a different message, M', in an attempt to fool a receiver into believing that C sent M'. The intruder can succeed in this attack if it can construct M' such that $f(M) = f(M')$. To prevent this attack, f is required to be a **one-way function**: f has the property that, given an output, y, constructing an argument, x, such that $f(x) = y$ is computationally infeasible. For example, a one-way message digest function might produce an output string that satisfies the following properties:

   (a) All values in the range of f are equally likely.
   (b) If any bit of the message is changed, every bit in the message digest has a 50% chance of changing.

   Property (a) guards against the possibility of finding an M' such that $f(M) = f(M')$ simply because f maps a large percentage of messages to $f(M)$. Property (b) ensures that $f(M)$ and $f(M')$ are not the same simply because M and M' are related or similar messages.

   Under these conditions, it is extremely difficult for the intruder to construct a message M' such that $f(M') = f(M)$ and hence to find a message, M', to which the signature $K_C^{priv}[f(M)]$ can be attached. Furthermore, the intruder cannot forge the signature that can be used with M', $K_C^{priv}[f(M')]$, since it does not know K_C^{priv}.

2. The intruder might attempt to copy and then resend a signed message a second time,[3] in what is referred to as a **replay attack**. A replay attack can be dealt with by having the signer construct a timestamp (using the technique described in Section 24.4) and include it in M. Since the digital signature is calculated over the entire message, the intruder cannot change the timestamp. Assuming that clocks at all sites in the network are roughly synchronized, if the receiver keeps a list of the timestamps of all recently received messages and rejects arriving messages containing timestamps in the list (recall that timestamps are globally unique), it can detect a message's second arrival. The key point here is that a particular timestamp is never used twice. Hence, a replay attack can also be dealt with if each message has a unique sequence number.

It should now be clear how a digital signature guarantees the integrity of the message. Although the message is transmitted in the clear, and hence can be read by an intrude, it cannot be changed by the intruder since the signature of the changed message would be different. (If privacy is desired, the signed message can be encrypted with another key.) Similarly, nonrepudiation is guaranteed. The signer cannot deny having constructed the message since the digital signature accompanying the message could have been constructed only with the signer's private key. For these reasons, digital signatures are often used in commercial security protocols.

26.4 Key Distribution and Authentication

With both symmetric and asymmetric cryptography, before two parties can communicate they must agree on the encryption/decryption key(s) to be used. Since doing so often involves communicating keys in messages, this phase of a protocol is called **key distribution**. In most situations, key distribution also involves authentication. At the same time that the parties agree on a key, they also make sure of each other's identity.

One might think that key distribution is easy for asymmetric algorithms since the receiver's encryption key is public knowledge. That is, if C wants to send an encrypted message to S, it simply sends a request in the clear (unencrypted) to S requesting S's public key. S can then send its public key (in the clear) to C. Life is not so simple, however. An intruder might intercept S's message to C and substitute its own public key. If C uses that key, the intruder can decrypt all messages sent from C to S. For this reason, key distribution is complicated by authentication when public-key encryption is used. C must be able to authenticate the sender of the key.

---

[3] This attack might be of some value if the message were a request by C to transfer money into the intruder's bank account.

The problem of key distribution with asymmetric encryption is generally dealt with using certificates, which we discuss in Section 26.8.

A similar situation exists with symmetric encryption. A session key must be created and distributed to the two communicating processes before a session can be started. It becomes a part of the communication context and is discarded when the session completes. Once again, a process using a session key wants to be certain of the identity of the other process that has a copy of that key.

It follows that, in addition to addressing the key distribution problem, we must also be concerned with authentication. Intuitively, when we speak of a client, we think of the individual on whose behalf the client process is running, and we use these concepts interchangeably.

One goal of authentication is to enable a server to positively identify the client that is the source of a message that it has received so that it can decide whether to grant the requested service. For example, should the requestor be allowed to withdraw money from Jody's bank account? Another goal is to enable a client to authenticate the server before sending it any important information. For example, am I sending my credit card number to Macy's or to a Macy's impersonator?

To model these situations, we speak of **principals**. A principal might be a person or a process, and the purpose of authentication is to demonstrate that a principal is who it claims to be. Generally, a person demonstrates that she is who she claims to be by providing something that only she possesses. The simplest, and least secure, of these is a password, in which case the individual possesses some unique knowledge. Unfortunately, passwords often have to be short and relevant (e.g., a pet's name) to be remembered and therefore can frequently be compromised by an intruder willing to try enough candidates. Also, if a password is sent over the network, it might be intercepted and thereby compromised.

Security can be enhanced by requiring a *physical* item that only the individual possesses, for example a token card. An even more secure technique involves the use of some biological identifier such as a fingerprint or voiceprint. Unfortunately, the cost of biological mechanisms is high, and any computer representation of such characteristics might be copied.

Although passwords play a role in key distribution and authentication protocols, the protocols involve a number of new techniques that employ the exchange of encrypted messages. Since the protocols involve the exchange of only a few short messages, the cost of encrypting and decrypting them is generally not significant. Hence, the protocols can be based on either symmetric encryption (e.g., Kerberos, as discussed in Section 26.4.1) or public-key encryption (e.g., SSL, as discussed in Section 26.8). However, because of the heavy computational requirements of public-key encryption, the actual exchange of data generally uses symmetric techniques based on session keys.

26.4.1 The Kerberos Protocol: Tickets

As an example of a protocol that uses symmetric cryptography to authenticate a client to a server and distribute a (symmetric) session key for subsequent data exchange, we describe a simplified version of the widely used **Kerberos** system designed at MIT [Steiner et al. 1988; Neuman and Ts'o 1994]. Kerberos is an off-the-shelf middleware module that can be incorporated into a distributed computing system and might be provided by a TP monitor or a Web application server.

The Kerberos protocol involves the use of an intermediary process, called a **key server**. (Actually Kerberos calls its key server the Key Distribution Server, or KDS.) The key server creates session keys on demand and distributes them in such a way that they are known only to the communicating processes. For this reason, it is referred to as a **trusted third party**.

Each user wishing to participate in the protocol registers a symmetric **user key** with the key server, *KS*. User keys are not session keys. They are used only in the key distribution protocol at the start of a session.

Assume that a client, C, wants to communicate with a server, S. C and S have previously registered user keys $K_{C,KS}$ and $K_{S,KS}$, respectively, with KS. $K_{C,KS}$ is known only to C and KS. Similarly, $K_{S,KS}$ is known only to S and KS. KS is trusted by C in the sense that C assumes that KS will never communicate $K_{C,KS}$ to any other process and that the data structure it uses to store $K_{C,KS}$ is protected from unauthorized access. Similarly, KS is trusted by S.

Kerberos introduces the concept of a **ticket** to distribute a session key. To understand the role of a ticket, consider the following sequence of steps, illustrated in Figure 26.4, which forms the heart of the protocol. (As with the other protocols described here, we omit some minor details.)

1. C sends to KS a message, $M1$ (in the clear), requesting a ticket to be used to authenticate C to S. $M1$ contains the names of the intended communicants (C, S).

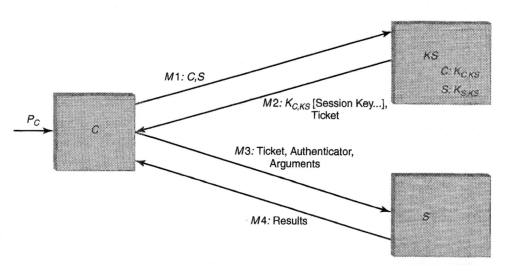

FIGURE 26.4 Sequence of messages used to authenticate a client in symmetric encryption.

2. When KS receives $M1$, the following takes place:

    (a) KS (randomly) constructs a session key, $K_{sess,C\&S}$.
    (b) KS sends to C a message, $M2$, containing two items:
        (i) $K_{C,KS}[K_{sess,C\&S}, S, LT]$
        (ii) $K_{S,KS}[K_{sess,C\&S}, C, LT]$—the actual ticket
        where LT is the *lifetime* (the time interval) over which the ticket is valid.

3. When C receives $M2$, it performs the following steps:

    (a) C recovers $K_{sess,C\&S}$ from the first item using $K_{C,KS}$ (it cannot decrypt the ticket).
    (b) C saves the ticket until it is ready to request some service from S.

Observe that KS does not know the actual source of $M1$: it could have been sent by an intruder, I, posing as C. However, KS encrypts $M2$, making the information returned accessible only to C and S.

Rather than store its user key, $K_{C,KS}$, in some protected way, C constructs it when needed using the principal's password, P_C, which is supplied to C at login time. This is done with the help of a one-way function, f.

$$K_{C,KS} = f(P_C)$$

Thus, only C (using f) can construct $K_{C,KS}$, and hence only C can retrieve $K_{sess,C\&S}$ from the first item in $M2$: the message sent by KS to the process claiming to be C. Note that the protocol does not send P_C across the network and so avoids the possibility that it might be copied. Furthermore, since C does not store $K_{C,KS}$ in the system, the possibility that it might be stolen is reduced.

Later, when C wants to request service from S, the following takes place:

4. C sends to S a message, $M3$, containing the arguments of the request, (which might or might not be encrypted using $K_{sess,C\&S}$), the ticket, and an authenticator (see below).

Only S can decrypt the ticket and recover the items it contains. However, the ticket (containing C) alone is not sufficient to authenticate C to S since I could have copied it in step 2 and replayed it to S with its own request. A timestamp might be useful in preventing a replay, but the timestamp cannot be stored in the ticket because the ticket is meant to be used by C multiple times during its lifetime. C therefore sends an authenticator along with its ticket. An **authenticator** consists of C's name together with a (current) timestamp, TS, encrypted with $K_{sess,C\&S}$:

$$authenticator = K_{sess,C\&S}[C, TS]$$

and is meant to be used only once. S can decrypt the authenticator by using $K_{sess,C\&S}$ (which it determines by decrypting the ticket).

At this point, S knows that the ticket could have been constructed only by KS since only KS knows $K_{S,KS}$. Furthermore, since S trusts KS and since each time $K_{sess,C\&S}$ is transmitted it is encrypted by either $K_{C,KS}$ or $K_{S,KS}$, S knows that only C (and KS) knows $K_{sess,C\&S}$. The authenticator contains some plaintext (e.g., C)

encrypted by $K_{sess, C\&S}$, that can be compared with the contents of the ticket (which also contains C). If they match, S concludes that C must have constructed the authenticator. To authenticate C to S (i.e., to be sure that the invocation actually comes from C), however, several possible attacks must be ruled out.

1. I attempts a replay attack in which it copies both the ticket and the authenticator from $M3$ and uses them at a later time. To combat this, we must make it impossible for an authenticator (in contrast to a ticket) to be used more than once. A new authenticator (with a unique timestamp) is constructed by C for each of its requests. The authenticator is *live* if its timestamp is within the lifetime (LT) of the accompanying ticket. To ensure that a copy of an authenticator is of no value, and that S can defend itself against a replay, S uses the following protocol:

    (a) If the received authenticator is not live, S rejects it.
    (b) S maintains a list of authenticators it has received that are still live. If the received authenticator is live, S compares it against the list and rejects it if a copy is found. By maintaining lifetime information, S can limit the number of authenticators it has to keep on the list.

2. I intercepts $M3$ (it does not reach S) and tries to use the ticket and authenticator for its own request for service. However, if C has chosen to encrypt the arguments of its request with $K_{sess, C\&S}$, then I cannot substitute its own arguments because it does not know $K_{sess, C\&S}$. Sending the entire intercepted message at a later time accomplishes nothing for I since it simply causes C's original request to be serviced.

3. I intercepts $M1$ (it does not reach KS) and substitutes the message (C, I). KS responds to C with a ticket encrypted with $K_{I, KS}$. I's goal in this attack is to copy the message $M3$ that it hopes that C will subsequently send to S. Since the ticket is encrypted with I's private key, I can extract the session key. In this case S will not be able to decrypt the ticket, but I can determine private information about C contained in the arguments that C sends to S. The protocol defends against this attack by including the server's name in the first item of $M2$, which in this case will be I instead of S. C uses this information to determine the identity of the process that can decrypt its request message.

A number of distinct levels of protection can be offered by this protocol. The client can request that authentication occur only when a connection to the server is first established. Or it can request authentication on each call for service. Or it can request that $K_{sess, C\&S}$ be used to encrypt the arguments of the invocation (in $M3$) and the results returned (in $M4$) as well as to encrypt the authenticator.

We have given arguments to demonstrate how Kerberos defends against a variety of attacks an intruder might attempt. Be under no illusions as to whether our discussion constitutes a proof that Kerberos is secure—it does not. Such proofs are the subject of ongoing research.

Single sign-on. Kerberos provides a property, referred to as **single sign-on**, that is becoming important as client interactions become increasingly complex. Complex interactions frequently involve access to multiple resources and hence multiple servers. Each server needs to authenticate the client and, in the worst case, has its own interface for doing so. If the client uses the same password for all servers, security can be compromised; if the client uses different passwords, he must remember all of them. In either case he must engage in multiple authentication protocols, and the system administrator must keep the authentication information associated with each server current as client information changes.

With single sign-on, the client needs to authenticate itself only once. Kerberos provides this property by concentrating authentication in an **authentication server**, AS (similar to KS), which authenticates C at login time using the password supplied by the client, as described earlier. Since the identity of the servers the client intends to access might not be known at this time, it is not possible for AS to construct the appropriate tickets (since each ticket must be encrypted with a particular server's key). Instead, it returns a **ticket-granting ticket** to C, which is used for requesting service from a particular server, called the **ticket-granting server**, TGS—also part of Kerberos. Later C can request the specific tickets it needs (for example, a ticket for S) from TGS using the ticket-granting ticket.

The authentication server generates a session key, $K_{sess,C\&TGS}$, that C can use to communicate with TGS, and returns to C (in a format similar to that of $M2$ in the simplified protocol).

- $K_{C,AS}[K_{sess,C\&TGS}, TGS, LT]$—$K_{sess,C\&TGS}$ is a session key for communicating with TGS

- $K_{TGS,AS}[K_{sess,C\&TGS}, C, LT]$—the ticket-granting ticket for TGS

where $K_{C,AS}$ and $K_{TGS,AS}$ are keys that AS and TGS have registered with AS.

Later, when C wants to access a particular server, S, it sends a copy of the ticket-granting ticket together with the server's name (and an authenticator) to TGS. TGS then returns to C (again in a format similar to that of $M2$).

- $K_{sess,C\&TGS}[K_{sess,C\&S}, S, LT]$—$K_{sess,C\&S}$ is a session key for communicating with S.

- $K_{S,AS}[K_{sess,C\&S}, C, LT]$—This is the ticket for S (note that S's private key, $K_{S,AS}$, is available to TGS).

C thus obtains a different ticket for each server it accesses. It engages in a single authentication protocol, and since the use of tickets is invisible at the user level, the user interface is simplified. Also, since authentication is concentrated in a single server, the administration of authentication information is simplified.

26.4.2 Nonces

Suppose two processes, P_1 and P_2, share a session key, K_{sess}, and P_1 sends an encrypted message, $M1$, to P_2 and expects an encrypted reply, $M2$. When P_1 receives $M2$, how can P_1 be sure that it was constructed by P_2? It might seem that P_1 can just decrypt $M2$

using K_{sess} and see if the result makes sense. Often, however, determining whether a string makes sense requires human intervention, and in some cases even that does not help. Consider the case in which $M2$ simply contains a data string (an arbitrary string of bits—perhaps the weight of some device) calculated by P_2. An intruder might substitute a random string for $M2$. When P_1 decrypts that string using K_{sess}, it might produce another string that looks like a data string. Unfortunately, P_1 cannot determine whether or not the string is correct without repeating P_2's calculation (which it is not in a position to do). Alternatively, the intruder might replay an earlier message sent during the same session and hence encrypted with K_{sess}. In some cases, such a replay might be a possible correct response to $M1$ (two devices could have the same weight), and hence P_1 is fooled into accepting it.

A nonce can be used to solve this problem. A **nonce** is a bit string created by one process in a way that makes it highly unlikely that another process can create the same string. For example, a randomly created bit string of sufficient length created in one process probably will not be created later by another process. Nonces have a variety of uses, one of which is related to authentication.

To solve the above problem, P_1 includes a nonce, N, in $M1$, and P_2 includes $N + 1$ in $M2$. On receipt of $M2$, P_1 knows that the sender must have decrypted $M1$, since $N + 1$, not a simple replay of N, is returned. This implies that the sender knows K_{sess} and is therefore P_2.

In Kerberos, the timestamp TS (which is already part of the authenticator) can be used as a nonce so that no additional items need be added. The server can include $TS + 1$ in $M4$.

Nonces are often used in cryptographic protocols for a completely different reason. Appending a large random number to the plaintext before encrypting a message makes it considerably harder for an intruder to decrypt the message by guessing parts of its contents—for example, guessing the expiration date or some of the redundant information in a credit card number—and using that information to reduce the cost of a brute-force search to discover the key. This use of a nonce is sometimes referred to as adding **salt** to a message. A number of the protocols we discuss later use salted messages, but we omit that part of the protocol in our discussion. In some protocols, a nonce used for this purpose is called a **confounder**.

26.5 Authorization

Having authenticated a client, the server must next decide whether the requested service should be granted. Thus, when a request arrives from a client to access a particular object, the authorization component of the system must decide whether the principal should be allowed the requested access to that object. This is referred to as an **authorization policy**. The modes in which an object can be accessed depend on the type of the object being protected.

If, for example, the resource is a file, the modes of access might be read, write, append, and execute. Operating systems typically control access to files stored in their file system by first requiring that principals authenticate themselves (at login

Id	r	w	a	x
11011	1	1	0	0
00000	1	0	0	0

FIGURE 26.5 Access control list for a file.

time) and then checking that each access to a file has been previously authorized by the file's owner. The data structure that is generally used to record the system's protection policy (in Windows and many versions of UNIX) is the **access control list** (ACL).

Each file has an associated ACL, and each entry on the ACL identifies a principal and contains a bit for each possible access mode. The ith bit corresponds to the ith access mode and indicates whether or not that principal is allowed to access the file in that way. Figure 26.5 shows an ACL for a file. The first five bits contain an Id. Each of the following bits corresponds to an access mode: read, write, append, and execute. The figure indicates that the user with Id 11011 has permission to read and write the file associated with the list.

As a practical matter, it is necessary to introduce the notion of a **group**. For example, it would be awkward to list all principals separately in the ACL of a file that is universally readable. A group is simply a set of principals, and an ACL entry can correspond to it. The access permissions contained in the entry are allowed to all group members. Thus, as illustrated in Figure 26.5, a file that is universally readable but writable only by its owner might have an ACL consisting of two entries: one for the owner with Id 11011 and read and write bits set and one for the group containing all principals with only the read bit set. The Id 00000 identifies the group consisting of all users. With the introduction of groups, several entries in an ACL might refer to a particular principal (e.g., a principal might belong to several groups). In this case, the principal is granted the union of the permissions in each such entry.

The structure for storing and enforcing an authorization policy in a transaction processing system is only a minor generalization of the ACL/group structure used by operating systems to protect files. Resources are controlled by servers, so a server (instead of the operating system) is responsible for storing the ACL and enforcing the authorization policy on the resources it controls. Servers export certain methods, making them available for invocation by clients. These methods constitute the modes of access to the resources encapsulated within the server. In short, the authorization policy is formulated in terms of the methods a particular principal can invoke and the particular resources on which to invoke them. In the Student Registration System, for example, the method that changes a grade cannot be invoked by a student, the method that changes the personal information describing a student (e.g., a student's address) can be invoked only by that student, and the method that sets a limit on class enrollment can be invoked by any faculty member.

ACLs can be used in support of this generalization. In one approach, the Student Registration System server might use a single ACL containing an entry for the student group and an entry for the faculty group. The permission bits in each entry correspond to the methods that can be invoked by the clients. An entry needs to have only enough bits so that each exported method can be associated with a distinct bit. In this case, the faculty group is granted permission for the grade change and class enrollment methods, and the student group is granted permission for the personal information method. The additional requirement that the personal information of a particular student be changed only by that student has to be checked separately. The ACL is checked by the server when a method is invoked, and, if the necessary permission has not been granted, an error code is returned to the caller.

Alternatively, we might regard the server as managing a number of distinct resources—class records, personal records—and allocate a separate ACL for each record. In this case, a finer granularity of protection can be enforced. For example, the ACL for a student's personal record contains an entry for that student only.

The SQL GRANT statement is one way that a client can specify an authorization policy for a table. In this case, the access modes correspond to various types of SQL statements. An SQL server might implement the policy using ACLs, in which case the GRANT statement causes a modification to the ACL associated with the table specified in the statement.

Each server is generally responsible for providing its own authorization module because the objects it controls and the access to them are specific to that server. By contrast, a principal's identity and group membership can be general to all servers. The authorization module within each server, referred to as a **reference monitor**, is responsible for constructing, retrieving, and interpreting access control lists. Middleware modules for doing this might be provided by a TP monitor.

26.6 Authenticated Remote Procedure Call

A goal of many distributed applications that require authentication and authorization is to hide the complexities of the required protocols from the principal. Once the principal has executed the login procedure, service invocation should be simple, and authentication and authorization should be invisible (unless a violation is detected). One way to achieve this goal is by implementing authentication in the RPC stubs, as shown in Figure 26.6, and by presenting the abstraction of an **authenticated RPC** to clients and servers. This is the approach used in the DCE (distributed computing environment) model of distributed computation.

In this approach, middleware provides an API that the client can use to log in and to invoke servers. The API interfaces to the stub, which engages in the exchange of messages (for example, the messages of Figure 26.4). The key server is now referred to as the **security server** since it implements authentication and plays a role in implementing authorization as well. It keeps track of all groups to which each principal belongs and includes (in a ticket sent to a principal) a list of that principal's group Ids. Security servers can be obtained as off-the-shelf middleware modules.

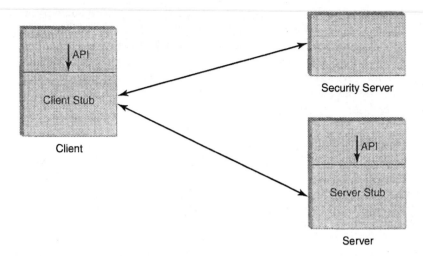

FIGURE 26.6 Relationship between stubs and authentication.

Each server is responsible for securely storing a copy of its server key, $K_{S,KS}$, locally and making it available to the server stub when an invocation message arrives. The stub can then decrypt the ticket contained in the message to determine the client's identity and the groups to which the client belongs.

The server stub API provides calls that the server can use to retrieve the client's identity and group membership information contained in the ticket from the server stub. Authorization for each client call is provided within the server proper (not the server's stub) by the reference monitor, using the client's (authenticated) identity and group membership information and the access control lists contained within the server.

26.7 Electronic Commerce

Security issues are particularly critical when transactions are executed over the Internet. Authentication is important to prevent one site from successfully impersonating another. Encryption is important to prevent eavesdropping. In addition, there is a general sense of suspicion between the parties participating in Internet transactions, perhaps because there is no face-to-face interaction and because impressive looking Web sites can be produced by fly-by-night operations.

In Chapter 25 we distinguished two kinds of electronic commerce transactions: customer-to-business (C2B) and business-to-business (B2B). The security requirements of the two are similar, but we assume that customers have only the security software that comes with their browsers, while businesses can have more sophisticated and specialized protection, such as their own public and private encryption keys, which customers (usually) do not have.

26.8 The Secure Sockets Layer Protocol: Certificates

Servers (perhaps representing businesses) that want to authenticate themselves to other parties as part of an Internet transaction can use a **certification authority** (**CA**), which acts as a trusted third party. A number of companies are in the business of being certification authorities.

A CA uses public-key encryption to generate **certificates**, which certify the association between a principal's name (e.g., Macy's) and its public key. The certificate contains (among other items) the principal's name and public key, and it is signed with the private key of the CA. Since the CA's public key is well known (and is most likely prestored in the user's browser), any process in the system can determine the validity of the certificate. Hence, if a client wants to communicate securely with Macy's, it can encrypt a message using the public key found in a valid certificate containing the name "Macy's" and be certain that only a process with knowledge of Macy's private key will be able to decrypt the message. Certificates thus solve the problem of distributing public keys reliably, which is the key distribution problem for asymmetric encryption. They are used in the protocols described below.

Any Internet server, S, that wants to obtain a certificate from a CA first generates a public and private key and then sends the public key, plus other information, to the CA. The CA uses various means to verify the server's identity (perhaps looking it up in Dun and Bradstreet and communicating with personnel at the server's place of business by phone and ordinary mail) and then issues it a certificate containing, among other items,

- The CA's name
- S's name
- S's URL
- S's public key
- Timestamp and expiration information

The CA signs the certificate and sends the signed certificate to S in the clear, perhaps by e-mail. S then verifies its correctness (for example, that the public key stored in the certificate is S's public key). Note that a certificate is public information readily available to an intruder. It is, however, of no use to an intruder because a client who wishes to communicate with S will use S's public key to encrypt a message. Since S's private key is not contained in the certificate, only S can decrypt the message.

The SSL protocol. The **Secure Sockets Layer** (**SSL**) protocol [Netscape 2000] uses certificates to support secure communication and authentication over the Internet between a client and an Internet server (or between servers). By using certificates, SSL is able to eliminate the need for an online key server (as in Kerberos), which can be a bottleneck in transaction systems that process thousands of transactions per second.[4]

A goal of SSL is to authenticate a server to a client. Since this is done using a certificate, each server that wants to be authenticated must first obtain a certificate. Clients, on the other hand, are not generally registered with certification authorities and hence do not have certificates or the encryption keys associated with them.[5] A logged-in client is typically represented by a browser, which (usually) does not have a private key of its own. Rather, the browser contains the public keys of all certification authorities that have made arrangements with that browser's vendor. The browser does not actually communicate with a CA during the SSL protocol; nor does a CA know any private information about a browser.

The SSL protocol authenticates the server to the client and establishes a session key for their use. A browser engages in the SSL protocol when it connects to a server whose URL begins with *https:* (instead of *http:*), which indicates an SSL-encrypted HTTP protocol.

Assume that a browser, C, connects to a server, S, that claims to represent a particular enterprise, E (for example, Macy's). In this case, the protocol consists of the following steps:

1. S sends C a copy of its certificate signed by the CA—in the clear.

2. C validates the certificate's signature using the CA's public key (included in its browser) and hence knows that the public key in the certificate belongs to the enterprise named in the certificate.

3. C generates and sends to S a session key encrypted with the public key in the certificate.[6]

Note that C, not S, generates the session key because, at this point in the protocol, C can communicate securely with S using the public key in the certificate, but S cannot communicate securely with C (nor is there an online key server, as in Kerberos, to generate the session key). Once the session key has been established, C and S can use it to exchange encrypted messages.

The steps in the protocol described above are performed invisibly to the application program in a layer of the communication hierarchy between the data transport (TCP/IP) and application levels. However, one small problem remains that requires user participation. Suppose an intruder intervenes and supplies its own (valid) certificate. Before sending any messages encrypted with the public key contained in the certificate, the user should verify that it describes the correct server. This is eas-

---

[4] Note, however, that certificates have a potentially significant disadvantage in that, once a certificate has been granted to a server by a CA, it is difficult to revoke it later if necessary. By contrast, an online key server can easily stop providing keys for a particular server.

[5] SSL has an optional authentication protocol for clients that do have certificates.

[6] SSL is actually slightly more complex. C generates and sends to S a **pre-master secret** from which C and S independently, using the same algorithm, generate two session keys—one for communication in each direction. This adds an additional measure of security. The pre-master secret is also used by C and S to verify the integrity of messages in the application part of the protocol.

ily done since the name of the certificate owner is contained in the certificate itself (and has not been altered because the certificate was signed by the CA). The user can determine the name by clicking on the security icon displayed by the browser.

If the browser uses the session key to communicate a credit card number to S, the user can have considerable confidence that that communication is secure. The browser itself generated the session key, which it communicated to S using E's public key, and the user knows that E's public key is genuine because it was obtained from a certificate that could have been generated only by the CA. The user trusts the CA to have verified E's identity and included the correct information about E in the certificate and trusts the browser vendor to have included the correct public key for each CA and a correct implementation of the SSL protocol in the browser. The user must also trust that its browser has not been corrupted, perhaps by some malicious program it downloaded at some earlier time.

At this point, the protocol has authenticated the server to the client, but the client has not been authenticated to the server. For many applications, client authentication is not necessary. For example, most servers will accept a credit card purchase from any browser that can supply the credit card number, without determining that the browser actually represents the card owner. (Most telephone-order catalog companies accept orders under similar conditions.)

For other applications, S does want to ensure that it is talking to a particular client (for example, before a stock broker's server sends a client its private portfolio information or accepts a stock trading transaction). One way to provide such authentication is for client and server to agree on a password, which the server stores and the client supplies after the session key has been established. Another way is for the client to have a certificate as well so that both client and server can be authenticated.

26.9 Passport: Single Sign-On

In Section 26.4.1 we discussed the difficulty that arises when a user has to interact with several different applications that require password authentication. Kerberos is an example of a protocol that implements single sign-on to solve this problem. Similarly, Microsoft Passport is an Internet protocol that uses an authentication server, A, to implement single sign-on. A stores the password of each customer, C, and a symmetric encryption key, $K_{S,A}$, for each server, S, that has registered for its service. It also stores a symmetric key, K_A for its own use. In simplified form, the protocol consists of the following steps:

1. When S wants to authenticate C, it sends a page to C's browser that contains A's address. The page is **redirected** (redirected pages are not displayed) from C to A (by setting the attribute `http-equiv= "refresh"`). In other words, the effect is as if, after receiving the page, C had clicked on A's address, forwarding the page to A.

2. A sends a page to C's browser requesting C's password.

3. *C* enters its password and clicks the submit button. An SSL session is established between *C* and *A*, and *C* sends its password to *A* using the session key established as a part of the SSL protocol.

4. *A* verifies that the password is correct.

5. *A* sends a page and a cookie to *C*. The page states that *C* has been authenticated and is redirected to *S*. It is encrypted with $K_{S,A}$, and hence *S* can verify that it came from *A*. The cookie also states that *C* has been authenticated. It is encrypted with K_A and placed on *C*'s browser. Its use will be explained below.

6. *S* sends a page to *C* that includes a (second) cookie to be placed on *C*'s browser encrypted with a key known only to *S*. Thus if *C* returns to *S*'s site, *S* can retrieve the cookie and determine that *C* was previously authenticated.

Suppose that *C* later visits a different server, *S'*, that also offers Passport authentication, and *S'* asks *A* to authenticate *C*. After step 1 of the procedure, *A* can retrieve the cookie it previously put in *C*'s browser and hence knows that *C* has been previously authenticated. *A* can now implement single sign-on. *A* skips steps 2 through 4 (it does not have to ask again for *C*'s password) and executes an abbreviated version of step 5 (it does not have to place another cookie on *C*'s browser).

A's cookie is similar to a Kerberos ticket, but the Passport protocol does not have the extra security offered by a Kerberos authenticator and hence is subject to some of the attacks that the authenticator addresses.

For example, *A* leaves a cookie on *C*'s browser after *C* completes its interaction with *S*. If *C*'s interaction originates from a public terminal (for example in a public library), a subsequent user of the terminal might (perhaps inadvertently) be authenticated as *C*. Kerberos deals with this type of threat by requiring that the client construct an authenticator, and this requires that the client know information contained in the ticket (the session key). In Passport, however, the cookie can be used on behalf of a client without the client demonstrating any knowledge of its contents. To circumvent this problem, most sites have a button that *C* can use to remove *A*'s cookie from the browser.

Paying with a credit card using single sign-on. Microsoft also has a related service, called E-Wallet, by which a user can store information, including a credit card number, mailing address, etc., on an E-Wallet server. Then the procedure described above is used to authenticate *C* to both *S* and the E-Wallet server. (Only a single password need be entered.) After the authentication has been completed, specified items from the E-Wallet server are sent to the merchant (in encrypted form) as a part of the purchase interaction. Thus the user does not have to re-enter credit card information and mailing address for each purchase with each merchant.

Verified by Visa is another protocol that provides single sign-on for paying with a credit card. In this protocol, the customer first enters a credit card number on the merchant's Web page. The page is sent (in an SSL session) to the merchant who initiates an authentication protocol similar to the first four steps of the Passport protocol. The goal of the protocol is to authenticate to the merchant that the customer is authorized to use that credit card. In this case, the authentication is performed by an authentication server operated by the bank that issued the card. That server checks that the password corresponds to the credit card number and that the credit card number is valid. One advantage of the system is that the customer can use the same password for all Visa purchases.

Note that in both the E-Wallet and Verified by Visa protocols, the merchant learns the credit card number of the customer.

26.10 Keeping Credit Card Numbers Private

Many merchants use the SSL protocol in customer purchase transactions. After the session key is established, the customer sends the details of the items to be purchased and the credit card information to the merchant's server, which completes the transaction by having the credit card approved at some other site representing the credit card company. One drawback of this protocol is that the merchant learns the client's credit card number. We saw that this was the case in both the Passport and Verified by Visa protocols.

Of course, in most non-Internet customer-merchant transactions, the merchant learns the customer's credit card number as well. When you go to a restaurant, for example, you give your credit card to a waitress who gets the transaction approved and returns a receipt for you to sign. How do you know she has not copied your credit card number?

However, revealing the credit card number to the merchant is particularly problematic in electronic commerce because only the number, not the card itself, is needed to make a purchase. This makes it easier for a criminal to make purchases without the cardholder's knowledge. Furthermore, the anonymous nature of electronic commerce does not promote a trusting relationship between merchant and customer. Hence Internet customers are more comfortable if merchants do not learn their credit card numbers. Also, on many sites, such as eBay, the "merchant" is not an established company but just an ordinary person who is selling, for example, her old record collection. The customer does not want that person to learn her credit card number.

One simple approach to this problem is to use a trusted third party to whom the customer has already given her credit card number and the merchant has already set up an account. When the customer wants to make a purchase, she tells the trusted third party to make a charge against her credit card and credit the merchant with the money. The most popular trusted third party of this type is PayPal, which currently has millions of registered users who execute hundreds of thousands of transactions per day, corresponding to billions of dollars in payments.

The PayPal protocol handles customer-to-customer (C2C) interactions. It allows one customer, C_1, to send money to another customer, C_2, who she identifies to PayPal by his email address. Perhaps C_1 just purchased an item from C_2 on an auction site. An important requirement is that the money can be transferred using C_1's credit card without C_2 seeing any of C_1's credit card information.

C_1 and C_2 must have previously registered with PayPal, which maintains accounts for them. Registration is accomplished at the PayPal site by submitting SSL encrypted forms that contain, among other information, C_1's name, email address, credit card information, and a password. To send money to C_2

1. C_1 logs onto the PayPal site, authenticates herself with her password (using SSL), and requests that PayPal use her credit card account to send the money to C_2, who she identifies with an email address.

2. PayPal executes a transaction that takes money from C_1's credit card account, deposits the money in C_2's PayPal account, and sends C_2 an email notifying him of the transaction. (This notification is why the protocol has been characterized, somewhat inaccurately, as "sending money by email.")

Once the money is in C_2's PayPal account, he can leave it there to use for later purchases through PayPal or he can request that PayPal send him a check for the amount.

26.11 The Secure Electronic Transaction Protocol: Dual Signatures

Another protocol in which the merchant does not learn the credit card number of the customer is the **Secure Electronic Transaction (SET)** protocol [VISA 2000], jointly developed by Visa and MasterCard. SET is particularly oriented toward customer-to-business (C2B) interactions. While SSL is a **session-level security protocol**, which guarantees secure communication for the duration of a session, SET is a **transaction-level security protocol**, which guarantees security for a purchasing transaction, including an atomic commit.

The SET protocol is quite complex, with many signatures and much cross checking to increase overall security. Here we present a simplified version that demonstrates the mechanisms by which the credit card number is hidden from the merchant and how the purchasing transaction is committed atomically.

The protocol involves two new ideas:

1. Each customer has his own certificate and hence his own public and private keys. These keys are used to provide one of the unique features of the protocol, the **dual signature**, which considerably increases the security of the transaction. The customer's certificate also contains a message digest of his credit card number and its expiration date. Recall that information in the certificate is unencrypted. Hence, only the digest (not the credit card number itself) can be included. The digest is used to verify that the credit card number supplied by the customer corresponds to a card belonging to the customer.

2. A new server, the **payment gateway**, G, operates on behalf of the credit card company. Thus, SET is a three-way protocol, involving the customer, the mer-

chant, and the payment gateway, which acts as a trusted third party during the protocol and performs the commit operation at the end of the transaction.

The basic idea of the protocol is that customer C sends merchant M a two-part message: the first part contains the purchase amount and C's credit card information encrypted with G's public key (so that M cannot see the credit card information); the second part contains the purchase amount and the details of the purchase (but not the credit card information) encrypted with M's public key. M then forwards the first part of the message to G, which decrypts it, approves the credit card purchase, and commits the transaction.

In one possible attack on a protocol such as this in which there is a two-part message, an intruder attaches the first part of one message to the second part of another. For example, having intercepted the messages for Joe's and Mary's purchases, an intruder can attach the first part of Joe's message to the second part of Mary's, hoping to force Joe to pay for Mary's goods. One way to thwart this type of attack is to have M associate a unique Id with each transaction and to require that C include it in both parts of the message. An attempt to unite the parts of different messages then becomes easily detectable. This does not solve the problem of a dishonest merchant, however, who associates the same Id with two different purchases so that the parts of the two resulting messages can be combined. A new mechanism is needed to overcome this type of problem. That mechanism is the dual signature, described next.

Before SET begins, C and M negotiate the terms of a purchase. The protocol begins with a handshake in which C and M exchange certificates and authenticate each other. C sends its certificate to M, and M sends both its certificate and G's certificate to C, at which point C and M know each other's and G's public key. Then the purchase transaction begins.

1. M sends a signed message to C containing a (unique) transaction Id (which is used to guard against replay attacks). C uses the public key in M's certificate to check the signature and hence knows that the message came from M and was not altered in transit.

2. C sends a message to M containing two parts plus the dual signature:

    (a) The transaction Id, C's credit card information, and the dollar amount of the order (but not a description of the items purchased)—encrypted with G's public key:

    $$m_1 = K_G^{pub}[trans\_Id,\ credit\_card\_inf,\ \$\_amount]$$

    (b) The transaction Id, the dollar amount of the order, a description of the items purchased (but not C's credit card information)—encrypted with M's public key:

    $$m_2 = K_M^{pub}[trans\_Id,\ \$\_amount,\ desc]$$

OPTIONAL

The dual signature has three fields:

(a) The message digest, MD_1, of the first part of the message:

$$MD_1 = f(m_1)$$

where $f()$ is the message digest function

(b) The message digest, MD_2, of the second part of the message:

$$MD_2 = f(m_2)$$

(c) C's signature of the concatenation of MD_1 and MD_2:

$$K_C^{pri}[f(MD_1 \cdot MD_2)]$$

Thus, the complete dual signature is

$$dual\_signature = MD_1, \ MD_2, \ K_C^{pri}[f(MD_1 \cdot MD_2)]$$

and the complete message sent from C to M is (m_1, m_2, $dual\_signature$).

The dual signature binds the two parts of the message. So, for example, an attempt by an intruder or M to associate m_2' with m_1 does not work since its message digest, MD_2', will be different from MD_2. Although MD_2' can be substituted for MD_2 in the dual signature, $K_C^{pri}[f(MD_1 \cdot MD_2)]$ cannot be used as the signature for $MD_1 \cdot MD_2'$, and only C can compute the correct dual signature for the reconstructed message.

3. M decrypts the second part of the message with its private key (but it cannot decrypt the first part, which contains the credit card number). The merchant then

(a) Uses the dual signature to verify that m_2 has not been altered in transit. It first computes the message digest of m_2 and checks that it is the same as the second field of the digital signature (MD_2). It then uses the public key in C's certificate to check that the third field is the correct signature for the concatenation of the first two fields.

(b) Verifies the transaction Id, the dollar amount of the order, and the description of the items purchased.

Next M sends a message to G containing two parts:

(a) m_1 and the dual signature it received from C:

$$m_3 = m_1, \ dual\_signature$$

(b) The transaction Id and the dollar amount of the order—signed with M's private key and encrypted with G's public key:

$$m_4 = K_G^{pub}[trans\_Id, \ \$\_amount, \ K_M^{pri}[f(trans\_Id, \ \$\_amount)]]$$

The complete message sent from M to G is (m_3, m_4), together with copies of C's and M's certificates.

4. G decrypts the message using its private key.

   (a) It uses the dual signature and the public key in C's certificate to verify that m_1 was prepared by C and was not altered (as in step 3a).

   (b) It uses the message digest of the credit card information in C's certificate to verify the credit card information supplied in m_1.

   (c) It uses M's signature in m_4 and the public key in M's certificate to verify that m_4 was not altered.

   (d) It checks that the transaction Id and the dollar amount are the same in m_1 and m_4 (to verify that M and C agreed on the purchase).

   (e) It checks that the Transaction Id was never submitted before (to prevent a replay attack).

   (f) It does whatever is necessary to approve the credit card request.

   Then G returns a signed *approved* message to M. At this point, the transaction is committed.

5. When M receives the *approved* message, it knows that the transaction has committed. It sends a signed message to C: *transaction complete*. C then knows that the transaction has committed.

Note how the protocol deals with some other attacks.

1. M cannot attempt to substitute different goods since the dual signature is over the description agreed to by C. By forwarding the dual signature on to G, M has committed itself to that description.

2. C cannot use m_1', copied from a message submitted by a different customer in an attempt to get that customer to pay for C's purchase by attaching it to m_2. In that case, the dual signature does not help since it is computed by C. However, m_1' and m_2 would have different transaction Ids, so the transaction will be rejected by G.

The atomic commit protocol for SET. When G commits the transaction, it logs appropriate data to make the transaction durable. M might also wish to commit its subtransaction when it receives the approved message from G. Many customers might not want to perform a formal commit, but the exchange of messages between C, M, and G can be viewed as a linear commit protocol and in that context

- The messages sent from C to M in step 2 and from M to G in step 3 are *vote messages*. Before sending them, C and M must be in a prepared state.

- The messages sent from G to M in step 4 and from M to C in step 5 are *commit messages*. G and M must enter appropriate *commit records* into their logs before sending those messages.

Note that G is a trusted third party, trusted by the other two participants to perform the commit.

26.12 Goods Atomicity, Certified Delivery, and Escrow

Some Internet transactions involve the actual delivery of the purchased items. Transactions involving the purchase of downloaded software are in this category. Such transactions[7] should be **goods atomic** in that the goods are delivered if and only if they have been paid for. In the context of the SET protocol, "paid for" means that the purchase has been approved by the payment gateway; in the context of the electronic cash protocols described in Section 26.13, it means that the electronic cash has been delivered to the merchant and accepted by the bank.

Transactions involving the purchase of physical goods are usually not goods atomic. The customer orders the goods, and the transaction commits, after which (in most cases) the merchant ships the goods. In Internet commerce, however, the customer might not trust the merchant to send (download) the goods after the transaction commits.

Goods atomicity is not really a new concept. The only original idea is that the event of delivering the goods is part of the transaction in which the goods are paid for. The requirement that the goods be delivered if and only if they are paid for is just the usual definition of atomic transaction execution. The hard part of implementing goods atomicity is that delivery cannot be rolled back, which means that if the goods are delivered before the transaction commits and the transaction subsequently aborts, there is no way to undo the delivery, and the execution is not atomic.

In Section 19.3.5, we considered a situation similar to goods atomicity in which cash is dispensed by an ATM if and only if the withdraw transaction at the bank commits. We discussed how a recoverable queue could be used for that purpose. Both cash dispensing and goods atomicity involve an external event that is supposed to take place if and only if the transaction commits.

The concept of goods atomicity and a protocol for implementing it were developed in connection with the NetBill system [Cox et al. 1995]. The protocol is in some ways similar to SET in that it involves a client, a merchant, and a trusted third party that effectively consummates a credit card transaction through a linear commit protocol. Rather than describe NetBill, we describe how to implement goods atomicity as an enhancement of the SET protocol.

After C and M have agreed on the terms of a transaction, but before C sends a confirmation to M (step 2 of SET), M sends (downloads) the goods to C, encrypted with a new symmetric key, $K_{C,M}$, that M has constructed for this purpose. M also sends a message digest of the encrypted goods so that C can verify that the encrypted goods were correctly received. Note that C cannot use the goods at this point since it does not know $K_{C,M}$.

The description, *desc*, that C sends to M (in m_2) includes both a specification of the goods and the message digest of the encrypted goods, signed with C's private key. In effect, C is acknowledging that it has received (in encrypted form) the

---

[7] The term "transaction" is used loosely in this context. The actual delivery of the goods might occur after the transaction commits but is part of the protocol in which the transaction is embedded.

goods corresponding to the digest. As in step 2 of SET, the complete message is $(m_1, m_2, dual\_signature)$, and this is C's vote to commit. If, on receiving the message from C, M agrees that the description it has received from C is accurate, it constructs the message (m_3, m_4) as in step 3 of SET, but includes two additional items in m_4:

1. $K_{C,M}$

2. The message digest of the encrypted goods signed with C's private key, which it received from C in step 2, signed again (countersigned) with M's private key

M then sends the message to G (step 3 of SET).

An unscrupulous merchant cannot change the terms of the transaction (perhaps to show a higher price) since the dual signature constructed by C contains the price information. By adding its signature to the message (in m_4) and forwarding it to G, M commits itself to the transaction. Once again, this message is M's vote to commit.

When G receives the doubly signed message from M (step 4 of SET), it knows that both parties are prepared to commit to the terms of the transaction. As with SET, if G is satisfied with the credit card information supplied by C, it commits the transaction, durably stores m_3, m_4, and the dual signature, and sends an *approved* message to M. M, in turn, sends a *transaction complete* message containing $K_{C,M}$ to C, so C can decrypt the goods.

This protocol is goods atomic for the following reasons:

- If a failure occurs before G commits the transaction, no money is transferred and C does not get the goods since it does not get $K_{C,M}$.

- If a failure occurs after the commit, the money is transferred, G has a (durable) copy of $K_{C,M}$, and C has an encrypted copy of the goods. C can get $K_{C,M}$ either from M or—if for some reason M does not send $K_{C,M}$—from G since G knows that the transaction has committed and C's certificate identifies it as the principal who constructed the dual signature.

An important feature of the protocol is that when the transaction commits, G has a copy of $K_{C,M}$, and hence C can decrypt the goods even if M "forgets" to send the *transaction complete* message containing $K_{C,M}$.

Certified delivery. Another issue in the delivery of goods over the Internet is **certified delivery**. A goods-atomic transaction guarantees delivery to the customer, but we would like to have the additional assurance that the right goods are delivered. How can M defend itself against a charge that the goods it sent do not meet the agreed-upon specifications, and how can C be assured that the specific goods ordered are received? In particular, if there is a dispute between M and C about the delivered goods and that dispute is to be resolved by an arbiter, how can M and C present their respective cases to the arbiter? For example,

- Suppose that after decrypting the delivered goods, C finds that they do not meet their specifications and wants her money back. C can demonstrate to the arbiter that the software does not work, but how can she show that this software is in fact the same software that M sent?

■ Suppose that C is trying to cheat M, and the nonworking software she demonstrates to the arbiter is not the same software that M sent. How can M unmask this attempted fraud?

The enhanced SET protocol meets the requirements of certified delivery. Recall that G durably stored m_3, m_4, and the dual signature when the transaction committed. The dual signature constructed by C was over the specification of the goods contained in m_2. By forwarding the signature on to G, M confirms that the specification is accurate (since it can decrypt m_2 to examine the specification and it can check that the signature is over m_2).

■ C can demonstrate to an arbiter that the encrypted goods she claims to have received from M are actually the goods that were sent by M by simply running the digest function against the goods and comparing the result to the digest in m_4 stored by G. The arbiter can then decrypt the goods using $K_{C,M}$ and test them. C can also provide m_2 (containing the specifications) and demonstrate that the dual signature was on m_2 and hence agreed to by M. The arbiter is now in a position to judge C's claim.

■ M can defend himself against a claim that the received goods do not meet their specifications since M can also produce m_2. Once again the arbiter can determine that the goods have not been tampered with and then test them against their specifications.

Escrow services. Another application requiring goods atomicity is the purchase of actual (nonelectronic) goods over the Internet from an unknown person or an auction site. The goods cannot be downloaded but must be sent by a shipping agent. One participant in the transaction might be suspicious that the other will not abide by the conditions of the purchasing agreement. How can both parties be sure that the transaction is goods atomic and that the goods will be delivered if and only if they are paid for?

One approach that comes close to meeting these requirements uses a trusted third party called an **escrow agent**. A number of companies are in the business of being escrow agents on the Internet. The basic idea is that, after the customer and the merchant have agreed on the terms of the purchase, instead of paying the merchant, the customer pays the escrow agent, which holds the money until the goods have been delivered and accepted by the customer. Only then does the escrow agent forward the payment to the merchant.

We sketch a simplified form of an escrow protocol,[8] leaving out many of the details involving authentication, encryption, and so forth. The protocol involves a customer, C, a merchant, M, and an escrow agent, E. It begins after C and M have reached agreement on the terms of the purchase.

1. C sends E the agreed-upon payment, perhaps using one of the secure payment methods described in this chapter.

---

[8] The protocol described is based on the i-Escrow protocol [i-Escrow 2000].

2. *E* durably stores the payment and other information needed for the rest of the protocol and commits the transaction.

3. *E* notifies *M* that the payment has been made.

4. *M* sends *C* the goods using some traceable shipping agent (such as FedEx or UPS), which agrees to make available to *E* the status information on the shipment (including confirmation of delivery).

5. When *C* receives the goods, she inspects them to see if they match her order. This inspection must be completed by the end of a stipulated period, which starts when the goods have been delivered as documented by the shipping agent's tracking mechanism.

   (a) If *C* is satisfied with the goods, the following take place:
      (i) *C* notifies *E* that the goods have been received and are satisfactory.
      (ii) *E* forwards the payment to *M*.

   (b) If *C* is not satisfied with the goods, the following take place:
      (i) *C* notifies *E* that the goods have been received and are not satisfactory.
      (ii) *C* returns the goods to *M* using some traceable shipping agent.
      (iii) *M* receives the goods and notifies *E*.[9]
      (iv) *E* returns the payment to *C*.

   (c) If, by the end of the inspection period, *C* does not notify *E* as to whether or not she is satisfied with the goods, *E* forwards the payment to *M*.[10]

This protocol reasonably approximates both goods atomicity and certified delivery. For example, *C* has a stipulated inspection period to determine whether or not the goods delivered are the goods ordered. As with the previous goods-atomicity protocol, this one relies on a third party, which is trusted by both *C* and *M*, to perform certain specified activities after the transaction commits.

26.13 Electronic Cash: Blind Signatures

The Internet purchasing transactions we have discussed so far use a credit card, which, along with a check, is an example of **notational money**. That is, your actual assets are represented by the balance in your bank account; your credit card or check is a *notation* against those assets. At the time you make a purchase, you provide a notation that identifies you and the cost of the goods you are purchasing; the merchant trusts that you will abide by the purchasing agreement and eventually pay for the purchases with real money—that there is enough money in your checking account or that you are in good standing with your credit card company. In either case, your bank balance will eventually be decremented to reflect your purchase.

---

[9] *M* can inspect the returned goods to see if they are as specified and must complete this inspection by the end of a stipulated inspection period. We omit what happens if *M* finds the returned goods unsatisfactory.

[10] *M* might not send the goods to *C* in step 4, or *C* might not return the goods to *E* in step 5b(ii). Again, these situations can be resolved using the shipping agent's tracking mechanism.

In contrast to notational money, cash is backed by the government. Although it does not have intrinsic value (it is, after all, just a piece of paper) the public's trust in the stability of the government causes it to be treated as if it had intrinsic value (i.e., as if it were gold). Thus, the merchant knows that he can deposit cash in his account or use it to purchase other goods without having to trust the customer. Cash is often referred to as **token money**. In the world of the Internet, token money is **electronic** or **digital** cash.

Token money offers the participants in a transaction certain advantages over notational money.

- *Anonymity.* Since the customer is not required to provide a signed record to complete a cash transaction, such a transaction can be performed anonymously. Neither the bank nor the credit card company knows the customer's identity. By contrast, a credit card company keeps records of all customers' purchases, and a bank has access to canceled checks. These records might be made available at a later time to the government, to a court proceeding, or even to someone hoping to pry into an individual's personal life.

- *Small-denomination purchases.* For each credit card transaction, the credit card company charges a fixed fee plus a percentage of the purchase price. Thus, credit cards are not appropriate for purchases involving only a small amount of money, yet many Internet vendors would like to charge a few cents for a page of information they supply to browsers. Small-denomination electronic cash would be useful for such transactions.

Hence, there is a need to support transactions based on electronic cash. Such transactions should satisfy the requirement of **money atomicity**: money should not be created or destroyed. However, since electronic cash is represented by a data structure in the system, there are several ways in which money atomicity might be violated. For example,

- A dishonest customer or merchant can make a copy of the data structure and use both the original and the copy.

- Money can be created or destroyed if a failure occurs (e.g., a message is lost or the system crashes). For example, a customer who has sent a copy of the data structure to a merchant cannot determine whether the message was received by the merchant and so decides to reuse the data structure in a different purchase—even though the money was actually received. Alternatively, the message might not have been received, but the customer does not reuse the data structure, failing to realize that the payment has not been made.

What follows is a discussion of an electronic cash protocol designed to support the purchase of arbitrary (not necessarily electronic) goods. Goods atomicity is not a feature of this protocol; instead, the customer trusts that the merchant will send the goods after the transaction commits.

Tokens and redundancy predicates. This protocol is based on the Ecash protocol [Chaum et al. 1988]. Cash is represented by electronic tokens of various denominations. Each token consists of a unique serial number, n, encrypted with a private key known only to the bank. The terminology here is confusing since it is often said that, in electronic cash protocols, the bank "signs" the serial number to create the token. Here, the meaning of signing differs from that given in Section 26.3, in which a signed item consists of the item followed by an encryption of its digest. In this section, when we say that the bank signs a serial number, we mean that the bank encrypts the serial number with a private key, and the result is a token.

How does this scheme prevent intruders from creating counterfeit tokens? After all, a token is just a bit string of a certain length. The fact that the bit string is the encryption of a serial number provides no protection. You might think that we could test the token for validity by decrypting it with the bank's public key and examining the result. However, that key can be applied to any valid or invalid token, yielding a bit string, and we have no way of distinguishing a bit string that is a valid serial number from one that is not.

To prevent intruders from creating counterfeit tokens, we use a technique that requires serial numbers to be bit strings that have some special property that distinguishes them from arbitrary bit strings. For example, it might be required that the first half of the serial number be created at random and the second half be a scrambled form of the first half using a fixed and known scrambling function. Formally, we say that there is some well-known predicate, *valid*, called a **redundancy predicate**, such that, for all valid serial numbers, n, the predicate *valid*(n) is true.

Although it is assumed that the counterfeiter knows the redundancy predicate and the bank's public key for decrypting tokens, she does not know the bank's private key and so cannot produce tokens by encrypting a valid serial number. Hence, in counterfeiting tokens she faces the problem of finding a (fake) token that decrypts to a bit string that satisfies *valid*. The counterfeiter can use a trial-and-error technique to do this, but it is extremely unlikely that the result of decrypting an arbitrarily chosen bit string will satisfy *valid* if the bit string is long enough and if *valid* is such that the number of bit strings of that length that satisfy *valid* is a small percentage of the total number of bit strings of that length.

In its scheme for minting tokens, the bank keeps a set of public/private key pairs and chooses serial numbers that satisfy *valid*. It signs all serial numbers used in creating tokens of a particular denomination, j, with the same private key, K_j^{priv}, from the set and uses a different private key for each denomination. The bank does not keep a list of the serial numbers of the tokens that it has created, but if the numbers are large enough and the number of tokens minted at each denomination is limited, the probability that the bank will choose the same serial number twice can be made vanishingly small. The bank does keep a list of the serial numbers of all tokens deposited and therefore can reject a copy of a token that was deposited already. In this way, it can detect an attempt to use a duplicated token. Any customer or merchant can check the validity and denomination of a token by decrypting it with K_j^{pub} and applying *valid* to the result.

OPTIONAL

A simple digital cash protocol.   If anonymity is not an issue, the customer, C, the merchant, M, and the bank, B, can use the following simple digital cash protocol.

Creating tokens

1. C authenticates himself to B and sends a message requesting to withdraw some specified amount of cash, in the form of tokens, from his account.

2. B debits C's account and mints the requested tokens by making up a serial number, n_i, for each token, such that $valid(n_i)$ is true. It then encrypts n_i with the private key, K_j^{priv}, corresponding to the token's denomination j, to produce the token $K_j^{priv}[n_i]$.

3. B sends the tokens to C, encrypted with a session key generated for B and C's use in the usual manner. A token cannot be sent in the clear because an intruder can copy it and spend the copy before C has a chance to spend the original. (In that case, the original token will be rejected by B when it is later deposited by C). At this point, the token-creation transaction is committed.

4. C receives the tokens and stores them in his "electronic wallet."

Spending tokens

1. When C wants to use some of his tokens to purchase goods from M, he establishes a session with M and generates a session key in the usual manner. He then sends a message to M containing a purchase order for the goods and the appropriate number of tokens, all encrypted with the session key.

2. Upon receiving the message from C, M decrypts the tokens and checks that they are valid and are sufficient to purchase the requested goods. M then sends the tokens to B, encrypted with a session key.

3. Upon receiving the message from M, B decrypts the tokens and checks that they are valid. It then checks its list of deposited tokens to ensure that the received tokens have not already been deposited. B then adds the received tokens to its list of deposited tokens, credits M's account with the amount of the tokens, commits the transaction, and sends a *complete* message to M.

4. Upon receiving the *complete* message from B, M performs local commit actions and then sends a *complete* message (and the goods purchased) to C.

(This protocol does not guarantee goods atomicity or certified delivery. M might not send the goods to C.) As with the SET protocol, the exchange of messages among B, M, and C can be viewed as a linear commit protocol.

An anonymous protocol and blinding functions.   The simple digital cash protocol does not provide anonymity to the customer because the bank can record the serial numbers of the tokens withdrawn by the customer. When those tokens are deposited by a merchant, the bank could conclude that the merchant sold something to that customer. This exposes some information about the customer's activities that she might prefer to keep private. To provide anonymity, the protocol is modified so that the customer (not the bank) makes up a serial number, n, that satisfies $valid(n)$, scrambles it, and then submits it to the bank. The bank creates the token by signing the scrambled serial number (it does not know what the serial number is), using a private key appropriate to the denomination being withdrawn. Such a signature is called a **blind signature** [Chaum et al. 1988]. The bank does not know the serial number, so it cannot trace it back to the customer when the token is later deposited by the merchant. When the customer receives the blinded token from the bank, it unscrambles it to obtain the token.

To implement a blind signature, the protocol uses a **blinding function**, b (sometimes called a **commuting function**). The function b and its inverse, b^{-1}, have two properties:

1. Given $b(n)$, it is very difficult to determine n.

2. b commutes with the encryption function used by the bank involving the (private) denomination key K_j^{priv}. That is,

$$K_j^{priv}[b(n)] = b(K_j^{priv}[n])$$

and as a result

$$b^{-1}(K_j^{priv}[b(n)]) = b^{-1}(b(K_j^{priv}[n])) = K_j^{priv}[n]$$

Therefore C can recover the token from the blinded token.

Creating tokens

1. C creates a valid serial number, n, satisfying $valid(n)$.

2. C selects a blinding function, b (known only to C), and **blinds** the serial number by computing $b(n)$.

3. C authenticates himself to B and sends a message containing $b(n)$, requesting to withdraw from his account some specified amount of cash in the form of tokens. (As in the simple digital cash protocol, the message is encrypted with a session key.) Since B does not know the blinding function, it cannot determine n.

4. B signs $b(n)$ with a private key, K_j^{priv}, appropriate to the token's denomination, creating the blinded token $K_j^{priv}[b(n)]$. It debits C's account accordingly and then returns the blinded token to C, again using a session key. Although B cannot check that C had selected a valid serial number (satisfying $valid(n)$), C has no reason to construct an invalid number because he knows that B will debit his account by the amount of the token and that the token's validity will be checked when he attempts to spend it. At this point, the token creation transaction is committed.

5. C **unblinds** the blinded token by using $b^{-1}(K_j^{priv}[b(n)])$ to obtain $K_j^{priv}[n]$, which is the requested token consisting of a signed valid serial number.

OPTIONAL

Creating a blinding function. The protocol requires that C create his own blinding function, b, unknown to B. This might seem a difficult task, but it is actually quite easy in the context of the RSA algorithm for public key cryptography. In one scheme for doing this, C first generates a random number, u, that is relatively prime[11] to the modulus N of the bank's keys (see Section 26.2). Because u is relatively prime to N, it has a **multiplicative inverse**, u^{-1}, with respect to N, such that

$$u * u^{-1} \equiv 1 \ (mod \ N)$$

To blind the serial number, n, C computes

$$K_j^{pub}[u] * n \ (mod \ N)$$

and sends the result to B. Hence, the blinding function can be viewed simply as multiplication by a random number.

The signed result, sr, returned by B to C is

$$sr = K_j^{pri}[K_j^{pub}[u] * n]$$

Using equation (26.1) on page 1141, it follows that

$$sr = u * K_j^{pri}[n] \ (mod \ N)$$

Informally, we can say that, to unblind the token, C "divides sr by u," but actually C uses the multiplicative inverse, u^{-1}, to recover the token

$$K_j^{pri}[n] = u^{-1} * sr \ (mod \ N)$$

The serial number n can now be obtained using K_j^{pub}.

Spending tokens. The protocol for spending and validating tokens involves the same steps as those in the simple protocol previously described. Fortunately, we did not assume that B kept a list of the serial numbers of the tokens it generated because, with the anonymous protocol, it does not know what these numbers are. When M submits the token to B for redemption, B simply assumes that, if the serial number satisfies *valid*, it earlier (blindly) signed that serial number. As before, B keeps a list of the serial numbers of tokens that have been deposited, so it will not accept the same token twice.

Money atomicity. The question is whether the electronic cash protocols achieve money atomicity. Money atomicity has two aspects:

1. Money might be created (outside of any transaction) if a process can make a copy of a token and then spend it. However, the bank will uncover this attempted fraud when it checks the serial number against its list of previously submitted

---

[11] Euclid's algorithm can be used to test whether the random number is relatively prime to N (see [Stalling 1997]).

tokens. Counterfeiting is another way of creating money, but, as we saw earlier, success in this is unlikely.

2. Money might be destroyed as the result of a failure, but such problems can generally be dealt with.

   (a) In the token generation transaction, the bank debits the customer's account, sends the token, and then commits, but the communication system loses the token, and it is never delivered to the customer. However, these protocols have the interesting property that, if the customer claims never to have received a token that the bank sent, the bank can simply send the customer a copy of the (blinded) token that it retrieves from its log. Even if the customer is dishonest and now has two copies of the token, only one can be spent.

   (b) In the token-spending transaction, the system crashes after the customer sent the token but before she received a message that the transaction committed. The customer does not know whether the transaction committed before the crash and hence whether the token was actually spent. If she attempts to spend the token again, she might be accused of fraud. However, she can later ask the bank whether a particular token was spent (i.e., is in the list of spent tokens), but this might compromise her anonymity.

26.14 Security in XML-Based Web Services

Increasingly, Web services require security. The integrity and privacy of data might have to be guaranteed, and principals might have to be authenticated. Many of these proposals for security protocols are still in an early stage of development and are likely to change. In this section we briefly discuss the basic ideas underlying some of them, leaving out details and a number of possible variations and optional features.

Web services security is built on the techniques described in previous sections. For example, public-key and symmetric encryption techniques, digital signatures, certificates, and Kerberos are used. The new issue is how to integrate them into the Web environment, and this means expressing them in XML and developing standards that all the players in the Web services world agree on. We consider two related problems: First, how do you encrypt and/or sign information contained in an XML document or a SOAP message? And second, how do you exchange security related information?

26.14.1 Encryption and Signatures—XML Encryption and XML Signature

XML Encryption. *XML Encryption*[12] is concerned with the encryption of XML data. It addresses a number of problems. How do we fit encrypted data into the XML model? How do we transmit to the receiver of encrypted XML data information

---

[12] We describe the *W3C Recommendation* of December 10, 2002, which can be found at *http://www.w3.org/TR/2002/REC-xmlenc-core-20021210*.

about how the encryption was done? Finally, an XML document will generally contain a variety of elements describing many aspects of an interaction. The elements are supplied by and directed to a variety of different entities. To make sure a receiver accesses only information relevant to it, each element might have to be encrypted in a different way. How is this to be done?

Suppose an XML document describing a purchase contains the buyer's name and credit card information:

```
<Payment xmlns = "http:// ...">
    <Name>John Doe</Name>
    <CreditCard Limit="5000" Currency="USD">
        <Number>1234 5678 9012 3456</Number>
        <Issuer>Bank of XY</Issuer>
        <Expiration>04/09</Expiration>
    </CreditCard>
</Payment>
```

While the name must be accessible to the merchant, we might want to reserve for the credit card company access to the credit card information. The result of encrypting the credit card information using XML Encryption is shown in Figure 26.7.

The credit card element has been replaced by an EncryptedData element. Its Type attribute indicates that an entire element (including its tag) within the document has been encrypted. The actual encrypted value of the credit card element is in the CipherValue element. The EncryptionMethod element gives information about the method used for encryption. The value of its Algorithm attribute is a URI that identifies the encryption algorithm, in this case a Triple DES algorithm. The KeyName element gives information that can be used to identify the

FIGURE 26.7 An encrypted element within an XML document.

```
<PaymentInfo xmlns = "http:// ...">
  <Name>John Doe</Name>
  <EncryptedData Type="http://www.w3.org/2001/04/xmlenc#Element"
      xmlns="http://www.w3.org/2001/04/xmlenc#"/>
    <EncryptionMethod
      Algorithm="http://www.w3.org/2001/04/xmlenc#tripledes-cbc"/>
    <ds:KeyInfo xmlns:ds="http://www.w3.org/2000/09/xmldsig#">
      <ds:KeyName>keyABC</ds:KeyName>
    </ds:KeyInfo>
    <CipherData>
      <CipherValue>Zx23XAbc4</CipherValue>
    </CipherData>
  </EncryptedData>
</PaymentInfo>
```

decryption key (perhaps the name of a file accessible to the receiver containing the key). The assumption is that the key is properly protected, and the receiver can produce the key given this information. The EncryptionMethod and KeyName elements are both optional and can be omitted if the user is expected to know that information.

In this example, the entire element has been encrypted, including its tag. In some circumstances it is desirable not to encrypt the tag. For example, executing an XPath search might be inhibited if tags are encrypted. More interestingly, since an intruder might be able to guess the tag, security is compromised. The intruder knows the clear text corresponding to a portion of the cipher text. Hence, among the possible values of the Type attribute is one which indicates that tags are not encrypted.

In some situations the same element might be encrypted more than once. For example, in a medical record the details of a particular malady might be accessible to the medical staff only while more general medical information might be accessible to the accounting department (for billing purposes) as well. To handle this, the details might be encrypted using a particular key or technique known only to the medical staff and then all the medical information (including the details) might be encrypted using a different key or technique known to both the medical staff and the accountants. As a result, the details are doubly encrypted and accessible only to the medical staff. For example, in Figure 26.7 we might encrypt both the Name element and the EncryptedData element and embed the result as CipherData in another EncryptedData element.

In Figure 26.7 the symmetric key used to decrypt the element is known to the receiver, and the sender simply identifies it using the KeyName child. Alternatively, the sender might transmit the key, in encrypted form, along with the element. In this case the key might be encrypted using the public key of the receiver. The EncryptedKey element defined in XML Encryption is used for this purpose. An example of this case will be given shortly. These alternatives illustrate the fact that the basic encryption techniques can be used in a variety of ways to satisfy the needs of different applications.

XML Signature. *XML Signature*[13] is concerned with signatures on XML data. As with XML Encryption, either an entire XML document or an individual element in a document can be signed. A simple signature element is shown in Figure 26.8

The SignedInfo element groups together all the information about the signature except the signature itself. A single signature can be used to sign multiple data items stored in different places. To do this, SignedInfo contains one or more Reference elements, each of which identifies an item through its URI attribute.

In Figure 26.8 the initial character of the value of the URI attribute of the Reference element, #, indicates that the data is an element elsewhere in the same document: the element with tag MsgBody. (In Figure 26.10 we present a complete

---

[13] We describe the *W3C Recommendation* of February 12, 2002, which can be found at *http://www.w3 .org/TR/2002/REC-xmldsig-core-20020212.*

FIGURE **26.8** A simple signature element.

```
<Signature Id="A Simple Signature"
      xmlns="http://www.w3.org/2000/09/xmldsig#">
  <SignedInfo>
    <CanonicalizationMethod
      Algorithm="http://www.w3.org/TR/2001/REC-xml-c14n-20010315"/>
    <SignatureMethod
      Algorithm="http://www.w3.org/2000/09/xmldsig#rsa-sha1"/>
    <Reference URI="#MsgBody">
      <Transforms ··· </Transforms>
      <DigestMethod
        Algorithm="http://www.w3.org/2000/09/xmldsig#sha1"/>
      <DigestValue>dER4boXp453tr56Y</DigestValue>
    </Reference>
  </SignedInfo>
  <SignatureValue>zi990CrnT9zoprOo</SignatureValue>
</Signature>
```

SOAP message containing both the data and its signature. It includes the element MsgBody being referred to here.) In other cases we might be signing data external to the document—for example a file attached to a message of a page accessible on the Web. For example, the attribute value *http://www.mycompany.audit#personnel* indicates that the personnel element contained in the indicated Web page has been signed.

The Reference element also gives us the first step used to compute the signature: the method used to compute the digest of the data is specified as the value of the Algorithm attribute of the DigestMethod child element, and the resulting digest value is given in the DigestValue child. (Since the Transforms element is a distraction from our description of the signature algorithm, we defer discussing it until later in this section on page 1175.)

The second step of the signature algorithm signs the SignedInfo element (*not* the data) in the traditional way. A digest of the SignedInfo element is computed, and the result is signed with the private key of the sender. The specific algorithm that does this is the value of the Algorithm attribute of the SignatureMethod element.

Hence, XML Signature uses *two* digests to compute a signature. Note that the double digest has all the properties of a digest as described in Section 26.3: all digest values are equally likely, and if any bit of the data is changed, all bits of the digest have a 50% chance of changing.

A nice feature of the double digest algorithm is that by signing the SignedInfo element instead of just the data, the sender guarantees that an intruder cannot change the information describing the signature algorithm that was used to sign the data. What would be the point of such an attack? Suppose an intruder could substitute in the SignedInfo element the name of a different digest function, D_2, for the digest function, D_1, used by the sender, and suppose that D_1 maps the item to be signed to the digest value dv. If the set of items mapped to dv by D_1 is a subset of the set mapped by D_2 to dv, then the receiver will not be able to detect the substitution (since the value dv will be encrypted in both cases). However, the likelihood that the intruder will be able to attach the signature to different data successfully is increased. Hence, the intruder has weakened the integrity guarantee provided by the digital signature.

Producing a digest of the `SignedInfo` element is not as simple as it appears. The element is embedded within an XML document. When computing the signature, the sender must extract the data first and, in the process, spaces or tab characters might be inserted or deleted. Similarly, when the receiver checks the signature, the data must be extracted from the received document. If this extraction is done differently, the string checked by the receiver might not be the same as the string signed by the sender. Although semantically the XML content of the data will be the same, the digest function is sensitive to the exact string. Two strings that differ by only a single space character will have completely different digests (see Section 26.3). Hence the digest computed by the receiver will not match the digest computed by the sender.

One way to deal with this problem is to convert the `SignedInfo` element into a canonical form—**canonicalize** it. This guarantees a unique representation of the element with respect to these issues. Both the sender and the receiver canonicalize the element using the algorithm specified in the element `CanonicalizationMethod` before computing the digest.

Reading from the top of the `Signature` element

- The `CanonicalizationMethod` element identifies the canonicalization algorithm to be applied to the `SignedInfo` element.
- The `SignatureMethod` element identifies the signature algorithm to be used to sign the `signedInfo` element (for example RSA-SHA1).
- The `Reference` element identifies the data to be signed and contains the `DigestMethod` and the `DigestValue`.
- The `DigestMethod` element identifies the digest algorithm to be used on the data.
- The `DigestValue` element gives the result of executing the digest algorithm on the data to be signed.
- The `SignatureValue` element gives the result of signing the `SignedInfo` element.

Note that the `SignatureValue` element is not a child of the `SignedInfo` element. This is fortunate because otherwise we would be in the awkward situation of having to know the value of the signature before we actually compute it.

Finally, in more complicated applications, certain transformations might have been performed by the sender on the data referenced by a `Reference` element *before* the message digest was computed. In other words, the received data is not exactly the data that the sender signed. For example, the data might bave been canonicalized (do not be confused here—we are talking about the data itself, not the `SignedInfo` element) before being digested. Or, the data might have been compressed or encrypted. Another case occurs when an XML document includes an element that was not digested. For example, the element might contain information that is subject to modification as the data is moved from one site to another. If the element is processed by the digest function, then any subsequent change to its value will invalidate the signature. In order to accommodate this problem the sender might have deleted the element before computing the digest—although the element is contained in the data sent.

In order to validate the signature, the receiver must know what transformations were performed when the signature was computed by the sender. It can then repeat those transformations, in the same order, to the received data as a first step (before computing the digest) of the signature validation process. The transformations are identified in the `Transforms` child of a `Reference` element. `Transforms` contains an ordered list of `Transform` children, each one of which describes a particular transformation that was performed.

One last point needs to be considered: suppose the receiver does not know the public key to be used in checking the signature. The sender might want to transmit this information, and XML Signature provides several ways in which this can be done. For example, the sender might provide a string that identifies the key. This might be the case if the receiver has several public keys on file and uses the string to identify the appropriate one. This type of information is transmitted in a `KeyInfo` child of the `Signature` element

```
<KeyInfo>
  <KeyName>
     · · · the identifier goes here · · ·
  </KeyName>
</KeyInfo>
```

Another alternative is to send a certificate. We will see an example of that shortly.

26.14.2 Encrypting and Signing SOAP Messages— WS-Security

XML Encryption and XML Signature supply a complete solution to the problem of encrypting and signing an XML document. However, if the document in question is a SOAP message, additional conventions must be introduced so that a SOAP processor can utilize these tools. The protocol that we describe is referred to as **WS-Security**.[14] WS-Security defines a security header block, tagged `wsse:Security`, which can be placed in the header of a SOAP message and which contains security related information. For example, the information might be a security token (which might contain a certificate or a Kerberos ticket), a timestamp (which can be used for dealing with replays), a signature, or an encrypted key. These items can be used in

---

[14] The discussion is based on the *OASIS Standard 200401*, March 2004.

a variety of ways to create a level of security appropriate to a particular application. We discuss two simple examples.

▣ **Sending encrypted data.** In Figure 26.9 the encrypted data is the entire child element (including its tag) of the body of a SOAP message. The header block contains an EncryptedKey element describing the key that was used to encrypt

FIGURE 26.9 An encrypted SOAP message.

```
<s:Envelope
    xmlns:s="http://www.w3.org/2001/12/soap-envelope"
    xmlns:ds="http://www.w3.org/2000/09/xmldsig#"
    xmlns:wsse="http://schemas.xmlsoap.org/ws/2002/04/secext"
    xmlns:xenc="http://www.w3.org/2001/04/xmlenc#">
  <s:Header>
    <wsse:Security>
      <xenc:EncryptedKey>
        <xenc:EncryptionMethod Algorithm="..."/>
        <ds:KeyInfo>
          <wsse:KeyIdentifier
            MnH5x7...
          </wsse:KeyIdentifier>
        </ds:KeyInfo>
        <xenc:CipherData>
          <xenc:CipherValue>jh54Da...</xenc:CipherValue>
        </xenc:CipherData>
        <xenc:ReferenceList>
          <xenc:DataReference URI="#bodyID"/>
        </xenc:ReferenceList>
      </xenc:EncryptedKey>
    </wsse:Security>
  </s:Header>
  <s:Body>
    <xenc:EncryptedData Id="bodyID"
        Type="http://www.w3.org/2001/04/xmlenc#Element">
      <xenc:EncryptionMethod
        Algorithm="http://www.w3.org/2001/04/xmlenc#tripledes-cbc"/>
      <xenc:CipherData>
        <xenc:CipherValue>Kiu87Cde...</xenc:CipherValue>
      </xenc:CipherData>
    </xenc:EncryptedData>
  </s:Body>
</s:Envelope>
```

the data. In this case, the data was encrypted with a symmetric key. The `Algorithm` attribute of the `EncryptionMethod` child of `encryptedKey` identifies the method that was used to encrypt the key. The `CipherData` element contains the key in encrypted form. So, in order to decrypt the data, the receiver must first decrypt the key. Fortunately, the sender has supplied some information about how that can be done using the `KeyIdentifier` child of the `KeyInfo` element. The value of that child uniquely identifies a key that the receiver can access to decrypt the encrypted key. So the assumption here is that the sender and receiver have exchanged some key information prior to the sending of this message.

The `ReferenceList` child contains a list of items encrypted by the (encrypted) key. In this case, the list contains a single `DataReference` child whose URI refers to the `EncryptedData` element in the message with `Id` value `BodyID` (recall that the # means that the data is an element within the same XML document).

■ **Sending signed data.** In Figure 26.10 the body contains the (unencrypted) data, and the header contains its signature. The `Signature` element is the same as that shown in Figure 26.8 with the exception that a `KeyInfo` child that contains information about the key to be used by the receiver to check the signature has been added. The assumption is that in this application the receiver does not know the public key to use. Hence, a certificate containing that key is included in a `BinarySecurityToken` header block, and a reference to it is included in the `SecurityTokenReference` element. Both of these elements are defined in the WS-Security schema. A security token might simply contain a user's name, or it might contain binary information like a certificate or a Kerberos ticket. A token reference might involve a URI (as in this case) or a `KeyIdentifier` (as described in connection with Figure 26.9 and embedded in a `KeyInfo` element).

The `Id` attribute of Body assigns the name `MsgBody` to the data, and the signature shown in Figure 26.8 refers to that item.

General considerations.   A SOAP message can pass through a number of intermediaries before getting to its final destination. A header block is addressed to an intermediary using the `role` attribute and contains individual processing instructions for the intermediary. This allows different security header blocks to be addressed to different intermediaries. For example, an intermediary might be a signature verifier, which verifies the signature of the data in the body. The signature would be included as a `Security` header block addressed to that site. After verifying the signature, the verifier might add an additional header block asserting that verification was successful and pass the message on to the final destination.

Alternatively, different intermediaries along a path might sign or encrypt different (perhaps overlapping) portions of a message, adding new security header blocks as the message progresses. For example, a salesperson might send an order in the body of a SOAP message and include a security header block with his signature. When the order is processed in the shipping department, a shipping header might be added and the shipping department might sign both that header and the body.

FIGURE 26.10 A signed SOAP message.

```
<s:Envelope xmlns:S="http://www.w3.org/2001/12/soap-envelope"
    xmlns:ds="http://www.w3.org/2000/09/xmldsig#">
  <s:Header>
    <wsse:Security
      xmlns:wsse="http://schemas.xmlsoap.org/ws/2002/04/secext"
      xmlns:wsu="...">
      <wsse:BinarySecurityToken>
        ValueType="...#X509v3"
        wsu:Id="X509Token"
        EncodingType="...">
        AsD4Fg567...
      </wsse:BinarySecurityToken>
      <ds:Signature>
        <!-- The SignedInfo and SignatureValue elements in Figure 26.8 appear here. -->
        <KeyInfo>
          <wsse:SecurityTokenReference>
            <wsse:Reference URI="#X509Token"/>
          </wsse:SecurityTokenReference>
        </KeyInfo>
      </ds:Signature>
    </wsse:Security>
  <s:Header>
  <s:Body Id="MsgBody">
    <!-- The data being signed appears here -->
  </s:Body>
</s:Envelope>
```

The message might then be passed to another department that functions in a similar way, adding new information, signatures, and perhaps encryption. The new blocks should be prepended so that the order in which these operations have taken place is implicit in the order of the blocks, making it possible to reverse the operations at a later time. In addition, care should be taken if modifications to previously signed data are made.

An interesting security breach may be possible if an element that is embedded in a larger XML document and that uses globally defined namespace prefixes is signed. If the global information (that is not included in the signature) is tampered with, the meaning of the signed element might change even though its integrity is guaranteed by the signature. The problem can be avoided if the prefixes are declared within the signed element.

A `Timestamp` element can be included in a security header block to indicate to the receiver the freshness of the message. Alternatively, it might be used in detecting replay attacks. In that case it should be signed by the sender to prevent alteration.

The important thing to note about WS-Security is that it does not specify a particular security policy. Rather, it supplies a toolbox of mechanisms that an application can use to convey security-related information and thereby to construct a policy suitable to its needs.

26.14.3 SAML: Authentication, Authorization, and Single Sign-On

SAML (Security Assertion Markup Language)[15] addresses the issue of specifying and exchanging security-related data—called **statements**—in a loosely coupled environment. Statements currently fall into three categories:

1. **Authentication statement.** Describes an authentication event that happened sometime in the past. For example, Joe was authenticated using method M at time T.

2. **Attribute assertion.** Provides the value of an attribute that describes a particular subject. For example, the value of the attribute "department" associated with Joe is Accounting.

3. **Authorization decision statement.** Gives the result of an authorization decision concerning a particular subject. For example, Joe is authorized to take action A with respect to resource R.

A number of use cases have been identified which illustrate the role SAML can play. Some of these are illustrated in Figure 26.11. The single sign-on use case is shown in (a). The user is authenticated at *site* 1, and an authentication statement is created. Later the user contacts *site* 2 and uses the statement to avoid re-authenticating. An authorization use case is shown in (b). The user requests access to a resource at *site* 1, and authorization decisions are made at *site* 2. *Site* 1 requests an authorization decision statement from *site* 2. Since *site* 2 is making decisions about *site* 1's resources and understands its access modes, it is likely that the two sites are in the same security domain. In (c) *site* 1 invokes a transaction at *site* 2 on behalf of the user. For example, *site* 1 might maintain credit information about the user that it passes to *site* 2 in an attribute statement.

In all of these cases, SAML distinguishes between the **asserting party**, the party that creates the statement, and the **relying party**, the party that uses the statement. The asserting party is referred to as a **SAML authority**.

To get a better idea of how SAML works, look at Figure 26.12. It shows a SAML **assertion**, which is an element that contains one or more SAML statements all pertaining to a single subject. In this case. a single authentication statement is included. In addition to the statements themselves, the assertion provides a number of other items of information. The time the assertion was constructed is an attribute of the Assertion element. The SAML authority that created the assertion is given as an Issuer child. The Subject child identifies the entity the statements describe:

---

[15] The discussion is based on the description of SAML V2.0 contained in *OASIS Draft 10,* April 2004

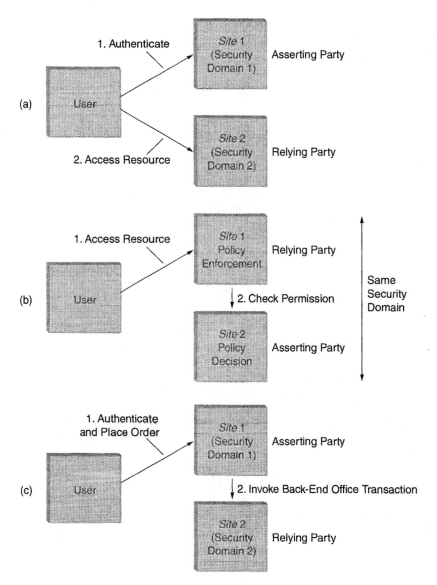

FIGURE 26.11 Use cases for SAML protocol: (a) single sign-on; (b) authorization; (c) invoking a transaction.

in this case, John Doe. The `Conditions` child specifies conditions on the use of the assertion: in this case, the time interval during which the assertion can be used.

Note that the `Signature` child contains the authority's signature. It guarantees the integrity of the assertion and allows the relying party to authenticate the authority using the authority's public key. A good question that you might ask at this

FIGURE 26.12 An example of a SAML authentication assertion.

```
<saml:Assertion
    AssertionID="ABCE-123"
    IssueInstant="2004-03-21T113:13:00-05:00"
    <!- other attributes go here -->
    <saml:Issuer> www.somecompany.com </saml:Issuer>
    <ds:Signature> ... </ds:Signature>
    <saml:Subject>
        <saml:NameIdentifier> John Doe </saml:NameIdentifier>
        <saml:SubjectConfirmation>
            <saml:ConfirmationMethod> ... </saml:ConfirmationMethod>
            <saml:SubjectConfirmationData> ... </saml:SubjectConfirmationData>
        <saml:SubjectConfirmation>
    </saml:Subject>
    <saml:Conditions
        NotBefore="2004-03-21T113:13:00-05:00"
        NotAfter="2004-03-21T113:18:00-05:00"/>
    <saml:AuthenticationStatement
        AuthenticationMethod="urn:oasis:names:tc:SAML:1.0:am:password"
        AuthenticationInstant="2004-03-21T113:13:00-05:00"/>
</saml:Assertion>
```

point is, how can a signature be contained within the element that it signs (such signatures are referred to as enveloped signatures)? That is, how can you compute the digest of the Assertion element without knowing the value of the signature that is contained within it? The solution to this problem lies in the use of a transform. The **enveloped signature transform** is used to delete the signature element from the assertion before computing the signature. We discussed this issue on page 1175.

In the example of Figure 26.12, the assertion contains an authentication statement. The statement specifies the time at which authentication took place and the method that was used to do the job. The method is outside the scope of SAML and is specified by a URI. Authentication might or might not have taken place at the authority's site. An additional (optional) child element is provided to specify the location. Note that SAML itself is not doing the authentication; an assertion simply reports on an authentication event that occurred sometime in the past.

One additional feature is needed if assertions are to be useful The relying party receives the assertion from a sender. For example, the assertion might state that its subject has been authenticated in some way. How does the relying party know that the sender represents that subject? The assertion might have been copied by an intruder who is now trying to use it to masquerade as the subject.

The additional feature is provided by the SubjectConfirmation child of the Subject element. This child element provides information that can be used by the relying party to confirm that the assertion was received from a sender representing the subject and that therefore the relying party can use the assertion in satisfying the sender's request. The ConfirmationMethod identifies the method that the relying party can use for this purpose, and the SubjectConfirmationData optionally provides some information that the method will use. For example, the data might be the public key of the subject, and the method might involve requiring the sender to demonstrate knowledge of the corresponding private key (by some specified interchange of encrypted messages using those keys).

The SubjectConfirmation element is required, independent of the type of SAML statements contained in the assertion. If the protocol is being used for single sign-on, however, you might legitimately ask if the required confirmation does not defeat the purpose of single sign-on since the subject is being asked to confirm its identity at each site despite the fact that the assertion already contains an authentication statement. The answer to this question is twofold. First, the same confirmation procedure is used at all sites so that the problem of requiring the subject to authenticate itself differently at each site—possibly with different passwords—is avoided. Hence, once the authentication statement has been created, subsequent confirmations can be hidden below the application level. This is also the approach used by Kerberos, where the use of the ticket-granting ticket need not be part of the application. Secondly, the confirmation method need not be a complete authentication protocol. In the above example, the sender does not have to present a certificate. The relying party has the authentication statement and hence already knows the association between the public key and the subject's identity. It can simply request the sending site to demonstrate knowledge of the private key.

SAML envisions that there will ultimately be **SAML Authority sites** on the Web: Authentication Authorities, Authorization Authorities, and Assertion Authorities, among others. Authority sites will act as trusted third parties that maintain repositories of authentication, authorization, and attribute assertions. For example, a site such as Yahoo, MSN, or AOL could act as an authentication authority with various servers acting as relying parties.

A site can send an assertion it has created to an appropriate Authority, which can store it in its repository. For example, when a user is authenticated by some site, the site can send the authentication assertion to an Authentication Authority. Later, other sites can query the Authentication Authority to obtain the assertion.

Alternatively, a client might authenticate itself with a vendor, who creates an authentication statement that it later sends to a supplier. After receiving the statement, the supplier might query an Authorization or Attribute Authority to obtain additional information about a customer.

As with the other proposed standards introduced in this section, we have discussed only a small fraction of the SAML protocol. A complete description would include SAML bindings (in particular, the conventions for embedding assertions in SOAP messages) and SAML protocols (the conventions used for communicating assertions). We refer the interested reader to the latest SAML document available on the Web. (See Bibliographic Notes.)

Discussion: single sign-on. Why do we need SAML single sign-on? A number of approaches to single sign-on already exist. For example, Passport centralizes authentication in an authentication server, a trusted third party that uses passwords for authentication. The server places and retrieves an encrypted cookie containing authentication information at the user's site and uses the cookie to avoid re-authentication each time the user accesses a new server.

In contrast, SAML does not actually do authentication and hence does not enforce a particular authentication procedure. A server can use an arbitrary procedure and then create an authentication statement that identifies the procedure used. The statement is passed in an assertion directly from one server to another, and the second server can judge from the assertion whether to trust the authentication done by the first. If not, it performs its own authentication. Hence, a trusted third party is not required.

Kerberos is similar to Passport in that it uses a trusted third party and stores tickets—which roughly correspond to encrypted cookies—at user sites. It is an integrated protocol that implements two-way authentication, key distribution, and encryption. SAML does not do any of these things. It simply provides an XML framework within which other protocols can be used to provide authentication.

Finally, SSL does not support single sign-on. If a client has a certificate, it supports client authentication as well as server authentication. However, a server that has authenticated a client cannot transfer that authentication to a different server. This is one of the use cases for which SAML was designed.

BIBLIOGRAPHIC NOTES

Much of the material in this chapter is well covered by [Stallings 1999]. The concept of public-key cryptography was first presented by [Diffie and Hellman 1976], but almost all public-key cryptography systems are based on the RSA algorithm [Rivest et al. 1978]. [Schneier 1995] does a good job of describing the mathematics underlying the RSA algorithm and of many other cryptographic algorithms and protocols. Like public-key cryptography, the concept of digital signatures was introduced in [Diffie and Hellman 1976], but, again, most digital-signature systems are based on the RSA algorithm [Rivest et al. 1978] or on other algorithms developed specifically for signatures and not appropriate for encryption. The Kerberos system is discussed in [Steiner et al. 1988; Neuman and Ts'o 1994] and forms the basis of security as provided in DCE [Hu 1995].

Descriptions of the SET and SSL protocols can be found at appropriate sites on the Web, which at publication time were [Netscape 2000] for SSL and [VISA 2000] for SET. The NetBill system was introduced in [Cox et al. 1995]. [Chaum et al. 1988] introduced the Ecash protocol and blind signatures. The escrow agent protocol is based on the i-Escrow system available through eBay and described at publication time on its Web site [i-Escrow 2000].

Material on Web security can be found on the Web sites of the standards committees or the companies developing them. For XML Encryption: *http://www.w3*

.org/TR/xmlenc-core/. For XML Signature: *http://www.w3.org/TR/xmldsig-core/*. For WS-Security: *http://www.oasis-open.org/committees/tc_home.php?wg_abbrev=wss*. For SAML: *http://www.oasis-open.org/committees/tc_home.php?wg_abbrev=security*.

EXERCISES

26.1 Discuss some security issues involved in executing transactions over the Internet.

26.2 Anyone who uses a computer keyboard should be able to easily solve the following simple substitution cipher:

Rsvj ;ryyrt od vjsmhrf yp yjr pmr pm oyd tohjy pm yjr lrunpstf/

26.3 Explain why, in general, short encryption keys are less secure than long keys.

26.4 Why is it necessary, in the Kerberos protocol, to include S in the message sent from KS to C (i.e., message $M2$)? Describe an attack that an intruder can use if S is not included.

26.5 Explain how timestamps are used to defend against a replay attack in a security protocol.

26.6 Explain how nonces are used to increase security when encrypting messages that are short or that include fields for which the plaintext might be known to an intruder.

26.7 In a system using public-key cryptography, site B wants to fool C by impersonating A. B waits until A requests to communicate with B. A does this by sending an "I want to communicate" message to B, stating its name (A) and encrypted with B's public key. Then B springs the trap. It sends an "I want to communicate" message to C claiming it is A and encrypted with C's public key. To ensure that it is actually communicating with A, C replies (to B) with a message obtained by encrypting a large random number, N, with A's public key. If C gets a response containing $N + 1$ encrypted with C's public key, it would like to conclude that the responder is A because only A could have decrypted C's message. C gets such a response. However, this conclusion is wrong because the response comes from B. Explain how this could have happened. (*Hint:* The protocol can be corrected if the encrypted text of each message includes the name of the sender.)

26.8 Suppose an intruder obtains a copy of a merchant's certificate.

a. Explain why the intruder cannot simply use that certificate and pretend he is the merchant.

b. Explain why the intruder cannot replace the merchant's public key with his own in the certificate.

26.9 Suppose that you use the SSL protocol and connect to a merchant site, M. The site sends you M's certificate. When the SSL protocol completes, how can you be sure that the new session key can be known only to M (perhaps an intruder has sent you a copy of M's certificate)? Can you be sure that you are connected to M?

26.10 Using your local Internet Browser

a. Describe how you can tell when you are connected to a site that is using the SSL protocol.

    b. Suppose you are connected to a site that is using the SSL protocol. Describe how you can determine the name of the CA that supplied the certificate used by that site.

    c. Determine how many bits are in the keys that your browser uses for SSL encryption.

26.11 Suppose that you obtained a certificate of your own. Explain how you could use that certificate to deal with situations in which an intruder might steal your credit card number.

26.12 Suppose that an intruder puts a virus on your computer that alters your browser. Describe two different ways that the intruder could then impersonate some server site S that you might attempt to communicate with—even though you use the SSL protocol—and obtain your credit card number.

26.13 A merchant using the SSL protocol (without SET) might implement a credit card transaction as follows: The customer purchases an item, and the merchant asks him to send his credit card information encrypted using the session key established with the SSL protocol. When the merchant receives that information, she initiates a separate transaction with the credit card company to have the purchase approved. When that transaction commits, the merchant commits the transaction with the customer.

    Explain the similarities and differences of this protocol to SET.

26.14 Assume that the merchant in the SET protocol is dishonest. Explain why he cannot cheat the customer.

26.15 Explain why a trusted third party is used in the certified delivery protocol.

26.16 Describe a restart procedure that the merchant's computer can use to deal with crashes during the SET protocol.

26.17 Explain why MD_2 in the SET protocol (Section 26.11) must be a part of the dual signature.

26.18 Explain why a forger could not simply submit an arbitrary random number as a token in the electronic cash protocol.

26.19 Assume that, in the anonymous electronic cash protocol, the bank is honest but the customer and the merchant might not be.

    a. After receiving the tokens from the bank, the customer later claims that she never received them. Explain what the bank should then do and why it is correct.

    b. After receiving the message containing the purchase order and the tokens from the customer, the merchant claims never to have received the message. Explain what the customer should do and why.

26.20 Describe the methods used in each of the following protocols to prevent a replay attack:

    a. Kerberos authentication

    b. SET

    c. Electronic cash

Bibliography

Abiteboul, S., Buneman, P., and Suciu, D. (2000). *Data on the Web*. Morgan Kaufmann, San Francisco.

Abiteboul, S., Hull, R., and Vianu, V. (1995). *Foundations of Databases*. Addison-Wesley, Boston, MA.

Abiteboul, S., and Kanellakis, P. (1998). Object identity as a query language primitive. *Journal of the ACM* **45**(5): 798–842.

Abiteboul, S., Quass, D., McHugh, J., Widom, J., and Wiener, J. (1997). The Lorel query language for semistructured data. *International Journal on Digital Libraries* **1**(1): 68–88.

Adam, N., Atluri, V., and Huang, W. (1998). Modeling and analysis of workflows using Petri nets. *Journal of Intelligent Information Systems* **10**(2): 131–158.

Agrawal, D., Bernstein, A., Gupta, P., and Sengupta, S. (1987). Distributed optimistic concurrency control with reduced rollback. *Distributed Computing* **2**(1): 45–59.

Agrawal, R., Imielinski, T., and Swami, A. (1993). Database mining: A performance perspective. *IEEE Transactions on Knowledge and Data Engineering* **5**(6): 914–925.

Agrawal, S., Agrawal, R., Deshpande, P., Gupta, A., Naughton, J., Ramakrishnan, R., and Sarawagi, S. (1996). On the computation of multidimensional aggregates. *Proceedings of the International Conference on Very Large Data Bases (VLDB)*, Mombai, India, 506–521.

Aho, A., and Ullman, J. (1979). Universality of data retrieval languages. *ACM Symposium on Principles of Programming Languages (POPL)*, 110–120.

Alagic, S. (1999). Type-checking OQL queries in the ODMG type systems. *ACM Transactions on Database Systems* **24**(3): 319–360.

Alonso, G., Agrawal, D., Abbadi, A. E., Kamath, M., Günthör, R., and Mohan, C. (1996). Advanced transaction models in workflow contexts. *Proceedings of the International Conference on Data Engineering (ICDE)*, New Orleans, LA, 574–581.

Alonso, G., Agrawal, D., Abbadi, A. E., and Mohan., C. (1997). Functionality and limitations of current workflow management systems. *IEEE-Expert, Special Issue on Cooperative Information Systems* **1**(9).

Andrade, J. M., Carges, M. T., Dwyer, T. J., and Felts, S. D. (1996). *The TUXEDO System, Software for Constructing and Managing Distributed Business Applications*. Addison-Wesley, Boston, MA.

Apt, K., Blair, H., and Walker, A. (1988). Towards a theory of declarative knowledge. In *Foundations of Deductive Databases and Logic Programming*, ed. J. Minker. Morgan Kaufmann, San Francisco, 89–148.

Arisawa, H., Moriya, K., and Miura, T. (1983). Operations and the properties of non-first-normal-form relational databases. *Proceedings of the International Conference on Very Large Data Bases (VLDB)*, Florence, 197–204.

Armstrong, W. (1974). Dependency structures of database relations. *IFIP Congress*, Stockholm, 580–583.

Astrahan, M., Blasgen, M., Chamberlin, D., Eswaran, K., Gray, J., Griffiths, P., King, W., Lorie, R., McJones, P., Mehl, J., Putzolu, G., Traiger, I., and Watson, V. (1976). System R: A relational approach to database management. *ACM Transactions on Database Systems* 1(2): 97–137.

Astrahan, M., Blasgen, M., Gray, J., King, W., Lindsay, B., Lorie, R., Mehl, J., Price, T., Selinger, P., Schkolnick, M., Traiger, D. S. I., and Yost, R. (1981). A history and evaluation of System R. *Communications of the ACM* 24(10): 632–646.

Attie, P., Singh, M., Emerson, E., Sheth, A., and Rusinkiewicz, M. (1996). Scheduling workflows by enforcing intertask dependencies. *Distributed Systems Engineering Journal* 3(4): 222–238.

Attie, P., Singh, M., Sheth, A., and Rusinkiewicz, M. (1993). Specifying and enforcing intertask dependencies. *Proceedings of the International Conference on Very Large Data Bases (VLDB)*, Dublin, 134–145.

Atzeni, P., and Antonellis, V. D. (1993). *Relational Database Theory*. Benjamin-Cummings, San Francisco.

Avron, A., and Hirshfeld, J. (1994). Query evaluation, relative safety, and domain independence in first-order databases. *Methods of Logic in Computer Science* 1: 261–278.

Bancilhon, F., Delobel, C., and Kanellakis, P., eds. (1990). *Building an Object-Oriented Database System: The Story of O2*. Morgan Kaufmann, San Francisco.

Bancilhon, F., and Spyratos, N. (1981). Update semantics of relational views. *ACM Transactions on Database Systems* 6(4): 557–575.

Batini, C., Ceri, S., and Navathe, S. (1992). *Database Design: An Entity-Relationship Approach*. Benjamin-Cummings, San Francisco.

Bayer, R., and McCreight, E. (1972). Organization and maintenance of large ordered indices. *Acta Informatica* 1(3): 173–189.

Beeri, C., and Bernstein, P. (1979). Computational problems related to the design of normal form relational schemes. *ACM Transactions on Database Systems* 4(1): 30–59.

Beeri, C., Bernstein, P., and Goodman, N. (1978). A sophisticate's introduction to database normalization theory. *Proceedings of the International Conference on Very Large Data Bases (VLDB)*, San Mateo, CA, 113–124.

Beeri, C., Bernstein, P., and Goodman, N. (1989). A model for concurrency in nested transaction systems. *Journal of the ACM* 36(2): 230–269.

Beeri, C., Bernstein, P., Goodman, N., Lai, M.-Y., and Shasha, D. (1983). A concurrency control theory for nested transactions. *Proceedings of the 2nd ACM Symposium on Principles of Distributed Computing*, Montreal, Canada, 45–62.

Beeri, C., Fagin, R., and Howard, J. (1977). A complete axiomatization for functional and multivalued dependencies in database relations. *Proceedings of the ACM SIGMOD International Conference on Management of Data*, Toronto, Canada, 47–61.

Beeri, C., and Kifer, M. (1986a). Elimination of intersection anomalies from database schemes. *Journal of the ACM* 33(3): 423–450.

Beeri, C., and Kifer, M. (1986b). An integrated approach to logical design of relational database schemes. *ACM Transactions on Database Systems* 11(2): 134–158.

Beeri, C., and Kifer, M. (1987). A theory of intersection anomalies in relational database schemes. *Journal of the ACM* 34(3): 544–577.

Beeri, C., Mendelson, A., Sagiv, Y., and Ullman, J. (1981). Equivalence of relational database schemes. *SIAM Journal of Computing* 10(2): 352–370.

Bell, D., and Grimson, J. (1992). *Distributed Database Systems*. Addison-Wesley, Boston, MA.

Berenson, H., Bernstein, P., Gray, J., Melton, J., O'Neil, E., and O'Neil, P. (1995). A critique of ANSI SQL isolation levels. *Proceedings of the ACM SIGMOD International Conference on Management of Data*, San Jose, CA, 1–10.

Berg, C., and Virginia, C. (2000). *Advanced Java 2 Development for Enterprise Applications*, 2nd ed. Prentice Hall, Englewood Cliffs, NJ.

Bernstein, A. J., Gerstl, D., Leung, W.-H., and Lewis, P. M. (1998). Design and performance of an assertional concurrency control system. *Proceedings of the International Conference on Data Engineering* (ICDE), Orlando, FL, 436–445.

Bernstein, A. J., Gerstl, D., and Lewis, P. (1999). Concurrency control for step decomposed transactions. *Information Systems* 24(8): 673–698.

Bernstein, A. J., Gerstl, D., Lewis, P., and Lu, S. (1999). Using transaction semantics to increase performance. *International Workshop on High Performance Transaction Systems*, Pacific Grove, CA, 26–29.

Bernstein, A. J., and Lewis, P. M. (1996). High-performance transaction systems using transaction semantics. *Distributed and Parallel Databases* 4(1).

Bernstein, A. J., Lewis, P., and Lu, S. (2000). Semantic conditions for correctness at different isolation levels. *Proceedings of the International Conference on Data Engineering*, San Diego, CA, 507–566.

Bernstein, P. (1976). Synthesizing third normal form from functional dependencies. *ACM Transactions on Database Systems* 1(4): 277–298.

Bernstein, P., and Chiu, D. (1981). Using semi-joins to solve relational queries. *Journal of the ACM* 28(1): 28–40.

Bernstein, P., and Goodman, N. (1983). Multiversion concurrency control—Theory and algorithms. *ACM Transactions on Database Systems* 8(4): 465–483.

Bernstein, P., Goodman, N., Wong, E., Reeve, C., and Rothnie, J. (1981). Query processing in a system for distributed databases (SDD-1). *ACM Transactions on Database Systems* 6(4): 602–625.

Bernstein, P., Hadzilacos, V., and Goodman, N. (1987). *Concurrency Control and Recovery in Database Systems*. Addison-Wesley, Boston, MA.

Bernstein, P., and Newcomer, E. (1997). *Principles of Transaction Processing*. Morgan Kaufmann, San Francisco.

Birrell, A., and Nelson, B. (1984). Implementing remote procedure calls. *ACM Transactions on Computer Systems* 2(1): 39–59.

Biskup, J., Menzel, R., and Polle, T. (1996). Transforming an entity-relationship schema into object-oriented database schemas. In *Advances in Databases and Information Systems, Workshops in Computing*, eds. J. Eder and L. Kalinichenko. Springer-Verlag, Moscow, Russia, 109–136.

Biskup, J., Menzel, R., Polle, T., and Sagiv, Y. (1996). Decomposition of relationships through pivoting. *Proceedings of the 15th International Conference on Conceptual Modeling*. In vol. 1157 of *Lecture Notes in Computer Science*. Springer-Verlag, Heidelberg, Germany, 28–41.

Biskup, J., and Polle, T. (2000a). *Constraints in Object-Oriented Databases* (manuscript).

Biskup, J., and Polle, T. (2000b). Decomposition of database classes under path functional dependencies and onto constraints. *Proceedings of the Foundations of Information and Knowledge-Base Systems*. In vol. 1762 of *Lecture Notes in Computer Science*. Springer-Verlag, Heidelberg, Germany, 31–49.

Blaha, M., and Premerlani, W. (1998). *Object-Oriented Modeling and Design for Database Applications*. Prentice Hall, Englewood Cliffs, NJ.

Blakeley, J., and Martin, N. (1990). Join index, materialized view, and hybrid-hash join: A performance analysis. *Proceedings of the International Conference on Data Engineering (ICDE)*, Los Angeles, 256–263.

Blasgen, M., and Eswaran, K. (1977). Storage access in relational databases. *IBM Systems Journal* **16**(4): 363–378.

Bonner, A. (1999). Workflow, transactions, and datalog. *ACM SIGACT-SIGMOD-SIGART Symposium on Principles of Database Systems (PODS)*, Philadelphia, PA, 294–305.

Booch, G. (1994). *Object-oriented Analysis and Design with Applications*. Addison-Wesley, Boston, MA.

Booch, G., Rumbaugh, J., and Jacobson, I. (1999). *The Unified Modeling Language User Guide*. Addison-Wesley, Boston, MA.

Bourret, R. (2000). Namespace myths exploded. *http://www.xml.com/pub/a/2000/03/08/namespaces/index.html*.

Bradley, N. (2000a). *The XML Companion*. Addison-Wesley, Boston, MA.

Bradley, N. (2000b). *The XSL Companion*. Addison-Wesley, Boston, MA.

Bray, T., Hollander, D., and Layman A. (1999). Namespaces in XML. *http://www.w3.org/TR/1999/REC-xml-names-19990114/*.

Breiman, L., Freidman, J. J., Olshen, R. A., and Stone, C. L. (1984). *Classification and Regression Trees Technical Report*. Wadsworth International, Monterey, CA.

Breitbart, Y., Garcia-Molina, H., and Silberschatz, A. (1992). Overview of multidatabase transaction management. *VLDB Journal* **1**(2): 181–240.

Bukhres, O., and Kueshn, E., eds. (1995). *Distributed and Parallel Databases—An International Journal*, Special Issue on Software Support for Workflow Management.

Buneman, P., Davidson, S., Hillebrand, G., and Suciu, D. (1996). A query language and optimization techniques for unstructured data. *Proceedings of the ACM SIGMOD International Conference on Management of Data*, Montreal, Canada, 505–516.

Cattell, R. (1994). *Object Database Management* (rev. ed.). Addison-Wesley, Boston, MA.

Cattell, R., and Barry, D., eds. (2000). *The Object Database Standard: ODMG 3.0*. Morgan Kaufmann, San Francisco.

Ceri, S., Negri, M., and Pelagatti, G. (1982). Horizontal partitioning in database design. *Proceedings of the International ACM SIGMOD Conference on Management of Data*, Orlando, FL, 128–136.

Ceri, S., and Pelagatti, G. (1984). *Distributed Databases: Principles and Systems*. McGraw-Hill, New York.

Chamberlin, D., Robie, J., and Florescu, D. (2000). Quilt: An XML query language for heterogeneous data sources. In *Lecture Notes in Computer Science*. Springer-Verlag, Heidelberg, Germany. *http://www.almaden.ibm.com/cs/people/chamberlin/quilt_lncs.pdf*.

Chang, S., and Cheng, W. (1980). A methodology for structured database decomposition. *IEEE-TSE* **6**(2): 205–218.

Chaudhuri, S. (1998). An overview of query optimization in relational databases. *ACM SIGACT-SIGMOD-SIGART Symposium on Principles of Database Systems (PODS)*, Seattle, 34–43.

Chaudhuri, S., and Dayal, U. (1997). An overview of data warehousing and OLAP technology. *SIGMOD Record* **26**(1): 65–74.

Chaudhuri, S., Krishnamurthy, R., Potamianos, S., and Shim, K. (1995). Optimizing queries with materialized views. *Proceedings of the International Conference on Data Engineering (ICDE)*, Taipei, Taiwan, 190–200.

Chaum, D., Fiat, A., and Noar, M. (1988). Untraceable electronic cash. *Advances in Cryptology: Crypto'88 Proceedings*. In *Lecture Notes in Computer Science*. Springer-Verlag, Heidelberg, Germany, 319–327.

Chen, I.-M., Hull, R., and McLeod, D. (1995). An execution model for limited ambiguity rules and its application to derived data update. *ACM Transactions on Database Systems* **20**(4): 365–413.

Chen, P. (1976). The entity-relationship model—Towards a unified view of data. *ACM Transactions on Database Systems* **1**(1): 9–36.

Chrysanthis, P., and Ramaritham, K. (1990). ACTA: A framework for specifying and reasoning about transaction structure and behavior. *Proceedings of the ACM SIGMOD International Conference on Management of Data*, Atlantic City, NJ, 194–205.

CLIPS (2003). CLIPS: A tool for building expert systems. *http://www.ghg.net/clips/CLIPS.html*.

Cochrane, R., Pirahesh, H., and Mattos, N. (1996). Integrating triggers and declarative constraints in SQL database systems. *Proceedings of the International Conference on Very Large Data Bases (VLDB)*, Bombay, India, 567–578.

Codd, E. (1970). A relational model of data for large shared data banks. *Communications of the ACM* **13**(6): 377–387.

Codd, E. (1972). Relational completeness of data base sublanguages. *Data Base Systems*. In vol. 6 of *Courant Computer Science Symposia Series*. Prentice Hall, Englewood Cliffs, NJ.

Codd, E. (1979). Extending the database relational model to capture more meaning. *ACM Transactions on Database Systems* **4**(4): 397–434.

Codd, E. (1990). *The Relational Model for Database Management, Version 2*. Addison-Wesley, Boston, MA.

Codd, E. (1995). Twelve rules for on-line analytic processing. *Computerworld*, April 13.

Copeland, G., and Maier, D. (1984). Making Smalltalk a database system. *Proceedings of the ACM SIGMOD International Conference on Management of Data*, Boston, 316–325.

Cosmadakis, S., and Papadimitriou, C. (1983). Updates of relational views. *ACM SIGACT-SIGMOD-SIGART Symposium on Principles of Database Systems (PODS)*, Atlanta, GA, 317–331.

Cox, B., Tygar, J., and Sirbu, M. (1995). Netbill security and transaction protocol. *Proceedings of the 1st USENIX Workshop on Electronic Commerce*, New York, vol. 1.

Date, C. (1992). Relational calculus as an aid to effective query formulation. In *Relational Database Writings*, eds. C. Date and H. Darwen. Addison-Wesley, Boston, MA.

Date, C., and Darwen, H. (1997). *A Guide to the SQL Standard*, 4th ed. Addison-Wesley, Boston, MA.

Davulcu, H., Kifer, M., Ramakrishnan, C. R., and Ramakrishnan, I. V. (1998). Logic based modeling and analysis of workflows. *ACM SIGACT-SIGMOD-SIGART Symposium on Principles of Database Systems (PODS)*, Seattle, WA, 25–33.

Deutsch, A., Fernandez, M., Florescu, D., Levy, A., and Suciu, D. (1998). XML-QL: A query language for XML. *Technical Report W3C. http://www.w3.org/TR/1998/NOTE-xml-ql-19980819/*.

Deutsch, A., Fernandez, M., and Suciu, D. (1999). Storing semistructured data with stored. *Proceedings of the ACM SIGMOD International Conference on Management of Data*, Philadelphia, PA, 431–442.

DeWitt, D., Katz, R., Olken, F., Shapiro, L., Stonebraker, M., and Wood, D. (1984). Implementation techniques for main-memory database systems. *Proceedings of the ACM SIGMOD International Conference on Management of Data*, Boston, 1–8.

Diffie, W., and Hellman, M. (1976). New directions in cryptography. *IEEE Transactions on Information Theory* IT-22(6): 644–654.

Di Paola, R. A. (1969). The recursive unsolvability of the decision problem for the class of definite formulas. *Journal of ACM* 16(2): 324–327.

DOM (2000). Document Object Model (DOM). *http://www.w3.org/DOM/*.

Eisenberg, A. (1996). New standard for stored procedures in SQL. *SIGMOD Record* 25(4): 81–88.

Elmagarmid, A., ed. (1992). *Database Transaction Models for Advanced Applications*. Morgan Kaufmann, San Francisco.

Elmagarmid, A., Leu, Y., Litwin, W., and Rusinkiewicz, M. (1990). A multidatabase transaction model for interbase. *Proceedings of the International Conference on Very Large Data Bases (VLDB)*, Brisbane, Australia, 507–518.

Eswaran, K., Gray, J., Lorie, R., and Traiger, I. (1976). The notions of consistency and predicate locks in a database system. *Communications of the ACM* 19(11): 624–633.

Fagin, R. (1977). Multivalued dependencies and a new normal form for relational databases. *ACM Transactions on Database Systems* 2(3): 262–278.

Fagin, R., Nievergelt, J., Pippenger, N., and Strong, H. (1979). Extendible hashing—A fast access method for dynamic files. *ACM Transactions on Database Systems* 4(3): 315–344.

Fayyad, U., Piatetsky-Shapiro, G., Smyth, P., and Uthurusamy, R., eds. (1996). *Advances in Knowledge Discovery and Data Mining*. The MIT Press, Cambridge, MA.

Fekete, A., Liarokapis, D., O'Neil, E., O'Neil, P., and Shasha, D. (2000). Making snapshot isolation serializable. *http://www.cs.umb.edu/ poneil/publist.html*.

Fekete, A., Lynch, N., Merritt, M., and Weihl, W. (1989). Commutativity-based locking for nested transactions. *Technical Report MIT/LCS/TM-370.b*. Laboratory for Computer Science, Massachusetts Institute of Technology, Cambridge, MA.

Flach, P. A., and Savnik, I. (1999). Database dependency discovery: A machine learning approach. *AI Communications* 12(3): 139–160.

Florescu, D., Deutsch, A., Levy, A., Suciu, D., and Fernandez, M. (1999). A query language for XML. *Proceedings of the Eighth International World Wide Web Conference*, Toronto, Canada.

Fowler, M., and Scott, K. (2003). *UML Distilled*, 3rd ed. Addison-Wesley, Boston, MA.

Frohn, J., Lausen, G., and Uphoff, H. (1994). Access to objects by path expressions and rules. *Proceedings of the International Conference on Very Large Data Bases (VLDB)*, Santiago, Chile, 273–284.

Fuh, Y.-C., Dessloch, S., Chen, W., Mattos, N., Tran, B., Lindsay, B., DeMichiel, L., Rielau, S., and Mannhaupt, D. (1999). Implementation of SQL3 structured types with inheritance and value substitutability. *Proceedings of the International Conference on Very Large Data Bases (VLDB)*, Edinburgh, Scotland, 565–574.

Garcia-Molina, H., Gawlick, D., Klien, J., Kleissner, K., and Salem, K. (1991). Modeling long-running activities as nested Sagas. *Quarterly Bulletin of the IEEE Computer Society Technical Committee on Data Engineering* 14(1): 14–18.

Garcia-Molina, H., and Salem, K. (1987). Sagas. *Proceedings of the ACM SIGMOD International Conference on Management of Data*, San Francisco, 249–259.

Garcia-Molina, H., Ullman, J., and Widom, J. (2000). *Database System Implementation*, Prentice Hall, Englewood Cliffs, NJ.

Georgakopoulos, D., Hornick, M., Krychniak, P., and Manola, F. (1994). Specification and management of extended transactions in a programmable transaction environment. *Proceedings of the International Conference on Data Engineering (ICDE)*, Houston, 462–473.

Georgakopoulos, D., Hornick, M., and Sheth, A. (1995). An overview of workflow management: From process modeling to infrastructure for automation. *Journal on Distributed and Parallel Database Systems* 3(2): 119–153.

Gifford, D. (1979). Weighted voting for replicated data. *Proceedings of the ACM 7th Symposium on Operating Systems Principles*, Pacific Grove, CA, 150–162.

Gogola, M., Herzig, R., Conrad, S., Denker, G., and Vlachantonis, N. (1993). Integrating the E-R approach in an object-oriented environment. *Proceedings of the 12th International Conference on the Entity-Relationship Approach*, Arlington, TX, 376–389.

Gottlob, G., Paolini, P., and Zicari, R. (1988). Properties and update semantics of consistent views. *ACM Transactions on Database Systems* 13(4): 486–524.

Graefe, G. (1993). Query evaluation techniques for large databases. *ACM Computing Surveys* 25(2): 73–170.

Gray, J. (1978). Notes on database operating systems. *Operating Systems: An Advanced Course*. In vol. 60 of *Lecture Notes in Computer Science*, Springer-Verlag, Berlin, 393–481.

Gray, J. (1981). The transaction concept: Virtues and limitations. *Proceedings of the International Conference on Very Large Data Bases (VLDB)*, Cannes, 144–154.

Gray, J., Chaudhuri, S., Bosworth, A., Layman, A., Reichart, D., and Venkatrao, M. (1997). Data cube: A relational aggregation operator generalizing group-by, cross-tab, and sub-totals. In *Data Mining and Knowledge Discovery*, eds. Fayyad et al., The MIT Press, Cambridge, MA.

Gray, J., Laurie, R., Putzolu, G., and Traiger, I. (1976). Granularity of locks and degrees of consistency in a shared database. *Modeling in Data Base Management Systems*, Elsevier, North Holland.

Gray, J., McJones, P., and Blasgen, M. (1981). The recovery manager of the System R database manager. *Computer Surveys* 13(2): 223–242.

Gray, J., and Reuter, A. (1993). *Transaction Processing: Concepts and Techniques*. Morgan Kaufmann, San Francisco.

Griffiths-Selinger, P., and Adiba, M. (1980). Access path selection in distributed database management systems. *Proceedings of the International Conference on Data Bases*, Aberdeen, Scotland, 204–215.

Griffiths-Selinger, P., Astrahan, M., Chamberlin, D., Lorie, R., and Price, T. (1979). Access path selection in a relational database system. *Proceedings of the ACM SIGMOD International Conference on Management of Data*, Boston, 23–34.

Gulutzan, P., and Pelzer, T. (1999). *SQL-99 Complete, Really*. R&D Books, Gilroy, CA.

Gupta, A., and Mumick, I. (1995). Maintenance of materialized views: Problems, techniques, and applications. *Data Engineering Bulletin* 18(2): 3–18.

Gupta, A., Mumick, I., and Ross, K. (1995). Adapting materialized views after redefinitions. *Proceedings of the ACM SIGMOD International Conference on Management of Data*, San Jose, CA, 211–222.

Gupta, A., Mumick, I., and Subrahmanian, V. (1993). Maintaining views incrementally. *Proceedings of the ACM SIGMOD International Conference on Management of Data*, Washington, DC, 157–166.

Hadzilacos, V. (1983). An operational model for database system reliability. *SIGACT-SIGMOD-SIGART Symposium on Principles of Database Systems (PODS)*, Atlanta, 244–256.

Hadzilacos, V., and Papadimitriou, C. (1985). Algorithmic aspects of multiversion concurrency control. *SIGACT-SIGMOD-SIGART Symposium on Principles of Database Systems (PODS)*, Portland, OR, 96–104.

Haerder, T., and Reuter, A. (1983). Principles of transaction-oriented database recovery. *ACM Computing Surveys* 15(4): 287–317.

Hall, M. (2000). *Core Servlets and JavaServer Pages (JSP)*. Prentice Hall, Englewood Cliffs, NJ.

Han, J., and Kamber, M. (2001). *Data Mining: Concepts and Techniques*. Morgan Kaufmann, San Francisco.

Hand, D. J., Mannila, H., and Smyth, P. (2001) *Principles of Data Mining*. MIT Press, Cambridge, MA.

Harinarayan, V., Rajaraman, A., and Ullman, J. (1996). Implementing data cubes efficiently. *Proceedings of the ACM SIGMOD International Conference on Management of Data*, Montreal, Canada, 205–216.

Harrison, G. (2001) *Oracle SQL: High-Performance Tuning*, 2nd ed. Prentice Hall, Upper Saddle River, NJ.

Henning, M., and Vinoski, S. (1999). *Advanced CORBA Programming with C++*. Addison-Wesley, Boston, MA.

Hsu, M. (1995). Letter from the special issues editor. *Quarterly Bulletin of the IEEE Computer Society Technical Committee on Data Engineering,* Special Issue on Workflow Systems. 18(1): 2–3.

Hu, W. (1995). *DCE Security Programming*. O'Reilly and Associates, Sebastopol, CA.

Huhtala, Y., Karkkainen, J., Porkka, P., and Toivonen, H. (1999). TANE: An efficient algorithm for discovery of functional and approximate dependencies. *The Computer Journal* 42(2): 100–111.

Hull, R., Llirbat, F., Simon, E., Su, J., Dong, G., Kumar, B., and Zhou, G. (1999). Declarative workflows that support easy modification and dynamic browsing. *Proceedings of the ACM International Joint Conference on Work Activities Coordination and Collaboration (WACC)*, San Francisco, 69–78.

Hunter, J., and Crawford, W. (1998). *Java Servlet Programming*. O'Reilly and Associates, Sebastopol, CA.

IBM (1991). System network architecture (SNA) logical unit 6.2 (LU6.2): Transaction programmer's reference manual for LU6.2. *Technical Report GC30-3084*. IBM, White Plains, NY.

i-Escrow (2000). i-Escrow. *http://www.iescrow.com*.

ILOG (2003). ILOG JRules. *http://www.ilog.com/products/jrules/*.

Ioannidis, Y. (1996). Query optimization. *ACM Computing Surveys* 28(1): 121–123.

Ito, M., and Weddell, G. (1994). Implication problems for functional constraints on databases supporting complex objects. *Journal of Computer and System Sciences* 49(3): 726–768.

Jacobson, I., Christerson, M., Jonsson, P., and Övergaard, G. (1992). *Object-Oriented Software Engineering: A Use Case Driven Approach*. Addison-Wesley, Boston, MA.

Jaeschke, G., and Schek, H.-J. (1982). Remarks on the algebra of non-first-normal-form-relations. *ACM SIGACT-SIGMOD-SIGART Symposium on Principles of Database Systems (PODS)*, Los Angeles, 124–138.

Jajodia, S., and Kerschberg, L., eds. (1997). *Advanced Transaction Models and Architectures*, Kluwer Academic Publishers, Dordrecht, Netherlands.

Jess (2003). The Rule Engine for the Java Platform. *http://herzberg.ca.sandia.gov/jess/*.

Kamath, M., and Ramamritham, K. (1996). Correctness issues in workflow management. *Distributed Systems Engineering Journal* 3(4): 213–221.

Kanellakis, P. (1990). Elements of relational database theory. In *Handbook of Theoretical Computer Science*, vol. B, *Formal Models and Semantics*, ed. J. V. Leeuwen. Elsevier, Amsterdam, 1073–1156.

Kantola, M., Mannila, H., Raäihä, K.-J., and Siirtola, H. (1992). Discovering functional and inclusion dependencies in relational databases. *International Journal of Intelligent Systems* 7(7): 591–607.

Kay, M. (2000). *XSLT Programmer's Reference*. Wrox Press, Paris.

Keller, A. (1985). Algorithms for translating view updates to database updates for views involving selections, projections, and joins. *ACM SIGACT-SIGMOD-SIGART Symposium on Principles of Database Systems (PODS)*, Portland, OR, 154–163.

Khoshafian, S., and Buckiewicz, M. (1995). *Introduction to Groupware, Workflow, and Workgroup Computing*. John Wiley & Sons, New York.

Kifer, M. (1988). On safety, domain independence, and capturability of database queries. *Proceedings of the 3rd International Conference on Data and Knowledge Bases*, Jerusalem, Israel, 405–415.

Kifer, M., Bernstein, A. J., and Lewis, P. M. (2004). *Databases and Transaction Processing: An Application-Oriented Approach*. Addison-Wesley, Boston, MA.

Kifer, M., Kim, W., and Sagiv, Y. (1992). Querying object-oriented databases. *Proceedings of the ACM SIGMOD International Conference on Management of Data*, Washington, DC, 393–402.

Kifer, M., and Lausen, G. (1989). F-Logic: A higher-order language for reasoning about objects, inheritance and schema. *Proceedings of the ACM SIGMOD International Conference on Management of Data*, Portland, OR, 134–146.

Kifer, M., Lausen, G., and Wu, J. (1995). Logical foundations of object-oriented and frame-based languages. *Journal of the ACM* **42**(4): 741–843.

Kitsuregawa, M., Tanaka, H., and Moto-oka, T. (1983). Application of hash to database machine and its architecture. *New Generation Computing* **1**(1): 66–74.

Knuth, D. (1973). *The Art of Computer Programming: Vol III, Sorting and Searching*, 1st ed., Addison-Wesley, Boston, MA.

Knuth, D. (1998). *The Art of Computer Programming: Vol III, Sorting and Searching*, 3rd ed., Addison-Wesley, Boston, MA.

Korth, H., Levy, E., and Silberschatz, A. (1990). A formal approach to recovery by compensating transactions. *Proceedings of the International Conference on Very Large Data Bases*, Brisbane, Australia, 95–106.

Kung, H., and Robinson, J. (1981). On optimistic methods for concurrency control. *ACM Transactions on Database Systems* **6**(2): 213–226.

Lacroix, M., and Pirotte, A. (1977). Domain-oriented relational languages. *Proceedings of the International Conference on Very Large Data Bases (VLDB)*, Tokyo, Japan, 370–378.

Lampson, B., Paul, M., and Seigert, H. (1981). *Distributed Systems: Architecture and Implementation (An Advanced Course)*. Springer-Verlag, Heidelberg, Germany.

Lampson, B., and Sturgis, H. (1979). Crash recovery in a distributed data storage system. *Technical Report*. Xerox Palo Alto Research Center, Palo Alto, CA.

Langerak, R. (1990). View updates in relational databases with an independent scheme. *ACM Transactions on Database Systems* **15**(1): 40–66.

Larson, P. (1981). Analysis of index sequential files with overflow chaining. *ACM Transactions on Database Systems* **6**(4): 671–680.

Litwin, W. (1980). Linear hashing: A new tool for file and table addressing. *Proceedings of the International Conference on Very Large Databases (VLDB)*, Montreal, Canada, 212–223.

Lynch, N., Merritt, M., Weihl, W., and Fekete, A. (1994). *Atomic Transactions*. Morgan Kaufmann, San Francisco.

Maier, D. (1983). *The Theory of Relational Databases*. Computer Science Press. Rockville, MD. (Available through Books on Demand: *http://www.umi.com/hp/Support/BOD /index.html*.)

Makinouchi, A. (1977). A consideration on normal form of not-necessarily-normalized relations in the relational data model. *Proceedings of the International Conference on Very Large Data Bases (VLDB)*, Tokyo, Japan, 447–453.

Mannila, H., and Raäihä, K.-J. (1992). *The Design of Relational Databases*. Addison-Wesley, Workingham, UK.

Mannila, H., and Raäihä, K.-J. (1994). Algorithms for inferring functional dependencies. *Knowledge Engineering* **12**(1): 83–99.

Maslak, B., Showalter, J., and Szczygielski, T. (1991). Coordinated resource recovery in VM/ESA. *IBM Systems Journal* **30**(1): 72–89.

Masunaga, Y. (1984). A relational database view update translation mechanism. *Proceedings of the International Conference on Very Large Data Bases (VLDB)*, Singapore, 309–320.

Melton, J. (1997). *Understanding SQL's Persistent Stored Modules*. Morgan Kaufmann, San Francisco.

Melton, J., Eisenberg, A., and Cattell, R. (2000). *Understanding SQL and Java Together: A Guide to SQLJ, JDBC, and Related Technologies*. Morgan Kaufmann, San Francisco.

Melton, J., and Simon, A. (1992). *Understanding the New SQL: A Complete Guide*. Morgan Kaufmann, San Francisco.

Microsoft (1997). *Microsoft ODBC 3.0 Software Development Kit and Programmer's Reference*. Microsoft Press, Seattle.

Minker, J. (1997). *Logic and databases: past, present, and future. AI Magazine* **18**(3): 21-47.

Missaoui, R., Gagnon, J.-M., and Godin, R. (1995). Mapping an extended entity-relationship schema into a schema of complex objects. *Proceedings of the 14th International Conference on Object-Oriented and Entity Relationship Modeling*, Brisbane, Australia, 205–215.

Mohan, C., Haderle, D., Lindsay, B., Pirahesh, H., and Schwartz, P. (1992). Aries: A transaction recovery method supporting fine-granularity locking and partial rollbacks using write-ahead logging. *ACM Transactions on Database Systems* **17**(1): 94–162.

Mohan, C., Lindsay, B., and Obermarck, R. (1986). Transaction management in the R* distributed database management system. *ACM Transactions on Database Systems* **11**(4): 378–396.

Mohania, M., Konomi, S., and Kambayashi, Y. (1997). Incremental maintenance of materialized views. *Database and Expert Systems Applications (DEXA)*. Springer-Verlag, Heidelberg, Germany.

Mok, W., Ng, Y.-K., and Embley, D. (1996). A normal form for precisely characterizing redundancy in nested relations. *ACM Transactions on Database Systems* **21**(1): 77–106.

Moss, J. (1985). *Nested Transactions: An Approach to Reliable Computing*. The MIT Press, Cambridge, MA.

Netscape (2000). SSL-3 specifications. *http://home.netscape.com/eng/ssl3/index.html*.

Neuman, B. C., and Ts'o, T. (1994). Kerberos: An authentication service for computer networks. *IEEE Communications* **32**(9): 33–38.

Novikoff, A. (1962). On Convergence Proofs for Perceptrons. *Proceedings of the Symposium on Mathematical Theory of Automata*, New York, 615–621.

O'Neil, P. (1987). Model 204: Architecture and performance. *Proceedings of the International Workshop on High Performance Transaction Systems*. In vol. 359 of *Lecture Notes in Computer Science*. Springer-Verlag, Heidelberg, Germany, 40–59.

O'Neil, P., and Graefe, G. (1995). Multi-table joins through bitmapped join indices. *SIGMOD Record* **24**(3): 8–11.

O'Neil, P., and Quass, D. (1997). Improved query performance with variant indexes. *Proceedings of the ACM SIGMOD International Conference on Management of Data*, Tucson, AZ, 38–49.

Orfali, R., and Harkey, D. (1998). *Client/Server Programing with Java and CORBA*. John Wiley, New York.

Orlowska, M., Rajapakse, J., and ter Hofstede, A. (1996). Verification problems in conceptual workflow specifications. *Proceedings of the International Conference on Conceptual Modeling*. In vol. 1157 of *Lecture Notes in Computer Science*, Springer-Verlag, Heidelberg, Germany.

Ozsoyoglu, Z., and Yuan, L.-Y. (1985). A normal form for nested relations. *ACM SIGACT-SIGMOD-SIGART Symposium on Principles of Database Systems (PODS)*, Portland, OR, 251–260.

Ozsu, M., and Valduriez, P. (1999). *Principles of Distributed Database Systems* (2nd ed.) Prentice Hall, Englewood Cliffs, NJ.

Papadimitriou, C. (1986). *The Theory of Concurrency Control*. Computer Science Press, Rockville, MD.

Paton, N., Diaz, O., Williams, M., Campin, J., Dinn, A., and Jaime, A. (1993). Dimensions of active behavior. *Proceedings of the Workshop on Rules in Database Systems*, Heidelberg, Germany, 40–57.

Peterson, L., and Davies, B. (2000). *Computer Networks: A Systems Approach*, 2nd ed. Morgan Kaufmann, San Francisco.

Peterson, W. (1957). Addressing for random access storage. *IBM Journal of Research and Development* **1**(2): 130–146.

Pope, A. (1998). *The CORBA Reference Guide*. Addison-Wesley, Boston, MA.

PostgreSQL. (2000). PostgreSQL. *http://www.postgresql.org*.

Pressman, R. (2002). *Software Engineering: A Practitioner's Approach*, 5th ed. McGraw-Hill, New York.

Przymusinski, T. C. (1988). *On The Declarative Semantics of Deductive Databases and Logic Programs*. In *Foundations of Deductive Databases and Logic Programming*, ed. J. Minker. Morgan Kaufmann, Los Altos, CA, 193–216.

Quinlan, J. (1986). Induction of Decision Trees. *Machine Learning* **1**(1): 81–106.

Ram, S. (1995). Deriving functional dependencies from the entity-relationship model. *Communications of the ACM* **38**(9): 95–107.

Ramakrishnan, R., Srivastava, D., Sudarshan, S., and Seshadri, P. (1994). The CORAL deductive database system. *VLDB Journal* **3**(2): 161–210.

Ramakrishnan, R., and Ullman, J. (1995). A survey of deductive databases. *Journal of Logic Programming* **23**(2): 125–149.

Ray, E. (2001). *Learning XML.* O'Reilly and Associates, Sebastopol, CA.

Reese, G. (2000). *Database Programming with JDBC and Java.* O'Reilly and Associates, Sebastopol, CA.

Reuter, A., and Wachter, H. (1991). The contract model. *Quarterly Bulletin of the IEEE Computer Society Technical Commmttee on Data Engineering* **14**(1): 39–43.

Rivest, R., Shamir, A., and Adelman, L. (1978). On digital signatures and public-key cryptosystems. *Communications of the ACM* **21**(2): 120–126.

Robie, J., Chamberlin, D., and Florescu, D. (2000). Quilt: An XML query language. *XML Europe.* http://www.almaden.ibm.com/cs/people/chamberlin/robie_XML_Europe.pdf.

Robie, J., Lapp, J., and Schach, D. (1998). XML query language (XQL). *Proceedings of the Query Languages Workshop,* Boston. http://www.w3.org/TandS/QL/QL98/pp/xql.html.

Rosenberry, W., Kenney, D., and Fisher, G. (1992). *Understanding DCE.* O'Reilly and Associates, Sebastopol, CA.

Rosenkrantz, D., Stearns, R., and Lewis, P. (1978). System level concurrency control for distributed database systems. *ACM Transactions on Database Systems* **3**(2): 178–198.

Rosenkrantz, D., Stearns, R., and Lewis, P. (1984). Consistency and serializability in concurrent database systems. *SIAM Journal of Computing* **13**(3): 505–530.

Ross, K., and Srivastava, D. (1997). Fast computation of sparse datacubes. *Proceedings of the International Conference on Very Large Data Bases (VLDB),* Athens, Greece, 116–125.

Roth, M., and Korth, H. (1987). The design of non-1nf relational databases into nested normal form. *Proceedings of the ACM SIGMOD International Conference on Management of Data,* San Francisco, 143–159.

Rumbaugh, J., Blaha, M., Premerlani, W., Eddy, F., and Lorenzen, W. (1991). *Object-Oriented Modeling and Design.* Prentice Hall, Englewood Cliffs, NJ.

Rusinkiewicz, M., and Sheth, A. (1994). Specification and execution of transactional workflows. In *Modern Database Systems: The Object Model, Interoperability, and Beyond,* ed. W. Kim. ACM Press, New York, 592–620.

Sagonas, K., Swift, T., and Warren, D. (1994). XSB as an efficient deductive database engine. *Proceedings of the ACM SIGMOD International Conference on Management of Data,* Minneapolis, MN, 442–453.

Savnik, I., and Flach, P. (1993). Bottom-up induction of functional dependencies from relations. *Proceedings of the AAAI Knowledge Discovery in Databases Workshop (KDD),* Ljubliana, Slovenija, 174–185.

Schach, S. (1999). *Software Engineering,* 5th ed. Aksen Associates, Homewood, IL.

Schek, H.-J., Weikum, G., and Ye, H. (1993). Towards a unified theory of concurrency control and recovery. *ACM SIGACT-SIGMOD-SIGART Conference on Principles of Database Systems (PODS),* Washington, DC, 300–311.

Schneier, B. (1995). *Applied Cryptography: Protocols, Algorithms, and Source Code in C.* John Wiley, New York.

Sciore, E. (1983). Improving database schemes by adding attributes. *ACM SIGACT-SIGMOD-SIGART Symposium on Principles of Database Systems (PODS),* New York, 379–383.

Sebesta, R. (2001). *Programming the World Wide Web.* Addison-Wesley, Boston, MA.

SGML (1986). Information processing—Text and office systems—Standard Generalized Markup Language (SGML). *ISO Standard 8879*. International Standards Organization, Geneva, Switzerland.

Shasha, D., and Bonnet, P. (2003). *Database Tuning: Principles, Experiments, and Troubleshooting Techniques*. Morgan Kaufman, San Francisco.

Shipman, D. (1981). The functional data model and the data language DAPLEX. *ACM Transactions on Database Systems* 6(1): 140–173.

Shoshani, A., and Bernstein, A. J. (1969). Synchronization in a parallel accessed data base. *Communications of the ACM* 12(11).

Signore, R., Creamer, J., and Stegman, M. (1995). *The ODBC Solution: Open Database Connectivity in Distributed Environments*. McGraw-Hill, New York.

Singh, M. (1996). Synthesizing distributed constrained events from transactional workflow specifications. *Proceedings of the International Conference on Data Engineering*, New Orleans, LA, 616–623.

Skeen, D. (1981). Nonblocking commit protocols. *Proceedings of the ACM SIGMOD International Conference on Management of Data*, Ann Arbor, MI, 133–142.

Spaccapietra, S., ed. (1987). *Entity-Relationship Approach: Ten Years of Experience in Information Modeling, Proceedings of the Entity-Relationship Conference*, Elsevier, North Holland.

SQL (1992). ANSI X3.135-1992, *American National Standard for Information Systems—Database Language—SQL*. American National Standards Institute, Washington, DC.

SQLJ (2000). SQLJ. *http://www.sqlj.org*.

Stallings, W. (1999). *Cryptography and Network Security: Principles and Practice*, 2nd ed. Prentice Hall, Englewood Cliffs, NJ.

Stallman, R. (2000). GNU coding standards. *http://www.gnu.org/prep/standards.html*.

Standish (2000). Chaos. *http://standishgroup.com/visitor/chaos.htm*.

Staudt, M., and Jarke, M. (1996). Incremental maintenance of externally materialized views. *Proceedings of the International Conference on Very Large Data Bases (VLDB)*, Bombay, India, 75–86.

Steiner, J. G., Neuman, B. C., and Schiller, J. I. (1988). Kerberos: An authentication service for open network systems. *USENIX Conference Proceedings*, Dallas, TX, 191–202.

Stonebraker, M. (1979). Concurrency control and consistency of multiple copies of data in INGRES. *IEEE Transactions on Software Engineering* 5(3): 188–194.

Stonebraker, M. (1986). *The INGRES Papers: Anatomy of a Relational Database System*. Addison-Wesley, Boston, MA.

Stonebreaker, M., and Kemnitz, G. (1991). The POSTGRES next generation database management system. *Communications of the ACM* 10(34): 78–92.

Summerville, I. (2000). *Software Engineering*, 5th ed. Addison-Wesley, Boston, MA.

Sun (2000). JDBC data access API. *http://java.sun.com/products/jdbc/*.

Sybase (1999). Sybase adaptive server enterprise performance and tuning guide. *http://sybooks.sybase.com/onlinebooks/group-as/asg1200e/aseperf*.

Teorey, T. (1999). *Database Modeling and Design: The E-R Approach*. Morgan Kaufmann, San Francisco.

Thalheim, B. (1992). *Fundamentals of Entity-Relationship Modeling*. Springer-Verlag, Berlin.

Thomas, R. (1979). A majority consensus approach to concurrency control for multiple copy databases. *ACM Transactions on Database Systems* **4**(2): 180–209.

Topor, R., and Sonenberg, E. (1988). On domain independent databases. In *Foundations of Deductive Databases and Logic Programming*, ed. J. Minker. Morgan Kaufmann, Los Altos, CA, 217–240.

Transarc (1996). Encina monitor programmer's guide and reference. *Technical Report ENC-D5008-06.* Transarc Corporation, Pittsburgh, PA.

Ullman, J. (1982). *Priniciples of Database Systems.* Computer Science Press, Rockville, MD.

Ullman, J. (1988). *Principles of Database and Knowledge-Base Systems,* volumes 1 and 2. Computer Science Press, Rockville, MD.

Vaghani, J., Ramamohanarao, K., Kemp, D., Somogyi, Z., Stuckey, P., Leask, T., and Harland, J. (1994). The Aditi deductive database system. *The VLDB Journal* **3**(2): 245–288.

Valduriez, P. (1987). Join indices. *ACM Transactions on Database Systems* **12**(2): 218–246.

Van Gelder, A. (1992). The Well-Founded Semantics of Aggregation. *ACM SIGACT-SIGMOD-SIGART Symposium on Principles of Database Systems (PODS)*, San Diego, CA, 127–138.

Van Gelder, A., Ross, K. A., and Schlipf, J. S. (1991). The well-founded semantics for general logic programs. *Journal of the ACM* **38**(3): 620–650.

Van Gelder, A., and Topor, R. (1991). Safety and translation of relational calculus queries. *ACM Transactions on Database Systems* **16**(2): 235–278.

Venkatrao, M., and Pizzo, M. (1995). SQL/CLI—A new binding style for SQL. *SIGMOD Record* **24**(4): 72–77.

Vincent, M. (1999). Semantic foundations of 4nf in relational database design. *Acta Informatica* **36**(3): 173–213.

Vincent, M., and Srinivasan, B. (1993). Redundancy and the justification for fourth normal form in relational databases. *International Journal of Foundations of Computer Science* **4**(4): 355–365.

VISA (2000). SET specifications. *http://www.visa.com/nt/ecomm/set/intro.html.*

Weddell, G. (1992). Reasoning about functional dependencies generalized for semantic data models. *ACM Transactions on Database Systems* **17**(1): 32–64.

Weihl, W. (1984). *Specification and Implementation of Atomic Data Types.* Ph.D. thesis, Department of Computer Science, Massachusetts Institute of Technology, Cambridge, MA.

Weihl, W. (1988). Commutativity-based concurrency control for abstract data types. *IEEE Transactions on Computers* **37**(12): 1488–1505.

Weikum, G. (1991). Principles and realization strategies of multilevel transaction management. *ACM Transactions on Database Systems* **16**(1): 132–180.

Weikum, G., and Schek, H. (1991). Multi-level transactions and open nested transactions. *Quarterly Bulletin of the IEEE Computer Society Technical Committee on Data Engineering* **14**(1): 55–66.

Whalen, G., Garcia, M., DeLuca, S., and Thompson, D. (2001). *Microsoft SQL Server 2000 Performance Tuning Technical Reference.* Microsoft Press, Redmond, WA.

Widom, J., and Ceri, S. (1996). *Active Database Systems.* Morgan Kaufmann, San Francisco.

Wodtke, D., and Weikum, G. (1997). A formal foundation for distributed workflow execution based on state charts. *Proceedings of the International Conference on Database Theory (ICDT)*, Delphi, Greece, 230–246.

Wong, E. (1977). Retrieving dispersed data from SDD-1: A system for distributed databases. *Proceedings of the 2nd International Berkeley Workshop on Distributed Data Management and Data Networks*, Berkeley, CA, 217–235.

Wong, E., and Youssefi, K. (1976). Decomposition—A strategy for query processing. *ACM Transactions on Database Systems* 1(3): 223–241.

Worah, D., and Sheth, A. (1997). Transactions in transactional workflows. In *Advanced Transaction Models and Architectures*, eds. S. Jajodia and L. Kerschberg. Kluwer Academic Publishers, Dordrecht, Netherlands, 3–45.

Workflow Management Coalition (2000). WfMC standards. *http://www.aiim.org/wfmc /standards/docs.htm*.

XML (1998). Extensible Markup Language (XML) 1.0. *http://www.w3.org/TR/REC-xml*.

XMLSchema (2000a). XML Schema, part 0: Primer. *http://www.w3.org/TR/xmlschema-0/*.

XMLSchema (2000b). XML Schema, parts 1 and 2. *http://www.w3.org/XML/Schema*.

X/Open (1996a). *X/Open CAE Specification Structured Transaction Definition Language (STDL)*. X/Open Co., Ltd., London.

X/Open (1996b). *X/Open Guide Distributed Transaction Processing: Reference Model, Version 3*. X/Open Co., Ltd., London.

XPath (2003). XML Path Language (XPath), version 2.0. *http://www.w3.org/TR/xpath/*.

XPointer (2000). XML pointer language (XPointer), version 1.0. *http://www.w3.org/TR /xptr/*.

XQuery (2004). XQuery 1.0: An XML query language. Eds. S. Boag, D. Chamberlin, M. F. Fenrandez, D. Florescu, T. Robie, and T. Simeon. *http://www.w3.org/TR/xquery*.

XSB (2003). The XSB system. *http://xsb.sourceforge.net/*.

XSLT (1999). XSL transformations (XSLT), version 1.0. *http://www.w3.org/TR/xslt/*.

Zaniolo, C. (1983). The database language GEM. *Proceedings of the ACM SIGMOD International Conference on Management of Data*, San Jose, CA, 423–434.

Zaniolo, C., and Melkanoff, M. (1981). On the design of relational database schemata. *ACM Transactions on Database Systems* 6(1): 1–47.

Zhao, B., and Joseph, A. (2000). XSet: A lightweight XML search engine for Internet applications. *http://www.cs.berkeley.edu/~ravenben/xset/*.

Zhao, Y., Deshpande, P., Naughton, J., and Shukla, A. (1998). Simultaneous optimization and evaluation of multiple dimensional queries. *Proceedings of the ACM SIGMOD International Conference on Management of Data*, Seattle, WA, 271–282.

Zloof, M. (1975). Query by example. *NCC*. AFIPS Press, Montvale, NJ.

Index